STRATEGIC
HUMAN RESOURCE
MANAGEMENT

STRATEGIC HUMAN RESOURCE MANAGEMENT

An INTERNATIONAL PERSPECTIVE

Edited by

Gary Rees &
Paul E. Smith

Los Angeles | London | New Delhi
Singapore | Washington DC

SAGE

Los Angeles | London | New Delhi
Singapore | Washington DC

SAGE Publications Ltd
1 Oliver's Yard
55 City Road
London EC1Y 1SP

SAGE Publications Inc.
2455 Teller Road
Thousand Oaks, California 91320

SAGE Publications India Pvt Ltd
B 1/I 1 Mohan Cooperative Industrial Area
Mathura Road
New Delhi 110 044

SAGE Publications Asia-Pacific Pte Ltd
3 Church Street
#10-04 Samsung Hub
Singapore 049483

Editor: Kirsty Smy
Editorial assistant: Nina Smith
Production editor: Sarah Cooke
Marketing manager: Alison Borg
Cover design: Francis Kenney
Typeset by: C&M Digitals (P) Ltd, Chennai, India
Printed and bound in Great Britain by Ashford
Colour Press Ltd

MIX
Paper from
responsible sources
FSC® C011748
www.fsc.org

Library of Congress Control Number: 2013942708

British Library Cataloguing in Publication data

A catalogue record for this book is available from
the British Library

ISBN 978-1-4462-5585-8
ISBN 978-1-4462-5586-5 (pbk)

CONTENTS

ABOUT THE CONTRIBUTORS

Gary Rees is MBA Director and Principal Lecturer in HRM/OB at Portsmouth University. Previous to this, Gary successfully managed the suite of postgraduate HR Programmes for a decade at Portsmouth Business School, taking the programmes through various internal and external (professional body) validation events. He has edited books and written chapters in bestsellers such as *Organisational Behaviour* (Wiley) and *Leading, Managing and Developing People* (CIPD). Gary has also published in several academic and practitioner journals in the area of burnout and engagement and has presented his research at international conferences in Australia, Spain, the UAE, the USA and the Cayman Islands. He has held a range of external examiner appointments across both undergraduate and postgraduate programmes in the UK and Europe, and is an examiner for the CIPD Organizational Design and Development module and holds Chartered Fellowship of the CIPD and membership of the British Psychological Society, including the Occupational Psychology Division.

Paul E. Smith is Head of the HR Subject Group, Programme Director for MSc Global Business, and Principal Lecturer in HRM at the University of Hertfordshire Business School. He teaches strategic human resource management at both undergraduate and postgraduate level. Paul has edited books and contributed chapters and case studies to a variety of books in the field of HR and organizational behaviour, including *Organizational Behaviour* (Routledge), *Leadership and Management for HR Professionals* (Butterworth-Heinemann) and *People Management and Development: A Revision Guide* (CIPD). Paul is a member of the Work and Employment Research Unit at Hertfordshire Business School and has contributed to a number of conference papers, journal articles and reports. His research interests encompass diversity in organizations, leadership, and the application of management theory to practice in HR. He has held a number of external examiner appointments and contributed to internal and external validation and reviews events. Paul is a Chartered Fellow of the CIPD.

David Allsop is a Principal Lecturer in Human Resource Management and Industrial Relations and a member of the Work Employment Research Unit at Hertfordshire Business School, University of Hertfordshire. David is an ex-coal miner and his research interests are employment relations within the coal industry and human resource management and international human resource management.

Moira Calveley is a Principal Lecturer in Human Resource Management and a member of the Work Employment Research Unit at Hertfordshire Business School, University of Hertfordshire. Moira's main areas of research interest are employment relations in the public sector and equality and diversity.

Dr Linda Holbeche is an independent developer, consultant, researcher and writer in the fields of HRM, OD and leadership. She is co-director of The Holbeche Partnership and of The Centre for Progressive Leadership at the City of London Business School where she is visiting professor. She also holds visiting professorships at Bedfordshire and Cass business schools and is Adjunct Professor at Imperial College, Fellow of Roffey Park and Associate of Ashridge. Linda has authored or co-edited 12 books, numerous book chapters and articles in the field, and works with a number of organizations in the UK and overseas on consulting projects. She was previously Director of Research and Policy for the CIPD.

Sue Hutchinson is Associate Professor in HRM at the University of the West of England, where she is also Associate Head of the HRM teaching and research group. She teaches on a range of HRM postgraduate modules including performance management, and is actively involved in research. Her main research interests focus on the link between people management and performance, the role of line managers in HRM, and involvement and consultation. Previous work experiences include research and teaching at Bath University, policy advisor for the CIPD and industrial relations advisor in the paper industry.

Paul Iles is a Professor of Leadership and HRM at Glasgow School for Business and Society, Glasgow Caledonian University. He was previously at the universities of Salford, Leeds Metropolitan, Teesside, Liverpool John Moores and the Open University. He has a BA in PPP from the University of Oxford, an MSc in Organizational Psychology from UMIST (University of Manchester) and a PhD from the University of Salford.

Paul is a chartered psychologist, Associate Fellow of the British Psychological Society, and Chartered Fellow of the Chartered Institute for Personnel and Development. He has a particular interest in leadership development, international HRM and talent management. His recent work on talent management in China and in regional structures in Asia has been published in the *Journal of World Business* and the *International Journal of Human Resource Management*. In addition he is the co-author of a new textbook published in 2013, *International Human Resource Management: A Cross-cultural and Comparative Approach*.

Zsuzsanna Kispál-Vitai is an Associate Professor at the Faculty of Business and Economics of the University of Pécs, Hungary. She teaches a number of management subjects for undergraduate and graduate students. Her research interest is new institutional economics and human resource management, and how theory appears in managerial practice.

Natalia Rocha Lawton is a Lecturer in Human Resource Management and a member of the Work Employment Research Unit at Hertfordshire Business School, University of Hertfordshire. Natalia's research interests are in equality and diversity and international employment relations, with a particular focus on Latin America.

Charles Leatherbarrow is a Senior Lecturer at the University of Wolverhampton Business School. He has extensive operational experience in HRM, working in the oil and gas industry in Europe, Africa, the Middle East and Kazakhstan. He writes textbooks on HR and has a specific interest in HR's contribution to organizational effectiveness.

Dr John Neugebauer FCIPD is a Client Director at Bristol Business School, University of the West of England. He has taught with the Open University, Bath University and Bristol University. Previously Head of HR for a national organization, he continues to consult in private, public, and third-sector organizations.

Marco Pironti was a visiting scholar at the Center for Computational Research NS Management Science, MIT, Boston (MA), at the Institute of Management, Innovation and Organization, Haas School of Business, Berkeley, and at the CEBIz of Columbia University. He is an Associate Professor in Innovation and Entrepreneurship at the University of Torino – Computer Science Department, and Scientific Chief of the E-Business Lab. He is an author of more than 80 articles and other publications.

Paola Pisano is visiting scholar at Westminster University, Glasgow Caledonia University and Assistant Professor of Innovation and Entrepreneurship at the University of Torino – Computer Science Department. She is involved in several projects on innovation and start-up with national and international research groups, such as the E-Business Lab and the Ideas Research Group. She is an author of books and several articles.

Alison Rieple teaches strategic management and the management of innovation and change at the University of Westminster in London, UK. She is in demand as a lecturer at international workshops, most recently in the USA, South Korea, Ireland, Iran and Denmark. She is the co-author of two strategic management textbooks and many articles on the subject of strategy, design and innovation management. She is on the editorial board of the *International Journal of Entrepreneurship and Management*, and *Management Decision*, and is co-editor of a special issue of the *Design Management Journal* and a special issue of the *International Journal of Entrepreneurship and Management*.

Kate Rowlands is currently a Lecturer in Human Resource Management at Salford Business School. Before taking up a full-time position within the University of Salford she worked as a senior manager within the retail sector for over ten years. It was this work background that led to her focus on teaching and research activities within the field of HRM policy and practice with particular relevance in developing and transitional countries. She is currently a member of the International Strategy and People Management discipline group within Salford Business School. This cluster manages a number of key postgraduate programmes within the School, including the MSc Human Resource Management and Development.

Jim Stewart is Professor of Human Resource Development at Coventry Business School where he leads on research in the Department of HRM and OB. He is CIPD Chief Examiner for Learning and Development and Chair of the University Forum for HRD. Jim has been researching HRD for over 20 years and is the author, co-author and co-editor of over 20 books on the subject. These have been informed by consultancy and research projects funded by the UK Government, the EC, CIPD, ESRC and employers in all sectors of the economy.

Stephen Taylor is a Senior Lecturer in Human Resource Management at the University of Exeter Business School and a Chief Examiner for the Chartered Institute of Personnel and Development (CIPD). He previously taught at Manchester Business School, at Manchester Metropolitan University, and worked in a variety of HR management roles in the hotel industry and in the NHS. He teaches courses in employment law, employee resourcing, employee relations and the business context at postgraduate and undergraduate level. Research interests include employee retention, occupational pensions and regulatory issues. He is the author/co-author of several books including six editions of *Resourcing and Talent Management* (CIPD Publications), three editions of *Employment Law: An Introduction* (with Astra Emir) (Oxford University Press), *The Employee Retention Handbook*, six editions of *Human Resource Management* (with Derek Torrington, Laura Hall and Carol Atkinson) (FT Prentice Hall) and *Contemporary Issues in HRM* (CIPD Publications). He regularly represents parties in employment tribunals.

Geoff White is Professor of Human Resource Management at the University of Greenwich Business School. He was until 2010 also Director of Research in the Business School. Prior to becoming an academic, Geoff worked for over ten years for the major pay research organization, Incomes Data Services (IDS). He has acted as an advisor on pay systems and data to the Low Pay Commission, the Local Government Pay Commission, the NHS Staff Council and the Universities and Colleges Employers Association. He has written extensively around work and employment issues, especially reward management and public sector pay, and is joint author of the CIPD textbook on reward management. He is currently completing research on the employment relations arrangements on the 2012 London Olympics construction site and research into the impact of the introduction of a new minimum wage in Hong Kong in 2011.

Geoffrey Wood is Professor of International Business, Associate Dean Research Excellence Framework, and Programme Quality at Warwick Business School, University of Warwick. He also holds honorary professorships at Griffith University (Australia), Nelson Mandela Metropolitan University, University of Witwatersrand (both in South Africa) and Pécs University (Hungary), and is an academic Fellow of the CIPD. He has authored/edited 12 books and over 100 peer-reviewed articles.

Dr Crystal Zhang, Academic MCIPD, is a Senior Lecturer in HRM and Organizational Behaviour (OB) at Leeds Business School and teaches at executive level in the UK, China and Africa. She has also delivered the management development programme for SINOPEC in China and the MAHRM for the NHS in the UK and has worked on applied research programmes with the UK Commission for Employment and Skills.

Dr Zhang received her doctoral and Master's degree in HRM and OB from Leeds University Business School. Her research interests lie in international HRM, cross-cultural learning, cognitive style, talent management in China and career development for ethnic minorities in the UK. Her current publications are in the areas of learning theories and training practice, cross-cultural HRD, graduate employment, global leadership, and talent management in China and HRM in India. She has also contributed to book reviews in professional and academic journals, and currently acts as a reviewer and referee for a number of publishers and academic journals.

PREFACE

The impetus for this textbook came from a desire to produce a cogent and coherent explanation of human resource management from a strategic perspective. The economic crisis post-2008 redefined the rules of the game as far as global competition and how organizations operated. The value and use of human resources remain paramount to the continuing success of any organization.

This strategic HRM book has been designed so that, if so desired, it can be delivered in one semester for both final year undergraduate and postgraduate programmes. The book includes UK, European and international case studies. The approach adopted is one of building up the student's confidence in various complex terminologies and models by exploring current academic models, perspectives and research, and then applying these through practical examples across the three industry sectors. A series of reflective activities allow the reader to pause for thought and consider a range of relevant and topical HR issues.

The text is structured into three distinct sections:

Part 1 includes the organization, the organizational context and strategy (Chapters 1 to 4)
Part 2 incorporates the functional aspects of HR (Chapters 5 to 10)
Part 3 includes the organizational culture, the global/international perspective and where HR is heading in the future (Chapters 11 to 13)

The perspective adopted can be seen in Figure 1.

This textbook starts by introducing the concepts of organization, the organizational context and HRM in Chapter 1. Three core concepts, namely strategy, structure and culture, are addressed throughout the text, as is the emphasis upon applying an international perspective to both Human Resource Management (HRM) and Strategic Human Resource Management (SHRM) (see Figure 2).

A range of key features is included within chapters in order to support the reader through a variety of activities, including:

- An opening vignette with a short or long case study/case example to stimulate student thinking or understanding
- A bulleted list of learning objectives at the beginning of each chapter
- A chapter overview for each chapter
- An introductory section for each chapter

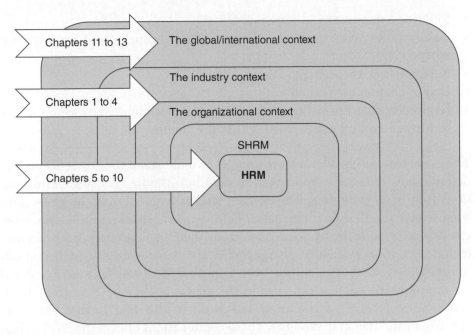

Figure 1 Book chapters and the various perspectives

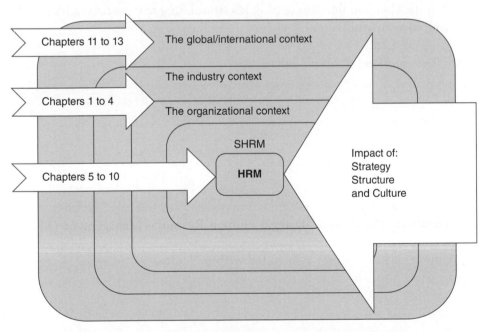

Figure 2 Strategy, structure and culture impacting upon HRM and SHRM

- Reflective questions and activities
- Case studies with questions (from a UK, European and international perspective)
- Key academic theories and frameworks
- End of chapter conclusion
- Explore further (a reading list which gives the student guidance on where to further explore issues raised within the chapter)

The pedagogic design allows for the reader to understand the key concepts and definitions within the introduction, leading into the key debates and discussions from a range of perspectives. Case studies from all over the globe have been selected so that international students who are studying for a UK degree can associate more freely with cases from their own country. Each chapter includes a critical evaluation of approaches and debates, clearly pitched at UK Master's-level study. The authors who contributed to this text were selected for their specific subject expertise in the area that they have written about, come from a range of countries, and work in differing English, Scottish, Hungarian and Italian universities. These combinations of expertise add a great deal of value over and above traditional texts which may have been written by a single author.

We hope that you find this textbook a stimulating and useful read, and wish you well in your studies.

Gary Rees and Paul E. Smith, Editors

COMPANION WEBSITE

Strategic Human Resource Management: An International Perspective edited by Gary Rees and Paul E. Smith is supported by a companion website.

Visit www.sagepub.co.uk/rees to take advantage of the learning resources for students and lecturers.

For students
Free selected SAGE journal articles
Podcasts

For lecturers
Instructors manual
PowerPoint slides

GUIDED TOUR

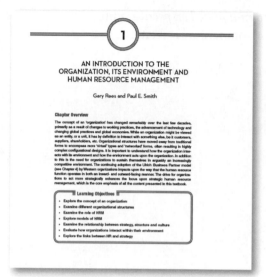

Chapter Overview
Introduces and makes connections between each chapter

Learning Objectives
Highlight at a glance the key content that will be covered in each chapter to focus your learning

Case Studies with questions
Taken from a range of countries and different types of organization, linking theory to practice

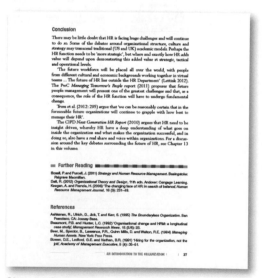

Pit Stop: Reflective Activities
Questions and activities test your understanding of important issues and build relevant skills

Chapter Conclusion
Summarizes the key points covered in the chapter, ideal for revision

Further Reading
Lists of books, journals and websites to explore for a deeper understanding of the issues raised

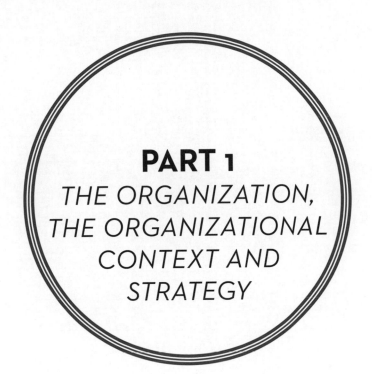

PART 1
THE ORGANIZATION, THE ORGANIZATIONAL CONTEXT AND STRATEGY

AN INTRODUCTION TO THE ORGANIZATION, ITS ENVIRONMENT AND HUMAN RESOURCE MANAGEMENT

Gary Rees and Paul E. Smith

Chapter Overview

The concept of an 'organization' has changed remarkably over the last few decades, primarily as a result of changes to working practices, the advancement of technology and changing global practices and global economies. While an organization might be viewed as an entity, or a unit, it has by definition to interact with something else, be it customers, suppliers, shareholders, etc. Organizational structures have moved away from traditional forms to encompass more 'virtual' types and 'networked' forms, often resulting in highly complex configurational designs. It is important to understand how the organization interacts with its environment and how the environment acts upon the organization. In addition to this is the need for organizations to sustain themselves in arguably an increasingly competitive environment. The continuing adoption of the Ulrich Business Partner model (see Chapter 4) by Western organizations impacts upon the way that the human resource function operates in both an inward- and outward-facing manner. The drive for organizations to act more strategically enhances the focus upon strategic human resource management, which is the core emphasis of all the content presented in this textbook.

≣ Learning Objectives ≣

- **Explore the concept of an organization**
- **Examine different organizational structures**
- **Examine the role of HRM**
- **Explore models of HRM**
- **Examine the relationship between strategy, structure and culture**
- **Evaluate how organizations interact within their environment**
- **Explore the links between HR and strategy**

OXFAM

Oxfam is currently responding to emergencies in 30 countries, from the conflict in Darfur, Sudan, to the humanitarian crisis caused by waterlogging in Bangladesh. The demands of having to recruit people fast in a crisis situation and of sustaining long-term development work mean that HR is key to the success of Oxfam's programmes. Catherine Layton, the HR adviser in the employee relations team at Oxfam, explains how the charity manages its people around the globe.

Oxfam is a highly devolved organization, with HR, financial management and programme management led by eight regional management teams around the world, which span regions as large as South America or the Middle East, Eastern Europe and the Commonwealth of Independent States. Layton explains: 'There has been a deliberate strategy over the past five years to build up regional management and have fewer people based in Oxford.' This means that when an emergency occurs in Haiti, for example, it would be the responsibility of the team in the Central America, Mexico and the Caribbean region to take the lead in organizing the response.

Reporting lines for HR staff at Oxfam reflect the organization's devolved approach. Country-based HR staff report to HR managers in each region, who in turn are managed by their regional director, but also have a 'dotted' reporting line to the organization's head of international HR. Regional HR practices and initiatives are sometimes not 'rubber-stamped' by head office, but they are monitored and recorded. The organization has an international people strategy to set principles for HR management in every region; the process differs from Oxfam's HR strategy for other divisions, such as the trading or finance divisions in the UK.

This means that while regions will follow Oxfam's international people strategy, pay and benefits framework and other HR procedures, they ultimately decide how to implement policies and pay their staff within regional budgets. Layton says:

> In Afghanistan, for example, pay has been agreed regionally, using local labour market information, and the reward team here in Oxford are notified of the salary scales. If they wanted to increase salaries by x per cent in order for them to remain competitive in that country, they could contact our international reward person based here in Oxford for assistance.

In general, Layton says, this approach works well. 'If we find out that something has been agreed which goes against a policy, then that could be escalated to the HR director or reward manager, but that doesn't tend to be a major issue,' she says.

The role of the country programme manager (CPM) – the most senior management post in each country where Oxfam operates – is key to the charity's work. Layton notes that the make-up of the country manager workforce is closely studied and monitored by Oxfam, saying: 'If they are doing their job well it makes a massive difference to how our programmes work.' She estimates that just below half (48 per cent) of the country manager workforce is from Organization for Economic Cooperation and Development countries with the remaining 52 per cent from developing countries.

While CPMs may come from any country in the world, the organization endeavours to employ and develop local staff. 'We recruit locally where we can,' Layton says, 'because immediately that person can speak the language, can understand the culture and they may have useful connections in that country – that's our preferred way of working.' For example, after the earth-quake in Pakistan in October 2005, the vast majority of the 500 staff recruited by Oxfam were Pakistani nationals, as is the CPM there. 'Some of these people were community workers, and we needed people from the community to do that work,' she says. However, work permits can cause problems in recruiting outside staff, particularly for junior roles. 'For certain levels of job you won't be able to get a work permit so there's no point in recruiting someone outside the country,' Layton says.

For some specialist roles, Layton acknowledges that there are countries where it is difficult to recruit people with certain skills. 'So in a country which doesn't have a proper education infra-structure, it's harder to get a qualified accountant or a senior finance manager, for example,' she says. However, Layton makes the distinction that the labour pool is from a global labour market rather than a Western one. 'There's international mobility but it's not all from Europe to Africa,' she says. 'For example, we may have an Ethiopian working for us in Zimbabwe, or a Zimbabwean who works in South Africa.'

In addition to regional and country-based staff, a team of emergency staff coordinated from the Oxford headquarters, known as humanitarian support personnel (HSP), are ready to be sent anywhere in the world at a moment's notice. Some of these professionals are human resources HSPs, who can be deployed, for example, to assist where a large number of local people need to be recruited in a very short space of time, preventing local HR staff from having to drop all of their ongoing HR work.

Because of the devolved nature of programmes and budgets at Oxfam, there are wide varia-tions in HR practice around the globe. However, the organization has an international people strategy and policies covering pay, benefits, performance appraisal and the whole range of HR practices that apply in every region. In each country, decisions need to be taken on the extent to which Oxfam's policies may conflict with local employment laws. As an organization that is acutely conscious of the need to avoid being perceived as telling local people what to do, Oxfam's approach is that its principles will apply unless they are contradicted by local legislation, in which case local legislation will take precedent. 'It's a challenge, and one that you have to go about very carefully, you don't just want to muscle in and say this is the way it should be done, because then you don't actually achieve what you want to achieve,' Layton says.

While Oxfam is best known for its emergency response work, much of the work undertaken by Oxfam is longer-term disaster prevention and development work. Asked which HR issues crop up most frequently, Layton says management training and development is an important priority. 'We want to grow our own staff and develop people so that they are able to progress from being a local project manager to a CPM, for example, but it is difficult to make people take time out for training when they are reluctant to take time out from programme work,' she says. A second ongoing issue is cross-cultural awareness: the difficulties for staff in trying to understand that differences in behaviour may be down to differences in culture.

For the future, Layton says that priorities include embedding a variety of global policies and procedures that have not yet filtered down across all regions. For example, Oxfam introduced a performance management system in 2000, setting out a common procedure for setting objec-tives and awarding performance ratings, which has yet to fully bed down in every country. Other plans for the future include the introduction of a global, web-based HR information system, which Layton anticipates will take some time to develop and implement.

Source: Adapted from Welfare (2006).

■ **Questions**

1. What would you anticipate are some of the difficulties for Oxfam when managing staff across different countries?
2. How much autonomy do you consider should the CPMs be given when deciding upon human resource management practices in their respective countries?

Introduction

This chapter starts by exploring the intricate links between organizational structure, strategy and culture and how all of these three aspects influence and are influenced by the HR function. Understanding the internal aspects is critical before expanding through to consider the external context. This chapter considers what an organization is, and how strategy, structure and culture fit together before considering the organizational environment. Furthermore, the role and function of HR are then considered in terms of both the internal (intra-organizational) context and the external (extra-organizational) context. It could be argued that any consideration of strategic human resource management needs to consider the latter, as the business strategy and human resource strategy will need to be aligned. Chapter 1 simply introduces these concepts, with Chapter 2 (Strategic Approaches), Chapter 3 on HR and Strategic HRM and Chapter 4 on how the HR function adds value (within the business context) further developing these ideas. Chapters 11 and 12 explore the intricate nature of organizational culture (and national culture) and how this relates to the global and international context, while Chapter 13 considers possible future trends in HR.

The concept of organization

The immediate context for human resource management is the organization. Buchanan and Huczynski define an organization as 'A social arrangement for achieving controlled performance in pursuit of collective goals' (2010: 8). They also point out the pervasive influence of organizations on our lives.

Mullins outlines the common factors that organizations share: 'interactions and efforts of people in order to achieve objectives channelled and co-ordinated through structure directed and controlled via management' (2010: 79). Sharing these broad common features are a large number of different organizational types and classifications, differentiated by such contingent factors as size, purpose, sector, and structure. As regards functions such as

HRM, this also adds to the complexity in terms of the sheer variety of practice, with different organizations applying HRM in different ways.

Although in our mind's eye when we think of the term 'organization' we may picture an office building or factory, with a definite physical entity and designated departments and hierarchy, in practice the spectrum is much wider than that. Francesco and Gold (2005) suggest that globalization of the economy has led to what they term the 'boundaryless organization' (Ashkenas et al. 1995) with widespread use of project teams and networks that reduce the boundaries that typically separate functions and hierarchical levels, thus leading to greater flexibility. Others have suggested a blurring of boundaries between organizations, based on loosely coupled arrangements between suppliers, contractors and other providers and making use of a flexible workforce, with such flexibility extending to employment arrangements. These trends are further explored below.

Critique of the concept of an organization

If an organization does not have to rely on occupying a physical space, such as a corporate headquarters, is communication (through whatever medium) the key factor in determining the existence of an organization? To what extent are people even aware of fellow employees in large and diverse global organizations? This point is particularly relevant to technology-based companies.

PIT STOP: REFLECTIVE ACTIVITY 1.1

1. Think of any large organization that comes to mind, and this may be from any country. What defines the organization? To what extent does the product, the brand, the reputation, or any other relevant factor(s) define what the organization is?
2. Is this an organization that you would like to work for, and if so why?

What is HR?

It could be argued that HR has travelled a considerable distance since the 1970s, moving from personnel administration through to personnel management, through to human resource management and now, in some quarters, 'people management'. Within this journey, it is possible to track the move from very much an administrative function (keeping personnel records, processing pay etc., often referred to as a 'transactional' approach) to a transformational function, through to utilization of human resources for specific goals, such as profit maximization, shareholder value etc. The degree to which HR functions are 'strategic' remains questionable, and may vary tremendously across industry sectors (public, private and not-for-profit), across countries and across sizes of companies.

When someone thinks of what HR actually does, recruitment and selection, arranging employment contracts, communicating employment terms and conditions and dismissal come to mind. However, the HR function may deal with a multitude of aspects, for example, dealing with promotion and career structures, job design, performance assessment, employee welfare, employment relations, management development and communication to employees. Chapters 5 to 10 address a range of functional HR aspects evident in many organizations.

While there are no universally accepted definitions of HRM, Storey defines HRM as 'a distinctive approach to employment management which seeks to achieve competitive advantage through the strategic development of a highly committed and capable workforce, using an integrated array of cultural, structural and personnel techniques' (1995: 5).

Boxall and Purcell (2003: 184) argue that HRM includes 'anything and everything associated with the management of the employment relationship in the firm'. If we accept that a HRM function has a range of offerings that it can contribute to an organization, the quality and added value of these offerings could be the acid test as to what offerings continue to be made, based on the logic that they only exist if they offer value (see Chapter 4).

As a starting point, an organization may wish to consider whether it actually wants a HR department or function. Robert Townsend (1970), the former CEO of Avis, likened the HR function (then known as 'personnel') to a cancerous growth, which had to be dealt with and if spotted in any small measure was to be removed for fear that it may grow back. While Townsend may have drawn attention to the functional aspect of HR, with an office, dedicated people, job descriptions etc., the question also remains as to who carries out the 'HR' work. Many aspects of the HR function could be outsourced, but with outsourcing comes a range of problems and challenges. To what extent could line management take up the jobs carried out by HR professionals? It could be argued that specialist expertise could then be 'bought in' where necessary.

Within the field of HR work there are specialist experts, such as compensation and remuneration experts, who may specialize in this area for the span of their career. In contrast, a HR generalist may work in a multitude of areas within their HR career (for example, start in recruitment and selection, then move to the training and development function, then work in job evaluation, and work their way through various HR managerial roles to become a senior HR professional).

In order to gain an understanding of what HR is all about, it is necessary to explore the theory underpinning HR in order to provide greater meaning and understanding to the topic area.

Models of HRM

Although the term 'human resources' had been used before then, human resource management as a distinctive term emerged in the early 1980s. Conceptually HRM could be differentiated from the 'old' personnel management, even if the degree and extent of its application have been somewhat variable. The work of Beer and colleagues at Harvard (Beer et al. 1984) and that of Fombrun et al. (1984) at Michigan University can be seen as central to this conceptualization.

One of the key differentiating factors of HRM propounded in such models was that it was linked to the strategic goals of the organization and provided a vital input into achieving competitive advantage. This can be contrasted with characterizations of personnel management, which could be viewed as being rather removed from the needs of the business, largely administrative and tasked with ensuring the compliance of policies and procedures. To this extent it could be argued that the 'strategic' in strategic human resource management is somewhat redundant, since a key attribute of HRM itself is its strategic nature. The addition of the 'S' in the term, as for example in this book title, does however serve both to highlight that the focus will be on these strategic aspects rather than the operational, and that in practice HRM may be applied to functions and activities that have very little link to strategic considerations.

The key models of HRM are concerned with strategic issues, however those sometimes termed 'hard' models, such as Fombrun et al.'s matching model illustrated in Figure 1.1, typically have a stronger focus on ensuring that the HRM strategy 'fits' and is driven by the overall corporate strategy (Fombrun et al. 1984).

This model introduced the concept of strategic human resource management by which HRM policies are inextricably linked to the 'formulation and implementation of strategic corporate and/or business objectives' (Fombrun et al. 1984: 34). It emphasizes a 'tight fit' or vertical integration between HR strategy and business strategy and the use of a set of HR policies and practices that are integrated with each other and with the goals of the organization. Two key assumptions underlie the model: that the most effective way of managing people will vary from one organization to the other and be dependent upon the organizational context; and the assumption of unitarism, i.e. working together for common goals. The 'hard' tag comes partly from the fact that if

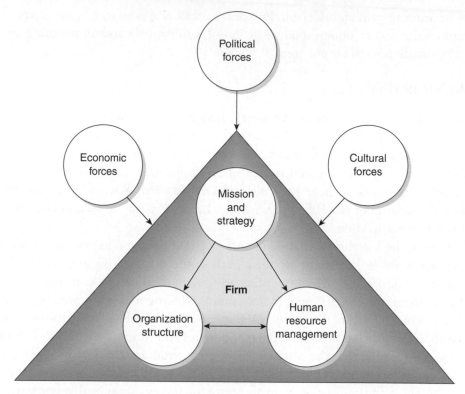

Figure 1.1 The matching model of HRM

Source: Fombrun et al. (1984).

the strategy required in a competitive environment denotes tight performance measures or cost-cutting, then these will be reflected in the approach adopted by HR. A differentiation or quality enhancement strategy, however, would result in an approach to HR that mirrors the high commitment approach of the 'soft' models.

Beer et al.'s Harvard framework depicted in Figure 1.2 can be seen as such a 'softer' model. It recognizes that there are a variety of 'stakeholders' in the organization. The model shows the legitimate interests of different groups, and assumes that the creation of HRM strategies will have to reflect these interests and fuse them as much as possible into the HR strategy and ultimately the business strategy. A key feature of the Harvard framework is its treatment of HRM as an entire system, with the various sub-elements of HRM combining to accomplish the stated outcomes, including high commitment. Although the link to organizational strategy is made, as well as being mediated by a recognition of differing interest groups as outlined above, the

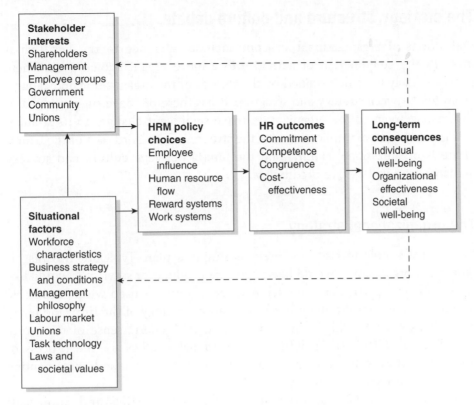

Figure 1.2 The map of the HRM territory

Source: Beer et al. (1984).

focus is also arguably more on *horizontal* alignment or integration as opposed to vertical (Marchington and Wilkinson 2012).

Guest (1989, 1997) discusses six key components including an HR strategy, a set of HR policies, a set of HR outcomes, behavioural outcomes, performance outcomes and financial outcomes. Guest acknowledges that the context in which HR operates may have a significant impact upon the effectiveness of HR.

There is a range of other prominent models (such as the Warwick Model of HRM) which is not addressed within this chapter. Ulrich's Business Partner model is explored in Chapter 4.

All of these models have one thing in common – they are trying to provide a useful conceptual model to address how HR operates in relation to the salient issues with which it interacts. All of these models provide useful additions to the formulation of key questions that we have to ask when understanding what the HR function is, what it does and how we can evaluate the HR function's contribution (within its particular context).

The strategy, structure and culture debate

Definitions of organizational *structure* include reference to the fact that it involves the coordination of activities to achieve organizational goals. These goals are likely to be determined by the *strategy* of the organization, indicating a clear link between strategy and structure. It has therefore been suggested that if the management of the organization make significant changes to its strategy, this is likely to have implications for the structure. The third part of the triumvirate is organizational *culture*, and the link(s) between culture and strategy and structure will be explored below.

The organizational strategy

In its most simple format, a strategy is simply a plan. Typically, this plan is where the organization would like to go (the products or services it would like to provide in a particular context). A range of terms is used within academic literature – corporate strategy, business strategy, strategy of the firm, and many more. This chapter will consider strategy in the generic sense of the word. French et al. (2011: 667) define organizational strategy as 'the process of positioning the organization in its competitive environment and implementing actions to compete successfully'.

Robbins et al. (2010: 442) make reference to Miles and Snow and other authors on strategic types. A typical approach is to categorize firms as to whether they primarily have an innovation, cost minimization or imitation strategy and then suggest suitable structural types to match (see Table 1.1).

An innovation strategy focuses on exploring new opportunities and creating new products or services. A cost minimization strategy seeks to tightly control costs and keep prices low. Organizations taking an imitation strategy

Table 1.1 The relationship between strategy and structure

Strategy	Suggested structure
Innovation	Organic, loose structure: decentralized, low specialization, low formalization
Cost minimization	Mechanistic, tight control: centralized, high work specialization, high formalization
Imitation	Mechanistic and organic, mix of loose and tight properties: tight control over established activities, looser controls over new undertakings

Source: Adapted from Robbins et al. (2010: 443).

fall somewhere in between these two. They move into new products or markets only after the innovator firms have proved them to be viable.

To support the strategy, an organization will usually have strategic objectives set out in order to assist it to achieve its overall plan. These objectives should be definable and measurable in order to ascertain later on whether they have been met. For an explanation of various strategic models and approaches, see Chapters 2 and 3.

A strategy by itself is not enough and therefore needs to be supported by a range of activities that may include the following: vision, mission, strategic plans, goals/objectives, and taken in the context of organizational culture, as demonstrated in case study 1.2.

CASE STUDY 1.2

SPECTRE (Special Executive for Counter-intelligence, Terrorism, Revenge and Extortion*)

Vision:	Global domination
Mission:	To eliminate all opposition forever
Strategy:	To reduce, and then eliminate all opposition by 2020
Goals/objectives:	To reduce and exterminate Western opposition completely by 2017, Eastern opposition by 2019 and eliminate the rest of the world opposition by 2020.
Values and culture:	Values based on power and domination. Extreme adoption of the Deal and Kennedy (1982) 'Work hard/play hard' culture, with the mantra of 'Failure is not an option'.

*Loosely based upon Ian Fleming's fictional global terrorist organization

 Questions

1. If you were an agent of SPECTRE, to what extent would the strategy, vision, mission, goals and culture assist you in your day-to-day work?
2. Both with regards to SPECTRE and any organization, what happens when employees' views don't necessarily reflect what the organization states as its strategy, vision, mission, goals and culture?

Organizational structure

Mintzberg (1979: 2) provides a useful definition: 'The structure of an organization can be defined simply as the sum total of the ways in which it divides its labour into distinct tasks and then achieves coordination among them.'

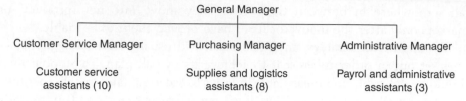

Figure 1.3 Functional structure
Source: author.

Similarly, Buchanan and Huczynski (2010: 453) define structure as 'The formal system of task and reporting relationships that control, co-ordinate and motivate employees to work together to achieve organizational goals.'

Traditional forms of structure

Organizational charts typically provide an indication of the organizational structure, demonstrating the various formal relationships and reporting patterns within an organization. One of the more popular forms is the functional structure (see Figure 1.3).

There are numerous other organizational designs, such as product/service, matrix, geographical or, possibly, combinations of these.

See Figure 1.4 for an example of a basic matrix structure.

A more complex design may incorporate both a geographical and functional design (see Figure 1.5).

While the design of the organizational structure is important, formal reporting structures are required, based upon job roles, span of control, authority and

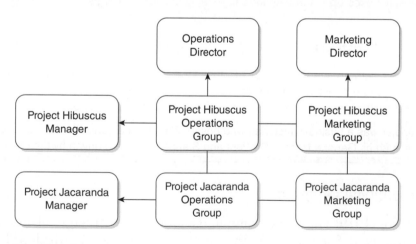

Figure 1.4 Matrix structure
Source: author.

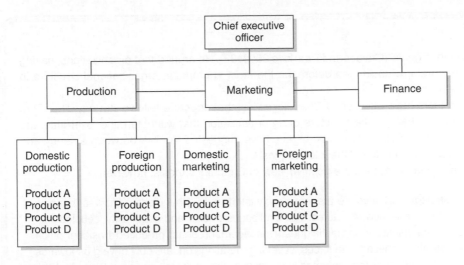

Figure 1.5 A complex structure
Source: Hodgetts and Luthans (1997).

responsibility. The degree to which managerial control exists may be based upon the employment contract, job descriptions, HR policies and procedures etc.

Mintzberg (1980) extends thinking beyond structural aspects by considering work constellations, flow of informal communication, flow of formal authority, flow of regulated activity, and the flow of an ad hoc decision process (see Mintzberg 1980). The usefulness of Mintzberg's model is found when applied beyond the simplistic formal/informal structure argument.

CASE STUDY 1.3

Alfred Chandler

Chandler was a business historian who observed that the organizational structures of organizations such as General Motors, Du Pont and Standard Oil were driven by the changing demands and pressures of the marketplace. This saw moves from rigid functional organizational forms to more loosely coupled divisional structures and Chandler was influential in the decentralization of companies in the 1960s and 1970s.

Chandler defined strategy as 'the determination of the long-term goals and objectives of an enterprise and the adoption of courses of action and the allocation of resources necessary for

(Continued)

(Continued)

carrying out those goals' (Crainer and Dearlove 2003: 32). He argued that organizations, having identified their strategy, could then determine the most appropriate organizational structure in order to achieve this.

Various authors have questioned Chandler's view that structure follows strategy. Thus Tom Peters has argued that it is the structure of an organization that will determine, over time, the choice of markets it chooses to attack. Others have suggested the link between strategy and structure is more complex than Chandler suggests.

Gary Hamel has offered a more positive view of Chandler's thesis, however:

Of course, strategy and structure are inextricably intertwined. Chandler's point was that new challenges give rise to new structures. The challenges of size and complexity, coupled with advances in communications and techniques of management control, produced divisionalization and decentralization. These same forces, several generations on, are now driving us towards new structural solutions – the federated organization, the multi-company coalition, and the virtual company. Few historians are prescient. Chandler was. (Crainer and Dearlove 2003: 32)

Source: author.

 Question

1. To what extent is looking for the 'ideal' organizational structure a waste of time? Is it possible to have several suitable structural designs?

PIT STOP: REFLECTIVE ACTIVITY 1.2

The debate about whether strategy precedes structure (or vice-versa) has been in existence for over half a century. Perhaps this is analogous to the chicken and egg debate, and may prove to be a rather futile discussion. However, consider the extent to which an organization decides its strategy from its internal capability (the resources that it has in order to achieve goals), or the extent to which it scans the external environment, then marries up the internal requirements in order to meet this. It could be argued that an internally driven organization is contingent upon structural configurations, while an externally driven organization is contingent upon strategic planning.

Argue the case for:

1. Strategy preceding structure.
2. Structure preceding strategy.

Modern forms of structure

The continuum of organizational structures depicted by Morgan (1989) raises questions as to what constitutes 'the organization' or where an organization begins or ends. The combination of outsourcing and subcontracting of activities with new electronic communication methods (information communication technologies or ICTs) gives rise to the possibility of organizations with very little in terms of physical presence and has also given rise to the term 'the virtual organization'.

Writers such as Castells (2001) explore these trends, suggesting a 'new economy' in tandem with new technologies has important implications for the structuring of organizations. He characterizes the new economy as being knowledge-based, global and networked and suggests that organizations too are affected by similar trends. Networked organizations will be decentralized and make use of subcontractors, freelancers and a variety of other flexible and non-standard types of workers. In any particular such organization, a worker will be connected to the network of that specific organization, but is also likely to be part of other networks and other organizations (based on Castells 2001; Mullins 2010).

Storey (2009: 90) argues that in recent years many organizations have been seeking a greater degree of agility and flexibility, which has resulted in a greater reliance on market and market-like forms and the mechanisms in which work activities and contributions are brought together and coordinated becoming looser and more variegated. He suggests that alternatives to the classic form of organization are still emerging and points to the process-oriented company, network organization, joint ventures and strategic alliances, the boundaryless organization and the virtual organization.

In terms of the possible implications for human resource management of such developments a positive picture can be painted, in that many of the resulting challenges of such trends will require a greater degree of strategic thinking about human resource issues. As a counter argument, such structural developments could be seen as running counter to a strategic approach to human resource management, given the flexible nature of employment relationships and the primacy of short-term financial goals.

In 1982, Peters and Waterman utilized the McKinsey model in order to demonstrate the components that make organizations successful. Seven aspects (the seven S's) were highlighted: strategy, structure, staff (employees), shared values (primarily organizational culture), systems, skills and style (primarily leadership). Within this model, shared values were central, highlighting the importance of culture to business success.

Organizational culture

Within an organization, what drives employees to work in particular ways, make certain types of decisions, maintain working relationships etc.? The norms (or standards of behaviour) within organizations determine to some extent what is permissible in terms of behaviours and attitudes within organizations. (See Chapter 11 for an in-depth explanation of organizational culture.) For the purposes of this chapter, organizational culture will be considered simply as 'how things are done' and to some extent 'why things are done' in a particular organization.

When visiting an organization known for its traditional and professional client relationships, based in the exclusive area of Mayfair in London, you may expect to see employees wearing expensive suits, well-groomed and attentive in their appearance. However, when you visit, you come across staff wearing jeans and T-shirts. When it is explained that there is a 'dress down Fridays' code, it becomes apparent why employees have dressed in this manner. The impact of organizational culture cannot be underestimated. However, more importantly, what role does HR play in dealing with strategy, structure and culture?

Understanding the eternal triangle

It could be argued that HR needs to play a critical role in decisions made around organizational direction, organizational design, organizational policies, procedure and practices, and importantly, shaping and developing organizational culture (through a range of methods, including human resource development, management development etc.). The authors argue that HR should undertake a strategic role in managing the relationship between these three vital aspects (see Figure 1.6).

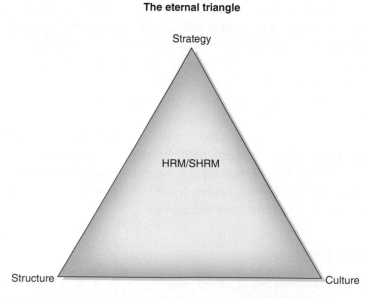

Figure 1.6 The relationship between strategy, structure, culture and HR
Source: author.

Part of the difficulty in applying Figure 1.6 to practice is due to the complexity and involvement of the HR function and HR-related activities and whether decisions are driven from within or responding to external forces. The HR function can adopt a 'business' (strategic) type approach where the focus is primarily external, and resources are utilized, bought in where necessary, and the overall aim is driven by commercial reasoning. Alternatively, the HR function can utilize internal resources and make decisions on strategy based purely upon internal capability, not looking outside for additional resources (perhaps more of a HR-level response).

The environment

While an organization will have its own environment in terms of buildings and facilities, to what extent is there a clear organizational boundary? With increasingly complex technologies it could be argued that organizational boundaries are not always clear. Every organization has to interface with some aspect of customer, supplier, etc.

Within this chapter, the industry context includes the arena in which an organization operates within a competitive or supply capacity. Some organizations may trade locally (within a few kilometres) in terms of suppliers and customers, while other organizations may trade around the world and have supply chains from many countries, operating at a national and local level in many countries. In relation to Figure 1.7, the environment considers both the global/international context and the industry context.

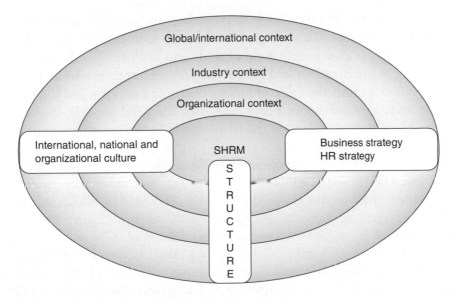

Figure 1.7 SHRM, the organization and its environment
Source: author.

The organization and environment fit: structural emphasis

Various studies have shown a link between the structure and management of an organization and the external environment within which the firm operates, specifically in relation to the degree of uncertainty and change in the environment.

Burns and Stalker (1961) studied a number of UK firms in different industries and their settings. They characterized these settings or environments into five types, ranging from stable to unpredictable. Two main types of structure and management practice were also identified: the mechanistic and the organic. The mechanistic structure was one with a high degree of task specialization and formalization, tight specification of individual responsibility and authority, centralized decision-making and formal rules and procedures. It can be likened to Weber's bureaucratic structure. The organic structure possessed little task specialization, a low degree of formalization, delegated decision-making and a high degree of individual responsibility.

Neither form of organizational structure was viewed as being better than the other; what was suggested is that either could be the most appropriate and efficient depending on the circumstances. Thus in their study, for a textile mill facing a stable and predictable environment, the mechanistic structure was found to be most suitable, while for an electronics firm operating in an unpredictable and rapidly changing environment, the organic structure suited best.

Linking HR to organizational strategy

The subject matter of this book is strategic human resource management or, to put it another way, the strategic management of human resources. This is examined both as an academic field of study and as an applied discipline that takes place in organizations and that managers attempt to implement. Storey (2009) points to both the value of linking theory and practice and the relative lack of such connectivity in reality and thus the need for this application. Legge (2005) also reminds us of the frequent gap between rhetoric and reality when it comes to HRM.

Defining strategic human resource management (SHRM) is not straightforward. Just as there are a number of competing definitions of human resource management itself, so this is also the case with SHRM. As Collings and Wood (2009: 1) point out: 'since its emergence HRM has been dogged by the still largely unresolved ambiguity surrounding its definition'. (These issues will be further explored in Chapter 3.) Broadly speaking, however, SHRM can be viewed as being about attempts to link HR practice to an explicit HR strategy, which is in turn linked to the strategy of the organization. As Greer (1995) suggests, HR strategies focus on the alignment of the organization's HR practices, policies and programmes with corporate and strategic business unit plans.

An example may serve to both illustrate this conceptual link and question the extent of its application in practice.

Consider an organization's recruitment and selection (R&S). Assuming that this approach was not solely ad hoc and that the organization in question purported to some sort of good practice in this area, then traditionally the approach adopted would be a systematic and psychometric one based around person–job fit, i.e. predicting the best candidate(s) based on predicted subsequent job performance.

A *strategic* approach, however, would consider how best human resource practices, in this case R&S, could best support the particular organizational strategy, for example in response to particular environmental pressures to maintain leading edge competitive positions (Sparrow and Pettigrew 1988). Millmore et al. (2007) point to research by Bowen et al. (1991) showing examples where R&S is directed at organizational and not specific job requirements, while Beaumont and Hunter (1992) found examples of R&S being used strategically to engender the more flexible workforce that the organizational strategy required.

Kew and Stredwick (2010) first set out a two-way model of the relationship between the environment and HR. One way of analysing the external environment is by the use of a political, economic, sociological and technical (PEST) or political, economic, sociological and technical, legal and environmental (PESTLE) analysis. Each categorization – political, economic, social or technological – and changes in these will influence HR. Examples would be changes in the law, or economic fluctuations. We are also reminded that the arrow is two-way, in that HR will also attempt to exert some influence on the environment. An example of this would be the professional body, the Chartered Institute of Personnel and Development (CIPD), attempting to influence government policy of proposed changes in employment law. This is illustrated in Figure 1.8.

Figure 1.8 The relationship between the environment and HR
Source: Kew and Stredwick (2010).

In addition to this relationship to the external environment, rather than HR practices being ad hoc and purely focused on day-to-day problem-solving, SHRM attempts to relate what the HR function does to an explicit HR strategy (Figure 1.9).

Figure 1.9 HR practice and HR strategy
Source: Kew and Stredwick (2010).

Figure 1.10 HR strategy and organizational strategy
Source: author.

The next stage is to relate the HR strategy to the overall organizational strategy, as depicted in Figure 1.10. In this, HR strategy is integrated into the organization's overall strategy.

Torrington et al. (2005) provide a useful diagrammatic representation of the potential relationships between organizational strategy and HR strategy, ranging from separation, in which the activities of HR are removed from that of the organizational strategy, if such a thing exists at all, through to increased levels of fit or integration, as shown in Figure 1.11.

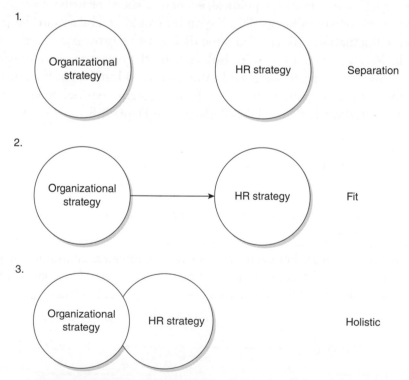

Figure 1.11 Different levels of integration between HR strategy and organizational strategy
Source: Adapted from Torrington et al. (2005).

The second example, that of fit, mirrors that of the Matching model (see Figure 1.1) in which recognition is given to the importance of human resources in achieving the organizational strategy. However, the direction of influence is rather one way, with HR responding to organizational strategic imperatives as determined by the market. This approach depends on a traditional classical approach to strategy formulation as a logical, top-down process. Of course the directional arrow could be matched by a dotted arrow the other way, with HR having at least some input into strategic decisions at board level.

The third example, that of a holistic model, views people as a key resource for the achievement of competitive advantage rather than just something downstream of organizational strategy. Human resource strategy then becomes of prime importance, particularly in situations where it is recognized that people (employees) form the key resource for a particular organization. Such thinking can be found in the work of Boxall (1996, 1998) and the idea of the resource-based firm, with such conceptions of strategy being broader than merely reflecting positioning in the marketplace.

As Millmore et al. (2007) point out, the latter part of the twentieth century saw a burgeoning interest in strategic management, concerned with how organizations could best utilize their resources strategically in pursuit of organizational goals. As such it is not surprising that the focus also fell on what is sometimes termed by some to be an organization's key resource, their employees. Arguably, however, this focus is still somewhat limited, with even today little direct reference being made in the mainstream strategic management literature to human resources and which has seen the literature on strategic human resource management being somewhat separate, if parallel, to that of strategy in general. This may reflect the HR function's ongoing battle to be considered as truly central to organizational success.

Farnham (2010), however, questions the assumption that historically business strategies simply defined the nature of competition in the marketplace, leaving personnel management/HR's input to be operational and pragmatic. Thomason (1991) argues that the resourcing and utilization of human resources in organizations have been approached in a variety of ways at different times. He argues that at each stage in the development of HRM some relationship did exist between the business strategies adopted and HR's responses to the external labour market, even if the link between the HR strategy and business strategy was not always made explicit.

Farnham (2010) argues that organizations need overall strategies to survive and prosper in a competitive environment. For firms in the private sector, such organizational strategies are likely to be couched in terms of how best to tackle their competitors. The strategies of public sector organizations currently are more likely to be expressed in terms of maximizing revenues and reducing costs at a time of cuts in government spending. However, for any organization, the strategy adopted will not just be a result of taking into account the opportunities and threats offered by the external environment in general, and the marketplace specifically; it will also be an outcome of the strengths and weaknesses of the organization's own resources, including human resources.

Porter (1998) suggests that organizations have three basic strategic options in order to gain competitive advantage: cost reduction, quality enhancement, and innovation. Yet as Porter (1998) points out, competitive advantage depends not only on conditions in product or service markets but also on the availability of factors of production. Thomason (1991) suggests a number of shifts in predominant business strategy over time since the Industrial Revolution, each placing different demands on HR in terms of labour acquisition and utilization. Returning to Porter's classification, an organizational strategy of differentiation (quality enhancement), for example, will depend on the availability of a core of skilled workforce in the labour market. In periods where skills are job-specific and non-transferrable between organizations and industries, then internal labour markets will be developed. Other conceptions of strategy, such as the resource-based view, place much greater importance on internal factors of the organization, including human resources.

This chapter has considered the nature of organizations in terms of strategy, structure and culture and the relative placement of HR within these, extending to the place of strategic HRM too. Figure 1.7 demonstrates the complex interrelationships between the key factors discussed within this chapter.

PIT STOP: REFLECTIVE ACTIVITY 1.3

1. To what extent is there a difference between HRM and Strategic HRM (SHRM)? What are the critical differentiating points between HRM and SHRM? Discuss.

CASE STUDY 1.4

Low-Cost Airlines

Southwest Airlines, based in Dallas, Texas, the largest airline in the United States based on domestic passengers carried, can be seen as one of the first low-cost airlines and providing a business model for others such as easyJet and Ryanair. Their competitive strategy combines high employee and aircraft productivity with low costs resulting from reducing aircraft turnaround time.

Michael Porter (2011) contrasts this strategy with that of full-service airlines. These are based around the aim of getting passengers from almost any point to another, reaching numerous destinations and providing connecting flights via a hub-and-spoke system centred on major airports. They provide a full range of service, including first and business class. And, to accommodate passengers who want to change planes, they coordinate the timetables and offer check-in and transfer of luggage. They also provide full-service meals.

In contrast, Southwest Airlines concentrate on short-haul, low-cost, point-to-point service between medium-sized cities and secondary airports in large cities. They offer frequent departures and low fares and tailor their activities around this. They do not offer meals, assigned seats, interline baggage checking or premium classes of service. Automated ticketing at the gate allows the airline to avoid the commission charged by travel agents. Fast turnaround of aircraft of only 15 minutes makes the most economical use of aircraft and their planes flying longer and providing more frequent departures than rivals, again reducing costs. A modern fleet of standardized aircraft also boosts the efficiency of maintenance.

Source: Adapted from O'Reilly (2001).

 ■ Questions

1. Within the context of cost-cutting, what could motivate employees working for low-cost airlines, such as those described above?
2. How would these airlines formulate a strategic HR approach?

Globalization and internationalization

Chapter 12 provides a detailed explanation as to how HRM and SHRM adjusts to global and international contexts. While organizations may wish for a one size fits all HR toolbox, this may not be particularly appropriate in some contexts. Similarly, HR policies, procedure and practices may vary significantly across countries and within multinational organizations.

CASE STUDY 1.5

Oracle

In Europe, the Middle East and Africa, Oracle has 14,000 employees in 32 countries, whose needs are met by an HR department of around 140 people. For the past four years, the HR department has been devolving certain HR functions to the line, using its own Oracle HR system.

'We started with pay slips on the Web, instead of having hard copy pay slips,' says Vance Kearney, European HR director. 'Then we enabled employees to access and update their own data, and since then we have introduced more and more Internet-based processes.' The full range of HR activities now available on the Internet includes:

(Continued)

(Continued)

- employee data
- pay slips
- salary reviews
- flexible benefits
- management of purchasing of products and services bought from internal departments of the company.

'It has given us far more flexibility,' says Kearney. 'And it has ended the linear relationship between the number of people in the HR department and the number of people in the organization as a whole. We could probably increase overall staffing levels by 50 per cent without adding more HR people.'

To work effectively, stresses Kearney, a devolved HR system needs to be thought through in detail before implementation starts. It will need to be updated and added to over the years, but getting the system right in the first instance is essential if the organic process is to work properly.

'You need to work out what needs to be different and what needs to be standardized,' he warns:

It doesn't make sense to have 32 different systems to do one thing. But there will be a slight difference in the way that things are done in each country. For instance, when we started, we had 32 different telephone systems in operation, and now we have one global system. That is a process that can be standardized.

Other functions need more careful handling as well. Kearney cites the example of updating records – a simple process in the UK, but in Switzerland, where citizens are taxed according to the canton in which they live, the line manager must inform the tax authorities if an employee has moved from one canton to another.

As far as the role of HR is concerned, Kearney says staff at all levels have benefited. 'Admin staff have been trained in dealing with people, rather than keyboards – they come in when there are specific problems to be dealt with,' he says:

Before this system was set up, we couldn't answer a simple question like 'What is the staff turnover across the company?' because each country had a different way of deciding what this meant. It only took one computer to blow up in Kazakhstan for the whole thing to be out. Now we have one system which works across the world.

Source: Adapted from O'Reilly (2001).

 ■ **Questions**

1. To what extent does standardization of processes devalue the way in which employees work within their local environment and organizational culture?
2. Can a 'one size fits all' apply to all of the functions that HR carries out? If not, why not?

Conclusion

There may be little doubt that HR is facing huge challenges and will continue to do so. Some of the debates around organizational structure, culture and strategy may transcend traditional (US and UK) academic models. Perhaps the HR function needs to be 'more strategic', but where and exactly how HR adds value will depend upon demonstrating this added value at strategic, tactical and operational levels.

'The future workforce will be placed all over the world, with people from different cultural and economic backgrounds working together in virtual teams ... The future of HR lies outside the HR Department' (Lettink 2012). The PwC *Managing Tomorrow's People* report (2011) proposes that future people management will present one of the greatest challenges and that, as a consequence, the role of the HR function will have to undergo fundamental change.

Truss et al. (2012: 295) argue that 'we can be reasonably certain that in the foreseeable future organizations will continue to grapple with how best to manage their HR'.

The CIPD *Next Generation HR Report* (2010) argues that HR need to be insight driven, whereby HR have a deep understanding of what goes on inside the organization and what makes the organization successful, and in doing so, also have a real share and voice within organizations. For a discussion around the key debates surrounding the future of HR, see Chapter 13 in this volume.

■ Further Reading ■ ■ ■ ■ ■ ■ ■ ■ ■ ■ ■ ■

Boxall, P. and Purcell, J. (2011) *Strategy and Human Resource Management*. Basingstoke: Palgrave Macmillan.
Daft, R. (2012) *Organizational Theory and Design*, 11th edn. Andover: Cengage Learning.
Keegan, A. and Francis, H. (2006) 'The changing face of HR: in search of balance', *Human Resource Management Journal*, 16 (3): 231–49.

References

Ashkenas, R., Ulrich, D., Jick, T. and Kerr, S. (1995) *The Boundaryless Organization*. San Francisco, CA: Jossey-Bass.
Beaumont, P.B. and Hunter, L.C. (1992) 'Organisational change and HRM: a longitudinal case study', *Management Research News*, 15 (5/6): 23.
Beer, M., Spector, B., Lawrence, P.R., Quinn Mills, D. and Walton, R.E. (1984) *Managing Human Assets*. New York: Free Press.
Bowen, D.E., Ledford, G.E. and Nathan, B.R. (1991) 'Hiring for the organization, not the job', *Academy of Management Executive*, 5 (4): 35–51.

Boxall, P. (1996) 'The strategic HRM debate and the resource-based view of the firm', *Human Resource Management Journal*, 6 (3): 59–75.

Boxall, P. (1998) 'Achieving competitive advantage through human resource strategy: towards a theory of industry dynamics', *Human Resource Management Review*, 8 (3): 265–88.

Boxall, P. and Purcell, J. (2003) *Strategy and Human Resource Management*. Basingstoke: Palgrave-Macmillan.

Buchanan, D.A. and Huczynski, A.A. (2010) *Organizational Behaviour*, 7th edn. Harlow: Pearson Education.

Burns, T. and Stalker, G.M. (1961) *The Management of Innovation*. London: Tavistock Publications.

Castells, M. (2001) *The Internet Galaxy*. Oxford: Oxford University Press.

CIPD (2012) *Next Generation Report*, available at http://www.cipd.co.uk/research/_next-gen-hr/, accessed 5 June 2013.

Collings, G.D. and Wood, G. (2009) *Human Resource Management: A Critical Approach*. Abingdon: Routledge.

Crainer, S. and Dearlove, D. (2003) *The Ultimate Business Guru Book*. Oxford: Capstone Publishing.

Deal, T.E. and Kennedy, A.A. (1982) *Organization Cultures: The Rites and Rituals of Organizational Life*. Reading, MA: Addison Wesley.

Farnham, D. (2010) *Human Resource Management in Context: Strategy, Insights and Solutions*. London: CIPD.

Fombrun, C.J., Tichy, N.M. and Devanna, M.A. (eds) (1984) *Strategic Human Resource Management*. New York: Wiley.

Francesco, A.M. and Gold, B.A. (2005) *International Organizational Behaviour*, 2nd edn. Harlow: Pearson.

French, R., Rayner, C., Rees, G. and Rumbles, S. (2011) *Organisational Behaviour*, 2nd edn. Chichester: Wiley.

Greer, C.R. (1995) *Strategy and Human Resources*. Englewood Cliffs, NJ: Prentice-Hall.

Guest, D.E. (1989) 'HRM: implications for industrial relations', in J. Storey (ed.), *New Perspectives on Human Resource Management*. London: Routledge. pp. 41–55.

Guest, D.E. (1997) 'Human resource management and performance: a review and research agenda', *International Journal of Human Resource Management*, 8 (3): 263–76.

Hodgett, R. and Luthans, F. (1997) *International Management*, New York: McGraw Hill Companies Inc.

Kew, J. and Stredwick, J. (2010) *Human Resource Management in a Business Context*. London: CIPD.

Legge, K. (2005) *Human Resource Management; Rhetorics and Realities*. Basingstoke: Palgrave Macmillan.

Lettink, A. (2012) *What is the future of HR?*, available at http://www.xperthr.co.uk/blogs/employment-intelligence/2012/02/anita-lettink-what-is-the-futu.html, accessed 5 June 2013.

Marchington, M. and Wilkinson, A. (2012) *Human Resource Management at Work*. London: CIPD.

Millmore, M., Lewis, P., Saunders, M., Thornhill, A. and Morrow, T. (2007) *Strategic Human Resource Management: Contemporary Issues*. Harlow: Pearson Education.

Mintzberg, H. (1979) *The Structuring of Organizations*. London: Prentice-Hall.

Mintzberg, H. (1980) 'Structure in 5's: a synthesis of the research on organization design', *Management Science*, 6 (3): 322–41.

Morgan, G. (1989) *Creative Organization Theory*. London: Sage.

Mullins, L.J. (2010) *Management and Organisational Behaviour*, 9th edn. Harlow: Pearson Education.

O'Reilly, S. (2001) 'Hand it all over', *Global HR*, 1 June. Available at http://www.xperthr.
co.uk/article/16810/hand-it-all-over.aspx?searchwords=In+Europe%2c+the+Middle+Ea
st+and+Africa%2c+Oracle+has+14%2c000+employees+in+32+countries%2c+whose+
needs+are+met+by+an+HR+department+of+around+140+people, accessed 29 August
2013.

Peters, T.J. and Waterman, R.H. (1982) *In Search of Excellence*. New York: Harper & Row.

Porter, M. (1998) *Competitive Advantage: Creating and Sustaining Superior Performance*.
New York: Free Press.

Porter, M. (2011) 'What is strategy?', In *HBR's 10 Must Reads*. Boston, MA: Harvard
Review Press, pp. 1–76.

PwC (2011) Managing Tomorrow's People: The Future of Work 2020. Available at http://
www.google.co.uk/url?sa=t&rct=j&q=&esrc=s&source=web&cd=1&ved=0CC0QFjAA&u
rl=http%3A%2F%2Fwww.pwc.com%2Fgx%2Fen%2Fmanaging-tomorrows-
people%2Ffuture-of-work%2Fpdf%2Fmtp-future-of-work.pdf&ei=tjQfUsfnFcWQ0AX8k
4DwAQ&usg=AFQjCNGZnTzw7NFqIRBbCoYBVE_ZHobMIw&sig2=KFEjjvnt1lgPYO7v
I3lh6A, accessed 29 August 2013.

Robbins, S.P., Judge, T.A. and Campbell, T.T. (2010) *Organizational Behaviour*, 14th edn.
Harlow: Pearson Education.

Sparrow, P.R. and Pettigrew, A.M. (1988) 'Strategic human resource management in the
UK computer supplier industry', *Journal of Occupational Psychology*, 61: 25–42.

Storey, J. (ed.) (1995) *Human Resource Management: a Critical Text*. London: Routledge.

Storey, J. (2009) 'New organizational structures and forms', in J. Storey, P. M. Wright and D.
Ulrich (eds), *The Routledge Companion to Strategic Human Resource Management*.
Abingdon: Routledge, pp. 90–105.

Thomason, G. (1991) 'The management of personnel', *Personnel Review*, 20 (2): 3–10.

Torrington, D., Hall, L. and Taylor, S. (2005) *Human Resource Management*. Harlow:
Pearson Education.

Townsend, R. (1970) *Up the Organization: How to Stop the Corporation from Stifling
People and Strangling Profits*. Greenwich, CT: Fawcett.

Truss, C., Mankin, D. and Kelliher, C. (2012) *Strategic Human Resource Management*.
Oxford: Oxford University Press.

Welfare, S. (2006) *A Whole World out There: Managing HR*. Available at http://www.
xperthr.co.uk/article/72688/a-whole-world-out-there--managing-global-hr.
aspx?searchwords=welfare+oxfam, accessed 4 June 2013.

2

STRATEGIC APPROACHES

Paola Pisano, Alison Rieple
and Marco Pironti

Chapter Overview

Defining the concept of strategy is both challenging and complicated at the same time. From the strategy definition depend the fundamental decisions about the future direction of an organization: its purpose, its resources and how it interacts with the environment in which it operates. Every aspect of the organization plays a role in this strategy: people, finance, production method, environment, customers, and so on. Moreover, changes in markets, regulations, technology, customers, competition and other factors mean that strategy formulation and implementation is an ongoing process that can be judged only from a historical perspective in the context of the organization's past events, resources and experience. In this chapter we would like to analyse the new trend of modern strategies. Starting from the meaning of strategy and its definition, the authors will introduce the general formulation and implementation of strategies within the organization and the new framework that the organization has to consider to manage national and global strategies. As the ultimate objective of every strategy is to increase the profit inside the organization, an analysis of the type of resources, objectives and activities the organization has to consider and exploit in order to achieve the best result is provided.

Learning Objectives

- **Explore the concepts of strategy and its core areas**
- **Examine the different types of corporate strategy**
- **Examine the different types of business strategy**
- **Define the role of HR in strategic management**

Subway world franchise

In 1965 17-year-old Fred DeLuca opened his first sandwich store in Bridgeport, Connecticut, on the suggestion of family friend Dr Peter Buck and a loan from him of US$ 1,000. It was called 'Pete's Super Submarines'. Fred himself ran the store and drove regularly to market to buy fresh vegetables and meat, obtaining the right quality at the right prices. A second store followed after one year and a third in 1967. This was in a more visible location and really a 'restaurant'.

For the next few years, the store/restaurant experimented with different approaches to the product range, marketing, purchase of fresh produce and in-store production. The company name was changed to 'Subway' and adopted a yellow logo. The founders developed a business formula for their restaurant:

- Low capital costs, around US$ 80–120,000
- Around 6–8 employees per store
- Clean and simple design with strong logo – name changed to 'Subway'
- Clear and simple in-store pricing and product presentation – hygiene factors and training are important to ensure that all food is fresh and clean.

This was the basis of the Subway franchise first offered in 1974. Over the next 30 years, Subway grew its operations mainly through franchising. It began to experiment with different locations: it found that its franchise could be operated in smaller and more specialist outlets – such as schools and factories – because of its smaller-scale business formula.

The strategic problem for Subway in North America was that sales growth was beginning to slow in the mid-1990s. To tackle this Fred DeLuca went back to his customers: he learned that an increasing number came to Subway because it offered a low-fat alternative to others' fast food. Using this, the company boosted its sales significantly. In 2000 the company decided to attract customers who wanted a full-calorie meal: by 2004, Subway had around 20,000 outlets in the USA and Canada.

The company opened its first franchise operation outside North America in 1984, and by 2004 it had opened 2,000 outlets in 75 countries.

Source: Adapted from Lynch (2006).

 ■ **Questions**

1. What are the important characteristics of Subway's strategy?
2. What makes the development of Subway's strategy both prescriptive and emergent?
3. Do you think that it's possible to mix two different types of strategy?

Introduction: Strategy in the twenty-first century

The last 20 years have witnessed further environmental developments that have had considerable effects on strategy (see Chapter 1). Free market competition has been one element in supporting and encouraging growth in many newly developing countries. The lower labour costs and greater wealth in countries such as China and India have put pressure on Western and Japanese companies to cut costs or move to those countries. In addition to economic growth, the world marketplace has become more complex in cultural and social terms: markets have become more international (Chapters 11 and 12), thus making it necessary to balance global interests and local demand variations. Furthermore, the rapid development of technology and new forms of communication have revolutionized strategy. The big change in the business environment has coincided with the higher level of training and deeper skill levels of employees (see Chapter 10) on one side and the higher capability and knowledge of the customers on the other side. The previous two forces (employees and customers) have increased the level of competition, developing more innovation into the market.

Tough revolutions in the external environment impact on the organization's strategy, which changes as the environment surrounding the organization changes: this in turn alters the way the organization's strategy is created and developed.

Corporate strategy and business-level strategy

Corporate strategy defines the scope of the firm in terms of the industries and markets in which it competes. A list of corporate strategy decisions could include investment in diversification, vertical integration, acquisition, new ventures, allocation of resources, etc. Corporate strategy is the responsibility of both the top management team and the corporate strategy staff.

> Corporate strategy is the pattern of major objectives, purposes or goals and essential policies or plans for achieving those goals, stated in such a way as to define what business the company is in or is to be in and the kind of company it is or is to be. (Andrews 1971: 28)

Corporate strategy is not a cohesive subject, but a different vision of corporate strategy has been developed because of its breadth and complexity. Two main approaches can be summarized:

1. *The prescriptive approach:* some researchers and scholars have judged corporate strategy to be essentially a linear and rational process starting with where we are now and then developing new strategies for the future (see Jauch and Glueck 1988; Argenti 1965). A prescriptive corporate strategy is one whose objective has been defined in advance and whose main elements have been developed before the strategy commences.
2. *The emergent approach:* other scholars and commentators take the view that corporate strategy emerges, adapting to human needs and continuing

to develop over time. It is evolving, incremental and continuous and therefore cannot be usefully or easily summarized in a plan (Mintzberg 1987). An emergent corporate strategy is one whose final object is unclear and whose elements are developed during the course of its life as the strategy proceeds. Figure 2.1 shows the two contrasting models.

At the business level strategy is concerned with competing for customers, generating value from your resources and the underlying principle of achieving a sustainable competitive advantage over rival companies using those resources.

The common elements in a successful strategy can be assumed as follows:

1. Simple, consistent and long-term goals
2. Profound understanding of the competitive environment
3. Objective appraisal of resources
4. Effective implementation of the strategy (Grant 2008).

As shown in Figure 2.1, the firm embodies three of the previous elements: goals and values (simple, consistent, long-term goals), resources and capabilities (objective appraisal of the resources) and structure and systems (effective implementation). The industry environment (a profound understanding of the competitive environment) is defined as the firm's relationships with customers, competitors and suppliers. The task of the business strategy, which represents a link between the firm and its environment, is to determine how the firm will deploy its resources within its environment and how it will organize itself to reach its long-term objective. To be successful, a strategy must be consistent with the firm's external and internal environment, which includes goals and values, resources and capabilities, and structure and systems.

Figure 2.1 Grant's strategic vision
Source: Adapted from Grant (2008).

1. One of the main disputes in corporate strategy over the last 20 years concerns the difference between prescriptive and emergent forms of strategy process. What is your view? Which approach is better and why?
2. What do you think is important in developing a winning strategy?

The core areas of corporate strategy

The three core areas of corporate strategy are strategic analysis, strategic formulation and strategic implementation (see Figure 2.2).

1. *Strategic analysis.* The organization, its mission and objectives have to be analysed in order to provide value for the people involved in the organization – its stakeholders.
2. *Strategic formulation.* Strategy options have to be formulated and then selected. The formulation has to be done according to the particular skills of the organization and the special relationships that it has or can develop with those outside – supplier, customer, distributor and government.
3. *Strategic implementation.* The selected options now have to be implemented.

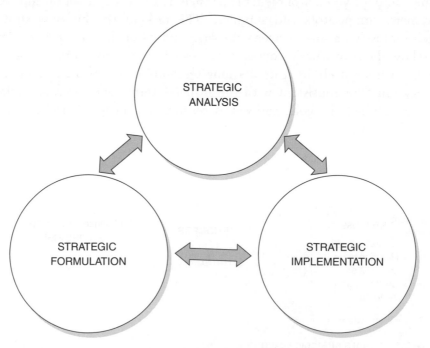

Figure 2.2 The core areas of corporate strategy
Source: author.

More research has shown that in most situations strategy is not simply a matter of taking a strategic decision and then implementing it; it takes a considerable time to make the decision itself and there is further delay before it comes into effect. There are two reasons for this: first, people are involved: managers, employees, suppliers and customers. Any of these may choose to apply their own business judgement to the chosen corporate strategy, influencing both the initial decision and the subsequent actions that will be implemented. Second, the environment may change radically as the strategy is being implemented. This will invalidate the chosen strategy and mean that the process of strategy development needs to start again.

For these reasons it's important to distinguish between context, content and process. While the context is the environment within which the strategy operates and is developed, the content consists of the main actions of the proposed strategy. Finally, the process is how to make actions link together or interact to each other.

As we can see in Figure 2.3, the intersection between context, content and process defines who affects the evaluation and who evaluates the strategy.

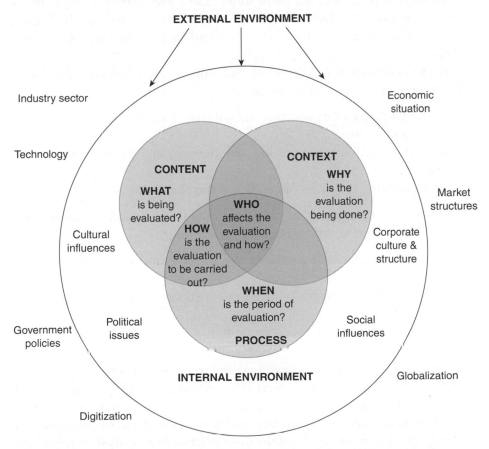

Figure 2.3 The content, context and process framework: internal and external environmental factors

Source: Adapted from Stockdale and Standing (2006: 1090–1102).

In most corporate strategy situations context and content are reasonably clear: it is the way in which strategy is developed and enacted – the process – that usually causes the most problems.

The process of strategic analysis

The two different approaches to the core areas of corporate strategy underline important details.

Strategic analysis, in both the prescriptive and emergent approach, can be divided into:

- *Identification of vision, mission and objectives*: developing or reviewing the strategic directions and the more specific objectives, e.g. the maximization of profit or return on capital or in some cases a social service. Some strategies place this third element before the other two, arguing that the organization should first set out the objectives and then analyse how to achieve them.
- *Analysis of the external environment*: examining what is happening or likely to happen outside the organization, or:
  - understanding factors affecting the industry, economy, communities and the environment
  - surveying participants regarding the purpose and performance of the organization
  - understanding the views of additional stakeholders.

- *Analysis of the internal environment*: exploring the skills and resources available besides those in the organization, which means:
  - surveying stakeholders regarding the purpose and performance of the organization
  - understanding the maturity of the organization in terms of deriving and supporting strategy
  - deriving an agreed purpose statement.

The analysis of the internal and external environment helps the organization to apply a SWOT analysis – Strengths, Weaknesses, Opportunities and Threats – an important tool used to define strengths and weaknesses internal to the organization and opportunities and threats external to the organization (see Chapter 1). Compiling the information from this analysis is useful for deriving the key strategic issues that the organization must address in order to satisfy the purpose statement over the following years.

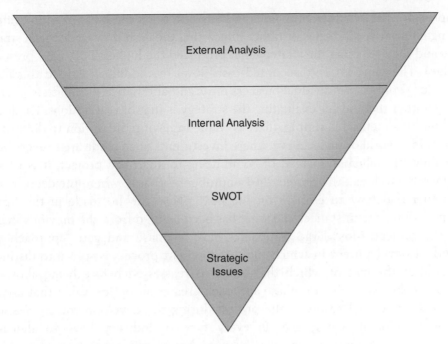

Figure 2.4 The process of strategic analysis
Source: author.

Strategy development and implementation

The prescriptive and emerging approaches clearly diverge in the development and implementation of strategy.

According to the prescriptive approach, once the objectives are set the next step is the formal consideration of the options available to achieve them. This is followed by selecting from those options according to identified criteria in order to arrive at the prescriptive strategy.

The emerging approach takes a much more experimental view of the strategy choice and its implementation. It seeks to learn by trial, experimentation and discussion as strategies are developed. There is no final agreed strategy, rather a series of experimental approaches that are considered by those involved and then developed further: strategy emerges during a process of crafting and testing. There is therefore no clear distinction in the emergent approach between the two stages of developing the strategy and its implementation: what is important is the strong link back to the earlier analytical phase, enabling the change in the environment and resources to be reflected quickly in the adaptive learning strategy.

When an organization needs to choose a strategy, the best approach would be to evaluate the strategy itself and then an alternative. The same approach used to value companies and business units can be applied to evaluating alternative strategies or rather forecasting the cash flow under each strategy and then selecting the strategy that produced the highest NPV (net present value). The same DCF (discounted cash flow) methodology is used to value individual projects, individual business units and alternative business strategies.

Another method for evaluating the strategy is that of real options. The idea behind this method is simple: there is value in having the option to do something. In a world of uncertainty, where investments once made are irreversible, flexibility is valuable. Instead of committing to an entire project, it is more favourable to break the project into a number of phases, where the decision of whether and how to embark on the next phase can be made in the light of prevailing circumstances and what has been learned from the previous stage of the project. Most large companies have a 'phase and gate' approach to product development in which the development process is split into distinct phases, at the end of which the project is reassessed before being allowed through the 'gate'. Such a phase approach creates an option value that arises from the potential to revise the project during the development process, or even abandon it. Companies in every type of industry have to allocate resources to competing opportunities; whether in existing businesses or new ventures they have to decide whether to invest at that moment, take preliminary steps reserving the right to invest in the future, or do nothing. Each of these choices creates a set of pay-offs linked to future choices.

This method is also used by venture capitalists to assess new business proposals when looking for the business's scalability, or rather the potential to scale up or replicate the business if it proves successful. Scalability is a source of option values. The adoption of real option valuations to evaluate investment projects and strategies has been limited by the complexity of the techniques for modelling uncertainty and the consideration of multiple scenarios in relation to the use of probability and/or the use of resources.

The core areas of business-level strategy

One of the classic questions that managers are supposed to ask themselves about their organization's strategy is 'Which business are we in?' The answer to this question – and to the related questions, 'How many businesses are we in, and how do they connect to one another?' – is what we term the organization's competitive stance. Companies cannot do everything: their value chains, cultures, architectures, and resources are not infinitely versatile, and will be more suited to one type of operation or market than another. This makes an organization's choices of competitive stance – which customers to serve and which products or services to offer them – the most fundamental of its strategic decisions (the term 'competitive stance' is our own, but forceful arguments for the importance of product and market selection in strategy can be found in Ohmae (1982) and Kim and Mauborgne (1999, 2004, 2005)).

In some cases, the starting point is an idea of how the value chain will be distinctive; the organization then works out which kinds of product and market will fit it. For example, Amazon, the world's leading Internet retailer, began in 1995 when its founder Jeff Bezos realized that the World Wide Web, then in its early days, presented commercial opportunities. He concluded that books, which people did not need to touch or see before they bought them, would be the ideal product to sell via the Internet, and would appeal to the affluent, educated people who were the early users of the Web. Later, Amazon was able to expand its product range to include CDs, electronic goods and a large range of other items, while the numbers of potential customers expanded as more people acquired Internet connections at work and at home.

Products and customer analysis

The concept of competitive stance also embraces decisions as to *how many* segments to serve and *how many* products to put on the market, and at a corporate level, how many businesses to be in. Should an organization concentrate on one product in one market, or spread itself more broadly across a number of different products, markets or even industries? There are clear attractions to being bigger, and more diverse. By offering a broader range of choices to its customers, an organization can make itself attractive to them. If it can make the different parts of the company work well together, then it may become a more formidable competitor in other ways as well: more efficient, and with a broader range of skills to call upon. Less obvious, however, are the very real risks that the sales from the new products or markets will not be profitable, or that any profits will not justify the extra investment involved.

There are potent forces that drive organizations, particularly successful ones, to consider broadening the scope of their activities. One force is the fear of being dependent upon one small set of customers or technologies. Probably more important is the fact that good entrepreneurs will, once they have found customers and developed the value chain to serve them, spot other ways that they can use their resources to generate profits.

Sometimes this expansion goes too far. Unilever, the Anglo-Dutch consumer goods conglomerate, found itself in 1999 with 1,600 brands (products, or variants of products), of which just 400 'power brands' accounted for 90 per cent of sales. It decided that by disposing of some of the 1,600 and focusing its marketing, research and personnel, it could raise its profit margins closer to those of its leading competitors (Smith 1999; Willman 1999a, 1999b).

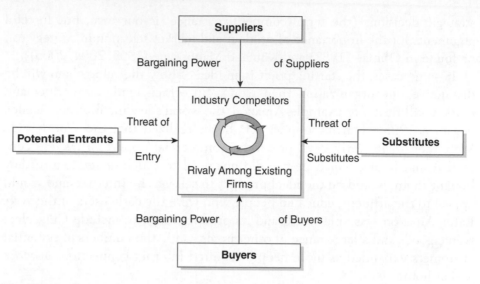

Figure 2.5   Porter's five forces of competition framework
Source: Adapted from Porter (1980).

Competitor analysis

The organization has to understand the competition in order to achieve 'competitor advantage' to outperform its rivals and capture a greater share of an existing market space.

To understand the competitor it is useful to apply Porter's (1980) framework to classify and analyse those features of an industry that quantify the intensity of competition and the level of profitability (see Chapter 3). He defined the five forces of competition (see Figure 2.5) as follows:

- competition from substitutes, from entrants, and from established rivals as sources of 'horizontal' competition
- the bargaining power of suppliers and buyers as sources of 'vertical' competition.

Horizontal competition

- Substitutes are products or services of a firm's rivals that meet approximately the same customer needs in the same ways, but do so in different ways, like the products or services provided by the firm itself.
- New entrants are firms that have recently begun operations in an industry or that threaten to begin operations in an industry soon. They are motivated by the above-normal economic profits that some incumbent firms in an industry may be earning.

Vertical competition

- Bargaining power of buyers: companies always appear on two markets. The first is the market in which they acquire the inputs for production (raw materials, components, financial and labour services) from the suppliers of these factors of production. The second is the market where they sell their output of production (goods, services) to customers (distributors, consumers, other manufacturers). In both cases, the relative profitability of buyers and suppliers in a transaction depends on their economic power.
- Bargaining power of suppliers: the analysis of suppliers' threat is similar to that of buyers. The determining factors for the effectiveness of the bargaining power of the supplier against the buying power in an industry are the same as those that decide the power of the industry against the power of their customers.

As Porter highlights, an industry structure that is stable and externally determined does not give a complete picture of industry competition. Competition is a dynamic process in which the industry structure changes through evolution and transformation. In the end, competition is not some constrained process that determines prices and profits and leaves the industry structure unchanged. Competition is a dynamic process in which a balance is never reached and in the course of which industry structures are continually reformed.

The dynamic interaction between competition and industry was first recognized and analysed by Joseph A. Schumpeter. He was of the opinion that the fight for market shares compels companies to enforce both new production technologies and new products. These innovations are made by dynamic firms or trailblazer companies in the first place. They would be motivated by the chance to earn temporary monopoly profits. Such temporary profits draw imitators, which leads to the diffusion and establishment of innovations. In this way a dynamic competition gets going, which is identified with an incessant search of innovations connected with a process of 'creative destruction'.

The question is whether current structures can be used as a solid base for forecasting competition and industry performance in the future. This depends on the speed of structural change in the industry. In the event that transformation is rapid, and innovations transubstantiate industry structure fast by changing the process technology, creating new substitutes and so on, then industry structure is not a useful basis for analysing competition and profit.

There are appropriate industries (computers, telecommunication, Internet access) where the relationship between competition and industry structure is unstable. These changes in the structure of industry are rapid and difficult to forecast. In such an industry it is not advisable to use current trends in industry structure to predict profitability several years ahead. However, most empirical studies have shown that Schumpeter's process of 'creative destruction' does not have excessive significance for most industries. In the modern economy such competition is classified as 'hyper-competition'.

Hyper-competition is an industrial environment identified with intense and rapid competitive moves. Competitors must move quickly to build advantages and erode those of their rivals. This quickens the dynamic strategic interactions between competitors. Hyper-competitive behaviour is defined as a process of continuously generating new competitive advantages and destroying, obsolescing, or neutralizing the competitive advantage of adversaries, thereby creating disequilibrium, destroying perfect competition, and disrupting the status quo of the marketplace. This is possible for dynamic firms moving up their escalation ladders faster than competitors, restarting the cycles, or switching to new markets. The quest for profit by establishing competitive advantages is the driving force of competition. Such attained competitive advantages are transitory, and only by continually recreating and renewing competitive advantages can firms sustain market dominance and superior performance over the long run.

How to diversify different businesses

Substantial changes to the range of offerings or to the markets served, or both, are known as **diversification**. This term was originally reserved for moves involving both new offerings and new markets (Ansoff 1965). However, it has come to denote any extension of an organization's activities into new areas.

It is now generally agreed that spreading risk is, of itself, an inadequate reason for a corporation to diversify in new markets, new costumers, and new offerings, as Figure 2.6 illustrates. Investors can achieve their desired spread of investment risks by diversifying their own shareholdings, at less cost than a corporation incurs in entering and leaving businesses and markets. There are exceptions to this where corporations are involved in businesses or geographical locations (the former Soviet Union, or China, for example) that have less well-developed capital or stock markets, and where the opportunities for buying a spread of shares are limited or risky because of a lack of information.

Whatever the reasons for expansion into new areas, the benefits may come at a price. Organizations that do not focus adequately on the needs of particular customers or segments risk losing business to firms that do. Senior managers in firms which diversify too much appear to lose the ability to oversee the different products or businesses in their portfolio. Their management attention and expertise are diluted, allowing competitors who are specialists (and therefore more likely to have deep knowledge which is unique and inimitable) to gain advantage – a process which happens individually in each product or market in which the diversified firm competes.

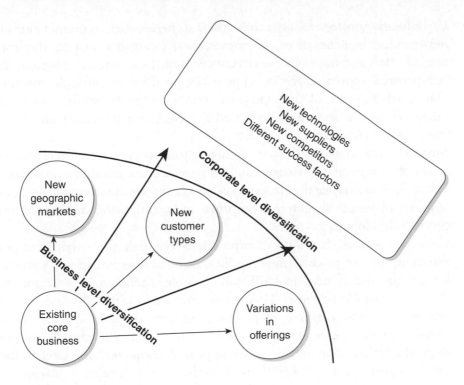

Figure 2.6 Diversification
Source: author.

The risk of dilution of management attention can be reduced, and the chances of success in diversification increased, if the elements in a portfolio are *strategically related*: that is, if the industry success factors are similar. This is particularly important in the case of corporate-level diversification.

How to balance different businesses

As a firm's degree of product and market diversity increases, it loses some economies of scale, but may be compensated by what are known at the business level as **economies of scope**, and at corporate level as **synergies**. These take six main forms (Goold and Campbell, 1998):

- *Sharing tangible resources*, such as manufacturing, research or head office or IT facilities. Having such facilities fully utilized across a range of products makes more economic sense than having them specialized but half-used.
- *Pooling negotiating power*, primarily vis-à-vis suppliers, to obtain lower prices, better quality or more responsive service, but also to obtain better treatment from retailers (more prominent displays of the firm's products) customers, regulators or even investors.

- *Co-ordinating strategic business unit (SBU) strategies,* such as market entries, new product launches or pricing moves, so as to avoid a wasteful duplication of effort and improve the effectiveness of the company's response to competitors' moves. Large conglomerates involved in multiple market-places, where some of their products may even be substitutes for each other, can benefit from a co-ordinated approach to product pricing across the divisions (Besanko et al. 1996).
- Margins across all their divisions are likely to increase – something known as the *efficiency effect.* Divisions can also cross-sell one another's products.
- *Vertically co-ordinating* the provision of goods and services across SBUs can help to minimize inventories, improve asset utilization and speed up product development.
- *Creating combined businesses.* Corporations can link the expertise from different SBUs to produce new products or businesses or can pull particular activities out of individual SBUs and combine them into a new business.
- *Sharing intangible resources.* Hamel and Prahalad (1994) showed how a number of, mostly Japanese, corporations discovered that knowledge about particular technologies or markets could profitably be applied to businesses or products that, to an outsider, often appeared completely unrelated to the firm's original sphere of operations. Nonetheless, the genuine similarities in terms of market needs, technological characteristics, or manufacturing processes justified a move into them. Businesses may also exchange information on customers – their details and preferences for the cross-selling of products, for example. When intangible resources are shared in this way, they are sometimes said to be **leveraged** across businesses – their power is multiplied by being shared, in the same way that a lever multiplies the force applied by a person or machine. Virgin, a London-based conglomerate, has a brand name and corporate identity that is distinctive and recognizable to a specific group of its potential target customers, mainly younger people. It attaches that brand to around 50 businesses, including airlines, mobile phone services, financial services, cosmetics, saucy underwear and space travel, whose products might be attractive to those target customers. Virgin's understanding of those customers' needs is an intangible resource that it leverages across all those businesses. The brand is similarly leveraged. Every time the group's charismatic founder, Richard Branson, generates favourable press coverage – as he has a gift for doing – he boosts the brand image of every single one of those businesses, at no greater cost than if Virgin were a small firm with just a single product.

Many strategy writers, particularly in the 1970s, felt that it was important for a portfolio to be 'balanced' – displaying a mixture of different characteristics. Balance might be achieved across a number of dimensions:

- Size – a mix of small and large businesses.
- The age or the life-cycle stage of the industry – a mix of young, fast-growing businesses and more mature ones (see Chapter 3).
- The extent to which the businesses are net producers or consumers of cash.

One theoretical benefit of a balanced portfolio is a reduction of risk, since it would minimize the likelihood of all the businesses facing severe problems at the same time. A second potential benefit is that resources can be redistributed from the businesses that have them to those that need them – for example, a mature business can become a source of cash and of marketing and production expertise for a younger one. However, there is absolutely no evidence that firms that have balanced portfolios perform any better (or worse) than those that have not.

The main tools used to assess balance in a portfolio are the well-known matrices developed by the Boston Consulting Group (the BCG growth-share matrix) and General Electric (the Business Attractiveness Screen).

However, empirical studies have not found any systematic differences in the way in which businesses appearing in different parts of these matrices need to be managed. This implies that it may not be valid to make investment decisions on the basis of such a simple piece of two-dimensional analysis, without, for example, taking account of an SBU's or product's relationship with the others in the portfolio. Moreover, certain of the assumptions behind the frameworks are false, notably the assumption that 'dogs' – low-growth, low-share products or businesses – are likely to consume rather than generate cash. In fact, the limited amount of testing that has been conducted on these frameworks suggests that managers who employ them make *worse* investment decisions than those who do not (Armstrong and Brodie 1994; Capon et al. 1987; Slater and Zwirlein 1992).

The importance of HRM in strategy

Organizations cannot achieve sustainable competitive advantage just by selecting the right combination of products and services, and positioning them to appeal to attractive target market segments. Although these decisions are a vital part of strategy, and may lead to desirable economies of scale and scope, they are not sufficient in themselves because they are too easy for competitors to notice and copy. The munificence, dynamism, and complexity of an industry environment also are not enough to explain the very real differences in profitability between firms in the same industry. After all, if the industry was the only factor, then all the firms in an industry would have similar levels of profits – and they do not. The 'resource-based view of the firm' (RBV), which emerged towards the end of the twentieth century, focuses on organizational features – resources – that are the basis of competitive strength if exploited properly (see Chapter 3). Edith Penrose (1959) showed how, over time, firms built up human and physical resources and the capability to use them to provide different kinds of services, some of which could be used in different products and markets from the ones for which they were developed. Subsequent developments of this theory (Amit and Schoemaker 1993; Nelson and Winter 1982; Peteraf 1993) focused on the importance of the unique, often hidden, aspects of an organization, such as tacit knowledge, or the things that it has learnt to do, in understanding differences between firms.

These differences arise because two firms can start from a common base, yet end up over time with very different sets of routines, capabilities, and knowledge, something now known as path dependence. Time also means that competitors find it difficult to copy a firm's resources, because they may not be able to understand precisely how and when they were developed – in other words there is causal ambiguity. These resources may also be part of a complex interaction with a number of other, *complementary*, resources within the firm that make them more effective than they would be if used on their own.

The human resource is a complex and important resource inside the organization that has to be managed in a close relationship with the strategy to create competitive advantage.

Recruitment, selection (Chapter 5), training and development (Chapter 10) are all aimed at bringing in or building certain skills, enabling employees to effectively perform their jobs. In addition, their experience with these practices, along with rewards, performance management (Chapter 7) and communication (Chapter 8), shape workers' perceptions of the company's fairness and desirability. And those perceptions then influence their commitment, motivation and engagement.

Researchers have found a significant relationship between HR strategies and profitability (see Chapters 3 and 13). However, this research has seldom identified how this relationship works.

Investing in employee management not only delivers administrative cost savings but is also in fact one of the best performance-enhancing investments a company can make. Research overwhelmingly indicates that effective employee management can and does lead to a competitive advantage in the form of a more motivated workforce and improved operational and business performance. By sharpening our focus on the relationship between employee management and business performance in the management of the strategy it is important to identify practices that will maximize the return on the investment in employee management practices and achieve the positive business results experienced by other companies. It is also important to align people management practice with the business objective.

The purpose of employee management is to solidify and enhance the advantage of human resources to motivate, develop and retain employees more effectively than your competitors.

The practices that apply to managing employees can be summarized as follows:

- *Hiring practices*: ensure that employees hired for different positions have the necessary skills and background to be successful in their individual jobs (Chapter 5).
- *Evaluation practices*: ensure that employees are being provided with useful feedback about their performance (Chapter 7).
- *Compensation practices*: provide employees with what they consider to be fair pay for their work (Chapter 7).
- *Training and development practices*: provide employees with opportunities to grow through job training, job rotation and promotions (Chapter 10).

CASE STUDY 2.2

Egg 2.0

Egg 2.0 is a communication and research laboratory developed from an idea of Guido Avigdor, Giorgio Risi and Pietro Dotti in 2009. These are a group of young talents who express their expertise in every area of communication including editorial art direction, video-making and various digital activities, the pursuit of new trends, the organization of events, innovations in the app market, and social marketing.

Every year since 2009 a contest is launched – in Italian universities, on the Web and in social networks – with the aim of selecting the best talent. Participants are given a theme which they have to develop using the kind of media they believe will be the most suitable to express their talent. The members and employees of Egg 2.0 and the Eggers in their last year will preselect the works taking part in the contest, which will then be judged by a quality jury made up of different members every year. The jury can consist of people who have start-ups, newspaper editors, movie directors, musicians, advertisers, university professors, etc.

Egg 2.0 is a limited company that subsists thanks to its own work in the market: it has never received any government funds.

Their main activity is to study cross-media and non-conventional communication campaigns including Web 2.0, the organization of events, the development of apps on smartphones and tablets, and the study of image positioning and commercials.

The main milestones of Egg 2.0 are summarized in the following list:

- Mission: to train new creative talents and launch them in the working world and, at the same time, give the working world the young talents' innovative answers.
- Team selection: this is carried out by an external jury that selects the future members of the factory.

(Continued)

(Continued)

- The working area: a loft that everyone shares without having fixed working spaces.
- Work management: a horizontal model which is transparent and inclusive.
- Sharing company challenges: sharing challenges and results.
- Factory life: paying attention to activities outside of work.
- Absence of hierarchy.
- Alternating work and appointments with personalities from the arts and communication world.

Every Egger takes part in the creative, executive and control phases. This is because one of the hinges of the experience at Egg 2.0 is understanding one's own role in connection with others, whether these are the group, the customer or the outside world.

Teamwork is focused on understanding the problem so that it can be handled in the best way, not just in terms of creativity but also in terms of strategy. One of the most acknowledged qualities of the projects carried out by clients is the attention given to finding good cross-media solutions in the short and long term.

This approach is inevitably more demanding both in terms of time dedication and mental application, but much more stimulating for everybody.

In a field of application such as creativity, linked with communication, it is hard to determine what the new trends and developments will be, and thus decide which expertise to invest in.

However, Egg 2.0 aims at steady growth through a continuous consolidation of the company, determined not only by its members' technical skills but also and especially by their aptitude.

The most important resource is the ability to become interested in the future, being aware that our role within the factory is not just functional but also motivational and that the co-responsibility for choices is the winning card that makes the individual or group evolve. With this approach we are training professional people who are completely different from those found in the market, or educated by universities: cross-media, multitasking, cool-hunting are the keywords that give everyone's profile extra points.

Egg 2.0 has decided to bet on young people alone and their ability to imagine the future by reinventing the present.

Doing this periodically, renewing the investment every year by using a considerable part of our turnover, and spending great energy on the creation and training of a new team are the strategic choices of Egg 2.0.

In only three years Egg 2.0 has seen the generation of as many as 64 young talents. Fortunately, this constant work has resulted in finding a job right away for more than 80 per cent of our young people: some by consolidating their role within the factory, some by co-operating in specific activities, and others by joining organizations closely linked with Egg 2.0 (customers, suppliers, partners).

This is a remarkable result for everyone: for the factory who can show with figures that their mission is valuable; for the young who, besides having training of a high quality, can really find a job; for the customers who can measure up to a world which is dynamic, fresh, full of ideas, and without structural barriers.

Nevertheless, in order to keep this approach reliable there are very few rules to follow and many choices to make, in most cases determined by common sense and the ability to understand everyone's talent and personality and take them along a path where the single individual can learn how to be part of a bigger group which is very close and competitive, and able to meet the challenges of the world around them with a more clear and confident attitude.

Human resources have a centralized role in the company, they contribute to its development and enable it to adapt to the changes of the knowledge society.

While computer development brings a dematerialization of work and some trends lead to thinking that teamwork and direct and continuous co-operation are no longer an essential qualification, Egg 2.0 bets on sharing spaces, projects and emotions so that young people can start a professional growth which helps them measure up to their own talents as well as to those of others.

Source: author. With thanks to Dr Guido Avigdor – Creative Director and Partner at Egg 2.0.

 ■ Questions

1. What do you think about the Egg 2.0 strategy?
2. Could it be a profitable strategy?
3. What is your opinion about Egg's management of the human resources? Does it seem to be a profitable model?

Emergent corporate strategy

In the following paragraphs we will examine different kinds of corporate strategy and analyse:

- The open business model strategy.
- The network strategy.

Open business model strategy

Johnson et al. (2008) defined a business model as the union of four blocks that, taken together, create and deliver value: customer value proposition, a profit formula, key resources and processes. The most important to get right, by far, is the first.

- *Customer value proposition (CVP).* A successful company is one that has found a way to create value for customers – that is, a way to help customers get an important job done. By 'job' the authors mean a fundamental problem in a given situation that needs a solution.
- *Profit formula.* The profit formula is the blueprint that defines how the company creates value for itself while providing value to the customer. It consists of the following:

- o Revenue model: price × volume.
- o Cost structure: direct costs, indirect costs, economies of scale. Cost structure will be predominantly driven by the cost of the key resources required by the business model.
- o Margin model: given the expected volume and cost structure, the contribution needed from each transaction to achieve desired profits.
- o Resource velocity: how fast we need to turn over inventory, fixed assets, and other assets – and, overall, how well we need to utilize resources – to support our expected volume and achieve our anticipated profits.

- *Key resources.* The key resources are assets such as the people, technology, products, facilities, equipment, channels, and brand required to deliver the value proposition to the targeted customer. The focus here is on the key elements that create value for the customer and the company, and the way those elements interact. (Every company also has generic resources that do not create competitive differentiation.)
- *Key processes.* Successful companies have operational and managerial processes that allow them to deliver value in such a way that they can successfully repeat and increase in scale. These may include such recurrent tasks as training, development, manufacturing, budgeting, planning, sales, and service. Key processes also include a company's rules, metrics, and norms.

These four elements form the building blocks of any business. The customer value proposition and the profit formula define value for the customer and the company, respectively; key resources and key processes describe how that value will be delivered to both the customer and the company. As simple as this framework may seem, its power lies in the complex interdependencies of its parts.

An open system model is a model in which the firm creates and captures value by taking advantage of both the internal and external resources (see Chapter 1). Chesbrough, in his book *Open Business Models: How to Thrive in the Innovation Landscape* (2006b), analysed the characteristics that a firm should have to create an open organization.

In the old model of *closed organization*, companies must generate their own ideas which they will then develop, manufacture, market, distribute and service themselves. For years, this was the 'right way' to bring new ideas to the market and successful companies were those who invested more heavily in internal research and development (R&D) than their competitors and attracted the brightest employees. Thanks to such investments, they were able to discover the best and greatest number of ideas which allowed them to get to the market first. This, in turn, enabled them to gather most of the profits, which they protected by aggressively controlling their intellectual property (IP) to prevent competitors from exploiting it. Closed organizations then reinvested the profits in conducting more R&D, which then led to additional breakthrough discoveries, creating a virtuous inner cycle of innovation. For most of the twentieth century the model worked – and it worked well.

The passage from closed organizations to open organizations depends on some factors that Chesbrough (2006) summarized. The most critical of these was the dramatic rise in the number and mobility of knowledge workers, making it increasingly difficult for companies to control their proprietary ideas and expertise. In other words, nowadays knowledge and ideas are spread out in different knots of social and productive networks. Another important factor was the growing availability of private venture capital, which helped to finance new firms and their efforts to commercialize ideas that spilled outside the silos of corporate research labs. Moreover, globalization, the increasing cost and complexity of R&D, the shortening of the technology life cycle, the improvement of ICT technology and the increase of competition and uncertainty inside industry moved the organization from a closed model to an inevitable open model.

The open organization model goes through some organizational characteristics. Chesbrough (2006) underlined the importance of having a new management capable of innovation which includes the process of acquiring and integrating such ideas into the organization and commercializing them: 'Valuable ideas can come from inside or outside the company and can go to market from inside or outside the company as well' (Chesbrough 2006). In the open organization model, firms commercialize external and internal ideas by deploying both outside and in-house pathways to the market. Specifically, companies can commercialize internal ideas through channels outside their current businesses as well as external ideas through channels inside their current businesses in order to generate value for the organization.

Some vehicles for accomplishing this include start-up companies (which might be financed and staffed with some of the company's own personnel) and licensing agreements.

Within this mechanism the number of ideas that can be potentially produced increases massively, so companies have to be able to screen their ideas and separate bad proposals from good ones so that they can discard the former while pursuing and commercializing the latter. While both closed and open models are adept at weeding out 'false positives' (that is, bad ideas that initially look promising), open innovation also incorporates the ability to rescue 'false negatives' (projects that initially seem to lack promise but turn out to be surprisingly valuable). A company that is too focused on the inside misses all the opportunities placed outside the organization's current businesses or those external technologies that, combined with internal ideas, could create a successful innovation. From this point of view the profit for a company does not only come from using the patents they have developed, but also from selling these patents to other companies.

The firm's value is contingent upon its ability to create and lay claim to the knowledge derived from participating in various kinds of collaborations with other actors.

It has been shown that connectivity with external actors is important in order for firms to remain innovative (Freeman 1991), and in the network literature it is commonly argued that firms benefit from the social landscapes in which they are embedded. Scholars writing along these lines have developed important findings in terms of how certain network structures (see Chapter 1) influence a firm's behaviour and performance (Ahuja 2000; Baum et al. 2000a; Gulati et al. 2000). Relationships with other actors help firms to absorb different knowledge technology (Ahuja 2000), improve survival rates (Baum and Oliver 1991), increase innovativeness (Baum et al. 2000b; Stuart 2000), improve performance (Hagedoorn and Schakenraad 1994; Shan et al. 1994) and in general grow faster (Powell et al. 1996; Stuart 2000).

Beyond the relation with the network's partners there are two important capabilities needing to be set up and developed by the organization. The first is the capability to absorb the external knowledge and skill to create and develop internal core competence beneficial to those firms that master it (Lorenzoni and Lipparini 1999), and the second is the capability to choose and manage the relationships within the network.

Some of the literature underlines the fact that firms need to increase processes that ensure the assimilation of developments in the external environment through the progress of absorptive capacity (Cohen and Levinthal 1990; Lane and Lubatkin 1998; Zahra and George 2002). Research has shown that firms need to have competencies in areas related to their partners' in order to assimilate external sources (Brusoni et al. 2001; Granstrand et al. 1997; Mowery et al. 1996). Internal capabilities and external relations must therefore be seen not as substitutes but as complements. The ability to absorb external inputs depends on what the firm knows. Another important point is related to the similarity of knowledge bases and how they facilitate the integration of ideas from distant realms (Kogut and Zander 1992), because shared languages, common norms and cognitive configurations enable communication (Cohen and Levinthal 1990). In absorbing new knowledge, the firm also increases its possibilities for making novel re-combinations. Incorporating knowledge bases too close to what the firm already knows will hamper the positive effect of assimilating external inputs. For instance, Ahuja and Katila (2001) suggested that knowledge relatedness between the acquiring and acquired firms is curvilinearly related to innovative performance. Too-distant inputs are harder to align with existing practices, and if knowledge bases are too similar, it is difficult to come up with novel combinations (Sapienza et al. 2004). In other words, the effectiveness of openness is also contingent upon the resource endowments of the partnering organization.

For the second point – the set-up and management of the relationship – Chesbrough's (2006) work underlined that the larger the number of external sources of innovation the more open the firm's search strategy will be, because innovation is often about leveraging on the discoveries of others. Firms that manage to create a synergy between what the firm does and the external environment are able to benefit from the creative ideas of outsiders: available resources become greater than what a single firm could handle, but enable innovative ways to market, or the creation of standards in emerging markets.

Lakhani et al. (2007) examined a new form of increasing the value of external sources of innovation through knowledge-brokering, by exploring how the firm InnoCentive adopted openness to broadcast problems to a large pool of diverse individuals. They argued that openness and transparency are necessary to increase the value of the entire accumulation of scientific knowledge available and present evidence that problem-solving success is associated with the ability to attract specialized solvers with a range of diverse scientific interests. This 'broadcast search' can attract solutions from external actors who have experience with the problem from a different domain of expertise.

CASE STUDY 2.3

InnoCentive

InnoCentive is the global leader in crowdsourcing innovation problems to the world's smartest people who compete to provide ideas and solutions to important business, social, policy, scientific, and technical challenges.

Its global network of millions of problem-solvers, proven challenge methodology, and cloud-based technology combine to help the clients transform their economics of innovation through rapid solution delivery and the development of sustainable open innovation programs.

Since 2001, InnoCentive has been making a profound impact on the world:

- Total registered solvers: more than 270,000 from nearly 200 countries
- Total solver reach: 12+ million through our strategic partners (e.g., Nature Publishing Group, *Popular Science*, *The Economist*)
- Total challenges posted: 1,500+ external challenges and hundreds of internal challenges (employee-facing)
- Project rooms opened to date: 450,000+
- Total solution submissions: 34,000+
- Total awards given: 1,300+
- Total award dollars posted: $37+ million
- Range of awards: $500 to $1+ million based on the complexity of the problem and nature of the challenge
- Average award rate: 57 per cent.

(Continued)

(Continued)

InnoCentive adopts the electronic marketplace business model. Through its open innovation marketplace, InnoCentive seeks to match a global network of solvers with R&D challenges faced by a number of seeker organizations.

Seekers post challenges, along with the associated financial award, by paying InnoCentive a fee of $35,000 and are allowed to post challenges anonymously to avoid competition-related issues. Solvers can view the challenges and submit solutions to any challenge without being charged anything. If the seeker is satisfied with the workability of the solution to a challenge provided by a solver, then the seeker provides this solver with the pre-specified award in exchange for the acquisition to the intellectual property (IP) rights to the winning solution. The seeker also pays InnoCentive a commission on the amount awarded. InnoCentive ensures IP protection for both seekers and solvers and facilitates the transfer of IP rights from the solver to the seeker.

The value proposition that the business model offers is twofold:

- First, InnoCentive allows seeker organizations to reduce their R&D budget by tapping into the wisdom and innovative capacity of a network of more than 200,000 solvers in order to find solutions to their difficult problems (challenges).
- Second, InnoCentive gives solvers the opportunity to focus on a range of challenging problems that are of interest with the hope of receiving a financial reward.

Source: author.

 ■ Questions

1. Which characteristics of an 'open system model' does InnoCentive demonstrate?
2. How does InnoCentive deliver value to its customers?
3. What do you think about crowdsourcing?
4. Why does the company have to post their problems on a blog?
5. How do you define the relationship between the organization and its network?

Network strategy

Even if the network model is not a recent strategic discovery, the increasing cost and complexity of R&D, the shortening of the technology life cycle, the improvement of ICT technology and the increase in competition and uncertainty inside the industry drive the organization toward a network model where partner selection and relationship management become important strategic variables. The early Schumpeterian model of the lone entrepreneur bringing innovations to markets has been superseded by a rich picture of different actors working together in iterative processes of trial and error to bring about the successful commercial exploitation of a new idea (Freeman and Soete 1997; Rosenberg 1982; Schumpeter 1942/87; Tidd et al. 2000; von Hippel 1988). As many authors underlined (Chesbrough 2006), being inside a network is not enough if the organization is not able to perceive the business opportunities of the environment, exploiting the network potentiality and management generally (Coles et al. 2003; Ritter and Gemünden 2003). The evidence on the management of networks (see Chapter 1) shows that managing informal and formal agreements while establishing trust means that the management of network relationships is inherently difficult (Biemans 1991). Those responsible for managing network relationships need to learn core network competencies over time, for example, being able to identify when an agreement needs a contract or should be based on good faith, the role that friendship or reputation plays in the identification of partners and the kinds of milestones or interventions that are needed to ensure a project stays on course (Shaw 1998). Knowledge of how to collaborate accumulates over time through experience, reflection, and interpretation (Lorenzoni and Lipparini 1999). The degree to which firms learn about new opportunities is of course a function of the extent of their existing participation in networks (Powell et al. 1996) as well as their actual level of knowledge, skill and competence. Gulati (1999; Gulati et al. 2000) argues that a firm's position in a network provides 'network resources' that are difficult to imitate and thus potentially provide an enduring competitive advantage.

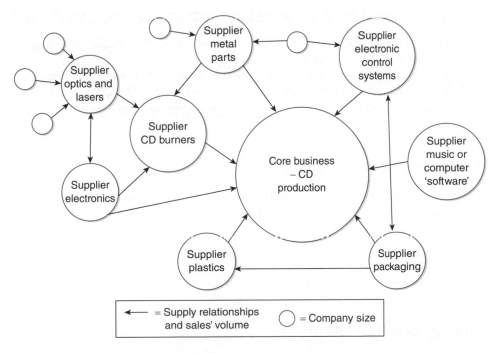

Figure 2.7 A networked value system
Source: author.

Networks like the one in Figure 2.7 enable small firms to appear to clients as if they are large corporations, with access to a wide range of resources. If one firm in the network receives an enquiry for some business that it cannot handle itself, it calls in one of its partners, or passes the enquiry on to them. Sometimes a single firm acts as the 'server' at the centre of the network, taking in the work and allocating it to the other partners. In other types of network, firms are part of a confederation of more equal alliance partners – some of whom will have alliances with only one firm in the network, others with several. Each partner may specialize in a certain part of the value chain (product development, marketing), have a particular expertise (website maintenance, computer network installation) or specialize in particular market segments (retailers or local governments). But it is not just small firms that feel the need to build such networks. For complex or technologically sophisticated products, it is very unlikely that one firm can contain all the necessary resources in-house.

Companies which, like Merck and H&M, sit at the centre of networks of suppliers, specifying the outputs and determining which supplier should do what, are called *orchestrators* or *servers* (Figure 2.8). There are even companies, like Hong Kong's Li and Fung, whose only role is as orchestrators: they specialize in finding and managing suppliers for whatever product their client may choose to offer, but have no product brands of their own.

PIT STOP: REFLECTIVE ACTIVITY 2.2

1. In which marketplace are networks developing more quickly and effectively: in the Internet or in the real marketplace?
2. Do you think that the industry characteristics influence the network formation?
3. Which kind of links and/or partners are more effective in strategy development?

Emergent business strategy

In the following paragraphs we will examine different kinds of business-level strategies.

In the business strategy we will analyse:

- The strategy based on customers.
- The strategy based on competitors.

Strategy based on customers

There is a general consensus in the literature about the positive role of customer orientation for short-term performance. Market-oriented businesses focus on

In 2005 the firm signed 44 agreements for external alliances (according to its 2005 annual report)

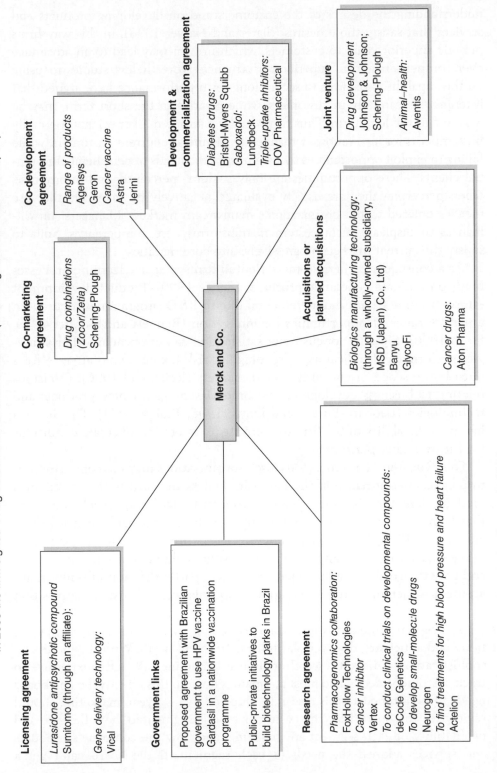

Figure 2.8 Merck's network of strategic alliances in 2006

Source: Numerous industry reports.

understanding the desires of the customers and on developing products and services that satisfy those desires (Slater and Narver 1998). In this way firms provide superior value to customers, which in turn may lead to an advantage over competitors and to superior performance. Nevertheless, studies focusing on the capabilities of firms to secure long-term performance have argued that listening too carefully to customers, while positive in the short term, may be negative in the long term. Thus firms led by a strong market orientation easily find impetus for innovations demanded by significant current customers, while failing to exploit opportunities that stem from the needs of peripheral or potential clients. These opportunities are only seldom perceived, and in any case, when perceived, they are usually evaluated negatively by managers that use metrics tailored to the organization's mainstream markets. Managers' unwillingness to displease main customers transforms core competences, built to satisfy the current markets progressively, into core rigidities.

As a consequence, in customer-oriented firms adaptive learning processes tend to dominate generative processes (Senge 1990). Product development efforts become trivial and incremental due to R&D programmes focused on a narrow range of opportunities for innovation (Bennett and Cooper 1979; Frosh 1996). Measures of customer satisfaction can overwhelm other strategic performance indicators, discouraging risk-taking explorative efforts outside the scope of currently served markets (Reichheld 1996). Decisions relating to business development become biased against new products and technologies (Leonard-Burton and Doyle 1996; Tauber 1974). This in turn hampers the ability of the firm to renovate its assets and to create conditions for future higher performance.

Following their customers too closely, organizations may miss opportunities to increase performance in the long run. Unless the firm is able to adopt a market orientation that goes beyond a strict customer-led approach, it is likely that being customer-oriented will hamper its long-term performance (Slater and Narver 1998). Too often, product managers simply launch line extensions or repackaged 'new and improved' products that fail to advance the innovation and growth agenda over the long term. This is partly the fault of senior management, which often responds coolly to speculative, high-risk initiatives that have long payback periods but that could secure longer-term growth.

To keep customers it is important to delight them, exceed their expectations, and anticipate, discover, and fulfil their latent needs. With the increasing sophistication of market research tools, it is becoming easy and inexpensive to track customers' needs, and most companies now do this effectively. The board needs to be attuned to this research. Once or twice a year, marketing should review for the board how the customer base is segmented, how the size and profitability of each segment are changing, and how the company's products and services address the needs of each segment. If the board can't get a succinct answer to the question 'How are your customers' needs changing?', marketing aren't doing their job.

Strategy based on competitors

If we think about the industry in this historical period we will quickly realize the plethora of new industries than only a few years ago didn't exist: cellular phones, biotechnology, nanotechnology, tablets and snowboards, to name a few. Just three decades ago, none of these industries existed, and if we think about the next ten years new industries will be created and existing ones will probably be recreated. If we start to look inside the different industries we can perceive a common phenomenon: a huge number of companies struggling to achieve more market share in a market where the population is declining. The result is that the number of organizations is overtaking the product demand. Thanks to the technological advances that have improved industrial productivity, suppliers can produce an unprecedented array of products and services free to move between nations and regions, wiping out niche markets. As Kim and Mauborgne held in an article in the *Harvard Business Review*:

> This situation has inevitably hastened the commoditization of products and services, stoked price wars, and shrunk profit margins. According to recent studies, major American brands in a variety of product and service categories have become more and more alike. And as brands become more similar, people increasingly base purchase choices on price. People no longer insist, as in the past, that their laundry detergent be Tide. Nor do they necessarily stick to Colgate when there is a special promotion for Crest, and vice versa. In overcrowded industries, differentiating brands *becomes harder both in economic upturns and in downturns.* (2004: 78)

In this framework organizations can choose to compete by following two macro types of strategies: the *red ocean strategy* or the *blue ocean strategy* (see Figure 2.9).

With the red ocean strategy, companies try to outperform rivals in order to grab bigger slices of existing demand using the same competitive leverage of the competitor's, while in the blue ocean strategy the organization moves the competition on different variables that are difficult to imitate. In the following we describe the two different strategies.

The red ocean strategy

The red ocean strategy can't consider the competitive interactions between firms: the entity of strategic competition is the interaction between players. A decision made by one player is dependent on the actual and anticipated decisions

Red Ocean Strategy	Blue Ocean Strategy
Compete in existing market space	Create uncontested market space
Beat the competition	Make the competition irrelevant
Exploit existing demand	Create and capture new demand
Make the value/cost trade-off	Break the value/cost trade-off
Align the whole system of a company's activities with its strategic choice of differentiation or low cost	Align the whole system of a company's activities in pursuit of differentiation and low cost

Figure 2.9 Red ocean and blue ocean strategy

Source: author.

of the other players. In Five Forces analysis competition is a mediating variable that links industry structure with profitability. Thus, it gives only a small insight into the firms' selection of whether to compete or to co-operate, the sequential competitive moves, and the role of threats, promises, and commitments.

Game theory makes it possible for us to prognosticate the balance results of competitive situations and the consequences of strategic moves by any one player because it makes it possible to recognize central issues of strategy. Simple game models like 'prisoner's dilemma' forecast co-operative versus competitive consequences, whereas more complex games, especially within the context of multi-period games, allow analysis of the effects of reputation, deterrence, information and commitment. With game theory, you have the ability to view business interactions as comprising both competition and co-operation. The Five Forces framework has the deficiency to view rivalry and bargaining as competitive in nature. Business relationships have a competitive (co-operative) duality. For example, Coca-Cola's relationship with Pepsi Cola is essentially competitive, but the relationship between Intel and Microsoft is primarily complementary. It follows that if customers value your product more when they have the other player's product than when they have your product alone, the other player is your complementor. And if customers value your product less when they have the other player's product than when they have your product alone, the other player is your competitor. However, it is very important to realize that a player may hold multiple roles. Figure 2.10 shows the value net which recognizes the relationship of both competition and co-operation.

Microsoft and Netscape are a good example of duality and multiple roles. On the one hand they compete fiercely to dominate the market for Internet

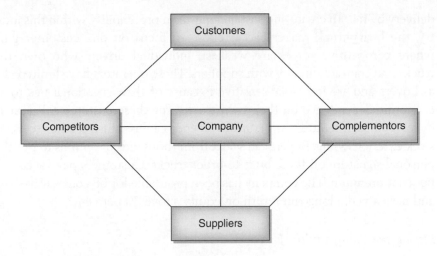

Figure 2.10 The value net

Source: Adapted from Brandenburger and Nalebuff (1996).

browsers. However, the two companies co-operate in establishing security proto-
cols for protecting privacy and guarding against credit card fraud on the Internet.

In summary, game theory offers the possibility of understanding the nature of
situations involving interactions among multiple players. It explains the structure
of relationships and nature of interactions among players and identifies the alternative actions available to different players and relates these to possible outcomes.

Game theory could be a valuable decision support, because it provides
excellent insights and understanding, though it has been less valuable in forecasting outcomes and designing strategies. In highly stylized situations involving few external variables and highly restrictive assumptions, game theory
provides clear prognostications. However, in more complex and more realistic
situations, it often results in either no balance or multiple balances. Even these
results are highly sensitive to small changes in assumptions.

The red ocean strategy in practice

To set up the red ocean strategy in practice the organization's management
need to:

Position the company where forces are weaker

Example:

In the heavy-truck industry, many buyers operate large fleets and are highly
motivated to drive down truck prices. Trucks are built to regulated standards
and offer similar features, so the price competition is stiff; unions exercise
considerable supplier power; and buyers can use substitutes such as cargo

delivery by rail. To create and sustain long-term profitability within this industry, the heavy-truck maker Paccar chose to focus on one customer group where competitive forces are weakest: individual drivers who own their trucks and contract directly with suppliers. These operators have limited clout as buyers and are less price-sensitive because of their emotional ties to and economic dependence on their own trucks. For these customers, Paccar has developed such features as luxurious sleeper cabins, plush leather seats, and sleek exterior styling. Buyers can select from thousands of options to put their personal signature on these built-to-order trucks. Customers pay Paccar a 10 per cent premium. The company has been profitable for 68 consecutive years and has earned a long-run return on equity above 20 per cent.

Exploit the changes in the forces

Example:

With the advent of the Internet and digital distribution of music, unauthorized downloading created an illegal but potent substitute for record companies' services. The record companies tried to develop technical platforms for digital distribution themselves, but major labels didn't want to sell their music through a platform owned by a rival. Into this vacuum stepped Apple, with its iTunes music store supporting its iPod music player. The birth of this powerful new gatekeeper has whittled down the number of major labels from six in 1997 to four today.

Reshape the forces in your favour

Use tactics designed specifically to reduce the share of profits leaking to other players.

Example:

To neutralize supplier power, standardize specifications for parts so your company can switch more easily among vendors.

To counter customer power, expand your services so it's harder for customers to leave you for a rival.

To temper price wars initiated by established rivals, invest more heavily in products that differ significantly from competitors' offerings.

To scare off new entrants, elevate the fixed costs of competing; for instance, by escalating your R&D expenditure.

To limit the threat of substitutes, offer better value through wider product accessibility.

Lavazza

The history of Lavazza started in 1895 when Luigi Lavazza took over a small grocery store in the old centre of Turin (Italy). He decided to produce a new coffee concept, 'the coffee blend', where different types of coffee were mixed together to achieve a more tasty and harmonious flavour. Today Lavazza is the leader in Italy in the mass market channel with a market share of 48 per cent; 40 per cent of the company's turnover is generated outside of Italy; and Lavazza is also ranked seventh as a green coffee importer worldwide. The current dimension of the company is defined by the following data:

- 17 billion cups consumed worldwide each year;
- the turnover is €1276 million;
- six industrial facilities;
- 3800 employees;
- geographical coverage is over 90 countries.

In 2010 the net revenue of the Lavazza Company amounted to €1147 million and earnings before interest, taxes, depreciation and amortization (EBITDA) were €145 million.

Lavazza makes coffee for home use, institutional customers, and restaurants: its objective is to expand the aroma, quality and culture of Italian espresso worldwide. The core values of Lavazza are based on two fundamental concepts:

- The internationalization of the business and consequentially of its human resources.
- The development capabilities to bring innovation inside the organization.

Lavazza has created a business model based on direct distribution through its own subsidiaries in 12 countries and indirect distribution through a wide network of distributors – specialized in different channels – in about 80 countries.

In general the concern for emerging markets shows an interesting potential in the growth of coffee consumption in Asia, South America and Eastern Europe.

Innovation is of fundamental importance if Lavazza is to continue to contend in a competitive international market.

Innovation activities are conducted by joining the exploration of new alternatives and the evolution of existing ones with a creative communication strategy. Since 2006 the company has enhanced several partnerships with universities by organizing MBA training programmes for their employees and setting up specific 'company projects' such as case studies for university students.

The link with the university makes it possible for the company to improve the capability of its employees and increase the potential resources of new ideas, strengthening relationships between 'potential employees and the company' and reinforcing the image of the company.

Collaboration with universities of international fame has been essential in guaranteeing an up to date research base and that personnel are able to take on market challenges.

Source: author. With thanks to Dr Anna Abbate – Human Resources Management and Development Manager, Lavazza Spa.

 ■ Questions

1. Which features of red ocean strategy does Lavazza demonstrate?
2. What are the key strategic factors that have led to the firm's success?

Blue ocean strategy

The blue ocean strategy is based on moving competition from overcrowded industries to uncontested market spaces where competition is irrelevant. Organizations will invent and capture new demands by offering their customers new values while shrinking costs.

As Kim and Mauborgne held in their article in the *Harvard Business Review* in 2004, the blue ocean strategy is not about technology innovation. Blue oceans seldom result from technological innovation. Often, the underlying technology already exists – and blue ocean creators will then link it to what buyers value. Compaq, for example, used existing technologies to create its ProSignia server, which gave buyers twice the file and print capability of the minicomputer at one-third the price.

Another important feature of the blue ocean strategy is that the incumbents are not at a disadvantage: still better are those who *create* a blue ocean strategy, usually within their core businesses. GM, Japanese car makers and Chrysler used to be established players when they created blue oceans in the auto industry, and so were CTR and IBM, and Compaq in the computer industry. This suggests that incumbents are not at a disadvantage in creating new market spaces. Moreover, the blue oceans made by incumbents are usually within their core businesses.

In the blue ocean strategy the traditional units of strategic analysis – company and industry – have little explanatory power when it comes to analysing how and why blue oceans are created.

There is no consistently excellent company; the same company can be brilliant at one time and wrong-headed at another. The most appropriate unit of analysis for explaining the creation of blue oceans is the strategic move – the set of managerial actions and decisions involved in making a major market-creating business offering. Kim and Mauborgne showed in their article how the blue ocean strategy can create brand equity that lasts for decades, using examples of companies such as Ford or IBM, established corporations that are traditionally seen as the victims of the new market space creation, as important players for this kind of strategy. What they reveal is that large R&D budgets are not the key to creating a new market space: the key is making the right strategic moves. What's more, companies that understand what drives a good strategic move will be well placed to create multiple blue oceans over time, thereby continuing to deliver high growth and profits over a sustained period. The creation of blue oceans, in other words, is a product of strategy and as such is also very much a product of managerial action.

The general characteristics of the blue ocean strategy

The most important feature of the blue ocean strategy is that it rejects the fundamental tenet of conventional strategy: that a trade-off exists between value and cost. According to this thesis, companies can either create greater value for customers at a higher cost or create reasonable value at a lower cost. In other words, strategy is essentially a choice between differentiation and low cost, but when it comes to creating blue oceans, the evidence shows that successful companies pursue differentiation and low cost simultaneously. A rejection of the trade-off between low cost and differentiation implies a fundamental change in the strategic mindset – we cannot emphasize enough how fundamental a shift it is. The red ocean assumption that industry structural conditions are a given and firms are forced to compete within them is based on an intellectual worldview that academics call the *structuralist view*, or *environmental determinism*. According to this, companies and managers are largely at the mercy of economic forces greater than themselves. Blue ocean strategies, by contrast, are based on a worldview in which market boundaries and industries can be reconstructed by the actions and beliefs of industry players. Kim and Mauborgne call this the *reconstructionist view*.

Adopting a blue ocean strategy is difficult to imagine and create but attracts customers in large volumes, generating scale economies very rapidly, putting the imitator in a continuing cost disadvantage. Moreover when a company offers a leap in value it rapidly earns a brand buzz and a loyal following in the marketplace.

CASE STUDY 2.5

Ferrero

Ferrero is a multinational corporation which originated in Italy and was founded in 1946 in Alba (Piedmont) by the family of the current owner, Mr Michele Ferrero. The total production of chocolate confectionery products is in excess of 800,000 tons. Ferrero has local companies in 38 countries and operates 19 factories around the world with 23,000 employees, 30 per cent of which are based in Italy. As an organization, Ferrero has enjoyed growth of 9 per cent during 2012 with a particular contribution from the extra-European countries such as Russia, the United States, Brazil and Asia, while in Europe growth was close to 5 per cent. Turnover is around €7.3 billion.

Since its origins the company has grown using exclusively self-generated financial resources and has never made acquisitions: 100 per cent of the shares are still owned by the Ferrero family. Ferrero is the major Italian-owned food group, the first chocolate confectionery company in Europe, and the fourth in the world. It is a brand-based company, marketing- and consumer-oriented, with outstanding innovation capabilities, and devotes considerable attention to human resources.

The company's strategy is strongly linked with its products, following the highest quality standards and with a strong tradition of innovation streamed in product ideas and underpinned technology, widely distributed and supported by major marketing investments.

(Continued)

(Continued)

Ferrero develops and launches only products that will deliver unique benefits to the consumer. All the products allow, thanks to some of their features, a unique selling proposition (USP) which is able to generate new distinctive niches or change the rules of the markets by redesigning the segmentation. Nutella, Kinder Sorpresa, Rocher, Mon Cheri, Kinder Cioccolato and Kinder Bueno, etc., are only some of Ferrero's products that are recognized by consumers to be unique and not imitable by any competitor. Ferrero competes against competitors by delivering a high level of product quality not only inside the factories (through a high level of process quality) but also outside, concentrating on the freshness and protection of the products all the way through to the final customer. This means shorter shelf-lives, lower stocks, caring about sell-out more than sell-in, monitoring the freshness of products, ensuring refrigerated transport and appropriate stocking conditions even when the product is out of their control, stopping sales and withdrawal during summer. The management of a product and distribution process controlled in this way means the company achieve something close to hand-crafted products. Ferrero does not only compete on differentiation of products but also makes the price of its products affordable because they are able to produce at a cost lower than others thanks to a strong business relationship with their suppliers (Ferrero buys 23 per cent of the world's production of nuts).

Finally, one of Ferrero's most important milestones is their human resource strategy, based on a long-term vision and an employee branding strategy. Starting from the *employment experience*, Ferrero invests time and resources in understanding the employees' needs and creating a high-quality work environment. Their great attention towards human resources means a low turnover rate and a high rate of *employment experience* satisfaction inside the organization.

Source: author. With thanks to Dr Dioguardi – Global Employer Branding and Talent Acquisition Director at Ferrero International S.A.

PIT STOP: REFLECTIVE ACTIVITY 2.3

1. Which would be the correct strategy to choose in case of a radical innovation market introduction?
2. Which, in your opinion, is the strategy most frequently followed by organizations and why?
3. Are you able to create a list of organizations that could apply the blue ocean strategy?

Conclusion

According to Leavy (1999), Samli (2006), and Perrott (2008), industries where the organizations have to compete are turbulent and dynamic due to different factors such as economic crisis, technology, globalization, competition, speed, changing power structure and lifestyles, downsizing, shareholders, trade unions, government policy, relevant legislation, etc. Turbulent environments can create uncertainty for firms in terms of both the supply side and demand side. The increase of uncertainty increases the actors' heterogeneity, the array of activities, the linkages and interaction that define the firm's environment (Dess and Beard 1984).

Managers that guide the organizations have to develop more than the well-known capability to think outside of the box. They must have the dynamic capability to manage the different sources and resources of creativity and innovation that surround the organization, the skill and core competence in a better execution of the creativity strategy called 'creative problem-solving', and speed in understanding and solving internal and external potential or effective problems. There is no list of practical actions that help to achieve these objectives, only some clues to consider, for example identifying unsolved problems, mapping the wider system that influences the results, and determining which weak links need strengthening and which gaps need filling. To continually identify gaps in the market, firms need real-time data and the ability to share these widely throughout the organization. These hard data must be supplemented with a direct observation from the field. But to do all this effectively, we must take into consideration a long-term vision on setting up and developing the right team inside the organization and the right partners outside.

Megginson (1963: 4), in remarks based on Charles Darwin's theory of natural selection, claimed: 'It is not the strongest of the species that survives, nor the most intelligent that survives. It is the one that is the most adaptable to change.' If we look at this concept today and at the new economic-productive scenario, we will find an evolution of enterprises based on a natural selection similar to that claimed by Darwin on animal species. This is what we call 'co-operative Darwinism', and it applies to a great many enterprises.

Many of these new enterprises will not be able to survive: they will either die or be absorbed by predators who are actually market giants with large financial resources. Others will consolidate their position of power. But all of them will have to face the environmental threats brought on by organizational and technological evolution. Recent studies have underlined that the traditional competitive view of relationships between enterprises is inadequate for a market structure which, on the contrary, shows the will of enterprises to co-operate. Co-operation reveals a new competitive profile: from firm-to-firm competition to a network-to-network competition. Co-operative relationships are the result of a compromise between competition and co-operation at the same time. Thus co-operation defines a new form of a more complex interdependence: co-opetition (Brandenburger and Nalebuff 1996).

The performance of the network leans on a principle of complementarity between internal ability and external co-operation so that the ability inside the enterprise is a sort of trading currency which, on the one hand, can contribute to co-operation and thus participate in having co-operative relationships with other enterprises, and on the other hand it can benefit from the co-operation itself (Park and Russo 1996).

This new economy founded on knowledge and information diffusion is affected not only by the changes in technology, but also by the changes in the behaviour of people who live and work in a new way.

The size of a company is no longer a key point, nor does it justify its success. As already stated above, it is rather the ability to innovate, to establish solid relationships with customers, to anticipate their needs or 'be there' at the right moment (time to market) that makes a company successful and, consequently, earns greater profits. It is because of these needs that more and more enterprises focus on their core business, so they can enhance their distinguishing skills (value added activities) and outsource all the other activities, creating particular and new organization models as a result.

■ Further Reading ■ ■ ■ ■ ■ ■ ■ ■ ■ ■ ■ ■

Anthony, Scott D., Johnson, M., Sinfield, Joseph V. and Altman, Elizabeth J. (2008) *The Innovator's Guide to Growth: Putting Disruptive Innovation to Work*. Boston, MA: Harvard Business Press Books.

Chan Kim, W. and Mauborgne, Renee A. (2005) *Blue Ocean Strategy: How to Create Uncontested Market Space and Make the Competition Irrelevant*. Boston, MA: Harvard Business Press Books.

Grant, R. (2008) *Contemporary Strategic Management*. Oxford: Blackwell Publishing.

Hitt, M.A., Hoskisson, R.E. and Duane Ireland, R. (2007) *Management of Strategy*. Mason, OH: Thomson, South-Western.

Lynch, R. (2003) *Corporate Strategy*. Upper Saddle River, NJ: FT Prentice Hall.

References

Ahuja, G. (2000) 'Collaboration networks, structural holes and innovation: a longitudinal study', *Administrative Science Quarterly*, 45: 425–55.

Ahuja, G. and Katila, R. (2001) 'Technological acquisitions and the innovation performance of acquiring firms: a longitudinal study', *Strategic Management Journal*, 22: 197–220.

Amit, R. and Schoemaker, P.J.H. (1993) 'Strategic assets and organizational rent', *Strategic Management Journal*, 14: 33–46.

Andrews, K. (1971) *The Concept of Corporate Strategy*. Homewood, IL: Irwin.

Ansoff, H.I. (1965) *Corporate Strategy*. New York: McGraw-Hill.

Argenti, J. (1965) *Corporate Planning*. London: Allen and Unwin.

Armstrong, J. and Brodie, R. (1994) 'Effects of portfolio planning methods on decision making: experimental results', *International Journal of Research in Marketing*, 11 (1): 73–84.

Barney, J. (1997) *Gaining and Sustaining Competitive Advantage*. Upper Saddle River, NJ: Prentice Hall.

Baum, J.A.C. and Oliver, C. (1991) 'Institutional linkages and organisational mortality', *Administrative Science Quarterly*, 31: 187–218.

Baum, J.A.C., Calabrese, T. and Silverman, B.S. (2000a) 'Don't go it alone: alliance network composition and startups' performance in Canadian biotechnology', *Strategic Management Journal*, 21: 267–94.

Baum, J.A.C., Stan Li, X. and Usher, J.M. (2000b) 'Making the next move: how experiential and vicarious learning shape the locations of chains' acquisitions', *Administrative Science Quarterly*, 45 (4): 766–801.

Bennett, R.C. and Cooper, R.G. (1979) 'Beyond the marketing concept', *Business Horizon*, 22 (5): 238–46.

Besanko, D., Dranove, D. and Shanley, M. (1996) *The Economics of Strategy*. New York: Wiley.

Biemans, W. (1991) 'User and third-party involvement in developing medical equipment innovations', *Technovation*, 11 (3): 163.

Brandenburger, A.M. and Nalebuff, B.J. (1996) *Co-opetition*. London: Profile Books.

Brusoni, S., Prencipe, A. and Pavitt, K. (2001) 'Knowledge specialization, organizational coupling, and the boundaries of the firm: why do firms know more than they make?', *Administrative Science Quarterly*, 46 (4): 597–621.

Capon, N., Farley, J. and Hulbert, J. (1987) 'A comparative analysis of the strategy and structure of United States and Australian corporations', *Journal of International Business Studies*, 8 (1): 51–74.

Chesbrough, H. (2006) *Open Business Models: How to Thrive in the New Innovation Landscape*. Boston, MA: Harvard Business School Press.

Cohen, W.M. and Levinthal, D.A. (1990) 'Absorptive capacity: a new perspective on learning and innovation', *Administrative Science Quarterly*, 35: 128–52.

Coles, A., Harris, L. and Dickson, K. (2003) 'Testing goodwill: conflict and cooperation in new product development networks', *International Journal of Technology Management*, 25 (1): 51.

Dess, G.G. and Beard D.W. (1984) 'Dimensions of organisational task environments', *Administrative Science Quarterly*, 29: 52–73.

Freeman, C. (1991) 'Networks of innovators: a synthesis of research issues', *Research Policy*, 20: 499–514.

Freeman, C. and Soete, L. (1997) *The Economics of Industrial Innovation*, 3rd edn. Cambridge, MA: MIT Press Books.

Frosch, R.A. (1996) 'The customer for R&D is always wrong!', *Research Technology Management*, 39 (6): 22–7.

Goold, M. and Campbell, A. (1998) 'Desperately seeking synergy', *Harvard Business Review*, 76 (5): 131–43.

Granstrand, O., Patel, P. and Pavitt, K. (1997) 'Multi-technology corporations: why they have "distributed" rather than "distinctive core" competences', *California Management Review*, 39 (4): 8–27.

Grant, R. (2008) *Contemporary Strategy Analysis*. Oxford: Blackwell.

Gulati, R. (1999) 'Network location and learning: the influence of network resources and firm capabilities on alliance formation', *Strategic Management Journal*, 20 (5): 397–420.

Gulati, R., Nohria, N. and Zaheer, A. (2000) 'Strategic networks', *Strategic Management Journal*, 21, 203–15.

Hagedoorn, J. and Schakenraad, J. (1994) 'The effect of strategic technology alliances on company performance', *Strategic Management Journal*, 15 (4): 291–309.

Hamel, G. and Prahalad, C.K. (1994) *Competing for the Future*. Boston, MA: Harvard Business School Press.

Jauch, L.R. and Glueck, W. (1988) *Business Policy and Strategic Management*. New York: McGraw-Hill.

Johnson, M.W., Christensen, C.M. and Kagermann, H. (2008) 'Reinventing your business model', *Harvard Business Review*, December, available at http://hbr.org/2008/12/reinventing-your-business-model/ar/1, accessed 6 June 2013.

Kim, W. and Mauborgne, R. (1999) 'Creating new market space', *Harvard Business Review*, 77 (1): 83–93.

Kim, W. and Mauborgne, R. (2004) 'Blue ocean strategy', *Harvard Business Review*, 82 (10): 76–84.

Kim, W. and Mauborgne, R. (2005) 'Blue ocean strategy: from theory to practice', *California Management Review*, 47 (3): 105–21.

Kogut, B. and Zander, U. (1992) 'Knowledge of the firm, combinative capabilities, and the replication of technology', *Organization Science*, 3: 383–97.

Lakhani, K., Lars, R., Jeppsen, B., Lohse, P.A. and Panetta, J.A. (2007) *The Value of Openness in Scientific Problem Solving*. Boston, MA: Harvard Business School Working Paper, No. 07-050.

Lane, P.J. and Lubatkin, M. (1998) 'Relative absorptive capacity and interorganizational learning', *Strategic Management Journal*, 19: 461–77.

Leavy, A. (1999) *Population and Employment Change in Rural Areas in Ireland 1971 to 1996*. Paper presented to the ERSA Conference, Dublin.

Leonard-Burton, D. and Doyle, J.L. (1996) 'Commercializing technology: imaginative understanding of user needs', in R.S. Rosenbloom and W.J. Spencer (eds), *Engines of Innovation*. Boston, MA: Harvard Business School Press, pp. 177–207.

Lorenzoni, G. and Lipparini, A. (1999) 'The leveraging of interfirm relationships as a distinctive organizational capability: a longitudinal study', *Strategic Management Journal*, 20 (4): 317.

Lynch, R. (2006) *Corporate Strategy*, 4th edn. Harlow: Financial Times/Prentice Hall.

Megginson, L. C. (1963) 'Lessons from Europe for American Business', *Southwestern Social Science Quarterly*, 44 (1): 3–13.

Mintzberg, H. (1987) 'Crafting strategy', *Harvard Business Review*, July and August: 65.

Mowery, D.C., Oxley, J.E. and Silverman, B.S. (1996) 'Strategic alliances and interfirm knowledge transfer', *Strategic Management Journal*, 17: 77–91.

Nelson, R.R. and Winter, S.G. (1982) *An Evolutionary Theory of Economic Change*. Cambridge, MA: Harvard University Press.

Ohmae, K. (1982) *The Mind of the Strategist*. New York: McGraw-Hill.

Park, S.H. and Russo, M.V. (1996) 'When competition eclipses cooperation: an event history analysis of joint venture failure', *Management Science*, 42: 875–90.

Penrose, E. (1959) *The Theory of the Growth of the Firm*. New York: Wiley.

Perrott, B. (2008) 'Managing strategy in turbulent environments', *Journal of General Management*, 33 (3): 21–30.

Peteraf, M.A. (1993) 'The cornerstones of competitive advantage: a resource-based view', *Strategic Management Journal*, 14 (3): 179–91.

Porter, M.E. (1980) *Competitive Strategy*. New York: The Free Press.

Powell, W. W., Koput, K. W. and Smith-Doerr, L. (1996) 'Interorganisational collaboration and the locus of innovation: networks of learning in biotechnology', *Administrative Science Quarterly*, 41 (March): 116–45.

Reichheld, F.F. (1996) *The Loyalty Effect*. Boston, MA: Harvard Business School Press.

Ritter, T. and Gemünden, H. (2003) 'Network competence: its impact on innovation success and its antecedents', *Journal of Business Research*, 56 (9): 745–55.

Rosenberg, N. (1982) *Inside the Black Box: Technology and Economics*. Cambridge: Cambridge University Press.

Samli, A.C. (2006) 'Surviving in chaotic modern markets: strategic considerations in turbulent times', *Journal of Marketing Theory and Practice*, 14 (4): 315–22.

Sapienza, H.J., Parhankangas, A. and Autio, E. (2004) 'Knowledge relatedness and post-spinoff growth', *Journal of Business Venturing*, 19 (6): 809–29.

Schumpeter, J.A. (1942/87) *Capitalism, Socialism and Democracy*. London: Unwin.

Senge, P.M. (1990) *The Fifth Discipline: The Art and Practice of the Learning Organization*. New York: Doubleday Currency.

Shan, W., Walker, G. and Kogut, B. (1994) 'Interfirm cooperation and startup innovation in the biotechnology industry', *Strategic Management Journal*, 15 (5): 387–94.

Shaw, B. (1998) 'Innovation and new product development in the UK medical equipment industry', *International Journal of Technology Management*, 15: 433.

Slater, S. and Narver, J.C. (1998) 'Customer-led and market-oriented: let's not confuse the two', *Strategic Management Journal*, 19: 1001–06.

Slater, S. and Zwirlein, T. (1992) 'Shareholder value and investment strategy using the general portfolio model', *Journal of Management*, 18 (4): 717–32.

Smith, A. (1999) 'Unilever steps up brand sales', *Financial Times*, 5 May: 28.

Stockdale, R. and Standing, C. (2006) 'An interpretive approach to evaluating information systems: a content, context, process framework', *European Journal of Operational Research*, 173 (3): 1090–102.

Stuart, T.E. (2000) 'Interorganizational alliances and the performance of firms: a study of growth and innovation rates in high-technology industry', *Strategic Management Journal*, 21 (8): 791–811.

Tauber, E.M. (1974) 'How market-research discourages major innovation', *Business Horizons*, 17 (June): 22–6.

Tidd, J., Bessant, J, and Pavitt, K.L.R. (2000) *Managing Innovation: Integrating Technological, Market and Organisational Change*, 2nd edn. Chichester: Wiley.

Von Hippel, E. (1988) *The Sources of Innovation*. New York: Oxford University Press.

Willman, J. (1999a) 'Unilever to focus on core "power brands"', *Financial Times*, 22 September: 25.

Willman, J. (1999b) 'Unilever thinks the unthinkable to accelerate its growth', *Financial Times*, 24 September: 27.

Zahra, S.A. and George, G. (2002) 'Absorptive capacity: a review, reconceptualisation, and extension', *Academy of Management Review*, 27 (2): 185–203.

3

STRATEGIC HUMAN RESOURCE MANAGEMENT

Geoffrey Wood and Zsuzsanna Kispál-Vitai

Chapter Overview

In this chapter we explore the origins of strategic HRM, the principle approaches to strategic HRM, and their possibilities and limitations, both in theory and practice. We evaluate the reasons behind the rise of strategic HRM in the 1990s, the main different approaches to managing people strategically, and link these to wider debates and controversies surrounding the role of the organization in society.

≣ **Learning Objectives** ≣

- **Understand what comprises strategic HRM**
- **Introduce and critically discuss shareholder-orientated/harder approaches to best practice HRM**
- **Identify the main ways HR strategy can be conceived to operate in practice**
- **Introduce and critically discuss stakeholder-orientated/softer approaches to best practice HRM**
- **Introduce and critically discuss the broad contingency approach**
- **Identify and compare and contrast the different forms of contingent HR strategy**

≣ **CASE STUDY 3.1** ≣

The South African motor industry

The South African motor industry originally emerged through the assembly of knock-down kits of parts from abroad. Over the years, these developed into fully fledged manufacturers. This was largely due to the active industrial policies of the apartheid government (in power from 1948 to

1994), which aggressively promoted import substitution. Under apartheid, racial discrimination in the communities was mirrored by racial Fordism: blacks were largely condemned to poorly paid unskilled work. This led to many industries relying on cheap labour to solve systemically imposed inefficiencies. In the 1970s, a wave of unionization of blacks took place, eclipsing the older, white-dominated trade unions. By the early 1980s, the new ('independent') unions became increasingly outspoken in opposing the apartheid order. Mass resistance in communities was paralleled by an upsurge in strike action. In the Mercedes-Benz plant in East London, the resistance became so intense that large areas of the factory were rendered no-go areas for management. Finally, a grouping of workers occupied the plant, damaging inventories and machinery.

The close of the apartheid era alleviated much of the underlying tensions; at the same time, managers began to forge cooperative deals with unions. At Mercedes-Benz, these included very much better pay and working conditions, new opportunities for up-skilling and career advancement, and a range of participative mechanisms, giving workers a real say in the process of production. Today, the plant is one of the most productive car plants in the world, and its products have the fewest defects of any Mercedes-Benz plant. While previously the plant was marginal, and by the late 1980s under threat of closure, today it is an integral part of the Mercedes-Benz worldwide production network.

Source: author.

 ■ Questions

1. What lessons does the Mercedes-Benz East London plant hold for HR managers worldwide?
2. Is the experience of Mercedes-Benz in East London relevant to other industries? If not, why not?

Introduction

We could regard HRM as a process where activities are depicted as a circle and the beginning of this circle is a matter of academic choice. If we think about how a business starts, then logic would dictate this starting point is staffing. When we think about already existing businesses and take into consideration the need of the practitioner, this starting point can be HRM strategy. Even the very definition of HRM assumes a strong link between the strategy of the business and the practice of people management (Redman and Wilkinson 2001). In this chapter we define what strategic human resource management is, and link models of HRM to strategic HRM practice with a special emphasis on the resource-based view of the firm. Based on research evidence we evaluate the strategic approach to HRM in adding value to business operations.

The rise of strategic HRM

It has been argued that if the 1980s saw the rise of HRM, the 1990s saw an increased emphasis on the strategic management of people (Kramer and Syed 2012). While the former focused on the recognition of the importance of human assets other than passive entities to be administered, the latter focused on the need to more closely align people with wider organizational objectives. In other words, strategic HRM focused on outcomes and the path towards optimizing a firm's performance, and hence its success; people were not only assets but also potential value creators, if they were more closely aligned to the architecture of the firm (ibid.). Indeed, it has been argued that as a result of structural changes in the global economy, people management has become ever more important (Bratton and Gold 2012: 50). It is suggested that, contrary to the traditional view of the firm, strategic HRM holds that the manner in which people are managed holds the key to competitive advantage; more traditional views focus on the physical factors of production such as plant and machinery (see Storey 2007). Strategic HRM is based on the assumption that internal resources provide the basis of competitive advantage, in contrast to the traditional economic focus on factors of production (Kramer and Syed 2012: 129).

A problem with this is that it suggests that people were somehow less important in the past, and/or that firms were in previous decades oblivious to the strategic advantages people could confer. Nonetheless, there is little doubt that even if this is the case, there has been an increasing focus on espoused rather than emergent strategy; in other words, there has been more emphasis on formal top-down strategies in words, if not in actual deeds, than in strategies emerging from a pattern of choices in HR actual practice, which has been the traditional approach of many firms (Bratton and Gold 2012: 51).

When looking for definitions of SHRM there is no shortage of different concepts, ranging from simple definitions such as the one in Mathis and Jackson (2008: 36):

> Use of employees to gain or keep competitive advantage.

to

> the intentions of the corporation both explicit and covert, toward the management of its employees, expressed through philosophies, policies and practices. (Torrington et al. 2005: 28)

or

> the pattern of planned human resource deployments and activities intended to enable the firm to achieve its goals. (Wright and McMahan 1992: 298)

A recent, and perhaps the clearest, definition is Mello's:

> the development of a consistent aligned collection of practices, programs and policies to facilitate the achievement of the organization's strategic objectives. (2006: 152)

Strategic human resource management is a relatively new field of research and exists at the intersection of strategy and HRM (Allen and Wright 2006). It has the ambition of creating models that encompass, and holistically incorporate, both the strategy a business should follow and also those HR activities that support this strategy. In SHRM the micro perspective that usually prevails in HRM – that is, examining people relationships, behaviours, or organizational policies – shifts towards a more meso or macro perspective, where researchers look at systems in the organizations and also look for relationships that enhance and complement each other.

Schuler and Jackson (2005) define SHRM as a complex system which has a number of characteristics. These are:

- *Vertical integration*: working together with line managers, HR managers have to understand the organization and its environment.
- *Horizontal integration*: the practices in the organization are harmonized into coherent systems, where elements mutually reinforce each other.
- *Effectiveness*: there is a way of showing how HRM contributes to the main activities of the organization.
- *Partnership*: working closely together with non-HR professionals, such as line managers, and other players within the firm, toward a common goal.

HR strategy in practice

There are several ideal types of HR strategy in practice.

Strategic models of competitive advantage

According to Mello (2006) models of strategy fall into two broad categories, those that examine the external environment and concentrate on external influences of the business, and those that look for defining factors in strategy in the inside of the firm. Among the outside-in or industrial organization models we look at two: the Miles and Snow typologies, and Porter's frequently mentioned model of generic strategies (see Chapter 2).

The Miles and Snow typology

Miles et al. (1978) created a typology of how firms deal with strategy challenges, and, later in 1984, they added human resources strategies to their systems. According to this framework there are four types of organizations:

- Defenders.
- Prospectors.
- Analysers.
- Reactors.

The first three are original strategies, the fourth is an unsuccessful residual strategy. Defenders look for stability and try to capture a narrow segment of the total potential market. Prospectors try to find new products and new market opportunities, they are the innovators. Analysers combine both the above strategies by getting into new markets or new products after their viability has been proved. They are the imitators. The last group, reactors, represents a mixed and inconsistent strategy. The three different clear strategies require different human resource management systems in the organization (Miles and Snow 1984). This framework can be regarded as the predecessor of the 'best practice' models created later.

Porter's generic strategies

In this model management of the firm should concentrate on what gives the business sustainable competitive advantage. According to Porter no business can perform at a high level if it does not choose a specific way of competing. He suggests three basic strategies:

- *Cost leadership*. Here the business produces at low cost, but low cost does not mean low quality as well. What they offer has to be acceptable quality or at least acceptable enough for the customer. The successful low-cost competitor should be the one who has the low*est* cost and is not just trying to be inexpensive. A firm has several ways to achieve cost advantage, such as economizing on efficiency of operations, low labour cost, using techno-logical innovations, or utilizing economies of scale, for example. This strategy seeks advantage in a broad range of industry segments.
- *Differentiation*. Here the business offers something that the others cannot, it tries to be unique in some way that is valued by the customer. This can be high quality, good service, or unique brand image. What the firm offers has to be very different from that of the competition, or at least should be perceived so. Differentiation can also focus at broad industry segments, where there can be a number of strategies to follow.
- *Focus*. This strategy seeks advantage in a narrow range of industry, and focuses on a specific issue, such as a special customer, or a specific distribution channel, or a geographical segment. The feasibility of this strategy depends on the size of the segment and that the income they earn can support the additional costs created by this focusing.

Porter calls organizations that do not use a specific strategy 'stuck in the middle'. These start with a certain strategy then deviate towards another one and then cannot decide which of these they represent. Such organizations can be profitable if they compete where there are plenty of resources, or when the competitors are similarly stuck in the middle (Porter 1998; Robbins and Barnwell 2006).

The resource-based view of the firm

If Porter's model represented the industrial and outside-in approach towards strategy then the resource-based view is the opposite as that goes inside-out and represents more micro aspects.

In the resource-based view of the firm (see also Chapter 13) we look inside and examine the resources and capabilities that are at the firm's disposal (Barney and Hesterly 2006). There are two key assumptions regarding these resources:

1. Firms may be heterogeneous in terms of what resources they own.
2. These resources may not be completely mobile so the heterogeneity may last long. There may not be a possibility for resources to be equalized by mobility.

Firm resources are classified into four basic categories:

1. Financial resources, such as capital, earnings.
2. Physical resources, such as equipment, machinery, buildings.
3. Human resources, and here they think about the experience, training, and intelligence of the individuals who work for the firm
4. Organizational resources, such as the formal structure, systems, informal relationships, teamwork inside the organization (Barney and Hesterly 2006).

This view suggests that the resource will represent a competitive advantage if it has four attributes. It must be:

1. *Valuable* in the strategic sense (it must enable the firm to take advantage of opportunities and neutralize threats in the environment).
2. *Rare* (not easily found among competitors).
3. *Imperfectly imitable* (for the other firms in the industry).
4. *Without good substitutes.*

General issues

A lot depends on the manner in which the firm is governed. It can be argued that, for example, the more a firm is insulated from shareholder pressures, the more viable the resource-based view will be in practice (Purcell 2001: 59). Hence, it can be argued that the relative viability of these models and how they work out in practice will depend on fundamental assumptions as to the organization, and its relationship with key parties. A key issue is whether there are certain best practices that have universal validity, or whether certain practices will work best in certain settings, rather than others.

Best practice approaches

Best practice approaches (see also Chapter 13) hold that there is one specific set of optimal HR practices. In practice, there are two strands of thinking that comprise this school, based on very different assumptions, shareholder-dominant and more stakeholder-orientated approaches. The first believes the task of the firm is to maximize shareholder value: people are a resource deployed to meet this end, and all aspects of people management should be narrowly orientated towards this agenda. The second believes that firms are most likely to succeed if they empower their workers: unlike a range of exter-nal pressures that have simply to be coped with, people are a uniquely flexible resource and can supply a firm with a genuine competitive advantage over competitors battling under similar circumstances.

PIT STOP: REFLECTIVE ACTIVITY 3.1

1. Try and identify an organization whose HR strategy follows the hard/shareholder-dominant approach to best practice HRM. What benefits does this strategy confer, and do you think it is sustainable?

Best practice: shareholder-dominant accounts

Structural changes in the global economy since the 1970s undermined the basis of competitiveness of many established firms, and greatly strengthened the hands of more fungible sections of capital, in other words, more mobile and speculative investors. The accession to power of right-wing governments in the UK and the US in the 1980s, and the subsequent deregulation of finan-cial markets, accelerated this process (see Chapter 8). Sometimes referred to as the shareholder revolution, this process reversed the relative empowerment of professional managers, under the so-called managerial revolution. Rather, firms were now expected to concentrate on maximizing returns to investors: anything else was cast as the misappropriation of organizational resources (cf.

Solomon 1992). In practice, it could be argued that the main beneficiaries of this process were not long-term investors, but rather financial intermediaries (Erturk et al. 2008).

Inspired by this, a particularly influential strand of theory, inspired by rational-choice economics, cast the role of managers simply as agents of shareholders. Ways needed to be found to closely align the former with the latter. It was held that if left to their own devices, managers would engage in 'empire building', misappropriating and misdirecting organizational resources in the interests of their personal glory (La Porta et al. 2002). Quite simply, it was held that managers would naturally prefer to work for larger organizations on account of the prestige these conferred, and would conspire with employees and other stakeholder interests to attain this agenda (ibid.).

To resolve this problem, two fundamental changes were necessary in HR practices. The first concerns senior managers. What was needed here was to more closely align their rewards with the share price of the firm (Dore 2009). As individuals were cast as rational profit-maximizing individuals, they would naturally respond by abandoning any plans for empire building in favour of maximizing shareholder value. In practice, many firms – again, particularly within liberal market economies such as those of the US and the UK – did indeed follow this prescription. In practice, the results have been mixed. First, it is possible – and indeed, likely – that managers may conspire with financial intermediaries to maximize returns through measures such as share buy-backs, that add little to the real value of the firm (Erturk et al. 2008). Intermediaries may also back excessive managerial incentives, even if normal investors suffer from the diversion of resources away from them. It may also lead to a rise in managerial 'irresponsibility', in that the firm may be viewed as little more than a debt vehicle, or a set of assets to be liquidated, rather than something that might add value to long-term investors and other stakeholders over many years.

Again, the consequences for the firm itself may be debilitating. First, the new managerial pay has led to rising inequality within firms: this is likely to undermine employee morale and sense of well-being. Second, agency approaches assume that leaner organizations are naturally more efficient. Indeed, proponents of agency theory, such as Jensen (1993), have argued that downsizing is a natural tendency in contemporary economies, and that organizations that downsize the most effectively will ultimately be the most efficient (see Chapter 1). Many institutional investors have indeed bought into this logic; as a result, firms that embark on redundancies or other forms of downsizing often benefit from short-term improvements in their stock market performance. Again, as labour is seen as a readily interchangeable commodity, deregulated labour markets will allow firms to readily access (and if need be, dispose of) skills as and when needed. In order to gain employment, job seekers will have a personal interest in gaining particularly needed skills. Again, weak tenure means that employees will be under pressure to upgrade their skills according to organizational need. Hence, training and development costs are shifted on to job seekers and existing employees.

What about employee well-being? Here the view is very simple. The purpose of business is, ultimately, to make money for shareholders (Friedman 1970). It is held that, if firms concentrate on maximizing shareholder returns, they will perform optimally. In turn, employees will benefit from working for a successful organization as opposed to a failing one: if all firms follow suit, the economy will grow. A problem with this view is that it relies on benefits trickling down. However, in a situation of cut-throat competition, firms may seize a short-term advantage through paying very low wages: if competitors follow suit, this will depress consumer demand, and all firms will ultimately suffer. Again, low job security and high internal inequality between top managers and the rest of the workforce have been proven to undermine staff morale and well-being (Dore 2000).

Once more, as Aoki (2010) notes, it is difficult to accurately gauge the worth of the collective cognitive capabilities of the organization and its people. In practice, there has been a tendency to systematically undervalue these, with waves of downsizing resulting in a considerable loss of accumulated knowledge and experience, and, indeed, existing synergies between groups of employees working together. In looking at the consequences of private equity takeovers in the UK, Goergen et al. (2011) found that such takeovers did tend to lead to downsizing, but rather than disciplining remaining staff, and making the organization more efficient, the ultimate result was lower productivity and reduced organizational performance. Finally, high staff turnover rates can lead to firms spending relatively large amounts on basic induction training, when higher levels of mutual commitment between a firm and its employees mean that training costs may be spread over many years (Brewster et al. 2012).

Although it is clear that this best practice approach brings with it serious practical problems, it remains highly influential. Indeed, it is the only set of HR strategies commonly recognized within financial markets to be of any value whatsoever. Although this hard approach to best practice is the minority view within the HRM academic community in Britain and continental Europe, it has achieved some impact among their US counterparts.

Best practice models resemble expectancy theory (Pilbeam and Corbridge 2010) in that *if* you implement a certain practice *then* you can expect higher profitability, less turnover, but only on condition that HRM is fully integrated into the strategic planning process of the company. Moreover all best-practice models are universalist and prescriptive in their approach; they claim that using the same best practices of HRM will be instrumental in improving performance. These models rely less on context and instead downplay its significance (Schuler and Jackson 2005). The factors that have to be present are:

- competence,
- commitment,
- motivation and effective job design (Pilbeam and Corbridge, 2010).

Best practice: stakeholder perspectives

If the above approach to best practice is dominant within the economics and finance literature, and indeed within the investor community, an alternative, softer, stakeholder-orientated view is rather more popular in the HRM academic community, in particular in Europe. There were two main causes behind the rise of this viewpoint. First, in the 1970s and 1980s, liberal market economies such as those of the United Kingdom and the United States performed rather worse than economies subject to a higher degree of coordination (that is, greater state intervention in mediating the interests of different groups of stakeholders), such as in Germany and Japan. This led to a proliferation of research aimed at identifying the secrets of managerial success in such contexts, with a particular interest in Japan (see Dore 2000). The result of such endeavours led to the view that what set practices apart in such contexts was a stronger focus on employee involvement (Japan) and participation (Germany) (Dore 2000). Hence, it could be argued that optimal HR practices were ones that gave employees a greater say in how their work was organized, and, potentially, in the terms and conditions of their service (see Chapter 8).

This led to arguments that softer more stakeholder-orientated approaches to HRM are generally likely to yield better results than harder, more shareholder-orientated ones. In other words, firms were urged to adopt softer policies in order to enhance their competitive position. A problem with this argument is that it assumes that firms that are associated with softer HR policies are likely to make more money. In practice, some of the most successful firms in the world have become enmeshed in controversy on account of their labour standards. These include Apple (labour conditions in Apple's suppliers in mainland China have been subject to much media attention), McDonalds (refer to the word 'McJob' encountered in the *Oxford English Dictionary*), and Wal-Mart. Again, if firms are enticed to engage in good conduct on account of the fact that it may be more profitable, then, it could be argued, such choices are devoid of moral worth (Mellahi et al. 2010).

In best practice HRM it is a common argument that people practices cannot influence operations in isolation. Rather, they have to be harmonized with each other and the company has to create a system where elements are related to each other and also have to be related to the main processes, such as for example manufacturing policies. The horizontal integration of HRM elements is what theorists call 'bundles' (McDuffie 1995). Bundles of human resource practices represent a view of the HR function where these are interrelated as elements of a system. The interrelated logical system of HRM practices will improve performance; one practice used in isolation will not have the same effect as when it works in combination with others. There has been empirical evidence that systematic improvement of HR practices improved performance while those that were adopted in isolation did not (Ichniowski and Shaw 1999). Moreover, practices can be introduced not just to complement each other, but also to neutralize each other's effects. If we are selectively hiring but do not remunerate our high-quality workforce according to company performance then these two conflicting effects will counteract each other and we will have lower performance. Consequently if we consciously design our HR system and pay attention to building it so that elements such as selection, training and performance evaluation, for example, are dependent upon each other, and support each other, overall company performance will be significantly better.

But if firms move towards a more stakeholder-friendly orientation to HRM, what practices should they adopt? Here, there are a number of alternative approaches.

The Harvard model

This model is called a stakeholder model by Huczynski and Buchanan (2007) because the decisions inside the organization are not made independent of stakeholder interests. Managers have to take into consideration these and the context where the organization operates. In this respect this model deviates from the universalism of the best-practice model, because it regards context as a moderating variable. HR policies adopted by the organization are influenced by:

- Shareholders.
- Management.
- Employees.
- Government.
- Community.
- Trade unions as *stakeholders*. And:

  - Workforce characteristics.
  - Business strategy.
  - Economic climate.
  - Management philosophy.
  - Labour market conditions.
  - Trade union policy.
  - Technology.
  - Legislation.
  - Social values as the *context*.

The four policies are:

- Employee influence.
- Human resource flow.
- Reward systems.
- Work systems.

Which also cause four outcomes, the four 'C's':

- Commitment.
- Competence.
- Congruence.
- Cost-effectiveness.

As Huczynski and Buchanan (2007) note, this model was not prepared to be a model of HRM in practice, but rather was a structure for the Harvard MBA syllabus in human resource management! It is not prescriptive, though if management implements these policies then the outcomes of the four 'C's' are bound to happen.

The Harvard model of HRM can be considered a 'soft' model (see also Chapter 13), because it emphasizes commitment, employee influence, competence and values. It looks at people in a humanistic way, and if we think about McGregor's Theory Y, it describes the approach. The soft model does not treat employees as a 'resource', but it is associated with commitment, communication and utilization of human talent. Truss et al. (1997) stress that although this dichotomy is implicitly based on the Harvard model of HRM it is not mentioned in American literature and the debates about it were exclusively British. The soft model can be regarded as a predecessor of the resource-based view because it emphasizes that a competitive advantage can be gained by building and supporting capabilities and commitment inside the firm (Storey 2007).

Pfeffer's high-commitment HR practices

Pfeffer first identified 16 universal HR practices which he later compressed to seven. This is also a US-orientated approach where the one practice that supports the others is employment security, inspired by the fact that the majority of workers in the US have very insecure tenure. It is perhaps a little difficult to propagate employment security in difficult times, when companies lay off people by the hundreds. However, it is logical that employees will not be very committed towards their organization and definitely are not so willing to exert organization citizenship behaviours if their jobs are insecure. The practices are:

- Employment security.
- Selective hiring of new personnel.
- Self-managed teams and decentralization of decision-making as the basic principles of organizational design.
- Comparatively high compensation contingent on organizational performance.
- Extensive training.
- Reduced status distinctions and barriers, including dress, language, office arrangements, and wage differences across levels.
- Extensive sharing of financial and performance information throughout the organization (Pfeffer 1998).

Still, if we just list our best practices the question remains: in which way will best practices contribute to competitive advantage? What are the mechanisms that lead towards productivity and quality because we adopt the bundles of practices? This is called the 'black box' problem, and research about it led to the AMO model of SHRM.

Best process – the AMO people and performance model

Purcell (2003) carried out research in 12 organizations from a wide range of sectors from manufacturing, through retail, to finance services for a 30-month period. The aim was to find out what are the processes through which the best-practice approaches work (Huczynski and Buchanan 2007). In this model HR policies are linked to organizational performance through the mediating AMO factors:

- Ability.
- Motivation.
- Opportunity.

For employees to contribute the maximum they must have the requisite knowledge, skills and abilities (KSAs). They also have to feel energized to do the job well and must have an opportunity to use their skills and knowledge in the interests of the organization.

HRM policies will provide the opportunity to employees to use their ability, and enhance motivation. The policies will be implemented by line managers who have to communicate trust, respect and encouragement – that is, they operate with best practices. The implemented HRM policies and the best practices used by line managers will lead to the required feelings of commitment and job satisfaction. If employees have these feelings then it will encourage them to perform better and do more than is expected.

The model is a straight continuation and development of the best practice models, because it identifies 11 core HR policies that can reinforce each other if introduced in a positive bundle. Practices should be positive and reinforcing: if not, the combination will reduce and not increase performance (Purcell 2003; Huczynski and Buchanan 2007).

Best-fit approaches: the Michigan model

This approach is not, strictly speaking, a best-practice model, in that it is held that HR should closely 'fit' the overall organizational strategy; however, it is somewhat inward-looking, and discounts the possible impact of wider societal features and relations. In practice, what is prescribed is little more than very hard-line HRM; stakeholder-orientated HR practices are seen as having little worth. Hence, it shares much in common with conservative best-practice approaches. In this model the internal 'fit' or horizontal integration (Torrington et al. 2005) can reinforce, emphasize, and create, high performance. The key practices they mention are:

- Selection.
- Performance.
- Appraisal.
- Rewards.
- Training.

The model is based on a rational strategy formulation that there is a strategy towards HRM strategies that can be aligned, and it does not address emergent strategy (Torrington et al. 2005).

It represents the 'hard' approach towards HRM, which is the rational, calculative approach that looks at people in the same way as at any other resource. The alignment with strategy also stresses using the workforce according to the needs of the business. It has been argued that this approach need not be regarded as 'inhuman' or 'exploitative'. Hollingworth (2009) poses the question of what would happen if managers mistreated their physical assets in the way they exploit their workforce, such as, for example, with 24/7 requirements, or expectations of putting in unpaid long hours in the name of commitment. A resource has to be treated well in order to function, so a human resource has to be treated in a way that satisfies not just the organization's requirement but also the employee's as well. One of the problems with the Michigan model is that it does not take into consideration the free will of employees and that they may not want to change (and nor may it be in their interests to change) their behaviour with the changes in the company's strategy (Torrington et al. 2005). As such, it takes little account of the political dimension of organizational processes, and, indeed, the impact of broader political processes on corporate governance and strategy formulation.

1. Try and identify an organization whose HR strategy follows the soft/stakeholder-dominant approach to best-practice HRM. What benefits does this strategy confer, and do you think it is sustainable?

≡ CASE STUDY 3.2 ≡

Postal workers in the UK

Postal workers in the UK have traditionally worked on a basis whereby they have considerable discretion over their labour time. They determine when precisely letters are delivered to individual houses, and how quickly they work. This has allowed them to have longer breaks in return for rapid working. In turn, postal workers are expected to cope with seasonal and unexpected fluctuations in the volume of letters to be delivered, again within broad parameters. This informal agreement – only partially defined in the employment contract – makes for speedy and reliable postal deliveries, but has always been the bane of consultants and managers seeking to 'modernize' the postal service. Modernization, in these terms, would imply bringing work and employment relations closer to those encountered in jobs with similar skill levels elsewhere in the economy. Understandably, postal workers have interpreted such interventions as challenging or undermining the existing employment contract and have resisted them, a good example being the 2010 Royal Mail dispute.

Source: author.

■ Questions

1. Postal workers appear to have traditionally had quite a lot of discretion in how they choose to deliver mail. How did this help the delivery of post?
2. What, do you think, are the costs associated with reducing the discretion available to workers?

Contingency approaches

The 1990s led to a resurgence of growth within liberal markets. Meanwhile Germany faced the enormous financial costs of integrating the former East Germany, while Japan entered a long period of stagnation. This led to proponents of the liberal market model loudly proclaiming its inherent superiority, with a blithe disregard for its historical track record. In response, a growing body of work suggested that each model had inherent strengths, although, implicitly, more coordinated models provided better outcomes for a wider range of stakeholder interests (Hall and Soskice 2001).

More specifically, it was held that within countries falling into each category, specific sets of institutions conferred specific advantages on firms if they followed specific practices (Hall and Soskice 2001; Hancke et al. 2007). Sets of mutually supportive practices were likely to work better together than individually, and if they were compatible with broader institutional arrangements. For example, stronger job security (in turn, a product both of law and convention) in coordinated markets would mean employees were likely to stay in specific jobs for longer: in turn, both firms and workers have an interest in developing their organization-specific skills, as adverse to those which are easily vendible on the external labour market. Conversely, situations of low job security in liberal markets might work well with generic tertiary skills bases (such as those encountered in Silicon Valley): the latter allows incumbents to more readily swap jobs, with firms benefiting from the diffusion of knowledge across an economy (see Hall and Soskice 2001). Again, a large unskilled pool of workers in liberal markets provides a good source of labour for low value added work in the service sector: weak job security allows firms to readily swap workers as a means of reining in poor performance and keeping wage costs down.

Of course, which HR policies work best does not only depend on the national context in which the firm operates (see Chapter 11), but also, inter alia, on the type of organization, its relative size, the industry it operates in, and its stage in the organizational life cycle (Wood and Lane 2012). In other words, strategy works best if it is closely integrated with context (Kramer and Syed 2012: 41). There are a number of different approaches within the broad contingency framework.

The competitive advantage model

Schuler and Jackson (1987) used the above-mentioned Porter strategic framework as a starting point, and identified certain employee behaviours that they suggested were required for the different strategic orientations. It stresses the usage of different behaviours that fit different strategic orientations. It proposes, for example, creative and innovative behaviours for the innovation strategy, but repetitive and predictable behaviour for the cost leadership strategy, high job involvement for innovation and low job involvement for cost leadership. Hence, they put together a 'menu' of HR practices which are continua ranging from one extreme to the other. For example, in training and development the company could have choices ranging from short-term to long-term, from productivity emphasis to quality of life emphasis. The choice depends on the strategy adopted by the organization. The model supposes there is a clear organizational strategy so the choices can be made, and if the strategy changes the choices have to change with it. The authors stress that the components of the system of practices have to be implemented simultaneously, otherwise the effect will be the opposite from what we want to achieve. This approach closely harmonizes with the HRM bundles concepts that emerged in research later.

Life-cycle models

These fit HRM strategy with the stage where the organization or the product life cycle rests (see Chapter 2). The logic here is that different HRM policies and practices will be effective at different stages of the organization. When a firm is at the beginning of its life cycle entrepreneurial flexibility is needed, while arriving at the growth stage it needs more stable and increasingly bureaucratic policies and practices. In the mature stage HR may concentrate on cost control, and in the declining stage again different issues come to the fore such as downsizing and related activities (Beardwell and Claydon 2010).

The resource-based view in practice

As noted above, the resource-based view represents the inside-out aspect of strategy where competitive advantage comes not from adaptation to the environment but is originated in the firm. In practical terms, for human resources, the conditions of the model have to be fulfilled, that is: they have to be valuable, rare, inimitable, and the human resource must be organized to be exploited. Barney and Wright (1997) argue HR can add value to business operations by either cutting costs or creating revenues. A firm's employees provide competitive advantage if they have specific characteristics that other firms' employees do not have. These may be, for example, enthusiasm or special knowledge or service orientation. Resources also have to be unique and difficult to imitate. According to Barney and Wright (1997) the social complexity is the factor that is created by the firm's unique history and development that render resources inimitable. The last condition of this model is similar to those of the configurational models in that resources have to be organized, that is, the organization must have policies and practices that are special and that enable them to exploit the resources.

The implications of this framework are that a sustainable competitive advantage comes from:

- Firm-specific rather than general skills.
- More from teams than individuals.
- More from HR systems than isolated HR practices.

PIT STOP: REFLECTIVE ACTIVITY 3.3

1. Which external factors, do you think, are likely to impact on the range of viable HR strategies open to managers?

Commodity chains in Chinese, Japanese and Korean plants

The following is a summary of some of the key findings of an investigation into HR strategy in manufacturing organizations in China.

Plants in Chinese firms tended to follow a cost-reduction strategy:

Plants, in general, were large mass production units seeking scale efficiencies and, to an extent, organizational power is centralized in a number of ways. Foreign-owned plants, for example, were staffed by expatriates, materials and production equipment were supplied for assembly by the parent company and production output and quality were closely monitored. In subcontractors, output and quality were similarly closely monitored. Work organization processes were carefully planned by engineers from the parent company and work, particularly in electronics, was broken down into simple tasks which were closely monitored and measured. Job design was fairly narrow, relatively few resources were invested in recruitment, selection and induction, and training and development was limited. Wage levels, meanwhile, were extremely low by comparison with those in parent company plants. Centralized organizational power was also expressed by relatively weak levels of communications (which were largely one-way), consultation and worker involvement. Quality demands were relatively high, albeit of standardized mature products, which is a reflection of the total-quality-control philosophy of the Japanese and Korean parent plants in electronics, and the demands of western and Japanese retail customers in clothing.

By contrast, the Japanese, Korean and Hong Kong-based plants employed a set of HRM strategies which were closer to quality enhancement and innovation strategies with, for example, high levels of participation, job security and extensive training and development. In a number of cases in our study, therefore, the same organization was pursuing different HRM strategies at different points in the commodity chain and at different locations.

Source: Morris et al. (2009: 367–8).

 ■ **Questions** ══════════════════════

1. To what extent does there appear to be a consistent HR strategy in place?
2. How can you explain the difference in practices between Mainland Chinese, Hong-Kong, Japanese and Korean-based plants?

Configurational approaches

A variation on the contingency approach are configurational approaches which assume that outcomes will be optimized through a close fit between internal HR policies and practices and the wider external dimension (Kramer and Syed 2012). In other words, it is argued that the firm needs to closely match outward business strategy and what actually goes on within the firm (Bratton and Gold 2012: 56).

Schuler and Jackson (2005) claim that the configurational perspective is 'conceptually indistinguishable' from the contingency perspective. However, Beardwell and Claydon (2010) argue that, according to this point of view, inside the firm horizontal integration is achieved by using a consistent set of HRM practices focused on a specific level of staff, and these are fitted to the strategy of the business vertically. So the configuration approach is not only about seeking a 'fit' with overall strategy and external context, but also with internal circumstances. The advantage of this approach is that it realizes firms may not use ideal strategies, and allows deviation from them.

CASE STUDY 3.4

Approaches to HRM in the hotel sector

HRM in the hotel sector is strongly influenced by the variability of customer demand, particularly in those establishments serving the seasonal tourism industry. The hotel sector is also heavily dependent on the external labour market as staff turnover is typically high and, therefore, a ready supply of both skilled and unskilled labour is often required to meet customer demand. This high turnover often results in problems of skills shortages in key operational areas, such as among waiting or kitchen staff. However, whilst the hotel industry context often acts to constrain managers' choice in HRM strategy, policies and practices, evidence suggests a variety of approaches to staffing and managing the workforce. The following case studies contrast the employment practices adopted in two 'similar' hotels operating in the same city.

The Mercury Hotel

'The Mercury' is a franchise establishment of a large US hotel chain. It is 4-star rated and mainly serves the commercial market, catering for business clients, including the hosting of conferences and seminars. It has almost 300 guestrooms, is located in the centre of a large UK city and directly employs more than 200 members of staff. Two-thirds of employees are employed full-time on 39-hour contracts with working patterns varying from week to week. Any hours worked beyond this are paid as overtime. The remaining third of employees are part-time (up to 25 hours per week). This structure appears to provide a balance between the need for flexibility in predictably busier periods throughout the year and as cover for short-term increases in demand. Management also make extensive use of return staff, mainly students who live in the area during term time or holiday periods to provide a further element of labour flexibility. Such employees are seen as a ready supply of trained labour but who have no claim to minimum hours, who can be shed with limited notice and who are most willing to work unsociable hours. Further, shortfalls in labour supply are met either by contracted or non-contracted casuals or by increasing permanent staff hours at short notice. Contracted casual employees are 'on-call' so that managers can demand that employees work 'as and when required', principally being used for functions such as wedding receptions. Management seek to minimize the potentially damaging effects on service quality by minimizing the use of non-contracted casuals and ensuring that, whilst providing a degree of flexibility, most employees are a 'known quantity' and have received at least some training. Moreover, rather than relying solely on numerical forms of flexibility (altering staffing levels in line with demand), The Mercury attempts to meet the challenge of variable demand by training members of staff across a range of different areas; a rudimentary form of skills flexibility. The approach to staffing adopted at The Mercury appears to reflect a compromise between the need for labour flexibility and employee stability, with management attempting not to overly manipulate employee hours simply to meet the direct needs of the organization.

In terms of employee involvement and communication, formal departmental meetings are held weekly for staff to discuss operational aspects of the hotel. Open staff meetings are held monthly, for both permanent and casual employees, the purpose of which is twofold. First, to pass on information on the performance of the hotel and, second, to act as a forum in which staff can ask questions directly of the general manager. Most importantly, a consultative committee, known as the 'Employee Forum', meets monthly and is chaired by the general and personnel manager. This forum is comprised of elected staff representatives from each department and allows staff to raise issues related to their working environment. It is also where recognition is passed on to staff for good service and employee representatives vote for 'employee of the month'.

Staff turnover is not considered a significant problem at The Mercury within the context of the industry. Management reported an annual turnover rate of approximately 35 per cent (the company target is 25 per cent). However, the HR manager claimed to do a significant amount of work to reduce this figure, particularly in the recruitment process. For example, department managers received training in interviewing techniques and ensured that candidates are made aware of the idiosyncrasies and demands of the industry. In addition, staff retention is addressed through ensuring staff development is offered to 'capable' employees and good performance is rewarded and recognized. Turnover is mainly attributed to mistakes made in recruitment and candidates' misconceptions about the industry generally, specifically pay levels and working hours. This is reflected in the fact that departing staff rarely left to work in other hotels, unless at a higher level, but tended to leave the industry. Absenteeism at The Mercury is considered acceptable. The personnel manager at the hotel suggested that an environment in which 'team-working' has evolved at the hotel and a degree of peer pressure discourages unnecessary absence.

Management at The Mercury considered skills shortages to be a huge problem in the industry, compounded by the highly competitive nature of the local labour market where it is felt that during most of the year employees would be able to leave employment at one hotel and gain employment 'five minutes down the road' in another. The HR manager claims that the inherent skills shortages in the local labour market are not felt as keenly in this hotel as in others because their image as a 'good employer' is useful in attracting and retaining staff. The package of benefits available to staff are described, by management, as 'exceptional' and are claimed to be central in recruiting and retaining high-quality, skilled employees and reducing problems of skills shortages, albeit within the context of moderate levels of staff turnover.

The Luna Hotel

'The Luna' is located approximately one mile from The Mercury and is part of a large UK hotel chain. It has 201 rooms, is also 4-star rated and employs 128 members of staff. The hotel was

(Continued)

(Continued)

subject to a takeover six months ago and is in a period of transition, not least in the way in which HRM is conducted. Again, two-thirds of the workforce is full-time, but the current management are seeking to significantly reduce this figure, having claimed they are overstaffed with permanent employees. They plan not to replace leavers in certain departments or replace them by offering workers flexible contracts; they express a willingness to rely heavily on casuals and agency staff to plug gaps in the workforce. Even permanent employees are now employed on significantly less favourable terms than prior to the takeover. Management claimed that this provided 'working-time flexibility' for both employer and employee. The number of hours and shift patterns are adjusted and planned on a weekly basis according to business levels, with both parties able to request more or less hours in a given period. No attempt had been made to train employees across a range of tasks to provide greater skills flexibility nor is there any intention to do so, given the stated desire to keep training costs to a minimum.

Employee communication at The Luna is predominantly one-way. General manager's briefings are held for all staff every quarter to inform them about organizational and establishment strategy and managerial decisions. Managerial meetings and communication between heads of department and employees is limited to one-to-one meetings as and when required, instigated by either party, usually to deal with grievance or disciplinary issues. There is no dedicated structure or schedule to these intra-departmental meetings although some departments imposed some formality by holding five-minute 'chats' between departmental heads and staff every month. Other departmental managers preferred employees to approach heads of department to raise issues. These one-to-one meetings appeared to be the only means of upward communication. There is no other provision for employee consultation, suggestion or participation in decision-making. It appeared that even the general manager's briefing is merely a communicative device with little provision for employee feedback.

The hotel had experienced high levels of labour turnover since the takeover, some of which was likely to be as a result of the upheaval caused. Regardless, labour turnover is reported to be both problematic and beneficial at The Luna, depending on the staff involved. On the one hand, employee turnover is considered undesirable because of the costs involved in recruiting new members of staff, especially skilled workers such as chefs and maintenance workers. On the other hand, however, employee turnover is considered a source of employment flexibility and 'natural wastage' of staff viewed as positive, especially where poor performing staff are concerned. The general manager claimed that the large labour market in which the hotel operated meant that staff are readily available, albeit often lacking required skills. Management coped with this apparent skills shortage by minimizing reliance on particular skills or providing rudimentary training. The high level of staff turnover often required management to adopt expedient approaches to filling vacancies, even in important frontline operational (for example, waiting and front of house) or skilled areas of work. As the HR and training manager suggested, *'When someone leaves just like that … you're in a hole and you have to get someone in, then you can't afford to wait a week or so for references to come through, when you've got a job to fill. You take a chance.'*

Source: Wilton (2013)

 ■ **Questions**

1. In what ways does the environmental context of the two hotels constrain or present opportunities for strategic choice?

2. Why do you think the two hotels have contrasting approaches to the management of their employees?
3. From a 'best fit' perspective, which of these hotels would appear to have best tailored its HR policies and practices to its competitive strategy?
4. What elements of 'best practice' HRM has The Mercury Hotel adopted and why might it have done so?
5. Drawing on the resource-based view, what elements of people resources could be exploited to create competitive advantage in the hotel industry?

Conclusion

There has been a growing consensus around the importance of managing people in a strategic manner. However, what is rather less clear is the extent to which specific sets of HR practices really lead to better organizational performance. Nonetheless, there is growing evidence that firms that engage in radical downsizing often do lasting damage to themselves, and that in some settings, more pluralist HR policies do indeed work better.

Here, a caveat is in order. There is an increasing assumption that all HRM is necessarily strategic, and/or that firms will increasingly be impelled to take a more strategic approach in managing their people owing to structural changes in the global economy. More critical approaches have pointed to the absence of strategic thinking in people management in many firms, and/or the great difficulties encountered in imparting strategic unity to HR activities within the real world. Many firms – particularly small- and medium-sized enterprises – manage people by 'muddling through', following traditional tried and tested policies, and adapting where this is necessary in the light of unforeseen pressures.

CASE STUDY 3.5

Dolphin Steel

Dolphin Steel traditionally made wire baskets for the deep frying or boiling of food, such as French fries and bagels. The firm used to employ a largely unskilled workforce of about 90 employees, and would supply the catering industry on a bulk basis, competing on cost grounds. Prior to the transformation of the organization, the firm would typically charge $6 for a basket; relatively low pay for workers made the operation viable at this cost basis.

Two major issues undercut the basis of the firm's competitiveness. First, the Atkins diet and other fad diets in the US led to reduced demand for foodstuffs that were high in carbohydrates, leading, in turn, to less demand by the catering industry. Second, new

(Continued)

(Continued)

competitors emerged in China, who were able to offer wire baskets at $3 or less. The firm was looking at a bleak future.

The situation changed dramatically one day when a representative from a major passenger aircraft manufacturer visited the factory. They wished to purchase a very small number of metal baskets suitable for dipping a key component into a tank of coating. They wished for the baskets to be of an exact specification, but were, in turn, willing to pay a premium for this. A final price of $3500 was agreed per basket.

Word got out among premium manufacturers of precision goods as to the suitability of the baskets for a wide range of uses in the process of production, and the willingness of Dolphin to supply a high-quality product according to the exact needs of the client. However, many of the new customers did not want to go to the difficulty of supplying exact specifications themselves, but asked Dolphin to do this for them, simply supplying details as to the process and components involved. In turn, this forced Dolphin to hire engineers. As nobody would pay $3500 for a wire basket that was not of the highest quality, the company soon increased the wages and upgraded the skills base of the workforce. A low-paying organization composed mostly of unskilled workers had been transformed to a high-paying organization with many skilled workers. Even basic administrative jobs such as dispatch now accrued premium wages: high-paying customers wished to be assured of the most reliable delivery schedules.

Source: author.

 ■ Questions

1. How central was strategic HRM to Dolphin's transformation?
2. Would the organization's new approach to people management be suitable to all organizations? Why?

Note: the name of the case study organization has been changed.

≡ CASE STUDY 3.6 ≡

Red Digital Cinema

The entire process of movie-making was revolutionized in the 2000s, with digital gradually replacing film as the primary recording medium. Digital allowed for very much easier editing and image manipulation, considerably less bulk, and greater cost-effectiveness, while the quality gap with conventional film has gradually closed. Red Digital Cinema was founded in the USA by Oakley sunglasses' founder Jim Jannard, shipping their first digital cinema camera in 2007, the RED One (http://www.red.com/). Unusually, product development involved involving prospective customers via a discussion board, on which Jannard regularly personally participates (see http://

reduser.net/). This has resulted in a great deal of interest and customer buy-in, and, by the more enthusiastic users, hero worship of the founder of the firm. This is an official account:

> Disruptive, revolutionary, game changing, paradigm shifting, visionary, challenging, rule breaking, irreverent. All are adjectives used to describe the technology and the pioneers that envisioned a true digital evolution of film, the minds behind RED. HD was a step backwards, offering less, not more, resolution than 35mm film. Modest steps along the path of innovation had to be leap-frogged. When the RED ONE was first conceptualized, the technology didn't exist to build it, recording solutions didn't exist to capture it and no one thought it was possible. No one except for a small band of people not smart enough to know that it couldn't be done. As with all revolutions, the RED revolution came with new rules, new solutions, and best of all, a new community of followers. One of the most significant departures from conventional marketing, pioneered by RED, was the concept of direct communication with its leaders. Here, unlike any camera company before it, a two-way dialogue has been established between the customer and the people responsible for the development of the product, most notably the owner and visionary himself, Jim Jannard. To have a finger on the pulse of the company, to engage in direct conversation with Jim and to learn the latest news at RED, your first stop should be the RECON thread on REDUSER. This extraordinary online relationship, creating a virtual roundtable of discussion, has been instrumental in the development and the advance of the art that is RED.

Source: http://www.red.com/learn

There is little doubt that RED shook up the somewhat conservative and closed world of cinema camera manufacturers. At roughly a similar time, a further threat to the latter emerged. Conventional 35mm single lens reflex (SLR) camera-makers such as Nikon and Canon had moved into the digital world, replacing film with digital sensors. As digital recording eliminates the need for bulky film stocks, it was soon possible for Nikon and Canon to offer motion picture recording facilities as an integral feature of their new digital single lens reflexes (DSLRs). While high-quality DSLRs were very much cheaper than professional cine cameras, they still came at a premium, and proved a very lucrative line for Nikon and Canon.

Spotting an opportunity, Jannard announced a digital slr (DSLR) 'killer', which metamorphosed into the Scarlet and Epic camera family. The new camera prototypes soon exhibited difficult to solve 'bugs'.

However, more serious was their original decision to outsource actual production to Foxconn, a Taiwanese firm that employs almost a million workers at its electronic factories in China (see the case study in Chapter 8). Foxconn were, and remain, the main manufacturer for Apple. To a large extent, their competitiveness is based on very low manufacturing costs, in turn due to low wages and large-scale mass production. Foxconn have been embroiled in numerous labour scandals in recent years, including the usage of child labour, low wages and long hours, and allegedly high levels of stress being imposed on workers by demanding working conditions.

(Continued)

Finally, a string of worker suicides and other protests rocked Foxconn plants. While Apple appear to have been undaunted by the reputational risks posed by such developments – periodic stated commitments to promoting better labour standards notwithstanding – RED were more deterred. Not only was the usage of labour under such conditions seen as detrimental to RED's brand and ethos, but prospective RED customers were pressing for deliveries of the Scarlet camera, at a time when it looked as if the protests would make Foxconn a less than perfectly reliable partner.

In a web forum, Jannard stated:

I have started two companies … Oakley and RED … and have never seen anything like this in 35 years of business. We will get past these obstacles. No question about it. But we are going to need patience from our customers … We have been a 'lucky' company up to this point … Trust me when I tell you that we have been humbled … So what does this mean? Obviously another delay … To compound matters, the company (Foxconn) that was to make Scarlet has made an incredible announcement recently and has significant issues ... RED has pushed the envelop in every way. We have pushed ourselves and our competitors. We have laid out a roadmap for everyone what the future of image capture should be. I can only hope that counts for a bit of your consideration.

This highlighted a major problem of RED against the likes of Nikon and Canon; its HR strategy had centred on a small highly skilled design and technical staff in the US, and had hoped to outsource the bulk of production, saving on labour costs and the challenges of managing a large workforce. In turn, this made their goal of humbling Canon and Nikon somewhat over-ambitious, especially as the latter continued to make headway into the cinema market in the interim.

Jannard has acknowledged 'The past couple of years we have been on a roll. Humility has now set in. Until we solve this one … we are heads down and nose to the grindstone. Probably not a bad lesson for us to learn.'

After the Foxconn debacle, RED decided to produce its new cameras in the USA, a move that will allow very much closer oversight of production process and labour standards, and a tighter integration between design and actual manufacture, a valuable advantage in a rapidly changing industry.

The inevitable increases in production costs have meant the new Scarlet camera was rather more expensive than initial estimates. Jannard has responded by saying that those using (significantly cheaper) DSLRs for filming 'should be ashamed of themselves', and that Red will not seek to cater to 'hockey moms'. However, somewhat disturbingly, two of the world's most prominent lens makers, Carl Zeiss and Schneider-Kreuznach, have begun to make cinematic quality prime lenses designed to be used with Canon and Nikon DSLRs. Against this, RED has begun to make slow inroads into the premium still photography market, with photographs shot with RED cameras appearing on the covers of leading fashion magazines.

Red's main competitor in terms of professional movie cameras is the industry leader, Arri (http://www.arri.de/). Arri is in many respects a traditional German-based manufacturing company, with much of the process of production being conducted in-house; the firm has over 12,000 employees. Arri's main supplier of lenses is Carl Zeiss, again a German company, with much of the production again taking place using a highly paid workforce in Germany. Outsourcing to China would have enabled Red to seize an advantage in cost terms. Over the years, the secret of Arri's success has been incremental innovation, gradually improving the reliability of the quality of its core products, aimed at professional cinema photographers, not 'computer geeks'. The digital revolution posed major challenges to Arri. Its initial response was to develop one of its existing camera platforms into a digital one, and offer scanning services from film. However, rapid inroads by Red into its market share led to it to develop a new digital camera, Alexa. Taking a leaf out of Red's book, the new product has its own website, with associated discussion forums (http://www.arridigital.com/). Arri has demonstrated no wish, however, to compete against considerably cheaper DSLRs, and remains committed to its highly paid workforce in Germany.

 ■ **Questions**

1. An attempt to outsource production to China did not work for Red. Why do you think this was the case? Is outsourcing the only option for other hi-tech companies making consumer electronics, such as Apple? If so why, and if not, why not?
2. What do you think are the benefits and costs of the alternative approach by Arri, of building much expertise and manufacturing capabilities in house? Which organization do you think is likely to be more successful in the long term and why?

■ Further Reading ■ ■ ■ ■ ■ ■ ■ ■ ■ ■ ■ ■ ■ ■

Key readings on the relationship between setting and specific HR strategies include:

Dore, R. (2000) *Stock Market Capitalism: Welfare Capitalism*. Cambridge: Cambridge University Press.

Hall, P. and Soskice, D. (eds) (2001) *Varieties of Capitalism: The Institutional Basis of Competitive Advantage*. Oxford: Oxford University Press.

There is a very extensive literature on agency theory. A good place to start will be the works of Michael Jensen:

Jensen, M. (1993) 'The modern Industrial Revolution, exit, and the failure of internal control systems', *Journal of Finance*, 48: 831–80.

In looking at existing research on both HR strategies in theory and practice, a good place to start is the *Emerald* stable of journals. These are available online at many universities, and they have an excellent keyword search facility.

In looking at examples of HR strategies in practice, a good place to start will be quality newspapers (e.g. *The Guardian* guardian.co.uk, *The Independent* www.independent.co.uk

and the *Financial Times* www.ft.com). Their archives are easily searchable online, and one can gain good evidence on the HR practices of major firms (e.g. Walmart, McDonalds, Apple, etc.). More detailed articles can be found in practitioner-orientated journals such as *Management Today* and through the CIPD website.

References

Allen, M.R. and Wright, P.M. (2006) *Strategic Management and HRM*, CAHRS Working Paper # 06-04. Ithaca, NY: Cornell University, School of Industrial and Labor Relations, Center for Advanced Human Resource Studies, available at http://digitalcommons.ilr.cornell.edu/cahrswp/404, accessed 25 November 2012.

Aoki, M. (2010) *Corporations in Evolving Diversity: Cognition, Governance and Institutions*. Oxford: Oxford University Press.

Barney, J.B. (1991) 'Firm resources and sustained competitive advantage', *Journal of Management*, 17 (1): 99–120.

Barney, J.B. and Hesterly, W. (2006) 'Organizational economics: understanding the relationship between organizations and economic analysis', in S.R. Clegg, C. Hardy, T.B. Lawrence and W.R. Nord (eds), *The SAGE Handbook of Organization Studies*, 2nd edn. London: Sage, pp. 111–49.

Barney, J.B. and Wright, P.M. (1997) *On Becoming a Strategic Partner: The Role of Human Resources in Gaining Competitive Advantage*, CAHRS Working Paper Series. Paper 150. Ithaca, NY: Cornell University, School of Industrial and Labor Relations, Center for Advanced Human Resource Studies, available at http://digitalcommons.ilr.cornell.edu/cahrswp/150, accessed 25 November 2012.

Beardwell, J. and Claydon, T. (2010) *Human Resource Management: A Contemporary Approach*, 6th edn. London: Financial Times/Prentice Hall.

Bratton, J. and Gold, J. (2012) *Human Resource Management: Theory and Practice*, 5th edn. London: Palgrave.

Brewster, C., Goergen, M., Wood, G. and Wilkinson, A. (2012) 'Varieties of capitalism and investments in human capital', *Industrial Relations*, 51 (s1): 501–27.

Dore, R. (2000) *Stock Market Capitalism: Welfare Capitalism*. Cambridge: Cambridge University Press.

Dore, R. (2009) 'Financialization of the global economy', *Industrial and Corporate Change*, 17 (6): 1097–112.

Erturk, I., Froud, J., Johal, S., Leaver, A. and Williams, K. (eds) (2008) *Financialization at Work: Key Texts and Commentary*. Abingdon: Routledge.

Friedman, M. (1970) 'The social responsibility of business is to increase its profits', *New York Times*, 13 September: 122–6.

Goergen, M., O'Sullivan, N. and Wood, G. (2011) 'Private equity takeovers and employment in the UK', *Corporate Governance: An International Review*, 19 (1): 259–75.

Hall, P. and Soskice, D. (2001) 'An introduction to the varieties of capitalism', in P. Hall and D. Soskice (eds), *Varieties of Capitalism: The Institutional Basis of Competitive Advantage*. Oxford: Oxford University Press, pp. 1–70.

Hancke, B., Rhodes, M. and Thatcher, M. (2007) 'Introduction: beyond varieties of capitalism', in B. Hancke, M. Rhodes and M. Thatcher (eds), *Beyond Varieties of Capitalism*. Oxford: Oxford University Press, pp. 3–38.

Hollingworth, M. (2009) 'Building 360 organizational sustainability', available at http://www.iveybusinessjournal.com/topics/global-business/building-360-organizational-sustainability, accessed 14 January 2012.

Huczynski, A. and Buchanan, D.A. (2007) *Organizational Behaviour*. London: Financial Times/Prentice Hall.

Huselid, M.A. (2009) *The HR Scorecard*, available at http://www.markhuselid.com/hr.html, accessed 4 January 2013.

Ichniowski, C. and Shaw, K. (1999) 'The effects of human resource management systems on economic performance: an international comparison of U.S. and Japanese plants', *Management Science,* 45 (5): 704–72.

Jensen, M. C. (1993) 'The modern industrial revolution, exit, and the failure of internal control systems', *Journal of Finance*, 48: 831–880.

Kramer, R. and Syed, J. (2012) *Human Resource Management in Global Context*. London: Palgrave.

La Porta, R., Lopez-de-Silanes, F., Shleifer, A. and Vishny, R. (2002) 'Investor protection and corporate valuation', *Journal of Finance*, 57 (3): 1147–70.

Mathis, R. and Jackson, J.H. (2008) *Human Resource Management*, 12th edn. Andover: South Western Cengage Learning.

McDuffie, J.P. (1995) 'Human resource bundles and manufacturing performance: organizational logic and flexible production systems in the world auto industry', *Industrial and Labor Relations Review*, 48 (2): 197–221.

Mellahi, K., Morrell, K. and Wood, G. (2010) *The Ethical Business: Challenges and Controversies*, 2nd edn. London: Palgrave.

Mello, J.A. (2006) *Strategic Management of Human Resources*, 3rd edn. Cincinnati, OH: South Western Cengage Learning.

Miles, R.E. and Snow, C.C. (1984) 'Designing strategic human resources systems', *Organizational Dynamics*, 13 (1): 36–52.

Miles, R.E., Snow, C.C., Meyer, A.D. and Coleman, Jr. H.J. (1978) 'Organizational strategy, structure and process', *The Academy of Management Review*, 3 (3): 546–62.

Morris, S.S., Wright, P.M., Trevor, J., Stiles, P., Stahl, G.K., Snell, S. and Farndale, E. (2009) 'Global challenges to replicating HR: the role of people, processes, and systems', *Human Resource Management*, 48 (6): 973–95.

Pfeffer, J. (1998) 'Seven practices of successful organizations', *California Management Review*, 40 (2): 96–124.

Pilbeam, S. and Corbridge, M. (2010) *People Resourcing and Talent Planning*, 4th edn. London: Financial Times.

Porter, M.E. (1998) *Competitive Advantage: Creating and Sustaining Superior Performance*. New York: The Free Press.

Purcell, J. (2001) 'The meaning of strategy in human resource management', in J. Storey (ed.), *Human Resource Management: A Critical Text*, 2nd edn. Thomson Learning, p. 59.

Purcell, J. (2003) *Understanding the People and Performance Link, Unlocking the Black Box*. London: Chartered Institute of Personnel and Development

Redman, T. and Wilkinson, A. (2001) *Contemporary Human Resource Management Text and Cases*. London: Financial Times/Prentice Hall.

Robbins, S. P. and Barnwell, N. (2006) *Organisation Theory*. Sydney: Pearson Education Australia.

Rutherford, M.W., Buller, P.F. and McMullen, P.R. (2003) 'Human resource management problems over the life cycle of small to medium-sized firms', *Human Resource Management*, 42 (4): 321–35.

Schuler, R.S. and Jackson, S.E. (1987) 'Linking competitive strategies with human resource management practices', *The Academy of Management Executive*, 1 (3): 207–19.

Schuler, R.S. and Jackson, S.E. (2005) 'A quarter-century review of human resource management in the U.S.: the growth in importance of the international perspective', *Management Revue*, 16: 1.

Solomon, R. (1992) *Ethics and Excellence: Co-Operation and Integrity in Business*. Oxford: Oxford University Press.

Storey, J. (2007) *Human Resource Management: A Critical Text*, 3rd edn. London: Thomson.

Torrington, D., Hall, L. and Taylor, S. (2005) *Human Resource Management*, 6th edn. London: FT/Prentice Hall.

Truss, C., Gratton, L., Hope-Hailey, W., McGovern, P. and Stiles, P. (1997) 'Soft and hard models of HRM – a reappraisal', *Journal of Management Studies*, 34 (1): 53–73.

Way, S.A. (2002) 'High performance work systems and intermediate indicators of firm performance within the US small business sector', *Journal of Management*, 28 (6): 765–85.

Wilton, N. (2013) *An Introduction to Human Resource Management*, 2nd edn. London: Sage Publications.

Wood, G. and Lane, C. (2012) 'Institutions, change and diversity', in C. Lane and G. Wood (eds), *Capitalist Diversity and Diversity within Capitalism*. London: Routledge, pp. 1–31.

Wright, P.M. and McMahan, G.C. (1992) 'Theoretical perspectives for strategic human resource management', *Journal of Management*, 18 (2): 295–320.

4

HRM: THE ADDED VALUE DEBATE

Charles Leatherbarrow

Chapter Overview

This chapter addresses the vexing issue of valuing the contribution that the human resource (HR) function adds to an organization. Any function (such as marketing, finance or purchasing) may be scrutinized for its added value, but HR is particularly prone to being questioned, and more so in stringent economic circumstances and contexts. Newer forms of HR delivery, such as the Ulrich Business Partner model, that attempt to move the HR function away from a simple transactional function to a business-focused transformational model, will also be explored.

Learning Objectives

- **To gain an appreciation of where HR can add value**
- **To consider how the Ulrich HR model applies to current HR contexts**
- **To consider some of the tools available for use by the HR function**
- **To evaluate the extent to whether the HR function can be measured**
- **To consider how the use of the Balanced Scorecard can add value to HR**
- **To consider what an effective HR function is**

CASE STUDY 4.1

Really Best Foods

In 2010 one of the UK factories of Really Best Foods, which specializes in the packaging of edible food powders such as beverages and desserts, lost a significant contract from a major customer. The factory normally operates on a 24-hour, 7 days a week basis. The demand for the packaging of foods can be very seasonal, which in turn has an impact upon how many production lines are required. In 2010 the workforce consisted of a mix of core directly employed staff together with temporary agency staff who were used to 'peak shave' the workload. Peak shaving is a term that refers to the process of employing temporary staff when work demand is high and releasing them when work demand reduces.

The main operational costs for such a continuous processing plant tend to be associated with the cost of labour. In 2010 the loss of the packaging contract caused the small human resources (HR) team to consider how best they could support the business. Clearly a reduction of headcount would be an obvious, and sadly very common, solution to the reduction of costs. Headcount reduction, a euphemism for loss of livelihood, has a social dimension. It impacts upon the ability of an individual to pay the rent or a mortgage, to maintain a standard of living, and may in the long term not be in the factory's best economic interests. Whenever staff leave an organization they take with them human capital, their knowledge and skills and sometimes tacit skills, which all can add up to give a competitive advantage. The factory has a long-standing and loyal workforce, and therefore the HR team did not wish to make compulsory redundancies. They were well aware of the impact that compulsory redundancies would have on the psychological contract, especially in a factory that could trace its roots to Quaker ownership and industrial welfarism.

The fluctuation in demands on the factory is one of the key factors which impacts upon effective workforce utilization. Clearly having people at work when there is little for them to do is not an option. A complex negotiation process developed that involved factory management and union representation. The discussion centred on improvements in staff utilization while minimizing likely redundancies in the factory's core workforce and the factory's ability to operate around the clock. The emerging solution moved towards a demand on the core workforce for more operational flexibility coupled with a reduction in the number of agency workers and overtime worked. The weight of negotiations was transferred to consideration of 'annualized hours' working, and since the beginning of 2012 this has become the norm. The introduction of annualized hours working demands the measurement of staff attendance over a 12-month period; how shifts and people work was analysed in minute detail. Consideration of working practices in terms of numbers of staff on each shift, methodologies of how many hours staff could 'bank' (i.e. extra hours worked to be taken off work at a later stage) and minimum 'notice periods' to request time off shift, compliance with the Working Time Directive, etc. all became the occupation of the HR team. All this was undertaken while still responding to the current operational demands of the business.

The net result of the negotiations was a minimal reduction in headcount of core company staff through voluntary severance. Original plans demanded a headcount reduction of 50 staff but as a result of negotiations with unions, which agreed the introduction of annualized hours and working practices, this was reduced to 20 employees who eventually left the company on voluntary terms.

Clearly the HR team, with staff and with local union support, has improved the business health of the Really Best Foods' site. The loss, and potential loss of contracts, focused the minds of all those employed at this rurally located factory. When considered within a European and global context of a significant economic downturn perhaps, in hindsight, the time was right to tackle the issue of effective workforce deployment.

Source: author.

Introduction

Key to being able to determine the value of human resource management (HRM) interventions is having a clear understanding of the nature of HRM, which is shown through a discussion of the Storey (1992, 2007) and Guest et al. (2003) models of HRM to be a subject still open to an ongoing debate (see Chapters 1, 3 and 13 for more on this). The work of Dave Ulrich (1996, 1998, 2011) and Ulrich and Brockbank (2005a, 2005b) is chosen as a vehicle to introduce how HRM can be structured to contribute strategically to organizational outcomes before going on to explore how HRM interventions can be focused and measured using a variety of strategic 'tools'.

Some of the tools which the HR professional has at their disposal and which are taken off the shelf and dusted down for use are: benchmarking; the quality approach as identified in the work of Jamrog and Overholt (2004); the concept of key performance indicators (KPIs) and the Balanced Scorecard approach initially developed by Kaplan and Norton (1996a, 1996b, 1996c) and subsequently modified as the HR Scorecard by Lockwood (2006); the notion of HR accounting, found in Cunningham and Kempling (2011); and finally a discussion of the dangers and dilemmas of trying to measure the degree of contribution of specific HR interventions to a measurable organizational performance outcome through a discussion of the work of Paauwe and Boselie (2005), and concluding with a review of the research of Ait Razouk (2011), who offers a glimmer of hope in this daunting task.

Throughout the course of this chapter the emphasis is placed upon discussing the perceived, and real, weaknesses in approaches to the various models of structuring HR delivery, i.e. Ulrich's work and the tools and techniques of valuing HR and HR measurement.

HRM and its contribution _____

Chapter 1 addressed the nature of HRM and strategic HRM. There is no doubt that the HR function has evolved over the years, and to a greater and lesser extent in some organizations. Ultimately, what does the HRM function add to an organization?

Storey (2007: 5) argues that 'HRM is a distinctive approach to employment management which seeks to achieve competitive advantage through a strategic deployment of a highly committed and capable workforce, using an integrated array of cultural, structural and personnel techniques'.

The focus of attention in terms of how employees are managed was shifted from the enforcement of rules and regulations to the alignment of employees with the business culture (see Chapter 11), its objectives and encouragement to work beyond contract. This alignment of employees with the organization's norms and objectives is associated with a unitarist rather than a pluralist perspective on the work relationship. The *unitarist's* perspective assumes that all the members of an organization have the same viewpoint; they accept the organization's goals and so do not require any convincing to focus their efforts on the achievement of these goals. On the other hand the *pluralist* viewpoint recognizes that there will be differences of opinion amongst an organization's employees; such is the natural order of life. As in life there will be conflict and this will have to be managed. In the context of an organization's long-term health and survival it may be worth reflecting upon whether unitarism or pluralism should be encouraged (see Chapter 8 on the employment relationship for a further discussion of these concepts).

Guest (1987: 511–13) offers a classical top-down normative model (*this is how things are done or should be done*) of human resource management. It is beguiling in its simplicity and inferred causality of outcome. Guest introduces his views by offering some of the thinking on HRM (op. cit.: 511), 'a comprehensive corporate strategy is essential to continuing business success' (Alpander 1982; Tichy and Devanna 1986). However, in many cases, human resource planning is not an integral part of strategic planning, but rather flows from it (see Chapter 1). One consequence is a weakening of strategic planning because, by emphasizing the quantitative dimensions of marketing, finance and production, it fails to take account of more complex issues such as values, power and company culture. Therefore, Alpander (1982) and Tichy and Devanna (1986) make the case that effective utilization of human resources is likely to give organizations a significant competitive advantage. The human resource dimension must therefore be fully integrated into the strategic planning process.

Guest (1987) argues that integration in four ways is key to a successful organization: to achieve the integration of an effective HR strategy with corporate strategy (new thinking at the time), the 'goal of employee commitment', the 'goal of flexibility and adaptability (implying organization structures and the flexible use of staff)', and the 'goal of quality' (implying staff quality, employer brand and performance excellence) (see Chapter 1).

Arguably it may be a sterile activity to try to define HRM because it is a concept which is dynamic. Torrington et al. (2011: 13), referring to the work of Bach, suggest that HR is evolving and the 'HR' approach focuses on

> the employment relationship [Chapter 8 this volume] which views employees and potential employees very much as individuals emotionally. It is associated with a move away from an expectation that staff will demonstrate commitment to a set of corporate values which are determined by senior management and towards a philosophy which is far more customer focused. Customers are defined explicitly as the ultimate employers and staff are empowered in such a way as to meet their requirements. (2011: 13)

The idea of fulfilling customer expectation will be a recurring feature in this chapter, as was the case in relation to strategy in Chapter 2.

With foresight Ulrich, in the preface to his text *Human Resource Champions*, offers the following as a portent of the future of HR:

> The future of HR includes new initiatives, programs, and agendas [see Chapter 13 this volume]. An HR professional from the 1940s would find it difficult to recognize the HR function of the year 2000, when the focus will be on global management, organizational capabilities, culture change, and intellectual capital. I also believe, however, that our past holds lessons for our future. HR issues of the past (for example, fair treatment of employees, shaping firms' values, sourcing talent) will continue to be central in the future. (1996: ix)

His prediction, made only four years before the millennium, was perhaps not so unreasonable when one considers the rate of change happening in the world. The collapse of the international banking system in 2008 epitomized the extent of the interconnections of the world's economic and business systems.

In his analysis of the way HR can add value to an organization Ulrich (1996) suggests that there are some key questions which need to be answered; in fact he argues that perhaps the questions are more important than the answers (see also Chapter 13).

The evolving nature of the HR function

Previously, the role of the HR function was undertaken by what was then termed the personnel department. The tasks were typically transactional: salary administration, absence management, recruitment, the general administration role required to enable the business to employ people. The role was described in metaphorical terms as a 'handmaiden', an ancient term implying someone, usually a female servant, who does menial tasks. However, the reason for the existence of the role was evident.

Since the mid 1980s the role of the personnel department has changed, from a lowly and very transactional role, to one where its stature has grown; its name has also changed in many organizations from 'personnel management' to 'human resource management', reflecting the new focus on employees as a resource rather than a cost centre and thus a key contributor to company profitability. As Jamrog and Overholt (2004: 56) write, 'As a result, during the '70s and '80s the HR profession was put under the microscope.'

While many companies still viewed HR professionals as personnel administrators, a growing number of professionals (implying HR professionals) were responding to their changing environment, and in their firms they were seen as 'people who were truly adding value to the company and giving the company a competitive advantage' (Jamrog and Overholt, 2004: 56). Critically in this context, Jamrog and Overholt (2004: 56) offer this advice: 'Human resource professionals must think of themselves as business people first and HR people second. HR professionals should be so well-versed in the operations side of the business, these experts argue, that the HR department is taken seriously when it offers insights.' The newfound role of HR elevated its status to one where, in some organizations, HR became represented on the 'board' of company directors (Drinan, cited in Jamrog and Overholt 2004: 56).

Jamrog and Overholt (2004: 60) argue that the HR professional needs a number of competencies: '[1] knowledge of business (which includes financial, strategic and technological capability), [2] knowledge of HR practices (which includes staffing, rewards, organizational planning, and communication) and [3] management of change (creating meaning, problem-solving, innovation and transformation, relationship influence, and role influence)'. However, they point out that a fourth domain is essential and should be added to Ulrich's framework: the ability to measure organizational effectiveness in the context of 'demonstrating the linkages between strategy, people and daily work, and the influence and interaction of these components'. Here they introduce the notion that by measuring these factors in an effective way the true value of HR's contribution can be measured.

Ulrich's powerful and very influential approach is to give the HR professional ideas and concepts of how HR should function and the role paradigm to which it should aspire. However, as Ulrich himself points out, issues of culture and organizational context influence how the HR professional should approach their role (see Chapter 1). If the approach is flawed, because of a misreading of the context or culture, then the HR department may not add value.

Ulrich (1996, 1998) proposed that the administrative expert role, subsequently redefined as the functional expert, should for large organizations be delivered through a 'shared-services' model, centrally driven and as is predominantly practised through call centres which, as multinational organizations, can be geographically distributed to accommodate 24-hour working across the globe. Brockbank (1999) argues that HRM needs to be strategically proactive and entrepreneurial in order to be a driver of strategy. Over the years, since Ulrich proffered his model of service delivery, a number of organizations have restructured their administrative HR services to reflect his concept. Additions and modifications have reflected the opportunities offered by advances in information technology and communication by combining the shared services concept with 'e' delivery systems.

There are, according to Reilly, cited in Cooke (2006: 213), a number of very good reasons why such organizations should adopt the model:

> to be part of a wider business change introducing the concept of 'professional' or functional services; to achieve a greater degree of structural flexibility; to respond to business change; to improve organizational learning across organizational boundaries; . . . to allow HR to reposition itself as more strategic; to reduce involvement in administrative trivia.

Centralizing delivery services does bring with it issues, not all of which are easily resolved. There are a number of criticisms which derive from the changing nature of the relationship between HR and their clients. Broadly, according to Cooke (2006), the criticisms can be grouped into the following areas:

- Loss of face-to-face contact
- Lack of employee representation
- Lack of clear ownership of HR problems
- Negative perceptions of the shared services centre (this can be compounded by information technology problems)
- Impact upon line managers in terms of work intensification
- Dampening of HR staff morale because of the reduced development routes and the 'dumbing-down' of the service.

Speedy (2008) makes the following point by quoting Phil Ainsley, head of employee share plans at Equiniti:

> Employing the shared services model for benefits can also mean running the risk of depersonalizing the organization to staff. You still need people out in the regions. You still need face-to-face communications. You still need the champions for the policy that the firm is trying to put in place.

Cooke (2006: 232) makes the following observation on Ulrich's model:

> The HR function cannot be neatly carved into four squared blocks to be delivered from different sources based on the *prima facie* evidence of cost-effectiveness. The intertwined nature of HR activities and the intangible role of the HR should not be divided simplistically, as they are the core threads that form the HR fabric of the firm.

Ulrich's contribution to the development of the HR function

The message that Ulrich confers and continues to argue is one of adding value (see Chapter 13) to the growth of the business and underlying profitability (Ulrich 1996, 2009, 2011). The notion of HR as a mature component arm of the business sets its role alongside that of any other business function and thus it must contribute its share of profitability; it cannot be a passenger. HR has matured from its early beginnings, as the 'handmaiden' to the organization. In HR's case the handmaiden role would be the administrative and transactional jobs associated with a service function. However, with the (relatively) freshly gained rights come responsibilities, HR must take an active stance and be proactive in adding value.

Ulrich offers guidance as to how HR can provide this added value in response to the competitive challenges faced by an organization: globalization, a value chain for business competitiveness (see Chapter 2) and HR services, profitability through cost control and growth, capability focus, change, change and change some more, technology, attracting, retaining and measuring competence and intellectual capital, and turnaround are not transformation (Ulrich 1996).

Ulrich (1996: 17, 24) is clear what HR must do: 'They must learn to measure results in terms of business competiveness . . . rather than to consolidate, to reengineer, or downsize when a company needs to turn around . . . it is time to perform and not to preach.' He goes on to write:

> To create value and deliver results, HR professionals must begin not by focusing on the activities or work of HR but by defining the deliverables of that work . . . With deliverables defined, the roles and activities of business partners may be stipulated.

Conceptualizing how HR can best structure itself to meet the demands placed upon it, he introduces a four-pronged 'business-partner' role (Ulrich 1996: 27):

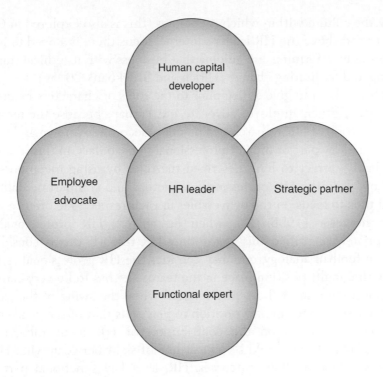

Figure 4.1 The Ulrich Business Partner Model

Source: Ulrich (1996).

1. Management of strategic human resources – the alignment of HR and business strategy. He calls this role the *strategic partner*.
2. Management of the firm infrastructure – re-engineering organization processes, 'shared services'. He calls this role the *administrative expert*.
3. Management of employee contribution – listening and responding to employees. He calls this role the *employee champion*.
4. Management of the transformation of change – he translates this roll into 'Ensuring the capacity for change'. He calls this role the *change agent*.

In an article for *People Management*, Ulrich and Brockbank (2005b) considered the evolution, as they called it, of the HR role. They depicted the model into which they believed HR had metamorphosed as shown in Figure 4.1.

The employee champion (Ulrich 1996) he splits into two roles, the employee advocate and the human capital developer. The administrative expert has expanded its remit to become the functional expert and the change agent role is now encompassed by that of the strategic partner, a role emphasizing the nature of HR's contribution: it becomes enmeshed within business and cannot be separated from an effectively run organization. The nature of the leadership role is one of role model to their own HR team and defining the culture within which it operates (this is also explored in Chapter 13). Over and above the HR leader's internal focus there is a need to focus on the business by informing and guiding that business with its ethical stance and managing and facilitating change (Ulrich and Brockbank 2005a).

Ulrich was keen to give a metaphor to the roles or characters he describes: the strategic partner, employee advocate, etc. Perhaps because the terms have, within the world of HR research and practice, become so known and accepted that they are now part of the HR professional's vocabulary, in this sense Ulrich was probably correct to have described the roles by using metaphors. These 'metaphors' help the HR professional to picture and compartmentalize their role and thus to focus on the deliverables in each respect. He offers a word of warning however (1996: 27), when he writes: 'HR professionals have inappropriately identified this as the only HR role'. If this is considered in terms of a football analogy, one may consider the HR professional as being a player with a multi-position place in the team: one has to be very careful not to remain in the role of the centre forward when the swing of the game has moved to defence and the key position to play in is that of the goalkeeper!

Ulrich's perspective on the contribution of HR is unambiguous. He emphasizes that there should be a clear line of sight between what HR does and business 'bottom-line' outcomes. HR, as a key functional part of the organization, is not altruistic per se. The improvement in the welfare of others (employees) is achieved through contributing to the wealth of the organization by developing and delivering better service. He offers many examples of what organizations do to achieve performance and competitive improvements and offers models against which HR professionals can align their functions. Specifically he suggests:

1. Translating business strategies into HR priorities
2. Administrative efficiency
3. Increased employee commitment and competence
4. The ability and capacity to manage change.

Implicit in Ulrich's model is that when translating and creating meaning and subsequently enacting the components of the model into reality for an organization, those responsible must perpetually balance priorities; they must multi-task. Giving unequal weight to creating administrative efficiencies (the functional expert role) at the expense of managing employee commitment and competence (the employee advocate role) may impact negatively on, for example, the psychological contract. The psychological contract is the relational, the emotional link between management and employee; it is indefinable but is core to a positive working environment and employee engagement. Where the psychological contract is positive staff are more likely to work beyond their written contract and job description. However, once 'punctured' the psychological contract is difficult to repair.

━━━━━━━━━━ **PIT STOP: REFLECTIVE ACTIVITY 4.1** ━━━━━━━━━━

What's in a name, employee champion or advocate?

When defining the role of employee champion Ulrich gives meaning to it by reflecting upon the need to view it in the context of employee commitment and contribution by matching the demands of the job to an employee or employees' capacity (to do the job) (Ulrich 1996: 126). Only by listening to employees can their experiences be understood. Improving capacity can be tackled from two directions. One way is to give the employee better skills and knowledge. Another way is to improve the techniques for doing the job, which may involve re-engineering or the better use of IT systems.

By splitting the employee champion role there is an overt recognition that the task of human capital developer is one of significance in itself, and arguably there is clarity of purpose in the activities related to this role.

 **■ Questions**

1. To what extent is Ulrich making assumptions about the way people orient themselves towards work?
2. Do employees and employers share similar goals and aspirations?

The three-legged stool or three-legged table?

Is Ulrich suggesting here that the introduction of the advocacy role is part of a more 'cuddly side' to HRM? On face value this appears to be the case, especially if one considers the dictionary definition of the word. *Harper Collins English Dictionary* defines advocate as, 'a person who upholds or defends a cause; a person who intercedes on behalf of another' (HarperCollins 2007). Is this what Ulrich and Brockbank mean? The understanding of their intention is in the detail of how *they* define advocate.

Ulrich and Brockbank (2005a: 27) suggest that caring for employees is very important because the employee is the organization's primary asset and increasingly more so in a world where technological advances are short lived. Part of the focus, in the context of the advocate role, is on employee engagement through which loyalty is developed and nurtured. At the strategy level the importance of employee representation by HR is stressed, and that the fact that representation has been made at a senior level is communicated to employees.

The preceding narrative fits tightly with what would be expected from a common-sense notion of advocacy. However, Ulrich and Brockbank expand upon the concept of advocacy and in a bizarre twist of logic suggest that it can be used to justify the release from the organization of poor performers:

> The employee advocacy role requires HR to establish a transparent and fair process for reproving and removing employees for whatever reason, and then to help implement the process equitably throughout the organization. Employee advocacy clearly adds value for employees. At the same time, it allows HR to add value for other stakeholder groups. (2005a: 27)

The moral of the above discussion centres on perceived and actual meaning. It is essential to look deeper than the obvious and not to take matters at face value. Ulrich and Brockbank's writing centres on and around adding value through HR. Employees are important, a key asset, but the asset must perform and to do so HR must be at the sharp end of the business and thus be willing to remove those who are not contributing. This is a completely reasonable position to take, but it is difficult to reconcile this stance under the aegis of employee advocacy.

Thematically, throughout his writing, Ulrich defines and identifies value as being outside the HR group and organization. It lies with what the customer perceives as value (Ulrich 1996, 2009, 2011). In Ulrich et al. (2012) he further explores the competencies which the HR professional needs to develop to deliver on customer expectations.

The strength of Ulrich's position lies in his experience and acknowledged competence as a consultant and researcher in the field of HR. Ulrich's (1996; Ulrich and Brockbank 2005c) argument and approach are based upon analysing how HR can add value using the roles he and Brockbank define as pathways, as conduits, to guide HR practitioners. They offer, in a structured way, guidance that allows the HR practitioner to dissect and to reflect upon how the HR function can best support the business to deliver what the customer wants and thus to make a profit. Interestingly, Ulrich (1996) does not explore, in any of his examples, his thesis in the context of public sector and not-for-profit organizations.

Developing a strategic approach to HRM

Ulrich (1996: 189) defines strategic human resources 'as the process of linking HR practices to business strategy'. He states that 'Strategic HR is owned, directed and used by line managers to make HR strategies happen' (ibid.). Key to the delivery of Ulrich's model is that business strategy is turned into an effective strategic HR model.

In terms of strategy creation, Ulrich is unequivocal in his view about the meaning of strategic HR (1996: 191). Strategic HR is owned by the line managers and is focused upon turning business strategies into a strategy which is both meaningful to those who have to deliver and is capable of delivery. The HR professional can then take the outcomes of the strategic HR formulation and convert them into a HR strategy.

Exploring the practicalities of strategic HRM

This chapter will use the fictional case of Motorway Aggregates to explore the practicalities of strategic HRM. Consider the case facing many UK manufacturing organizations at present. The executive team of Motorway Aggregates decided to expand its sales operation into South America to improve sales turnover. The organization was medium-sized which means, according to the European Commission (2003), it employs less than 250 people and has a financial turnover of less than €50 million. The countries Motorway Aggregates decides to target for its sales drive are Brazil and Mexico because both have massive natural resources. These countries will need to further develop their industrial infrastructures so their vast natural resources can be efficiently and effectively exploited. Motorway Aggregates can offer its expertise and the specialist rock-crushing equipment the firm manufactures.

The company's business strategy is clear; it is one of expansion into the South American market. To deliver this strategy will require a sales and servicing centre or centres in both countries.

Once the business strategy is formulated it can be translated into strategic HR (line management) and a HR strategy (HR executive) and can shape the HR organization (HR executive).

The line management, with the support of the HR directorate, will have to translate the decision to expand into a South American market into organizational capabilities. What does this mean in reality, in practical terms, for strategic HRM? In essence the answer to this question can be found by considering the capabilities the organization will need to develop. There will be a requirement for some UK staff to be expatriated – to work and to live overseas. They will have to work with and develop Brazilian and Mexican nationals and sell equipment into the indigenous mineral extraction business. The company's expatriates will also have to understand the complexities and comply with Brazilian and Mexican taxation and customs (import) duty requirements as well as employment legislation. There will also be a requirement to recruit and develop 'in-country' sales and support and maintenance teams.

Defining the capabilities of the 'in-country' teams is not always straightforward. The finance manager, assuming one will be nominated for Brazil and another separately for Mexico, will, over and above the need to deal with the respective country's accounting systems, have cause to manage large amounts of monies, millions of dollars equivalent, when buying and selling goods and services. In this respect a comprehensive understanding of exchange rate mechanisms and mechanisms associated with the short-term banking of uncommitted capital to 'lever' the best returns (interest) on the available capital is essential.

The UK-based organization has to be able to support their expatriated colleagues both in terms of product supply and technical support.

Once the components of strategic HRM have been verbalized, the HR executive can begin to develop and make sense of the HR strategy. In our case study the HR strategy can conveniently be split into two component parts, the first dealing with the overseas requirements and the other dealing with the UK-based operations.

The HR strategy will have to address both the 'hard' and the 'soft' HR issues (see Chapter 13). The hard-type issues are those matters that, literally, can readily be accounted for: for example, the number of staff required to deliver the business strategy in terms of indigenous, Brazilian and Mexican, and UK expatriate staff. Vital to the venture's success will be the quality of the expatriate staff – the soft HR issues. This implies that the parent company needs to consider how to address the selection of UK national staff for a prolonged expatriate experience.

Defining the totality of softer qualities, the capabilities which an expatriate manager or member of staff must possess (see Chapters 11 and 12), over and above the key technical requirements and company savvy which is assumed fundamental to the role, is not straightforward. The assumption that a competent UK manager can also be effective in a foreign environment is too simplistic an approach. Expatriates will be required to operate in a culture which is significantly different from their Anglo-Saxon or Celtic cultural origins. Consideration has to be given to personal traits, such as being open to experience and having empathy for and the ability to understand a foreign culture, as key to expatriate survival and corporate effectiveness. Although limited in scope by the lack of full and detailed information from the case study, it would be advantageous to group, to bring together in a holistic way, the issues surfaced so far, together with other issues that would need to be addressed. The following bullet points, though general, may be used to stimulate debate about the underlying HR issues which impact upon the successful delivery of the business:

- Development of new products
- A focus on cost-effective operations and the reward of performance
- Developing the South American operation

- Developing the UK operation to meet the challenges of working with new cultures
- Maintaining and nurturing the existing business
- The identification and development of talent (UK and overseas)
- The maintenance of a supportive work culture.

Clearly it is possible to further identify topics for consideration, for example, should health and safety be on the list, or health, safety and environmental protection? It is possible to debate at length what should and should not be included. There will be some imperatives for inclusion, for example the 'how' of expanding operations while still supporting the existing operation. There will also be other factors/issues, which perhaps are peripheral to the immediate perceived needs but may have a disproportionate effect upon the long-term viability of the business. Ulrich offers the view that too many HR strategies remain just that – strategies. A HR strategy should help, not hinder; it is a map which guides the HR team in their decision-making process. It should reflect the objectives of the business strategy and just like that business strategy it will change; it is not cast in stone, it has a malleable quality.

The UK-based organization must be able to support, both in technical terms and HR terms, the overseas business outposts; at least and until it becomes, in capability terms, self-sufficient. This means much more than having staff who can speak Spanish or Portuguese working in its UK-based headquarters. The organization must develop a capacity to do business across the UK–South American time zones. Staff must have the capacity to develop and operate an expatriate payroll system, to create and manage a whole raft of terms and conditions of expatriate service, which meet the needs of the business in terms of attracting, retaining and motivating its overseas staff as well as meeting the needs of these (expatriated) staff and their families (see Chapter 12).

Finally, according to the Ulrich model, the HR executives will need to focus on the HR organization (function).

The HR strategy defines what HR has to focus upon, and thus will need to do, to deliver its desired outcomes. The review of the HR organization addresses how it will need to be structured to both meet the needs of the newly expanded business and the existing operation. As well as structure, Ulrich et al. (2012) further suggest a range of competencies which HR professionals should develop for twenty-first century business.

How a HR function is structured can help or hinder the way it provides and, perhaps as equally important, is perceived by the line management to provide a service to its home- and overseas-based sales and engineering teams. A current and common model, especially for multinational organizations, would be to structure HR along the lines of Ulrich's three-legged stool model of shared services together with business partners and centres of expertise. However, this may not be suitable in all cases. In a recent CIPD survey on the changing nature of the HR function a panel of academic staff and HR practitioners commented on the 'model' in the following manner:

> Our panel of practitioners and academics expressed a certain frustration with what they saw as a fixation with one particular model. They argued that HR's structure should reflect the business it is in and what business customers want. Professor Chris Brewster, for example, made the point that HR teams in SMEs have to be all-rounders, dealing with both the operational and strategic. (CIPD 2007)

In this sense, the HR team at Motorway Aggregates would be wise to engage with their line management colleagues to consider how best to organize.

Critical to the review of the HR organization will be a determination of the measures against which the HR organization will be assessed, sometimes called key performance indicators (KPIs) (see Kaplan and Norton 1996a, 1996b). Ulrich's focus in his work on the provision of human resources as a service function begs the question of how the quality of service should or could be measured. Interestingly, Ulrich uses Eastman Kodak as an exemplar when explaining the concept of Strategic HR. He writes, in 1996, of George Fisher, the then Chief Executive officer, when changing company performance but also redefining the company culture (1996: 193): 'He [George Fisher] revised the company portfolio by selling non-core businesses, and he adapted the corporate culture to fully integrate Kodak's five core values: respect for the individual, uncompromising integrity, trust, credibility, and continuous improvement and personal renewal'. Sadly, on 20 January 2012, the headline in *The Times* was, 'Kodak puts up shutters and files for bankruptcy'. What, according to Ulrich, did Fisher, this paragon of HR virtue, do wrong? As *The Times* correspondent, Rhys Blakey, writes:

> In 1890 Kodak revealed the Brownie, a cardboard camera that sold for a dollar and was designed to be so simple that anyone could use it. Launched with the promise 'you push the button, we do the rest', it created the concept of the 'snapshot'. A Kodak camera captured the Moon landing in 1969, and at its peak the company employed 145,000 people as Eastman's home town of Rochester, New York, became a hub of high-tech engineering. (Blakey 2012)

Kodak lacked insight into the fact that technology and society were changing and that KPIs were critical to its future survival, thereby allowing for the company to adapt to latest technologies and innovations.

Measurement within HR

Tootell et al. (2009: 378), referring to Yeung and Berman, argue that 'HR measures should be impact rather than activity orientated, forward looking rather than backward looking, and should focus on the entire HR system not just on individual HR practices.' In essence they make the point that the time-consuming action of measuring parameters, which may offer some insight into how HR is functioning, should be clearly targeted at relevant outcomes and should not focus upon how HR has contributed but how best it *can* contribute. Weiss and Finn (2005: 36) argue a similar point:

> Organizations are tending to focus on background, functional measures, and efficiency measures. These operational metrics . . . do not provide information that enables the senior executives to make grounded decisions about business strategy. Monitoring headcount changes, for example, makes sense. Business leaders need to have this information, but it will not give them clear direction on the key people issues that drive the business forward, such as leadership team capability, change management capability, motivation, and levels of relevant competencies.

The concept of Human Resource Accounting (HRA), which is the subject of the work of Tootell et al. (2009) and Flamholtz (2007), is an enticing concept because, in principle, it offers a set of quasi-financial measures to which senior management can relate. However, there are problems with this approach. The problems, which in reality should not be unexpected, revolve around the measurement of such concepts as knowledge and leadership qualities:

> The 'hidden value' of an organisation is that hard-to-define property, where common knowledge understands that it is worth a lot, but there is difficulty in expressing this value in purely monetary terms . . . knowledge is intangible, it is not captured well by traditional accounting measures, so managers underestimate the value and contribution of intangible assets. (Tootell et al. 2009: 378, citing Hauser and Katz)

The crux of the issue of HR accounting is that there are no widely agreed HR accounting standards; therefore, whatever the methodology for measuring the contribution of HR, the issue becomes one of acceptance by those in senior positions of responsibility. Getting this 'buy-in' is further compounded when those who are tasked with developing relevant metrics do not have the knowledge or skill in designing metrics nor the analytic skills to interpret the outcome of a measurement exercise (Tootell et al. 2009).

A model that helps to explore measurement is that of Jamrog and Overholt (2004), whose proposal is based upon the Six Sigma quality approach which considers the systems involved in the process. Consider the case of a supermarket which wishes to introduce a clothing section into a local store. This decision sets off a train of actions. For HR, one action would be to train, initially, one supervisor for the newly created clothing section but with the potential to recruit and train a second. Assessing the quality of training his staff member has received would be important to the store manager. At one level there is the quality of training received by the prospective clothing section manager; feedback on this aspect would be from the individual in terms of: how they perceived the quality and

Table 4.1 Building a strategic HR function

	Strategic HR	HR strategy	HR organization
	Translates business strategies into organizational capabilities and then into HR practices	Building a strategy and action plan – focus to make the HR function more effective	Crafting, designing, and improving a HR function to deliver HR services
Owner	Line managers	HR executives	HR executives

Source: After Jamrog and Overholt (2004).

relevance of information they were given, the pace of the training, the quality of the on-the-job trainer, etc. However, the true effectiveness and relevance of the decision both to promote and train a second section manager (clothing) would be measured by the ultimate feedback of increased footfall and sales of clothes.

The approach in Table 4.1 has significant advantages. It is a logical step forward from Ulrich's focus on the giving of guidance on, and about, how to structure and focus the levels of activity of the HR function. In the case of Motorway Aggregates, the business strategy of increasing sales is linked to HR activity at an operational level, HR feedback upon the quality of training and, in addition, there is feedback on business outcomes. It was possible to apply a 'systems', quality-based approach, as initially proposed by Juran (1951) and later adopted and subsequently modified by quality management consultancy organizations. However, the added value of HR cannot always be perceived so readily. HR added value is not always transparent, it can be hidden and so hard to quantify; yet there is still a need to try and identify, or at least recognize, where HR is adding value. This is imperative if HR is to become more central to the organization, because of its shift towards having a strategic rather than a transactional focus for the discipline. The CIPD emphasize that the focus should be on efficiency, effectiveness and impact in order for organizations to understand how such an important and elusive asset makes an impact (CIPD 2007; Lockwood 2006).

In a recent CIPD report on using HR metrics for maximum impact (2012), they outline four key internal aspects that HR should measure:

- Employee engagement
- Alignment, agility and shared purpose
- Capability and talent
- Performance measurement and metrics.

These four aspects focus on internal aspects of the organization, which in themselves then impact upon sustained organizational performance (the external impact). The CIPD's 2012 report argues that there are three critical aspects that underpin effective measurement: aligning measurement and goals, taking a business partner perspective and adding value by focusing on building capability.

Lockwood (2006) argues the importance of monitoring and measuring HR metrics. However, she recognizes, as has been previously indicated in this chapter, that it is a very complex undertaking. The difficulty arises because of the plethora of parameters that can be monitored. These range from employee absence figures to turnover rates, employee headcount as percentage of sales turnover, return on capital employed, profit after tax, etc. However, she points out that:

> With a clear line of sight on workforce and organizational performance, effective use of KPIs [Key Performance Indicators] also illustrates HR's in-depth understanding of the links to business success. KPIs help build the credibility of the HR department, demonstrate HR value and foster respect and partnership with senior management. (Lockwood 2006: 10)

In essence, Lockwood is offering a 'double whammy' for HR by demonstrating the links to business success while, at the same time, gaining a 'street credibility' with senior management. Unfortunately, as Lockwood points out, not all HR executive directors consider that they are seen as full partners by their co-board members and conversely not all non-HR directors perceive that their counterpart HR directors are working at an equivalent strategic level.

The problem with any KPI-type indicator is the 'line of sight' linkage between its implementation and the desired outcome. Tapping into a new talent pool (see Chapters 5 and 13), for example by forming a link with a university by providing summer holiday work for undergraduates and thus recognizing and gradually nurturing potential quality recruits, does not immediately lead to such outcomes as reduced staff turnover, improved leadership and decision-making, product innovation or greater customer satisfaction. In this sense, the activity and process of tapping into a new talent-pool would be defined as a 'leading indicator' and the measures of the remaining outcomes listed above would be labeled as 'lagging indicators'. Lockwood does recognize, however, that one of the problems with the notion of lead and lagging indicators is attributing, with any degree of confidence, the influence that any changes in the lead indicator has on changes in the lagging indicator. The time lag is so great that other factors such as a recession or a glut of talent in a particular skill or knowledge set, thus making it difficult for staff to job hop, can also impact positively on attrition rates. In essence a KPI, although readily measured, as would be the case with a reduction in staff turnover, may not be easily attributed with any confidence to a direct cause.

If one of the organizational KPIs is employee turnover, and over a period of time this can be shown to have dramatically fallen, one might argue that the lead indicator, the identification, measurement and recruitment of new talent, could reasonably be perceived to have a causal link with the desired outcome of a reduction in turnover. However, business life, particularly in the modeling of business activities, is never straightforward. For there to be a causal link between the leading and lagging indicators one would need to show that there were no other factors which could have impacted upon the reduction in staff turnover. There are a number of key questions that must be asked before drawing a conclusion between perceived cause and desired effect:

- How clear or murky was the line of sight between the perceived causal action and the outcome?
- What other factors could have impacted upon the outcome?

If, for example, the business environment had entered into a recession between starting the initiative of developing a pipeline of graduate intakes and the output measurement of turnover, it would be difficult to argue with any conviction that the strategic recruitment initiative had been solely responsible for the desired and somewhat longer-term effect of reduced employee turnover. Similarly, should the company have modified or materially altered the way it manages its reward systems during the intervening period this would further impair the logic of trying to reason between cause and effect. The number and variety of leading variables would be too many to enable, with any degree of confidence, linkages to be made between lead and lagging indicators.

▰▰▰ PIT STOP: REFLECTIVE ACTIVITY 4.2 ▰▰▰

Key performance indicators: cause and effect

Reflecting upon the previous discussion about the difficulty of demonstrating, with a reasonable level of confidence, the linkage between a lead and lagging indicator, consider what activity could be considered to be a lead indicator to:

1. Improve the quality of technical business graduates attracted to apply for positions in a large organization which has several hi-tech factories throughout the country.
2. Encourage managers to improve the speed of their decision-making by empowering them to take greater ownership of their departments or business units.

Lockwood (2006) offers a word of caution. Because of the abundance of possible measures she emphasizes that it is important to select both activities and measures which reflect 'deliverables' that promote and lead to organizational success such as financial outcome measures. She suggests, for example, 'customer satisfaction, process technology innovation . . . globalization' (Lockwood 2006: 2). The difficulty is in defining relevant KPIs as they will not be the same for every organization. In her exploration of how and where HR can add value to business Lockwood (2006) promotes the use of the HR Balanced Scorecard.

The Balanced Scorecard

The Balanced Scorecard as a strategic management system was first proposed by Kaplan and Norton in 1996 (1996a, 1996b, 1996c). They suggest that the Balanced Scorecard emphasizes that financial and non-financial measurement must be part of the information system for employees at all levels of the organization. Front-line employees must understand the financial consequences of their decisions and actions; senior executives must understand the long-term financial success. The objectives and the measures are derived from a top-down process driven by the mission and strategy of the business unit.

The Balanced Scorecard, because it breaks down the complex strategic objectives and translates them into identifiable targets that can be measured, helps:

1. Clarify and translate vision and strategy
2. Communicate and link strategic objectives and measures
3. Plan, set targets, and align strategic initiatives
4. Enhance strategic feedback and learning (Kaplan and Norton 1996a: 10).

The clarity that this strategic tool offers is powerful in its simplicity: by asking one question about each of the four outcomes of vision and strategy, business objectives become less elusive and thus take on a structured form for those who have to deliver business outcomes; in reality this means every employee. Kaplan and Norton (1996a: 9) suggest the following:

- Financial – 'To succeed financially, how should we appear to our shareholders?'
- Internal business process – 'To satisfy our shareholders and customers, what business processes must we excel at?'
- Learning and growth – 'To achieve our vision, how will we sustain our ability to change and improve?'
- Customer – 'To achieve our vision, how should we appear to our customers?'

Driving the vision and strategy, objectives, measures, targets and initiatives, all of which can be linked to appraisal outcomes, can be clearly defined.

Based upon the work of Kaplan and Norton the HR Balanced Scorecard can, in a similar manner, be defined and applied to any organization, private, public or not-for-profit.

Figure 4.2 Kaplan and Norton's Balanced Scorecard
Source: Kaplan and Norton (1996a).

≣ CASE STUDY 4.2 ≣

Charity begins at home (using the HR Scorecard)

The Glowhome Housing Association is a not-for-profit (charitable) organization which buys, renovates, lets and maintains houses and flats. It employs 200 full-time staff (coworkers) and, at the last count, over 400 volunteer coworkers who work part-time to manage a stock of 2,500 properties, mainly old but, after some tender loving care by coworkers, habitable for another 50 years.

The origins of the organization can be traced to a small cooperative of 15 people who came together, over 30 years ago, to build their own houses. The group of friends realized that between them they had the necessary mix of skills to build and finish houses to a habitable state. Over a three-year period they built eight modest houses.

From these early beginnings, and urged on by their successes in building their own properties, the group, who were like-minded and with a strong moral compass that emphasized helping those less fortunate, realized that they could expand upon their original concept. They believed that by exploiting the benevolent nature of individuals who were willing to volunteer, all the better if they had useful skills, the group could build or renovate houses and flats suitable for the low rent market; thus affording, to those less fortunate, an opportunity to live in a safe and welcoming home. The initial 'deal' for those wishing to rent one of the properties was that they, in turn, help either to build or renovate the house or flat they would eventually be allocated and then commit to work on one further property which the organization was in the process of preparing for inclusion in its rental stock.

Funding for Glowhome's first property came from three local philanthropists and also local government, who considered it was a worthwhile investment. If the concept worked, the outcome blended well with the local government's long-term strategic housing plan. From acorns great oak trees grow and so, after several years, 10 of the first 15 cooperative members had become employees of what had become Glowhome, a partnership-type organization but with charitable status. The philosophy of build and renovate has remained the same but the newly named (Glowhome) organization also found itself with a group of several hundred volunteers who, for whatever reason, wished to use their skills as builders, carpenters, electricians, plumbers, administrators, solicitors etc., in a voluntary capacity. The volunteers had become core to the business model; without them the low cost rental philosophy and cooperative philosophy could not work. Glowhome now has a chief executive, three offices in different regions of the UK, a network of collectors, 'tin shakers' who seek public donations, high street charity shops, a small group of individuals led by a senior colleague whose sole task is to raise funds from corporate donors, celebrity supporters, a clerk of works who plans and schedules tasks, teams of tradesmen and women, and a small centrally based HR section consisting of a HR manager and two assistants. The organization has plans to expand into further UK regions.

The aim of the association is:

- To build, acquire and manage safe, energy-efficient and affordable housing predominately for those who are unable to pay market rates.
- To encourage, through a cooperative spirit of self and mutual help, people to contribute to the provision of good accommodation for themselves and for others who have been in a similar economic situation.
- To provide work and training in a range of skills for out of work people.
- As an aspirational goal, to make a difference in neighbourhoods by using its reputation to 'lever into the community' resources and to use its experience in social projects to give some focus to community activity.

Let us consider how the HR Scorecard can be developed as a means to improve the way HRM contributes to the successful accomplishment of the organization's strategies, goals and objectives. The (HR) Balanced Scorecard should be a tool to give direction and focus to HRM so that the strategic aims of Glowhome are translated into clear HRM departmental strategies, objectives, measures, targets, and initiatives.

Source: author.

 ■ **Question**

1. How can the Kaplan and Norton model be employed to develop an effective HR Balanced Scorecard at Glowhome?

HR Balanced Scorecard measures

So what does the HR Balanced Scorecard look like for Glowhome? A range of factors included are listed below.

The financial perspective

Financial data, which are both timely and accurate, are important. Financial objectives and subsequent measures are valuable in summarizing the consequences of budgetary expenditure. In charitable organizations, financial objectives typically highlight activities, outputs and outcomes. For example, financial measures related to HRM might include cost per hire, cost of turnover, cost per head of training, legal costs related to HRM, HRM expenditures as a percentage of overall operating budget and the like.

The focus is on how HR services can help internal clients, and the organization, save money and improve decision-making.

The internal business process perspective

In the context of the internal business process perspective, the HR manager's role is to identify the critical internal processes at which the HR organization must excel. It goes without saying that it is these processes which enable the organization to help make sure it delivers, in an efficient and effective manner, the services for which it is responsible. For example, dealing with emergencies in companies, HRM-specific measures might be associated with: how work is structured in terms of team and teamworking, and the reward system which compensates and motivates its technicians to do their work as well as to be prepared to work unsocial hours. In a broader context the concept could encompass the quality of staff recruitment, time to fill staff vacancies, costs of grievances and other employee relations issues. From an HR perspective it could also relate to the effectiveness of how knowledge and competence are managed.

The learning and growth perspective

The reason why Kaplan and Norton suggest that there should be a focus on learning and growth is because this recognizes essential employee capabilities. Organizational learning comes from three potential sources: people, systems, and organizational procedures. Specific to HRM might be the training related to performance management for managers, facilitation skills, teamworking skills, and, of course, skills training at all levels, whether this be competency-related or problem-solving (see Chapter 10). Also from an HR perspective it will relate to how knowledge and competence are managed and how people are prepared (nurtured) to take over senior positions within the organization. This is a process issue which flows into the internal business process arena as a critical area to measure.

HR's role is first to review its processes, policies and procedures to ensure that, in one sense, they do not hamper or impede growth, and in another, foster the appropriate environment to encourage growth yet ensure compliance with legal requirements. The HR manager has to be politically shrewd in this respect. Consider the hypothetical situation where the partnership desperately requires a second legal adviser, a solicitor, to support the increasing activity in land and property purchase. Let us assume that a coworker's spouse is a conveyancing solicitor and wishes to join the organization. The expedient move would be to rubber-stamp the recruitment of the individual. This would support the drive for HR to be seen as facilitating the work of its internal customers, by providing a resource at minimal (recruitment) cost, in a very timely manner. However, one would need to consider how this, namely recruiting a colleague's spouse, would chime with the policies on recruitment in terms of the transparency of process and compliance with the organization's values and policies and procedures. Quick fixes are not necessarily the best fixes.

HR's role is not always linear and straightforward, and there can be contradictions in interpreting the quality of the perceived outcome of the service.

The customer perspective

It may be important to consider both external as well as internal clients as customers. External clients may be represented by citizens and key stakeholder groups. Internal clients may include groups of managers and employees.

The focus is on and about the type of service which HR can deliver to enable, for example, a fund-raising group to go about their role of attracting corporate sponsors, effectively supporting the management of its high street charity shops and the various volunteer groups.

The HR section cannot define, in isolation, how it should respond to each of the four areas of the scorecard. Common sense demands that there should be consultation with its customers to define what they wish HR to be able to do for them and the business.

Cunningham and Kempling (2011: 199–200) suggest that the following questions are asked of the internal and external customers:

1. What key roles can HRM best perform to help you achieve your objectives?
2. What are some positive ways that HRM has helped you in the past? What are examples of these?
3. What are some functions or activities where you have needed HRM to perform better? What are examples of times when you were frustrated with HRM activities in this organization?
4. What are the roles and practices you would like to see HRM do in the future to help you achieve your objectives?

The relevance of the HR Balanced Scorecard

The development of HR Balanced Scorecard measures is very organization-specific, as Cunningham and Kempling (2011: 194) point out:

The nature of the 'fit' between HRM and strategic objectives is very specific and idiosyncratic to any organization. As such, HRM processes for recruiting, selecting, training, evaluating and rewarding employees might depend on the nature of the organization's objectives. A strategic objective like improving customer relations would need to be supported by HRM policies, processes, programs, practices, skills, and behaviours which encouraged client or customer relations.

It would not be relevant to expect, for example, a range of organizational measures developed for one UK-operating tyre manufacturing company to be copied and employed in total or in part in another UK tyre manufacturing company with the same degree of success. Similarly one charitable housing trust would not be able to adopt the operational measures developed by another.

The thinking behind the concept of 'fit' is that an organization is likely to operate better if each part of its operational structure – HR, finance, engineering etc. – is woven together in such a way that HR policy development is informed by and supports the overarching organization's strategic objectives as well as those of each of its component parts; this is the idea of vertical and horizontal integration. The HR Balanced Scorecard extends this thinking into practice by teasing out and thus exploring the potential for a causal relationship between one part of the organization and another.

Fit can be considered in two ways, internal and external. Internal fit is influenced by such factors as organizational culture and business strategy, for example cost reduction, quality enhancement or innovation (Schuler and Jackson 1987). External fit, which is associated with how an organization responds to factors in the external environment, is both environmentally sensitive in its broader sense (economic, political and social climate, legal etc.) and affected by the sector in which the organization functions (process industry, manufacturing, service and public administration sectors, etc.).

Critics of the 'fit' approach opine that no organization can define and control every factor which impacts upon its business (see Chapter 3). Boxall and Purcell (2008) point out that no firm can completely control its own HRM; there are too many impingeing factors which can affect outcomes. For example, one could imagine an organization enjoying the luxury of being able to recruit, set its conditions of service etc. without having to consider competitive (external) pressures because of its unique position as the only major manufacturer of electric light bulbs within a geographical location. In essence the company has a monopolistic control of the local labour market. However, this position would change dramatically if a credible competitor were to open a factory within the region. In this sense the fit, for both organizations, would be influenced by external factors.

Diversity at Ford

When thinking about best practice examples of diversity and women's rights (see Chapter 9), Ford's manufacturing plant in Dagenham doesn't immediately spring to mind. With a workforce that is still 92 per cent male, the traditional stereotypes of a politically incorrect factory floor are still predominant.

But Jenny Ball and three other female colleagues have broken the mould with their recent appointments to lead HR functions in the four business units at the plant.

'We all do our jobs as managers first and foremost, but we also have ambassadorial roles too,' said Ball, who went on to aver that 'I suppose as the first all-woman HR team in Dagenham, we are role models, but really we don't think about that most of the time.'

Ford at Dagenham has had a patchy history concerning equality. In 1968, a group of female sewing machinists went on strike against a sex-biased grading structure. The 1970 Equal Pay Act followed shortly after (the movie, *Made in Dagenham*, highlights the plight of some female employees seeking equality).

In the late 1960s, investigations into race discrimination complaints were a regular part of the Ford HR territory, though the company was among the first with ethnic monitoring.

Matters came to a head in the 1990s when Sukhjit Parmar, a Dagenham engine plant worker, won a claim of racial discrimination and victimization, and an advertisement showing Ford workers with faces changed to disguise ethnic origins provoked unfavourable publicity. Global president Jacques Nasser flew in from Detroit to take personal control of the growing crisis.

The result was a comprehensive agreement with unions to stamp out discrimination and harassment. Among other things, it provided for joint equal opportunities committees in every Ford plant and business throughout the UK, backed up by anti-racist policies for promotion, recruitment and corporate image-making. At the time, union leader Bill Morris hailed it as 'the fresh start that Dagenham needs'.

However, Ball (2006) has a different take:

Without trying to be defensive or anything, diversity has been part of our approach for a long time at Ford. We were conducting ethnic monitoring back in 1967 and had equal opportunities policies in the 1980s. These incidents were flagged up and prompted the company to move forward. It's part of our history.

Inclusive approach

In 2000, Ford embarked upon an approach to diversity and inclusion, which Ball claimed put Ford at the leading edge of HR practice.

The foundation was an audit of policies and practices, conducted with the collaboration of the Commission for Racial Equality and known as the Diversity and Equality Assessment Review (Dear). 'Dear has absolutely become part of our business, and that is not a cliche,' Ball said.

One way or another, it seems, Ford has arrived pretty much where it ought to be. The joint equality committees and national equality committee have a life of their own.

(Continued)

(Continued)

'There are too many of them to be controlled by HR,' said Ball. 'The Dear approach and a system of annual audits by the national equalities committee have put a rigour into equality and inclusion.'

But where pressing issues of output, quality, change and skill levels are on every manager's agenda, how does the company make space for diversity?

'As plant managers, we have a set of objectives known as SQDCME,' said Ball. 'It stands for safety, quality, delivery, costs, morale and environment.'

> That's six priorities in all plants, not just in the UK but throughout the world, and they are followed through right down to work group level. It's a wonderfully effective process and you have a scorecard, with the whole thing cascading down from senior management level. Within the 'morale' heading there is 'diversity' without question. (Ball 2006)

Dear identified recruitment selection, development, communication, corporate citizenship, policy and planning and auditing for equality as the priorities for action. Each of these is assessed in every plant and sub-unit of the company. In manufacturing plants, the objectives are incorporated into the SQDCME system. Each heading has five or six criteria that are examined and measured against a descriptive, evaluative framework. Managers collect evidence folders during the year to demonstrate how they are meeting their specific targets, and the metrics of equality auditing are built onto that.

Going green

Managers are assessed by the audit and metrics, which give rise to a traffic light red, yellow or green indicator of how things stand on each of the six headings in each small part of the organization. Getting your colours to green is important.

After each annual audit, you end up with your six areas and have quite a detailed breakdown of what you will have to do to turn that level to a green [said Ball]. So you then produce your action plan, based on the audit and your previous audit's recommendations for improvements.

Diversity, it seems, is being tackled with the logistics of line control, which Ford used to revolutionize commercial motor production in the twentieth century. Henry would be proud.

Source: Ball (2006).

 **Question**

1. Why does the concept of a 'scorecard' make line managers pay attention and take the issue more seriously?

The effective HR function

So what does an effective HR function look like, or is it more about what makes a HR function effective? Research conducted by Murphy for the IRS (2012) highlighted the following areas that HR use to measure effectiveness:

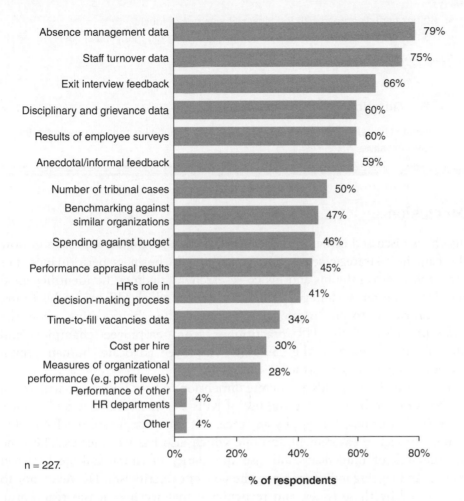

Absence management data — 79%
Staff turnover data — 75%
Exit interview feedback — 66%
Disciplinary and grievance data — 60%
Results of employee surveys — 60%
Anecdotal/informal feedback — 59%
Number of tribunal cases — 50%
Benchmarking against similar organizations — 47%
Spending against budget — 46%
Performance appraisal results — 45%
HR's role in decision-making process — 41%
Time-to-fill vacancies data — 34%
Cost per hire — 30%
Measures of organizational performance (e.g. profit levels) — 28%
Performance of other HR departments — 4%
Other — 4%

n = 227.

% of respondents

Figure 4.3 Measures taken into account when assessing HR effectiveness
Source: XpertHR.

While the measures included here are commonplace, the HR function has to actively demonstrate where it made a significant contribution.

PIT STOP: REFLECTIVE ACTIVITY 4.3

In an IRS survey of 253 employers, published by XpertHR, two-thirds thought the influence of the HR function has increased over the past two years.

Almost three-quarters of the employers surveyed (72 per cent) rated their HR function as 'very effective'. The HR roles and responsibilities survey covered a combined workforce of 355,000 people.

What managers think of HR:

- 68 per cent said HR added value to the business.
- 69 per cent agreed that HR was influential.

- 60 per cent disagreed with the view HR was out of touch.
- 75 per cent disagreed that HR was busy producing too many initiatives.

Source: Woolf (2012).

 ■ **Question**

1. Despite HR being viewed as very efficient, why might it be seen as producing too many initiatives?

Conclusion

Ulrich, as discussed earlier in this chapter, takes a pragmatic approach to how HR can, in a strategic sense, best contribute to business performance. His approach is driven by his and his co-researchers' findings; he identifies good practice and offers a strategic framework against which HR can, in his terms, best contribute to the organization's bottom line by focusing upon the different roles of the HR practitioner, from employee champion and administrative expert in the 1990s to employee advocate, human capital developer and strategic partner in the 2000s.

Lockwood (2006) adds a concrete dimension to how HR can contribute to the bottom line by exploring the use of KPIs as a measurement tool – not a revolutionary or new concept by any means. It is a strategic approach to value adding through measurement and one which also has weaknesses. The time lag, the lack of immediacy and also the clarity of causal linkage between leading and lagging indicators open the concept to criticism. However, not to be daunted by these issues, and recognizing that we live in the real world, Lockwood espouses the use of Kaplan and Norton's Balanced Scorecard model, but with a focus on HR. In adopting a model which recognizes multiple outcomes from human resource management practice, there is an overt acceptance that business outcomes are not simply measured in financial terms.

Defining and measuring how HR can add value to an organization are fraught with problems. Paauwe and Boselie (2005: 68) give some insight into the nature of the problems surrounding the issues of how HR adds value. They ask three questions: 'What is HRM? What is performance? What is the nature of the link between HRM and performance?' In essence these three questions have been, in part, the guiding themes of this chapter.

Peter Lieskovsky, HR director at Oracle, claims that HR needs to adjust its metrics to reflect more accurately where the organization is heading:

> HR is the only function in the corporate world fighting to justify its own importance. HR must talk business, do business and take responsibility for business results as

There is a lack of consensus of and about the nature of HRM: 'There is not one fixed list of generally applicable HR practices or systems of practices that define or construct HRM' (Paauwe and Boselie 2005: 69). There are some practices which appear to reflect the core elements of strategic HRM – careful recruitment and selection, training and development, reward schemes based upon a contingent approach and performance management systems – but there is no overall consensus. Even with a consensus there is no guarantee that implementation is carried out in the same manner with similar degrees of diligence.

Strategic HRM tends to be constructed around the 'best fit' approach. This further compounds the problem of teasing out, from the strategic intent of a set of practices, a commonality of approach because of the variable nature of both internal and external contextual factors which impact upon how organizations operate. Internal in terms of, for example, structure, culture etc., and external such as the nature of the relationship with a dominant union, stakeholder, shareholder and possibly government influence. The nature of these external influences may arise sometimes because of organizational sectoral influences, as would be the case in banking, mineral extraction, manufacturing, education etc.

As we have seen, there is a problem in defining the relevant parameters that should be measured and which represent HRM's contribution to business success. This is an important consideration. Imagine asking an engineer to measure the output from a Porsche 911 motor car. The engineer would consider and reflect upon your request and then, perhaps, ask you to be more specific. They may ask, 'is it the power available at the road wheels? Is it the zero to sixty miles per hour time? Is it the car's urban driving fuel consumption figures? Is it the CO_2 emissions per km travelled?' All of these measures, and many more, are accepted, and are well-known, clearly defined and understood throughout the motor industry and also by those non-specialists interested in comparing models of vehicles. The problem with HRM, in terms of how its contribution to how business is measured, is that there are no universally accepted measurable parameters. As Paauwe and Boselie (2005) argue, there are many organizational measures of performance which are in common usage. Some are based on financial outcomes, such as profits and sales, and others are based upon organizational outcomes, which tend to be factors such as quality and productivity and customer satisfaction. The HRM outcomes though, such as employee satisfaction and motivation (behavioural measures), can only be linked to the organizational and financial outcomes in a very tenuous way because, as they point out, the distance between some of the performance indicators (e.g. profits, market value) and HR interventions is simply too large and potentially subject to other business interventions (e.g. research and development activities, marketing strategies). For example, having smart policies for managing working capital can increase earnings substantially, but have nothing to do with the proclaimed effect of HR practices (apart from apparently having selected the right treasury manager). (Paauwe and Boselie 2005: 71)

There is little evidence which examines the time to effect of the introduction of a new policy or procedure. Initial evidence suggests that with the exception of the introduction of something like a performance related pay policy (see Chapter 7), most HR strategic interventions take one to three years to come to fruition (Guest et al. 2003). Thus the line of sight between cause and effect becomes very unclear and it is difficult to demonstrate with any confidence that a change in a business performance measure was as a result of the now almost forgotten change in conditions of employee service, introduction of performance-related pay scheme, family-friendly policy, etc.

To conclude, it is worth considering the notion of reverse causality. Consider a highly profitable organization, which has an HR director, engages in strategic thinking and has adopted sophisticated HR practices and monitors a variety of HR outcomes, mapping these against business measurement metrics. One might legitimately reflect upon why the organization is profitable. Is the organization profitable because it has a strategic presence on the board and develops, uses and monitors a range of HR practices, for example: employee engagement surveys, has a platform for 'employee-voice', which is actively monitored and feedback given, has adopted high-performance work systems (HPWS) etc.? Or is the organization already successful and so can afford to introduce, or indulge itself in, a range of HR practices? Most people enjoy being part of a winning team, and high firm performance also signals organizational health and thus employment security (Paauwe and Boselie 2005: 77).

In the context of the debate about reverse causality, Ait Razouk (2011) offers a word of caution, and perhaps hope, before we all walk away, shaking our heads in despair from the complex and thorny issues associated with linking HRM practices to business outcomes. In a longitudinal study conducted into the impact of HPWSs within 275 French small- and medium-sized enterprises (SMEs), in the findings of research Ait Razouk (2011: 322) 'counters the hypothesis of reversed causality. Our results indicated that a causal relation exists between HPWS and performance indicators retained for the purposes of our study.' However, rather than think 'job done, let's go home', Ait Razouk also offers a caveat. The research team of which he was a member chose to monitor 12 HR variables, which included appraisal, compensation participation, etc., but of course there are other variables which they could have chosen but were not monitored. In summarizing the research, he says: 'Finally, although our research attests that HPWSs allow predicting firm's performance, the link between HRM and performance is not direct. Several authors propose to test intermediate variables such as behaviours, skills, social capital, work relationship, employees groups, psychological contract' (Ait Razouk 2011: 323).

The transparency of how strategic HRM and HR practices can bring added value to an organization is very complex and contextually affected. The HR department does not deliver human resource management practices: they may develop policy, organize training, but the delivery is done by line management and in many cases it is how these people (line managers) interpret and implement those practices and policies. HR's role is to be aware of these deficiencies, as discussed throughout this chapter, yet strive, in an imperfect world, to seek relevant practices and to monitor their outcomes.

The problem, usually attributed to Cameron (1963), in our case assessing the value and relevance of HR interventions, can be summed up in the following way:

> It would be nice if all of the data which sociologists require could be enumerated because then we could run them through IBM machines and draw charts as the economists do. However, not everything that can be counted counts, and not everything that counts can be counted. (1963: 3)

CASE STUDY 4.4

Securitas

Business consultant Paul Kearns recently carried out some work with a European arm of the security firm Securitas.

This involved working with a team made up of both operational and HR managers with the aim of aligning a new HR strategy to the business strategy of the company, by getting the best out of every employee to gain competitive advantage. Kearns says the approach taken flies in the face of regular personnel methods, where traditionally HR has been trained to follow HR best practice:

> This leads HR departments to follow what other HR teams are doing rather than introducing initiatives that are practical and focused on the specific issues in their organization (he says). It also means HR starts off thinking about what training would be suitable, what competencies need developing, or how they can improve employee engagement. But this should be an end point, not a starting point.

(Continued)

(Continued)

Kearns says what he did with the Securitas team was to look at the long-term strategic aims of the company, break them down into operational measures – and then consider practical ways HR can help in these areas.

One area the company wanted to improve was the time each Securitas team took to respond to call-outs. 'To get the best evidence possible, we didn't break down the analysis into groups of security guards, but looked at each individual and how they were performing,' explains Kearns.

As a result, a performance chart was developed where every employee could see how they performed in terms of response times in relation to everyone else. 'This provided evidence on an individual level and highlighted what each person had to do to improve, and wasn't the sheep-dip approach that you often find in HR projects,' Kearns says.

Source: Bentley (2008).

 ■ **Question**

1. To what extent does HR have to move away from a one size fits all approach and consider the context and everything pertinent within that context rather than looking for an off the shelf approach?

■ **Further Reading** ■ ■ ■ ■ ■ ■ ■ ■ ■ ■ ■ ■ ■

Becker, B.R., Huselid, M.A. and Ulrich, D. (2001) *The HR Scorecard: Linking People, Strategy, and Performance*. Boston, MA: Harvard Business School Press.

Rousseau, D.M. and Barends. E.G.R. (2011) 'HRM in the 21st century: becoming an evidence-based HR practitioner', *Human Resource Management Journal*, 21 (3): 221–35.

Storey, J. (1995) 'Is HRM catching on?', *International Journal of Manpower*, 16 (4): 3–10.

Ulrich, D. and Smallwood, N. (2004) 'Capitalizing on capabilities', *Harvard Business Review*, June: 119–27.

References

Ait Razouk, A. (2011) 'High-performance work systems and performance of French small and medium-sized enterprises: examining causal order', *International Journal of Human Resource Management*, 22 (2): 311–30.

Alpander, G. G. (1982) *Human Resources Management Planning*. New York: Amacom.

Ball, C. (2006) 'HR leads Ford's diversity drive', *Personnel Today*, 21 February, RBI, available at http://www.personneltoday.com/articles/21/02/2006/34005/hr-leads-ford39s-diversity-drive.htm, accessed 12 September 2013.

Bentley, R. (2008) 'HR strategy: how HR can make a difference', *Personnel Today*, 30 June, available at http://www.personneltoday.com/articles/30/06/2008/46469/hr-strategy-how-hr-can-make-a-difference.htm, accessed 12 September 2013.

Blakey, R. (2012) 'Kodak puts up shutters and files for bankruptcy', *The Times*, 20 January, 30.

Boxall, P. and Purcell, J. (2008) *Strategy and Human Resource Management*. Basingstoke: Palgrave Macmillan.

Brockbank, W. (1999) 'If HR were really strategically proactive: present and future directions in HR's contribution to competitive advantage', *Human Resource Management*, 38: 337–52.

Cameron, W.B. (1963) *Informal Sociology: A Casual Introduction to Sociological Thinking*. New York: Random House.

CIPD (2007) *The Changing HR Function. CIPD Survey Report*. Available at http://www.cipd.co.uk/hr-resources/survey-reports/changing-hr-function.aspx, accessed 13 September 2013.

CIPD (2012) *Using HR Metrics for Maximum Impact, Part of the 'Shaping the Future' Reports*. London: CIPD Publications.

Cooke, F.L. (2006) 'Modeling an HR shared services center: experience of an MNC in the United Kingdom', *Human Resource Management*, 45 (2): 211–27.

Cunningham, J.B. and Kempling, J. (2011) 'Promoting organisational fit in strategic HRM: applying the HR scorecard in pubic service organizations', *Public Personnel Management*, 410 (3): 193–213.

Faragher, J. (2012) 'HR needs to invest in its own development', *Personnel Today*, 13 July.

Fisher, S. (2012) *HR's True Position in the Boardroom*. Cartoon. Stafford, Staffordshire

Flamholtz, E. (2007) 'Human resource accounting: a review of theory and research', *Journal of Management Studies*, 11 (1): 44–61.

Guest, D.E (1987) 'Human resource management and industrial relations', *Journal of Management Studies*, 24: 503–21.

Guest, D.E., Michie, J., Conway, N. and Sheehan, M. (2003) 'Human resource management and corporate performance in the UK', *British Journal of Industrial Relations*, 41 (2): 291–314.

Hackman, G.R. (1978) 'The design of work in the 1980s', *Organizational Dynamics*, 7 (1): 3–17.

Hackman, J.R. and Oldham, G.R. (1975) 'Development of the job diagnostic survey', *Journal of Applied Psychology*, 60, 159–70.

Harper Collins English Dictionary (2007) London: HarperCollins.

Jamrog, J.J. and Overholt, M.H. (2004) 'Building a strategic HR function: continuing the revolution', *Human Resource Planning*, 31 (1): 29–38.

Juran, J.M. (1951) *Quality Control Handbook*. New York: McGraw-Hill.

Kaplan, R.S. and Norton, D.P. (1996a) *Translating Strategy into Action: The Balanced Scorecard*. Boston, MA: Harvard Business School Press.

Kaplan, R.S. and Norton, D.P. (1996b) 'Linking the balanced scorecard to strategy', *California Management Review*, 39 (1): 53.

Kaplan, R.S. and Norton, D.P. (1996c) 'Using the balanced scorecard as a strategic management system', *Harvard Business Review*, January–February (76): 68–83.

Lockwood, N. (2006) 'Maximising human capital: demonstrating HR value with key performance indicators', *HR Magazine*, 51 (9): 1 10.

Mayo, E. (1945) *The Human Problems of an Industrial Civilization*. New York: Macmillan

Murphy, N. (2012) 'HR roles and responsibilities: the 2012 XPertHR survey', IRS Employment Review, IRS Publishers, available at http://www.xperthr.co.uk/survey-analysis/hr-roles-and-responsibilities-2013-xperthr-survey/115436/, accessed 14 September 2013.

Paauwe, J. and Boselie, P. (2005) 'HRM and performance: what next?', *Human Resource Management Journal*, 15 (4): 68–83.

Schuler, R.S. and Jackson, R.E. (1987) 'Linking competitive strategy with human resource management', *Academy of Management Executive*, 1 (3): 207–19.

Speedy, S. (2008) 'Central perks', *Employee Benefits*, 48–9.

Storey, J. (1992) *Developments in the Management of Human Resources: An Analytical Review*. Oxford: Blackwell.

Storey, J. (2007) 'Human resource management today: an assessment', in J. Storey (ed.), *Human Resource Management: A Critical Text*. London: Thomson Learning, pp. 1–400.

Tichy, N.M and Devanna, M.A. (1986) *Transformational Leadership*. New York: John Wiley.

Tootell, B., Blackler, M., Toulson, P. and Dewe, P. (2009) 'Metrics: HRM's Holy Grail? A New Zealand case study', *Human Resource Management Journal*, 19 (4): 375–92.

Torrington, D., Hall, L., Taylor, S. and Atkinson, C. (2011) *Human Resource Management*, 8th edn. Harlow: Pearson Education.

Ulrich, D. (1996) *Human Resource Champions: The Next Agenda for Adding Value and Delivering Results*. Boston, MA: Harvard Business School Press.

Ulrich, D. (1998) 'A new mandate for human resources', *Harvard Business Review*, 76 (1): 124–34.

Ulrich, D. (2009) 'The HR business-partner model: past learnings and future challenges', 32 (2): 5–7.

Ulrich, D. (2011) 'Celebrating 50 years and anniversary reflection', *Human Resource Management*, 50 (1): 3–7.

Ulrich, D. and Brockbank, W. (2005a) 'Employee advocate role drives business results too', *Canadian HR Reporter*, 18 (7): 27.

Ulrich, D. and Brockbank, W. (2005b) 'Role call', *People Management*, 11 (12): 24–8.

Ulrich, D. and Brockbank, W. (2005c) *The HR Value Proposition*. Boston, MA: Harvard Business School Press.

Ulrich, D., Younger, J., Brockbank, W. and Ulrich, M. (2012) *HR from the Outside In*. New York: McGraw Hill.

Walton, R. (1972) 'How to counter alienation in the plant', *Harvard Business Review*, November–December: 70–81.

Weiss, D.S. and Finn, R. (2005) 'HR metrics that count: aligning human capital management to business results', *Human Resource Planning*, 28 (1): 33–8.

Woolf, C. (2012) 'How employees align HR with business', available at http://www.xperthr.co.uk/survey-analysis/how-employers-align-hr-with-the-business-2012-xperthr-survey/113740/, accessed 14 September 2013.

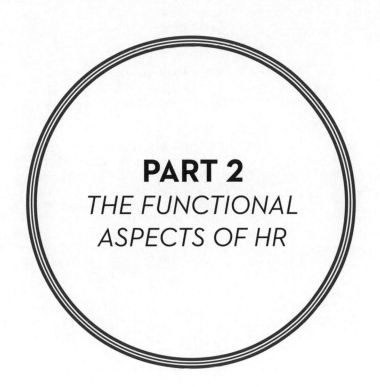

PART 2
*THE FUNCTIONAL
ASPECTS OF HR*

5

RECRUITMENT AND SELECTION

Stephen Taylor

Chapter Overview

This chapter surveys the range of different ways that organizations recruit and select staff. We start with an overview of the approach that is generally considered to constitute 'good practice', partly because it is fairest from the candidates' point of view and partly because it is widely agreed to provide the organization with the best possible recruit in terms of likely subsequent performance. The second part of the chapter then reviews all the major tools, techniques and approaches that are commonly used by organizations through the prism of this good practice model. In the process questions are raised about whether good practice is always appropriate for organizations to adopt. This section also aims to introduce you to some of the more significant contemporary developments in the field, particularly employer branding and recruitment and selection in global organizations. Finally we briefly consider how an organization can develop a strategic approach to the management of its recruitment and selection activities. Throughout examples from both the UK and overseas are used to illustrate key points.

≡ Learning Objectives ≡

- **Explain and evaluate 'good practice' thinking in the field of recruitment and selection**
- **Debate the advantages and disadvantages of replacing job analysis processes with competency frameworks**
- **Evaluate the effectiveness of internal and informal methods of recruitment**
- **Discuss the concept of employer branding and its potential to improve established approaches to recruitment**
- **Identify the benefits and dangers associated with the employment of headhunters and recruitment consultants**
- **Assess the arguments for and against selecting new staff using traditional interviews**
- **Review the use of ability tests, personality tests and assessment centres in personnel selection**
- **Appreciate what taking a strategic approach to recruitment and selection involves**

McDonalds at the London Olympics

In the months running up to the London Olympic Games of 2012 two large companies had to undertake major recruitment exercises. They took totally different approaches with very different results.

In 2010 security company G4S won the contract to become the official provider of security services to the Games. At that stage the requirement was for 2,000 staff to check tickets, patrol sites, operate X-ray machines, monitor CCTV and search bags and vehicles. However, late in 2011 the requirement was suddenly increased to 10,400 staff – all to work for a maximum of just seven weeks. This meant that G4S had to change its initial strategy of targeting people with experience of security work. Instead, in addition, it sought applications from unemployed people and students with a view to providing them with appropriate training. A five-month recruitment campaign was run between November 2011 and April 2012 using a wide variety of methods including online ads, local radio, billboards, ads in buses, on trains and in football programmes. Over 100,000 people expressed an interest, but many withdrew when they were informed about the 12-hour shifts, lack of assistance with transportation, the £8.50 an hour pay rate and the complex screening and vetting procedures they would have to go through. In the end, with a few weeks to go before the start of the Games, G4S managed to make the required 10,400 appointments. But it was not easy.

Major problems then started to develop as large numbers of the recruits failed to turn up for their training sessions and first shifts. Views vary on why this happened. G4S claims that it kept in touch with everyone it had recruited using a dedicated intranet site, but press reports suggest that these efforts were inadequate. Early recruits heard nothing from the company for weeks on end and either lost interest or took up other employment opportunities. The upshot was a shortfall of around 3,500 staff just two weeks before the games started. This required the government to draft in troops at very late notice to cover for the absent G4S recruits. A media storm then developed, with newspapers heaping scorn on G4S and particularly on its Chief Executive, Nick Buckles, who was given a torrid time by MPs when summoned to give evidence to a Select Committee in the House of Commons. Huge reputational damage was done to G4S, putting in doubt its capacity to secure public sector contracts in the future, while the value of the company's shares plummeted.

At around the same time McDonalds was appointed as the official provider of restaurant services to the London Games by the International Olympic Committee, a task it has performed at every Olympics since 1976. The UK company was charged with establishing four restaurants on the main Olympic park (including one for the athletes) and several more at other Games' venues. A total of 1,900 staff would be required for the duration of the main games and the Paralympics that followed.

Managers at McDonalds took a completely different approach from G4S, preferring to recruit internally rather than externally. They ran a competition among staff at all existing restaurants in the UK, the aim being to reward their best people with an opportunity to work at the Olympics as part of what they labelled their 'Olympic Champion Crew Super Team'. As official sponsors of the games, McDonalds were able to give the selected staff tickets to many of the events. Mobile phones were also given to successful recruits, who were accommodated in a large, central London hotel for the duration of the Games. The key attributes that they sought were:

- The ability to work at speed
- Outstanding customer service skills
- The ability to work well in a team.

The company was determined to ensure that its Olympic restaurants ran to the highest standards of quality and efficiency as it expected that one in every ten visitors to the Olympics would make use of them. In the event 6,800 staff from across the UK made it through to the final selection event in London, from whom the final 1,900 were selected. McDonalds also won the contract to recruit and train 70,000 volunteers to work on the Olympic sites and 12,000 further staff were directly employed by the London Organising Committee (LOCOG). Both tasks were accomplished smoothly and in good time.

Sources: Gabb (2012), Woods (2012) and press reports.

 ■ **Question**

1. What key R&S lessons can be learned from this case?

Introduction

Recruiting and selecting new members of staff is a core HRM activity that is of considerable significance in organizations. The more substantial the potential impact of a role, the more important it is to ensure that the individual who carries it out is well-qualified, highly motivated, able to work well alongside colleagues and likely to remain in post for a reasonable period of time. These objectives are achieved first by attracting a sizeable pool of suitable candidates and second by taking steps to maximize the chances that the best candidate is appointed. However, when labour markets are tight and skills are in relatively short supply, recruiting and selecting strong performers can be difficult. As much energy often has to be put into persuading good candidates to apply or to take up a post, as it does shortlisting and selecting.

Recruitment and selection have always been controversial topics in HRM because there are so many different approaches available. Over time a fairly well-defined good practice approach has become established, but it is by no means always used by organizations, and in some respects it is only used by a minority. It thus remains itself a topic of considerable controversy and debate. In this chapter we explore the major alternative methods used to recruit and select staff, analysing each through the prism of the good practice model.

Good practice in recruitment and selection

In the UK and in most industrialized countries, HR managers have tended for many years to advocate an approach to recruitment and selection which is widely believed to constitute good practice. Its purpose is to secure the best qualified and highest performing staff for the employer, while also being scrupulously fair to job applicants. The approach is set out clearly and concisely by ACAS (2009) and CIPD (2012) in their advisory publications. It also forms the basis of numerous accounts of recruitment and selection in management handbooks and textbooks (see Rankin 2003; Hall et al. 2008; Smith 2011; Armstrong 2012). The good practice model is typically conceived as a process with a number of distinct stages (see Figure 5.1):

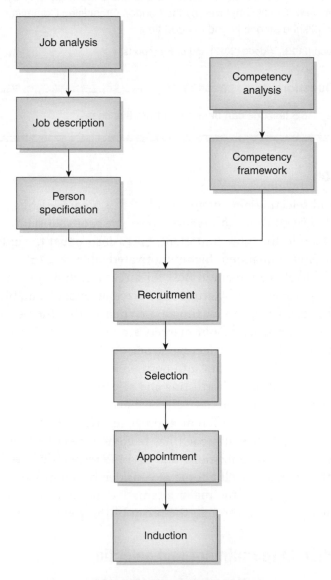

Figure 5.1   Stages in good practice recruitment and selection
Source: author.

Job analysis and design

The process starts with a systematic assessment of the organization's recruitment needs. First of all, managers are urged to consider whether a vacancy needs to be filled at all, and if so, whether it should be redesigned in order to better meet organizational needs. Further questions are then asked and answered after thought and consultation. What will the job require of its holder? How will the job relate to others in the organization? To whom will the job holder report? What kind of attributes should the job holder possess in order to perform to a high level?

Two key documents are then produced – a job description and a person specification. Job descriptions aim to summarize the major duties and accountabilities of job holders. Employers following the good practice model typically provide copies to all their employees so that they know precisely what is expected of them and where they fit in to the wider organizational design. They are also made available to would-be candidates for job vacancies to help them to prepare their applications effectively. Person specifications are derived from job descriptions. Their purpose is to set out concisely the characteristics and experience that a successful job applicant will be expected to have. Person specifications typically distinguish between 'desirable' and 'essential' characteristics. Both the job description and the person specification then inform subsequent stages of the good practice approach.

Recruitment

In the good practice model, the recruitment stage is concerned with attracting applications from as many suitably qualified candidates as possible, thus maximizing the organization's ability to employ the best available person. While the precise tools used will vary depending on the job and the size of the pool of potential applicants, the assumption is that all jobs are advertised in such a way as to reach the target audience and to encourage them to apply. This involves actively 'selling' the job by stressing its positive aspects in the advertisement and the potential advantages of working for the employer.

Recruitment advertisements can be placed in a number of different places in order to achieve wide dissemination. While many fewer now appear in national and local newspapers than was once the case, many employers continue to source staff in this way. The recruitment pages of trade journals also remain a key recruitment method, as do job centres and careers services. Increasingly, however, we are seeing recruitment advertising moving online, as employers make use of corporate websites and a variety of cyber-agencies to advertise the jobs they have available.

A feature of the good practice approach to recruitment is an understanding that it is underpinned by a commitment to fairness. Applications are encouraged from everyone who is qualified to do the job, irrespective of personal characteristics (gender, race, age, religion sexuality, disability etc.) or of whether or not they are already known in the organization (see Chapter 9 on equal opportunities and diversity). Everyone will be considered on their merits in a fair and objective way. To that end it is normal for job advertisements to specify a 'closing date' after which no further applications will be considered.

Selection

The first task that has to be accomplished during the selection stage is short-listing. The applications that have been received need to be sifted by managers in order to establish which candidates they wish to give serious consideration to employing. When there is just one vacancy to be filled, a shortlist of five or six people is typical. This allows a reasonable choice, while also being manage-able and cost-effective. However, where larger numbers are being recruited at the same time, as happens when larger employers are recruiting cohorts of graduate trainees, shortlists can consist of dozens of candidates. In the good practice model shortlisting is undertaken in a highly objective fashion. Each application form or CV is given careful consideration and is matched up with the person specification. Those who 'fit' best in terms of the essential and desirable characteristics needed for the role are those who get shortlisted.

Shortlisting is followed by some form of selection testing. Traditionally, of course, managers have interviewed candidates (often quite informally) before deciding who to appoint. However, this approach is rejected by advocates of good practice because it is insufficiently systematic and too susceptible to personal bias. Interviewing, particularly when it is little more than a chat in which different candidates may be asked different questions, often leads to poor selection deci-sions. In short, managers tend to choose who they like most personally, rather than thinking analytically about who is most likely to perform best in the role.

Good practice thinking about employee selection tends to downplay the importance of references from former employers and of giving them any sub-stantial role in selecting new staff. This is partly because they are judged to be poor tools to use when trying to predict future performance, and partly because they are by their nature very subjective assessments of someone's ability. Not only therefore are they thought to have the potential to mislead and misinform, but their use is also seen as being potentially unfair. The best person for the job may not be in a position to provide an excellent reference from a current manager for the very good reason that they do not want their employer to know that they are looking for alternative employment.

The good practice approach therefore stresses the benefits of the most objective selection methods. When selection interviews are used they should be structured so that all are asked the same set of questions derived from the job description and person specification, and should involve a panel of inter-viewers. Ideally, though, interviews should be supplemented with more sophis-ticated selection tools such as personality and ability tests, or when possible, with assessment centres. Later in the chapter we will discuss each of these approaches and their rationale in further depth.

Induction

The final stages of the good practice model go beyond the appointment of candidates, taking in the subsequent processes during which they prepare to start the new job and start working. Here too an emphasis is placed on formality and the need for some kind of standardized induction programme. Typically this will involve some formal training supplemented by meetings with managers and colleagues. However, good practice approaches also stress the potential role played by more formal socialization and orientation practices in helping people to settle in and perform well at an early stage.

There are many very positive features of this traditional, good practice approach to recruitment and selection which will endure for many years to come. However, in a wide range of respects it has started to attract scepticism and some criticism too. Alternative thinking has begun to influence practice in many organizations, while more innovative approaches are being widely adopted often in order to supplement aspects of established good practice. In the rest of the chapter we will introduce these debates and consider how far different aspects of the good practice model can be both re-thought and enhanced by organizations seeking to maximize their effectiveness in the contemporary business environment.

PIT STOP: REFLECTIVE ACTIVITY 5.1

1. Think about your own experience of working and that of your close friends and relations. To what extent was the recruitment and selection process you or they have experienced similar to the good practice model? In what ways was it different? What might account for the differences?
2. It is often argued that good practice approaches to recruitment and selection have much more to offer larger companies and public sector organizations than smaller employers. To what extent do you agree with this point of view and why?
3. Walley and Smith (1998) argue that many job applicants actively deceive employers when applying for jobs by making misleading claims about themselves and generally engaging in 'impression management' in order to present a more positive image of their capabilities than is really justified. How far can the adoption of a good practice approach help to reduce the effectiveness of deception on the part of candidates?

Competency frameworks

In recent years the major challenge to the use of job descriptions and person specifications in recruitment and selection has come from advocates of an alternative competency-based approach. The term 'competency' was defined by Boyzatis (1982) in one of the most influential books yet to be published in the field of HRM:

an underlying characteristic of a person which results in effective and superior performance in a job.

On the surface a 'competency framework' looks quite similar to a person specification. It comprises a list of personal attributes that can be used by HR managers to inform both their recruitment campaigns and selection processes. There are typically around a dozen competencies listed, the aim being to try to ensure that only those who possess a good number of them are hired by the organization. Competencies are typically expressed in terms of what people can do or how they prefer to conduct themselves at work. Examples are as follows:

- Focuses on delivering a high quality customer experience
- Takes responsibility for managing /their own learning and development
- Motivates others to innovate effectively.

What makes competency frameworks different from person specifications is the methodology used to develop them. The starting point is neither job analysis nor a written job description. Indeed, the whole idea behind competencies is that they are not specific to any one job or even, usually, any defined group of jobs. Instead they aim to cover a wide range of divisions or even a whole organization. In their purest form they are generic in nature, acting as a concise statement of the characteristics the organization seeks in its new recruits. The process for developing a robust competency framework starts by identifying existing employees who are the most effective and contribute most. A variety of tests are then conducted that establish which underlying characteristics these superior performers share which make them so effective. Various methods can be used including interviews with individuals and their colleagues, personality tests and direct observation of the superior performers at work. The outcome is a framework of competencies that can then be used for a variety of HR purposes including performance management (see Chapter 7), employee development (see Chapter 10), and as is our concern here, recruitment and selection.

In recent years competency frameworks have tended to become more distinct from person specifications by including statements which are clearly value-laden (see Milsom 2009). They move beyond a simple statement of the attributes required to do a good job to encompass language which reflects the organization's core values (see the discussion of organizational culture in Chapter 11) .

It is not unusual now to come across competency frameworks that refer to personal integrity, to commercial awareness and, above all, to effective team-working. How people go about doing their jobs, their motivations and also their ethics are thus incorporated into the recruitment and selection process.

The spread of competency frameworks that are derived from an analysis of characteristics shared by superior performers in an organization has provoked a significant debate between those who support them and those who prefer the traditional approach rooted in job analysis (see Wood and Payne 1998; Voskuijl and Evers 2008). The major arguments in favour of using competency frameworks to underpin recruitment and selection are as follows:

- In the contemporary business context it is not appropriate to define jobs too narrowly. People have to be flexible, expecting their duties and responsibilities to evolve and change over shorter and shorter timescales. It thus makes sense for organizations to recruit people who have the competencies required by the organization rather than those who meet a narrowly defined job description and person specification. They are recruited 'to a team' rather than 'to do a job'.
- All-pervasive change driven by globalization, new technologies and less predictable market conditions means that job descriptions, and hence person specifications, need to be continually updated, reviewed and re-written. This is both costly and disruptive, providing people with an opportunity to challenge and object to proposed changes. It is thus more effective to dispense with a job-based approach altogether and replace it with a person-based approach that sets out expectations in more general terms.
- It is increasingly recognized that what makes people effective as performers is less their skill sets and more their attitudes towards work and their personal values. People can be trained to improve their skills, but should be selected primarily for their attitudes which are harder for an organization to influence. This is the approach that has long been used successfully by global Japanese corporations and is increasingly being imitated by others. Desired attitudes are generic rather than job-specific and are best expressed in a competency framework.

Competency-based approaches have themselves been subjected to criticism by people who support the established good practice approach to recruitment and selection rooted in thorough job analysis. The key points made are as follows:

- When used as the basis for recruitment decisions competencies have a strong tendency to produce 'clones'. Because they are derived from an analysis of the characteristics shared by effective performers, competency frameworks inevitably lead to the selection of candidates who are very similar to one another. The result is reduced diversity, particularly among management teams (Kandola et al. 2000). Everyone thinks in the same way, comes at problems with the same mindset and shares the same values. People who have a different outlook and may have a lot to offer are put off from applying when they read competency-based recruitment literature. Without diversity there is less creative tension, less innovation and ultimately a loss of competitive advantage.
- The use of competency frameworks across international organizations has been particularly criticized because the approach fails to take account of profound cultural differences between the customary approaches to work found in people with different cultural backgrounds (see Chapter 11). Numerous studies have demonstrated that the type of competencies that are

associated with effective performance in one country are often very different from those associated with effective performance in others. This is particularly true of people employed in leadership roles. It follows that recruiting internationally using competency frameworks can damage an organization's long-term prospects.

- Competency frameworks have a strong tendency to reflect the characteristics that made people working for organizations effective in the past. They do not therefore adequately reflect the attributes organizations need to start developing for the future. New recruits are brought in who are wonderfully placed to perform well in circumstances that are changing and are likely to change further and faster in the future.

Perhaps, as is so often the case in HRM, the best approach is to blend the two approaches together and to draw the best features from competency frameworks as well as job analysis. Job descriptions and person specifications still have a role to play, but in order to ensure that they are compatible with flexibility, they have to be made more generic and less precise. There is room for them to incorporate competencies alongside points that are role-specific. At the same time organizations need to be less inclined to recruit purely on the basis of competencies derived from an analysis of the characteristics shared by their current high performers. More thought needs to be given to likely future requirements and to the potential benefits of recruiting diverse teams who have different contributions to make.

≣ CASE STUDY 5.2 ≣

Recruiting expatriate staff: culture shock

According to Black and Gregerson (1999) a substantial minority (20–30 per cent) of Americans who take up expatriate postings overseas either return home early or fail to meet their original objectives. There are many reasons for this 'expatriate failure', but it is often due to culture shock. As is the case with other nationalities, a good proportion of Americans who take up work abroad find it very difficult to adjust to living in overseas locations, and particularly those which are culturally very different from the USA.

Kuwait, like the other Gulf states, has become extremely wealthy in recent decades thanks to its prodigious supplies of oil. As a result it has been able to develop quickly, with Kuwaitis enjoying standards of living that are among the highest in the world without having to work very hard. In fact most of the jobs in Kuwait are carried out by expatriate workers who are recruited from all over the world: 63 per cent of the population is made up of immigrant workers (the figures are even higher in Qatar and the UAE) employed to manage businesses, to provide professional services, as labourers on the many large-scale construction sites, to work in shops, hotels and restaurants, and also to work as maids in private homes.

The biggest culture shock for Americans arriving in Kuwait for the first time arises when they witness the way that many expatriate workers are treated by the Kuwaitis. Rudeness and arrogance are standard, but bullying and abusive treatment of a kind that would not be tolerated in the USA is also very common. The maids, many of whom originate in the Philippines, have a particularly tough time. In some cases they are treated like slaves, in effect being 'owned' by the households they work in. What is more it is very difficult for them to leave as their passports are taken from them when they take up residence. From an American perspective Kuwaiti society appears to be highly racist, seriously anti-Semitic and class-ridden. Sexism is also a major issue for female expatriates, many of whom report being treated with disrespect by Kuwaiti men in ways that would be seen as wholly unacceptable in American society. Expatriates from the USA are also deeply shocked by the way that Kuwaitis treat their domestic pets. This appears to be appallingly cruel to Americans brought up in a dog-loving, cat-loving society.

The other major cultural difference that American expatriates notice is the lack of any rule of law in Kuwait. There appears to be one law for the Kuwaitis and one for the expatriate workers. The police and criminal justice system is entirely biased towards the Kuwaitis whenever legal disputes arise. What appears in American eyes to be open and rampant corruption is also part and parcel of Kuwaiti culture. People who are particularly wealthy and influential, along with their friends and families, are treated much more favourably by state officials than everyone else. Finally many also remark on the lack of labour laws to protect workers from abuse. The absence of health and safety regulations is particularly shocking for Americans, while many are appalled by the number of hours that the construction workers and maids are required to work.

Source: www.internationschoolreview.com/non-members/Kuwait-culture-shock.htm

 ■ **Questions**

1. Would someone born and brought up in Kuwait find it equally difficult to adjust to working in the USA? What kind of culture shock would they experience?
2. What steps can be taken by those who recruit people to work overseas to minimize the extent of culture shock? What business case can be advanced for investing resources in addressing this issue?

Internal and informal recruitment

The term 'internal recruitment' refers to situations in which existing staff are given preference when new job opportunities arise in an organization. Sometimes jobs are only advertised internally, there being no external considered candidates at all. More commonly internal candidates are obliged to compete with external applicants, but are favoured by recruiters and, in practice, tend to get selected. A third approach involves advertising jobs internally first, the organization only advertising externally when they struggle to make a good internal appointment.

'Informal recruitment' refers to situations in which jobs are not formally advertised at all, with successful recruits hearing about them through word of mouth. Many are friends and family of existing employees, with others being recruited after making unsolicited applications to an organization on the off-chance that they may have suitable vacancies.

Those who adhere to good practice thinking about recruitment and selection tend to be uneasy about internal recruitment and actively hostile to informal recruitment. Their objections stem partly from a belief that these approaches are unfair (see Chapter 9) because they exclude so many would-be candidates from the recruitment process, particularly in the case of more senior jobs. The result tends to benefit groups in society who are already relatively powerful, while operating against the interests of women and members of ethnic minorities. In addition many argue that organizations are themselves disadvantaged when they recruit internally or informally because they are excluding from the field of potential candidates many people who might actually turn out to be better performers than the people they actually recruit.

These are sound points rooted in the concepts of fairness and objectivity that underpin the good practice model, but there are plenty of strong arguments that can be advanced in support of both the informal and internal approaches to recruitment. In short, several research studies now appear to demonstrate that a lack of formality can bring considerable benefits to organizations. It follows that a good business case can be advanced which challenges good practice, provided of course that the organization's actions do not breach any anti-discrimination laws.

This explains why internal and informal recruitment is very common, even in countries such as the UK, where an acceptance of good practice principles is widespread (Taylor 2010: 178–80).

The major arguments in favour of internal recruitment are as follows:

- *Low costs.* Jobs can be advertised on staff intranets, via e-mail or internal newsletters. Appointees are also able to take up their new jobs quickly, avoiding the need to appoint temps or agency workers while an external recruit works their notice.
- *Low risk.* Internal recruits may not be as strong in performance terms as potential external recruits, but they are known quantities. The employer is familiar with their strengths and weaknesses. Appointing them thus reduces the risk of appointing an external candidate who appears plausible at interview, but who disappoints in practice once appointed.
- *Speed of adjustment.* Internal recruits typically require less training and support than external recruits when they take up their new posts. Not only are training costs lower, but they are also able to get up to speed more quickly and start performing at an optimum level faster because they

already possess a great deal of organization-specific knowledge. They are also likely to have a very high level of understanding about what the work involves and are thus less likely than external recruits either to become disillusioned early on or to take up an unsuitable job offer in error.

- *Incentive and motivation*. If internal candidates know that they will be favoured when new opportunities arise and that the organization likes to promote from within when it can, there is inevitably going to be a strong positive motivational effect. Internal recruitment sends out a clear signal that existing staff are valued and will be provided with career development opportunities.

- *Return on investment*. If internal promotion opportunities are few and far between because external candidates are preferred, it is inevitable that ambitious employees will look outside the organization to develop their careers. Moreover, they will never even consider the prospect of staying in the organization over the long term. The result is not only the loss of strong performers to other organizations, but a considerable waste of the money invested in their development over the time that they are employed.

There has been very little research published that specifically evaluates the impact of internal recruitment on organizations or which compares its use to external recruitment. A study of European companies carried out by Sparrow and Hiltrop (1994) is one of few to provide robust evidence to support the benefits set out above. However, the presence or absence of internal promotion opportunities has been extensively studied in the wider context of 'high performance working' and the development of HR practices which enhance organizational performance in more general terms (Pfeffer 1994; Delaney and Huselid 1996; Delery and Doty 1996). These studies, all based on American data, strongly suggest that the presence of a strong internal labour market (i.e. plenty of promotion opportunities for staff), at least when combined with a bundle of other sophisticated, employee-centred HR practices, is associated with superior organizational performance (see Chapter 3).

However, not all the research evidence points in this direction. Cho et al. (2006) in their study of HR practices in American hotels found that organizations which promoted internally suffered higher levels of employee turnover among non-managerial staff than those that preferred to recruit externally. Their study reminds us that there are potential disadvantages associated with internal recruitment as well as advantages, particularly when people are promoted without being given sufficient training and support to carry out their new roles effectively. There is also the tricky problem of how to handle situations in which internal candidates are unsuccessful in their applications or are discouraged from applying in the first place. Thwarted ambition can be very demotivating and have a negative impact both on individual performance and team harmony. Rejecting applications from external applicants is a great deal less problematic.

Having a heavy reliance on internal recruitment for senior personnel can also be criticized on the grounds that it tends to perpetuate existing ways of doing things. Senior management teams need regular infusions of fresh blood in the form of external recruits if they are to avoid becoming stale and reluctant to innovate.

Informal recruitment shares some potential advantages in common with internal recruitment. Friends and family of existing employees are, for example, more likely than unknown external recruits to possess a reasonable level of knowledge about the job they are applying for and of what working for the organization is like. They thus benefit from what the research on recruitment terms 'a realistic job preview'. They enter their new job with realistic expectations and are thus less likely to become disillusioned or to suffer from dashed expectations. Informal recruitment is also much less expensive than formal recruitment. This is why many organizations pay their employees 'referral fees' when they recommend a friend as a potential recruit and that person is subsequently appointed. It is further argued that existing staff are positively motivated by the opportunity to refer their friends and family members and to work alongside them (Reed 2001: 23–6).

There is now a considerable body of robust research evidence which strongly suggests that informal recruits, on average, turn out to be stronger performers than external recruits, and that they are also less likely to leave at an early date.

Some studies also demonstrate that informal recruits, particularly those who are appointed after they have directly approached the organization to ask for a job, are better qualified on average than applicants who respond to formal job advertisements (see Kirnan et al. 1989; Blau 1990; Iles and Robertson 1991; Barber 1998: 22–32; Castilla 2005; Breaugh 2008: 109–10).

A final important point to make about informal recruitment is that in many parts of the world it is not only common, but is also seen as being the norm as far as recruitment is concerned. Cultural norms (see Chapter 11) require people to look after the interests of their families and their friends by helping them to secure jobs. In Western cultures nepotism of this kind is generally seen as being a form of corruption which the law seeks to discourage, but this is far from the case in many African countries, in India, Pakistan, parts of Southern Europe and some East Asian countries. Hofstede's (1980, 1991) research offers an explanation for this difference. He found that countries such as the UK, the USA and those in Northern Europe have cultures which are both individualistic in nature and also relatively comfortable with risk. Across much of the world the opposite is the case, cultural norms being characterized by high levels of collectivism and a strong aversion to risk-taking. Informal recruitment is prevalent in countries with collectivist cultures where people have close ties to others through family and social connections, and feel obliged to one another. Moreover, where what Hofstede refers to as 'uncertainty avoidance' is high, there is a tendency to appoint friends and family and people who are recommended by those who are trusted. There is a preference for 'known' internal candidates rather than unknown external recruits. Informal recruitment is also associated with cultures in which 'power distance' is relatively high; that is to say cultures in which senior managers are relatively autocratic in their approach and do not expect any interference when making decisions. Here leaders appoint who they want to a job, on whatever grounds they choose, and do not expect to be restricted or to have their judgement questioned at all.

PIT STOP: REFLECTIVE ACTIVITY 5.2

1. It is common for larger UK-based organizations, including those in the public sector, to advertise jobs externally despite there being an internal candidate who is highly qualified and all but certain to get the job. Why do they do this? What are the advantages and disadvantages of the practice?
2. What lessons can multinational organizations learn from research on different attitudes to informal recruitment across the world?
3. Evaluate the strengths and weaknesses of the case for restricting the ability to apply for jobs to internal candidates.

Employer branding

The traditional good practice model of recruitment and selection is not especially strategic in its approach. Its starting point is an organization identifying a need for new staff, which then triggers various activities aimed at securing the best qualified recruits. In recent years, at least for organizations that are obliged to compete quite fiercely to secure the services of people with relatively rare skill sets or particular types of professional experience, it has become accepted that this traditional reactive approach to recruitment is inadequate. It needs to be supplemented with strategic approaches which aim, over a prolonged period of time, to build an organization's reputation as an employer. Employer branding, along with a range of associated activities, is now generally recognized as being effective in helping to achieve this.

There is nothing at all new about the idea that organizations need to compete actively in the labour market, or that they need sometimes to 'sell' jobs to would-be recruits in order to raise the quality of their applicant pools.

As long ago as the 1920s articles were being published that advocated this approach (e.g. Bulkley 1922). However, the term 'employer branding' only appears to have been coined for the first time in the 1990s by a London-based recruitment consultant called Simon Barrow (Ambler and Barrow 1996). Since then it has become very widely used by HR professionals, although there sometimes remains a lack of clarity about exactly how it should be defined and about precisely what purposes it serves (Taylor 2010: 196–8; Martin et al. 2011). All agree, however, that the basic idea has been borrowed from the marketing function and applied to HRM.

Commercial organizations build brand identities in order to gain and maintain competitive advantage in their markets. Over time, as a brand name and its associated image become well-known, consumers develop trust in that brand, identify with its perceived values and demonstrate a preference for branded products when making their purchasing decisions. This is a fundamental truth about consumer psychology which drives the marketing of most products and services. The reason that sales of Coca Cola and Pepsi Cola are so much higher than those for comparable products is that they have highly recognizable brand images which have been developed and enhanced over decades. In consumer markets brands are used to communicate to customers the ways in which a particular product or service is:

- better than those of its competitors
- distinct from those of its competitors.

Brands are thus hugely powerful, and when they become internationally known, are often worth a great deal more in financial terms than all the plant, equipment and other assets of the corporations which own them.

Employer branding applies the same principle to the labour market. The idea is that over time an organization can use branding techniques to build for itself a reputation as an employer which is both more positive than that of its major labour market competitors, and also clearly distinct. The term has become closely associated with two others which are also increasingly widely used in HRM:

- The term 'employer of choice' indicates an organization which is generally recognized as being the most desirable in the industry from an employee's perspective. It is an organization for which most of the target market would like to work if they could.
- The term 'employee value proposition' (EVP) indicates the package of terms and conditions (Chapter 7) as well as the potential experiences that an organization tries to offer its recruits in order both to attract and retain them.

In short, employer branding involves developing and communicating a compelling EVP in order to achieve employer-of-choice status in its industry.

Some commentators and managers erroneously take the view that employer branding is largely about the development of more sophisticated recruitment advertising. This is not the case. Recruitment advertising is often used as a means of communicating an employer brand, but the processes involved in its development are a great deal more strategic and long-term in their nature. In consumer marketing the following homily is widely quoted as a kind of golden rule: 'to thine own brand be true'.

This means that the claims you make about your product in any advertising or public relations activity must genuinely reflect consumer perceptions of their qualities. If you start making claims that are misleading in any way, trust in the brand is lost – a very expensive mistake to make when it is considered how much time, effort and investment go into building up credible branding. The same is true of employer branding. Employer branding will only yield dividends if the EVP that is communicated is firmly rooted in the real, lived experience of employees working for an organization.

The upshot is that an effective employer branding exercise must start with gaining a detailed understanding of what your existing employees perceive are the best things about their employment experience and, as importantly, the ways in which it is distinct from that offered by potential competitors. A variety of tools can be used to achieve this, and many organizations employ specialist consultants to advise them and to carry out the necessary research. Focus groups are commonly used, with most participants being people who started their employment relatively recently and who have worked for competitor organizations in the past.

Wider employee surveys can also provide data to support the building of a robust employer brand.

The next stage is the formulation of a compelling EVP. This aims to define in a few short sentences precisely what it is that is positive and distinct about the employment experience that is being offered. Cameron (2009) gives an excellent example of the EVP developed by Marks and Spencer to underpin their employer branding activities. This has ten points:

Join M&S and we will:

1. Make you feel valued and proud to work for M&S
2. Reward you well against our retail competitors
3. Make sure you have inspirational, effective line managers who value and support you
4. Tell you how the company is doing
5. Give you opportunities to share your ideas on improving the business
6. Listen and deal with your issues and concerns

7. Train you thoroughly to do your job
8. Offer you career opportunities and support to take advantage of them
9. Tell you how you are doing
10. Treat you fairly, using modern, transparent employment practices.

Finally, again taking a leaf out of the marketing specialist's textbooks, a successful employer branding exercise requires the development of a relatively short, snappy slogan which sums up the main points in the EVP and can be used in recruitment advertising, as well as in internal communication exercises which aim to improve employee engagement and retention. In the case of Marks and Spencer the following formulation was drawn up, making use of the expression 'Your M&S' which the company uses extensively in its consumer branding activities: 'Your M&S people are proud, committed, involved, challenged, valued and fairly treated.'

Another good example comes from recent efforts by the UK Prison Service to brand itself more effectively as an employer (Walker 2008). Extensive research among its staff led to the identification of six attributes which summed up the reality of day to day work as a prison officer. Some of these might surprise people who are unfamiliar with work of this kind:

- human insight
- thoughtfulness
- realism
- courage
- competence
- humour.

The following statement was then formulated for use in recruitment literature which emphasizes these attributes: 'If you are fascinated by people and can relate to them effectively, you'll find long-term interest and satisfaction in a career with the prison service'.

Another example of a company that used an employer branding exercise to start altering widespread but inaccurate perceptions of its EVP is Telstra, the large Australian telecommunications conglomerate (Macklin 2011). External research demonstrated that many people in key target groups had fairly negative views about the organization, perceiving it as being a large, monolithic corporation which is inflexible and conservative, providing only limited and unexciting career prospects. The response was to establish what existing staff liked most about their jobs, an exercise which established considerable enthusiasm for the experience of working alongside colleagues, with cutting edge technologies and with very considerable flexibility. This led to the development of a slogan aimed at persuading people that Telstra is a great place to work: 'A career at Telstra enables you to connect with what you love.'

The ideas behind employer branding are compelling and have been widely adopted in recent years by larger organizations with the resources available to undertake the necessary research and development activity. Moreover, there is also evidence to demonstrate that the approach is spreading internationally. However, as yet, there is only very limited robust evidence to demonstrate a good return on this investment. While it can be demonstrated that some companies have managed to improve their perception as employers, detailed data on the impact of employer branding exercises in general terms are not yet available.

It is widely argued that employer branding will become more significant in the future as a result of technological developments. Much recruitment activity is now carried out online, an increasing proportion of it using smartphones and other mobile communication devices. This opens up all kinds of possibilities for organizations to interact with potential job applicants in more sophisticated, creative and interactive ways. However, as yet the use of social networking, YouTube and applications such as Second Life in order to build an employer brand tends to be more of an aspiration than an active part of employer branding strategies.

There also remain some important, unresolved issues about which people have different views. One concerns the use of employer brands by multinational employers (see Chapter 12). The key question concerns the extent to which an international corporation which employs people in several very different cultural contexts can usefully develop a single EVP which is going to be equally compelling across its global operations. Surely if people in different countries have different expectations of work and of their employers, the EVP and the employer brand have to be tailored to meet local preferences. And if so, the concept of developing an international employer brand makes little if any sense.

While published research on this issue is limited, a consensus is beginning to emerge among employer branding specialists. First, it is clear that while some aspects of the expectations people have of employment vary very considerably from country to country (Hofstede 1980, 1991), there are some core requirements that apply pretty well everywhere. Towers Perrin (2005) identified three:

- ensuring adequate compensation and financial security
- achieving work/life balance
- having relevant learning and career opportunities.

So should international corporations simply develop global employer brands which stress these three basic features? They could, but were they to do so the result would be self-defeating because there would be precious little opportunity for differentiation, which is central to effective employer branding (Reilly and Williams 2012: 97). Moreover, of course, only some aspects of the EVP would ever be covered, hugely reducing their authenticity – another essential component of any successful employer branding exercise.

On the other hand, it makes little sense for international companies to develop wholly distinct EVPs and employer brands in each country that they recruit in. Not only would this be expensive, but it would also make it very difficult to convey any strong, compelling and authentic messages to employees across a corporation's global operations. There would be confusion among employees about exactly what their organization stood for and was aiming to achieve in terms of its employment practices.

The solution is therefore to take what Martin and Hetrick (2009) refer to as a 'glocal' approach or what Torrington et al. (2011) call 'thinking global, while acting local'. This involves making a clear distinction when developing the EVP between some core global employment principles that are applied universally across an organization's international operations, and a local EVP which reflects the lived reality of being employed in a particular country. The aim is to achieve the best of both worlds. Firm general principles are supplemented to provide the authentic local flavour which any effective branding exercise requires.

The research by Towers Perrin (2005) referred to above provides some useful guidance about how this might be done. The key is to understand what are the main 'attraction and retention drivers' in different countries. For example, they found that in the following countries the opportunity to carry out 'challenging work' tops the list of attraction drivers: Belgium, France, Germany, Italy, Japan and the Netherlands. It follows that any employer seeking to recruit top performers in those countries must build challenging work into their EVP.

Elsewhere, by contrast the opportunity to be challenged comes well down the list of priorities for job-seekers, if indeed it appears at all. This is true of China, Spain, Mexico, Brazil and South Korea. In these labour markets there is much more to be gained by focusing efforts on the provision of genuine career development opportunities. Another major difference in job-seekers' priorities across the world is the relative significance of base pay (i.e. a guaranteed monthly salary as opposed to benefits and incentives). Base pay comes top of the list of attraction drivers in the UK, USA and Canada, but matters much less in the Netherlands and Germany.

PIT STOP: REFLECTIVE ACTIVITY 5.3

In this chapter we have looked at the role played by employer branding in enhancing an organization's recruitment capability. It is often claimed, however, that the approach brings several other potential benefits to organizations too. In what ways do you think it might play a role in the following areas?

1. Reducing staff turnover levels?
2. Enhancing employee engagement?
3. Raising levels of performance?
4. Strengthening employee relations?
5. Improving a corporation's public image?

Headhunters and recruitment agencies

The use of headhunting companies to source recruits has always been a highly controversial aspect of HRM. It is seen by many as being wholly incompatible with good practice approaches as well as being a very expensive recruitment method. This is why it is hardly ever used in the public sector, and where it is, as was the case when the BBC appointed a new Director General in 2012, it attracts negative media comment.

Headhunting is a very competitive business in the UK, and because the industry is unregulated, on occasions headhunters can be guilty of misleading both recruitees and recruiters and also indulging in sharp practice of various other kinds. The level of competition arises from the ease with which anyone with some entrepreneurial flair and a reasonable number of contacts can set themselves up as a 'recruitment consultant'. All you need is a telephone, an e-mail address and some basic sales skills. In many ways the job has similarities to running a dating agency. The aim is simply to match recruits with employers, selling the job to the recruit and the recruit to the employer. When successful, headhunters typically command a commission worth 25–35 per cent of the first year's salary. This potentially makes headhunting very lucrative, particularly when the focus is on finding and placing professional and managerial staff in new roles.

Seen from an HRM perspective there are many serious drawbacks associated with sourcing new recruits through headhunters. Aside from the costs and the tendency for agents to exaggerate the qualities of their candidates in a bid to ensure that they are interviewed for a post (i.e. hard selling), recruiting through a headhunter means that only a very narrow field of candidates is ever considered when there is a vacancy. Agents typically put forward candidates who are already on their books, being reluctant to carry out a great deal of work sourcing potential candidates when no financial return is guaranteed. This makes it very difficult to argue that the use of headhunters is compatible with a genuine commitment either to equal opportunities (see Chapter 9) or with a policy of selecting new recruits from the widest possible field of talent.

Why then are headhunters used at all? How can it be that the recruitment industry in the UK and elsewhere has continued to thrive and grow during several years of slow economic growth and loose labour market conditions (Newell Brown and Swain 2012)? The answer is that there are many situations in which it makes good sense to recruit via headhunting firms, and some in which an organization has little choice if it is to source the best potential recruits. A common example occurs when an organization needs to find someone to fill a highly specialized role for which only a few dozen people in the country are truly qualified. Placing a job advertisement in the press or on a corporate website is unlikely to prove successful, as the key target group are unlikely to be aware of the opportunity. Headhunters thus need to be employed to make contact with people confidentially so as to let them know that a job is available which they might be interested in applying for. Another common example is a situation in which a company is expanding its operations into a new region or country and lacks the expertise required to recruit locally. In such a situation a headhunter who has the required contacts and understanding of the labour market can be an invaluable partner. Also reasonably common is a situation in which a company does not want its existing staff to know that it is recruiting a new person to fill a role. This happens when an individual is performing poorly and the intention is to dismiss them when, but only when, the services of a suitable replacement have been secured.

HR managers usually like to recruit externally without the assistance of headhunters, preferring where they can to advertise jobs and shortlist themselves. But there are plenty of labour markets where taking this good practice approach is unlikely to yield the strongest possible field of candidates. The reason is simply that there are some significant professional groups for whom seeking a job through an agent has become the norm. This is true in the UK of senior managers, finance and accountancy specialists, public relations people and some more specialized IT workers too. Indeed any job which is well paid and in which terms and conditions are negotiable ahead of appointment is potentially one in which job-seekers prefer to work through agents. Here, if an organization wishes to access the highest calibre potential recruits, it has no alternative but to consider applications submitted by headhunters. Furthermore it can make sense simply to subcontract the whole recruitment process to a firm of headhunters who can then open up confidential lines of communication with potential candidates who are working for competitors and present a shortlist of excellent potential employees.

In such circumstances there is everything to be gained from an HR perspective by developing strong links with one or two trusted headhunting companies and working with them over a long period of time. In return for a measure of exclusivity, the employer hopes to ensure that the consultant works for them, refraining either from talking up candidates' abilities without justification or from making an attempt to attract successful candidates away to further new jobs elsewhere soon after the commission has been paid.

The Chinese labour market

The World Bank estimates that growth rates in China will slow somewhat between now and 2020, but will continue to outpace global growth rates by a very substantial margin. This will see China's share of world gross domestic product (GDP) increase to 8 or 9 per cent. If a similar growth rate is maintained beyond 2020, by the middle of this century the Chinese economy will be as big as, if not bigger than, the US economy.

The lion's share of Chinese economic development has come from manufactured goods, which provide over half of China's GDP. The key has been the country's ability to export these around the world, using the currency earned to purchase raw materials, energy and capital equipment. The Chinese strategy has been based on its ability to undercut competitors in other countries via low wages – Chinese wages are the lowest of any major industrial country. This allows Chinese manufactured goods to be sold in the USA at 30 per cent less cost than comparable products from other countries. In 1980 China enjoyed a 0.8 per cent share of world exports in manufactured goods. It now has a 9 per cent share, including 16 per cent of all telecommunications equipment that is exported internationally and 25 per cent of all clothing exports.

Rapid growth has brought with it huge increases in living standards for many Chinese people, but it is those who have technical, managerial and professional skills who have seen their incomes rise the fastest. This is because very rapid economic growth brings with it significant skills shortages. The ability of the economy to grow outpaces people's capacity to gain the higher level skills that are required in order to succeed in more senior roles.

Skills shortages of this kind are common across the world as countries have restructured their economies in order to maintain growth in a globalizing economy, but the rapidity of the change experienced in China has made the situation worse. Moreover there is the additional problem of a brain drain as so many Chinese people choose either to study overseas or to take up job opportunities in other countries on graduation. Over 75 per cent of people graduating in hi-tech-related subjects from China's top universities (Tsinghua and Beijing) since 1985 have emigrated to the USA alone. However, Chinese students graduating from overseas universities and who return home to look for employment often find it difficult to secure highly paid positions. This is because they have good degrees, but tend to lack work experience and the 'China-specific knowledge' needed to take up senior roles in the growing industries.

The Chinese education system is often criticized for its failure to develop both practical skills and the capacity to think independently. It has traditionally placed great emphasis on rote learning and the acquisition of theoretical knowledge. The outcome is a cohort of young people who are bright, hard-working and well-educated, but not always suited to higher level managerial and professional work.

(Continued)

(Continued)

Labour markets for highly talented people in China are thus very tight indeed. Employee turnover levels are very high, while pressure to increase the pay packets of those who are able to fill senior roles is strengthening. Companies poach staff from one another regularly because they struggle to recruit in any other way.

Source: Cooke (2012).

 ■ **Questions**

1. Why are Chinese firms less prepared to invest in training and developing their staff than is the case in other countries? Why do they prefer to poach 'oven-ready' employees?
2. What steps would you advise a major Chinese company with international prospects to take in order to ease skills shortages at senior levels?
3. What steps could the Chinese government take?

Selection interviews

Once the recruitment stage is completed, usually resulting in the drawing up of a shortlist of candidates, organizations next need to undertake a process of selection. By far the most common method used is the selection interview involving a formal face-to-face encounter between candidates and the managers charged with deciding who to appoint. Most interviews are unstructured in nature and involve only one or two interviewers. Different questions may be asked of different candidates, selection decisions often being taken on grounds of who the interviewer thinks will best fit in with the existing team, is best able to fill existing skills gaps or simply who they most like personally.

Such approaches remain very common despite having been condemned pretty sharply by those who adhere to good practice principles of recruitment and selection. Traditional, unstructured interviewing falls foul of good practice thinking for two main reasons. First, there is a strong risk of unfair bias playing a role in the decision about which candidate to select. Interviewers have a tendency to favour people who are like themselves, for example, to make up their minds about someone very early on in the interview or to allow the experience of interviewing one candidate to affect the way they interview subsequent candidates. There is also a tendency to stereotype, with interviewers making unjust assumptions about candidates' suitability because of the way they look or speak. The process thus tends to disfavour members of ethnic minority groups as well as women, disabled people and older candidates (see Chapter 9). Prejudicial judgements of this kind are often unconscious, but nonetheless frequently result in largely irrelevant characteristics determining who gets a job and who does not.

Second, traditional interviewing has long been known to be a poor predictor of subsequent job performance. Over a century of research has clearly established that unstructured interviews are among the very worst selection tools when judged by their capacity to appoint people who go on to perform well in their jobs or stay with the organization for a good length of time.

Research undertaken by occupational psychologists compares selection methods in terms of their relative predictive validity, resulting in a 'score' on a scale of 0 to 1 (see Figure 5.2). A selection scored at 1 would be one that predicted future job performance perfectly. In other words the scores awarded to candidates at the selection stage would correlate perfectly with scores later awarded for performance when the same people are appraised in their job roles. By contrast a selection method with predictive validity of 0 is one which has no capacity whatever to predict future work performance. Pulling names out of a hat or deciding who to appoint on the throw of a die would be as effective. Traditional, unstructured interviews score very poorly indeed when judged in this way. Meta-analyses which aggregate the results of many small published surveys typically report correlation scores of between 0.1 and 0.2, making them barely more effective as predictors of future performance than methods based on pure chance (Schmitt and Fandre 2008: 182–7).

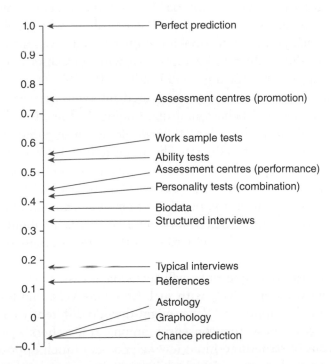

Figure 5.2 Meta-analyses, various selection methods

Source: Smith et al. (1989).

There are many potential explanations for why unstructured interviews are so poor as a tool to use when predicting likely future job performance (Cook 2004: 42–6). One is the opportunity the approach gives candidates to manage impressions through force of personality, personal charm or simply by presenting themselves professionally. People who 'give a good interview', possibly as a result of having been trained well, thus tend to get appointed, irrespective of whether their skills, abilities or attributes really justify their selection over and above others. At the same time, unstructured interviewing tends to mean that some candidates are given more of an opportunity than others to shine simply because they get asked more helpful questions or manage to steer the conversation on to ground that better suits their strengths.

Research into the predictive validity of interviews demonstrates that their capacity to estimate future job performance accurately is considerably enhanced by adopting a more rigorous and structured approach. Here every candidate is asked the same questions in the same way, enabling a clear comparison to be made between their answers. Moreover, the questions that are asked are derived directly from a person specification or competency framework, ensuring that their purpose is to establish how far each candidate meets the specific requirements for the job in question. Structured interviewing also requires the involvement of a panel of interviewers who are all tasked with scoring the candidates against the same set of selection criteria. After interviewing everyone, the panel then discusses its scores and reaches a consensus about who would be best to appoint. Meta-analyses of studies looking at the predictive validity of structured interviews have shown them to be impressive, with correlations in the range of 0.4 to 0.6 being reported (Schmitt and Fandre 2008: 182–7).

The most effective formats for structured interviews appear to be those based on situational and behavioural questioning. In the case of the former, candidates are all asked about how they would act in hypothetical situations which are directly relevant to the job. The aim is to help interviews to establish candidates' preferred approach in scenarios which they would face if appointed. Behavioural questions, by contrast, are focused on the candidates' past experiences. On what occasions in the past have they demonstrated effective use of relevant skills or attributes? Behavioural interviewing is all about seeking out hard evidence of someone's capacity to meet the core requirements of the job. So, for example, where dealing with difficult or demanding customers is a key requirement of the role, questions will focus on occasions in the past when candidates have dealt effectively with such situations. What did they do? Why did they choose that approach? What might they do differently another time?

For many years now the consensus among researchers has thus been firmly in favour of structured interviewing and very much opposed to traditional, unstructured interviewing. This is fairer, less open to unjustified bias and, above all, a much better approach to use in order to predict future performance accurately. It thus meets the requirements of good practice in a way that unstructured interviewing does not.

There are nonetheless some solid arguments in favour of traditional interviews which challenge this consensus view and suggest that traditional approaches may still have something to offer as part of a broader selection process. First, it can be argued that the problem with unstructured interviews lies less with the format itself and more with poor interviewers. Unfair bias and prejudice only creep in to the selection decision when interviewers allow them to. It follows that a well-trained interviewer can undertake unstructured interviews and reach a good, objective selection decision based on sound judgement. Moreover, recent research strongly suggests that interviewers who are trained to use their questions as a means of establishing whether or not a candidate has particular personality traits can do so just as effectively using unstructured as structured interview formats (Blackman 2008: 204–5). The unstructured interview can be particularly effective as a tool to use in establishing levels of personal integrity, with one study finding that the more informal the setting, the better it will be when it comes to enquiring about integrity (Townsend et al. 2007). This appears to be the case simply because candidates are given more of an opportunity in unstructured interviews to talk at some length and hence to say more, while interviewers seem more prepared to ask follow-up questions which elicit valuable information on which to base a judgement.

The other major argument in favour of traditional approaches to interviewing starts with the proposition that the prediction of future job performance is only one of a number of purposes that they are designed to fulfil. It follows that it is unwise to judge their effectiveness purely against that one criterion. For example, interviews are also used to supply information to candidates about the job and the organization which they can subsequently use when deciding whether or not to take up a job offer. The conversational nature of a traditional interview allows this purpose to be met more effectively than is the case within the more rigid and controlled environment of a structured interview. There is also, in many instances, a negotiation aspect to traditional interviews, the outcome of which can be an agreement on matters such as pay, hours, job duties, training opportunities, start dates and other conditions of employment. It is the two-way nature of exchanges in a traditional, unstructured interview, as well as their comparative naturalness and authenticity, that allows this kind of negotiation to occur. Finally, it is not only candidates who indulge in impression management when being interviewed. Interviewers do too, and for good reason. They want to leave all who are interviewed, whether they are ultimately successful or unsuccessful, impressed by the organization. One of their aims is quite properly to leave those who are not appointed happy with the way that they have been treated, happy to consider applying again in the future and disposed to pass on to others a positive impression of the organization. These public relations objectives can arguably be achieved more effectively in the relaxed and natural environment of a traditional conversational interview than in that of a highly structured one.

Ability testing

Ability tests come in different forms, with some very specialized in terms of which abilities they test and others much more general. Tests of cognitive or mental ability are widely used, particularly in graduate recruitment and in the selection of managerial staff. In the USA it is typical for general intelligence (IQ) tests to be administered to job applicants. In Europe, including the UK, the preference tends to be for ability tests that focus on particular aptitudes such as numeracy, verbal reasoning and analytical ability. All these tests take a similar form, with candidates being required to answer a battery of questions using a multiple-answer format. Tests are designed for different levels of mental ability, with those intended for senior managers being a good deal tougher than those designed for use in the selection of lower-paid staff. The questions themselves are not necessarily particularly difficult, but a test becomes more challenging when taken against the clock. How many correct answers a candidate manages in the time available is thus the key determinant of the final score. Contemporary tests are nearly always computer-based, allowing for programs which tailor the 'hardness' of questions to the capacity of a candidate to answer them. Hence if someone does well early on in a test, the computer will quickly start to generate more challenging questions. This allows the level of mental ability to be established much more rapidly and accurately than a traditional paper and pencil test. It also gives almost instant results which are 100 per cent accurate.

Tests of mental ability are not especially expensive, can be completed in half an hour or so, are straightforward to mark and do not require extensive training in order to interpret correctly. Once purchased they can be used again and again by an organization recruiting people to a variety of different jobs. There is also no need to invest in the development of different tests for different occupational groups. They have also been found by occupational psychologists to be relatively good predictors of future job performance across a wide range of roles. Correlations between test scores and future performance scores of 0.5 to 0.6 have been reported in the meta-analyses, putting them right at the top of the league table as far as predictive validity is concerned (see Figure 5.2). For this reason they tend to be favoured by proponents of 'good practice' in recruitment and selection, particularly those tests which have been developed over time and are regularly refined by their highly reputable producers.

There are also other good reasons for using ability tests in employee selection, along with personality tests which we are going to consider below. Wolf and Jenkins (2006), looking to explain the growth in testing over recent years in the UK, demonstrate that legal reasons underlie much of their spread. Organizations are increasingly keen to avoid having to defend claims of unlawful discrimination brought in employment tribunals (see Chapter 9). Such claims carry considerable risks not just in terms of the financial consequences should a case be lost, but also in terms of negative publicity which can affect corporate reputation. In addition simply defending a claim is a costly business. By incorporating testing into selection procedures, HR managers are often seeking simply to minimize these risks. The more objective and systematic selection processes become (or appear to become) the less likely decisions are to be challenged in the courts by disappointed candidates. Wolf and Jenkins (2006) also show that the growth in test use in the UK has also been associated more generally with the professionalization of the HR function and the adoption of more sophisticated, standardized approaches to HRM across organizations.

Despite these advantages, there are some major potential issues with mental ability tests which serve, at least in some people's eyes, to undermine their effectiveness and render them unsuitable for use in selection. First and foremost there are problems with most tests in terms of their fairness to people sitting them in a second language. Native speakers tend to score more highly, not least because they are able to answer more quickly and thus complete more questions in the allotted time. This poses very serious problems as labour markets internationalize and workforces become increasingly diverse culturally (see Chapter 11). Some tests also tend to favour different demographic groups. Questions which measure 'fluid intelligence', defined by Furnham (2005: 207) as 'the ability to perceive relationships, deal with unfamiliar problems and gain new types of knowledge', tend to favour younger people with fast brains. Our ability to answer these questions rapidly and accurately peaks at around the age of 20. By contrast questions which test 'crystallized intelligence', drawing on knowledge of the world, tend to favour older people with more and wider life experiences to draw on when answering them (Searle 2003).

There is also evidence to suggest that with extensive practice, people get better at ability tests, particularly at improving the speed with which they are able to answer questions written in the most common formats (Cook 2004: 125). Moreover, because there are only a limited number of reputable tests available on the market at any one time, the chances that a recent graduate, for example, may end up sitting the same test more than once as part of the recruitment processes operated by different companies is high (Silvester and Brown 1993). Others argue that underperformance rather than over-inflated performance is actually the bigger problem. Some very able candidates, either as a result of anxiety or mistaken test-taking strategies, score less highly than their true capability suggests they should (Walley and Smith 1998). A final major problem with tests of mental ability that some researchers have drawn attention to is the way that they sometimes put able candidates off from applying for jobs or from pursuing applications once shortlisted (Reeve and Schultz 2004).

Opinion is divided about how far it is possible for the producers of mental ability tests to refine their products so as to eliminate biases and about how far test-users can practically compensate for their potential deficiencies when interpreting the results. There are also major ongoing debates about whether or not a test of mental ability is always appropriate for use when selecting some groups of staff. Some argue, for example, that emotional intelligence is as important to test as mental ability when recruiting senior managers, while others take the view that for many routine jobs it is possible to be too intelligent. People with very high IQ scores are likely to get bored in such roles and under-perform as a result (see Cook 2004 for an excellent summary of these debates).

The conclusion that most have reached is that ability tests have a potentially important role to play in the selection of some groups of job applicants, largely because they can be shown to predict job performance more effectively than the other available methods. However, it is wise not to rely on them too heavily because of the weaknesses identified above. Care must be taken when interpreting results so that they play a supportive rather than a decisive role in determining which of the shortlisted candidates should be appointed. Wood and Payne (1998: 139–40) give sound advice when they argue that the best approach involves using data from tests of ability to screen out those who come over well at interview, but are revealed by their test scores to have rather lower levels of mental ability compared to other candidates.

One or two of the same kinds of problems are associated with other types of ability test. These mainly take the form of work samples (e.g. typing tests, shorthand speed tests, auditions etc.) or tests of physical fitness, but by and large these are free of controversy. The key here is to ensure that the right kinds of test are developed to support decision-making about selection for the right roles. There is a danger that testing for the ability to carry out a task which only takes up a proportion of the job-holder's role can assume too great a part of the selection process. Some also argue that for many jobs it is wise for managers to 'select for attitude and train for skill' and that consequently too much emphasis can be placed on the extent to which candidates already possess abilities that they could be trained to acquire cheaply and quickly. A potential solution is to develop tests which focus primarily on trainability (Chapter 10) rather than on skills that have already been acquired. Assessors need to focus on how quickly candidates are able to pick up a new skill or knowledge base when making decisions about who to recruit.

Personality testing

Personality tests are widely used as a selection tool in some industries and for some staff groups, notably graduate recruits (CIPD 2011: 18). There are a wide variety of tests on the markets, some of which are much more expensive than others. Price, however, generally reflects quality, and it is the more expensively developed tests that are the most reliable and which have the best record at helping employers to predict subsequent job performance. That said, validity scores for personality tests are not as impressive as they are for ability tests. Moreover, the meta-analyses show them to be a great deal more variable in their effectiveness (Schmitt and Fandre 2008: 173–6).

The vast majority of tests aim to map someone's personality by asking them many dozens of questions over a period of about an hour. While the approach taken varies, along with the format of questions, the reputable tests are all underpinned by extensive psychological research into the constructs of human personality that determine differences between individuals. There are widely agreed to be five major personality constructs which are both measurable and which remain stable over time. The five are:

- extroversion–introversion (the extent to which we enjoy socializing with others, as well as excitement and change)
- emotional stability (the extent to which we exhibit tension and anxiety)
- agreeableness (the extent to which we avoid conflict and exhibit good nature, warmth and compassion)
- conscientiousness (the extent to which we are well-organized, concerned with meeting deadlines and the making and implementation of plans)
- openness to experience (the extent to which we are imaginative, flexible and view new experiences positively).

Personality testing is used to establish where each person being tested sits on these five scales, or on others that are derived from them. Their usage in employee selection is thus concerned with helping to decide which of a field of candidates has the best mix of personality traits to succeed in the job concerned. Hence where extraversion and agreeableness are prominent requirements on a person specification, a personality test can be administered to establish which candidate exhibits those attributes.

Some tests contain questions that take the form of statements which candidates have to agree or disagree with. An example would be as follows:

I regularly find that I lose my temper when I am at work:

(a) agree
(b) in between
(c) disagree.

Five options are common too, as in the following example:

I prefer to work on projects alone rather than as part of a team:

(a) strongly agree
(b) agree
(c) unsure
(d) disagree
(e) strongly disagree.

A test needs to contain two hundred or so questions of this kind, some quite similar to others, in order to map someone's personality with any degree of accuracy. However, a major problem with the approach is the considerable ease with which candidates can guess which answers the employer is looking for, enabling them to fake the result and mislead. In order to address this problem, some tests take a more opaque approach which makes them much harder to fake unless the candidate is familiar with the methods used to devise the questions. A common format involves forcing candidates to choose between attributes which are apparently equally desirable and undesirable. An example might be as follows:

I prefer to work with people who are:

(a) generous
(b) hard-working
(c) confident
(d) flexible.

Such tests work by setting each of the major personality constructs against one another. When dozens of questions are answered a pattern emerges as to a candidate's preferences and a 'map' of their personality can then be generated.

Another method used to establish how far a candidate is faking their answers involves the inclusion in a test of questions which aim to test integrity, or at least the extent to which the person taking the test is acting with integrity as they do so. This involves including questions to which there is only one honest answer. Only people who are truly saint-like would be able with any degree of honesty to answer otherwise. One test which is widely used in the UK, for example, contains the following statement which candidates are invited to agree or disagree with: 'I sometimes talk about people behind their backs'.

The assumption of the test's designers is that everyone sometimes does this and that it therefore follows that anyone who denies doing so is giving a socially desirable (i.e. fake) answer rather than a truthful one.

The use of personality testing in selection has long been the source of vigorous debate among psychologists, not least because some have made a great deal of money developing tests, licensing organizations to use them and training managers to administer them properly. Some argue that commercial interests sometimes cloud scientific judgement. But for the most part the disagreements are about matters of detail rather than the fundamental principles which underpin the use of tests. For example, some recent studies have demonstrated that tests of relative conscientiousness provide a far more effective method of predicting future job performance than tests of the other personality traits. Emotional stability is also sometimes argued to have greater significance than the other traits when it comes to predicting performance (Johnson and Hezlett 2008: 75–6). It follows that questions in tests should primarily focus on these traits rather than on the others. However, this view has been widely criticized by psychologists who have found that highly conscientious people only perform better in jobs when their conscientiousness is combined with relatively high levels of extraversion and agreeableness (Lievens and Chapman 2010). Over time our knowledge of this field develops in new directions, requiring the test producers to adjust and refine their approaches.

As with ability testing, the consensus is that personality testing can only form part of a good practice approach to recruitment and selection when used professionally. There are a number of poorly designed instruments available on the market which are inexpensive and quick for candidates to complete, but which are only very limited in their capacity to map personalities at all effectively. Tests are only able genuinely to act as an aid to decision-making in selection if they are scientifically robust and when decision-makers have been properly trained to interpret the results.

PIT STOP: REFLECTIVE ACTIVITY 5.5

Recent research has found strong correlations between relative levels of self-esteem and effective job performance across many different types of jobs (Furnham 2005: 211–13).

1. Why do you think that people with high self-esteem appear to perform better in their jobs than those who have low self-esteem?
2. What questions could be developed for use in personality tests in order to establish relative levels of self-esteem?
3. How far do you agree with the proposition that a test exclusively devoted to testing self-esteem would be an effective tool to use in personnel selection? Justify your answer.

Assessment centres

The assessment centre has often been described as the Rolls-Royce of employee selection methods. They are very costly to organize, but produce excellent results if managed properly. They have received an excellent press in the HR and psychological literature and are unquestionably seen as constituting good practice when designed professionally (Cook 2004: 289). The approach was first used in the mid-twentieth century in the USA to recruit military personnel and to select civil servants in the UK. In recent decades it has become widely used across the world (Povah and Thornton 2011).

Assessment centres are best seen as events taking place over two to three days at which shortlisted candidates come together along with a team of assessors to participate in a range of different selection exercises. They are most commonly used in the selection of senior managers and graduate recruits, but it is not unusual for 'mini assessment centres' comprising three or four exercises carried out over a single day to be organized for candidates applying for all manner of different jobs. The exercises included in an assessment centre programme vary considerably depending on the type of competencies the organization is looking for, but the following are typical:

- structured interviews
- ability, personality and integrity tests
- presentations
- role plays
- fact-finding exercises
- group exercises and discussions
- report writing exercises
- work samples and simulations.

It is the inclusion of a dozen or so different exercises that gives well-designed assessment centres their apparent predictive power. Each of the key attributes or competencies required by the job holder can be tested two or three times and scored by a number of different assessors. Moreover, because the candidates interact with one another in many of the exercises, direct comparisons can be made between them in terms of how they perform. It is also often argued that the duration of an assessment centre makes it very much harder for candidates to fake their performance than is the case in an interview or shorter programme of exercises. Impression management is not at all easy to sustain over three days of considerable pressure. Strengths and weaknesses are bound to emerge, giving the assessors an excellent opportunity to decide who best meets the criteria for the post. Moreover, of course, the situations in which candidates are observed are directly relevant to the work that they would be doing if appointed.

The major disadvantage with assessment centres is the cost. If a centre is to be effective it has to be designed with great care so that the major competencies being sought are all effectively tested on at least two occasions. There are thus very considerable development costs. In addition there are sizeable administrative costs associated with pulling an assessment centre together, not to mention the need for food and accommodation to be provided for candidates and assessors. There are also significant training costs associated with training assessors, most of whom are likely to be relatively senior managers. Their time is also a major cost to take into account.

A well-run assessment centre which leaves all participants feeling that they have been treated fairly even if unsuccessful also needs to include opportunities for them to be provided with constructive feedback. This requires either further extensive training or the employment of qualified occupational psychologists to lead the feedback sessions.

While fairness and felt-fairness are major advantages of assessment centres (Cook 2004: 188–9), it can be argued that some potential candidates may be put off from applying for a job because they cannot spare the time to attend an assessment centre. The approach is likely to be particularly off-putting to people who have young children or caring responsibilities that make it hard for them to spend nights away from home. Single parents are particularly disadvantaged. There are thus questions to be asked about how far men are favoured by the method over women.

There are also likely to be people who are put off from applying for a job or from pursuing an application simply because they dislike the prospect of attending an assessment centre. In fact they are usually very enjoyable, if tiring affairs, but this is not always apparent to candidates before they start. Some will argue that if someone is put off in this way it shows that they are not sufficiently committed and should not therefore be appointed in any event. But this is a short-sighted view. People often have to be persuaded to apply for a new job that at first sight looks to have only limited appeal. Only later, after having attended an interview and meeting potential colleagues, do they decide that it is an opportunity they would like to take up. In situations where such candidates are the best for the job, assessment centres can act as a costly way of ensuring that the strongest performer is not appointed.

It is important to understand that most assessment centres are not run as straightforward selection exercises. In fact most are used within organizations as part of wider talent management programmes (see Chapter 10), their purpose being to establish whom among existing members of staff has the attributes required for promotion into senior management roles. When used in this way assessment centres are mostly concerned with identifying potential and then formulating individual plans for its further development. Assessment centres are particularly useful when determining who should be recruited onto a fast-track management development programme. They can also play a role in helping international organizations to decide who has the attributes required to succeed in an expatriate role (see Chapter 12).

While there are many different models used, most expatriate assignments last three to five years and involve a manager based in one country spending a period of time working in another, often at a relatively senior level. The prime purpose is to allow a global organization, over time, to develop a cadre of managers who have the international experience required to operate effectively at the most senior levels. Research shows that many expatriate assignments either fail or disappoint in practice (Black and Gregerson 1999; Reiche and Harzing 2011), largely because the people selected are either inappropriate for the job or are poorly prepared ahead of their assignments.

Successful expatriates require a relatively rare skill set as well as some specific personality traits. Tung (1981) identifies four key sets of attributes that organizations should take account of when selecting people for expatriate assignments:

1. Technical competence (i.e. the knowledge, skills and experience to undertake the technical aspects of the job without needing extensive support).
2. Relational ability (i.e. the ability to live and thrive in an overseas culture and to work effectively with others whose cultural norms and expectations differ from one's own).
3. Environmental coping ability (i.e. the ability to work effectively within systems and environmental constraints that are different from those that prevail in the parent country).
4. Family preparedness (i.e. the ability and willingness of spouses/partners and other family members to adjust well to a foreign living environment).

Mendenhall and Oddou (1985), by contrast, focus more on the personality traits that they believe are needed if an expatriate episode is to be successful:

- relatively high levels of self-esteem, self-confidence and mental health
- a capacity to interact well with people from a different cultural background
- a deep understanding of cultural differences and their roots/causes.

The attribute that is needed most of all from a would-be expatriate manager is the ability to adapt quickly and effectively to foreign surroundings. This requires what Ng et al. (2009) refer to as 'cultural intelligence', a concept which encompasses both sensitivity to cultural difference and the ability to learn how to adjust working methods accordingly (see Chapter 11). It is when selecting people for roles of this kind – highly paid and high-risk – that assessment centres are particularly useful. The costs are justified and the opportunity provided to test competency in quite specific areas using a variety of different exercises.

≡ CASE STUDY 5.4 ≡

Recruiting and selecting in Finland

Finland consistently scores very highly in comparative assessments of education quality around the world, topping most league tables year after year. There are many reasons for its success, but most informed opinion believes that its approach to the recruitment and selection of teachers plays a crucial role.

To become a teacher in Finland you have to go through a very vigorous process of selection and training. People apply when they leave school, seeking a place on the programmes offered by just 11 universities. There are many more applications than there are places available. Over 1200 apply every year to Helsinki University, of whom some 400 are interviewed. There are only 125 places available on the programme, meaning that around 90 per cent of applications are unsuccessful. Only the very best are selected. Interviews are notoriously tough and unpredictable, focusing as much on attitudes and the motivation to become a teacher as on skills and qualifications.

Teacher training in Finland lasts for a minimum of five years, all teachers being required to hold a Master's qualification. Many go on to complete doctorates too, making teachers in Finland as qualified as doctors, lawyers and architects. The training also includes plenty of practice in schools which are linked to the universities that provide the courses. Once trained, over 90 per cent of teachers remain in the profession throughout their careers.

Why is teaching so much more attractive as a career in Finland than in other countries? The answer is partly simply cultural. Teaching has always been a highly respected profession with extensive social prestige. Pay is no higher than it is for teachers elsewhere in the world, but because there is greater social equality in Finland generally, teachers' pay is not as far behind that of other leading professional groups as it tends to be elsewhere in the world.

The real attraction seems to be the work itself. Class sizes are small by international standards, ranging from 15 to 25. School hours are shorter than in most countries, and there are fewer examinations to prepare children for. Teachers enjoy very considerable autonomy to teach the curriculum in the way that they want to, while schools have a great deal of freedom to determine their curricula. Management styles in Finnish schools are democratic, teachers having a great deal of say in how their workplaces are run. The profession as a whole is also run on

(Continued)

relatively democratic lines, with teachers being trusted by government to deliver high standards without the need for much by way of inspection and the paperwork that accompanies it. There are no school league tables and only a limited core national curriculum which has been designed by the teachers themselves. The working environment in schools is also clean and attractive. Another attraction is the size of the profession. The total school population in Finland is only 600,000 (compared to seven million in the UK), allowing the teaching profession to be a genuine community in which long-term relationships are established.

Sources: Malaty (2006) and NCEE (2011).

 ■ **Questions**

1. What particular features of Finland's education system make teaching such an attractive career there?
2. What is the approach taken to the recruitment and selection of teachers in Finland?

Recruitment and selection strategy

It is generally considered that a good practice approach to HRM will be strategic in character, this being preferable in terms of outcomes to approaches which are, by contrast, 'reactive', 'ad-hoc' or 'unplanned'. It follows that an organization seeking to claim that its approach to recruitment and selection constitutes good practice should have in place and follow a coherent recruitment and selection strategy. What is a great deal less clear is what this entails in practical terms.

Definitional problems arise from the various different ways in which managers, writers, consultants and thinkers working in HRM have chosen to conceive of 'HR strategy' over the years (Taylor 2010: 424–45). For some a 'strategic approach' simply means one which is planned and evidence-based. For others an emphasis is placed on the concept of strategic alignment, the key test being the extent to which long-term organizational objectives are reflected in defined HR objectives (see Chapter 3). A third perspective is primarily concerned with environmental scanning and seeking to ensure that an organization is better placed than its competitors to cope with future challenges when they become present realities.

From a practical, operational point of view it makes sense to incorporate all of these into a working definition of HR strategy and to take the best ideas from each. Hence, as far as recruitment and selection activities are concerned the following criteria could be used to establish whether or not an organization is pursuing a strategic approach:

- When vacancies materialize managers take time to think through the organization's likely future personnel needs when deciding exactly how to design the job, what to include in the person specification and what approach to take to recruiting and selecting the job holder.
- Candidates are recruited and selected with an eye to their capacity to help the organization achieve its current and likely future strategic objectives.
- Recruitment and selection policy is well-aligned with other aspects of HRM, so that a consistent approach is used. So if claims are made in recruitment literature or on websites about excellent training and development opportunities being available, high levels of pay or the prospect of working overseas, these do actually materialize in practice once someone has been recruited.
- A long-term, planned approach is taken. If it is known that someone is going to retire on a set date or has given plenty of notice of their intention to leave a month or two ahead of time, a replacement is recruited ahead of schedule so that gaps are avoided between one person leaving and another starting. Ideally a planned handover period should be organized too so that a smooth transition can be affected.
- The organization takes active steps to manage its own labour market reputation rather than simply accepting whatever reputation it has developed in the past. The employment experience that it offers is communicated effectively as something clearly distinct and more attractive than that of its major competitors.

Millmore (2003) drew up a similar list of criteria when undertaking research into the extent that UK organizations were genuinely strategic in the approach they took to the management of recruitment and selection. In addition to stressing the importance of long-term thinking and thoughtful planning he also identified three further 'secondary' features of recruitment and selection policy which are typically associated with a strategic approach:

- The use of a wide range of diverse recruitment and selection tools as and when appropriate for different categories of job (i.e. a relatively sophisticated and complex approach).
- High status is accorded to recruitment and selection activities within the organization and to the people who carry it out. This is reflected in the devotion of reasonably high levels of expenditure and the active involvement of senior staff.
- The adoption of recruitment and selection practices which are sensitive to the perceptions and needs of candidates as well as to those of the organization. The aim is to facilitate 'informed self-selection decisions' so that unsuitable would-be candidates screen themselves out of the process at an early stage.

Having set his criteria, Millmore (2003) then went on to undertake a substantial survey of recruitment and selection practice in a wide range of UK organizations. His conclusion was that, in practice, there was only very limited evidence of a truly strategic approach to recruitment and selection being used consistently by organizations. He found no examples whatever of any organization meeting all of his criteria, and even his primary criteria were only all met in a small minority of cases. His conclusion was that 'taken together it could be argued, perhaps very generously, that 8 per cent of recruitment and selection exercises are being strategically driven' (Millmore 2003: 101).

Millmore's criteria for 'a strategic approach' clearly appear to have been influenced by thinking about 'good practice' in recruitment and selection as well as by more general debates about HR strategy. And in consequence it might be argued that he set rather too high a bar against which to judge organizational practice. His criteria, taken together, perhaps represent an ideal approach rather than one which is simply strategic in nature. Nonetheless his findings are very striking, particularly when it is considered how high a profile strategic HRM has achieved in recent years and how widely debated are the principles underpinning good practice approaches to recruitment and selection. Whatever theoretical advantages these principles can be said to have, it appears that most organizations, big and small, successful and unsuccessful, are reluctant to adopt them in practice.

PIT STOP: REFLECTIVE ACTIVITY 5.6

Think about your own experience of recruitment and selection in organizations and about the idea of 'a strategic approach to recruitment and selection'. Then give some consideration to Millmore's (2003) principal research findings.

1. What key defining features would you expect to find in recruitment and selection policies operated by an organization that claimed to take a strategic approach to HRM?
2. Can you think of any disadvantages associated with taking an approach to recruitment and selection that is clearly strategic in character? What about the advantages of a more reactive, ad hoc kind of approach?
3. Why do so many HR managers claim to have adopted a strategic approach to their activities, when in practice there is only limited evidence that this is really the case?

Conclusion

At the start of this chapter we introduced the good practice model of recruitment and selection which has long been seen by many as being the approach that organizations should follow if they are serious about recruiting the strongest performers while also adhering to principles of scrupulous fairness. The purpose of the chapter has not been to undermine these principles, but to question how far every aspect of the model is truly appropriate for all recruitment and selection scenarios. Hopefully, as you have read the chapter, you have thought about to what extent good practice is universally applicable in this field. Are there situations in which, for example, it might be entirely justifiable for an organization to recruit staff using headhunters, or to select using an unstructured interview, or to operate an approach which is 'unstrategic' in character? Are these approaches always likely to yield poor results or might they have something important to contribute?

A second purpose of this chapter has been to introduce you to a range of contemporary developments in the fields of recruitment and selection, notably to the use of underpinning competency frameworks, to employer branding and to the impact of globalization and the rise of international organizations on recruitment and selection practice. Each of these fields, like the more established approaches, is the subject of ongoing debates, each of which we have introduced.

Can we reach any general conclusions at the end of the chapter? The main one is that contrary to the assumptions that underlie the good practice model, there is no single, easily defined approach to recruitment and selection which will lead to superior performance across all organizations. What is appropriate in one scenario will not be appropriate elsewhere. The key from a practical management point of view is to choose the most suitable processes for the organization. And in doing so it is necessary to recognize that recruiting and selecting one group of staff may need a different approach from the recruitment and selection of another.

■ Further Reading ■ ■ ■ ■ ■ ■ ■ ■ ■ ■ ■

Barber, A. (1998) *Recruiting Employees*. Thousand Oaks, CA: Sage.
Chamorro-Premuzic, T. and Furnham, A. (2010) *The Psychology of Personnel Selection*. Cambridge: Cambridge University Press.
Taylor, S. (2010) *Resourcing and Talent Management*, 5th edn. London: CIPD.

References

ACAS (2009) *Recruitment and Induction*. London: Advisory, Conciliation and Arbitration Service.
Ambler, T. and Barrow, S. (1996) 'The employer brand', *Journal of Brand Management*, 4 (3): 185–206.
Armstrong, M. (2012) *Armstrong's Handbook of Human Resource Practice*, 12th edn. London: Kogan Page.

Barber, A. (1998) *Recruiting Employees*. Thousand Oaks, CA: Sage.

Black, J. and Gregerson, H. (1999) 'The right way to manage expats', *Harvard Business Review*, 77 (2): 52–60.

Blackman, M. (2008) 'The effective interview', in S. Cartwright and C. Cooper (eds), *The Oxford Handbook of Personnel Psychology*. Oxford: Oxford University Press, pp. 194–213.

Blau, G. (1990) 'An empirical analysis of employed and unemployed job search behavior', *Industrial and Labor Relations Review*, 45: 738–52.

Boyzatis, R.E. (1982) *The Competent Manager*. New York: Wiley.

Breaugh, J.A. (2008) 'Employee recruitment: current knowledge and important areas for future research', *Human Resource Management Review*, 18 (3): 103-18.

Bulkley, C.P. (1922) 'Selling the institution to its own personnel as well as the public', *Industrial Management*, 64: 278–9.

Cameron, K. (2009) 'From poor M&S to your M&S – the historical perspective', in H. Rosethorn (ed.), *The Employer Brand*. Aldershot: Gower Publishing, pp. 89–101.

Castilla, E.J. (2005) 'Social networks and employee performance in a call center', *American Journal of Sociology*, 110: 1243–83.

Cho, S., Woods, R. H., Jang, S. and Erdham, M. (2006) 'Measuring the impact of human resource management practices on hospitality firm's performances', *International Journal of Hospitality Management*, 25 (2): 262–77.

CIPD (2011) *Resourcing and Talent Planning: Annual Survey Report*. London: Chartered Institute of Personnel and Development.

CIPD (2012) *Recruitment Overview Factsheet*. London: Chartered Institute of Personnel and Development, available at www.cipd.co.uk/hr-resources/factsheets/recruitment-overview.aspx

Cook, M. (2004) *Personnel Selection: Adding Value Through People*, 4th edn. Chichester: Wiley.

Cooke, F.L. (2012) *Human Resource Management in China: New Trends and Practices*. Abingdon: Routledge.

Delaney, J. and Huselid, M. (1996) 'The impact of human resource management practices on perceptions of organisational performance', *Academy of Management Journal*, 39: 349–69.

Delery, J.E. and Doty, D.H. (1996) 'Modes of theorizing in strategic human resource management: tests of universalistic, contingency, and configuration performance predictions', *Academy of Management Journal*, 39 (4): 802–35.

Furnham, A. (2005) *The Psychology of Behaviour at Work*. Hove: The Psychology Press.

Gabb, A. (2012) 'Safety in numbers', *People Management Guide to Recruitment Marketing*, July.

Hall, D., Jones, R., Raffo, C. and Anderton, A. (2008) 'Recruitment', in I. Chambers and D.Gray (eds), *Business Studies*, 4th edn. Harlow: Pearson Education, pp. 350–55.

Hofstede, G. (1980) *Culture's Consequences: International Differences in Work-related Values*. Beverly Hills, CA: Sage.

Hofstede, G. (1991) *Cultures and Organizations: Software of the Mind*. London: McGraw Hill.

Iles, P. and Robertson, I. (1991) 'The impact of selection procedures on candidates', *Human Relations*, September (44): 963–82.

Johnson, J. and Hezlett, S. (2008) 'Modeling the influence of personality on individuals', in S. Cartwright and C. Cooper (eds), *The Oxford Handbook of Personnel Psychology*. Oxford: Oxford University Press, pp. 59–91.

Kandola, B., Stairs, M. and Sandford-Smith, R. (2000) 'Slim picking', *People Management*, 28 (December): 28–30.

Kirnan, J., Farley, J. and Geisinger, K. (1989) 'The relationship between recruiting source, applicant quality and hire performance: an analysis by sex, ethnicity and age', *Personnel Psychology*, 42: 293–308.

Lievens, F. and Chapman, D. (2010) 'Recruitment and selection', in A. Wilkinson, N. Bacon, T. Redman and S. Snell (eds), *The Sage Handbook of Human Resource Management*. London: Sage. pp. 135–53.

Macklin, B. (2011) 'Insights into the building of an employer brand at Telstra', in H. Davies and S. Moir (eds), *Employer Branding*. Bookpal, 88–98.

Malaty, G. (2006) What are the reasons behind the success of Finland in Pisa? University of Joensuu, www.cimt.plymouth.ac.uk/journal/malaty.pdf.

Martin, G. and Hetrick, S. (2009) 'Employer branding and corporate reputation management in an international context', in P. Sparrow (ed.), *Handbook of International Human Resource Management: Integrating People, Process and Context*. Chichester: Wiley, pp. 293–319.

Martin, G., Gollen, P.J. and Grigg, K. (2011) 'Is there a bigger and better future for employer branding: facing up to innovation, corporate reputations and wicked problems in SIHRM', *The International Journal of Human Resource Management*, 22 (7): 3618–37.

Mendenhall, M. and Oddou, G. (1985) 'The dimensions of expatriate acculturation: a review', *American Academy Review*, 10 (1): 39–47.

Millmore, M. (2003) 'Just how extensive is the practice of strategic recruitment and selection?', *Irish Journal of Management*, 24 (1): 87–108.

Milsom, J. (2009) 'Key trends and issues in employers' use of behavioural competencies', *IRS Employment Review*, 918, March.

NCEE (2011) *Finland: Teacher and Principal Quality*. Center on International Education Benchmarking, available at http://www.ncee.org/programs-affiliates/center-on-international-education-benchmarking/top-performing-countries/finland-overview/finland-teacher-and-principal-quality/.

Newell Brown, J. and Swain, A. (2012) *The Professional Recruiter's Handbook: Delivering Excellence in Recruitment Practice*, 2nd edn. London: Kogan Page.

Ng, K.-Y., Van Dyne, L. and Ang, S. (2009) 'Beyond international experience: the strategic role of cultural intelligence for executive selection in IHRM', in P. Sparrow (ed.), *Handbook of International Human Resource Management*. Chichester: Wiley, pp. 97–113.

Pfeffer, J. (1994) *Competitive Advantage Through People*. Boston, MA: Harvard University Press.

Povah, N. and Thornton, G.C. (eds) (2011) *Assessment Centres and Global Talent Management*. Farnham: Gower Publishing.

Rankin, N. (ed.) (2003) *Best Practice in HR Handbook*. London: LexisNexis/IRS.

Reed, A. (2001) *Innovation in Human Resource Management: Tooling up for the Talent Wars*. London: CIPD.

Reeve, C.L. and Schultz, L. (2004) 'Job-seeker reactions to selection process information in job ads', *International Journal of Selection and Assessment*, 12 (4): 258–70.

Roioho, B.C. and Harzing, A.W. (2011) 'International assignments', in A. W. Harzing and A. H. Pinnington (eds), *International Human Resource Management*, 3rd edn. London: Sage, pp. 183–223.

Reilly, P. and Williams, T. (2012) *Global HR: Challenges Facing the Function*. Farnham: Gower Publishing.

Schmitt, N. and Fandre, J. (2008) 'Validity of selection procedures', in S. Cartwright and C. Cooper (eds), *The Oxford Handbook of Personnel Psychology*. Oxford: Oxford University Press. pp. 163–93.

Searle, R. (2003) *Selection and Recruitment: A Critical Text*. Milton Keynes: Open University and Palgrave Macmillan.

Silvester, J. and Brown, A. (1993) 'Graduate recruitment: testing the impact', *Selection and Development Review*, 9 (1).

Smith, M., Gregg, M. and Andrews, D. (1989) *Selection and Assessment: A New Appraisal*. London: Pitman.

Smith, M. (2011) *Fundamentals of Management*, 2nd edn. London: McGraw Hill.

Sparrow, P.R. and Hiltrop, J. (1994) *European Human Resource Management in Transition*. London: Prentice-Hall.

Taylor, S. (2010) *Resourcing and Talent Management*, 5th edn. London: Chartered Institute of Personnel and Development.

Torrington, D., Hall, L., Taylor, S. and Atkinson, C. (2011) *Human Resource Management*, 8th edn. Harlow: FT/Prentice-Hall.

Towers Perrin (2005) *Winning Strategies for a Global Workforce*. London: Towers Perrin HR Services.

Townsend, R.J., Bacigalupi, S.C. and Blackman, M.C. (2007) 'The accuracy of lay integrity assessments in simulated employment interviews', *Journal of Research in Personality*, 41: 540–57.

Tung, R.L. (1981) 'Selection and training pf personnel for overseas assignments', *Columbia Journal of World Business*, 16 (2): 68–78.

Voskuijl, O. and Evers, A. (2008) 'Job analysis and competency modeling', in S. Cartwright and C. Cooper (eds), *The Oxford Handbook of Personnel Psychology*. Oxford: Oxford University Press. pp. 139–61.

Walker, P. (2008) *Employer Branding: A No-nonsense Approach*. London: Chartered Institute of Personnel and Development.

Walley L. and Smith, M. (1998) *Deception in Selection*. Chichester: Wiley.

Wolf, A. and Jenkins, A. (2006) 'Explaining greater test use for selection: the role of HR professionals in a world of expanding regulation', *Human Resource Management Journal*, 16 (2): 193–213.

Wood, R. and Payne, T. (1998) *Competency-based Recruitment and Selection*. Chichester: Wiley.

Woods, D. (2012) 'Olympics Special 6/7: interview with Jez Langhorn, Vice President People at McDonald's', *HR Magazine*, June: 10.

6

FLEXIBLE WORKING

Sue Hutchinson

Chapter Overview

This chapter explores a key issue in strategic human resource management, that of flexibility. Increasingly flexible working is being promoted as advantageous for both employers and employees. For the former, it is argued that it allows organizations to be more responsive and thus competitive in the marketplace; for the latter it is suggested that it can give employees greater control over how and when they work and lead to a better work–life balance. The chapter critically evaluates such arguments and highlights the associated debates. Flexibility/adaptability is seen as a key dimension of HRM and an important outcome in models of HRM (see Chapters 1 and 3) and the chapter evaluates such propositions. Definitions, meanings and types are also explored and reasons for the increased interest in flexibility are outlined. The concept is explored from both the employers' and employees' perspective, as is the link to the psychological contract. Overall the evidence suggests a fairly complex picture, with flexible working in practice able to have both positive and negative outcomes for both parties of the employment relationship.

≣ Learning Objectives ≣

At the end of this chapter you should be able to:

- **Understand the meaning of labour flexibility and its different dimensions**
- **Understand the relationship between employee attitudes and behaviour and flexibility**
- **Explain the growth in interest in flexibility**
- **Develop an understanding of the theoretical arguments that support flexibility from both the employer and employee perspective**
- **Critically evaluate the impact of numerical and functional flexibility on employers and employees**
- **Recognize some of the key constraints to implementing effective flexible working arrangements**

In September 2012, it was reported, amidst a great deal of controversy, that some NHS Trusts were using zero hours contracts for highly skilled health professionals, such as midwives, cardiologists, anaesthetists, and psychiatrists, rather than ordinary employment contracts. Zero hours contracts are designed to create an 'on call' arrangement between employer and employee, but do not guarantee a specified number of hours or income or employment rights (other than the fact that the minimum wage rate does apply when people work). The employer is under no obligation to offer an employee work and in an extreme case an individual can be in work but not paid for work. From the employers' perspective, these types of contracts are cost-effective and offer flexibility, allowing the employer to retain a pool of workers to fill positions as and when the need arises.

NHS Trusts are increasingly using these contracts because of government reforms in the health service which will allow patients more choice about where they will be treated, meaning increased competition for Trusts and private providers. In order to be an approved provider services must be able to demonstrate they have spare capacity to meet any unexpected increases in demand. The use of zero hours contracts allows Trusts to do just that by having a pool of experienced staff they are able to draw upon should patient demand rise. Proponents of this approach further argue that it is a cost-effective way of using public money and reduces the need to use more expensive agency staff.

Zero hours contracts became popular in the late 1980s and 1990s, and the use of such contracts has risen sharply in recent years as organizations look for more cost-effective ways of using staff. According to the 2011 Workplace Employment Relations Survey, the proportion of workplaces with some workers on zero hours contracts rose from 4 per cent in 2004 to 8 per cent in 2011; in larger workplaces (100 or more employees) this figure rose from 11 per cent to 23 per cent (van Wanrooy et al. 2013). Such contracts are typically associated with low-paid jobs in the hospitality and retail sector where there are seasonal fluctuations in demand – companies such as McDonald's, the world's biggest fast-food chain, employs the majority of its UK staff on this basis, allowing them to call in workers at short notice at busy periods or not at all if it is quiet. A similar approach was used by the private security firm, G4S, at the London Olympics but with disastrous results since key staff failed to turn up on the eve of the Games. The use of these contracts for core professional staff in the health service, however, is new, and been subject to huge criticism. Zero hours contracts are seen to represent the darker side of HRM, with the mutual security of an ordinary employment contract disappearing as the risk of employment shifts to the employee, making their lives less secure. It is seen as a key change to 'the fabric of NHS employment', and could result in damaging consequences for patients if a G4S-type situation arose.

This approach is in sharp contrast to ongoing initiatives in the NHS to adopt a range of good HR policies and practices as a means to enhance organizational performance (DoH 2000), and meet the Improvement in Working Lives Standard (IWLS) developed in 2001 to ensure that all NHS employers are committed to improving the working lives of their staff (see www.nhsemployers. org). This includes a raft of flexible working policies and practices, such as career breaks, job sharing, term time working and sabbaticals. In contrast to zero hours contracts, these practices have been found to have a range of mutually beneficial outcomes (Atkinson and Hall 2011). From the employers' perspective this includes enhanced patient care, reduced nurse turnover, and reduced use of temporary staff hours. For employees these initiatives have enabled greater control over working lives and resulted in improved job satisfaction, improved health and well-being, and the promotion of 'happiness'.

Sources: Inman (2013); Cusick (2012); BBC News (2012); Atkinson and Hall (2011).

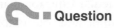 ■ **Question**

1. It could be argued that if an organization that requires critical resources (like the NHS) can effectively adopt a zero hours contract policy, then this could apply to any organization. What are the arguments for and against a zero hours policy applied to differing organizational sectors and types?

Introduction

Increasingly organizations and policy-makers are promoting flexible working initiatives as being 'good for business' and a means of enhancing organizational performance. Most recently in the UK the coalition government put forward new proposals to extend the right to request flexible working, which are seen to benefit not just employers, but also employees and the economy as a whole. A flexible organization can match the demand for labour with the supply (see Chapter 8) to ensure economic use of labour, and be responsive and competitive in the marketplace. Achieving flexibility in the use of labour is a desired outcome in models of HRM (Guest 1987; Boxall and Purcell 2011), and many flexible working practices are seen as key features of the high-performance workplace. Proponents of flexibility also argue that it is something employees want because it provides them with some control over how, when and where they work, and can give a greater sense of empowerment and enable a better work–life balance. As a result employees will be more satisfied, motivated and engaged, which in turn produces higher levels of productivity and performance (see Chapter 3). As such then, flexibility is a win–win situation for both employee and employer.

But there is a darker side to flexibility, as suggested in the introductory case study. Critics argue that in practice it means flexibility *of* the employee rather than flexibility *for* the employee (Alis et al. 2006), which has disadvantaged workers. Many of these debates have centred on the growing use of contingent labour, and the suggestion that this is a form of exploitation and has led to increased job insecurity, a growing sense of marginalization and less meaningful work. Forms of task flexibility, such as teamworking, have also been criticized for leading to work intensification, increased pressure and stress. Given this bleak scenario it is not unreasonable to assume that flexibility has a negative impact on employee attitudes and behaviour, with potentially damaging consequences for both individual and organizational performance. This suggests a more complex and highly ambiguous picture of flexibility.

This chapter considers these debates and asks who benefits from flexibility by examining the impact on the employer and the employee. Flexibility is a very broad and ill-defined concept and can be understood at different levels, but the focus of this chapter is on labour flexibility, in particular functional and numerical flexibility. The chapter starts by outlining the importance of flexibility in models of HRM, and introduces a framework of the HR causal chain which highlights the important role of employee attitudes and behaviour in determining organizational outcomes such as flexibility. The chapter then considers the meaning of flexibility, and the different forms it can take, before moving on to address some of the reasons for the recent rise in interest in the subject. The theoretical arguments are then developed to support the case for flexibility from an employers' and employees' perspective, including a model of the flexible firm and the psychological contract (see Chapter 13). The second part of the chapter reviews the empirical evidence, and explores in some detail developments and the impact of the main forms of functional and numerical flexibility, plus some possible explanations for the diverse findings.

Flexibility from a HRM perspective

In Guest's (1987) model of HRM flexibility/adapability is a key dimension of HRM, and seen as having three components relating to organizational design, job design and employee attitudes. The argument is that 'flexible organization structures together with flexible job content and flexible employees will result in a capacity to respond swiftly and effectively to changes and ensure the continuing high utilization of human and other resources' (1987: 515). This means organizations must avoid inflexible hierarchical and bureaucractic structures and demarcation, and seek organic structures, decentralization and delegation of control (see Chapter 1). This can be achieved through a job design which will enable functional flexibility and the relaxation of job demarcations. An important point, however, is that these flexibilities can only be achieved if employees display high organizational commitment, high trust and high levels of intrinsic motivation.

Similarly, Boxall and Purcell (2011) argue that organizational flexibility is one of the critical economic goals underpinning the management of work and people. In models of the HR causal chain (e.g. Wright and Nishii 2004; Purcell and Hutchinson 2007), which seek to explain how HRM impacts on performance, flexibility is often taken as a proximal measure of performance, because it is directly affected by HR policies and practice and an outcome over which employees have some influence (Boselie et al. 2005; Boselie 2010). This model argues that the effect of HR policies and practices on performance is not automatic and proposes a linked sequence of events to explain the connection (Figure 6.1) in which emphasis is given to the mediating role of employee attitudes and behaviours (see Purcell et al. 2009: 15–17 for a more detailed explanation). The achievement of flexibility, then, will be influenced by employee attitudes (as seen in job satisfaction, organizational commitment and motivation), which in turn will lead to employees exhibiting discretionary behaviours. These type of behaviours are key to driving performance, and refer to the degree of choice people have over how they perform their tasks and responsibilities, and involve working beyond the formal contractual requirements of the job (Appelbaum et al. 2000; Purcell et al. 2003). In the context of flexibility this might include employee discretion to change hours according to the demands of the job such as working beyond contractual hours to complete a job, or covering the tasks of an absent colleague. The model further argues that employee reactions will be influenced by how HR practices are implemented, and employee perceptions of such practices. Other research provides evidence that it is line managers who are largely responsible for the effectiveness of HR practices in the workplace. For example, Purcell et al.'s (2003) research shows that the way line managers implement and enact HRM (or 'bring policies to life') and show leadership strongly influences employee attitudes and behaviour (see also Chapter 3). Thus, the way line managers support and manage flexible working arrangements, and lead and manage teams, will impact on employees' satisfaction, motivation and discretionary effort. How employees perceive these practices will be judged through the lens of fairness, organizational justice, and the psychological contract. Both the psychological contract and the importance of line management behaviour are addressed later in the chapter. In sum, the model theorizes that any impact on flexibility will be determined partly by employee reactions to HR practices and the way these practices are implemented. Before considering this further, it is necessary to understand the meaning of flexibility.

What do we mean by flexibility?

The concept of (labour) flexibility is, as Legge notes, poorly specified (2005: 204) and has many different meanings, each holding different implications for employers and employees. The CIPD (2013) uses the term 'flexible working' to describe 'a type of working arrangement which gives some degree of flexibility on how long, where and when the employees work. The flexibility can be in terms of working time, working location or the pattern of working.'

Examples of practices associated with this definition are shown in Table 6.1. This interpretation is increasingly used in policy debates and the practitioner

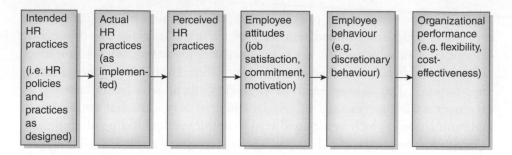

Figure 6.1 1 The HRM–performance causal chain

Sources: Wright and Nishii (2004); Purcell and Hutchinson (2007) (adapted).

Table 6.1   Flexible working practices

- **Part-time working**: when employees are contracted to work anything less than standard, basic, full-time hours.

- **Term-time working**: an employee remains on a permanent contract but can take paid/unpaid leave during school holidays.

- **Job-sharing**: a form of part-time working whereby a job designed for one person is undertaken by two or more people.

- **Flexitime**: refers to a situation where employees have some choice, normally around core times, over when to begin and end work.

- **Compressed hours**: work is reallocated into fewer and longer working days, for example by working normal weekly hours over 4 days or a 9-day fortnight. It does not normally involve a reduction in total hours.

- **Annual hours**: this is a situation where employees are contracted to work a set number of hours on an annual basis. Normally the employer has some flexibility to vary the hours worked over the year according to demand – for example requiring employees to work longer hours in a peak period (without recourse to overtime) and shorter hours when demand is low.

- **Homeworking**: employees spend all or part of their time working from home.

- **Mobile working/teleworking**: this allows employees to work all or part of their working week at a location remote from the employer's workplace.

- **Career breaks**: career breaks, or sabbaticals, are extended periods of leave which can be paid or unpaid.

Flexible working could also include practices such as employee self-rostering, shift swapping, or taking time off for training.

Sources: Adapted from BIS (2012); CIPD (2013).

literature and is often associated with practices that give a better work–life balance, suggesting that flexibility is about being more responsive to employee needs. Others refer to 'atypical working' (De Grip et al. 1997), 'non standard work' (Kalleberg 2000), and 'contingent employment' – a term commonly used in the USA to refer to 'any arrangement that differs from full time, permanent, wage and salary employment' (Polivka and Nardone 1989: 10). The main types of work usually identified here are part-time work, temporary jobs, fixed-term jobs, agency work, subcontract work, casual employment and sometimes self-employment. This more traditional view of flexibility (Brewster et al. 2011) centres on the employers' need for flexibility, and many of the debates have focused on the extent to which this type of work is less stable and secure than traditional work.

While these distinctions are useful, none capture all elements of labour flexibility. A more complete view of flexibility is to conceptualize it as having a number of dimensions as follows (Atkinson 1985; Blyton and Morris 1992):

- **Functional or task flexibility**, which concerns the ability to redeploy employees across a wide range of tasks according to changing patterns of demand. This can involve taking on tasks at a different or the same job level, such as lecturing staff taking on administrative roles (vertical functional flexibility), or electrical engineers taking on mechanical work (horizontal functional flexibility). Work practices associated with these types of flexibility include multi-skilling, job rotation and teamwork.
- **Numerical flexibility**, which allows employers to adjust the labour supply by increasing or decreasing the number of employees and/or the number of hours worked. This includes part-time working, temporary jobs, and job share, and is common in very cyclical businesses such as tourism, agriculture and retail which require more staff in the peak season and less at off peak times.
- **Temporal flexibility**, which allows employers to vary the number and pattern of working hours in response to work demands. The aim is to maximize productive time and minimize unproductive or idle time. Examples include annual hours, flexitime, overtime, and zero hours contracts.
- **Financial or wage flexibility**, which allows greater financial flexibility for the price of labour. Examples include performance-related pay, bonus schemes and profit-related pay (see Chapter 7).
- **Geographical or distance flexibility**, which is the ability to work remotely or at different locations.

Boxall and Purcell (2011) take a slightly different perspective, differentiating between short-run responsiveness and long-term agility. Short-term responsiveness includes numerical, functional, and financial flexibility, whereas long-term flexibility is concerned with the ability of a firm to survive in a rapidly changing environment by changing its products, costs and/or technologies (see Chapter 1). The example they give is Dyson, Britain's innovative technology company, which moved its production facilities from

Britain to Malaysia in 2000 where labour unit costs were cheaper and there was closer proximity to suppliers. As a result some 550 British workers were laid off and the focus in the UK is now on research and development. Outsourcing, or the transfer of products or services to an outside vendor or supplier (Haines 2009), is a variant of this. These long-term types of flexibility, which, as illustrated in the case of Dyson require making hard strategic decisions and can require quite radical changes in HRM, are not discussed in this chapter.

PIT STOP: REFLECTIVE ACTIVITY 6.1

Many commentators use the terms 'flexibility' and 'work–life balance' interchangeably, although the two do not necessarily mean the same thing. Work–life balance has been defined as 'individuals being able to have some control and autonomy over where, when and how they work' (Jones et al. 2007), and is primarily focused on accommodating employee needs. However, although flexibility can support work–life balance, not all flexible working practices may better employees' work–life balance.

1. Which flexible working arrangements are likely to enable employees to improve their work–life balance?
2. Which flexible working arrangements might negatively impact on an individual's work–life balance?
3. What problems might be encountered in implementing and sustaining work–life balance policies in an organization?

Why the increased interest in flexibility?

Growth in the interest and use of flexibility dates from the mid to late 1970s. In the UK a recent CIPD survey (2012) of employers and employees found that the vast majority of employers (96 per cent) offered some form of flexible working, and some three-quarters of employees made use of some form of flexible working. Research by the CBI/Harvey Nash in 2011 reported similar findings, with 96 per cent of employers offering at least one form of flexible working and 70 per cent offering three or more types.

Interest in a more flexible labour market is widespread (from government, business, academics and the media) and can be attributed to a number of factors (Blyton and Morris 1992; Kalleberg 2000; Jones et al. 2007; CIPD 2012):

- Intensified competition, globalization, and more volatile and unpredictable product markets (see Chapters 1 and 2). This encouraged organizations to look for ways of matching labour supply to demand so that they could be more responsive to the market conditions and become efficient and economic in their use of labour.

- The 'flexible specialization' thesis in the 1980s, which was seen as the alternative to Fordism, and associated with functional flexibility. (For a discussion see Legge 2005 and Tailby 2003.)
- Increasing need for businesses to be able to deliver services to customers on a 24/7 basis.
- Technology improvements in communication and information systems (facilitating, for example, remote working and relaxing job boundaries).
- Public policy and state intervention. In the 1980s the UK Conservative government were committed to making the labour market more flexible (see Chapter 8). Since that time there has been growing statutory regulation which has influenced employers' use of flexibility, some of which has been initiated in the EU and driven by European employment strategy. In the UK relevant legislation includes protecting the rights of part-time and temporary workers, the Working Time Directive, enhanced maternity and paternity leave and the right to request flexible working.
- Demographic changes in the composition of the labour force, such as an increase in female and older workers and a more diversified labour market.
- Changing employee expectations about the boundaries between work and personal life leading to an increased demand for a better work–life balance and more choice over work. The Third Work Life Balance Employee survey reports that half of all adults, including a higher proportion of men than women, said they would like to work more flexibly (Holmes et al. 2007). Long working hours in the UK and concerns about work intensification and overload are likely contributors to this demand.

More recently, flexible working arrangements have been used as a means of avoiding or minimizing job losses and cutting employment costs during the recession. A 2010 IRS survey reported that a quarter of respondents had used or were about to use flexible working to reduce job losses, for example through reduced hours, unpaid sabbaticals and job sharing schemes (Wolff 2010). Provided these measures are temporary they are likely to be well received by employees as alternatives to redundancy or pay cuts. One such example is KPMG (Case Study 6.2).

These factors suggest that flexibility is both supply- and demand-led. The considerable interest in the work–life balance agenda over the last decade was seen to be predominantly employee-led, but has increasingly been promoted as being of mutual benefit to employees and employers. In the UK a wide range of reports from government, business and professional bodies (e.g. CIPD 2007; Hooker et al. 2007; Family Friendly Working Hours Taskforce 2010) has heralded the business benefits of these types of flexible working. For example, a report by the Family Friendly Working Hours Taskforce set up in November 2009 by the UK government states that:

Flexibility in the workplace is about developing modern working practices to fit the needs of the 21st century. Both employers and employees can gain from flexible working opportunities as both parties have the flexibility to organize their working arrangements in a way that suits them. This can enable organizations to adapt to changing business conditions and individual employees to better balance their work and family life. (2010: 6)

The business benefits are broadly seen to be improved productivity, reduced absence, increased ability to recruit from a wider talent pool (see Chapter 5) and improved employee motivation, engagement and loyalty. According to Pabayo et al. (2010) many of the legislative changes in the UK and Europe have been explicitly or implicitly underpinned by the assumption that these types of flexibility will have a positive impact on employees in terms of their attitudes, well-being, work–life balance and performance (although in the UK flexible working is still treated as a concession rather than a right, in so far as there is a right to request flexible working but not to receive it).

Significantly, however, the benefits of these types of working have yet to be established in the academic literature. For example, Kelly et al. (2008, cited in Walsh 2013) observe that the empirical evidence on work–life balance initiatives is weak. In a review of the literature on flexible working arrangements which accommodate employees' preferences (e.g. part-time work, home work, flexitime, term time working, home working, compressed hours) De Menezes and Kelliher (2011) found no consistent evidence of a business case for these types of arrangements, although they recognize there are considerable methodical shortcomings with the studies reviewed. The following section examines the theoretical arguments for flexibility in more detail, beginning with a model of the flexible firm.

CASE STUDY 6.2

Avoiding redundancy through flexible futures

Faced with the economic global downturn in 2008/09, KPMG, the international professional services firm, introduced an innovative short-term flexible working scheme to preserve jobs and help retain talent. KPMG were unwilling to repeat the experiences of 2002/03, when the firm made redundancies which constrained growth when the upturn in the economy came, and in January 2009 launched a new scheme which provided for:

- The redeployment of employees to other international parts of the business where more resources are needed. This also fits with the firm's long-term aim of developing people to work across cultures and geographical boundaries (see Chapters 11 and 12).

- Retraining some employees so skills can be used across different parts of the business. This allows KPMG to build up 'response teams' comprising of individuals who have a mixed set of skills that can be used across different areas of work.
- Implementing 'Flexible Futures' – a scheme which involves agreed changes in working patterns during times when the business is quiet.

The flexible futures scheme includes one or both of the following options:

- A reduced working week (e.g. a four-day week or nine-day fortnight)
- A sabbatical of between four to twelve weeks' leave at 30 per cent of pay in 2009.

KPMG can invoke either option by giving one-week's notice for reduced hours working or four-week's notice for the sabbatical. The maximum salary loss in any calendar year is capped at 20 per cent of pay, and pay reductions are spread over a period of time (e.g. six months) to minimize the impact. Employees continue to receive full benefits throughout the period when they are on reduced hours or the sabbatical.

Following the launch of the initiative, employees had three weeks to decide whether to volunteer for the scheme, and by the end of the period, four out of five (85 per cent) of the 11,000 KPMG partners and staff had signed up. The changes required volunteers to agree to a variation in the terms and conditions of employees' contracts for a temporary period of 12 months. Individuals who have signed up for the scheme can be approached at any time by their manager with a request to reduce hours or take a sabbatical.

The scheme allows KPMG to respond in a proactive way to changes in the market, and reduce its labour costs very quickly if needed, and is reported to have saved the company £12.5 million. It also retains intellectual capital and avoids the costs of redundancies (estimated at five or six months' pay per individual). The firm also believes that motivation levels are retained and loyalty increased.

Sources: Wolff (2009); Churchyard (2009).

 ■ **Questions**

1. On the face of it, this appears to be a win–win situation for employer and employee. Do you agree with this view?
2. What are the problems of implementing such a scheme?
3. What other flexible working arrangements could be introduced during a downturn to avoid redundancies?

The flexible firm: the employers' perspective

Flexibility, from the employers' perspective, has often been theorized in terms of the core periphery model popularized by Atkinson (1984, 1985). Although old, the model remains influential and clearly articulates the choices available to employers to meet the need for flexibility.

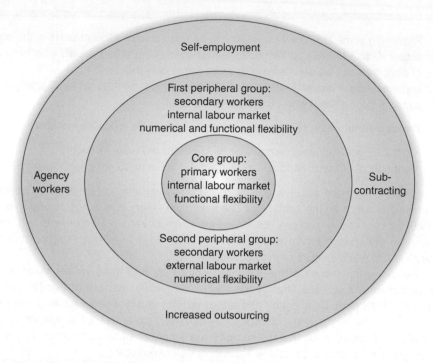

Figure 6.2 The flexible firm
Source: Adapted from Atkinson (1984).

The model argues for the segmentation of the workforce, distinguishing between two groups of workers: core and peripheral staff (see Figure 6.2). Core staff are the primary workers who are critical to the organization's success, and include anyone with key skills and knowledge. They are engaged on permanent full-time contracts and, because of their core status, are rewarded well, receive training and development opportunities and are expected to be functionally flexible, acquiring new skills as changes in the market demand. In return for this relative security and treatment their long-term commitment to the organization is expected to be secured.

Peripheral staff, on the other hand, are not critical to the business and occupy lower-skilled jobs which are more readily available in the external labour market, and offer numerical flexibility. The peripheral group effectively protect the core against insecurity. They receive little investment in training and development, have less attractive terms and conditions of employment compared to the core group, and less job security. It follows that they can be expected to be less committed to the organization in the long term. This group is subdivided into the first and second group. The first group are part of the internal market, have permanent contracts, but have a lower level of job security compared to that of the core workers. They may be full- or part-time and are also expected to show functional flexibility. The second group of peripheral workers are part of the external labour market, and include individuals who find it hard to break into the internal market, such as subcontract employees and temporary staff. They therefore provide numerical flexibility and minimize the firms' commitment to offer job security.

There is also a third group of workers, shown in the outer ring of the diagram, which comprise people who are not employees but employed by another employer or in self-employment, and are used as and when demand requires it (e.g. cleaners, security). It includes agency workers, subcontractors, and outsourced workers. Essentially the risk of employing these people is transferred to another organization or the individual.

The advantages of this approach are the ability to adjust labour supply to product or service demand, higher productivity from a protected and committed core, and lower and more flexible wage costs. Despite its intuitive appeal, however, the model has been subject to considerable criticism. The model's status and purpose were considered ambiguous – was it to be viewed as a description of what organizations do? Or a prescription of what organizations ought to do (Hunter et al. 1993)? The evidence that it reflected a discrete strategy to segment the workforce between a core and a periphery was limited (ibid.), and many argued that these developments were simply a pragmatic short-term reaction to intensified market pressures. The distinction between periphery and core has been questioned. For example, the model suggests part-timers are peripheral whereas many part-timers occupy key positions. Alternatively, employees doing 'core' tasks such as maintenance can be employed on an agency or freelance basis. Shifting boundaries of work between and within organizations add further confusion. Marchington and Wilkinson (2012) give the example of a management consultant working for a client who may be a peripheral worker for the client but a core worker for the consultancy. Functional flexibility means that job boundaries become more blurred and individuals may be taking on a combination of core and peripheral work. Furthermore, the model neglects the tensions and managerial problems in segmenting the workforce (Tailby 2003). Refinements have subsequently been made to this model, such as Handy's (1989) 'shamrock organisation' which also distinguishes between a core and peripheral workforce, although in a slightly different way. Nevertheless, as Tailby asserts, the model remains influential in that 'its concepts of core and periphery, numerical, functional and wage flexibility, have been absorbed into "everyday" practitioner and academic vocabularies' (2003: 499).

Flexibility from the employees' perspective

The case for flexibility from the employees' perspective can be found in the motivation theories of Maslow (1960), Alderfer (1972) and Herzberg (1959), theory on work design (Hackman and Oldham 1976: 1980), and sociotechnical theory which advocates group-based work design (e.g. De Sitter et al. 1997; Pasmore 1988). Some of these theories emerged in reaction to scientific management, pioneered by F. W. Taylor (see Taylor 1911), who advocated task specialization by organizing work into tightly defined, low discretion jobs – an approach which characterized many mass production jobs in 1920s, such as the Fordist production line system in the US automobile industry. Critics argued that this created product inflexibility and was 'dehumanizing' with negative implications for employees including de-skilling, removal of worker responsibility, increased management control, monotony and boredom (e.g. Braverman 1974). Many of the new ideas to counter these conditions centred on forms of job design and were seen 'as an antidote to the worse excesses of Taylorism', and a means of motivating and satisfying employees (Marchington 1992: 107). For example, job enlargement and job enrichment can help promote the motivators in Herzberg's two-factor theory, such as sense of achievement, responsibility, and the 'nature of the work' (similar to Maslow's esteem and self-actualization and Alderfer's 'growth'). Building on Herzberg's work, Hackman and Oldham's (1976, 1980) Job Characteristics theory tells us how job enrichment, job rotation, job enlargement and empowerment are important for intrinsic motivation, satisfaction with work and job performance. This can be met by horizontally and vertically expanding a person's job through multi-skilling, rotating work to reduce boredom, increasing task responsibility and discretion over decision-making through teamworking and delayering.

Many of these practices are commonly found in high-performance work systems (HPWS) on the grounds that they provide richer and more fulfilling jobs, promote a more collaborative and flexible approach to work and enhance employee involvement (see, for example, MacDuffie 1995; Ichniowksi et al. 1997; Wood and de Menezes 1998; Appelbaum et al. 2000). Enriched job design, for example, which allows employees some discretion over how they undertake and manage their tasks, has been shown to have predominantly positive associations with well-being, job satisfaction, and performance (Wood et al. 2012). Appelbaum et al.'s (2000) three-industry study of HPWSs finds that autonomy over task-level decision-making, off-line team membership (working in a team, committee, or task force), self-directed team membership (part of a team that work together and jointly make decision about task assignments) and communication with people outside the team enhance employee commitment and job satisfaction.

Although numerical and temporal forms of flexibility were excluded from early HPWS, more recent research (e.g. Purcell et al. 2003) suggests that these types of flexibility should also be included as a feature of high performance working. Macky and Boxall (2007) suggest that practices associated with work–life balance initiatives may moderate any work intensification arising from HPWS. Research by Atkinson and Hall (2011) in an acute NHS trust found that flexible time arrangements enabled employees to have greater control over their working lives and promoted active states of happiness, such as being pleased and cheerful, and passive states, reflected in feelings of contentment and calm. Furthermore, the promotion of happiness gave rise to discretionary behaviours and other desirable performance outcomes. This concurs with the work of others (e.g. Berg et al. 2004; Pabayo et al. 2010) who have found positive links between flexible working and employee health and well-being. Kelliher and Anderson (2008) found a positive relationship between flexible working and job quality (although there were perceived costs such as long-term opportunities for development and progression). Research on engagement finds that workers on flexible contracts tend to be more emotionally engaged, more satisfied with their work, more likely to speak positively about their organization and less likely to quit (Truss et al. 2006).

De Menezes and Kelliher's (2011) review of the literature on flexible working arrangements (FWAs) and indicators of performance, referred to earlier, finds that the evidence is supportive of a positive link between job satisfaction and these types of arrangements. For example, the Third Work Life Balance survey (Hooker et al. 2007) shows that flexible workers are more likely to be 'very satisfied' with their jobs compared to non-flexible workers. Similarly research by the Cranfield School of Management found those who had FWAs reported higher levels of job satisfaction than those who did not in four out of seven organizations studied. The research, however, is less clear on the link with organizational commitment, showing either a positive relationship or no relationship. They also find mixed evidence on the link with stress and well-being.

The impact of flexible working on employee attitudes and behaviour can also be viewed through the lens of the psychological contract (Chapter 13), which is now considered.

===== PIT STOP: REFLECTIVE ACTIVITY 6.2 =====

Hackman and Oldham's (1980) job characteristics model

This model identifies five job characteristics that promote three 'critical psychological states' (experienced meaningfulness, experienced responsibility, and knowledge of results):

- Skill variety: the extent to which the job requires a diverse set of skills.
- Task identity: the extent to which a job produces a whole identifiable piece of work.
- Task significance: the extent to which the job has an impact on others, either at work or outside the organization, such as service/product users.
- Autonomy: the extent to which the job allows individuals to exercise choice and discretion in their work.
- Feedback: the extent to which the job itself provides information on how well the individual is performing.

The first three are believed to influence the meaningfulness of the work, the fourth affects responsibility for work outcomes and the fifth impacts on knowledge of results of work activities. Collectively these three psychological states influence motivation, job satisfaction and work performance, and reduced absence and turnover.

Support for the theory can be found in Fried and Ferris's (1987) meta-analysis which found that the five job characteristics are strongly positively related to internal job motivation and job satisfaction, although the relationships with job performance were weaker. There is less support, however, for the mediating effects of the critical psychological states.

 ■ **Questions**

1. Thinking of a job you have performed, how can the characteristics of that job be changed to meet the three critical psychological states?
2. What are the implications of this from the organization's perspective?

The psychological contract

The psychological contract is a 'useful concept to describe, analyse and explain the feelings and reactions of employees' (Guest et al. 2010: 89) but interpretations of the concept vary. The term 'psychological contract' was first coined by Argyris in the 1960s who observed that there was an unspoken agreement between supervisors and employees which resulted in staff maintaining high performance, provided they received fair wages and had some control over the way they worked (in Conway and Briner 2004). This notion of shared expectations between employer and employee is reflected in early definitions of the psychological contract (see Chapter 13). For example, Schein defines it (1978: 48) as 'a set of unwritten reciprocal expectations between an individual employee and the organisation', arguing that successful employment relationships (see Chapter 8) involve matching organization needs with individual needs. Rousseau, however, takes a different perspective and views it from the employee perspective, defining is as 'individual beliefs, shaped by the organisation, regarding terms of an exchange agreement between individuals and their organisation' (Rousseau 1995: 6). Rousseau therefore positioned it as subjective, individual and 'in the eye of the beholder'. However, as Guest and others have argued, the problem with this approach is that the psychological contract, like the employment contract, involves two parties, and prefers to define it as 'the perceptions of both parties to the employment relationship, organization and individual, of the reciprocal promises and obligations implied in that relationship' (Guest 2007: 133).

Further distinctions are often made between transactional and relational contracts (e.g. Rousseau 1995). Transactional contracts are concerned with the tangibles of the employment relationship, and tend to be fairly explicit and for a specified time period with a clearly defined output for each party, such as pay in return for a particular level of employee performance. Relational contracts, on the other hand, are less tangible, less specific and more open-ended exchanges such as loyalty in return for job security. It is relational contracts that are often considered most important since they can signify increased commitment and strong identification with the organization and its goals (Tietze and Nadin 2011).

The psychological contract can therefore be formal and informal, explicit and implicit, written and unwritten. It can be developed over time and change, and usually begins during the recruitment process (see Chapter 5). An array of obligations and promises can form the contract, and there is no clear agreement as to what these might be. Examples could include an employee offering to be flexible with regard to the range of tasks performed in exchange for training and development opportunities (Chapter 10), or remaining loyal in exchange for a 'good' work–life balance. Other examples are given in Table 6.2.

Guest and Conway (2002) refer to the 'state of the psychological contract' (see Figure 6.3) which is influenced by an employee's sense of fairness and trust in whether obligations and promises have been met, plus a belief in 'delivering

Table 6.2   Implicit and explicit promises

Employees might promise to:

- work hard
- show loyalty to the company and uphold its reputation, make suggestions for improvement
- be punctual
- put in extra effort when necessary
- be flexible with regard to tasks and hours when required
- learn new skills and update existing ones
- be courteous to customers and colleagues
- treat property carefully
- be honest

Employers might promise to:

- pay commensurate with performance
- provide equitable pay
- provide training and development opportunities
- provide opportunities for promotion
- provide a good work–life balance
- provide reasonable job security
- provide interesting work
- provide a safe place to work
- ensure fairness of treatment
- allow time off to meet family and personal needs
- consult and communicate on matters that affect employees

Sources: Conway and Briner (2004), Sparrow and Cooper (2003).

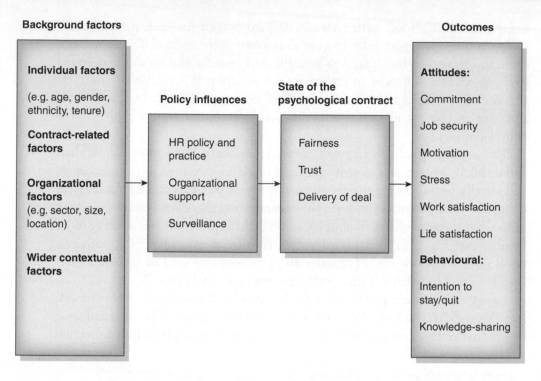

Figure 6.3 The psychological contract model
Source: Adapted from Guest and Conway 2002.

the deal'. This model also highlights the importance of organizational and individual factors and has implications for attitudes and behaviours. When the state of the psychological contract is positive (i.e. promises and obligations are met), employees will show high levels of commitment and satisfaction, but a failure to fulfil promises and obligations results in negative outcomes for both employee and employer, such as reduced commitment, lower job satisfaction, and increased turnover. Some distinguish between breach and violation; the former refers to less serious transgressions of obligation, the latter to more serious transgression of promises (Tietze and Nadin 2011). The greater the degree of perceived breach the stronger the negative outcomes. Conway and Briner's (2004) research found that broken and exceeded promises occur regularly at work and that line managers were the main agents for this.

Two studies on homeworkers highlight the importance and relevance of the psychological contract for one group of flexible workers. In both studies homeworkers sought this form of temporal flexibility and accepted demotion or gave up promotion in order to work from home and achieve a better work–life balance, suggesting a career may not be an important aspect of the psychological contract for homeworkers.

The relevance of this debate is also returned to later in the chapter.

The psychological contract

The psychological contract captures at any one point in time what the perceived 'deal' between the two parties is. The traditional view (or 'old deal') of the psychological contract is characterized as 'relational' and one in which employees offer their commitment and discretionary effort in exchange for career progression and job security. Some, however, have argued that the 'deal' is changing (e.g. Rousseau 1995; Herriot and Pemberton 1995), and employees no longer seek job security but want fair pay, opportunities for training and development and employability. In this sense the new contract is more transactional in nature.

Some researchers claim to have found evidence of a change, particularly regarding reduced loyalty (e.g. Coyle-Shapiro and Kessler 2000) whereas others, such as Guest and Conway, have found evidence of the persistence of the old relational contracts.

 ■ **Question**

1. Thinking about your own experiences, do you think the old psychological contract or the new one is more relevant?

Research also shows that expectations about work vary at different times in people's lives. Younger workers, for example, tend to want either part-time and reduced hours to combine work and study or exciting, creative, interesting jobs and expect career progression and personal development.

 ■ **Question**

1. What are some examples of other groups of workers who might have different expectations about work?

CASE STUDY 6.3

Homeworking and the psychological contract

Tietze and Nadin (2011) examined the impact of the transition from office-based to home-based working for clerical workers in a local authority. They found that participants chose homeworking in the expectation that it would allow them to combine work with domestic responsibilities and escape from the stressful contact of the office environment, even though this could negatively impact on promotion prospects. These employees had previously experienced contract violation in so far as their employer had failed to honour obligations relating to workload, pay and

(Continued)

(Continued)

promotion, and inadequately managed the office. This had contributed to a negative atmosphere at work, and resulted in reduced levels of trust, increased cynicism, and low job satisfaction. Homeworking allowed employees the opportunity to repair some of this damage done in the psychological contract by restoring equity in workload and pay, and removed them from the difficult office environment. This emphasizes both the transactional and relational elements of the psychological contract. The impact on these homeworkers was very positive (e.g. household relationships became less fraught) and the organization benefited from increased productivity. Thus, better flexibility resulted in a win–win situation. However, the authors caution that the impact on those left in the office should also be considered, as this might lead to feelings of resentment and create new problems for managers to deal with.

In another study of female clerical workers, Collins et al. show how the immediate manager represents the organization for homeworkers, acting as a 'gatekeeper in terms of whether expectations of clerical staff are met' (2013: 12–13). Homeworkers had been able to negotiate their own idiosyncratic deals with line managers in order to attain their desired level of temporal flexibility. However, the research also found that managers had developed different interpretations and perspectives regarding flexibility and differed in their implementation depending on how comfortable they were with allowing people to work from home. Some managers, for example, struggled to let go of control.

Source: author.

Key forms of flexible working

The following section considers developments and the impact of key forms of flexible working, beginning with functional flexibility.

Functional flexibility

Functional flexibility is associated with a variety of types of working practices, including:

- Multi-skilling or cross-training which involves reducing the demarcation between jobs and relaxing job boundaries.
- Teamworking, including problem-solving groups and continuous improvement teams.
- Flatter hierarchies.
- Job rotation.

The 2004 Workplace Employee Relations Survey (WERS) finds that two-thirds of UK workplaces (66 per cent) formally trained at least some core employees to be functionally flexible, and in 65 per cent of workplaces some core employees did jobs other than their own at least once a week, although this varied by sector. However, only a fifth (19 per cent) trained at least three-fifths of their core staff to do other jobs, and just 16 per cent of workplaces said that three-fifths of their core workers were doing other jobs (Kersley et al. 2006: 92). Three-quarters (72 per cent) of UK workplaces reported teamworking present for core employees, and problem-solving groups or continuous improvement groups were found in one-fifth of workplaces (21 per cent). The overall incidence of teamworking, multi-skilling and problem-solving groups has changed little since 1998, indicating that the diffusion of these 'so called high involvement management' practices has been rather muted in recent years (Kersley et al. 2006: 107). This leaves the UK with a lower level of functional flexibility than in many other northern European economies (Jones et al. 2007).

The theoretical case for these types of practices was outlined earlier in the chapter. Employees who are functionally flexible are expected to have more fulfilling and satisfying jobs and be more productive. Cross-training can also reduce anxiety about job security, by reducing an employee's reliance on one particular type of work. From the employers' perspective, functional flexibility allows organizations to reorganize, reallocate and retrain their employees to respond to contingencies presented by fluctuating markets (Cappelli and Neumark 2004). In a large supermarket, such as Tesco or Asda, if employees are multi-skilled they can quickly be redeployed to shelf stacking, the check-out or customer services as demand requires. To a customer like myself, who loathes doing the weekend shop and simply wants to buy the goods I need and move out of the store as quickly as possible, this is a key competitive advantage. Multi-skilling also makes it easier to cover absences and lateness. Presented in this way functional flexibility is a win–win situation with employers and employees simultaneously benefiting from the approach.

There are, however, disadvantages. Functional flexibility is expensive because training is required. It may result in a dilution of skill, and people not being able to carry out tasks as effectively as a highly specialized individual might. Some employees may not like to be 'jack of all trades and master of none', preferring to specialize, and some skills may be too complex to broaden out. Commentators have questioned the extent to which such practices result in increased management control, work intensification and stress rather than employee empowerment, arguing that employees have tasks added to their workload rather than being given increased autonomy (Legge 2005; Hyman and Mason 1995). Resistance to some forms of functional flexibility, in particular attempts to reduce demarcation and multi-skill, has resulted in industrial action in the UK. All of this suggests that functional flexibility is not the mutual gain assumed in the HRM literature (Wood et al. 2012).

These contradictions are well illustrated in teamworking.

Teamworking

In theory, teams represent an extensive form of job redesign, which can combine both vertical and horizontal additions to the job such that employees not only move between different tasks but also take on a responsibility for managing the team as well (Marchington 1992). A teamworking environment is often portrayed as one in which employees work together, share ideas and knowledge, jointly problem solve, and achieve greater control over tasks and management: 'Working in teams empowers people and helps develop autonomy, which is a source of profound job satisfaction and reduces stress' (Hayes 2005: 172, in Eurofound 2007a). It is seen as leading to better decision-making, more creative solutions (Pfeffer, 1998), and creating an environment in which employees are encouraged to work harder, and more smartly and efficiently (Delarue et al. 2008). Additionally, the introduction of teamworking can involve a rationalization of the production process and a decentralization of decision-making, resulting in further efficiencies such as cost savings and throughput times.

However, there is an alternative perspective on teamworking which shows it to be intrusive, to place increased demands on both employees and managers, and an attempt to strengthen management control and intensify work (Parker and Slaughter 1988; Berggren 1993). As a result employees experience higher levels of stress, increased work pressure and face a greater risk of health problems (Eurofound 2007a). Sewell and Wilkinson regard teamwork as producing 'horizontal disciplinary force, based on peer scrutiny, (which) operates throughout the team as members seek to identity and action those who may jeopardise overall performance' (1992: 110). Team working can also encourage 'social loafing' (Ringelmann 1913; Karau and Williams 1993) or 'shirking' which can have a negative impact on productivity. Teams can also be difficult to implement in practice, and just because people work in a team, this does not mean they will work as a team.

The reality is that teams come in different shapes and sizes and are used in a wide variety of ways (Geary 1994; Mueller et al. 2000). Teamworking varies from a loose group of employees simply sharing some skills and tasks to more sophisticated self-managed or autonomous teams. Marchington (1992) suggests analysing teams in terms of scope, the technical requirements of the work, and the extent of employee influence and control over these requirements. According to the Workplace Employment Relations Survey 2004 (Kersley et al. 2006) 83 per cent of teams are given responsibly for specific products or services, 81 per cent depend on each other's work, 66 per cent rotate tasks or roles, 61 per cent jointly decide how work is to be done and just 6 per cent can appoint their own leaders. Teamwork in a manufacturing operation, where it is part of the overall approach to production, is very different from teamworking in a call centre. Even in the same sector, the nature of teamwork can vary, as shown in Table 6.3 which contrasts two production systems in the automotive industry: the Japanese model of lean production (described as 'flexible Taylorism' by Berggren [1993]) and the Scandinavian model of semi-autonomous working associated with Saab and Volvo. These two models have their advantages and disadvantages with very different implications for management control and employee autonomy (Sisson and Storey 2000). For example, in the Scandinavian model roles and responsibilities are decided by team members, in contrast to the lean production model where such decisions are made unilaterally by management.

On balance, however, the evidence suggests that teamworking can contribute positively to improved performance and is a win–win scenario. In reviewing the empirical research evidence on the links between team-based working and various outcomes (operational, financial, structural and worker) Delarue et al. (2008) conclude that adopting team structures can yield positive outcomes for organizations on all four dimensions. Moreover, they found that 'any positive link between teamworking and performance can be explained by the impact of teamworking on employee attitudes and behaviours and/or organizational structure' (2008: 142). Other research also suggests that employees working in teams generally report higher levels of satisfaction, and are more motivated than their counterparts who work under more traditional systems (e.g. Edwards and Wright 1998). Analysis of the European Company Survey, for example, shows a positive link between adoption of teamworking and management perceptions of financial performance and productivity (Eurofound 2007a). However, as Delarue et al. (2008) point out, it is important to recognize that the effectiveness of teamworking will be influenced by a range of organizational factors including strategy, culture, size and industry. Furthermore, teamworking cannot be considered in isolation and will be most successful when integrated with a bundle of mutually reinforcing HR practices (see Chapters 3 and 13), such as training and development, job redesign and employee involvement schemes.

Table 6.3 Teamworking in the automobile industry

Dimensions	Scandinavian	Toyota/lean production
Membership	Voluntary	Mandatory
Selection of group members	By the group	By management
Selection of group leader	By the group	By management
Qualifications	Mixed	Generalists
Reward	Skill-dependent	Uniform (seniority)
Task	Complex	Simple
Technology	Independent of pace	Dependent on pace
Autonomy	Large	Narrow
Internal division of labour	Voluntary	Largely prescribed

Sources: Sisson and Storey (2000) based on Fröhlich and Pekruhl (1996).

Numerical flexibility

As suggested in the Atkinson model, numerical flexibility allows organizations to deploy employees where they are most needed at times when they are most needed. Using the supermarket analogy again, part-time, temporary and agency staff can be taken on at peak times such as Saturdays, Christmas and Easter. This section considers two quite different ways of achieving numerical flexibility: part-time work and temporary work.

Part-time contracts

Part-time work is the most rapidly expanding 'new' form of employment (Walsh 2007), and the most common form of numerical flexibility. According to the 2012 CIPD survey on flexible working, part-time working was provided by 88 per cent of respondent organizations. In the UK, 26.8 per cent of employees worked part-time (between July and September 2012) and 77 per cent of these were female (Office for National Statistics 2012), representing one of the highest levels of female part-time working in the OECD countries. Not surprisingly, part-time work has been characterized as a 'universally gendered' form of employment (Fagan and O'Reilly 1998: 1), although it is anticipated that in the UK more men will work part-time in the future, moving into previously female-dominated occupations such as the service sector (Lyonette et al. 2010). The characteristics of the part-time workforce are, however, more nuanced than that (see Table 6.4).

There has been a rise in both the number of men and women working part-time during the recent recession, reflecting historical trends which show an increase following periods of economic decline and a decrease during periods

Table 6.4 Who works part-time in the UK

Overall, part-time work is more likely to be undertaken by:

- women aged between 30 and 44, as well as younger and older men and women
- men and women in lower-level jobs
- men and women with no qualifications
- white women, and men from other ethnic groups
- men and women registered disabled and with a work-limiting disability
- men and women working in organizations with higher proportions of women overall
- men and women working in public sector organizations
- men and women working in wholesale, retail and motor trades, as well as hotels and restaurants.

The areas in which female part-time workers are found are also the most feminized and particularly in (low-paid) jobs frequently viewed as 'women's work'.

Source: Lyonette et al. (2010: 29).

of economic growth. The recent rise is mainly due to an increasing number working part-time because they could not find full-time employment (17.8 per cent of all those in part-time employment in the period July–September 2012), indicating that this shift has been involuntary.

Part-time working has also been increasing in Europe over the past two decades for both males and females, although the part-time rate for females (32 per cent) is four times that for males (8 per cent) (Eurofound 2011). In 2011, the proportion of the EU-27 workforce reporting that their main job was part-time was 19.5 per cent, although there are wide differences across countries in terms of the growth, proportion of part-timers (as shown in Table 6.6) and the characteristics of part-time jobs. It should, however, be noted that country comparisons are difficult because definitions vary. In France and Belgium, for example, part-time is defined as fourth-fifths or less of collectively agreed working time, in the Netherlands it is less than 35 hours, and in the UK less than 30 hours. In the main, differences in national part-time rates are due to various socioeconomic factors such as access to affordable childcare, differences in working hours cultures, quality of available part-time work, and differences in legislation (Eurofound 2011). This is illustrated in the comparison of three countries in Case Study 6.4.

The implications of part-time working, from a tripartite point of view, are summarized in Table 6.5 taken from the European Company Survey 2009.

Table 6.5 The importance of part-time work in a tripartite structure

Employer	Individual	Government
Positive aspects:		
• allows employers to adjust hours worked to cyclical conditions; adjustment of production and labour costs lead to productivity gains; may meet the preference of workers	• solution for better work–life balance • facilitates progressive entrance to or withdrawal from the labour market over the life course; may increase life satisfaction	• increases labour participation, especially for females
Negative aspect:		
• fixed costs (e.g. recruitment, training, social security) may increase overall labour costs	• hourly earnings for part-time are lower than those of full-time • reduced benefits • fewer possibilities for progressing career • transition to and from full-time work into part-time may be difficult • reduced job quality	• wastage of resources, under-use of investmont in human capital, as many part-time workers are highly educated part-time jobs may crowd out full-time positions

Source: Eurofound 2011.

Part-time working is generally considered to be demand-led. The fact that some two-thirds of people in part-time work in the UK say they chose to work on this basis because they did not want a full-time job can be interpreted as evidence that part-time work is something that is desired by employees, and therefore voluntary. Many people (men and women) prefer part-time working because it allows them to combine work with other responsibilities, such as caring for children or older relatives, or combining work with study. Buddelmeyer et al. (2008) found that the fertility rate is positively related to the part-time rate, suggesting that part-time work creates opportunities for women to continue working rather than leaving the labour market altogether by allowing them to combine work and childcare responsibilities. It can thus have a beneficial effect on the employment rate, for example through increased female participation. Part-time work can also produce less conflict, stress and exhaustion at work and generally offers employees a better work–life balance (Hakim 1996; Barnett and Gareis 2002). Beham et al.'s (2012) study in five western European countries found that part-time employees had higher levels of satisfaction with work–family balance than full-time employees, even after taking work demands and resources into account. From this perspective part-time work can be implemented as an organizational strategy to become an 'employer of choice' and a means of attracting and retaining human capital, particularly important in a tight labour market. It also enables employers to respond to cyclical peaks and troughs in demand and cover for less social hours such as night shifts. Reducing hours worked by staff (with agreement) when there is a downturn in business is an alternative to losing key staff through redundancy. Another argument is that it allows employers to pay only for the most productive hours of an employee's time (the longer one works the less productive per hour one becomes). It also helps keep the full-time equivalent (FTE) headcount down.

On the other hand, there are disadvantages to employing part-time workers. Overall labour costs may increase due to fixed costs such as training, particularly where two part-timers are employed rather than one full-time person. Part-timers can be inflexible, for example, restricted to working hours around caring responsibilities, and this can cause resentment amongst full-time employees. It has also been suggested that part-timers are unlikely to contribute greatly to functional flexibility (Gallie et al. 1998). Some also believe that the commitment and motivation of part-time workers is less than those working full-time, although this does not seem to be substantiated in the research.

From the employees' perspective, there can be less access to training, development, and promotion opportunities, and part-timers, on average, have lower earnings and lower-quality jobs (Lyonette et al. 2010). Part-timers are less likely to perform complex tasks compared to full-timers and full-timers are more likely to find their job intellectually demanding than part-time workers. Research in the UK (in Lyonette et al. 2010) found that 51 per cent of all part-time workers, both male and female, define themselves as working below their potential. This implies a wastage of resources and an underutilization of investments in human capital, with negative implications for the economy because of lost productivity. In the UK there are fewer part-time jobs available in higher-level occupations, meaning part-time working is a potential barrier obtaining more senior positions. The Women and Work Commission found that a shortage of high-quality part-time work across sectors and occupations in the UK means that many women are being crowded into a narrow range of low-paid part-time jobs which do not fully utilize their skills. There is also evidence of occupational downgrading when moving to part-time work which affects more women than men (Lyonette et al. 2010). For example, research shows that a minimum of 14 per cent and probably around 25 per cent of all women who move to part-time work change to an occupation where the average qualification level is below that of their previous full-time work (Connolly and Gregory 2008).

The research thus reveals a complicated and ambiguous picture of part-time work and highlights the 'dualism' of part-time work, which encompasses both good and bad work (Kalleberg 2000). Walsh's (2007) study of women part-time working in the banking sector makes this point well. In her study the vast majority of women were content with part-time work, and not concerned about pay or job security. Nevertheless, there was evidence of dissatisfaction with the work schedules, mandated overtime and difficulties in taking time off which created problems for some women at work and at home. Research among professional women in high-level jobs reports a positive link between part-time employment and their work–life balance (e.g. Hill et al. 2004) whereas reduced working hours have been found to have negative implications for the work–life balance of working-class employees (Lautsch and Scully 2007). However Beham et al.'s (2012) study, referred to earlier, found that those in marginal part-time employment with reduced working hours were the most satisfied.

In practice part-time working appears in many forms and plays different roles for different employee groups. A key conclusion, therefore, must be that part-timers cannot be treated as an homogeneous group.

 CASE STUDY 6.4

Three country comparisons on part-time working

Netherlands

Part-time work is embedded in mainstream employment, and not restricted to marginal jobs. The majority of working females have a part-time job. Although 40 per cent of female part-timers are mothers of young children, almost half are over 40 years old with no young children. Partnered women working part-time are reported to have high job satisfaction and only 3 per cent of

(Continued)

(Continued)

female part-timers would prefer to work full-time (Booth and Van Ours 2010). Most taxes in the Netherlands are neutral to working hours and social security payments are applied to part-time workers on a pro rata basis.

The Netherlands has gradually changed its policy to remove barriers to part-time work and make it more attractive. For example:

- In 1993 the minimum wage and social security applied to jobs with working hours below a third of normal working hours
- A 2000 law established the right to work part-time
- A 2001 reform resulted in women reducing their working hours to receive a higher hourly wage rate after tax.

As a result of these legislative changes, plus increased demand for non-standard hours by employers, part-time working since the 1990s has increased.

UK

The UK is characterized by a long working hours culture, while formal childcare is expensive. For these reasons the UK has one of the highest part-time rates in Europe and is highly gendered. Occupational downgrading for part-time working is common in the UK, and is one of the reasons for a significant gender pay gap.

Previously in the UK, part-timers where often subject to less favourable treatment than full timers. For example, between 1975 and 1995 those working less than eight hours a week were disqualified from many statutory rights, and those working between 8 and 16 hours had to have five years continuous employment to qualify for many employment rights. Part-timers were therefore 'crowded' into the low-wage economy. The Part-time Workers Regulations came into effect in 2000, giving equal contractual rights to part-timers, equal pay and equal benefits. Subsequent UK legislation has introduced the right of parents of young children to request flexible working hours.

Hungary

Until recently part-time working was almost non-existent in Hungary. However, the part-time rate has increased slightly since the Employment Promotion Act of 1991, which allows subsidies for part-time work, although the rate remains significantly below the EU average. There is little difference between male and female part-time rates. The labour market is relatively inflexible with demand and supply concentrated in either eight-hour full-time or four- to six-hour part-time jobs. It is also relatively common to work part-time while also working full-time and receiving full pay on an undeclared basis. This 'pseudo' part-time avoids the need to pay the minimum wage. It is often involuntary, carried out on the basis of oral agreements with the employer, and is found in low-wage industries.

The EU Part-time Directive took effect from 2003 prohibiting the discrimation against part-time workers and makes efforts to avoid the minimum wage legislation through employing 'pseudo' part-time workers illegal. Since 2010 it has been compulsory for public sector organizations to provide part-time employment on a 20 hours a week basis for females returning from maternity leave, until the child is three years old. Childcare provision is free in Hungary although there are concerns that the state-run childcare system will be unable to deal with increased demand as more mothers look to work part-time.

Source: Eurofound (2011).

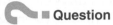 ■ **Question**

1. What are the key differences in part-time working across the Netherlands, UK and Hungary, and why do you think that these differences occur?

Temporary contracts

Many of the criticisms of flexible work concern temporary work. Although there is no universally accepted definition of temporary work, it is generally characterized as work of a limited or fixed duration, and covers a variety of arrangements, including fixed-term contracts, agency workers, and casual work. Zero hours contracts, or on-call workers with no regular or guaranteed hours, could also be included in this category. The growth in temporary employment which began in the 1980s and continued into the 1990s was heralded as 'one of the most spectacular and important evolutions in Western working life' (De Cuyper et al. 2008: 25), although growth since the 1990s has been more slow and recent evidence (presented below) suggests it has stabilized. The biggest growth has been in agency working, which some commentators have seen as the emergence of a 'regime of precarious employment' (e.g. Ward et al. 2001), with the risks of employment being transferred from the employer to the worker.

According to the WERS, 25 per cent of workplaces had some employees on fixed-term or temporary contracts in 2011, a slight increase from 22 per cent in 2004, suggesting some stability in the use of these types of contracts (van Wanrooy et al. 2013). There was also little change in the use of agency workers over these two points in time, with 10 per cent of workplaces using some agency workers in 2011 compared to 12 per cent in 2004. In the UK 6.4 per cent of all employees were contracted to work on a temporary or fixed term basis during the period July–September 2012: 46.9 per cent were males and 53.1 per cent females (Office for National Statistics 2012). Of these just over 40 per cent gave the reason for temporary working as 'could not find a permanent job', suggesting that for many this type of work is involuntary. Historically, the incidence of temporary work has fluctuated with economic conditions, increasing for example in the early 1980s, and reducing and then decreasing again sharply in the early 1990s. WERS 2011 reports that 16 per cent of managers felt that the recession had resulted in a decrease in the use of temporary and agency staff and 3 per cent reported that they had increased their use of these types of contracts (van Wanrooy et al. 2013). It is also seasonal, rising in the summer due to tourism and agriculture. The predictability of business levels also influences the use of temporary workers: where volumes are unpredictable, the proportion of temporary staff is generally higher. The use of temporary labour has also grown across the EU since the 1980s, although this varies across countries (Table 6.6). As with part-time work, however, international comparisons are difficult because of the lack of a universally accepted definition.

The growth in temporary employment has been driven mostly by employers' demands for greater flexibility, and a desire to reduce employment costs and administrative complexity (e.g. Matusik and Hill 1998; Kalleberg et al. 2003; Burgess and Connell 2006; Heywood, Siebert, Wei 2011). In particular, it provides employers with the flexibility to adjust staff levels to demand, cover for staffs short-term absences, deal with one-off tasks (e.g. a project), and provide specialist skills and screen for permanent jobs (Atkinson et al. 1984; EMAR 2008). Other reasons include 'unable to fill vacancies' and 'freeze on permanent staff numbers', reflecting the influence of the state of the economy and labour market. From the employers' perspective there are also disadvantages. Temporary workers are thought to be less reliable than permanent employees, need in-house training and can lack commitment.

Although there is a group of workers who seek temporary jobs, in the main this form of work is not initiated or desired by employees and hence has raised concerns about the impact of temporary work on individuals. The flexible firm model suggests that temporary workers are peripheral workers, and as such are marginalized and disadvantaged. These workers are often in fairly monotonous jobs, lack opportunities for training and development, may have little influence over the design and nature of their work, less involvement in workplace decisions, and receive limited support from co-workers or the union (see Chapter 8). Temporary workers are considered to be more vulnerable than permanent workers in terms of job stress, perceptions of fairness, and feelings of job insecurity (de Cuyper et al. 2008).

An alternative view, however, is that temporary workers have more discretion, choosing how much work and what kind of work they want. For this reason they could be less stressed or overloaded with work compared to permanent employees (Eurofound 2007b). Some employees seek temporary work not because there is no alternative but for other reasons, such as earning during a career break or while studying. Temporary jobs can act as a stepping stone to permanent work by providing an entry point to employment that might not otherwise be available. Research using panel data from the Labour Force survey between 1993 and 2000 (quoted in EMAR 2008) reports that almost half of agency workers make the transition to permanent employment over the course of a year.

Table 6.6 Proportion of persons working part-time and on a fixed-term contract in the EU 2011

	Part-time (All)	Part-time Male	Part-time Female	Employees with a contract of limited duration (age group 15–64)
EU-27	19.5	9	32.1	14
Belgium	25.1	9.8	43.4	8.9
Bulgaria	2.4	2.2	2.6	4.1
Czech Republic	5.5	2.5	9.4	8.0
Denmark	25.9	15.3	37.6	8.9
Germany	26.6	10.3	45.7	14.8
Estonia	10.6	5.6	15.4	4.5
Ireland	23.5	12.8	35.6	9.9
Greece	6.8	4.5	10.2	11.6
Spain	13.8	6.0	23.5	254
France	17.9	6.9	30.1	15.2
Italy	15.5	5.9	29.3	13.4
Cyprus	10	7.5	13.0	13.7
Latvia	9.2	7.5	10.8	6.5
Lithuania	8.7	6.9	10.5	2.8
Luxembourg	18.4	4.8	36.1	7.1
Hungary	6.8	4.7	9.2	8.9
Malta	13.2	6.7	25.7	6.5
Netherlands	49.1	25.4	76.7	18.2
Austria	25.2	8.9	44.0	9.6
Poland	8.0	5.5	11.1	26.9
Portugal	13.3	10.7	16.3	22.2
Romania	10.5	9.6	11.5	1.5
Slovenia	10.4	7.9	13.3	18.0
Slovakia	4.1	2.8	5.9	6.5
Finland	14.9	10.6	19.6	15.5
Sweden	26.0	13.7	39.6	15.9
United Kingdom	26.8	12.7	43.1	6.0
Iceland	20.8	10.4	32.2	12.4
Norway	28.1	14.8	42.8	8.0
Switzerland	35.3	14.5	60.1	12.9
Croatia	9.9	7.9	12.4	12.7
FYR Macedonia	6.3	5.8	7.1	14.8
Turkey	12.0	6.8	24.7	12.2

Source: Eurostat (2013).

De Cuyper et al.'s (2008) comprehensive review of empirical research on the psychological impact of temporary employment reveals inconclusive and contradictory results. For example, some studies show higher job satisfaction among permanent workers than among temporary workers, while others find the opposite pattern, and some find no differences. Similar mixed results are found for organizational commitment, well-being and productive behaviours (e.g. organizational citizenship behaviours). Research by EMAR (2008) on agency workers reports similarly mixed evidence for the satisfaction and well-being of agency works. The evidence on job security is also inconsistent, although it seems possible that those on contracts of choice are less worried about job security.

Various suggestions have been put forward for these puzzling findings, such as the heterogeneity of temporary workers, the methodological shortcomings of the research, and the psychological contract of temporary workers. It is also possible that the positive aspects of temporary work may buffer against the more negative ones. For example, reduced workload may ameloriate the potential negative effects of low autonomy.

Certainly, it is important to note that the category is extremely mixed. It includes skilled professional workers (e.g. doctors, engineers, accountants, teachers) who are likely to enjoy high wages and job autonomy, seek a 'boundaryless career', and are less concerned about job security. This contrasts with low-wage casual workers in agriculture and hospitality sectors who have little employment security. However, in reviewing the evidence on the consequences of contract flexibility, Guest finds that 'the state of the psychological contract of workers on flexible contracts is at least as positive and sometimes more positive than that reported by workers on permanent contracts' (2004: 15). One explanation is that the content of the psychological contract for temporary workers is narrower and more transactional and easier for both sides to monitor than more relational contracts, and that some on temporary contracts prefer it (Guest 2004: 16). It is possible, for example, that temporary workers know that they have no long-term employment security, and adjust their expectations accordingly. In later research comparing contingent and permanent employees Guest and Clinton (2006) found that those on temporary contracts reported better well-being, better general health, more positive attitudes towards work, better work behaviours and a more positive state of psychological contrast than permanent workers. In particular, they reported less violation by the employer of promises and commitments made to them, fairer treatment and more trusting relationships than their permanent counterparts. The interpretation offered for this is the deterioration of the relationship between permanent employees and their employer. Permanent workers reported higher levels of work overload, irritation, anxiety and depression and it is possible that temporary workers had not had long enough in the job to become disillusioned with their employer.

Public policy has also started to improve the position of these types of workers. For example, the EU's Fixed Term Workers Directive, introduced in 2002, protects temporary workers from adverse treatment at work. It also requires employers to give notice to their temporary workers of any permanent vacancies and limits the number of times a fixed-term contract can be renewed. The Agency Workers Regulations introduced in October 2011 give agency workers the same basic terms and conditions of employment as permanent employees after 12 weeks, and some comparable rights from day one.

PIT STOP: REFLECTIVE ACTIVITY 6.4

'Flexicurity'

There has been considerable debate in Europe (public policy and academia) concerning the ability to achieve a balance between labour market flexibility and the security needs of employees, sometimes referred to as the 'flexicurity' debate.

Security has several dimensions (Withagen et al. 2003, in Eurofound 2008). It can include:

- **Job security**, in other words the expectation of high job tenure in relation to a specific job.
- **Employment security**, or the degree of certainty that a worker will remain at work, but not necessarily with the same employer.
- **Income security,** which concerns having a guaranteed income, including protection in the case of, say, illness, unemployment or maternity.
- **Combination security**, which is associated with the possibility for workers to combine work with their private life and other social responsibilities.

 **Questions**

1. Which types of flexible working might meet the needs of each form of security?
2. What are the problems with trying to achieve a balance between the flexibility and security needs of employers and employees?

In summary, the research suggests a fairly complex picture of flexible working, with both positive and negative experiences for workers. Some possible explanations for this have already been put forward, and clearly attitudes will vary depending on individual circumstances and preferences. The example of flexitime in Japan (Case Study 6.5) suggests that this may be welcomed by females and has a positive impact on turnover, but matters less to males. People's reactions will also differ according to their national culture, as highlighted in Case Study 6.6 on work–life balance in China.

CASE STUDY 6.5

Flexitime in Japan

The use of flexitime is quite common in Japan, particularly in urban areas. Many employers have adopted flexitime schemes which have core hours, typically two to five, during which all workers must be at work, but others leave the allocation of working time to the discretion of the employee. Some organizations require employees to get a supervisor's approval in advance (e.g. in the national public service), and others require employees to simply submit their starting and completion times at the end of a given period to confirm that they have worked the predetermined hours. This practice is considered particularly beneficial to employees with small children who go to day care centres, and pregnant workers. The traditional work schedule does not suit many workers given that they can spend up to an hour commuting to their office by train after dropping their children off at a day care centre (on-site day care is not popular in urban areas because this would mean lengthy commutes for children). Pregnant female employees also benefit from flexitime because they can avoid travelling in crowded trains. During the rush hour passengers are packed in commuter trains in urban areas (e.g. Tokyo and its surrounding suburbs). According to one recent government report the average number of passengers in Tokyo reaches 1.7 times the riding capacity during this time.

In a study of family practices in Japan Yanadori and Kato found that flexitime and longer childcare are associated with a decreased turnover of female employees. The same survey, however, found no relationship between this rate and the male turnover rate.

Source: Yanadori and Kato (2009).

Another explanation for these contradictory findings is that the effectiveness of flexible working is contingent on organizational factors such as line management behaviour and organizational culture. These are now considered.

CASE STUDY 6.6

Work–life balance in China

The way that many eastern countries, particularly those in Asia, view work and family is quite different from the way that Western countries perceive them. This is due to cultural traditions, family structures and societal institutions (Hassan 2010). Lu et al.'s (2006) cross-cultural study of work–family demands for British and Taiwanese employees found that people from collectivist cultures (see Chapter 11) see work as a means of supporting the family rather than the self, and thus even when work demands are high they are less likely to generate work–family conflict issues. However, those from individualistic cultures tend to perceive work and family demands as competing for limited personal resources and are less likely to tolerate work–family conflict.

Cooke and Jing's (2009) study found that Chinese organizational leaders, and to a large extent workers, tend to accept work–life conflicts as a fact of life without feeling the need for organizations to address it and that individuals adopt various coping strategies of their own. Although organizations may introduce strategies to deal with long working hours, there is less sympathy towards childcare needs and other family commitments. The managers interviewed in their study held the view that work is important for both the organization and the individual and there is nothing wrong if family life has to be sacrificed. They report on one private accounting firm where the CEO believes that once a woman chooses work she cannot be a good housewife too. Female employees do not get any special treatment in the companies they work for except for the minimum maternity leave stipulated by law.

Money is considered not only the main motivator, but also de-stressor and financial and material rewards have been the mechanisms used to address any work–life conflict (WLC) created by work intensification. The provision of employee welfare and employee entertainment is also a traditional way of improving commitment and morale and enhances productivity. The collectivist and paternalistic culture in China means that the workplace plays an important role in providing social bonding activities to develop harmonious relationships among employees and between the company and its workforce (Chandra 2012). Individuals are also more willing to endure WLC partly because of the traditional Confucian work ethic, in which work and career achievement are more important than family life and self-enjoyment: 'Diligence and self sacrifice, including the family's well-being for public good are praised and glorified. Relaxation is encouraged only in the sense that it contributes to the regeneration of energy for one to work more efficiently' (Chandra 2012: 1043).

Source: author.

Constraints on implementing flexible working

The existence of flexible working policies does not guarantee that employees will take up flexible working, or the success of such arrangements. At the beginning of the chapter it was theorized that the effectiveness of HR practices (including flexible working arrangements) and their implementation were critical to how HRM impacts on performance. Recent research shows that line management behaviour in HRM mediates the effect of HR practices on attitudes and behaviour (Truss 2001; Purcell et al. 2003; Purcell and Hutchinson 2007), and is an important factor in determining the state of the psychological contract and managing employee expectations (Guest and Conway 2004). It follows that the extent to which line managers support and their ability to manage flexible working will partly determine the success of any flexible working policy initiatives, such as employee awareness, policy uptake and policy satisfaction. This is confirmed in surveys of both employers and employees, which point to line managers' attitudes being a significant barrier to flexible working (e.g. IRS 2009; CIPD 2012). Line management awareness of flexible working initiatives in terms of availability, eligibility and specific operational arrangements has been shown to be an important determinant of their intentions and behaviour towards such policies. Bond and Wise (2003) found that knowledge of statutory and company family leave policies is often lacking, partly because of inadequate training. Line managers' attitudes towards the instrumentality and value of such policies will also affect their behaviour (McCarthy et al. 2010). Managing flexible working is also challenging and requires good management skills to reorganize work and communicate with, involve, and empower people. More generally, a lack of time, work overload, role ambiguity and a lack of commitment may constrain line managers' ability to implement flexible working effectively (Hutchinson and Purcell 2010). Essentially this means organizations need to support line managers in managing flexible working.

Other barriers to improving flexible working are operational pressures, costs, maintaining customer requirements, cultural perceptions (e.g. misconceptions about people who want to work flexibly), poor communications, the impact on, and reactions of, staff who do not want to work flexibly, the attitudes of senior managers and an incompatability with the nature of the work itself (e.g. IRS 2009; CIPD 2012; van Wanrooy 2013).

Conclusion

Flexibility in the employment context has been a contentious concept, and there has been ongoing debate in academic circles about whose interests are at stake. The case study introduced at the beginning of this chapter highlighted the tensions in flexibility, raising the question of who (if anyone) benefits from flexible working. This chapter has explored the theoretical arguments for flexibility from both the employers' and the employees' perspective and examined what happens in practice. A model of the HRM causal chain and theory on the psychological contract have provided useful frameworks for this chapter and highlighted the important role of employee attitudes and behaviours in determining organizational outcomes, such as labour flexibility. This has been the focus of the empirical evidence studied in the chapter.

The chapter began by examining the definition of flexibility, which in itself is flexible (Jones et al. 2007). Flexibility is used as an umbrella term to cover a wide range of practices, and has come to mean many different things. But the definition is important because different interpretations have different implications for employers and employees. The narrow definition used in many of the recent reports from public bodies and business and professional groups tends to focus on employee preferences for flexibility and arguably presents a distorted view of practice. In this chapter the preferred definition of flexibility is more wide-ranging, covering working different hours (numerical), at different times (temporal), on different tasks, in different ways (functional), and in different places (geographical).

The evidence presented suggests a fairly complex picture of the practice of flexible working with positive and negative experiences for both employees and employers. Generally, flexible working practices are expected to enable organizations to become more responsive, make more efficient use of their labour and have a positive impact on employees by, for example, improving job satisfaction and commitment, and offering greater autonomy and control and a better work–life balance. But there is evidence of negative outcomes, including increased job insecurity, work intensification, lower-quality work and less access to training. A core conclusion is that these outcomes are shaped by a range of particular organizational and individual factors. These depend on the choices that people have, their expectations and their individual circumstances. Flexibility that gives workers more choice or control is likely to have more positive effects. It also depends on the form that flexible working takes and its implementation. Line managers in particular play a critical role in determining the success or failure of such practices and require support in managing flexible workers.

If employee attitudes are a predictor of performance, as theorized in the model of the HR causal chain, then negative employee reactions will result in negative organizational outcomes and any anticipated gains from implementing flexibility will not be realized. This suggests that rather than talking about flexibility from a singular point of view, it will only be effective if it is something that is shared, with mutual benefits for both employer and employee.

■ Further Reading ■ ■ ■ ■ ■ ■ ■ ■ ■ ■ ■ ■ ■ ■

De Cuyper, N., Jong, J., De Witte, H., Isaksson, K., Rogotti, T. and Schalk, R. (2008) 'Literature review of the theory and research on the psychological impact of temporary employment: towards a conceptual model', *International Journal of Management Reviews*, 10 (1): 25–51.

De Menezes, L.M. and Kelliher, C. (2011) 'Flexible working and performance: a systematic review of the evidence for a business case', *International Journal of Management Reviews*, 13: 452–74.

Delarue, A., Van Hootegem, G., Procter, S. and Burridge, M. (2008) 'Teamworking and organizational performance: a review of survey-based research', *International Journal of Management Reviews*, 10: 127–48.

Family Friendly Working Hours Taskforce (2010) *Flexible Working: Working for Families, Working for Business*. London: The Taskforce, available at http://www.dwp.gov.uk/publications/policy-publications/family-friendly-task-force.shtml, accessed 26 October 2012.

Guest, D. (2004) 'Flexible employment contracts, the psychological contract and employee outcomes: an analysis and review of the evidence', *International Journal of Management Reviews*, 5/6 (1): 1–19.

Kelliher, C. and Anderson, D. (2008) 'For better or for worse? An analysis of how flexible working practices influence employees' perceptions of job quality', *International Journal of Human Resource Management*, 19 (3): 419–31.

Legge, K. (2005) *Human Resource Management: Rhetoric and Realities*, 2nd edn. Basingstoke: Macmillan.

References

Alderfer, C.P. (1972) *Existence, Relatedness and Growth: Human Needs in Organisational Settings*. New York: Free Press.

Alis, D., Karsten, L. and Leopold, J. (2006) 'From gods to goddesses', *Time and Society*, 15 (1): 81–104.

Appelbaum, E., Bailey, T., Berg, P. and Kalleberg, A. (2000) *Manufacturing Advantage: Why High-performance Work Systems Pay Off*. Ithaca, NY: Cornell University Press.

Argyris, C. (1960) *Understanding Organisational Behaviour*. Homewood, IL: Dorsey Press.

Atkinson, C. and Hall, L. (2011) 'Flexible working and happiness in the NHS', *Employee Relations*, 33 (2): 88–105.

Atkinson, J. (1984) 'Manpower strategies for flexible organisations', *Personnel Management*, August, 28–31.

Atkinson, J. (1985) 'Flexibility: planning for the uncertain future', *Manpower Policy and Practice*, 1: 26–31.

Barnett, R.C. and Gareis, K.C. (2002) 'Full-time and reduced-hours work schedules and marital quality', *Work and Occupations*, 29: 364–79.

BBC News (2012) 'Zero hours contracts for NHS staff explained', http://www.bbc.co.uk/news/business-19592412, accessed 23 November 2012.

Beham, B., Prag, P. and Drobnic, S. (2012) 'Who's got the balance? A study of satisfaction with the work–family balance among part time service sector employee in five western European countries', *International Journal of Human Resource Management*, 23 (18): 3725–41.

Berggren, C. (1993) 'Lean production – the end of history?', *Work Employment and Society*, 7 (2): 163–88.

BIS (2012) *Flexible Working*, available at http://webarchive.nationalarchives.gov.uk/+/http://www.bis.gov.uk/policies/higher-education/access-to-professions/prg/latest-trends/flexible-working, accessed 5 December 2013.

Blyton, P. and Morris, J. (1992) 'HRM and the limits of flexibility', in P. Blyton and P. Turnbull (eds), *Reassessing Human Resource Management*. London: Sage, pp. 116–30.

Bond, S. and Wise, S. (2003) 'Family leave policies and devolution to the line', *Personnel Review*, 32 (1): 58–72.

Booth, A.L. and van Ours, J.C. (2010) *Part-time Jobs: What Women Want?*, IZA Discussion Paper 4686. Bonn: IZA.

Boselie, P. (2010) *Strategic Human Resource Management: A Balanced Approach*. London and Columbus, OH: McGraw-Hill.

Boselie. P., Dietz, G. and Boon, C. (2005) 'Commonalties and contradictions in research on human resource management and performance', *Human Resource Management Journal*, 15 (3): 67–94.

Boxall, P. and Purcell, J. (2011) *Strategy and Human Resource Management*, 3rd edn. Basingstoke: Palgrave Macmillan.

Braverman, H. (1974) *Labour and Monopoly Capital: The Degradation of Work in the Twentieth Century*. New York: Monthly Review Press.

Brewster, C., Sparrow, P., Vernon, G. and Houldsworth, E. (2011) *International Performance Management*, 4th edn. London: CIPD.

Buddelmeyer, H., Mourre, G. and Ward, M. (2008) 'Why do Europeans work part time? A cross country panel analysis', *Research in Labour Economics*, 28: 81–139.

Burgess, J. and Connell, J. (2006) 'Temporary work and human resource management issues, challenges and responses', *Personnel Review*, 35 (2): 129–40.

Cappelli, P. and Neumark, D. (2004) 'External churning and internal flexibility: evidence on the functional flexibility and core-periphery hypotheses', *Industrial Relations: A Journal of Economy and Society*, 43: 148–82.

CBI/Harvey Nash (2011) *Navigating Choppy Waters, CBI/Harvey Nash Employment Trends Survey*. London: CBI.

Chandra, V. (2012) 'Work life balance : eastern and western perspectives', *The International Journal of Human Resource Management*, 23 (5): 1040–56.

Churchyard, C. (2009) 'Employers follow KPMG's four day week', *People Management*, 18 June, available at http://www.cipd.co.uk/pm/peoplemanagement/b/weblog/archive/2013/01/29/employers-follow-kpmgs-four-day-week-example-2009-06.aspx, accessed 29 September 2013.

CIPD (2007) *Flexible Working: Good Business: How Small Firms are Doing it*. London: CIPD. Available at http://www.cipd.co.uk/hr-resources/guides/flexible-working-good-business-small-firms.aspx, accessed 5 November 2012.

CIPD (2012) *Flexible Working Provision and Uptake*. London: Chartered Institute of Personnel and Development.

CIPD (2013) *Flexible Working Factsheet*, available at http://www.cipd.co.uk/hr-resources/factsheets/flexible-working.aspx, accessed 16 April 2013.

Collins, A.M., Cartwright, S. and Hislop, D. (2013) 'Homeworking: negotiating the psychological contract', *Human Resource Management Journal*, 23: 211–25.

Connolly, M. and Gregory, M. (2008) 'The part-time pay penalty: earnings trajectories of British women', *Oxford Economic Papers*, 1–22.

Conway, N. and Briner, R. (2004) 'Promises, promises', *People Management*, 25 November.

Cooke, F.F. and Jing, X. (2009) 'Work–life balance in China: sources of conflicts and coping strategies', *NHRD Network Journal* (Work–life balance special issue) 2 (3): 18–28.

Coyle-Shapiro, J.A.-M. and Kessler, I. (2000) 'Consequences of the psychological contract for the employment relationship: a large scale survey', *Journal of Management Studies*, 37 (7): 903–30.

Cusick, J. (2012) 'Health warning over army of NHS "temps"', *The Independent*, 3 September.

De Cieri, H. and Bardoel, E.A. 'What does work life management mean in China and South East Asia for MNCs?', *Community Work and Family*, 12 (2): 179–96.

De Cuyper, N., Jong, J., De Witte, H., Isaksson, K., Rogotti, T. and Schalk, R. (2008) 'Literature review of the theory and research on the psychological impact of temporary employment: towards a conceptual model', *International Journal of Management Reviews*, 10 (1): 25–51.

De Grip, A., Hoevenberg, J. and Willems, E. (1997) 'Atypical employment in the European Union', *International Labor Review*, 136 (1): 49–71.

De Menezes, L.M. and Kelliher, C. (2011) 'Flexible working and performance: a systematic review of the evidence for a business case', *International Journal of Management Reviews*, 13: 452–74.

De Sitter, L.U., Den Hartog, J.F. and Dankbaar, B. (1997) 'From complex organizations with simple jobs to simple organisations with complex jobs', *Human Relations*, 50: 497–534.

Delarue, A., Van Hootegem, G., Procter, S. and Burridge, M. (2008) 'Teamworking and organizational performance: a review of survey-based research', *International Journal of Management Reviews*, 10: 127–48.

DoH (2000) *Working Lives: Programmes for Change*. Leeds: NHS Executive.

Edwards, P. (2006) Non-standard work and labour market re-structuring in the UK. Paper for Associazione Nuovi Lavori conference on 'The Latest in the Labour Market', Rome, 23 February.

Edwards, P. and Wright, M. (1998) 'Human resource management and commitment: a case study of teamworking', in P. Sparrow and M. Marchington (eds), *Human Resource Management: The New Agenda*. London: Pitman, pp. 272–85.

EMAR (Employment Markets Analysis and Research) (2008) *Agency Workers in the UK: A Review of the Evidence*, Employment Relations Research Series No. 93. London: Department for Business Enterprise & Regulatory Reform.

Eurofound (2007a) *Teamwork and High Performance Work Organisations*, available at http://www.eurofound.europa.eu/ewco/reports/TN0507TR01/TN0507TR01.htm, accessed 1 December 2012.

Eurofound (2007b) *Temporary Agency Work in the European Union*, available at http://www.eurofound.europa.eu/ewco/reports/TN0408TR01/TN0408TR01.pdf, accessed 1 December 2012.

Eurofound (2008) *Employment Security and Employability: A Contribution to the Flexicurity Debate*, available at http://www.eurofound.europa.eu/publications/htmlfiles/ef0836.htm, accessed 1 December 2012.

Eurofound (2011) *Part Time Work in Europe: European Company Survey 2009*, available at http://www.eurofound.europa.eu/pubdocs/2010/86/en/3/EF1086EN.pdf, accessed 1 December 2012.

Eurostat (2013) available at http://epp.eurostat.ec.europa.eu/statistics_explained/index.php/Employment_statistics, accessed 28 August 2013.

Fagan, C. and O'Reilly, J. (1998) 'Conceptualising part-time work: the value of an integrated perspective', in J. O'Reilly and C. Fagan (eds), *Part-Time Prospects*. London: Routledge, pp. 1–32.

Family Friendly Working Hours Taskforce (2010) *Flexible Working: Working for Families, Working for Business*. London: The Taskforce, available at http://www.dwp.gov.uk/publications/policy-publications/family-friendly-task-force.shtml, accessed 1 December 2012.

Fried, Y. and Ferris, G.R. (1987) 'The validity of the job characteristics model: A review and meta analysis', *Personnel Psychology*, 40 (2): 287–322.

Fröhlich, D. and Pekruhl, U. (1996) *Direct Participation and Organisational Change – Fashionable but misunderstood? An analysis of recent research in Europe, Japan and the USA*. EF/96/38EN. Luxemburg: Office for the Official Publications of the European Communities.

Gallie, D., White, M., Cheng, Y. and Tomlinson, M. (1998) *Restructuring the Employment Relationship*. Oxford: Oxford University Press.

Geary, J.F. (1994) 'Task participation: enabled or constrained?', in K. Sisson (ed.), *Personnel Management: A Comprehensive Guide to Theory and Practice in Britain*. Oxford: Blackwell, pp. 634–61.

Guest, D. (2004) 'Flexible employment contracts, the psychological contract and employee outcomes: an analysis and review of the evidence', *International Journal of Management Reviews*, 5/6 (1): 1–19.

Guest, D. (2007) 'Human resource management and the worker: towards a new psychological contract?', in P. Boxall, J. Purcell and P. Wright (eds), *The Oxford Handbook of Human Resource Management*. Oxford: Oxford University Press, pp. 128–46.

Guest, D.E. (1987) 'Human resource management and industrial relations', *Journal of Management Studies*, 24 (5): 503–21.

Guest, D.E. and Clinton, M. (2006) *Temporary Employment Contracts, Workers' Well-being and Behaviour: Evidence from the UK*. London: Department of Management Working Paper No. 38, King's College.

Guest, D.E. and Conway, N. (2002) *Pressure at Work and the Psychological Contract*. London: CIPD.

Guest, D. E. and Conway, N. (2004) *Employee Well-being and the Psychological Contract: A report for the CIPD*. London: CIPD

Guest, D.E., Isaksson, K. and De Witte, H. (2010) *Employment Contracts, Psychological Contracts, and Employee Well-being: An International Study*. Oxford: Oxford University Press.

Hackman, J. and Oldham, G. (1976) 'Motivation through design of work', *Organizational Behaviour and Human Performance*, 16 (2): 250–79.

Hackman, J.R. and Oldham, G.R. (1980) *Work Design*. Reading, MA: Addison-Wesley.

Haines, R. (2009) 'Organisational outsourcing and the implications for HRM', in D. G. Collings and G. Wood (eds), *Human Resource Management: A Critical Approach*. Abingdon: Routledge, pp. 92–112.

Hakim, C. (1996) *Key Issues in Women's Work: Female Heterogeneity and the Polarization of Women's Employment*. London: Athlone Press.

Handy, C. (1989) *The Age of Unreason*. London: Hutchinson.

Hassan, Z. (2010) 'Work family conflict in east vs western countries', *Cross Cultural Management: An International Journal*, 17 (1): 30–49.

Herzberg, F. (1959) *The Motivation to Work*. New York: Wiley.

Heywood, J.S., Siebert, W.S. and Wei, X. (2011) 'Estimating the use of agency workers: can family friendly practices reduce their use?', *Industrial Relations*, 50 (3): 535–64.

Hill, J.E., Märtinson, V. and Ferris, M. (2004) 'New-concept part-time employment as a work-family adaptive strategy for women professionals with small children', *Family Relations*, 53: 282–92.

Holmes, K., Ivins, C., Hansom, J., Smeaton, D. and Yaxley, D. (2007) *The Future of Work: Individuals and Workplace Transformation*, Working Paper Series. Manchester: EOC.

Hooker, H., Neathey, F., Casebourne, J. and Munro, M. (2007) *The Third Work–life Balance Employees' Survey: Main Findings*, Employment Relations Research Series No 58. London: Department for Trade and Industry.

Hunter, L., McGregor, A., MacInees, J. and Sproul, A. (1993) 'The flexible firm: strategy and segmentation', *British Journal of Industrial Relations*, 31 (3): 383–409.

Hutchinson, S. and Purcell, J. (2010) 'Managing ward managers for roles in HRM in the NHS: overworked and under-resourced', *Human Resource Management Journal*, 20 (4): 357–74.

Hyman, J. and Mason, B. (1995) *Managing Employee Involvement and Participation*. London: Sage.

Ichniowski, C., Shaw, K. and Prennushi, G. (1997) 'The effects of human resource management practices on productivity: a study of steel finishing lines', *American Economic Review*, 87, 291–313.

IDS (2012) *Flexible Working*, HR studies. London: IDS.

Inman, P. (2013) 'Big rise in firms hiring staff on zero-hours', *The Guardian*, available at www.guardian.co.uk/law/2013/apr/02/rise-staff-zero-hour-contracts, accessed 19 April 2013.

IRS (2009) 'IRS flexible working survey 2009: availability, take-up and impact', *IRS Employment Review*, 921. www. xperthr.co.uk/survey-analysis/its-flexible working-survey-2009-availability-take-up-and-impact/93627/, accessed 16 November 2013.

Jones, A., Visser, F, Coats, D., Bevan, S. and McVerry A. (2007) *Transforming Work: Reviewing the Case for Change and New Ways of Working*. Manchester: Equal Opportunities Commission.

Karau, S.I. and Williams, K.D. (1993) 'Social loafing: a meta-analytic review and theoretical integration', *Journal of Personality and Social Psychology*, 65 (4): 681–706.

Kalleberg, A. (2000) 'Nonstandard employment relations: part-time, temporary and contract work', *Annual Review of Sociology*, 26: 341–65.

Kalleberg, A. Reynolds, J. and Marsden, P.V. (2003) 'Externalizing employment: flexible staffing arrangements in US organisations', *Social Science Research*, 32: 525–52.

Kelliher, C. and Anderson, D. (2008) 'For better of for worse? An analysis of how flexible working practices influence employees' perceptions of job quality', *International Journal of Human Resource Management*, 19 (3): 419–31.

Kersley, B., Alpin, C., Forth, J., Bryson, A., Bewley, H., Dix, G. and Oxenbridge, S. (2006) *Inside the Workplace: Findings from the 2004 Workplace Employment Relations Survey*. London: Department of Trade and Industry.

Lautsch, B.A. and Scully, M.A. (2007) 'Restructuring time: implications of work-hours reductions for the working class', *Human Relations*, 60: 719–43.

Legge, K. (2005) *Human Resource Management: Rhetorics and Realities*. Basingstoke: Macmillan.

Lu, L., Gilmour, R., Kao, S.-F. and Huang, M.-T. (2006) 'A cross-cultural study of work family demands. Work family conflict and well-being: the Taiwanese vs. British', *Career Development International*, 11 (1): 9–27.

Lyonette, C., Badauf, B. and Behle, H. (2010) *'Quality' Part Time Work: A Review of the Evidence*. London: Government Equalities Office.

MacDuffie, J. (1995) 'Human resource bundles and manufacturing performance: organisational logic and flexibly production systems in the world auto industry', *Industrial and Labour Relations Review*, 48: 197–221.

Macky, K. and Boxall, J. (2007) 'The relationship between high performance work practices and employee attitudes: an investigation of additive and interaction effects', *International Journal of Human Resource Management*, 18: 537–67.

Marchington, M. (1992) *Managing the Team: A Guide to Successful Employee Involvement*. Oxford: Blackwell.

Marchington, M. and Wilkinson, A. (2012) *Human Resource Management at Work*. London: CIPD.

Maslow A. (1960) *Motivation and Personality*. New York: Harper Row.

Matusik, S.F. and Hill, C.W.L. (1998) 'The utilization of contingent work, knowledge creation and competitive advantage', *Academy of Management Review*, 23 (4): 680–97.

McCarthy, A., Darcy, C. and Grady, G. (2010) 'Work-life balance policy and practice: understanding line manager attitudes and behaviours', *Human Resource Management Review*, 20 (20): 158–167e.

Mueller, F., Procter, S. and Buchanan, D. (2000) 'Teamworking in its context(s): antecedents, nature and dimensions', *Human Relations*, 53: 1387–424.

Office for National Statistics (2012) *Labour Market Statistics, November*. London: Office for National Statistics.

Pabayo, J.K., Critchley, J.A. and Bambra, C. (2010) *Flexible Working Conditions and their Effects on Employee Health and Well Being*. The Cochrane Collaborations, Wiles.

Parker, M. and Slaughter, J. (1988) 'Management by stress', *Technology Review*, October: 37–44.

Pasmore, W.A. (1988) *Designing Effective Organizations: The Sociotechnical Systems Perspective*. New York: Wiley.

Pfeffer, J. (1998) *The Human Equation*. Boston, MA: Harvard Business School Press.

Polivka, A.E. and Nardonne, T. (1989) 'The definition of "contingent work"', *Monthly Labor Review*, 112: 9–16.

Purcell, J. and Hutchinson, S. (2007) 'Front-line managers as agents in the HRM–performance causal chain: theory, analysis and evidence', *Human Resource Management Journal*, 17 (1): 3–20.

Purcell, J., Kinnie, N., Hutchinson, S., Rayton, B. and Swart, J. (2003) *Understanding the People and Performance Link: Unlocking the Black Box*. London: Chartered Institute of Personnel and Development.

Purcell, J., Kinnie, N., Swart, J., Rayton, B. and Hutchinson, S. (2009) *People and Performance*. Abingdon: Routledge.

Ringelmann, M. (1913) 'Research on animate sources of power: the work of man', *Annales de l'Institut National Agronomique*, 12: 1–40.

Rousseau, D. (1995) *Psychological Contracts in Organizations: Understanding Written and Unwritten Agreements*. London: Sage.

Schein, E. (1978) *Career Dynamics: Matching the Individual and Organizational Needs*. Reading, MA: Addison-Wesley.

Sewell, G. and Wilkinson, B. (1992) 'Empowerment or emasculation? Shopfloor surveillance in a total quality organisation', in P. Blyton and P. Turnbull (eds), *Reassessing Human Resource Management*. London: Sage. pp. 97–115.

Sisson, K. and Storey, K. (2000) *The Realities of Human Resource Management: Managing the Employment Relationship*. Milton Keynes: Open University Press.

Sparrow, P.R. and Cooper, C.L. (2003) *The Employment Relationship: Key Challenges for HR*. Oxford: Butterworth Heinemann.

Tailby, S. (2003) 'Flexibility', in G. Hollinshead, P. Nicholls and S. Tailby (eds), *Employee Relations*, 2nd edn. Harlow: FT Prentice Hall. pp. 489–530.

Taylor, F.W. (1911) *Principles of Scientific Management*. New York: Harper.

Tietze, S. and Nadin, S. (2011) 'The psychological contract and the transition from office based to home based work', *Human Resource Management Journal*, 21 (3): 318–34.

Truss, C. (2001) 'Complexities and controversies in linking HRM with organisational outcomes', *Journal of Management Studies*, 38 (8): 1121–49.

Truss, C., Soane, E., Edwards, C., Wisdom, K., Croll, A. and Burnett, J. (2006) *Working Life: Employee attitudes and engagement 2006*. London: CIPD.

van Wanrooy, B., Bewley, H., Bryson, A., Forth, J., Freeth, S., Stokes L. and Wood, S. (2013) *The 2011 Workplace Employment Relations Study: First Findings*. London: Department for Innovation, Business and Skills.

Walsh, J. (2007) 'Experiencing part-time work: temporal tensions, social relations and the work family interface', *British Journal of Industrial Relations*, 45 (1): 155–77.

Walsh, J. (2013) 'Work-life balance: the end of the "overwork" culture?.' in S. Bach and M. R. Edwards (eds), *Managing Human Resources*, 5th edn. Chichester: Wiley

Ward, K. G., Grimshaw, D., Rubery, J. and Beynon, H. (2001) 'Dilemmas in the management of temporary work agency staff', *Human Resource Management Journal*, 11 (4): 3–21.

Wolff, C. (2009) 'KPMG avoids redundancies through flexible working', *IRS Employment Review*, 924. www.xperthr.co.uk/case-studies/kpmg-aviods-redundncies-through-flexible-working/947700/, accessed 16 November 2013.

Wolff, C. (2010) 'IRS flexible working survey 2010: combating the recession', *IRS Employment Review*. www.xperthr.co.uk/survey-analysis/its-flexible-working-survey-2010-combating-the-recession/100963/, accessed 16 November 2013.

Wood, S. and de Menezes, L.M. (1998) 'High-commitment management in the UK: evidence from the Workplace Industrial Relations Survey and the Employer's Manpower Skills Practices Survey', *Human Relations*, 51 (4): 485–515.

Wood, S., Van Veldhoven, M., Croon, M. and de Menezes, L.M. (2012) 'Enriched job design, high involvement management and organizational performance: the mediating roles of job satisfaction and well-being', *Human Relations*, 65 (4): 419–45.

Wright, P.M. and Nishii, L. (2004) *Strategic HRM and Organisational Behaviour: Integrating Multiple-level Analysis*. Paper presented at the What Next for HRM? Conference, Rotterdam.

Yanadori, Y. and Kato, T. (2009) 'Work and family practices in Japanese firms: their scope, nature and impact on employee turnover', *International Journal of Human Resource Management*, 20 (2): 439–56.

REWARD STRATEGY AND MANAGING PERFORMANCE

Geoff White

Chapter Overview

This chapter covers a major component of strategic human resource management – reward strategy and its link to managing performance. Since the 1990s the US 'New Pay' paradigm has had a major influence on HR practitioner thinking around the world concerning the role of remuneration and benefits in achieving organizational objectives. Reward management, a term coined by writers in the UK but meaning much the same as the 'New Pay', has certainly moved from being a largely administrative function to being seen as a significant lever to improve organizational effectiveness. In this chapter we consider the rise of the 'strategic reward' concept, whether this is largely a prescription for reward design or whether it is a description of actual practice, and review some of the theoretical support for this new approach to remuneration. The chapter then considers the importance of organizational and national cultures in the design of reward systems and describes the key reward components and how they are integrated into a 'total reward' approach, utilizing both intrinsic and extrinsic rewards. Finally the chapter considers the utility of the concept of strategic reward and concludes by reviewing recent research in the UK which has suggested that reward may actually be more about the management of organizational risk than a strategic tool.

≡ Learning Objectives ≡

- **To explore the concepts of reward management, the 'New Pay' and performance management**
- **To explore the theoretical base for reward management and the contribution of economics, psychology and sociology to the subject**
- **To explore the importance of organizational and national cultures in the design of reward systems**
- **To understand the key components of any reward system and how they relate to organizational objectives**
- **To understand and be able to critique the total reward paradigm**

The reform of UK police pay

Police officers provide a unique and vital public service in modern society. Because of the special relationship which the police have with society, the UK government has been keen to ensure their special status as public servants is protected. Arrangements were put in place many decades ago to take police pay and conditions out of contention so that, while police officers are prohibited from taking industrial action against their employers, their pay and conditions are negotiated with representative bodies from the Police Service – the Police Federations – through a Police Negotiating Board chaired by an independent nominee of the government.

In 2011, police pay and conditions remained based on a scheme devised in 1978 by a Committee of Enquiry chaired by Lord Edmund-Davies. This committee decided to index police pay to non-manual worker pay and while the pay formula has changed over time, police pay is still linked to external comparisons. Since 2001 the police service has enjoyed a sustained period of increased funding but that funding will not continue. Given the severity of the economic crisis facing the UK Government and the reduction in public spending, the growth in the police budget must therefore be constrained. The ability of the police service to absorb these savings without reducing effectiveness at the front line is a major challenge. Over 80 per cent of the police budget goes on pay, so the government expects the police service to take immediate and substantial steps to reduce its costs. In June 2010 the UK Government announced a two-year pay freeze for central government departments, including the police service.

In 2010 the government appointed Thomas Winsor to conduct a Review of Police Officer and Staff Remuneration and Conditions (Winsor 2011, 2012). Various attempts at reform of police pay were attempted during the twentieth century, although the last fully implemented review was the Edmund-Davies Review in 1978. Most of these subsequent reviews were prompted by crises in the recruitment and retention of police officers or severe discontent and unrest within the ranks of the police service. In contrast the Winsor Review was established with the clear objective of contributing to reducing the national budget deficit. In addition, the review was also established because police pay and conditions were seen by the Coalition Government as having developed 'a degree of rigidity and a distance from modern management instruments and practices' (Winsor 2011: 16). These rigidities 'inhibit the ability of the police service to adapt to the changing needs of the public and the demands properly made of the police' (Winsor 2011: 16). The terms of reference of the Review stated that it should make recommendations as to the means 'by which the police service might acquire the necessary management flexibility to structure, incentivise and remunerate their workforce in a way which will ensure the greatest efficiency, economy and effectiveness, providing value for money for the taxpayer' (Winsor 2011: 323).

Thomas Winsor adopted a number of principles in making his recommendations on reward changes:

- Fairness is an essential part of any new system of pay and conditions.
- The particular demands of policing work need to be taken into account.
- People should be paid for what they do, the skills they have and are applying in their work, and the weights of the jobs they do.
- People should be paid for how well they work.

(Continued)

(Continued)

- There should be a single police service and distinctions between the conditions of police officers and police staff should be objectively justified.
- The new system should be simple to implement and administer.
- The reforms should be introduced over time so police officers and police staff do not feel threatened and have time to adjust.

The main recommendations of the Winsor Review were as follows:

- Changes in payments for working unsocial hours (20.00 to 06.00).
- Reductions in overtime payments for some staff.
- New, shorter pay scales for constables and sergeants.
- Skills-based pay progression based on rigorous tests of skills, knowledge and experience.
- Contribution-based pay progression based on annual appraisals.
- Abolition of competence-related threshold payments.
- A new power to make police officers open to redundancy.
- A pension age of 60, rather than 55.

A Police Federation spokesman responding to the proposals said that:

Whilst these are merely proposals at this stage we remain extremely disappointed that Tom Winsor's report fails to demonstrate any evidence-based methodology or reasoning ... We expect the Police Negotiating Board will give each proposal the in-depth analysis and consideration it deserves before any decision on any of the proposals is made. To make any changes to police terms and conditions, the unique working arrangements and special relationship the police have in society must at all times be borne in mind. Whilst police officers understand that these are just proposals at this stage, they are putting their last ounce of faith in this government to honour the processes and procedures in place to protect their unique working status ... Many of the proposals put forward in the Winsor Report cause grave concern and consternation amongst the rank and file, particularly as some officers would suffer a pay cut of up to £4,000. It is clear that police officers will be the biggest victims of the financial cuts in the public sector as this would be in addition to a two-year pay freeze and possible increased pension costs. The 20 per cent budget cuts imposed by this government will not only see a reduction in the numbers of officers fighting crime but will also impact on the unique working arrangements of police officers which reflect the dangerous and often thankless job they do. (Police Federation Press release 8 March 2011)

Source: author.

 ■ **Questions**

1. What do you think of the principles adopted in undertaking the Winsor Review? Are they principles that could be applied when designing any reward system?
2. Do you think the suggested changes will meet the objectives of the review?
3. Why do you think the representatives of the police are less than enthusiastic? How could they be encouraged to accept these changes?

Introduction

The effective management of reward and employee performance is increasingly seen as key to any human resources strategy (see Chapter 3). Over the last 30 years there has been a distinct shift from traditional pay administration to a new concept of 'strategic reward', the view that reward systems can be managed in such a way as to provide important signalling mechanisms to employees about what is expected from them in terms of behaviours and what they can expect in return. Central to this is the view that the management of employee performance and the rewards that result must be linked to the strategic objectives of the organization. The concept of strategic remuneration management goes under a number of names – in the USA it has been termed the 'New Pay' or strategic compensation, while in the UK and the rest of Europe the term 'Reward Management' has become more fashionable. As Trevor (2011: 1) argues, 'strategic pay has very rapidly come to represent the "received wisdom" within practice, mirroring the equally rapid ascendancy of theory as the "new orthodoxy"'. This chapter investigates the development of the strategic reward concept and the major elements within a reward system.

In fact the relationship between performance and reward remains hotly debated but the 'effort bargain' (Behrend 1957) – the concept of the reward relationship being one of exchange between the buyers and sellers of labour – remains core. While much of the theoretical underpinning to reward systems increasingly comes from the economics and psychology literatures, the employee relations literature (see Chapter 8) offers equally important and often neglected insights. The potential for conflict in the reward relationship therefore remains inherent in this exchange relationship, and effective performance and reward management continues to be a major risk for employers that must be managed, not just by HR practitioners but by general managers as well. This chapter considers the major dimensions of any reward strategy – in particular issues of market positioning versus internal equity – and the major elements in any reward system, such as grading systems, pay progression methods, incentives and variable pay and employee benefits. The chapter questions the utility of the reward strategy paradigm and explores the concept of 'total reward', which embraces a much wider definition of workplace rewards. The chapter also touches on the importance of organizational and indeed national contexts for the design of reward systems and provides practical guidelines for the HR practitioner.

Definitions of strategic reward

Strategic reward has been defined by a number of writers. For Lawler (2000), the US writer who first popularized the concept of strategic pay, strategic pay

Table 7.1 Traditional versus New Pay

Item	Traditional	Strategic
Reward basis	Job	Person
Market position	High	Based on skills and knowledge
Equity focus	Internal and external	External
Hierarchy	Significant level differences	Minimal level differences
Contract	Loyalty and entitlement	Employability and performance

Source: Lawler (2000). Reproduced by kind permission of Jossey Bass Inc.

is defined in relation to traditional pay under five elements (see Table 7.1). Strategic pay is seen as person-centred rather than job-centred, based on the market value of skills and knowledge, externally referenced rather than internally, non-hierarchically focused, and with the emphasis on employability and performance rather than loyalty and entitlement. For Armstrong and Brown (2006: 7), strategic reward management is about the 'development and implementation of reward strategies and the philosophies and guiding principles that underpin them'. For Armstrong and Murlis (2007: 3), reward management is defined as: 'the formulation and implementation of strategies and policies that aim to reward people fairly, equitably and consistently in accordance with their value to the organisation'. For Trevor (2011: 8) the strategic pay concept is summarized as being 'positioned as a means of enhancing company performance and securing competitive advantage, through the alignment of pay strategies, systems practices and processes to the organisational strategy'.

All of these definitions indicate that strategic reward is different from previous pay policies and practices, but the concept of devising a pay system to meet organizational needs is nothing new. The debate between the contingency approach, which argues that the design of reward systems should be based on organizational context and requirements, as opposed to the concept of 'best practice' (see Chapter 3) under which there are favoured options which fit all circumstances, has been around for years.

In their seminal book *Selecting a Wage Payment System*, Lupton and Gowler (1969: 8) set out four questions to be asked when designing a reward system. These were:

- What should the objectives of a firm be when installing or modifying a payment scheme?
- What payment schemes are available to choose from?
- How should a firm go about deciding which of the available schemes is best suited to its circumstances?
- Which of the available schemes satisfies its objectives?

These questions seem to suggest a linkage of pay systems to organizational objectives (Chapter 1) and context (i.e. organizational strategy) but, interestingly, Lupton and Gowler went on to say that: 'Although a firm may have in mind to look for something suitable to its own circumstances, it is also rare for these circumstances to be sharply and fully defined, let alone measured' (Lupton and Gowler 1969: 8). This statement suggested that in the period in which that book was written, there was little evidence of employers taking such a strategic approach. As we will discuss later in this chapter, there is still debate as to how prevalent strategic reward is today, or indeed the utility of such a concept.

The change from traditional to strategic pay

In the period in which Lupton and Gowler (1969) were writing their book, remuneration systems were largely divided along traditional lines between those for manual or blue-collar workers (then the majority of the workforce) and those for staff or white-collar workers. The former emphasized contingent payment systems and payment by results, with little in the way of security of earnings and minimal employee benefits. The latter emphasized a more best practice approach – security of earnings, status, loyalty, seniority and substantial employee benefits. It was also a world in which the majority of the workforce had their pay determined through collective bargaining between employers and trade unions (see Chapter 8). Pay management was largely about administering the outcomes of these collective agreements and there was little concern about competitive advantage between employers. Because of the strength of trade unions, employers were more interested in working together in multi-employer negotiations with the unions to determine industry-wide pay levels and norms than in establishing remuneration systems that were unique to themselves. Even in non-union firms, there was often a strong concern for internal equity through the use of job evaluation and rigid grading schemes – sometimes as a means to keep unions out of the organization.

This relatively stable and settled picture began to change in the 1970s as the post-Second World War global economic system broke down. In most of the developed countries there was a substantial switch from manufacturing to service-based industries and international competition led to a substantial decline in the traditional manufacturing jobs for unskilled and semi-skilled workers. This in turn led to a considerable shift in the balance of employment for male and female workers, with a large increase in employment opportunities for women, especially in part-time work. This growth of female employment led in turn to new concerns about gender discrimination and equal pay for men and women (see Chapter 9).

The decline in manufacturing industry led to a decline in the membership of traditional trade unions organizing skilled and unskilled workers, although the growth of new jobs in an enlarged public sector and financial services compensated the unions to some extent. With the decline of trade unions the prevalence of industry-wide pay determination also declined and employers, at least in the private sector, increasingly began to see advantages in fixing pay at an organizational or workplace level, rather than in concert with other employers. There is evidence of a clear shift from pay being determined at the industry level in 1998 to unilateral pay determination by employers alone and increasingly centralizing pay decisions at a firm level.

The corollary of this decline in collectively bargaining pay has been a marked change in the power of employers to dictate the form of pay determination. As Trevor (2011: 6) comments: 'Never before in post-war Britain have employers enjoyed as much freedom to determine the basis of employee pay unilaterally and in the interests of achieving purely managerial ends.'

PIT STOP: REFLECTIVE ACTIVITY 7.1

1. What factors could explain the shift from traditional pay administration to a more strategic approach to reward over the last 30 years?

At the same time as this economic change was taking place, the Human Resource Management (HRM) concept was developing as a new guide to the management of people in enterprises (see Chapters 1 and 3). The HRM model emphasized the importance of effective management of employment to achieve competitive advantage and the importance of a strategic plan which linked organizational objectives with HR policies and practice (see Guest 1990; Storey 1992; Sisson 1994; Legge 1995 for a discussion of HRM concepts). The Michigan school of HRM (exemplified by Fombrun et al. 1984) in the USA argued the importance of linking organizational HR strategy to business strategy and prioritizing business needs over employee interests – so-called 'hard HRM'. In contrast the Harvard school (exemplified by Beer et al. 1984), also in the USA, argued that workers could not be treated as a 'resource' in the same way as other resources and needed to be engaged with the organizational strategy if it was to be effective – so-called 'soft HRM'. Both models, however, stressed the importance of HR strategy being linked to organizational strategy. The New Pay was an integral part of this new model of people management.

The term New Pay was first used by the US management writer Edward Lawler in 1990 (Lawler 1990) and later developed by others such as Schuster and Zingheim (1992) and Gomez-Mejia and Balkin (1993). The core message of the New Pay paradigm was that remuneration needed to be linked to business strategy and to corporate objectives. As Lawler (1995: 14), comments: 'The new pay argues in favour of a pay-design process that starts with business strategy and organizational design. It argues against an assumption that certain best practices must be incorporated into a company's approach to pay'.

The new approach was designed to challenge traditional approaches to pay management such as job evaluation, across the board cost of living increases and external referencing of pay levels (Schuster and Zingheim 1992). The New Pay, in contrast, begins with the premise that pay needs to vary in line with individual, group and organizational performance. Rewards should be contingent on the achievement of business objectives and risks should be shared between employers and employees. The key to this was the shift from traditional pay systems which were exemplified by the concept of the 'job' (through job evaluation, grading systems and 'rate for the job') to new 'person-related' structures which emphasized the value of the individual worker, rather than the job done. This concept fitted neatly with the decline of collectivist pay determination systems and the increasing use of employer discretion in setting pay levels. As Mahoney (1992: 338) argues, 'the concept of job was the unifying concept in the Scientific Management approach to organisation and management ... the development and application of a concept of job ownership expressed in the labour movement and collective bargaining'. Another key facet of the new pay paradigm is emphasized by Gomez-Mejia and Balkin (1993: 14) who argue that it is based on a strategic orientation 'where issues of internal equity and external equity are viewed as secondary to the firm's need to use pay as an essential integrating and signalling mechanism to achieve over-arching business objectives'.

Three important aspects of the new pay have been identified by Heery (1996) from the context of employee relations. First, the ratio of variable pay to fixed is shifted in favour of the former, reducing the amount of guaranteed pay for the worker. In 1994 the Confederation of British Industry (CBI) saw the great attraction in variable pay in that 'it can go up and, crucially, down in line with individual, group or company performance' (CBI/Wyatt 1994: 5). There was also an emphasis on reducing indirect remuneration (i.e. staff benefits) to free up more cash for variable pay. The second aspect identified by Heery was that the scope of variable pay could be expanded to reflect a number of levels of corporate performance. Lastly, New Pay emphasized the importance of the value of the individual employee rather than the content of the job done. Hence the New Pay writers see job evaluation and the associated narrow banded grading structures as inimical to strategic reward. Instead, they advocate systems where employers have much more freedom to appoint and progress individual workers in line with their market worth.

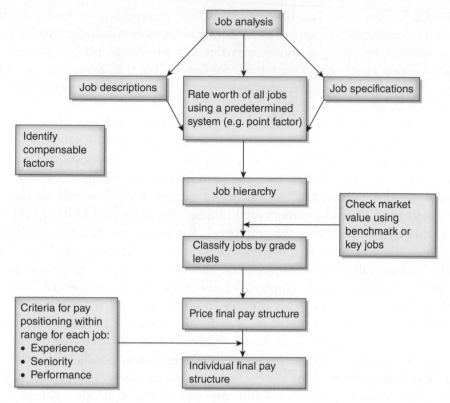

Figure 7.1 Traditional compensation model

Source: Gomez-Mejia et al. (2010). Reproduced by kind permission of M.E. Sharpe Inc.

≡≡≡ **PIT STOP: REFLECTIVE ACTIVITY 7.2** ≡≡≡

1. What is meant by 'New Pay' and what are the advantages for organizations of such an approach to pay?

In the UK the development of the 'reward management' concept is closely connected with the US New Pay paradigm. While the term 'reward management' was coined by Armstrong and Murlis (1988), John Child had used the term 'reward policies' earlier in his book *Organization* (Child 1984). In Child's words:

> For management the criterion of success for reward policies is that they motivate employees to commit high levels of physical or mental effort towards performing tasks well. A condition for their success is also that the employees concerned regard the rewards offered to them as attractive and fair, and any punishments as legitimate and merited.

The concept of reward management has been further developed by Brown (2001) and Armstrong and Brown (2006). For Armstrong and Brown the rationale for a strategic approach to pay is to ensure that results and behaviours are in line with the key goals and behavioural standards of the organization. According to Armstrong and Murlis (2007) the aims of strategic reward are as follows:

- To support the achievement of the organization's strategic and shorter-term objectives.
- To assist with the communication of organizational values and performance expectations.
- To promote the organization's culture and support change.
- To drive and support desired behaviours.
- To encourage value-added performance.
- To promote continuous development.
- To compete in the employment market.
- To motivate all members of the organization from the shopfloor to the boardroom.
- To promote teamwork.
- To promote flexibility.
- To provide value for money.
- To achieve fairness and equity.

Key underpinning reward theory

Reward management is based primarily on two bodies of theoretical literature – economics and social psychology. These two bodies of theory provide the twin pillars of reward strategy – on the one hand economics provides the theory of the labour market and its role in fixing pay levels between employers and employees, and on the other hand psychology provides its insights into human behaviour and how employees are motivated to perform in the employers' interests.

Key to our understanding is the concept of internal and external markets for labour. Classical economic theory argues that the price of labour is fixed where the supply of labour intersects with the demand for labour. Once all the demand has been met, wage equilibrium will result. Under this theory, workers in similar jobs with similar levels of skill will all end up being paid at the same wage level. No individual employer or employee has the power to disrupt this 'going rate'. In reality, however, such a system would require a perfect competition with both employers and employees knowing exactly what was being paid where and when. Observations of the labour market, however, show that there are wide variations in the price of labour for the same jobs within the same industry. Nonetheless, the power of the external labour market remains strong in reward design, and benchmarking pay data against competitors is a major part of the reward manager's role in ensuring that the organization continues to recruit and retain its workforce.

The alternative to the external labour market is the so-called internal 'labour market', although in reality this is a closed market and not really affected by external competition. In an internal labour market, employers seek to ensure the retention of labour by providing firm-specific training in skills (see Chapter 10) which are difficult to replicate elsewhere. Moreover, there is an emphasis on strong internal grading systems that provide equitable rewards for employees of the same level of skill or knowledge. In the internal market the emphasis is on equity, security of employment and career development within the firm. All of this is designed to protect the organization from having its staff 'poached' by competitors. Job evaluation and hierarchical career structures, with their emphasis on internal equity, are the product of such internal markets. Such internal markets became popular in large private sector firms in the 1920s and 1930s as employers sought to protect themselves and their workers from the effects of the external market, but in more recent times there has been a decline in such organizational forms. The external labour market has become more important in the private sector but such closed 'internal' labour markets remain for many public service professionals such as doctors, nurses and teachers where the state has more or less a monopoly on their employment.

Economists have attempted to explain why the simple supply and demand model does not appear to work in practice. Alternatives to the classical economic model of the labour market include human capital theory, exchange theory, efficiency wage theory and principal-agent theory. Human capital theory (Becker 1957) is based on the concept that individuals acquire human capital by investing time and money in education, training and experience that increase their productive capability and hence their value within the labour market. Competition between organizations for this skilled labour requires employers to pay more for the skills they wish to acquire and go beyond simple market-clearing mechanisms. In this model the employee becomes an investment for the employer. Exchange theory is based on the concept of a bargain struck between the employer and worker – traditionally the concept of 'a fair day's pay for a fair day's work'. The issues involved in valuing the different skills and the transaction costs incurred in using them have led to the concept of the flexible labour market (see Chapter 6), in which the core permanent workforce has more investment by the employer than the peripheral (casual) workforce, which can be dispensed with in hard economic times. Efficiency wage theory also attempts to explain why employers will often pay more than the market rate for particular skills. Under this theory, employers assume that employees will use their human capital to seek out the best possible pay rates, but this creates unacceptable transaction costs for the employer in having to constantly replace labour. Employers therefore seek to pay above market rates to ensure that their workers are retained. The argument is that workers will also perform better if they feel they are being better paid and will also be concerned not to lose this above-market pay, providing a disciplinary effect. Therefore paying more than is strictly necessary in the external market is seen as efficient in the longer term. Principal-agent theory or agency theory was originally based on the relationship between owners of enterprises and their managers but has now been extended to the relationship of managers with workers. The theory states that while base pay levels may be set at below-market levels, the employer (the principal) ensures the coalition of their own and the worker's (agent) interest through providing opportunities for above-market total pay via higher performance and meeting specific targets.

Turning to the psychology literature, its major contribution to reward practice has been its understanding of employee behaviour and particularly motivation. Unlike the economics literature, which views human behaviour as the rational pursuit of self-interest, the psychologists argue that human behaviour is based on more complex factors. Central to our understanding of motivation is the difference between intrinsic and extrinsic motivation. Herzberg's two-factor theory argued that these two forms of motivation were exclusive, and Maslow arranged them into a 'hierarchy of needs'. For Herzberg there were specific factors or conditions that led to motivation and others which, while necessary as 'hygiene factors', did not motivate. For Maslow there was a hierarchy of human needs that moved from basic 'extrinsic' rewards to higher level intrinsic rewards and finally 'self-actualization'. In general, these writers saw pay as a hygiene factor rather than a motivator. The issues of extrinsic versus intrinsic motivation and their relationship to reward continue to fuel debate, and the 'total reward' concept is the latest theoretical contribution to this controversy (Franco-Santos and Gomez-Mejia 2012).

These early 'content theories' were largely about explaining *what* motivates individuals. The later 'process theory' writers concentrated more on the process of *how* individuals are motivated. Some of this theory was based on early experiments on the conditioning of animals and concentrated on the concept of employees learning through experience that certain types of behaviour were rewarded while others were not. For example, Skinner's reinforcement theory (Skinner 1953) argued that employee behaviour could be shaped by positive reinforcement of the correct behaviours. According to this theory, managers can 'educate' employees into the required behaviours by means of rewards.

In contrast the cognitive theories of motivation argue that employees are conscious individuals who make rational choices based on their past lived experiences. Examples of such cognitive theories are goal-setting (Locke et al. 1981), expectancy theory (Vroom 1964) and equity theory (Adams 1965). Goal-setting theory argues that, in order to perform effectively, employees have

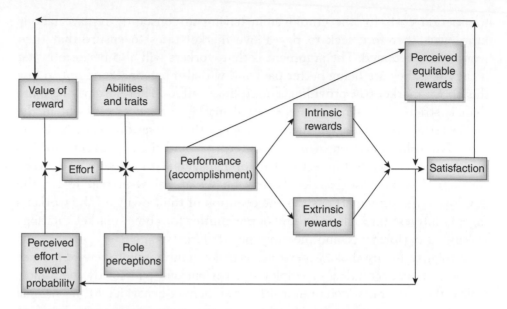

Figure 7.2 The Porter-Lawler expectancy model of work motivation
Source: Porter and Lawler (1968).

to have clear ideas about their role and the expectations of their managers. Expectancy theory argues that future expectations govern current behaviour and that employees can be incentivised to perform. For example, if employees perceive that high productivity will lead to personal goal achievement, then they will improve their performance (the reverse of course is also the case). Equity theory is based on the argument that humans have a perception of fair treatment and that the success of incentives to perform will depend on the degree to which the results are seen as congruent with the effort expended.

Porter and Lawler (1968) developed Vroom's expectancy theory to include other dimensions based on active self-reflection by individuals on their abilities and other traits, the perceived nature of the role or task to be performed, and the degree of equity attributed to both extrinsic and intrinsic rewards likely to result. The Porter and Lawler model is shown in diagrammatic form in Figure 7.2.

As Child (1984: 184) comments:

> From a practical point of view, the utility of the (expectancy) model lies in the way that it draws attention to basic conditions which have to be met for rewards to assist in matching motivation to contingent requirements ... these requirements are that: 1) employees must expect that additional effort leads to higher performance; 2) they must perceive that higher performance leads to greater rewards, and 3) they must attach value to some reward outcomes rather than others; that is, not be indifferent as to the rewards they receive.

Clearly strategic reward, with its aim that rewards should be managed in line with organizational objectives, draws heavily upon expectancy theory.

═══════════ **PIT STOP: REFLECTIVE ACTIVITY 7.3** ═══════════

1. How important a motivator would pay be for you in your working life?
2. How would it compare to other motivating factors?
3. How might your priorities change over your working life?

The major determinants of reward

Mahoney (1992) has argued that there are three main contingencies in making decisions about reward – job, person and performance. The job is the essential building block for designing reward structures – jobs are the major way in which value is attributed to particular skills or tasks. Hence the development of job analysis and job evaluation to value jobs or roles in the process of creating fair and equitable pay structures.

The process of creating a pay structure has been driven by the concept of internal equity, the need for pay levels to be linked in some way to the content of the job so that employees feel that their positioning within that structure is fair and expected. In the past, such grading structures were relatively simple and related to skill levels (usually skilled, semi-skilled and unskilled) but the development of job evaluation techniques in the USA in the 1920s and 1930s led to a much more complex codification of job levels, based on quasi-scientific methods. The development of job evaluation as a tool to rate jobs was very much a part of the creation of strong internal labour markets by large US corporations (see the earlier section on reward theories). It was also an attempt to thwart the rise of trade unions and bargaining over job prices, although in time unions came to embrace job evaluation as a means of enforcing job equity (the 'rate for the job'). In Europe job evaluation has also become associated with equal pay for work of equal value concerns – such schemes are seen as a defence against legal challenges about gender bias in the fixing of pay levels (see Chapter 9 on equality and diversity).

As Kessler (2005: 320) points out, however: 'If a job is the basis for establishing the grading structure, a pay system is the mechanism used to drive pay movements once the post and the individual filling it have been placed in the structure.' Kessler (2007: 161) also makes the useful distinction that 'the relationship between business strategy and pay can be seen to equate more directly to person and performance than to job'.

Traditionally reward systems have been required to meet two competing demands – on the one hand the creation of a method for allocating rewards that is seen as internally fair and equitable and, on the other hand, a method for maintaining pay levels at a sufficient level to attract, retain and motivate employees. These two demands create a dynamic tension between equity and market – one or other of these will predominate in different types of labour market at different times, but the tension is always present. Unfortunately, while an organization can use techniques such as job evaluation to rate the value of particular jobs or roles and then attach monetary values to each level, there is always a differential demand for different types of worker in the external market. For example, accountants and HR managers may be deemed to have the same job weight under a job evaluation scheme but they may have very different external salary levels for their work. The great skill of the HR practitioner is to balance these competing demands in the design of the reward system.

The other determinants of pay design relate to the external environment. The baseline for the design process in any country is the legal framework governing employment, especially that governing pay (e.g. minimum wage law, collective bargaining law, equal pay and discrimination law) but also tax law often plays a part in how benefits are treated. In the UK there are significant legal constraints in the design of reward systems but less in the form of legal requirements concerning collective bargaining. The major areas of regulation concerning reward in the UK are as follows:

- Contracts of employment
- The National Minimum Wage
- Hours of work, holidays and time off
- Equal pay for work of equal value
- Discrimination concerning gender, race, religion, disability, age and employment status
- The law affecting the employee benefits package
- The law affecting pension schemes and pension provision by employers.

In the USA there is a significant legal divide between those employees covered by collective agreements and the rest of the workforce who are covered by 'employment at will' (basically the employer and employee are free to end the employment relationship without contractual penalties). Much of Europe has significant legal regulation of the reward relationship, and much of this law is now determined at a European-wide level.

There are also significant differences in the approach to reward between different types of organization and industry, in particular between private for-profit organizations and those in the public and private not-for-profit sectors. Hence there tend to be sector and industry 'norms', although the barriers between the main sectors of the economy have gradually become more permeable. In general terms there are still, however, significant differences in the approach to reward for high-paid and low-paid workers, between industries (e.g. finance versus retail) and between different occupational groups (e.g. craft workers versus accountants).

Lastly, national culture (see Chapter 11) has also been found to have an influence over reward design. In a seminal article, Gomez-Mejia and Welbourne (1991) attempted to use Hofstede's (1980) cultural variables to theorize about how national cultures might influence the choice of reward strategies. They concluded that using cultural theory to design reward systems was problematic, and that corporate culture probably had more impact. This is especially the case in terms of differences between multinational corporations, which tend to reflect the home country's reward philosophy, and domestic employers who tend to reflect more the local culture and traditions (Guest and Hoque 1996; Ferner and Quintanilla 1998). Much of the reward literature emanates from North America, which may reflect values and traditions that differ from other societies, as evidenced by the clear philosophical dichotomy between American and European reward practices. As Sparrow and Hiltrop (1994) noted, the Anglo-Saxon approach to variable pay systems is rather different to the European – for example American and UK managers tend to assume a linkage between variable pay and corporate performance because of their cultural inclination towards short-termism while European managers, with a culture of longer-term perspectives, are more cautious about the claims for such pay systems. The Dutch management writer Fons Trompenars argues that, while it may be possible to have 'a universal rule that success must be rewarded commensurate with its size … the difficulty is that (managers) all mean different things by pay and different things by performance' (Trompenars 1993: 176). Mamman et al. (1996) found that there were clear differences in the perception of different reward components between countries. Research into how three international banks operated broad international reward strategies in London and Hong Kong found that while there was general alignment in terms of broad principles, a number of differences in interpretation of the strategy at a country level were evident, most importantly in the way in which performance was rewarded (White et al. 1998).

On the other hand, a literature review of the strategic HRM perspective on international compensation (Bloom and Milkovich 1998: 8) concluded that:

While studies of national culture and national business models may be an important first step in understanding international compensation and reward systems, they face the same serious limitations as traditional comparative models of HRM … that national borders largely define the important contextual features (e.g. national economic, demographic and cultural conditions) that the differences between nations are greater and more salient to understanding international compensation than differences within nations.

Performance management

Central to the strategic reward paradigm is the linkage between an organization's performance management system and its reward system. If no performance management system exists it is hard to envisage how reward can meet the strategic imperative.

A performance management system requires a system of clear performance targets, a system of measurement of performance and a clear linkage of performance results to reward. An important theoretical frame for understanding the importance of the performance management process is the concept of 'procedural justice' versus 'distributive justice' (Cropanzano and Folger 1996). Procedural justice is defined as the fairness of the procedures used to allocate rewards whereas distributive justice is the perception of the value of the actual rewards received. In general, if an employer manages to get the procedural justice right then it is more likely that employees will accept the distributive justice of the rewards received. Marsden comments that

> employees are more likely to withdraw performance if they feel that management violate procedural justice norms when operating their reward systems. This failure of alignment between procedural justice and distributive justice can be caused by a number of things: the inability of managers to set realizable goals and review employee's performance properly; when managers are not acting in good faith; when the performance criteria contradict employees' own values and experience; and when management's concept of motivation is not in alignment with employees' sense of value and achievement. (Marsden 2007: 112)

Bach (2005) indicates that in the UK there has been a general shift away from simply having individual staff appraisals towards a wider concept of performance management, with much more alignment with the organizational context and strategy and much more emphasis upon the role of line managers in managing performance.

Five objectives for a performance management system have been identified by Armstrong and Baron (2005: 17):

- To communicate a shared vision of the organization's purpose and values
- To define expectations of what employees need to deliver and how it should be delivered
- To ensure that employees are aware of what constitutes high performance and how it can be achieved
- To enhance motivation, engagement and commitment by providing a mechanism for recognizing endeavour and achievement through feedback
- To enable employees to monitor their own performance and encourage dialogue about what needs to be done to improve.

The use of performance appraisals in the UK has been increasing. According to the 2004 Workplace Employee Relations Survey (WERS), 78 per cent of workplaces reported undertaking performance appraisals in 2004, compared to 73 per cent in 1998 (Kersley et al. 2006). Two-thirds of all workplaces reported regularly conducting appraisals for most non-managerial employees. Most appraisals were conducted on an annual basis, and 16 per cent conducted them more frequently. These were undertaken by the employee's line manager in the great majority of workplaces and most included an appraisal of training needs (see Chapter 10). Only a third of workplaces linked their appraisals to pay.

There are usually four stages to the performance management process. The first stage is the performance planning meeting where objectives are agreed between the manager and employee. The agreed performance plan forms the basis for a later evaluation of the employee's performance. Such a plan usually includes individual objectives; competencies and behaviours; and personal development plans (IDS 2007). The second stage is about evaluating progress, involving an interim formal review and feedback to the employee by the manager and, if necessary, some adjustment of the plan. The third stage is the annual appraisal where the line manager and employee review the evidence. In general it is easier to evaluate performance against quantitative measures of achievement of agreed tasks or goals than against more qualitative evidence such as competences or behaviours. The latter is often subject to manager perceptions or those of colleagues, rather than 'hard evidence', although organizations may provide guidance on these issues. The fourth stage is the rating of individual performance, which is especially important if the outcomes of the appraisal are to be linked to reward. Research by IDS (2007) found that there are essentially three core levels of performance used in organizations:

- 'Exceptional' or 'exceeds expectations'
- 'Effective' or 'meets expectations'
- 'Not effective' or 'below expectations'.

The number of ratings on the performance scale usually range from four to five. In some cases there may be separate scales for the achievement of objectives and for competences displayed. Ratings can send important messages to staff about their performance but they have been recognized as potentially de-motivating, especially where the appraisal is poorly managed by the manager.

One popular method of measuring performance is the 'balanced scorecard' approach (see Chapter 4), developed by Kaplan and Norton (1996). This approach uses four related criteria for measuring performance: how should we appear to our customers, how should we appear to our shareholders, what business process must we excel at, and how will we sustain our ability to change and improve?

Performance management at Microsoft

Introduction

Microsoft once dominated the hi-tech industry and was the wealthiest corporation in the world. But since 2000, its competitors Apple, Facebook and Google have overtaken it and Microsoft has, according to ex-Microsoft executive Kurt Eichenwald, fallen flat in almost every new product area it entered. In January 2012 Microsoft's CEO Steve Ballmer announced at the International Consumer Electronics Show in Las Vegas that his company's presentation would be its final keynote at the show. He argued that the timing for announcements of its new products did not match the timetable of the annual show.

In the words of Kurt Eichenwald, Microsoft's swan song was 'nothing if not symbolic of of more than a decade littered with errors, missed opportunities and the devolution of one of the industry's innovators into a "me too" purveyor of other companies' products' (Eichenwald 2012). While other firms forged ahead with social media products, Microsoft relied on its established product range – Windows, Office and servers – for its financial performance.

This business performance was reflected in Microsoft's stock price – despite booming sales and profits from its flagship products, over the last decade Microsoft's stock barely shifted from around $30, while Apple's stock is now worth 20 times what it was ten years ago. In December 2000 Microsoft had a market capitalization of $510 billion, making it the world's most valuable company, but by June 2012 it was number three, worth $249 billion. In contrast Apple was worth $541 billion and had become number one. The Apple iPhone evidently brings in more revenue than the whole of Microsoft's entire product range.

In the words of Eichenwald, 'the story of Microsoft's lost decade could serve as a business school case study on the pitfalls of success' (Eichenwald 2012). In this case study, based on Eichenwald's 2012 *Vanity Fair* magazine article, we review the business decisions that may have led to the decline of Microsoft and especially the management of reward at the company.

The growth of Microsoft

Microsoft began when two friends, Paul Allen and Bill Gates, decided that their long-term desire to design an operating system using BASIC computer language was finally possible with the launch of the first minicomputer. They wrote a computer programme called Altair BASIC and persuaded the company that made the mini-computer – MITS – to license it. They named their new company Micro-soft, and as the market for personal computers grew rapidly they sold their product to bigger and bigger companies. Within two years Microsoft, as it was now named, was setting the standards for microprocessor programming. In 1980 IBM – then the world leader in computer manufacture – decided to use Microsoft to write the software for its new IBM PC.

The company started to double and triple in size every year as the operating systems grew increasingly sophisticated – from MS-DOS to Windows, which shifted from a text-based system to a graphic interface. In August 1995 the company reached its peak when it launched Windows 95. By the end of 1997 Windows 95, along with Microsoft's other operating systems, was running almost 90 per cent of the computers in the USA. Bill Gates had become the richest man in the world, worth $6.8 billion.

So what went wrong?

According to Eichenwald (2012), although Microsoft's problems stemmed from too much reliance on its successful products and a failure to embrace new emerging technologies such as the e-book and smartphone, a more important issue was corporate culture. In its early days, Microsoft had a corporate culture of employee involvement in the company. Almost every employee had a stake in the company through stock options so that everyone benefitted when the share price rose. Many of the long time executives grew wealthy and therefore let new employees take over their work while they rested and waited for the vesting period when they could exercise their share options.

Then, in December 1997, Microsoft stock reached its all-time high and then collapsed as part of the effect of the bursting of the 'dot-com bubble'. Bill Gates resigned as CEO and handed the reins to Steve Ballmer, the company's previous executive responsible for the financial and sales side of the business. Within a year the company had lost half its value and the stock options no longer worked as motivators for employees. An increasing divide emerged between the old guard of original Microsoft engineers and developers and the newer generation of employees. Major foci for staff dissatisfaction was the ending of the provision of towels in the company showers to save money and the abandoning of the company's 'gold-plated' health insurance plan. Whereas in the past employees had been able to enjoy job satisfaction and earn good money through creating innovations, now the only way to career advancement was through promotions. As one former senior executive is quoted as saying, 'They turned into people trying to move up the ladder, rather than people trying to a make a big contribution to the firm' (Eichenwald 2012). More employees seeking management roles led to more managers, more meetings and more memos, and more red tape led to less innovation.

One issue was that the technology stars who had joined the company in the 1980s in their 20s and 30s were now middle-aged managers in their 40s and 50s – and they were out of touch with the demands of an increasingly youth-oriented market for gadgets.

By 2002 a by-product of this bureaucracy had emerged at Microsoft – 'brutal corporate politics'. Employees were competing with each other – for promotions, bonuses or just survival – instead of working together for the good of the company. At the centre of this problem was a reward practice called 'stack ranking'.

The 'stack ranking model' and its effects

'Stack ranking' was seen by almost all Microsoft employees interviewed by Eichenwald as the most destructive process inside the company. The system – also known as the 'performance model', the 'bell curve' or the 'employee review' – worked as follows. Every unit was forced to declare a certain percentage of employees as top performers, good performers, average, below average or poor. This practice is known in reward management as 'forced distribution' and is

(Continued)

(Continued)

designed to ensure that managers discriminate between employees when awarding performance rankings, but it is also a method of ensuring that the budget for performance pay is not exceeded.

A former software developer described the system as follows:

If you were on a team of 10 people, you walked in the first day knowing that, no matter how good everyone was, two people were going to get a great review, seven were going to get mediocre reviews and one was going to get a terrible review ... it leads to employees focusing on competing with each other rather than competing with other companies. (cited in Eichenwald 2012)

A lot of Microsoft star performers therefore sought to avoid working with other top developers in the company because they feared it might hurt their performance rankings. The impact of the performance reviews was substantial – those who received the top ranking received bonuses and promotions while those at the bottom usually received no cash or were dismissed. Outcomes were unpredictable and, while some departments set business objectives for each staff member each year, meeting the objectives was no guarantee of a high ranking because somebody else might exceed the expectations. In Eichenwald's (2012) words, as a result Microsoft employees 'not only tried to do a good job but also worked hard to make sure colleagues did not'.

According to one Microsoft engineer:

The behaviour this engenders, people do everything they can to stay out of the bottom bucket ... People responsible for features will openly sabotage other people's efforts. One of the most valuable things I learned was to give the appearance of being courteous while withholding just enough information from colleagues to ensure they didn't get ahead of me on the rankings. (cited in Eichenwald 2012)

There was also a problem in the frequency of the reviews – every six months. Employees and their managers therefore focused on short-term performance, rather than on longer efforts to innovate.

One software designer commented that 'The six month reviews forced a lot of bad decision-making ... People planned their days and their years around the review, rather than around products' (cited in Eichenwald 2012).

Each year the team supervisors would meet to agree the distribution of the rankings across the company. Teams could have slightly higher proportions of higher ranked employees as long as the average across the department was within the required percentage. One Microsoft manager said that:

There are some pretty impassioned debates and the Post-it notes (used to put names of individual employees and their rankings on a board) end up being shuffled around for days so that we meet the bell curve ... It doesn't always work out well. I myself have had to give rankings to people that they didn't deserve because of this forced curve. (cited in Eichenwald 2012)

This process of meeting the departmental bell curve led to haggling between supervisors about which employees and which teams would benefit most. The result was that employees did not just have to impress their own team supervisor but other teams' bosses as well. One employee was told by his supervisor that that 'the political game' was more important than his actual performance. The advice was that he should work on the political game rather than focus on improving his actual performance. He commented that the corporate culture engendered by this system slowed everything down.

> Whenever I had a question for some other team, instead of going to the developer who had the answer, I would first touch base with that developer's manager, so that he knew what I was working on. That was the only way to be visible to other managers, which you needed for the review ... It was always much less about how I could become a better engineer and much more about my need to improve my visibility among other managers. (cited in Eichenwald 2012)

Staff surveys, conducted every six months, showed time and again that the reason for the lack of innovation at Microsoft stemmed from the 'stack ranking' system. But the company did nothing to change it.

By Autumn 2004 Microsoft was facing a huge challenge from Google because the smaller company was poaching so many of Microsoft's talented young software designers. Google was emerging as the leading IT company and had gone public in August 2004. Google now has almost the same amount of cash on its books as Microsoft – $50 billion to Microsoft's $58 billion. In contrast, Apple started the year with about $100 billion.

Source: Adapted from Eichenwald (2012).

 ■ **Questions**

1. What do you think were Microsoft's intentions in introducing the 'stack ranking' system for managing reward and promotion at the company?
2. Were there any advantages in this system?
3. What were the disadvantages of 'stack ranking' and how did this affect the performance of the company overall?
4. What could Microsoft have done to encourage more innovation and better teamworking at the company?
5. To what extent do you think the reward system was to blame for Microsoft's problems, or were there other more important business issues?

The major elements in reward

As mentioned earlier, three main contingencies for reward have been identified: job, person and performance (Mahoney 1992). The job contingency largely relates to the creation of a hierarchy of jobs or roles, namely a grading or banding structure, and these normally provide the framework for decisions about base pay levels for different levels of employee. As already discussed, the primary theoretical issue to be considered in the design of such base pay structures is the degree to which they will provide equity and at the same time the degree to which they can be flexible enough to accommodate market pressures. The traditional methods for allocating 'internal equity' value to jobs have been either job evaluation, a system of assessing the relative 'weight' of jobs, or the external market (through pay benchmarking individual roles against comparators in other organizations), although some patent job evaluation schemes allow both approaches (i.e. they use data collected via job evaluation consultancy exercises in different organizations to indicate market values).

However, according to Gomez-Mejia and Balkin (1993: 4): 'The emerging paradigm of the field is based on a strategic orientation where issues of internal and external equity are viewed as secondary to the firm's need to use pay as an essential integrating and signalling mechanism to achieve overarching business objectives' (see also Chapter 10 for a discussion of organizational culture). The argument is that strategy has now overtaken both equity and market as the major element in the design of reward systems. However, as Kessler (2007) has indicated, while it is relatively easy to find examples of reward practices that exemplify internal and external equity it is rather difficult to find examples of the link to business strategy. Kessler (2007) argues that the contingencies of person and performance probably relate more to business strategy than the internal equity 'job' contingency. The elements of person and performance in turn relate more to pay progression and variable pay than to base pay structures and levels. This is because pay progression and additional forms of variable reward relate more to the individual person's capabilities and contribution to the organization than to some concern for a 'felt fair' social order or how the job or role is paid in the wider labour market. This does not imply that issues of fairness and equity do not apply to individual pay progression and the allocation of variable pay, but rather that the normative view of reward strategy is concerned primarily with linkages between organizational objectives and individual performance or capabilities and hence to reward. Interestingly, looking at the UK reward scene, Kessler (2007) argues that, contrary to Gomez-Mejia's view, both internal and external equity have become central to organizational strategic imperatives, although the evidence indicates that there are differences between the public and private sectors. In the public sector the major concern over the last two decades has been internal equity, with major concerns about gender inequality being addressed in new pay structures (Bach et al. 2009; Perkins and White 2010). In contrast, in the private sector the emphasis has been upon the market and external benchmarking of salaries and benefits. The latter partly reflected the strength of the UK labour market in the 1990s and early 2000s, with record employment levels and tight competition for labour

(IDS 2004). This UK evidence does not appear to support the contention that either internal or external equity have become less important in the design of reward systems.

It is also interesting to note the findings of the latest UK and US pay practices surveys. In the UK the CIPD 2012 survey found that 'Organisations in our survey are making strategic choices about reward through competitive remuneration positioning relative to comparative organisations. In this survey, almost nine in ten employers are positioning reward levels ... between the median and upper decile for their sector' (CIPD 2012a: 6). The survey also found that nearly half of the respondents said their organizations used individual rates/ranges or spot salaries to manage base pay, with broad bands the next most common method for managers/professional staff while pay spines for other staff were common. In contrast the US WorldatWork organization, which conducts an annual survey of compensation programmes and practices, found in its latest 2012 survey that market pricing now far exceeds traditional points factor job evaluation as the method for determining base pay levels (WorldatWork 2012). On the other hand, it also discovered that the use of traditional salary structures had increased to 86 per cent of the sample, with a major decline in the use of broad banding (down to 8 per cent). The latter findings might indicate a retreat from a more strategic New Pay approach.

The shift to contingent or variable pay

It has been argued that pay systems are subject to two basic criteria: time and performance (Brown 1989). Employees may either be paid for the time they spend at work (or the time taken to perform a certain task) or they may be paid according to the quantity or quality of the work produced. Traditionally workers were paid (or compensated) for their time at work. Hence employees are often placed on an hourly rate of pay, a weekly wage or a monthly salary. Under such time-based systems, additional hours worked may be paid at premium rates (i.e. overtime rates). In terms of salary systems, pay progression through the grade has traditionally been related to service, rather than individual performance.

In contrast, while employees may still be paid in relation to their time at work, performance-based, variable or 'contingent' pay systems link the level of pay in some way to productivity, output or performance. In the past such 'payment by results' systems were common for production workers, not least in the use of piecework systems where the employee is paid by the quantity of work produced within a period of time, but in recent times there has been a decline in such systems for manual workers. Research by the UK Office for National Statistics (Grabham 2003: 398) found that incentive pay declined as a proportion of total pay between 1987 and 1990 but has remained fairly constant since. It appears to have declined in manufacturing but risen in services.

Evidence of a more strategic reward model might be indicated by a growth in individual performance-related or contingent reward. A key element of the US New Pay paradigm was its advocacy of more contingent or 'at-risk' elements within the reward package and there is indeed some evidence of this growth. The latest US survey of pay practices (WorldatWork 2012) shows that 84 per cent of respondents use variable pay. More than three-quarters award bonuses and two-thirds recognition payments such as 'spot' awards. A majority of organizations use some form of incentive plan but only 19 per cent use profit-sharing plans. Virtually all organizations assess employee performance and the most common criterion for determining pay increases continues to be individual performance against job standards, although individual performance against management objectives or personal objectives is gaining ground.

The evidence from the UK, however, is more mixed. The 2004 WERS, furthermore, indicated a significant growth in performance-related pay from 20 per cent of workplaces in 1998 to 32 per cent in 2004. Analysis of the WERS data over time indicates that the overall incidence of contingent pay grew considerably between 1984 and 1990 to 56 per cent, but then fell slightly to 55 per cent of workplaces by 2004. In the private sector the incidence of variable pay grew from 52 per cent in 1984 to 72 per cent of workplaces in 1990, falling back to 67 per cent in 2004 (Pendleton et al. 2009). The ONS research (Grabham 2003) found that incentive pay accounted for a quarter of gross pay in financial services in 2002. The interesting finding from the WERS analysis is that, while the prevailing view is that individual performance-related pay systems have become the major form of contingent reward in the UK, in fact between 1984 and 2004 there was a shift from individual forms of payment by results systems to more collective forms of contingent pay (e.g. profit-related pay and share ownership schemes).

The latest UK CIPD survey of reward practices indicates that individual performance is the most common criterion for pay progression within base pay structures (CIPD 2012b: 20). Over half use market rates and less than a third use length of service, but length of service is still the most common criterion for the public services.

================ **PIT STOP: REFLECTIVE ACTIVITY 7.4** ================

1. Outline the key arguments for and against performance-related pay.

Total remuneration and flexibility

In addition to base pay and any additional variable pay components (such as individual or team bonuses, profit-sharing or other gain-sharing programmes, and share ownership schemes), employers provide a range of other reward components broadly defined as employee benefits. The composition of benefits packages varies between organizations and indeed between countries. In many countries, notably the USA, health care is a vital part of the package, but in many European countries the social welfare system provides health care, rather than the employer. From an economic perspective, some employers may choose to provide more generous benefits to compensate for lower base pay levels and earnings (Forth and Millward 2000). On the other hand, there is evidence that benefits tend to be better in higher-paying organizations than lower-paying ones (Dale-Olson 2005). Robinson and Hudson (2008) suggest that benefits might encourage an alignment of employer and employee goals and encourage employees to volunteer additional effort.

The major benefits found in most systems tend to be paid annual leave, paid sick leave, paid maternity and paternity leave, some form of retirement savings benefit (usually a pension), life insurance and often medical insurance. In most countries, minimum terms for these benefits are laid down by law and in many European countries 'family-friendly' benefits, such as child care and health-related benefits, have become popular in recent years.

While most employers provide such benefits as part of their overall reward offer, there has been little research on whether the provision of such benefits is linked to improved performance. There are no clear answers to the question of whether effective benefit management contributes to organizational ability to recruit (see Chapter 5), retain and motivate employees (Milkovich and Newman 2008). As Lengnick-Hall and Bereman (1994: 102) state: 'benefits are not wages for time worked, nor are they normally viewed as performance-contingent'. The US New Pay writers advocate that there should be a reduction in indirect remuneration to free up more cash for incentives and variable pay elements. We would therefore expect a strategic reward management approach to include benefits within the strategy.

One indication that employers may be taking a more strategic approach to benefits design and provision might be increasing flexibility in provision. There is indeed some evidence of this in the 'flexible' or 'cafeteria' benefits paradigm, which has been promoted by reward consultants in the USA and elsewhere. In the late 1990s Barringer and Milkovich (1998) reported that around 70 per cent of firms in the USA offered flexible benefits. The cafeteria approach was a response to both the increasing cost of benefits provision in the USA (especially health care insurance) and increasing demands from employees for more choice in their benefits. The concept is based on the provision of a budget figure for the total benefits package to each employee. A 'menu' of benefits and their associated 'price' is then provided to the employee who then chooses which benefits to take from the menu and in what proportions. Another form of benefits flexibility has been the availability of employees in the UK to take more or less of a particular benefit by surrendering cash for more benefits or vice versa (i.e. giving up benefits for a higher salary). Armstrong and Murlis (2007) identify three approaches to flexibility:

- The introduction of new voluntary or discounted benefits funded by the employee out of post-tax income or by 'salary-sacrifice'.
- Variation in the level of existing benefits with a compensatory adjustment to cash pay
- Defining the benefits package in terms of a flex fund to be spent as the employee wishes (cafeteria benefits).

According to the Hay Group, the great majority of flexible benefits plans are limited in scope in the UK, with only certain benefits open to choice. This is largely due to differences in the taxation of benefits between the UK and the USA. In the USA most benefits are not taxable and hence there is no potential loss to the employee in switching benefits.

Total reward

The most recent development in reward theory and practice has been the development of the 'total reward' concept, and indeed some writers now interpret the total reward approach as de facto strategic reward. There is some lack of precision, however, in how the term is used. As Davis (2007: 2) comments: 'It is easy to see how people can use the term ... only to find that they are referring to very different notions.' The concept can expand to encompass everything that is 'rewarding' about working for a particular employer or everything employees get as a result of their employment (Corby and Lindop, 2009).

For some total reward equates to 'total remuneration', i.e. all elements of remuneration including pensions (Levy et al. 2010), while for others the term indicates a much wider definition of reward that embraces both extrinsic and intrinsic elements of the employer offer (Franco-Santos and Gomez-Mejia 2012). According to Levy et al. (2010):

> Total Reward can also be seen as the sum of current and deferred earnings which accumulate to be paid as a pension when the employee retires. From this perspective, deferred earnings include both employer pension contributions (on top of gross pay) and employee pension contributions, which are deducted from gross pay.

In contrast, for Franco-Santos and Gomez-Mejia (2012), total reward consists of 'extrinsic and intrinsic rewards within a single reward framework that comprises all the reward mechanisms available to the employer to motivate, attract and retain employees'. The CIPD defines total reward as 'a mindset that enables employers to look at the bigger picture' (Richards and Hogg, 2007: 2) with the implication that employers will actively manage those aspects of the work experience that are taken for granted by the employee.

The development of the total reward concept has been linked to two phenomena – (a) the increasing competition for highly skilled staff (the so-called 'war for talent') between organizations, and (b) the need to communicate the total value of the employment offer to employees, including both extrinsic and intrinsic rewards. Perkins and White (2011: 304) suggest that total reward has developed from a range of HR initiatives including 'high investment work systems', 'mutual gains', 'high involvement work practices', 'employee involvement programmes', notions of 'employee voice' (see Chapter 8) and 'partnership at work', 'emotionally intelligent' leadership, 'employee wellbeing' and the 'psychological contract' (see Chapter 13). Figure 7.3 indicates the inclusivity of the total reward concept.

According to WorldatWork in the USA the five components of total reward are compensation, benefits, work–life balance, performance and recognition, and development and career opportunities (Davis 2007: 4). Similarly, the CIPD in the UK describes the total reward concept as a 'reward strategy that brings additional components such as learning and development (see Chapter 10), together with aspects of the working environment into the benefits package' (Richards and Hogg 2007: 1). Given that a 'one size fits all' reward package often fails to meet the diverse needs of the workforce (see Kinnie et al. 2005), embracing a much wider range of rewards and allowing some flexibility and choice for employees may be a first step towards a total reward approach.

Given the importance attached to non-financial rewards in the psychological literature, it is these elements that provide the difference in approach in the total reward paradigm. It is of note that Franco-Santos and Gomez-Mejia (2012) include work environment and conditions, recognition, learning and development and leadership as extrinsic rewards while intrinsic rewards include meaningfulness of work, choice or autonomy, growth in role (competence and progress) and community. We look at each of these elements below.

Workplace environment and working conditions

Working environment covers both the provision of a safe workplace and congenial working conditions. The physical setting in which employees are located has been known to be a key variable in recruitment and retention (see Chapter 5) for some time. In some countries, employers have a legal duty of care to look after the health, safety and welfare of their employee while at work, but some employers have gone further by designing workplaces ergonomically to enhance employee comfort and hence productivity. Work environment includes job design, work–life balance and recognition (Heneman 2007).

Job design is more than about the physical characteristics of the job. It also relates to employees' perceptions of their jobs and whether the work is challenging or meaningful, whether it provides autonomy and whether the employee

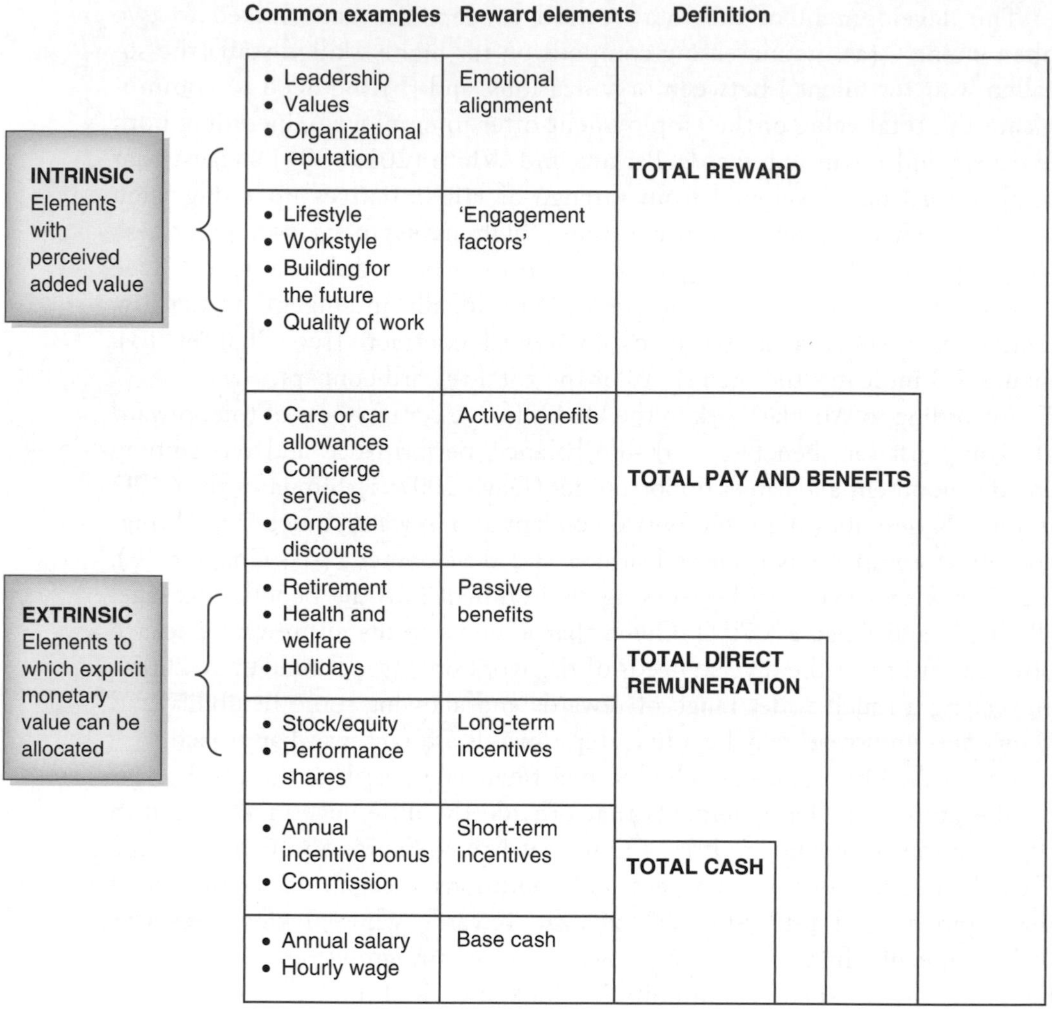

Common examples	Reward elements	Definition

Figure 7.3 An inclusive view of total reward

Source: Perkins and White (2011) Reproduced by kind permission of CIPD Publications.

identifies with the role. According to Hackman and Lawler (1971), positive perceptions of work lead to higher employee motivation and better performance.

Work–life balance (see Chapter 6) is also an integral part of total reward, and employers will seek to ensure that employees are able to balance their time and commitments at work with their family and community responsibilities. These programmes can include workplace flexibility, special leave, community involvement and caring for dependents (Franco-Santos and Gomez-Mejia 2012). Workplace flexibility covers a range of flexible work options (e.g. telecommuting, job sharing, part-time employment, flexible working arrangements, compressed working weeks etc.) that enable employees to have more control over where, when and how the work is delivered. Special leave covers arrangements such as maternity and paternity leave, adoption leave, sabbaticals and study leave. In some countries, paid maternity and paternity leave are statutory requirements but employers may offer more than the statutory minimum. Community involvement involves employees being given time off work to act as volunteers while caring for dependents and includes such elements as childcare, eldercare etc.

However, the workplace environment can have much wider connotations and can also relate to the psychological environment and culture of the organization. The ability of employees to be involved in decisions affecting their working lives has also been linked to workplace environment. According to research conducted by Truss et al. (2006), the two most important drivers of 'employee engagement' are having opportunities to feed upwards and feeling well-informed about what is happening in the organization. Cox et al. (2006) observe a statistically significant link between addressing these issues of employee voice and workforce commitment and reported satisfaction.

Another key element of the total reward concept is a recognition of employee effort in ways other than simply pay. Recognition reward programmes provide a formal acknowledgement of individual employee effort or service through cash or non-cash awards (e.g. gifts, prizes, vacations, 'employee of the month' awards, etc.). These programmes are designed to motivate employees and recognize their commitment to the organization. Such awards work best when they are provided close to the event being rewarded. According to Heneman (2007), most employee recognition schemes provide rewards that are relatively inexpensive compared to other elements in the reward package. Some research indicates that employees prefer non-financial rewards (Amabile et al. 1994) and such awards can exert a powerful impact on employee performance (Stajkovic and Luthans 2001).

Learning and development

Learning and development opportunities are also an element of total reward. Such provision is designed to support the employee's 'sense of competence, self-efficacy and achievement as well as encourage innovation' (Franco-Santos and Gomez-Mejia 2012). This can include on-the-job and off the job training as well as the time and funding to pursue further and higher education qualifications and challenging work assignments that allow new experience and expertise to be gained (see Chapter 10).

Intrinsic rewards of work

The intrinsic rewards of work include a sense of meaningfulness, choice, growth and community. Finding meaning in work is a major element in work satisfaction and when work is seen as meaningful it can lead to higher motivation and self-generated activity (see Chapter 3 for a discussion of high commitment and soft HRM). A sense of choice in how the work is conducted through autonomy or discretion being built into the job design is also seen as a major motivator (Ryan and Deci 2000). When employees feel that they can select the activities that best suit their goals and perform them in ways that they deem appropriate, this can also be seen as rewarding work. A sense of growth refers to how employees feel that their competence and efforts are achieving something important – what is often referred to as 'pride in one's work'. Lastly a sense of community – the feeling of belonging to a social group or community at work – also plays a role in reward. Environments that create strong interpersonal relationships and a feeling of belonging can be motivating and seen as a reward of work.

The reward mix

The contribution of the total reward concept to strategic reward comes from the ability to provide a mix of rewards that meet the needs of the organization and the employee. The strategic perspective on total rewards is based on two assumptions (Gomez-Mejia et al. 2010): (a) how responsive the reward system is to internal and external forces and (b) the choice of reward components. A number of critical reward choices have been identified in terms of the distribution of rewards, the design of rewards and the administration of rewards (Gomez-Mejia et al. 2010). The total reward approach provides a framework for selecting the type of rewards offered to employees. Amabile (1993) identified a choice between 'non-synergistic extrinsic rewards' (those rewards that do not combine well with intrinsic rewards because they undermine autonomy, growth and community) and 'extrinsic in service of intrinsics' rewards (those rewards that support and enhance an employee's intrinsic motivation). As Franco-Santos and Gomez-Mejia (2012: 18) argue:

> Non-synergistic extrinsic rewards are likely to generate a transactional-based relationship in which employees are mainly motivated to work for an economic return in exchange, whilst reliance on extrinsic rewards that are in the service of intrinsic is more likely to produce a commitment-based relationship where individuals are more willing to contribute high levels of discretionary behaviours and align their interest to those of the employer.

Can reward be strategic?

We conclude this chapter by considering the evidence for a strategic approach to reward management. Lewis (2001: 100) argues that while Lawler's model of strategic reward 'seems highly rational', it makes significant assumptions. His first objection is the notion of business strategy used by Lawler – i.e. that it is a rational top-down process rather than emerging as a result of a pattern of management actions over time, as suggested by Mintzberg and Waters in 1989 (see Chapters 2 and 3). Lewis argues that even if the strategy is clear there is no guarantee that the HRM strategy will follow this lead, especially as HR decisions are more likely to be incremental in scope. Second, Lewis argues that the model is essentially unitarist (see Chapter 8) in that it assumes that employees will endorse the reward strategy and comply with it. This may be problematic if the changes in reward envisaged are seen as a threat to employee interests. Third, the New Pay paradigm is 'highly deterministic' in that it 'assumes that an effective reward strategy will have a beneficial effect upon the performance of the organisation' (Lewis 2001: 101). This is a significant assumption in that it is difficult to provide an empirical test of effectiveness. Despite recent concerns to encourage evidence-based HRM based on evaluating the success of HR policies and practice against a battery of metrics, research by E-Reward and the UK Institute of Employment Studies found scant evidence of a linkage to improved delivery of reward goals between those organizations that evaluated and those that did not (E-Reward 2010). Lewis argues that 'the deterministic perspective is based on assumptions of rationality and unitarism which disregard the political realities of organisational life' (Lewis 2001: 101). Pfeffer (1998) suggests that an overreliance on pay to secure the motivation of employees may be at the cost of more powerful motivators such as meaningful work in a high-trust, friendly environment, although as we have seen the total reward paradigm has begun to address this disconnect between extrinsic and intrinsic rewards.

The annual surveys of reward policy and practice carried out by the CIPD in the UK indicate that only a minority of respondents had a formal reward strategy (35 per cent) and a similar proportion had adopted a total reward approach (CIPD 2010). The number with a formal reward strategy remained the same as in 2007 while the number planning to introduce one had actually gone down. On the other hand, over half the respondents stated that their total reward priority was to ensure alignment with the business strategy of their organization.

Recent research by the CIPD in the UK, however, using Miles and Snow's (1984) market competition typology of 'defenders' and 'prospectors' (see Chapter 3), found that there were indeed clear differences in reward policy and practice between the two types of organizations (CIPD 2012b). As the authors of the report state:

> Our results have shown that private sector firms using different business strategies in their chosen product/service sectors have also adopted markedly

different reward management practices ... Findings for Prospectors and Defenders in relation to human resources outcomes would suggest that their differing approaches to reward management do lead to different HR outcomes. (CIPD 2012b: 30–31)

Other recent research (Trevor 2008: 1) on organizations' implementation of reward strategies found that 'many organisations experience profound managerial difficulties when attempting to use compensation strategically' and as a result actual practice reflects neither espoused strategy nor policy. Negative outcomes from such strategies include high costs, greater administration and industrial conflict (see Chapter 8), as manifested in employee disengagement and demotivation. Trevor argues that strategic reward may be not so much about the value-creating mechanisms envisaged by the New Pay writers but 'rather a business risk that requires careful management and good governance' (2008: 1). Trevor also found that where reward decisions were centralized, 'standardised pay policies are rarely implemented as intended' (Trevor 2009: 3). Where decentralized, 'line management choose typically to continue to use pay in ways that are characteristic of traditional pay management, despite the aspirations of their superiors'. In conclusion, Trevor argues that 'strategic approaches to pay are not sufficiently grounded in the complex and messy reality of organisations to be achievable by the pure terms of standard theory' (2009: 35).

≋ CASE STUDY 7.3 ≋

RETCO changes reward strategy

RETCO is a communications network company supplying services to the public sector. It is a not-for-profit organization, owned by its public service clients who are charged for the company's services. The company also receives government grants towards its services. The services provided include web mail, web hosting, video-conferencing and wireless roaming, and high-capacity data transfer. It employs around 130 staff based mainly in its headquarters in the south-west of the UK but also has some staff in a London office. RETCO's staff are largely professional telecommunications engineers but there is also a range of support functions such as finance, marketing and general administration. In general, the company is seen as a good place to work with lots of autonomy and interesting work for the professional staff. While staff complain that salary levels are not competitive with other private sector firms, turnover of staff is less than average and the benefits package is generally generous when compared to those of the company's private sector competitors.

RETCO's public sector background means that it recruits many of its staff from the public sector organizations it serves and its terms and conditions tend to follow those in the public sector. There is a nine-band salary structure with fairly narrow pay ranges in each grade. There is a minimum for each band, a target point in the range and a maximum. New employees are normally appointed at the minimum of the band and are reviewed after a year. It is intended that staff move fairly quickly to the target salary, but exceptional performance can be rewarded through increases up to the maximum. In addition, one-off bonuses can be paid to those who have reached the top of their band. Staff can join a public sector-defined benefit pension scheme and annual leave is generous by comparison to its private sector competitors. Similarly the sick pay scheme follows public sector arrangements. The roles were subjected to a job evaluation exercise (using a civil service job evaluation scheme) several years ago but since then there has been considerable change in roles and the job evaluation has rather fallen into disuse.

Grading structure

Table 7.2   RETCO grading structure

Band	Job example	Min.	Target	Max.
1	Admin. support	£15,660	£16,480	£17,305
2	Admin. officer	£17,255	£18,155	£19,065
3	Marketing officer	£19,250	£20,255	£21,270
4	Service desk member	£20,580	£22,245	£23,360
5	PA to CEO	£24,495	£26,480	£27,805
6	Technical specialist, contracts manager	£29,380	£31,755	£33,345
7	Management accountant, project manager	£34,055	£37,850	39,745
8	Head of IT and corporate infrastructure	£42,395	£47,120	£49,475
9	Director	£59,790	£66,450	£69,775

The company had in the past a policy of benchmarking annually against external pay data, using a basket of comparator organizations. The pay levels were then set by reference to the median market rate data plus 5 per cent in order to set the target rate. Pay ranges were set around this target rate, but this system of pay benchmarking has now fallen into disuse.

Changing business context

The organization is now subject to a changing business context for its activities. The reductions in public spending introduced as part of the UK government's austerity policies mean that RETCO's clients have less money to spend on its services and pay levels have been frozen for two years, mirroring pay restraint among its client organizations. Some of its clients are now looking for cheaper private sector alternatives for the supply of its services. The company is now becoming subject to market competition for its services, while previously its market was more

(Continued)

(Continued)

or less guaranteed, and it is changing its business strategy from one of purely servicing guaranteed contracts to creating new markets for its services. This means that a more private sector model of business organization is being adopted to compete in the new market.

Review of reward system

As part of a general review of the company's business strategy, a consultant was engaged to review the reward system – both to benchmark the pay levels for the nine salary bands and to make recommendations on how the the entire reward package might be changed. The consultant noted a number of issues that needed to be addressed.

1. While the company has a nine-band salary structure, this appears to be a rather hierarchical structure for an organization of only 130 employees. There is little promotion from one band to another and little flexibility to reward individuals. The band ranges also appear rather arbitrary and in general are fairly narrow, allowing little scope for employee progression. Information on the populations of each pay band reveals that bands 1–3 have very few incumbents. Bands 1 and 3 currently have no incumbents and band 2 has only two.
2. There is a large gap (over £10,000) between the maximum of band 8 and the minimum of band 9. Unless the gap is justified by genuine market differentials between the two bands (which would suggest that band 9 roles are significantly larger than band 8 roles), this might indicate that either there is a need for an extra band or the two band ranges need to be widened.
3. The distribution of staff within the pay bands also indicates some issues. In band 4 only 7 per cent of staff are paid above target while in band 9 there are 78 per cent paid above target. In bands 5–7 there are 65 per cent who have reached target and in band 8 there are 51 per cent. It is not clear whether these differences between bands are due to market pay pressures, whether staff in the lower graded roles have shorter service (and hence have yet to reach the target salary) or whether a higher proportion of senior band staff are deemed to be exceptional performers. This could indicate potential equity issues but may also indicate that the maximum is being used to address external market demands rather than exceptional performance. This could be a particular issue if there was a gender difference between the staff on the maximum and those below target.
4. At present the company does little to monitor recruitment and resignation patterns so has no real understanding of where its labour market competitors might be. It is reported that most staff come from its client public sector organizations and hence they expect a similar reward package to that in their previous employment. But there is also anecdotal evidence that staff resigning tend to move to RETCO's private sector competitor firms which do not offer such generous benefits. The company needs to ensure its pay benchmarking exercises take account of these two separate markets – where staff are joining from and where staff are moving to.
5. The benefits structure is considerably more generous than the private sector competitor firms offer and hence more costly. In particular it is unusual for a small company such as RETCO to provide a defined benefit pension plan. If RETCO is looking to strip out costs, it may wish to review the benefits on offer, although clearly many of these will be contractual and difficult to simply withdraw.

6. After a pay benchmarking exercise by the consultant, comparing salary levels for similar job responsibilities and job size in comparable organizations through salary survey data and a job pricing exercise with a small number of competitor firms, it is found that RETCO's salaries are generally in line with the market for lower band roles but significantly behind those of the private sector comparators for mid-range and senior roles.

The consultant's recommendations

After due deliberation, the consultant presented a report making the following recommendations:

- RETCO needs to change its salary banding system to better provide for flexibility to reward staff and to better reflect the non-hierarchical organizational structure that will be needed to face future challenges. The nine-band structure should be reduced to just four bands with much wider salary ranges within each band. The current pay differential between the minimum and maximum of each band varies between 10.5 per cent at the lower level and 16.7 per cent in the higher bands. The range of pay that is covered by the structure results in pay gaps between the maximum of each band and the minimum of the band above for each band from band 4 upwards. There may be advantages in narrow salary bands, such as clearly defined pay relativities, good control of pay growth and being relatively easy to communicate to employees. Such structures, however, can create rigidity, be prone to grade drift (as the only way of getting a pay increase is to be promoted or be upgraded), be difficult to relate to external market differences between different types of staff, and provide less scope to reward individual performance.
- RETCO should move away from a rigid adherence to its policy of setting salaries at the median plus 5 per cent and introduce a more flexible approach. The current arrangement gives little scope to reflect changing business and economic conditions such as affordability. As long as the pay structure is flexible enough to accommodate specific market pressures and individual performance differences, it is usually sufficient to compare with mid-market salaries.
- Current RETCO reward policy envisages an annual full market analysis of salary levels. This is generally unusual and most organizations set their structures in line with the market data and then update each year in line with general labour market trends, the general level of pay increases for similar organizations in the same industry, inflation levels and ability to pay.
- If market concerns about particular roles or groups of roles emerge, these should be dealt with through the use of job families. While part of the same salary band, salary levels for the affected staff can be dealt with separately. An alternative is to pay a 'market supplement' for roles that appear difficult to recruit externally, although such supplements need to be regularly reviewed to ensure they are justified.
- Progression through the salary band should be related to rigorous reviews of individual performance and a transparent system of performance management.
- One-off bonuses should continue but the criteria for these must be clearly set out and communicated to staff.

(Continued)

(Continued)

- The benefits package should be reviewed to consider potential cost savings. If RETCO wishes to continue to provide what are seen as popular parts of the reward package for staff, then it should consider the implementation of a 'total remuneration' approach so that the cost of any above-market benefits are offset against salary levels. Employees need to be made aware of the overall cost of their reward package through annual benefit statements.
- Given that it appears that the professional staff at RETCO seem to be more than satisfied with their work, the company should consider adopting a 'total reward' approach where the non-financial rewards on offer from the company are made more explicit to potential recruits and existing staff.

Source: author.

 ■ **Question**

1. After considering the consultant's suggestions, what are the pros and cons of introducing greater pay band width in the light of a tightening financial market (with potentially less ability for the employer to increase financial rewards)?

Conclusion

This chapter has reviewed the growth of the strategic reward concept and the theory underpinning the design of reward systems. The major elements of reward have been described and the integration of intrinsic and extrinsic rewards into a total reward approach discussed. Reward management has always presented a risk of conflict in the workplace, but there can be no doubt that over the last 30 years there has been a steady increase in the belief among HR practitioners that reward systems can and must be designed to reflect and support organizational strategy. There is also evidence that practitioners are taking an increasingly holistic approach to the concept of reward so that it is no longer just about remuneration but rather the whole employment offer. The total reward approach reflects this increasing and more sophisticated understanding of work motivation. However, recent research has suggested that the operational reality of reward management may be less about a strategic approach and more about mitigating the very real risk of workplace conflict which can arise from the effort-bargain between employers and employees.

■ Further Reading ■■■■■■■■■■■■■■■■■■■

Gomez-Mejia, L.R., Berrone, P. and Franco-Santos, M. (2010) *Strategic Compensation and Performance*. New York: M. E. Sharp.

Heneman, R.L. (2007) *Implementing Total Rewards Strategies*, SHRM Foundation's Effective Practice Guidelines Series. Alexandria, VA: SHRM Foundation.

Kessler, I. (2005) 'Remuneration systems', in S. Bach (ed.), *Managing Human Resources: Personnel Management in Transition*. Oxford: Blackwell Publishing, pp. 317–45.

Lawler, E.E. (2000) *Rewarding Excellence: Pay Strategies for the New Economy*. San Francisco, CA: Jossey-Bass.

Perkins, S. and White, G. (2011) *Reward Management: Alternatives, Consequences and Contexts*, 2nd edn. London: CIPD.

Trevor, J. (2011) *Can Pay Be Strategic? A Critical Exploration of Strategic Pay in Practice*. Basingstoke: Palgrave Macmillan.

References

Adams, J.S. (1965) 'Inequity in social exchange', in L. Berkowitz (ed.), *Advances in Experimental Social Psychology*, vol. 2. New York: Academic Press.

Amabile, T.M. (1993) 'Motivational synergy: toward new conceptualizations of intrinsic and external motivation in the workplace', *Human Resource Management Review*, 3 (3): 185–201.

Amabile, T.M., Hill, K.G., Hennessey, B.A. and Tighe, E.M. (1994) 'The work preference inventory: assessing intrinsic and extrinsic motivational orientations', *Journal of Personality and Social Psychology*, 66 (5): 950–67.

Armstrong, M. and Baron, A. (2005) *Performance Management: The New Realities*. London: IPD.

Armstrong, M. and Brown, D. (2006) *Strategic Rewards: Making it Happen*. London: Kogan Page.

Armstrong, M. and Murlis, H. (1988) *Reward Management: A Handbook of Remuneration Strategy and Practice*. London: Kogan Page.

Armstrong M. and Murlis, H. (2007) *Reward Management: A Handbook of Remuneration Strategy and Practice*, revised 5th edn. London: Kogan Page.

Bach, S. (2005) 'New directions in performance management', in S. Bach (ed.), *Managing Human Resources. Personnel Management in Transition*, 4th edn. Oxford: Blackwell, pp: 289–316.

Bach, S., Givan, R.K. and Forth, J. (2009) 'The public sector in transition', in W. Brown, A. Bryson, J. Forth and K. Whitfield (eds), *The Evolution of the Modern Workplace*. Cambridge: Cambridge University Press. pp. 307–31.

Barringer, M. and Milkovich, G. (1998) 'A theoretical exploration of the adoption and design of flexible benefit plans: a case of human resource innovation', *Academy of Management Review*, 23 (2): 305–24.

Becker, G.S. (1957) *The Economics of Discrimination*. Chicago, IL: University of Chicago Press.

Beer, M., Spencer, B., Lawrence, P., Mills, Q. and Walton, R. (1984) *Managing Human Assets*. New York: Free Press.

Behrend, H. (1957) 'The effort bargain', *Industrial and Labour Relations Review*, 10 (4): 505–15.

Bloom, M. and Milkovich, G.T. (1998) *A SHRM Perspective on International Compensation and Reward Systems*, Working Paper 98-11. Ithaca, NY: Industrial Labor Relations School, Cornell University.

Brown, D. (2001) *Reward Strategies: From Intent to Impact*. London: Kogan Page.

Brown, W. (1989) 'Managing remuneration', in K. Sisson (ed.), *Personnel Management in Britain*. Oxford: Blackwell, pp. 249–70.

CBI/Wyatt (1994) *Variable Pay Systems*. London: Confederation of British Industry.

Child, J. (1984) *Organization: A Guide to Problems and Practice*, 2nd edn. London: Harper and Row.

CIPD (2010) *Reward Management Annual Survey Report 2010*. London: CIPD.

CIPD (2012a) *Reward Management Annual Survey Report 2012*. London: CIPD.

CIPD (2012b) *Aligning Strategy and Pay: Annual Survey Report Supplement 2012*. London: CIPD.

Corby, S. and Lindop, E. (2009) *Rethinking Reward*. Basingstoke: Palgrave Macmillan.

Cox, A., Zagelmeyer, S. and Marchington, M. (2006) 'Embedding employee involvement and participation at work', *Human Resource Management Journal*, 16 (3): 250–67.

Cropanzano, R. and Folger, R. (1996) 'Procedural justice and worker motivation', in R.M. Steers, L.W. Porter and G.A. Bigley (eds), *Motivation and Leadership at Work*, 6th edn. New York: McGraw-Hill, pp. 72–83.

Dale-Olson, H. (2005) *Using Linked Employer-employee Data to Analyse Fringe Benefit Policies. Norwegian Experiences*, Institute for Social Research Norway. Paper presented to Policy Studies Institute Seminar, July.

Davis, M.L. (ed.) (2007) 'Total rewards: everything that employees value in the employment relationship', in M.L. Davis (ed.), *World at Work Handbook of Compensation, Benefits and Total Rewards*. New York: Wiley.

E-Reward (2010) *Evaluating Reward Effectiveness: Survey Report*. Stockport: E-Reward.

Eichenwald, K. (2012) 'Microsoft's lost decade', *Vanity Fair Magazine*, July 8, available at http://www.vanityfair.com/business/2012/08/microsoft-lost-mojo-steve-ballmer#, accessed 12 January 2013.

Ferner, A. and Quintanilla, J. (1998) 'Multinationals, national business systems and HRM: the enduring influence of national identity or a process of "Anglo-Saxonisation"', *International Journal of Human Resource Management*, 9 (4): 710–31.

Fombrun, C., Tichy, N. and Devanna, M.A. (1984) *Strategic Human Resource Management*. New York: Wiley.

Forth, J. and Millward, N. (2000) *The Determinants of Pay Levels and Fringe Benefit Provision in Britain*, Discussion Paper 171. London: National Institute of Economic and Social Research.

Franco-Santos, M. and Gomez-Mejia, L. (2012) 'Developing a total reward system: a strategic approach', in D. Needle and D. Guest (eds), *Wiley Encyclopedia of Human Resource Management*. Chichester: Wiley.

Gomez-Mejia, L.R. and Balkin, D.B. (1993) *Compensation, Organisation and Firm Performance*. San Francisco, CA: Southwestern.

Gomez-Mejia, L.R. and Welbourne, T. (1991) 'Compensation strategies in a global context', *Human Resource Planning*, 14 (1): 29–42.

Gomez-Mejia, L.R., Berrone, P. and Franco-Santos, M. (2010) *Strategic Compensation and Performance*. New York: M. E. Sharp.

Grabham, A. (2003) 'Composition of pay', *Labour Market Trends*. London: ONS: 397–405.

Guest, D. (1990) 'Human resource management and the American dream', *Journal of Management Studies*, 27 (4): 387–97.

Guest, D. and Hoque, K. (1996) 'National ownership and HR practices in UK greenfield sites', *Human Resource Management Journal*, 6 (4): 50–74.

Hackman, J.R. and Lawler, E.E. (1971) 'Employee reactions to job characteristics', *Journal of Applied Psychology*, 55: 259–86.

Heery, E. (1996) 'Risk, reputation and the new pay', *Personnel Review*, 25 (6): 54–65.

Heneman, R.L. (2007) *Implementing Total Rewards Strategies*, SHRM Foundation's Effective Practice Guidelines Series. Alexandria, VA: SHRM Foundation.

Hofstede, G. (1980) *Culture's Consequences: International Differences in Work Related Values*. Beverley Hills, CA: Sage.

IDS (2004) 'The pros and cons of market-related pay', *IDS Pay Report*, 907 (June): 8–9.

IDS (2007) *Performance Management*, IDS HR Studies 839, February. London: Incomes Data Services.

Kaplan, R. and Norton, D. (1996) *The Balanced Scorecard*. Boston, MA: Harvard Business School Press.

Kersley, B., Alpin, C., Forth, J., Bryson, A., Bewley, H., Dix, G. and Oxenbridge, S. (2006) *Inside the Workplace: Findings from the 2004 Workplace Employment Relations Survey*. London: Routledge.

Kessler, I. (2005) 'Remuneration systems', in S. Bach (ed.), *Managing Human Resources: Personnel Management in Transition*. Oxford: Blackwell Publishing, pp. 317–45.

Kessler, I. (2007) 'Reward choices:strategy and equity', in J. Storey (ed.), *Human Resource Management: A Critical Text*, 3rd edn. London: Thomson. pp. 159–76.

Kinnie, N., Hutchinson, S., Purcell, J., Rayton, B. and Swart, J. (2005) 'Satisfaction with HR practices and commitment to the organisation: why one size does not fit all', *Human Resource Management Journal*, 15 (4): 9–29.

Lawler, E.E. (1990) *Strategic Pay: Aligning Organizational Strategies and Pay Systems*. San Francisco, CA: Jossey-Bass.

Lawler, E.E. (1995) 'The new pay: a strategic approach?', *Compensation and Benefits Review*, 27 (July-August): 14–22.

Lawler, E.E. (2000) *Rewarding Excellence: Pay Strategies for the New Economy*. San Francisco, CA: Jossey-Bass.

Legge, K. (1995) *Human Resource Management: Rhetorics and Realities*. Basingstoke: Macmillan.

Lengnick-Hall, M.L. and Bereman, N.A. (1994) 'A conceptual framework for the study of employee benefits', *Human Resource Management Review*, 4 (2): 101–15.

Levy, S., Mitchell, H., Guled, G. and Coleman, J. (2010) 'Total reward: pay and pension contributions in the private and public sectors', *Economic and Labour Market Review*, 4 (9): 22–8.

Lewis, P. (2001) 'Reward management', in T. Redman and A. Wilkinson (eds), *Contemporary human Resource Management. Text and Cases*. Harlow: Prentice Hall, pp. 98–127.

Locke, E. A., Shaw, K. N., Saari, L. M. and Latham, G. P. (1981) 'Goal setting and task performance: 1969–1980', *Psychological Bulletin,* 90 (1): 125–52.

Lupton, T. and Gowler, D. (1969) *Selecting a Wage Payment System*, Research Paper 111. London: Engineering Employers Federation.

Mahoney, T.A. (1992) 'Multiple pay contingencies: strategic design of compensation', in G. Salamon (ed.), *Human Resource Strategies*. London: Sage.

Mamman, A., Sulaiman, M. and Fadel, A. (1996) 'Attitudes to pay systems: an exploratory study within and across cultures', *International Journal of Human Resource Management*, 7 (1): 101–21.

Marsden, D. (2007) 'Pay and rewards in public services: fairness and equity', in P. Dibben, P. James, I. Roper and G. Wood (eds), *Modernising Work in Public Services: Redefining Roles and Relationships in Britain's Changing Workplace*. Basingstoke: Palgrave Macmillan, pp. 107–20.

Miles, R. and Snow, C.C. (1984) 'Designing strategic human resource systems', *Organisational Dynamics*, 13: 36–52.

Milkovich, G.T. and Newman, J.M. (2008) *Compensation*, 9th edn. Boston, MA: McGraw Hill International Edition.

Pendleton, A., Whitfield, K. and Bryson, A. (2009) 'The changing use of contingent pay at the modern workplace', in W. Brown, A. Bryson, J. Forth and K. Whitfield (eds), *The Evolution of the Modern Workplace*. Cambridge: Cambridge University Press, pp. 256–84.

Perkins, S. and White, G. (2010) 'Modernising pay in UK public services: trends and implications', *Human Resource Management Journal*, 20 (3): 244–57.

Perkins, S. and White, G. (2011) *Reward Management: Alternatives, Consequences and Contexts*, 2nd edn. London: CIPD.

Pfeffer, J. (1998) 'Six dangerous myths about pay', *Harvard Business Review*, 76 (May–June: 108–19.

Porter, L.W. and Lawler, E.E. (1968) *Managerial Attitudes and Performance*. Homewood, IL: Irwin.

Richards, J. and Hogg, C. (2007) *Total Reward: Factsheet*. London: Chartered Institute of Personnel and Development.

Robinson, A. and Hudson, R. (2008) 'From fringe to mainstream? A portrait of employee benefit provision in Britain', in M. Variainen, C. Antoni, X. Baeten, N. Hakonen, R. Lucas, and H. Thierry (eds), *Reward Management – Facts and Trends in Europe*. Lengerich: Pabst Science Publishers, pp. 211–29.

Ryan, R.M. and Deci, E.L. (2000) 'Intrinsic and extrinsic motivations: classic definitions and new directions', *Contemporary Educational Psychology*, 25: 54–67.

Schuster, J. and Zingheim, P. (1992) *The New Pay: Linking Employee and Organisational Performance*. New York: Lexington Books.

Sisson, K. (1994) 'Personnel management paradigms, practice and prospects', in K. Sisson (ed.), *Personnel Management: a Comprehensive Guide to Theory and Practice in Britain*. Oxford: Blackwell, pp. 3–52.

Skinner, B.F. (1953) *Science and Human Behavior*. New York: Macmillan.

Sparrow, P. and Hiltrop, J.M. (1994) *European Human Resource Management in Transition*. London: Prentice Hall.

Stajkovic, A.D. and Luthans, F. (2001) 'Differential effects of incentive motivators on work performance', *Academy of Management Journal*, 4 (3): 580–90.

Storey, J. (1992) *Developments in the Management of Human Resources*. Oxford: Blackwell.

Trevor, J. (2008) *Can Compensation be Strategic? A Review of Compensation Management Practice in Leading Multinational Firms*, Working paper. Cambridge: Judge Business School.

Trevor, J. (2009) *Exploring the Strategic Potential of Pay: Are We Expecting Too Much?*, Working paper. Cambridge: Judge Business School.

Trevor, J. (2011) *Can Pay be Strategic? A Critical Exploration of Strategic Pay in Practice*. Basingstoke: Palgrave Macmillan.

Trompenaars, F. (1993) *Riding the Waves of Culture: Understanding Cultural Diversity in Business*. London: Economist Books.

Truss, K., Soane, E., Edwards, Y., Wisdom, K., Croll, A. and Burnett, J. (2006) *Working Life: Employee Attitudes and Engagement*. London: CIPD.

Vroom, V.H. (1964) *Work and Motivation*. New York: John Wiley.

White, G., Luk, V., Druker, J. and Chiu, R. (1998) 'Paying their way: a comparison of managerial reward systems in the London and Hong Kong banking industries', *Asia Pacific Journal of Human Resources*, 36 (1): 54–71.

Winsor, T. (2011) *Independent Review of Police Officer and Staff Remuneration and Conditions, Part 1 report*. Cm 8024. March 2011. London: The Stationery Office.

Winsor, T. (2012) *Independent Review of Police Officer and Staff Remuneration and Conditions, Part 2 report*. Cm 8325-I. March 2012. London: The Stationery Office.

WorldatWork (2012) *Compensation Programs and Practices 2012: A report by WorldatWork, October 2012*. Scottsdale, AZ: WorldatWork.

8

MANAGING THE EMPLOYMENT RELATIONSHIP

Moira Calveley, David Allsop and Natalia Rocha Lawton

Chapter Overview

Previous chapters in this book have looked at human resource management (HRM) in the broader context, including how it relates and contributes to the business strategy of organizations. Other chapters have looked at the more functional aspects of HR, such as recruitment and selection and employee engagement and reward. This chapter will consider the management of the employment relationship.

The chapter begins by discussing what is meant by 'the employment relationship', a term that is often used in a simplistic way, obscuring the complexities of such a relationship. The chapter goes on to consider the different organizational perspectives with regard to managing the relationship before taking a look at the impact of the various 'actors' involved in the employment relationship. By taking a multi-level approach, the chapter allows us to explore the employment relationship from different perspectives. One section looks at the role that the state, and in particular government, has in various aspects of managing people. The next looks at employers' organizations and the extent to which they are able to influence employment matters at the local level. No discussion of the employment relationship is complete without a consideration of the power relations between management and workers and between workers and the government and this is covered in 'Employers and employers' associations'. The remaining sections of the chapter look at employee 'voice' and the individual and collective representation of workers; 'Employee voice' focuses on employee involvement, engagement and participation and looks at the role of trade unions and works councils. The final section of the chapter examines how the media are able to impact on the employment relationship.

≡ Learning Objectives ≡

- **To explore and consider the concept of the employment relationship**
- **To develop an understanding of the role of the actors or 'social partners' in the employment relationship**
- **To consider the notion of power within the employment relationship**
- **To develop an understanding of the extent to which employees are able to have a 'voice' in the workplace**

The employment relationship in Barrowton School[1]

Context

The English schooling system is heavily influenced by government policies to which school managers (school governors, head teachers and deputy head teachers) have to adhere. In some cases, legislation and directives formulated by the government mean that managers are obliged to implement certain people-management practices. For example, a formal performance appraisal of all of school-teachers is regulated by The Education (School Teachers' Appraisal) (England) Regulations 2012.

Since the implementation of the 1988 Education Reform Act (ERA) there has been a growth in marketization in schools (Calveley 2005a) with the introduction of school league tables or 'performance tables' as they are referred to by the government (http://www.education.gov.uk/schools/performance/). These tables, which are published annually by the government, draw on various data in order to rank schools according to their pupil success. The rationale behind the tables is that they allow parents to assess the school to which they are planning to send their child. The government promotes performance tables as being a transparent process, designed to push up the quality of teaching. Nonetheless, the value of the tables is disputed by critics who suggest that pupil success is partly related to socio-economic background (BBC 2013). By their very nature, league tables produce 'winners' and 'losers' with those schools at the bottom of the table often being marginalized and viewed as 'failing' their students (Calveley 2005a).

Barrowton School – the background

Barrowton is a secondary (11–16-year-olds) inner-city school which is situated at the bottom end of the school league tables. The school is in severe financial difficulties, losing pupil numbers as parents choose to send their children to other schools in the area. It is the view of the Local Education Authority (LEA) that bad management has greatly contributed to the school's poor league table performance and financial difficulties. In an attempt to put this right, a new head teacher is appointed.

The head teacher took on the role fully aware that the school is in a precarious situation and that it will be a mammoth task to improve the league table position of this school. Nonetheless, he is fully committed to what he sees as his mission in making the school a good, viable choice for local parents; he hopes to engage the commitment of the teaching staff to this mission. Many of the teachers, most of whom are members of the National Union of Teachers (NUT), the largest teachers' union in England and Wales (NUT 2013), have been at the school for a number of years. They are extremely committed to Barrowton School which caters for many under-privileged pupils (including a large proportion of refugee children) in a deprived area of a large city. It appears, therefore, that from the outset both management and staff are united in their desire to provide a good sound education for the children in the local area.

Shortly after the head teacher's appointment the school had an Ofsted (Office for Standards in Education, Children's Services and Skills[2]) inspection which deemed the school to have 'significant weaknesses' in the standard of education being delivered to the students. The senior management

---

1 This a pseudonym and not the real name of the school.

2 This is the official, government appointed body for inspecting schools.

team and the governing body[3] are charged by Ofsted to produce an Action Plan to address the school's problems. The development of the Action Plan is led by the head teacher who is determined to do all that he can to improve the school in the eyes of Ofsted. The school was warned that if it did not make substantial improvements within the next six months it would face closure. The teachers did not agree with the Ofsted report, claiming that the inspectors failed to take into account the number of students from refugee families who could speak no, or very little, English. In their opinion, the school should be assessed on its good work with these children, rather than examination results.

The employment relationship in Barrowton School

On his appointment the head teacher discovers that the previous head teacher had introduced a morning briefing session which took place in the staffroom every morning before the start of school. He decides to continue this process and sends a memorandum to all staff informing them that morning briefings will continue and they should, therefore, be in the staffroom by 8.30 a.m. each morning. Unlike the briefing sessions under the previous head teacher these meetings are compulsory. All staff are to attend and the meeting will be led by the head teacher and his two deputies. The head teacher views these meetings as an ideal time to communicate school issues (such as cover for absent colleagues, pupils excluded from school for bad behaviour etc.) to the staff. The head teacher sees these meetings as informal gatherings and encourages staff participation.

Although the head teacher believes in the use of both formal and informal communication, on the whole he tends to address his staff through the use of formal written memoranda. This is particularly the case if he has an issue which might be considered to be controversial, for example, matters of a possible disciplinary nature. Things that are written down are less likely to be misinterpreted or misunderstood. It is not unusual for teachers to receive memorandums in their pigeonholes when they arrive at school for the morning briefing.

When he arrives at the school the head teacher creates a 'management suite' consisting of his office, a meeting room, his secretary's office and the office of the senior deputy head teacher. Unlike the previous head teacher's office, which was situated close to the school's entrance, the new offices are at the rear of the school building. They are accessed via a key-coded security door, the code to which is kept closely guarded. The aim of the door is to discourage pupils and parents attempting to enter the head teacher's office unannounced. Teachers are always welcome to see him but need to make an appointment with his secretary beforehand.

In a similar way to the previous head teacher, both deputy head teachers practise 'walking the floor' and are often seen by the teaching staff during the school day. In contrast to this, the new head teacher is completely focused on producing the Action Plan and although he spends many long hours in the school (usually there well before and long after any of the teaching staff) his only visibility in the school is at the formal morning briefing sessions in the staff room. As a result, teachers feel that the head teacher has locked himself away, is non-communicative and has raised a barrier between himself and the teaching staff.

---

3 This is made up of volunteers from the local school community. School governors can include parents, teachers and local community members. Governors have 'a general responsibility for the conduct of the school with a view to promoting high standards of educational achievement' (Department for Education 2013).

(Continued)

(Continued)

The Action Plan is immensely important for the school. The head teacher is keen to have the input of his teaching staff to this and has sent a copy to all heads of departments for comment. He has received very little input back from them and feels that they are not very interested in helping to implement changes which may save the school.

At the same time, in what he sees as a measure to improve the school, the head teacher has asked the two deputy head teachers to start a process of observing teachers while they teach in class. He has also instigated formal disciplinary procedures against two teachers whom he has judged to be under-performing. Both of these teachers are popular with the rest of the teaching staff, who do not believe that the disciplinary procedures are fair. The two teachers have consulted with their trade union representative who is now representing them in discussions with the head teacher. Following a vote instigated by the trade union official, the teachers have all agreed to take action against the head teacher's decision to discipline their colleagues. Rather than enter into a strike they decide to withdraw their 'goodwill' in support of the two disciplined teachers. This means that none of the teachers are supervising children during school beaks (including lunch times) or engaging with after-school activities such as the photographic club or school trips. The atmosphere within the school is one of hostility and a lack of trust between the teachers and their head teacher. The situation is exacerbated because after the publication of the Ofsted report there were reports in the local press that the teachers are 'failing' the children.

Source: author.

 ■ **Questions**

1. Who do you see as being the main actors within this case study?
2. How would you describe the employment relationship in this case study? Give reasons for your answer.
3. What impact do the various actors have on the employment relationship?
4. With regard to people management, what are the benefits of:

   i 'walking the floor'?
   ii isolating oneself to get an important task completed?

5. Why do you think there is little feedback from the staff regarding the Action Plan?
6. If you were in the situation of the Barrowton head teacher, is there anything you might have done differently?

Introduction

A key factor underpinning the study of strategic HRM is the way in which the employment relationship is managed. As we have seen in previous chapters, people, i.e. employers and employees, play a significant part in the successful operation of organizations. The fulfilment of strategic organizational objectives largely depends upon the commitment and cooperation of the workforce and it is therefore a fundamental necessity for any company that the employment relationship runs smoothly. As has already been shown throughout this book, the management of people does not take place in a vacuum; organizations are not islands, operating in a sea of their own, and accordingly the employment relationship has a far-ranging contextual setting (see Chapter 1). As the chapter will go on to demonstrate, there are influences outside the organization that impact upon the people management policies, practices and processes.

In line with this, it is important to appreciate that contemporary organizations frequently operate across national boundaries (see Chapter 12). The globalization of business theorists suggests that economies are becoming globally integrated, with global trade making the more traditional national boundaries increasingly permeable. As a result, it is argued that there is a move towards a greater convergence of management practices based around notions of 'best practice' (Sera 1992), particularly with regard to multinational corporations (MNCs) who, due to the nature of their operations, are exposed to highly competitive international market forces. In order to enhance and maintain their competitiveness MNCs are often seen to pursue, or attempt to pursue, HRM policies integrated into their global HR strategy, processes and procedures in order to generate greater efficiencies and resist pressures to adopt localized management practices (Ashkenas et al. 1995). Conversely, it is similarly argued that MNCs may also follow localized employment policies. Hu (1992) argues that most MNCs cannot easily be defined as stateless because cultural differences and local context will inevitably promote a differentiation in people management practices. It is probable that the variation in country-specific institutional arrangements, such as the state and legislation, will dictate the maintenance of distinctive, localized, HR practices. It is within this context that the chapter will explore the nature of the employment relationship through the eyes of the key 'actors'. Examples from around the world are drawn upon to illustrate the complex and dynamic interrelationship between the various 'actors' engaged in the employment relationship.

The meaning of the employment relationship

Although the employment relationship is basically that which exists between the employer and the employee, it is a dynamic and multifaceted relationship. It is usually, but not always, governed by a contract of employment. Like most contracts, the employment contract is a bargain between two parties. In this case, the contract sets out the terms and conditions of employment that exist between the buyer of labour (the employer) and the seller (the employee). The employee sells their labour for a wage that is determined by the value put upon that labour by the employer and the employee themselves (as explored in Reflective Activity 8.1). This value can vary depending upon the type of labour that the employer is looking to purchase and also the availability.

In the current economic climate we could argue that it is a 'buyer's market' for employers as there are more people looking for jobs than there are jobs available; this is termed a 'loose labour market' (Torrington et al. 2008). The opposite position to this is when there is a 'tight labour market' and there are more jobs available than there are people seeking jobs. This clearly impacts on the HRM function because HR managers need to take availability of workforce into account when setting recruitment policies and practices and pay levels. In theory, under loose labour market conditions, employers are able to recruit more easily and set a lower wage while simultaneously demanding higher qualifications or more experience. Of course this is not always the case, as workers with certain skills and occupations are able to demand a higher wage (see Reflective Activity 8.1).

=== PIT STOP: REFLECTIVE ACTIVITY 8.1 ===

The labour market

It was reported in October 2010 that Premier League Manchester United's star football player, Wayne Rooney, had agreed a contract which paid him £90,000 a week (*Financial Times* 2010).

In August 2012 there were 2.56 million unemployed people in the UK: this equates to approximately 8 per cent of 'the economically actively population' (Office for National Statistics 2012).

The UK National Minimum Wage (NMW) for those over 21 is £6.19 per hour, based upon a 40-hour week: this equates to £247.60 per week.

1. Why, in the present economic climate, are Manchester United willing to pay Wayne Rooney 370 times more than the NMW?

Availability of labour is a macro-determinant of the employment relationship, but the nature of employment being 'sold' is also an important factor. In recent years we have seen a change in the composition of employment, with a decline in the traditionally male-dominated manufacturing industry and growth in the service sector. Simultaneously we have seen a change in the format of employment contracts with 'atypical' and flexible working patterns such as part-time and temporary jobs becoming the norm (see Chapter 6). This is a pattern that is not only occurring across Europe (Eurofound 2010) but also worldwide. Even in Japan, where lifetime employment was seen as a pillar upon which the employment relationship has been built, the government came under pressure to change legislation and allow firms to introduce atypical contracts (Kuroki 2012). Such employment is often precarious in nature and combined with the current worldwide economic downturn and resulting job cut-backs there is a heightened insecurity for workers (Noon and Blyton 2007; Kuroki 2012). Insecurity plays a significant factor in the wage bargain relationship.

While the employment contract is central to the employment relationship because it defines the general terms, conditions and rewards of the exchange between the employer and the employee, the relationship itself is a complex process. Underpinning the employment relationship is the transformation of the employee's labour power (best seen as the hours that employees 'sell' to the employer for a wage) into productive labour. To achieve this employers, through a managerial process, have to organize, direct and control employees' labour. How labour power is turned into actual productive labour is crucial to both parties as this part of the relationship might be contested. The environment in which this takes place can either be one which provides employees with rewarding and fulfilling jobs and input into decision-making, or it may be one whereby employees are under intense scrutiny, control and direction. The former might be seen as 'soft HRM' whilst the latter fits into the 'hard HRM' (Storey 2001) category (see Chapter 3). These working environments create dynamic and often unpredictable employment relationships which can lead to either cooperation or conflict within the workplace.

In a loose labour market the balance of power within the employment relationship tends to lie more with the employers, who have access to greater economic resources than employees. At such times, employers have more freedom to regulate wages and employment contracts and to choose from the pool of potential employees seeking employment, thus giving them far greater control over the employment relationship. In essence, they are able to replace unwanted workers more easily than during tight labour market periods. As we will see later in the chapter, if employees perceive management to be too controlling, they can draw upon their individual and collective power (the latter through the medium of trade unions – see below) in an attempt to constrain management actions and redress this asymmetrical balance of power (Blyton and Turnbull 2004). To understand the employment relationship, we need to take account of the various collective and shared interests of the employees (Blyton and Turnbull 2004).

The above has provided a brief overview of the employment relationship internal to an organization, however, this relationship does not take place in isolation. To fully understand the employment relationship we must situate it in a wider context, both nationally and globally. The strategic approach to people management is often governed by what is happening outside the organization, and it is to the political and economic perspectives of government that we now turn.

The employment relationship from different organizational perspectives

We have established that the employment relationship is broadly (but not exclusively) based around an exchange of employee labour for (usually) monetary reward and that the way in which this is managed and organized can be contested. To help understand and contextualize the employment relationship, it is helpful to have an awareness of some underpinning perspectives, that is, ways of viewing the relationship and how it should be managed. For this we go back to the influential work of Alan Fox (1966) who put forward two frames of reference, or perspectives, on the employment relationship – unitarist and pluralist. These perspectives are still widely referred to within the study of employment relations, and they help us to categorize the way in which the employment relationship is formulated within the workplace. Fox's perspectives are discussed below.

Unitarist perspective

This perspective sees the organization as an integrated, unified, group of people, with a common set of values and interests, working towards the same goals. There is a single source of authority and it is, therefore, management's right to manage and make decisions. Viewed as one big happy family, any conflict is seen as irrational and where this does occur it is presumed to be as 'a result of misunderstanding or mischief' (Crouch 1982: 18 quoted in Edwards 2003: 10).

Managers who approach the employment relationship from this perspective would view the collective representation of employees in the form of trade unions as being unnecessary. People identifying with this frame of reference are likely to perceive any disagreement between managers and workers as being minor, the fault of the employees, probably due to poor communication and easily resolved. Trade unions are viewed as intrusions into management's right to manage. Should any conflict occur then managers would resort to coercion, including the use of the law, as this is regarded as being a legitimate use of managerial power to gain employee consent. Blyton et al. provide us with a succinct summary of this perspective: 'the right employment policies and practices will align the interests of employers and employees' (2008: 103).

Managers adhering to the unitarist perspective would look for loyalty and commitment from their workforce while at the same time expecting complete and undisputed managerial control. Unitarism is sometimes viewed as a management ideology, and Dundon and Rollinson promote caution when they suggest that 'the capacity for a unitarist view to explain the reality of work-

...ents of this perspective are very much in ...ontemporary workplaces, particularly in ...actice of HRM and the idea of creating ...s. For example, a company like the retail ...xcludes trade unions, but also treats their ...010). This might not, however, be the case ...s who may actively exclude trade unions. ...concept of individualism.

...ns

...esents the interests of its members (employees)

...o regulate the employment relationship through ...rgaining.

...pluralist perspective recognizes that ...nt groups with different interests and ...pting to gain the maximum advantage ...example, employers may be seeking to ...costs down and production levels up, ...er share of the profits to be reflected ...e employment relationship from this ...t not only is workplace conflict likely to

...pluralist perspective accept that there is a ...nization of employees in trade unions and ...priate mechanism for agreeing wage rates. ...ndividualism, pluralism is associated with ...nent to manage rather than suppress con- ...engage in negotiation with the union. ...chapter, trade union representation is less strong in organizations than it was in the mid-1960s when Fox was putting forward his perspectives for understanding the employment relationship, we do still see a pluralist approach to management in some organizations, with trade unions recognized by employers as the collective representative voice for employees. This is particularly the case in the public sector in the UK.

Marxist perspective

In 1977, Fox critiqued his own pluralist perspective, a critique which was subsequently taken up by other authors. Fox's pluralist perspective provides the view that collective voice can help provide a balance of power within the employment relationship but he later argued that, due to managers controlling the capital resources, it was not possible for this to be the case. Indeed, he argued that there is a 'gross disparity of power between the employer and the employee' and that despite trade unions and collectivism 'a great imbalance [in the employment relationship] remains' (1977: 141).

Fox's (1977) 'radical critique' of pluralism was taken up by Marxist writers (for example Hyman 1975, 1978) who argue that the employment relationship has to be placed within the wider context of the imbalance of power between capital (business owners) and labour (employees). The Marxist perspective rests upon the view that '*profit* – the pursuit of economic returns to the owners – is the key influence on company policy . . . and that control over production is enforced *downwards* by the owners' managerial agents and functionaries' (Hyman 1975: 19, emphasis in original). The argument is, in effect, that workers are, and always will be, exploited by the owners of industry and business. Marxist writers argue that conflict in the workplace reflects not only the tensions between employer and employee at the workplace level but also the wider social and economic divisions – arguably class divisions – throughout society. Hence, in the struggle for class equality conflict is inevitable and this conflict will be reflected in the workplace.

For Marxists, within the pluralist perspective trade unions become part of the system of workplace government as they strive for compromise rather than engage in conflict (Marchington 1982). This view is likely to be rejected by some academics and practitioners who may see the *raison d'être* of trade unions to be resisting or contesting management's right to manage.

PIT STOP: REFLECTIVE ACTIVITY 8.2

Perspectives on the employment relationship

1. Think of an organization that you are familiar with. What are the overall management perspectives employed in that organization?
2. Why do you think managers have this approach in the organization?
3. Try looking at it from another perspective: how would the organization have to change to accommodate this perspective?

It is important to recognize that these perspectives are useful as tools of analysis; they help us to understand the context in which the employment relationship operates, however, they are not discrete entities and it is possible to see a merging of the boundaries between them. As Marchington (1982) argues, we must be prepared for a shift in individual views and opinions depending upon the issue that they are facing.

As discussed previously, the employment relationship is wider than the relationship between the employer and the employee and is influenced by a number of different factors and actors. The following sections will now move on to consider these wider institutional influences beginning with the state.

The role and scope of the state

Within the study of employment relations the state is normally taken to mean the elected government of the day, including all the agencies that implement its legislation and policies (Gospel and Palmer 1993, quoted in Dundon and Rollinson 2011).The state is, however, wider than this and state agencies include the police; the armed forces; and government. In the UK the state is headed by the Queen or King. The UK Government, which is democratically elected, is headed by the Prime Minister and there is an impartial Civil Service which remains constant and works for the elected government of the time; the government is able to influence and alter the way in which the Civil Service operates. In other societies, however, there may be a less democratic approach to governing the country. For example, in Saudi Arabia the King not only heads the government, he is also the Commander in Chief of the military and is the most senior person in the legal system (Saudi Embassy 2013). As we shall see below, the role of the government and their ideological approach to running the country can have an impact on the workplace employment relationship.

The role of government and the employment relationship

Governments around the world influence the employment relationship in many and varied ways. They are, for example, able to introduce legislation which, depending on their strategy, is geared towards providing greater or lesser protection for the employee and likewise for the employer. As we see in Case Study 8.3, they are also able to influence the outcomes of disputes between the employer and the employee. The government are also able to introduce economic policies which have an impact on taxation and the rate of pay an employer is obliged to pay their workers; for example, many countries now have a minimum wage which employers are legally bound to adhere to.

The extent of government intervention into the workings of industry and business does, however, vary between countries. Some governments are seen to take an interventionist approach, where they are heavily involved in regulating the labour market, as is the case in France (Calveley 2005b), while other governments in countries such as the USA and the UK may follow a voluntarist approach, whereby the parties involved in the regulation of employment (employers and trade unions) 'determine the nature and content of their relationship' and 'regulate it without governmental or legal integration' (Salamon 2000: 63). Japan provides us with an interesting example of how governments intervene in the employment relationship. Japanese workers enjoy strong legislative protection with regard to dismissal and redundancy, nonetheless, due to competitive pressures and lobbying from businesses, the government have relaxed part of the legislation in order to allow firms to employ temporary workers (Kuroki 2012).

Governments in most democratic societies are in office for only a limited period of time and thus subject to periodic elections to gain office; by definition they are transient in nature. Therefore the stance that governments take with regard to intervening in the employment relationship may vary over time and often changes dramatically with a change of government.

We shall discuss below how different governments hold different political ideological perspectives on how society and employment relationships should be ordered.

Ideological perspectives: neo-liberalism and neo-corporatism

It is important to recognize here that, as with the organizational perspectives of the employment relationship discussed above, the following ideological perspectives are indicative rather than discrete typologies. These perspectives represent the prevailing ideological frameworks of national governments and it is within these frameworks that the institutions within the country (for example, legislature; employer representatives; employee representatives) have to operate. They therefore influence the nature of the employment relationship and are important for those working within and studying employment relations and HR to understand. They are particularly relevant for MNCs as regards their HR policies, which emanate from the home country head office (see Chapter 12). Ideological perspectives develop over time and as we will see below, are influenced by the history and culture of a country.

Neo-liberalism

The rise of neo-liberalism in the Western world dates back to the 1980s when the British Prime Minister Margaret Thatcher and the American President Ronald Reagan promoted laissez-faire, free-market economic theories. Blaming economic problems on state interference in business and industry matters, both governments promoted deregulation of the labour market, removal of government interventions in market policies and the liberalization of trade and industry. They argued that the state should play a much smaller role within a country's economic and social well-being and that public spending (on the provision of social services and health care for example) should be kept to a minimum. Throughout the 1980s in the UK there was a mass privatization of state-owned industries, which was referred to as 'selling off the family silver' by those who were against it. During this period the UK government privatized the provision of energy (gas, electricity, coal), transport (British Rail) and telecommunications (British Telecommunications) allowing private enterprise to take this over. Similar actions occurred in other European countries.

Within the neo-liberalism philosophy, management should have the sole right to manage and there should be no interference whatsoever from the workforce, particularly through their collective representation by trade unions. In fact, Prime Minister Thatcher described trade unions as 'the enemy within'. Liberal within this context is used to describe a society of individuals who pursue their own best interests by entering freely into contracts without state or trade union help, with the latter viewed as being responsible for wage inflation. Neo-liberalism conviction follows classical economic theory: market forces will prevail and therefore wage levels should be set entirely by market demand. If there is high unemployment then wages will fall, on the other hand, if there is a demand for labour then wages will increase. The individual employee, rather than collective representation through trade union membership, is paramount within the employment relationship.

PIT STOP: REFLECTIVE ACTIVITY 8.3

Neo-liberalist philosophy and the employment relationship

1. The neo-liberalist ideological perspective fits comfortably with which of the organizational perspectives of the employment relationship discussed above?

Neo-corporatism

Neo-corporatism can be used to describe an employment relations model that has largely operated in parts of mainland Europe after the Second World War, most notably in Germany but also in France, Austria, the Netherlands and Sweden. It was also an influential perspective in the UK during the 1960s, when Conservative and Labour governments alike adopted some aspects of neo-corporatist policies. However, as discussed above, since the 1980s UK governments have taken a more neo-liberal ideological stance.

Hollinshead puts it succinctly: neo-corporatist ideology 'envisages an active role for the state in seeking to mediate and integrate the interests of various powerful societal groupings, particularly those representing capital and labour' (2010: 25). A government following this ideological perspective would work with the employers and trade unions at a macro level on industrial, economic and social policy aimed at producing growth, full employment and price stability. Such an approach is known as a tripartite approach to employment relations whereby the main actors become 'social partners'. Neo-corporatists would see the neo-liberal free market philosophy as leading to an unequal distribution of wealth and resources across society.

As opposed to the neo-liberal philosophy as discussed above, within the neo-corporatist ideology the government creates institutions to facilitate agreement between the parties within the employment relationship; the government would, for example, legislate for collective agreements on minimum wages and employment conditions.

According to Rose (2008), critics of neo-corporatism would argue that it is not possible for the state to be neutral when it comes to employment relations because a government 'will intervene either to bolster the power of capital or to support labour in order to redress the power imbalance' (2008: 37). In short, the government will act in a way that enhances their ideological position.

From corporatism to neo-liberalism

An example of an almost overnight shift in national government ideology from a corporatist stance to one of neo-liberalism is the UK.

Depending on their political stance, from 1945–1979 UK governments either tolerated (Conservative governments) or promoted (Labour governments) trade unions. Trade unions were seen as part of the democratic running of the country. Throughout this period, government viewed industry leaders and trade unions as having a stake in the social and economic development of the country and sought their input into policy-making decisions. This represented a corporatist ideological approach.

In 1979 all of that changed. The Conservative Government elected that year asserted their right to unilaterally govern the country. The views of the trade unions were no longer sought and emphasis was placed upon the needs of business owners. This represented a neo-liberalist ideological approach.

Summary

It is clear that not all countries fit into these ideological frameworks, but they are useful in helping us to understand the context in which organizations operate. Arguably the influence of globalization and the growth of large international and multinational organizations (see Chapter 12) have impacted upon the ideological perspectives of governments as they come under pressure to welcome these organizations, who bring with them often much needed employment opportunities. The latter is particularly the case with developing countries in Africa and Asia, who are beginning to engage with the neo-liberal perspective not only to encourage inward investment from MNCs but also as they begin to compete on a global basis. This is not a one-way process, however, and when thinking of expanding to countries outside their country of origin, organizations are obliged to consider the ideological framework of the host country.

An interesting consideration of how neo-liberalism might develop on a global basis (Kurtz and Brooks 2008; Schneider 2009) is that of the four major economies of Latin America: Argentina, Brazil, Chile and Mexico. As these economies have followed diverse trajectories (King 2010: 2) there has not been a single, universal pathway and implementation of neo-liberalism has depended upon the individual economic drivers within the countries.

It should be recognized that there are also variations to the neo-corporatist framework. We see throughout Europe differing interpretations of the neo-corporatist ideology as global influences have impacted on individual countries. As Hollinshead states, as a result of global competition and the search for employment flexibility, 'neo-corporatist tendencies in the EU . . . have tended to give way to a powerful agenda of de-regulation' (Hollinshead 2010: 26).

The above section has considered the role of the state and how this is influenced by the ideological perspectives within which governments operate. As we have seen, there are national and international influences to state policies and practices. As a main actor within the employment relationship the state generates a changing and dynamic variable which continuously influences the relationship from an external perspective.

Another dynamic that influences the employment relationship, in this case both externally and internally, is the power relationship between the various actors. For example, we see in Case Study 8.3 how the balance of power changes within the employment relationship and how this balance is influenced by the various actors. These issues are further explored below.

Employers and employers' associations

Clearly, major actors within the employment relationship are the employers themselves. As we stated at the start of the chapter, the employment relationship does not take place in a vacuum and neither do employers operate in this way. Employers are influenced by the state and have to adhere to statutory requirements and other institutional arrangements. For example, the state education and training policies can impact on employers. In some countries, for example Germany and France, there is a strong state intervention with regard to workplace learning, training and development (Calveley 2005b).

In order to help mediate the impact of state interventions and also as a result of the development of collectivism through trade unionism (see below) in many countries employers come together to create employers' associations. Individual companies belong to these associations, who act on their behalf to lobby government in order to influence policy making (see Case Study 8.3). They also provide advice and guidance to companies with regard to employment relations issues. Examples of employers' associations are the National Farmers' Union in the UK and LTO, the Dutch Confederation of Agriculture and Horticulture, in the Netherlands.

The following section turns to the influence of power with regard to the contestation, regulation and control of the employment relationship.

Power relations

The notion of power, and how this is contested, forms a central tenet to understanding the complex nature of the employment relationship. Power is a nebulous concept; it is multifaceted and can have different dimensions. Power may also be viewed in different ways by different people. In her work on gendered power, Bradley describes power relations as being 'complex and fluid' (1999: 32) and defines power as being 'the capacity to control patterns of social interaction' (1999: 33). In the employment relationship we see social interactions on a daily basis between employees (and their representatives) and management and these interactions need to be considered within the context of the power relationship. Bradley (1999: 34) provides us with a typology of nine different types of power 'resources', four of which are particularly relevant and are adapted here to help us to understand the complexity of the employment relationship:

1. Economic power: the control of economic resources. In the workplace this would usually lie in the hands of the business owner. However, this is an area that may well be contested as employees look to seek a greater share of these resources.
2. Positional power: power and authority gained by virtue of holding positions, which in the workplace would be that of employer, manager, supervisor or possibly trade union leader. We also see this outside the workplace when

governments intervene and introduce employment legislation. Depending on the ideological stance of the government, such legislation may be beneficial to the business owner/management (neo-liberal) or the employee and their representative (neo-corporatist).

3. **Symbolic power:** the ability to impose one's own definitions, meanings, values and rules on a situation. We might see this within the workplace when management promote a particular 'culture' (see Chapter 11).
4. **Collective power:** the mobilization of collective resources; the ability to organize groups of people to pursue common goals, e.g. trade unions.

We see in Case Study 8.3 how the power resources outlined above operate both independently and simultaneously when there is a dispute between employers and employees in the workplace. The outcome of such disputes frequently rests upon the strength, or – and often more importantly – the *perceived* strength, of the power resources of the various actors, including the role that the government plays. Indeed, as Blyton and Turnbull suggest, the nature of the employment relationship 'is not simply one of (management) control versus (worker) resistance, but a more problematic mix of dissent and accommodation, conflict and cooperation' (1994: 31).

The following sections will, in the context of power relations, explore the extent to which employees have a 'voice' within the employment relationship.

Employee voice

The extent to which employees have a 'voice' in the workplace is a fundamental element of the employment relationship, so much so that the concept has been central to academic literature on employment relations, organizational behaviour and HRM studies during the last 25 years (see for example: Ackers et al. 2004; Beardwell 1998; Benson and Brown 2010). Employee voice can be defined as the ability of employees to make a contribution to the main decisions in the organization (Lucas et al. 2006), and is understood in broad terms as 'a whole variety of processes and structures which enable, and at times empower, employees, directly and indirectly, to contribute to decision-making in the firm' (Boxall and Purcell 2003: 162). Writing from a people management perspective, the Chartered Institute of Personnel and Development in the UK describe employee voice as 'the two way communication between employer and employee. It is the process of the employer communicating to the employee as well as receiving and listening to communication from the employee' (CIPD 2011 [online]). This refers essentially to the formal and informal mechanisms of participation through information, communication, consultation between employers and employees and employees' active participation in the company decision-making processes. Voice is seen as an important part of organizational commitment where employees make decisions in voice and non-voice spaces (Walton 1985; Lewin and Mitchell 1992; Pfeffer 1998; Dundon 2002; Ackers et al. 2004).

Employee voice can take various formats and in organizations which operate from a pluralist perspective it is likely to be collective voice through trade unions and/or works councils, whereas in organizations which follow the unitarist HRM approach to people management it is more likely to be an individualistic approach through team meetings, management communications etc. Again, we need to take caution in making wide-ranging assumptions and these are broad generalizations.

Brewster et al. (2007: 1248) state that employee voice practices 'may be grouped by dimension (whether based on collective or individual voice) and depth (i.e. the extent to which a practice is likely to influence management decision making)' and this is something we will return to later in the chapter. Figure 8.1 provides a pictorial view of employee voice in organizations and shows the 'dimension' (Brewster et al. 2007) of voice and the relationship between collective participation and unitarist involvement as discussed above.

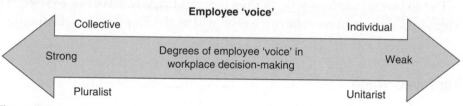

Employee 'voice'

Collective — Individual

Strong — Degrees of employee 'voice' in workplace decision-making — Weak

Pluralist — Unitarist

Figure 8.1
Source: author.

Armstrong (2006) argues that there are four objectives with regards to employee voice: the first is the articulation of employee dissatisfaction with the organization; second is the role of the voice of the employees as a form of expression in the collective management organization; third is the decision of management in relation to the organization of work, quality and productivity; finally, employee voice shows the correlation between the employer and the employees.

Within the unitarist versus pluralist debate, Freeman and Medoff (1984) argued that employee voice as a mechanism has both a consensual and a conflictual characteristic, where on the one hand, employee participation may have a favourable impact on quality and productivity while on the other hand, the collective voice provided by trade unions allows for a contestation of the asymmetrical power relations (Blyton and Turnbull 2004) as discussed above. Nonetheless, trade unions can be mediators between management and workers within the employment relationship; by giving employees voice, managers allow workers some autonomy within the workplace which ultimately can help to reduce the exit of workers (Ackers et al. 2004: 299). By allowing workplace dialogue and negotiation to take place, it is possible to alleviate issues which may otherwise fester and lead to greater discontent; voice mechanisms are able to 'reflect aggregated worker preferences' (Heywood and Jirjahn 2009: 125) and therefore help promote workplace harmony.

As can be seen from the discussion above, employee voice can be interpreted in different ways. Ackers et al. (2004), for example, provide a framework for employee voice where voice is distinguished along two dimensions: direct (based on employees) and indirect (based on a collective grouping), which represent shared interests and/or conflicting positions. For these authors, conception of voice is understood from a broad and systematic perspective, where direct and indirect dimensions operate in the changing patterns of employee voice organization. In their view employee voice is based on a shared or conflictive agenda, rather than being absolutely different or similar. Taking a different perspective, Freeman and Medoff's (1984) notion of employee voice is based mainly on the collective aspect and trade unions.

Although there is much written on employee voice there is a paucity of literature exploring employee voice with regard to employee diversity; the increase of the ethnic, gender and age diversity of the workforce has not been adequately represented in the literature (Rank 2009). If, as Beauregard et al. (2011) suggest, it is necessary to create new voice employment mechanisms which take account of diversity in order to develop a culture of inclusion, this omission in the literature requires immediate attention.

Clearly employee voice has a central role in the employment relationship and this is particularly relevant when taking an international perspective. Putting this into the context of the ideological frameworks followed by governments, as discussed above, in general – although not exclusively – organizations operating within a neo-liberalist framework (e.g. in the USA or UK) will follow the unitarist HR management approach. These companies will employ HR practices that promote employee 'engagement' (see below) through direct communication to workers with the main principle being to provide them with company specific information, rather than inviting discussion. In neo-corporatist settings (e.g. France and Germany), organizations are more likely to follow a pluralist management approach and give employees a collective voice in decision-making through trade union and/or works council representation. As we will see below, the unitarist, individual approach generally sits with management strategies of Employee Involvement (EI), while the pluralist, collective approach sits within the Employee Participation (EP) strategic approach to people management.

Working definition of individualism and collectivism

Individualism refers to the extent to which personnel policies are focused on the rights and capabilities of individual workers. Collectivism concerns the extent to which management policy is directed towards inhibiting or encouraging the development of collective representation by employees and allowing employees a collective voice in management decision-making. (Purcell 1987: 533)

Employee involvement, engagement and participation

The concepts of 'involvement' and 'participation' are used to refer to the scope of decision-making allowed by employee voice methods.

Employee involvement and employee engagement

Employee involvement is premised on the HRM unitarist view that managers and employees have common interests. This approach to managing the employment relationship promotes the concepts of teamwork, quality and 'quality circles', customer care and employee commitment, all of which are in line with US and Japanese approaches to management.

Employee involvement might be viewed by HR practitioners as a mechanism by which managers are able to engage the workforce in a way which secures their commitment and collaboration in achieving organizational objectives and to identify and resolve organizational problems. However, this is a rather simplistic view. Although it has been common to associate employee involvement with empowering employees we could view this as rhetoric; this management strategy arguably fails to take into account the real distribution of power in the workplace (Wilton 2010: 290). Without a collectivist orientation to management, managers retain control in making the strategic decisions in the workplace, such as those relating to wages, working conditions or issues on the more general policy of the organization. Therefore, EI can be viewed as a weak form of voice which seeks to involve the employee through channels of expression but which provides them with little opportunity to contest management decisions. Indeed, it has been argued that EI systems are designed to weaken and marginalize trade unions, or to motivate them to take more responsibility (Ramsey 1977).

From a neo-liberal perspective, this would be the normal order of the employment relationship, whereas the neo-corporatist view would give more say to the employees and their representatives. According to Kersley et al. (2006), in the UK the decline of union representation in the workplace has coincided with an increase in the direct participation of employees, but this should not be seen as a natural progression: in France, for example, there is very low trade union membership (around 8 per cent of the workforce) but there is strong trade union representation in the workplace (EIRO 2013).

There is much emphasis placed by HR practitioners on employee engagement (EE). It is seen as 'a combination of commitment to the organization and its values and a willingness to help colleagues' (CIPD 2012: 1). A useful conceptualization is that of Kahn who suggests it is 'the harnessing of organization members' selves to their work roles; in engagement, people employ and express themselves physically, cognitively, and emotionally during role performances' (Kahn 1990: 694). As such, it is a complex and ambiguous notion which in essence is about engaging the 'heart and soul' of the employee when they are at work.

Employee participation

Unlike employee involvement, employee participation (EP) is a stronger representation of employee voice: it allows employees greater access to the decision-making processes and consequently some degree of power-sharing is evident between employees and management. Rather than simply communicating information to employees, in this approach management actively seek input from the workforce. As Brewster et al. state, 'participation accords employees a genuine – clearly demarcated – input into how the firm is governed' (2007: 1248), which is why some management teams are seen to resist it (Wilton 2010).

Participation may be direct or indirect, with the indirect usually involving the use of elected representatives who represent the interests of all employees. This can be through management's engagement with trade unions or through established works councils. The latter are common features in continental Europe and, as discussed below, are usually supported by legislation.

PIT STOP: REFLECTIVE ACTIVITY 8.4

1. Consider Figure 8.1. Where do you see (a) employee engagement and (b) employee involvement fiting within this model? Provide reasons for your answer.

Working definition of employee voice

- Involvement: a unitarist approach to employee voice whereby managers seek the views of employees in a desire to gain their commitment.
- Participation: a pluralist approach to employee voice where management actively seek the input of employees into the decision-making processes.

Participation in action
Trade unions

A trade union is an organization made up of members who are working people. The main principles of a trade union are to represent workers and to protect their working conditions; they do this through negotiation and collective bargaining with management. Trade unionism, referred to as the labour movement in the USA, emerged as a workers' defence against management practices in the nineteenth century. Early trade unions were closely related to craft workers and developed in order to represent skilled workers, however, the twentieth century saw the growth of large industrial unions which represented all workers regardless of employment status. The strengthening of worker power to resist management initiatives was a natural development of trade union growth, however, a trade union's strength lies in the willingness of the membership to take industrial action (to withdraw their labour). Like all organizations, trade unions have leaders and it is important to remember that these leaders are generally elected from the union membership.

Trade unions continued to grow until the early 1980s, and then we begin to see a general decline of these institutions in the liberalized market economies. By the end of the twentieth century the globalization of the workforce (see Chapter 12) had brought new challenges to the labour movement, particularly in industries whose workers could be replaced by a cheaper labour force in a different part of the world. Trade unions have nevertheless had a lasting influence.

The principles and practices of trade unionism are embedded in the economic systems of most industrial countries, and we often see trade unions fighting for social justice as well as workers' rights. Positive legislation and, in some countries, direct political action have established collective bargaining as the principal means of settling disputes over wages, working conditions, and other issues. Unions are, however, sometimes resisted by management and governments alike because they have the potential to mobilize workers to disrupt production.

In China such conflictual relations are avoided because trade unions have been embedded within the framework of the market economy. Despite legislation giving them more freedom, Chinese unions are required to promote the interests of the state and their leaders are frequently senior managers in the companies they are representing (Zhao et al. 2012) so there can be no union/management negotiation in the true sense of the word (see Case Study 8.2).

Read the above section on trade unions

1. What, if any, are their benefits to workers?
2. What, if any, are their benefits to managers?
3. How might collective bargaining promote employee voice in the workplace?

Collective bargaining

This is the term given to the process whereby trade unions representatives consult and negotiate with management with regard to the terms and conditions of employment of their members.

Works councils

Throughout much of Western Europe works councils (WCs) are in operation. They are upheld in law in a number of countries particularly where they were introduced 'as an integral statutory part of the post-war industrial relations system to aid co-operative efforts for economic recovery' (Salamon 2000: 400). Hence we can view them as part of the neo-corporatist frame of reference. WCs are an instrument for giving employees a voice in the workplace, helping facilitate employee involvement in employment relations and management decision-making at company level.

Generally made up of elected employees, works councils have various rights, ranging from being provided with company information (e.g. financial), through consultation with regard to various company policies and practices, to decision-making. The latter may involve issues such as changes in working hours; criteria for hiring staff; and disciplinary procedures. It is important to recognize that WCs are completely different institutions to trade unions. They are enterprise-based and unlike trade unions, work councils have no right to instigate industrial action in any form. In that respect they might be viewed by management as being a less confrontational approach to employee voice. This may, however, be a misnomer as Bennett (1997) suggests that WCs can act as a countervailing influence on management decisions, delaying mergers and watering down management proposals.

Although elected from the workforce in general, evidence suggests that trade unionists are often elected as works council members (Klikauer 2004; Addison et al. 2006; Gumbrell-McCormick and Hyman 2006) which means that management beliefs that they are marginalizing trade unions by instigating works councils may be misguided.

The employment relationship at Foxconn China

The Tiawanese-owned FoxconnLonghua factory (or campus as it is often referred to), located in Shenzhen in China, is reported as being one of the largest contract manufacturers for electronic goods – and indeed the largest factory – in the world (Branigan 2010). Covering more than a square mile, the facility provides dormitories for workers as well as other everyday facilities such as shops, banks and swimming pools. In 2010 more than 8,000 people a day were reported to apply for jobs (Moore 2010) and currently around 240,000 people are employed there (*Economist* 2012). Across China, Foxconn is a huge employer, employing around 1.4 million workers on 28 different sites (*Economist* 2012). The workers in these factories are mainly migrant workers from rural areas. Wages are said to be above the National Minimum Wage (NMW) at 900 Yuan (approximately £91) per month in 2010 (Branigan 2010) and this is reported to have increased more recently, with one report suggesting an average 21.2 per cent increase in 2011 (Reuters 2012).

In 2010 news broke on a worldwide scale of suicides taking place in the factory. Reports suggested that around 18 workers had attempted suicide with 14 actually dying (Zhang 2012). Despite the tragic nature of these suicides they might have gone relatively unnoticed, except for the fact that Foxconn was manufacturing Apple products such as the iPhone and iPads. Hence we have 'newsworthiness'.

News reports suggested that factory workers were working very long hours in repetitive and monotonous jobs to make enough money to live. Although above the NMW, wages were insufficient and workers were working vast amounts of overtime to make enough money to survive, often working up to 120 hours extra a month and averaging 70 hours of work per week (Moore 2010). It was reported that staff were 'burning out' due to the long hours and repetitive nature of the work (Moore 2010). Workers were forbidden to talk during their long shifts and often felt lonely and isolated, working on a compound a long way from home (Zhang 2012), and there were reports of under-age workers (Smedley 2013).

Nevertheless, despite these apparently appalling conditions, some workers say that conditions and wages compare well with other manufacturers (Moore 2010) and writing in 2012, the *Economist* reported that workers appeared relatively content, despite sleeping eight to a dormitory and there being safety nets to prevent suicide attempts (*Economist* 2012). The 'better than average' working conditions may well provide a clue as to why workers continue to apply for jobs. It may also be due to the looseness of the labour market (Torrington et al. 2008 as discussed above) in rural areas of China; people desperate for employment will take what work they are able to get.

Since the suicides in 2010, there have been a number of protests at Foxconn campuses across China, with workers demanding better pay and working conditions. These protests have ranged from suicide threats (Reuters 2012; Zhang 2012) to demonstrations and strikes (Zhang 2012). The reports about the situation at Foxconn were so bad and the publicity so incriminating that Apple asked the Fair Labor Association (FLA) to set about investigating the situation. The FLA spent almost a month gathering both quantitative and qualitative data, including site visits. In March 2012, FLA produced a wide-ranging report identifying four main areas for improvement (Fair Labor Association 2012a):

1. *Working hours*. These were reported as exceeding the 'FLA Code Standard and Chinese legal limits' (2012a: 2) with some workers working more than seven consecutive days without a 24-hour break.

2. *Health and safety.* Workers 'felt generally insecure' (2012a: 2) and there was a concern about aluminium dust.
3. *Industrial relations and worker integration.* The FLA found workers were 'largely alienated, in fact or in perception, from factories' safety and health committees'. The FLA also suggested that as managers nominate the candidates for the worker representatives the committees, which tend to be reactive rather than proactive, 'may not be truly representative of the workers' (2012a: 3).
4. *Compensation and social security insurance.* Although wages were above the legal minimum, the FLA found that '14 percent of the workers may not receive fair compensation for unscheduled overtime' (2012a: 3) as overtime was paid in 30-minute blocks. Therefore 29 minutes and less went unpaid and workers completing 58 minutes would be paid for only 30 of these.

In August 2012 the FLA announced that progress had been made and that '[O]ver 280 action items [had been] completed on time or ahead of schedule' (Fair Labor Association 2012b). In September 2012, however, there had been more news of unrest at the company when fighting broke out amongst workers in the Taiyuan factory in Northern China, which employs around 79,000 workers, and the plant was temporarily closed (Arthur 2012). Managers and police were reported as saying that this was not work-related, however, this followed an earlier 'rampage' by workers in the Chengdu plant (Arthur 2012) and a refusal to work (the company denied reports of a strike) at its approximately 200,000 strong factory in Zhengzhou in October (Hille 2012).

In 2013, Foxconn announced that it was introducing measures to increase employee representatives (*China Post* 2013) and were described as the first Chinese company to introduce a truly independent labour union, the Foxconn Federation of Labour Unions Committee (Hille 2013). For Foxconn workers, this might be seen as a positive step forward, however it is debatable to what extent this new initiative will improve their representation in any meaningful way due to management involvement in the way in which representatives are chosen (*China Post* 2013; Reuters 2013). This is not unusual in China. We discussed earlier in the chapter how Chinese trade unions are embedded within the organization and there is little (if any) encouragement to resist management initiatives. Although the company was said to be seeking the help of the FLA to train the workers in how to vote for their union representatives, there is still some doubt as to the independence of the union. As Hille (2013) points out, the Chairman of the Union is apparently a close and trusted member of the management team.

Source: author.

 ■ Questions

1. Why do you think there is unrest at the Foxconn factories in China?
2. Discuss the extent to which having:

   i   a works council
   ii a trade union might improve workplace relations.

3. Consider the discussion of trade unions earlier in the chapter. To what extent does the Foxconn Federation of Labour Unions Committee fit with this description? Give examples in your answer.

(Continued)

(Continued)

4. Drawing upon your understanding of the ideological perspectives discussed, how can you interpret the policies and practices of the Chinese Government? Provide examples in your answer.
5. What role, if any, do the media play in pressurizing management to improve working conditions?
6. What might you as a HR manager do to improve the relationship between workers and management?

=== PIT STOP: REFLECTIVE ACTIVITY 8.6 ===

Works councils: the German model

The German model of a works council is frequently upheld as an exemplar. German legislation requires the establishment of works councils in companies with more than five employees. The scope of works councils covers information rights on financial issues, and consultation rights including: the implementation of new technologies; workforce planning; working conditions; and job specifications. German WCs also have joint decision-making rights with regard to remuneration, recruitment, and work plans covering 'social' matters such as the principles of remuneration, performance-related pay (PRP), work schedules, overtime, holidays and firing.

Works councils tend to be situated in larger organizations, with far less presence in smaller organizations (Addison et al. 2006; Gumbrell-McCormick and Hyman 2006).

1. To what extent do works councils promote employee participation and involvement in the workplace?
2. What, if any, are the benefits of works councils to managers?
3. What, if any, are the benefits of works councils to workers?

The media

Earlier we discussed the roles of various actors within the employment relationship and we followed this with a discussion of the importance of power resources, or the perception of power resources, on the employment relationship. One area that is often neglected when discussing both the role of actors impacting the employment relationship and the importance of power is that of the media and the impact that this institution might have.

Marchington (1982) explores Fox's (1973) pluralist perspective and the imbalance of power in the employment relationship. He points to the fact that employers are not only able 'to influence employees directly at work but also through the underlying ideological perspectives that permeate the media and society at large' (Marchington 1982: 47), and this is a useful starting point for us to discuss the role of the media within the employment relationship.

In many societies it is now viewed as important that the media, and in particular television and newspapers, are able to freely report on societal and economic events. More recently, with the advent of satellite broadcasting, Internet technology, 24-hour news channels on television and the World Wide Web with its social media websites, media coverage has become an instantaneous phenomenon. We, the 'general public', appear to have an unquenchable thirst for news and information and it is the role of the media to bring this information to us. The extent to which the media should remain impartial and unbiased in delivering such news has long been the subject of debate in societies which grant a freedom of reporting to their media institutions. In the USA, where the freedom of the press is protected by the US Constitution, the media are commonly known as 'the Fourth Estate'. This title demonstrates the significance given to the media in that country where they are seen as being of almost equal standing with the three official branches of government (legislature, judicial, executive). This gives us some idea of the power that the press may yield within a country. It is well-known that in many countries (including the USA), political parties are eager to encourage major newspapers to align themselves with their political views. For example, we often hear of newspapers as being aligned to 'the right' or 'the left' of the political spectrum.

We also need to remember that historically media sources were 'owned' by the state (for example the British Broadcasting Corporation [BBC] in the UK) and were therefore to some extent controlled in what they were allowed to put into the public domain. Although for many countries in the Western world this is no longer the case, there are still some countries where this remains the situation and as such media reporting should be followed with caution.

So what role might the media play in the employment relationship? The way in which the media report a news story can provide that story with a stance that favours one party or another. This is often the case with, for example, the coverage of employment disputes, particularly strikes. It may be that one section of the media supports the management and slants the reports in their favour, while another section of the media may be sympathetic to the workers and their trade unions. (See Reflective Activity 8.7 and Case Study 8.3 on the UK fuel tanker drivers' dispute.)

PIT STOP: REFLECTIVE ACTIVITY 8.7

The media

1. Read the political editorial of three different newspapers. Discuss whether they are to the left or the right of the political spectrum.

2. Find a news article which covers an employment relations issue and:

    i Consider whether the reporting can be seen as unbiased.
    ii Does it favour the employers or the employees?
    iii Why do you think this?
    iv What impact might this coverage have on the issue being reported?

3. Are you able to relate the coverage with neo-liberal or neo-corporatist ideological views?

CASE STUDY 8.3

'Fuelling the shortage?' The UK fuel tanker drivers' dispute

In March 2012, petrol station forecourts across the UK were flooded with customers queuing to buy fuel for their motor vehicles. This 'panic buying' spree lasted several days as the government, fuel providers, Acas (Advisory, Concilliation and Arbitration Service) and Unite, the union representing the tanker drivers who delivered the fuel, discussed, both publicly and privately, issues surrounding a possible strike by the tanker drivers. The threatened nationwide strike, which would be the first of its type in more than a decade, made headline news for several days.

This case study sets out the dispute and provides insight into the roles played by various actors, including highlighting the influential role that the press can have in such disputes. The case begins by providing an overview of the fuel distribution industry before moving on to consider how the dispute unfolded.

The fuel distribution industry[1]

In the UK, our everyday lives are heavily dependent on petroleum fuels (petrol and diesel), whether this is for our own personal motor vehicle use, for public transport, for government-owned vehicles (ambulances, fire engines, police vehicles etc.) or for the use of commercial vehicles which deliver to us the luxuries and necessities of our lives. Whether we are aware of it or not, the fuel delivery industry is an important and integral part of our lives.

According to the UK Petroleum Industry Association (UKPIA) 'over 75 million tonnes of petroleum products are moved around the UK' each year (UKPIA 2012d), with road transport being one method of several different fuel distribution systems. The fuel we buy for our motor vehicles in petrol stations is generally delivered by either 44- or 18-tonne road tankers and as consumers, UKPIA tell us that we buy approximately '56 million litres of petrol and 68 million litres of diesel per day'.

Delivery of fuel to the service stations where we buy it has undergone significant change over the past three decades with, according to UKPIA, supermarkets being a driving factor. During the 1980s supermarkets began to open petrol filling stations alongside their bigger stores and they now account for 40 per cent of petrol and diesel sales in the UK (UKPIA 2012a). There had been a reduction in petrol filing stations from 'over 26,000 in 1979 to 8,706' by the end of 2011 (UKPIA 2012a). UKPIA inform us that the closure of around 450 filling stations a year has led to the exit of major fuel providers from the market and we now see 'a multifaceted sector where the emergence of specialized independents, operating in all segments of the business, well reflects the increasingly competitive structure of the market in which they operate' (UKPIA 2012a).

Greater competition (arguably a bonus for us as consumers) and lower returns on capital have resulted in downsizing (reductions in staff) of organizations and the distribution of petrol and diesel being outsourced to specialized logistics companies (UKPIA 2012a). As a result of this, the big oil companies such as Shell and Esso use contractors to deliver petrol to filling stations such as Sainsbury's and Tesco. The contracts are regularly renegotiated and this has subsequently led to competition between the delivery companies; as we know, such competition inevitably results in downward pressure on the wages and working conditions of staff. As we shall see below, it is the fragmentation of delivery and, arguably, the change in working conditions that contextualize the tanker drivers' dispute.

The dispute

Like all employment relations disputes, the arguments behind the dispute vary depending upon which story one listens to. We will start by setting out the views and actions of the different 'social actors' within this dispute before.

The trade union[2]

The Unite union represents over 2,000, or approximately 90 per cent, of the drivers in the fuel distribution industry supplying fuel to petrol stations throughout the UK. In March 2012 the union, in line with UK legislation on strike action, balloted their members asking them whether they would be prepared to take strike action to demand national standards on working conditions and health and safety. The union argued that:

> Over the past 10 years, multiple contractors responsible for the delivery of oil and petrol supplies to petrol stations and supermarkets across the country have been consistently squeezing the terms and conditions of around 3,000 tanker drivers. The constant transfer of contracts between contractors has led to drivers' wages, pensions and working conditions being eroded. The pattern has become particularly pronounced over the last 18 months. The drivers' demands are reasonable. They are calling on the industry to introduce national standards to stop this race to the bottom (Unite 2012a).

According to the union they had made several unsuccessful attempts to speak with and discuss the concerns of their members with the oil companies and the retailers, and the ballot for strike action was therefore a last resort. In January 2012 the union stated that they were hoping to resolve the issues around the negotiation table with Len McCluskey, Unite general secretary-elect, stating:

> This is not about pay. Our demands are very reasonable. We are calling for national standards to bring stability to the industry. It would benefit our members but it would also benefit the multitude of contractors in the industry too. Time and workers' patience is running out, so we appeal to the key stakeholders to engage with Unite urgently to find a better way forward (Unite 2012a).

This negotiation did not take place and the ballot for strike action subsequently went ahead.

On 26 March 2012 Unite announced that the result of the ballot was 'overwhelmingly' in favour of strike action, with 69 per cent of the membership who voted backing the action; 77.7

(Continued)

(Continued)

per cent of the membership participated in the ballot (Unite 2012a). The tanker drivers worked for five major fuel distribution firms delivering petrol to service stations run by BP, Esso and Shell and the supermarket chains of Tesco and Sainsbury's. Clearly, consumers would be affected by the industrial action.

Following the ballot result Unite again categorically stated that the dispute was 'not about pay' but related to the deteriorating terms and conditions and health and safety concerns (Unite 2012a).

Under UK law covering industrial action, a strike has to take place within twenty-eight days of the result of the ballot being announced and the union also has to give seven days' notice of the strike. In the case of Unite and the tanker drivers, this period included the busy UK holiday period over Easter. A strike during this period would have a big impact on motorists wishing to use their cars for their holidays.

The fuel distribution industry and the distributors

In immediate response to Unite's 26 March announcement, UKPIA published a statement which said 'There is no current impact upon deliveries but UKPIA and its members are working with Government through the Dept (sic) for Energy and Climate Change (DECC) to minimise any potential impacts on customers that may arise from action by UNITE members' (UKPIA, 2012b).

They also urged motorists to 'stick to their normal fuel buying patterns and don't buy more fuel than they normally would' (UKPIA 2012b). The following day, UKPIA responded to Unite's call for improved health and safety by publishing a press release entitled 'Safety background to fuel deliveries to UKPIA's members' sites', stating that 'UKPIA and its members give high priority to safety issues within the industry' and 'UKPIA promotes the work of and participates in a number of industry and cross-sector groups established to improve safety and share best practice listing' (UKPIA 2012c). The statement went on to describe health and safety initiatives undertaken by their member organizations with regard to tanker drivers, therefore apparently refuting the claims made by Unite members.

One of the distribution companies involved in the dispute, HOYER UK limited, responded to the ballot result as follows:

> We are dismayed at the outcome of the Unite ballot for industrial action involving 650 drivers on our fuels contracts. Particularly as only 215 drivers out of the 650 voted for strike action and we therefore believe that this action is being driven by a small disaffected group of employees. HOYER has some of the best health, safety and training standards in the petroleum distribution sector. This has resulted in a health and safety record of which HOYER is proud. Pay and conditions for HOYER drivers are among the best in the

---

1 The information for this section, unless otherwise stated, is taken from the UK Petroleum Industry Association (UKPIA) website (www.ukpia.com/home.aspx). UKPIA is a representative body for nine member organizations who, between them, supply more than 30 per cent of energy used in the UK, own over 25 per cent of service stations in the UK and 'support the employment' of more than 150,000 people.

2 The information for this section, unless otherwise stated, is taken from the Unite website (www.unitetheunion.org).

industry. Our drivers earn on average £45,000 a year. They are well rewarded because they are professionals, highly trained and skilled in the work that they carry out particularly with regard to health and safety (HOYER UK 2012).

In the same statement the company went on to dispute the claim by Unite that employers were not prepared to negotiate:

We have been actively engaged in discussions with Unite through the Industry Forum to examine ways in which these high health safety and training standards can be applied across the industry but Unite walked away from those discussions.

By choosing to ballot the six companies who have supported the activity on minimum standards and shown their commitment through active participation in the Industry Forum, Unite has completely ignored the numerous low cost operators whose pay, terms and conditions, safety and training standards fall way short of ours. In doing so it risks shifting the market towards the lowest cost operators whose approach to safety is different to our own.

By leading its members to strike action now, we believe that safety is being used as a Trojan horse by Unite's leadership in its bid to seize control of the industrial relations agenda.

HOYER has a business to run and a duty to all its employees to see that business is sustainable – we believe that this industrial action will be damaging to all parties as well as the British economy (HOYER 2012).

The company went on to describe in some detail the terms and conditions under which their drivers worked. Clearly, this company disputed the claims of Unite.

The government

Following the announcement of the ballot result for industrial action, the immediate response from Prime Minister Cameron was that there was 'no justification for a strike'. The government had an emergency meeting to discuss contingency plans; these plans were reported to include the training of soldiers (BBC 2012) and employing foreign drivers (*The Telegraph* 2012) to deliver petrol. The Prime Minister was widely reported throughout the media when on the day after the ballot result was announced, he suggested that people who relied upon their cars to get to work should 'fill up their tanks'; on the same day Cabinet Minister Francis Maude suggested that people should store some petrol in their garages. The following day, petrol sales were reported to have risen by 170 per cent, diesel sales by almost 80 per cent and the price of petrol was said to have increased by over 45 per cent (*The Guardian* 2012a, 2012b). Although no strike had yet been called, the petrol stations were beginning to run out of fuel; some restricted sales to their regular customers and many closed. For a few days, it was not unusual to see petrol stations displaying 'Sorry, no fuel' signs.

At the same time, the Secretary of State for the Department of Energy and Climate Change, Ed Davey, called upon the union and employers to work with Acas to settle the dispute. Unite responded immediately to this call with an open letter, published on their website and subsequently reported by the media, suggesting that he should aim his comments

(Continued)

(Continued)

at the oil companies, retailers and employers rather than the union and stating again that the union was not intent on industrial action; Unite went on to ask the government to assist in bringing the parties to the negotiating table (Unite 2012c).

Advisory, Conciliation and Arbitration Service (Acas)

Although funded by the UK government, Acas is an independent organization, set up in 1975 to provide confidential and impartial advice to both employers and employees. It works with small and large organizations, individual employees and trade unions. The organization's main aim is to 'improve organisations and working life through better employment relations' (Acas 2012c). One of the functions of Acas is to mediate in disputes between employers and employees and their representatives and they became heavily involved in this dispute.

Two days after the ballot result was made public, Acas announced that they were

in urgent discussions with the parties involved on an individual basis: It is normal for us to do this to establish the format for talks. There are eight parties involved in this dispute – Unite and seven contractors (Acas 2012a).

Involving Acas at this stage was a clear declaration by the union and the employers that they were willing to negotiate a settlement.

The organization spoke independently with the different parties before engaging them in discussions which went on for several weeks, with Acas making frequent statements throughout the process. As might be expected in disputes of this kind, the statements from Acas were fairly vague as the sides continued discussions. It was important for Acas to demonstrate full impartiality but in a case which was so much in the public eye, it was not possible for them to remain completely silent.

Throughout April Acas continued to mediate in talks between Unite and the employer representatives. Then, following a prolonged and intensive 12-hour session, Acas announced that

a final set of proposals has been produced by the fuel distribution contractors and Unite. The industrial action mandate has been extended to 21 May 2012 to enable Unite to consult with its Oils Trade Conference and the membership on these proposals (Acas 2012b).

They again reiterated the confidential nature of these proposals, which were not disclosed to the press. This was, in effect, the end of Acas's role in the mediation process: now it was up to the negotiating parties.

The media

Every stage of the dispute was reported in the media and below is a sample of some headlines from television and newspapers:

Army on standby to deliver petrol in event of tanker strike: soldiers are being trained to deliver fuel to petrol stations in anticipation of a possible strike by tanker drivers (*Guardian*, 25 March 2012)

Soldiers on standby to get fuel to pumps (Sky News, 25 March 2012)

Fuel strike drivers vote yes in row over conditions (BBC, 26 March 2012)

Petrol pumps could run dry as tanker drivers vote for industrial action (*The Telegraph*, 26 March 2012)

Fuel strike threat: 'panic buying' at petrol stations: queues have formed at petrol stations as demand for fuel shot up after ministers called for people to top up in case of a tanker drivers' strike (BBC, 29 March 2012)

Queues and shortages as motorists told: 'don't panic' (ITV News, 29 March 2012)

No strike yet, but petrol sales jump 172% (Sky News, 30 March 2012)

The outcome

Following the Acas discussion, Unite again balloted their members. Despite recommending that they should reject the revised offer, on 11 May 2012 the drivers accepted the offer and industrial action was, at least in the short term, avoided.

Source: author.

 ■ **Questions**

1. How would you describe the balance of power in the dispute?
2. What role did the government play in the dispute?

   i. Did they demonstrate neo-liberal or neo-corporatist tendencies? Give reasons for your answer.

3. What was the role of Acas?
4. From the headlines displayed above, what impact do you think the media had on the situation?
5. To what extent do you think the way in which the dispute was reported contributed to the balance of the bargaining power of the different parties in the dispute?

Conclusion

This chapter has provided an insight into the complexity of the employment relationship. It has demonstrated how there is an ever-changing and dynamic interactive relationship between various actors and agencies, both within and outside the workplace, and how these are able to impact on the people management practices and processes within an organization.

Initially we saw how the ideological perspective of the government can influence the HR strategies of organizational leaders. If a government promotes a neo-corporatist, collective orientation towards worker representation, then organizations are more likely to accept and work with trade unions. On the other hand, if the government follows a more neo-liberal orientation then organizations are less likely to engage with trade unions. In some countries, specifically the USA and to some extent the UK, trade unions are actively discouraged. In these countries management may be seen to follow an individualistic and unitarist approach towards managing which is strongly related to HRM.

Despite feeling the lack of need for trade unions the contemporary thought in 'enlightened' organizations towards people management is that there is a need to engage the workforce in order to gain employee commitment to the culture and goals of the company. This chapter has demonstrated ways in which employee participation and involvement may help organizations achieve this engagement. It is important to consider, however, whether such engagement is superficial or does in fact give an active voice to worker representation.

The Foxconn case study allowed for a deeper exploration of worker voice, particularly – although not exclusively – from a collective orientation. This case highlighted the complexity of the Chinese model of employment relations. Although there is a trade union *in situ*, it is embedded within the company structure and therefore not given an independent voice. The Foxconn Federation of Labour Unions Committee is neither a trade union in the true sense of the meaning nor does it have the rights of a works council. The workers at Foxconn are faced with what Keller describes as a 'representation gap' (2004: 226) where employees have neither works council nor trade union representation, and hence no voice.

Although a neo-liberal approach to management promotes the right of the manager to manage, we can see how this can be affected by influences outside of their control. For example, government legislation can impact upon the equal opportunities and health and safety policies and practices within the organization, while the state of the labour market can make recruitment more or less difficult and also impact on the wage levels set. The strength of the labour market may also influence the balance of power within the employment relationship – a balance which we suggest is often asymmetrical (Blyton and Turnbull 2004). Nonetheless, as the tanker driver dispute in Case Study 8.3 demonstrates, even in an entrenched neo-liberal society when workers act collectively they are able to impact on, if not change, the power relations between workers and management, or workers and government.

A final external body that we considered was the media. Case Study 8.3 demonstrates how important the media can be when reporting a dispute. It is clear that they can help shift the balance of power and can become influential in promoting the settlement of a dispute. The media also played a crucial role in the Foxconn case because in highlighting the plight of the Chinese workers, pressure was put upon the organization to reconsider their employment practices.

■ Further Reading ■■■■■■■■■■■■

Benson, J. and Brown, M. (2010) 'Employee voice: does union membership matter?', *Human Resource Management Journal*, 20 (1): 80–99.

Blyton, P., Bacon, N., Fiorito, J. and Heery, E. (2008) *The SAGE Handbook of Industrial Relations*. London: Sage.

Dundon, T. and Rollinson, D. (2011) *Understanding Employment Relations*, 2nd edn. London: McGraw Hill.

Hollinshead, G. (2010) *International and Comparative Human Resource Management*. London: McGraw Hill.

Rollinson, D. and Dundon, T. (2011) *Understanding Employment Relations*, 2nd edn. London: McGraw Hill.

Zhao, S., Zhang, J. Zhao, W. and Shuk-Ching Poon, T. (2012) 'Changing employment relations in China: a comparative study of the auto and banking industries', *The International Journal of Human Resource Management*, 23 (10): 2051–64.

References

Acas (2012a) 'Statement on tanker drivers dispute', available at http://www.acas.org.uk/index.aspx?articleid=3736, accessed 14 July 2012.

Acas (2012b) 'Updated statement on the tanker drivers dispute', available at http://www.acas.org.uk/index.aspx?articleid=3785, accessed 14 July 2012.

Acas (2012c) 'About us', available at http://www.acas.org.uk/index.aspx?articleid=1342, accessed 14 July 2012.

Ackers, P., Marchington, M., Wilkinson, A. and Dundon, T. (2004) 'Partnership and voice, with or without trade unions: changing UK management approaches to organisational participation', in M. Stuart and M. Martinez-Lucio (eds), *Partnership and Modernisation in Employment Relations*. London: Routledge, pp. 23–45.

Addison, J.T., Schnabel, C. and Wagner, J. (2006) *The (Parlous) State of German Unions*, Discussion Paper No 2000. Bonn: IZA.

Armstrong, M. (2006) *A Handbook of Human Resource Management Practice*, 10th edn. London: Kogan Page Publishers.

Arthur, C. (2012) 'Foxconn closes China factory after brawl: reports suggest as many as 2,000 workers involved in fight in dormitory at Taiyuan plant, which makes Apple's iPhone 5', *The Guardian*, available at http://www.guardian.co.uk/technology/2012/sep/24/foxconn-closes-china-factory-brawl, accessed 19 March 2013.

Ashkenas, R., Ulrich, D., Jick, T. and Kerr, S. (1995) *The Boundaryless Organisation. Breaking the Chains of Organisational Structure*. San Francisco, CA: Jossey-Bass.

BBC (2012) 'Army training to deliver fuel in case of strike action', available at http://www.bbc.co.uk/news/uk-17502973, accessed 18 July 2012.

BBC (2013) 'Viewpoints: school league tables', available at http://www.bbc.co.uk/news/education-20628795, accessed 5 May 2013.

Beardwell, I. (1998) 'Voices on', *People Management*, May: 32–6.

Beauregard, A., Bell, M., Özbilgin, M. and Sürgevil, O. (2011) 'Voice, silence, and diversity in 21st century organizations: strategies for inclusion of gay, lesbian, bisexual, and transgender employees', *Human Resource Management, Special Issue: Special Section: Employee Voice*, 50 (1): 131–46. Available at http://www.wiley.com/bw/journal.asp?ref=0954-5395, accessed 1 September 2012.

Bennett, R. (1997) *Employee Relations*, 2nd edn. Harlow: FT/Prentice Hall.

Benson, J. and Brown, M. (2010) 'Employee voice: does union membership matter?', *Human Resource Management Journal*, 20 (1): 80–99.

Blyton, P. and Turnbull, P. (1994) *The Dynamics of Employee Relations*. Basingstoke: Macmillan.

Blyton, P. and Turnbull, P. (2004) *The Dynamics of Employee Relations*, 3rd edn. Basingstoke: Palgrave Macmillan.

Blyton, P., Bacon, N., Fiorito, J. and Heery, E. (2008) *The SAGE Handbook of Industrial Relations*. London: Sage.

Boxall, P. and Purcell, J. (2003) *Strategy and Human Resource Management*. Basingstoke: Palgrave Macmillan.

Bradley, H. (1999) *Gender and Power in the Workplace*. London: Macmillan.

Branigan, T. (2010) 'Tenth apparent suicide at Foxconn iPhone factory in China: death of 23-year-old comes only hours after parent company's chairman admitted fears of further incidents', *The Guardian*, available at http://www.guardian.co.uk/world/2010/may/27/foxconn-suicide-tenth-iphone-china, accessed 18 March 2013.

Brewster, C., Croucher, R., Wood, G. and Brookes, M. (2007) 'Collective and individual voice:convergence in Europe?', *International Journal of Human Resource Management*, 18 (7): 1246–62.

Calveley, M. (2005a) *Teaching in Britain Today: Working in the Relegation Zone*. Glasgow: humming earth.

Calveley, M. (2005b) 'National context of international human resource management', in M. Özbilgin (ed.), *International Human Resource Management: Theory and Practice*. London: Palgrave, pp. 63–81.

Calveley, M. (2010) 'Case study: Marks and Spencer', in G. Hollinshead (ed.), *International and Comparative Human Resource Management*. London: McGraw Hill, pp. 38–41.

Calveley, M. and Healy, G. (2003) 'Political activism and workplace industrial relations in a UK "failing" school', *British Journal of Industrial Relations*, 41: 1.

China Post (2013) 'Foxconn to bolster Chinese workers' union participation', available at http://www.chinapost.com.tw/taiwan-business/2013/02/05/369610/Foxconn-to.htm, accessed 18 March 2013.

CIPD (2011) *Employee Voice Factsheets*, available at http://www.cipd.co.uk/hr-resources/factsheets/employee-voice.aspx, accessed 15 September 2012.

CIPD (2012) *Employee Engagement Factsheets*, available at http://www.cipd.co.uk/hr-resources/factsheets/employee-engagement.aspx, accessed 22 March 2013.

CIPD (2013) *Employee Engagement Factsheets*, available at http://www.cipd.co.uk/hr-resources/factsheets/employee-engagement.aspx#link_0, accessed 19 February 2013.

Department for Education (2013) *Categories and Roles of School Governors*, available at http://www.education.gov.uk/a0056694/categories-and-roles-of-school-governors, accessed 5 May 2013.

Dundon, T. (2002) 'Employer opposition and union avoidance in the UK', *Industrial Relations Journal*, 33 (3): 234–5.

Dundon, T. and Rollinson, D. (2011) *Understanding Employment Relations*, 2nd edn. London: McGraw Hill.

Economist (2012) 'When workers dream of a life beyond the factory gates: can Foxconn, the world's largest contract manufacturer, keep growing and improve its margins now that cheap and willing hands are scarce?', available at http://www.economist.com/news/business/21568384-can-foxconn-worlds-largest-contract-manufacturer-keep-growing-and-improve-its-margins-now, accessed 18 March 2013.

Edwards, P. (2003) *Industrial Relations*, 2nd edn. Oxford: Blackwell Publishing.

EIRO (European Industrial Relations Observatory online) (2013) *France: Industrial Relations Profile*, http://www.eurofound.europa.eu/eiro/country/france.htm, accessed 17 February 2013.

Eurofound (2010) 'Flexible forms of work: "very atypical" contractual arrangements' available at http://www.eurofound.europa.eu/ewco/studies/tn0812019s/tn0812019s.htm, accessed 16 February 2013.

Fair Labor Association (2012a) 'Fair Labor Association finds progress at Apple Supplier Foxconn', available at http://www.fairlabor.org/press-release/foxconn_verification_report, accessed 19 March 2013.

Fair Labor Association (2012b) 'Independent investigation of Apple supplier, Foxconn', available at www.fairlabor.org, accessed 19 March 2013.

Financial Times (2010) 'Wayne Rooney stays at Manchester United', available at http://www.ft.com/cms/s/0/fa6f8ed2-ddd4-11df-8354-00144feabdc0.html#axzz24AWyglvf, accessed 21 August 2012.

Fox, A. (1966) *Industrial Sociology and Industrial Relations*. London: HMSO.

Fox, A. (1977) 'The myths of pluralism and a radical perspective: from "Man Mismanagement" (1974)', in T. Clarke and L. Clements (eds), *Trade Unions Under Capitalism*. London: Fontana, pp. 136–51.

Freeman, R.B. and Medoff, J.L. (1984) *What do Unions do?* New York: Basic Books.

Guardian (2012a) 'Petrol tanker drivers' strike: ministers accused of creating crisis', available at http://www.guardian.co.uk/politics/2012/mar/28/petrol-tanker-drivers-strike, accessed 14 July 2012.

Guardian (2012b) 'Francis Maude urged to quit over petrol panic as union rules out Easter strike', available at http://www.guardian.co.uk/uk/2012/mar/30/francis-maude-petrol-panic-strike?intcmp=239, accessed 14 July 2012.

Gumbrell-McCormick, R. and Hyman, R. (2006) 'Embedded collectivism? Workplace representation in France and Germany', *Industrial Relations Journal*, 37 (5): 473–91.

Heywood, J.S. and Jirjahn, U. (2009) 'Family-friendly practices and worker representation in Germany', *Industrial Relations*, 48 (1): 121–45.

Hille, K. (2012) 'Foxconn suffers unrest at iPhone factory', *Financial Times*, available at http://www.ft.com/cms/s/0/116dc2e8-105a-11e2-a5f7-00144feabdc0.html#axzz2Nv4fHNxs, accessed 19 March 2013.

Hille, K. (2013) 'Foxconn plans Chinese union vote', *Financial Times*, available at http://www.ft.com/cms/s/0/48091254-6c3e-11e2-b774-00144feab49a.html#axzz2Nv4fHNxs, accessed 19 March 2013.

Hollinshead, G. (2010) *International and Comparative Human Resource Management*. London: McGraw Hill.

Hoyer UK (2012) 'Hoyer statement in response to Unite ballot for industrial action', available at http://www.hoyer-group.com/en.php/contact/press.html?i1=669bd, accessed 14 July 2012.

Hu, Y.S. (1992) 'Global or stateless corporations are national firms with international operations', *California Management Review*, 34 (2): 107–26.

Hyman, R. (1975) *Industrial Relations: A Marxist Introduction*. London: Macmillan.

Hyman, R. (1978) 'Pluralism, procedural consensus and industrial relations', *British Journal of Industrial Relations*, 16: 16–40.

Kahn, W.A. (1990) 'Psychological conditions of personal engagement and disengagement at work', *Academy of Management Journal*, 33 (4): 692–724.

Keller, B.K. (2004) 'Employment relations in Germany', in G.L. Bamber, R.D. Lansbury and N. Wailes (eds), *International and Comparative Employment Relations*, 4th edn. London: Sage, pp. 211–30.

Kersley, B., Alpin, C., Forth, J., Bryson, A., Bewley, H., Dix, G. and Oxenbridge, S. (2006) *Inside the Workplace: First Findings from the 2004 Workplace Employment Relations Survey*. London: Routledge.

King, G. (2010) *Varieties of Neoliberalism in Latin America, Integrative Exercise Winter*, available at http://people.carleton.edu/~amontero/Geoff%20King.pdf, accessed 20 February 2013.

Klikauer, T. (2004) 'Trade union shop floor representation in Germany', *Industrial Relations Journal*, 35 (1): 2–18.

Kuroki, M. (2012) 'The deregulation of temporary employment and workers' perceptions of job insecurity', *Industrial and Labor Relations* Review, 65 (3): 560–77.

Kurtz, M.J. and Brooks, S. (2008) 'Embedding neoliberal reform in Latin America', *World Politics*, 60 (January): 231–80.

Lewin, D. and Mitchell, D. (1992) 'Systems of employee voice: theoretical and empirical perspectives', *California Management Review*, 34 (3): 95–111.

Lucas, R., Lupton, B. and Mathieson, H. (2006) *Human Resource Management in an International Context*. London: CIPD.

Marchington, M. (1982) *Managing Industrial Relations*. Maidenhead: McGraw-Hill.

Moore, M. (2010) 'Inside Foxconn's suicide factory', *The Telegraph*, available at http://www.telegraph.co.uk/finance/china-business/7773011/A-look-inside-the-Foxconn-suicide-factory.html, accessed 18 March 2013.

Noon, M. and Blyton, P. (2007) *The Realities of Work: Experiencing Work and Employment in Contemporary Society*, 3rd edn. Basingstoke: Palgrave Macmillan.

NUT (2013) 'NUT: The largest teachers' union', available at http://www.teachers.org.uk/, accessed 5 May 2013.

Office for National Statistics (2012) *Labour Market Statistics, August 2012*, available at http://www.ons.gov.uk/ons/rel/lms/labour-market-statistics/august-2012/statistical-bulletin.html, accessed 21 August 2012.

Pfeffer, J. (1998) *The Human Equation: Building Profitability by Putting People First*. Boston, MA: Harvard Business School Press.

Purcell, J. (1987) 'Mapping management styles in employee relations', *Journal of Management* Studies, 24 (5): 534–48.

Ramsey, H. (1977) 'Cycles of control: worker participation in sociological and historical perspective', *Sociology*, 11: 481–506.

Rank, J. (2009) 'Challenging the status quo: diversity, employee voice and proactive behaviour', in M. Özbilgin (ed.), *Equality, Diversity and Inclusion at Work: a Research Companion*. Cheltenham: Edward Elgar, pp: 195–215.

Reuters (2012) 'Workers protest at Foxconn plant in China', available at http://www.reuters.com/article/2012/04/27/us-china-foxconn-idUSBRE83Q0JV20120427, accessed 18 March 2013.

Reuters (2013) 'Foxconn says to boost China worker participation in union', available at http://www.reuters.com/article/2013/02/04/us-foxconn-china-idUSBRE9130EM20130204, accessed 18 March 2013.

Rose, E. (2008) *Employment Relations in the UK*, 3rd edn. London: Pearson Education.

Salamon, M. (2000) *Industrial Relations: Theory and Practice*, 4th edn. Harlow: Financial Times/Prentice Hall.

Saudi Embassy (2013) *About Saudi Arabia: Government*, available at http://www.saudiembassy.net/about/country-information/government/, accessed 25 February 2013.

Schneider, B.R. (2009) 'Hierarchical market economies and varieties of capitalism in Latin America', *Journal Latin American Studies*, 41: 553–75.

Sera, K. (1992) 'Corporate globalization: a new trend', *Academy of Management Executive*, 6: 89–96.

Smedley, T. (2013) 'Do you really? Global supply chains expose your company to searching questions – and working conditions that have been illegal for a century in the UK', *People Management*, February: 22–7.

Storey, J. (ed.) (2001) *Human Resource Management: A Critical Text*, 2nd edn. London: Thomson.

Telegraph, The (2012) 'Motorists should consider stockpiling fuel for strike, suggests No 10', available at http://www.telegraph.co.uk/motoring/9170200/Motorists-should-consider-stockpiling-fuel-for-strike-suggests-No-10.html, accessed 11 July 2012.

Torrington, D., Hall, L. and Taylor, S. (2008) *Human Resource Management*, 7th edn. Harlow: Pearson Education.

UKPIA (2012a) *Distribution and marketing in the Downstream Oil Industry'*, Available at: http://www.ukpia.com/files/pdf/distribution-and-marketing-2012.pdf Accessed 11th July 2012

UKPIA (2012b) 'Press release 26 March', available at http://www.ukpia.com/news_press/12-03-26/Tanker_drivers%e2%80%99_vote_for_strike_action.aspx, accessed 14 July 2012.

UKPIA (2012c) 'Press release: Safety background to fuel deliveries to UKPIA's members' sites', available at http://www.ukpia.com/news_press/12-03-27/Safety_background_to_fuel_deliveries_to_UKPIA_s_members_sites.aspx , accessed 14 July 2012.

UKPIA (2012d) 'Distribution', available at http://www.ukpia.com/industry_information/distribution.aspx, accessed 11 July 2012.

Unite (2012a) 'Tanker drivers warn oil industry bosses to take their heads out of the sand', available at http://www.unitetheunion.org/news__events/archived_news_releases/2011_archived_press_releases/tanker_drivers_warn_oil_indust.aspx, accessed 14 July 2012.

Unite (2012b) 'Tanker drivers say "enough is enough" and vote for action', available at http://www.unitetheunion.org/news__events/latest_news/tanker_drivers_say__enough_is.aspx, accessed 14 July 2012.

Unite (2012c) 'Unite calls on Ed Davey to intervene in tanker driver dispute', available at http://www.unitetheunion.org/news__events/latest_news/unite_calls_on_ed_davey_to_int.aspx, accessed 14 July 2012.

Walton, R.E. (1985) 'From control to commitment in the workplace', *Harvard Business Review*, March–April: 77–84.

Wilton, N. (2010) *An Introduction to HRM*. London: Sage.

Zhang, L. (2012) 'China's Foxconn workers: from suicide threats to a trade union?', *The Guardian*, available at http://www.guardian.co.uk/commentisfree/2012/jan/16/foxconn-suicide-china-society, accessed 18 March 2013.

Zhao, S., Zhang, J. Zhao, W. and Shuk-Ching Poon, T. (2012) 'Changing employment relations in China: a comparative study of the auto and banking industries', *The International Journal of Human Resource Management*, 23 (10): 2051–64.

9

EQUALITY AND DIVERSITY IN THE WORKPLACE

John Neugebauer

I don't want to be unkind, but really think about what you are asking me, and why you are asking it. Because you want me to play some game of stereotyping, and I don't want to.

Clare Balding on being questioned about her sexuality in Cochrane (2013)

Chapter Overview

This chapter will consider equality, diversity, and discrimination in the workplace. The workplace has become a highly regulated environment in which many forms of discrimination are made unlawful. Legal compliance is important, but there is ample evidence that seeking to avoid discrimination by legal means alone fails to understand the root causes and effects of workplace discrimination; fails to consider underlying workplace cultures; fails to consider the potential benefits of greater equality and diversity; and fails to recognize how the excessive imposition of legal remedies may even be counter-productive. Therefore, this chapter will critically examine the wider background to the causes and effects of discrimination, and how and why organizations attempt to address these. The focal point is Europe and the UK, but wherever possible, reference is also made to global diversity issues.

Inequalities within the workplace often reflect inequalities brought in from wider society. After a brief review of global inequality and discrimination, the chapter will consider how stereotype often forms the basis for subsequent discrimination. It will then review the impacts of inequalities on various minority groups within the workplace. This review of minority group impacts will look at gender and age inequality in depth. This is not to suggest that other forms of discrimination are any less important, but this will illustrate the range of complexity in understanding and addressing contemporary equality and diversity issues.

Following this review, the chapter will consider the legislative response to discrimination, followed by a discussion of how and why organizations may try to manage inequality.

≡ **CASE STUDY 9.1** ≡

High heels at the Geneva Motor Show

Cars best accessorised by tall women with high heels

The following is an extract from an article originally written by Matt Prior for *Autocar*.

Ah, the Geneva Motor Show. Proud showcase of all that is good about the motor industry. Home to the optimistic, the brilliant and the futuristic. And home, sadly, to the inevitable reminder that some parts of the car business are forever stuck in 1973.

Oh, it starts off okay. Executives – from Supervisory Boards, perhaps holding titles that include 'officer' and chief' – arrive to tell you about their latest car.

But then the men leave and the cars start pinning on their turntables behind cordons. The men are then replaced by models, who are young and beautiful and – here's the problem – exclusively women. And sometimes companies who resist models employ only women to attend the stand, giving out brochures and taking punters' contact details.

They don't all do this, of course, but at [the] Geneva [Motor Show] it was sufficiently widespread that you could call it common. The implication is clear: the men who make the decisions have visited, spoken, completed their important work and returned to the Boardroom. Now, girls, it's your turn. Stand here and look pretty. At least, that's what they're inferring. What's the alternative? What do they think they're trying to say?

And this, remember, is the motor industry's most public face. This is how it chooses to present itself to the world.

As in most industries, women are under-represented at management level, and it's hard enough to encourage girls and women into careers in engineering and sciences. Yet here's one of the world's biggest employers of technical staff making its most prominent female workers the ones whose job is to arrive looking waxed and pouty.

(Continued)

Having read this abstract by Matt Prior, consider the following questions:

1. Is there anything unlawful about using female models in the way described? Might there be?
2. What is the typical distribution of women on executive boards?
3. What is the underlying culture which is being identified here? How does it demonstrate horizontal and vertical segregation?
4. What are the issues in encouraging more women into careers in engineering and sciences?
5. If all this matters, how *can* it be changed?

Source: Prior (2013) (Reproduced with permission from *Autocar*).

Introduction

McCann and Giles (2002) argue that stereotypes in the workplace do not occur in isolation, but reflect stereotypes which are widespread within society. We may, therefore, expect that the inequalities which are seen within society are often then brought into the workplace. It is therefore important to gain some insight into the inequalities experienced across the world. One such study of global diversity was undertaken by the International Labour Office (2011). A brief summary of the results which give evidence of work and social inequality is shown in Table 9.1. Notice that HIV/AIDS is also a source of discrimination at a global level.

Overall, the ILO found that while there was more legislation worldwide to address workplace discrimination, not all the news was good. It considered that there was a growing awareness of the need to overcome discrimination, but that 'capacity does not keep pace with political will' (International Labour Office, 2011: ix). In part, this recognized global economic weaknesses, but the ILO also observed that the issue of discrimination in the workplace was ever-changing – and that 'new challenges arise where old ones remain at best only partially answered' (International Labour Office 2011: ix).

More detailed examples of the causes and effects of inequality and discrimination will be discussed in this chapter. First, we will consider what are meant by the terms equality and diversity.

Definitions of equality, diversity and discrimination

Equality and diversity are often used interchangeably as if they are the same concept. In fact, there are important differences both in what the terms mean, and the policies which are then pursued within the workplace.

Table 9.1 To show examples of worldwide inequality and discrimination

Women	Women are more likely to live in poverty Overall, women's pay is about 70–90% of that of men Progress in many areas, but still many challenges
Ethnicity	Remains a widespread problem, especially for those of African and Asian descent, and indigenous people Women are most likely to be affected within those groups
Disability	Estimated that 10% of the world's population has some form of disability (but 20% of the world's poor) Disabled people are more likely to suffer disadvantage in education, employment, and earnings
Sexuality	Violence, discrimination, and harassment still widely evident for gay, lesbian, bisexual or transgender workers Homosexuality still a criminal offence in some countries
Religion/belief	Reported increase in discrimination on grounds of religious belief
Migrant workers	Comprise 8–20% of workforce in many countries Widespread discrimination evidenced in access to and participation in employment
Age	Cites 2009 European Commission Report which considered age discrimination to be widespread
HIV/AIDS	In 2008, 33% of countries reported to UNAIDS that there was no legal protection against HIV/AIDS discrimination For example, in India employment may be denied if HIV positive; in Estonia, Georgia, Russian Federation, Ukraine and Uzbekistan employees with HIV and AIDS are likely to face discrimination. But elsewhere, compulsory HIV testing/discrimination for employment is unlawful – e.g. Namibia, Bahamas, Malawi, South Africa, Fiji

Source: International Labour Office (2011).

Equality is based on the intention that all individuals should have the same chance and opportunity. Straw (1989) categorized equalities as:

- Equal chance: having the same chance for opportunities within the workplace, for example, in training, selection, or promotion.
- Equal access: having the same opportunity to enter an organization.
- Equal share: having proportionate representation within all groups and all levels within the organization.

However, one of the underlying problems with the concept of equality is that each individual is … an individual, so that applying the same criteria to everyone may actually become a source of inequality, as people's needs, abilities, and life contexts differ so much. Therefore, the concept of diversity has evolved to recognize, respect, and accommodate, where possible, differences and different needs. The aim is still to offer the same opportunities to each

Table 9.2 Comparing approaches to equality and diversity

Equality	Diversity
Assumes that from a moral perspective, each individual should have an equal chance	Assumes that there is a social justice/moral argument for each individual to have an equal chance, but that differences between individuals can yield benefits to organizations
Aims to eliminate discrimination	Acknowledges that differences cannot be eliminated, but seeks to value difference and reduce discrimination
Presumes inequality is a disadvantage	Seeks to reduce conflict
Emphasis is on legal compliance (with anti-discrimination legislation)	Promotes the value and benefits of diversity – more than simply legal compliance
Critique of this approach: relies too heavily on legal sanctions/fines for non-compliance, rather than tackling the underlying cultures within workplaces	Critique of this approach: 'upbeat naivety' (Prasad and Mills, 1997) – difficult to tackle underlying cultures, beliefs, stereotypes and behaviours without sanctions

Source: Derived from Kirton and Greene (2005: 2–3).

individual, both to enrich the workplace with the business benefits of those differences, and to provide a society which has social justice of equality of opportunity.

In practice, these different interpretations of equality and diversity mean that policies which are framed either for equality, or for diversity, have different underpinning assumptions about how inequality may be addressed. Kirton and Greene (2005) summarize these differences as shown in Table 9.2.

In equal opportunity and diversity, managers have a key role in the design and implementation of policy, despite the differences in the points of emphasis of these concepts. For example, Kandola et al. (1995) argue in favour of managers adopting a managing diversity approach as more appropriate to the needs of business than equal opportunity.

With regard to employment discrimination, Gutek et al. (1996) describe this as existing 'When employment decisions such as selection, evaluation, promotion, or reward allocation are based on an individual's immutable characteristics such as age, appearance, sex, or skin color rather than on productivity or qualifications' (1996: 793).

With the introduction of employment law in many countries, discrimination has been defined in more precise legal terms, which provide employment rights for workers (and, in some cases, for service users as well). Further details and interpretations of various forms of discrimination under the UK Equality Act are discussed in the section 'Legislative response to diversity and equality' below.

The concept and implications of stereotyping

We may not think – or prefer not to recognize – that our own thought patterns are stereotyped, especially around workplace discrimination, but they probably are. To illustrate this, try Reflective Activity 9.1.

===== PIT STOP: REFLECTIVE ACTIVITY 9.1 =====

Challenging our thinking

A father and son are travelling together in a car. There is a terrible crash. The father, who was a famous surgeon, is killed instantly. The son is seriously injured and is flown by helicopter to hospital. In the operating theatre the surgeon says 'I cannot operate on this boy. He is my son.'

How can this have happened?

(Answer at the end of the chapter.)

If you got the answer right – well done ... but see how your friends do. If you did get it wrong, then you are in the majority – the author's experience is that typically only 10 per cent of any given population will get the answer right first time. For those who did not get the right answer, the problem is usually one of stereotyped thinking.

Stereotypes have been defined as 'Cognitive structures that store our beliefs, and expectations about the characteristics of members of social groups' (Cuddy and Fiske 2002: 4).

Stereotypes therefore reflect an 'automated' response to a person or a situation. The stereotype may be over-positive about the attributes of a person but too often, where there is difference, the stereotypes are negative and become the source of negative prejudices. In turn, these prejudices – often with little or no realistic foundations – both become the source of injustice towards the individual and fail to see the wider benefits and contributions which an individual can make.

Stereotypes are prevalent in society. To illustrate how they can affect the workplace, this section will consider stereotypes in relation to older workers. But similar principles (with different reasons for stereotyping) can apply to women, disabled people, ethnic monitories, etc.

To illustrate one form of stereotype, consider the position of older people in the workforce. Research has shown that older people tend to be viewed as less capable in cognitive skills, and are wordy, and irritable (Nuessel 1982; Braithwaite and Gibson 1987; Coupland et al. 1991; Gold et al. 1994). On the other hand, older people are seen as more likely to be friendly than younger people (Chasteen et al. 2002). In the workplace, older workers tend to have reduced training and development opportunities and older workers were seen as less trainable, less interested in developing their careers, and so more suitable for lower skill or lower responsibility roles (Taylor and Walker 1994).

But despite these stereotypes, empirical evidence shows that the advantages of older workers are often overlooked. For example, the potential benefits of older workers include that they are more experienced, mature, and stable, (Marshall 1995), with higher crystallized intelligence (applied experience/ wisdom) (Stuart-Hamilton 1991). Brosi and Kleiner (1999: 101) found older workers to be more loyal and more committed to the organization. Despite some perceptions that older workers are slower to embrace change, in a study of dental practitioners' response to change, Watt et al. noted that 'being older was not a barrier to change for some' (2004: 487). Overall research on older workers suggests that age rarely accounts for more than a 10 per cent variation in manual work performance – and none for clerical workers (Rhodes, 1983); while McCann and Giles (2002) saw little difference in work performance between younger and older people and may even favour the overall performance of older workers.

Therefore, one society approach to avoid stereotype and subsequent discrimination towards older workers is to introduce laws to prevent it. Indeed, this has happened in many countries. For example, in the USA, the Age Discrimination in Employment Act was originally introduced to protect employees in the 45–65 age range, but subsequently reduced to 40, since 'this was the age when most expert witnesses [to the US Senate] considered age discrimination in employment became evident' (Macnicol, 2006: 235–6). In Europe, the European Council Directive 2000/78 sought to eliminate workplace age discrimination, and in the UK there were voluntary measures, then subsequent legislation: the Employment Equality (Age) Regulations 2006, and the Equality Act 2010.

However, in considering the impact of stereotyping towards individuals or groups, it is also necessary to consider the impact on the individuals themselves. Sherif (1956) found that when we develop strong loyalty within one group, we tend to develop negative perceptions of groups to which we do not belong. A similar result was identified by Tajfel (1970), who found that being categorized as one group could produce negative attitudes and beliefs about other groups. All of these findings may obviously affect stereotypes and prejudices, with groups and individuals not working to their best. However, in addition to group impacts, it is also important to look at the impact on the individuals themselves who suffer stereotype attitudes.

Research has found that where individuals are aware of the negative stereotypes against them, it negatively affects their self-perception and scores in performance tests. Steele and Aronson's (1995) Stereotype Threat Theory suggests that implied or explicit inter-group comparison may impair performance if there is a threat of negative stereotype of the ability of the group. Furthermore, even the knowledge that a negative stereotype ('Stereotype Threat') exists towards an individual or group is sufficient for those individuals to feel a burden of suspicion and therefore to underperform, even if the stereotype is not believed (Steele 1997). Levy (1996) showed that subliminally believed stereotypes of older people by older people lowered self-perception judgements and cognitive performance. This was supported by Abrams et al. (2006) who found that a high stereotype threat reduced the cognitive test performance of older age groups. This important research demonstrates that legal sanctions against discrimination are not enough, and that the underlying culture and attitudes within a workplace need to be addressed.

However, where there had been previous contacts between groups which may otherwise have been subject to stereotype threat and prejudice (for example, older and younger people working together), this negative effect was moderated. Contact theory suggests that where we live and work with others who may be 'different' from us, we actually learn to value and respect those differences, so that contact between groups may reduce inter-group negative stereotypes (e.g. Allport 1954; Pettigrew 1998). This suggests that diverse organizations will tend to be more effective, flexible, and able to work internally and externally than non-diverse organizations. However, Rothbart and John (1985) found that in order for contact theory to help in reducing prejudice and stereotype, it was important that three criteria were met: that behaviours within the minority group were not consistent with their stereotype; that contact was relatively frequent and in a range of different social contexts; and that minority members are perceived as typical of their cultural group.

The impact of workplace discrimination for different groups

This section will consider the impact of workplace discrimination. It will consider gender and age in some detail, so as to demonstrate some of the complexity in addressing workplace issues. Other areas of discrimination (ethnicity, disability, and belief, sexuality, HIV/AIDS) will also be reviewed, but in less detail: this is not to imply that these topics are any less important, it merely reflects limitations as to the amount of detail which can be discussed in a single chapter.

Women

The following subsections will consider women and workplace discrimination in general terms, women and pay, and women and career. Women comprise 51 per cent of the UK population, and girls and women outperform boys and men at school and university (Equality and Human Rights Commission 2011: 7). Women are taking an increasing role in paid occupational employment, but still lack equality of career opportunities and reward compared with their male colleagues. Leaker (2008) demonstrated that 41 per cent of women were in part-time roles, compared with 10 per cent of men.

Broadbridge and Hearn (2008) noted that women have similarly high levels of education as their male counterparts, and a desire to advance in their personal careers. However, they are unlikely to reach comparable levels of management as men, nor to achieve pay equality with their male counterparts (2008: S44). Broadbridge and Hearn suggest that 'male homosociality' (the tendency for same-sex relationships to develop non-sexual/non-romantic friendships and social ease) may contribute to this, in which emotional detachment, competitiveness, and viewing women as sexual objects form a masculine work environment with a 'pecking order' amongst the men (2008: S44).

Much of the literature on women's careers has been from the perspective of women as sexually heterogeneous, although some (for example, Pringle 2008) have also considered women managers who may be lesbians. Here, the conclusion is that the challenges facing all women managers in the workplace are similar, irrespective of sexual orientation, and that 'strategies for success are represented by tactics for navigating the labyrinth of heterosexual attributions and innuendos' (Pringle 2008: S118).

Women and pay

The many differences between the workplace experiences of men and women have been the subject of a UK legislation programme dating back to the mid-1970s. The Sex Discrimination Act 1975 and Equal Pay Act 1970 were intended, respectively, to eliminate gender discrimination in selection and employment, and to achieve equality of pay between men and women.

Subsequent legislation, for example, the Maternity and Parental Leave etc. Regulations, 1999 and the Part Time Workers (Prevention of Less Favourable Terms) Regulations, 2000, have sought to refine and further develop women's rights in the workplace. However, despite the existence of this legislation, there remains extensive evidence of gender-based discrimination within the workplace in both pay and career.

In the UK, women's pay continues to lag behind male equivalents for both full-time employees. According to the Office for National Statistics (ONS) the mean difference between men and women's hourly rates of pay pay was 9.6 per cent (ONS 2012a). The gender pay gap also widens with advancing age. Leaker (2008) shows that while men and women may have comparable rates of pay when they enter the labour market at the ages of 18–21, the gender pay gap starts to be evidenced from ages 30–39, and then the gap increases for the

40–49 year age group (2008: 21). The ONS (2010) also finds that the pay gap is highest in the 40–49 age band, at 18.4 per cent for full-time employees, and 29.5 per cent for all employees (i.e. including part-time employees). Furthermore, there are gender pay differences between occupational groups. Leaker (2008) notes that the widest pay gaps amongst full-time employees are for skilled trades (25.4 per cent). The narrowest gender pay gaps are for professional occupations (3.8 per cent), and sales and customer services roles (5.9 per cent) (2008: 22). However, for the 'managers and senior officials' category, the pay gap is 23 per cent.

Women and career

Despite the progression, albeit slow, in closing the gap between pay for men and women, there remains inequality in the career experiences of women. Indeed, Duncan and Loretto (2004) observe that concepts of the chronology of career are male-dominated, and fail to take account of differences in women's careers and lives, most notably in relation to childbearing (2004: 99) and subsequent child care provision. Moen and Han (2001) note that while the idea of career is central to our social beliefs and behaviours, career has been 'a heavily male gendered [concept], rather than [reflecting] women's experiences' (2001: 426). While the male concept of career typically refers to moving through a series of related roles during the lifecourse, a female definition becomes narrower, and may include the woman moving into and out of the workforce (2001: 429).

≡ PIT STOP: REFLECTIVE ACTIVITY 9.2 ≡

In Norway, there is a requirement that at least 40 per cent of women are directors of corporate boards. It is claimed that where there are more women in a corporate board, organization performance improves (Equality and Human Rights Commission, 2011: 11).

1. Does this justify imposing quotas for women directors on UK boards?
2. How would you evidence whether the proportion of women actually made the difference in organizations' performance?
3. Are there wider arguments (other than corporate performance alone) for the inclusion of women on corporate boards?

Marshall (1989) suggested that the feminist perspective of career can be identified as three phases. In the first phase, it was noted that women were not included within career theory and models, and that this needed to be addressed. The second phase was one of reform, aimed at enabling women better access to 'career', even though the model of career remained male, white, and middle class. Finally, Marshall (1989) suggested a more radical approach, in which women did not accept the contemporary male view of career, and looked instead for a new model of career in which women's perspectives were more fully taken into account. Domestically, women tend to have significantly more home care responsibilities than their male counterparts (Alvesson and Due Billing 1997).

Evetts (2000) considered findings and literature from a range of organizations, including banking, and identified three explanatory theories for the ways in which women's careers could be considered as different from those for men:

1. Cultural dimensions: family and feminine ideologies, and organizational culture
2. Structural dimensions: family structures and organizational processes
3. Action dimensions: women's choices and strategies (2000: 58).

Evetts (2000) argues that all three dimensions are generally important and usually interconnected in understanding women's careers. The cultural dimensions refer to 'gendered cultural associations which make difficulties for women in senior positions in organization and professions' (2000: 60), so that organizational culture dimensions (see also Chapter 11) will tend to drive women's career choices and preferences. The second area which Evetts considers is the structural dimension of family life and organizational process (2000: 60). Here, the 'uncritical acceptance' of beliefs such as 'jobs ... most appropriately ... women's jobs', 'career success is merit-based', and 'women's family roles are more important anyway' (2000: 62) has therefore tended to emphasize the difficulties and determinants of women's careers (2000: 62). Finally, Evetts (200) also considered action choices – women's choices and strategies. Here, Evetts suggests that women's careers tend not to be determined in any causal way by structure and culture.

It may also be important to consider different levels of confidence in the role between women and men. Clance and Imes (1978) found that even successful women were inclined to experience impostor phenomenon, where:

> **Unlike men who tend to own success as attributable to a quality inherent in themselves, women are more likely either to project the cause of success outward to an external cause (luck), or to a temporary internal quality (effort) that they do not equate with inherent ability. (1978: 242)**

Even so, Evetts' observation that 'Careers also result from happenstance, serendipity and from chance encounters as well as from career planning, structural and organizational changes and changes in organizational conditions' (2000: 64) will surely resonate as strongly for men as for women. However, the difference is that women's career choices to date are more likely to be choices from decisions made earlier in paid employment, which will have tended to narrow the range of opportunity for women (2000: 64).

=== PIT STOP: REFLECTIVE ACTIVITY 9.3 ===

Flexible working

1. What types of Flexible Working arrangements are made available to employees?
2. How may these be used to support women in the workplace?

   (See also Chapter 6 on flexibility.)

Women remain under-represented in the most senior roles in the UK (see Table 9.3). By 2007, the UK Equal Opportunities Commission (EOC) reported that women were still under-represented in managerial roles, with 10.4 per cent of FTSE 100 directors being female, and only 18 per cent of small businesses having a majority of women directors (Equal Opportunities Commission, 2007: 4). Research about women and management has considered to what extent roles such as more senior management roles are 'gendered': where the perceived required behaviours of the role of manager are seen (whether or not for any objective reasons) as requiring masculine traits. For example, Schein et al. point out that the tendency to '"think manager – think male" is a global phenomenon, especially amongst males' (1996: 39). However, Pringle (2008) and Bruni and Gherardi (2002) noted that where women were in roles which tended to be perceived as masculine jobs, then they tended to believe they need to use masculine behaviours in their management roles in order to be seen as authoritative and credible. But where women aspire to more senior roles, there is a danger that they may do so with stereotypical masculine traits, which are not acceptable to either their male or female colleagues (Mavin, 2008: S76). Furthermore, Mavin also notes that 'forms of sexism mean that women are harder on other women than men are' (2008: S77), and that women may find it harder to deal with senior women (rather than senior men) because the strategies they use to deal with men (being flirtatious, generally supportive, admiring) do not work with senior women (2008: S77).

By 2011, the Davies Report (Women on Boards) found that the proportion of women on Corporate FTSE 100 boards had increased to 12.5 per cent, but that the rate of increase had been too slow, particularly when contrasted with Norway, Spain, and Australia. At the current rate of change, Davies suggests that it would take 70 years to have balanced male/female representation on boards. Davies (2011) suggests that the rationale for increasing women's board representation was that those companies with women on boards

Table 9.3 The proportion of women in key positions within the UK

The figures below show the proportion of women in key positions within the UK

Business:	12.5% of FTSE 100 board members; 7.8% of FTSE 250 board members
Politics:	22.2% of MPs; 17.4% of Cabinet members; 21.9% of House of Lords
Media:	6.9% of newspaper editors; 6.7% of media CEOs
Public sector:	12.9% of senior judiciary; 2.3% of local authority CEOs; 14.3% of university Vice Chancellors; 35.5% of secondary school head teachers

Source: Equality and Human Rights Commission (2011).

outperformed competitors with a 42 per cent higher return on sales, a 66 per cent higher return on capital, and a 53 per cent higher return on equity (2011: 7–8). Therefore, Davies suggests that greater gender diversity improves organizational performance, accesses a wider talent pool, enables a more responsive approach to the market, and achieves better corporate performance (2011: 8). (These arguments represent a 'business case' rationale for diversity, which is examined in more detail in the section 'Organization response to diversity and equality' below.) Amongst Davies' recommendations were increasing the proportion of women directors on FTSE 100 companies to 25 per cent by 2015, and that the UK Financial Reporting Council should amend the UK Corporate Governance Code for companies to establish a policy to include corporate boardroom diversity, with a requirement to report annually on progress.

This raises the question of how the UK glass ceiling – that invisible barrier which inhibits or blocks women's advancement to the most senior roles in an organization – continues to be a significant factor in UK organizations. The glass ceiling has been defined as the 'invisible barrier for women and minority groups, preventing them from moving up the corporate ladder' (Weyer 2007: 483). Morrison and Von Glinow described the glass ceiling as a barrier which was 'so subtle that it is transparent, yet so strong that it prevents women and minorities from moving up in the management hierarchy' (1990: 5). Oakley (2000) proposed that the glass ceiling could be accounted for on the basis of corporate practice, such as procedures for advancement or recruitment; culture and behaviour, such as leadership styles and [gender] stereotyping; and structure and culture, based on feminist theory.

═══ PIT STOP: REFLECTIVE ACTIVITY 9.4 ═══

1. What evidence do you see of the existence, or otherwise, of a glass ceiling in the workplace?
2. What do you observe to be the causes of that glass ceiling?

Age

There has been a gradual recognition that age is also a potential source of workplace discrimination, both in younger and older age groups (Giele and Elder, 1998). Age in the workplace matters for a broad range of 'social justice', and 'business case' reasons. For example, in the UK, unemployment for 16–24-year-olds is 21.6 per cent; in contrast the average unemployment rate in the UK is 8.1 per cent (ONS 2012). Across Europe, unemployment in some countries was even worse, with the highest unemployment for under-25-year-olds and the highest rates in Greece (57.0 per cent in August 2012) and Spain (55.9 per cent) (European Commission, Eurostat, 2012).

But if there are currently difficulties for younger people in entering the labour market, the experience of many workers is that to be considered 'older' comes at a comparatively early age, so squeezing the age range when some employers seem to consider an employee as not too young and not too old. In 2005, prior to the introduction of UK legislation on age in the workplace (Employment Equality (Age) Regulations, 2006) Lewis (2005), wrote in *The Times*: 'You may consider yourself young and in the prime of life. But think again if you are male and more than 45. Think again if you are female and more than 35' (2005: 3).

Arguments for greater age diversity in the workplace are, as with the need for wider inclusion of all disadvantaged groups, the need and opportunity to access a wider pool of talent and resource. But there are more direct financial pressures too, as the average age of the population increases both as a result of lower birth rates and longer life expectations (ONS 2007). Therefore, the cost of economic inactivity, unemployment and retirement pensions for older people places a considerable long-term burden on the UK economy: a reducing proportion of people at work will need to support an increased proportion who are older and economically inactive (Turner et al. 2006). Similar pressures apply across the Organisation for Economic Cooperation and Development (OECD). For example, Taylor and Walker (1994) in a study of five European countries found 'declining labour force participation among older people, with public policies being geared primarily to the labour market exit of this group, rather than its retention' (1994: 36). (It should be noted, however, that since this research, European economic austerity measures seek to retain the number of older people in the workforce and to increase retirement ages.)

But how do we define age, and what constitutes a younger or older age? It is clear that age does not simply relate to a person's chronological or calendar age. For example, Achenbaum (2005) sees age as much more than a number, and with associated meanings and expectations about the consequences of age:

Men and women throughout recorded history have ascribed a plethora of positive, negative, contradictory, ambiguous and ambivalent images and ideas, attitudes, traits and behaviours in ageing-related constructs which typically correlate with the process, problems, challenges, and opportunities of growing older. (2005: 21)

Age may also be considered as that person's location in the lifecourse, defined as a sequence of age-linked transitions that are embedded in social institutions and histories (Bengtson et al. 2005: 493). In other words, as we see the workplace as 'social institutions', we must consider the attitudes of organizations, and the people who work within them, as contributing to the understanding of age, together with how the individual interacts with family, labour market, and society, and how they themselves regard their own age.

Therefore, age can be seen as how an individual changes over time in biological, psychological, and social functioning, and how this affects that individual at the personal, organizational, and societal levels (Kooij et al. 2008: 365). Researchers have considered a variety of definitions of age, all of which go beyond simple chronological/calendar age, so that ageing may be seen as multidimensional. For example, Sterns and Doverspike (1989) identified five areas in which an individual's age could be considered:

1. Chronological age – based on calendar age and date of birth.
2. Functional or performance age – based on the employee's work performance, recognizing that as chronological age increases, employees' biology and psychology change, leading to differences in health, physical capacity, and cognitive abilities.
3. Psychosocial or subjective age – based on the individual's self-perception of age, and social perception of age. Social perception reflects age norms within an organization, profession, or wider society. Psychosocial age reflects the age when society perceives a person to be older; the social attitudes towards older workers, including stereotypes applied to older workers; and the impacts of HRM decisions from considering an employee to be older.
4. Organizational age – the ageing of employees within the organization, which may be framed as discussion about job seniority, or length of service in the organization, where older age may be either be detrimental or positive in its effects. Organizational age may also refer to career stage, skill obsolescence, and age norms within the organization.
5. Life – span and age – consider behavioural change at any point of the life cycle, based on normative behaviours, age-related biological changes, and age-related environmental determinants. Lifespan is also linked to life stage and family status (1989: 299–332).

Categorizations of age and ageing help us better understand the complexities of understanding 'age' and 'older'.

Age also affects individual workplace behaviours. For example, Barnes-Farrell and Piotrowski (1991) found that the discrepancy between subjective age (self-perception and social age) and chronological age was related to workplace stress: employees were likely to feel older (self-perception) where they felt higher workplace stress, but younger than their chronological age where workplace stress was lower.

This section on age discrimination has explored some of the issues in workplace age discrimination, with particular reference to older workers (although, as has been noted, younger workers also suffer workplace discrimination). The issues discussed have been seen to be different in their nature from the discussion on gender discrimination, but have the same effect of failing to provide social justice for groups in society, and potentially under-using available talent for the workplace. However, so far, this chapter has considered discrimination issues as single-issue discrimination. Complex as many of these discrimination circumstances may be, they fail to take account of multiple reasons for a person to be discriminated against (for example, the dual effects of gender and age). These combined grounds for discrimination will now be explored.

Discrimination in combination and intersectionality

There is extensive evidence that some types of discrimination against minority groups will have dual or multiple reasons (for example, gender and age; gender and ethnicity, and so on).

Women are considered to be more likely to suffer from age discrimination, and likely to be considered older and old at a younger age than their male colleagues. Furthermore, women may have less opportunity than men to offset the negative consequences of age: Vincent (1999) observes that men in later life are better able to access desirable images (for example, wealth and power) not available to women.

Bytheway (2005) draws attention to the importance which feminists have attached to visual images in the age/sexism experienced by women: 'Just as the anonymous fashion model represents a fantasy of womanhood, so her youth is perceived to be the ideal' (2005: 341).

Reinforcing these academic and media perspectives of women being regarded from the point of view of their physical attractiveness, Hearn and Parkin (1995) noted that 'Gender and sexuality do not exist in isolation, but in their specific conjunctions with such division as age, ethnicity, and bodily facility'.

De Beauvoir (1972) suggested that women were subject to the 'double jeopardy' of discrimination based on age and gender. Subsequent research (for example, Itzin and Phillipson, 1993, 1995) has continued to identify this double jeopardy for women, although it has not always been possible to identify whether the prime cause of that discrimination is gender, or age (or, for some, ethnicity and disability) (Biggs 1993; Duncan and Loretto 2004). The failure to identify a prime cause for discrimination towards older women may be because of insufficient theory in this area, as suggested by Bytheway (1995), or because of feminists seeking to demonstrate that the cause is sexism (Sontag 1978). Despite this lack of clarity, Duncan and Loretto observe:

> It is unclear, for instance, whether the dual effect of age and gender discrimination is simply additive or in some ways mutually reinforcing. The latter view is supported by some strands of feminist thought that hold that the origins and manifestations of ageism amongst older women are quite distinct from those affecting older men. (2004: 98)

Subsequent to De Beauvoir's original conceptualization of gender and double jeopardy, further investigation has centred on how different forms of social inequality may combine (for example, through a combination of gender, with ethnicity, disability, age, sexual orientation and class) to lead to 'intersectionality'. This concept was subsequently developed in the setting of employment (notably by Acker, 2006; Bradley, 2007; Bradley and Healy, 2008; Walby, 2007, 2009). In particular, Walby (2007) postulates that different inequalities change the nature and impact of the individual discrimination components, so that to add inequalities together to assume a total equality experienced by an individual is an oversimplification. Further analysis on double jeopardy and intersectionality in the workplace is still required, and in a review of the literature on development of thinking on intersectionality since the 1980s Durbin and Conley (2010) conclude that:

> As the workforce becomes more feminized, older and diverse, we have to think of innovative ways to both theoretically and empirically investigate multiple inequalities and how these impact upon diverse groups within and outside of the paid labour market. (2010: 198)

≡ **CASE STUDY 9.2** ≡

Discrimination in combination – an international example

In this example, two forms of discrimination are suggested against aboriginal women: one based on gender, the second based on ethnicity.

According to Cathy Eatok, a senior policy officer in state government, Australia's aboriginal female community experiences much higher rates of abuse than the rest of the population.

For why this should be the case, see www.unmultimedia.org/radio/english/2012/12/aboriginal-women-in-australia-face-abuse-says-an-aborigine/

Source: UN Radio (2012).

However, it is misleading to presume that age and gender disadvantages for women are based on physical appearance alone. Older women of working age may have domestic responsibilities, for the care of grandchildren or elderly relatives, and lower financial and intrinsic rewards than men. But despite these reasons, Arnold (1997) concluded on age and gender discrimination issues in occupational employment for women that 'After all the legitimate or potentially legitimate reasons for men's success being greater than women's, there is still a residual difference that can only be attributed to straightforward discrimination' (1997: 190).

 CASE STUDY 9.3

Intersectionality in workplace discrimination?

Praised by the BBC for winning a broadcasting award in 2008, Miriam O'Reilly then found herself dropped when *Countryfile* (a BBC TV programme) was moved to an evening slot for wider broadcasting. In the meantime, O'Reilly became 50 years old.

The new evening programme was to be fronted by younger broadcasters, in an attempt for the programme to be refreshed and reach out to a wider audience. Even so, another broadcaster on *Country file*, John Craven, male and aged 68, continued to have a place on the new programme.

O'Reilly claimed age and sex discrimination against the BBC. Following an employment tribunal, O'Reilly won her case on the grounds of age discrimination and victimization.

Source: Derived from *O'Reilly v BBC and Anor* 2200423/2010 (ET).

 ■ Question

1. It could be argued that age discrimination is identified more overtly as it is both factually measurable and comparative (when comparing two or more newsreaders' ages, for example). What are the difficulties in identifying aspects of age discrimination in an organization that appears to treat people of varying genders equally, but has an identifiable and differential treatment of employees when it comes to age?

The previous sections on gender, age, and intersectionality/discrimination in combination have given a detailed introduction to some of the complexities which underlie workplace discrimination. The following sections provide shorter introductions to other forms of workplace discrimination. Behind these introductions, it should be noted that each discrimination type has its own complex and different causes and effects.

Ethnicity

Ethnicity refers to colour, nationality, ethnicity, or national groupings. In a review of 27 countries in the European Union, ethnicity was regarded as the most widely perceived basis for discrimination at 64 per cent – contrasted with disability at 53 per cent, sexual orientation at 50 per cent, age at 46 per cent, religion at 44 per cent, and gender at 40 per cent (Eurobarometer 2007: 4).

Further study of employment and ethnicity suggests that there is a wide variety of workplace experiences for those who are other than white/British. For example, black people aged in their 20s are twice as likely as white/British to be not employed (Equality and Human Rights Commission 2010). Pakistani workers show high levels of occupational segregation, with 25 per cent of men primarily working as taxi drivers, and 83 per cent of working women in care/personal services. However, only one in four Bangladeshi and Pakistani women are in employment. In contrast, Caribbean women are more likely to be in employment than any other group of women, and those of Indian and Chinese ethnic origin are increasingly working in professional roles –already they are twice as likely as white/British to be employed in professional roles.

Women from ethnic minorities have even worse representation in managerial roles than we have already discussed for white/British women, despite them having similar aspirations at age 16 as white women. As a result, 11 per cent of white British women are in management roles, while for Black Caribbean women the number is 9 per cent, and for Pakistani women it is 6 per cent (Equal Opportunities Commission 2007: 9).

In ethnicity, as with other areas of diversity management, organizational culture (see Chapter 11) has been seen to have an important role in how that organization works internally and how it perceives and works with external stakeholders. The Macpherson Enquiry was established to look into delays in progressing the investigation and prosecution of suspects in the case of Stephen Lawrence, a young black man who was murdered in London. The enquiry found that the police case had been delayed by what was referred to as 'institutional racism', which was explained as:

> The collective failure of an organisation to provide an appropriate and professional service to people because of their colour, culture, or ethnic origin. It can be seen or detected in processes, attitudes and behaviour which amount to discrimination through unwitting prejudice, ignorance, thoughtlessness and racist stereotyping which disadvantage minority ethnic people. (Home Office 1999: para 6.34)

This tragic case serves as a reminder that diversity management is not simply a case of legal compliance but goes to the heart of an organization's culture, behaviours, and the service which that organization is charged with delivering. The case further underlines the earlier discussion in this chapter about stereotyping, and reinforces the challenges which organizations face when they seek to change workplace attitudes and behaviours on diversity issues.

Disability

The UK Equality Act (2010) defines disability as:

- a physical or mental impairment, and
- the impairment has a substantial and long-term adverse effect on their ability to carry out normal day-to-day activities.

It is estimated that about 20 per cent of the UK working population (approximately 8 million) may have some form of disability which could affect their employment. Laws to protect workers with disability are arguably the earliest in the UK to provide some protection for what we now regard as protected characteristics (see the Equality Act 2010, below). The Disabled Persons (Employment) Act of 1944 required employers with over 20 staff to provide at least 3 per cent of their vacancies for registered disabled staff.

Further statistics on the impact of disability on the workplace are shown in Table 9.4 below.

Table 9.4 To show disability and employment in the UK

The economically inactive rate for disabled people of working age is 46%, more than twice the rate for non-disabled people.

There are currently 1.3 million disabled people in the UK who are available for and want work.

The UK employment rate for disabled people of working age (aged 16 to 64) at the end of September 2010 was 48.1%, compared to 75.7% of non-disabled people. The employment rate gap between disabled people and non-disabled people is 27.6%.

Employment rates differ across impairments and are particularly poor for those with learning disabilities (less than 1 in 5), and mental health problems (just over 1 in 10).

The highest employment rates of over 6 in 10 exist for those with diabetes, skin conditions or chest/breathing problems.

1 in 6 of those who become disabled while in work lose their employment during the first year after becoming disabled.

80% of all those who become disabled are in employment at the time of the onset.

Long-term inactivity or unemployment can increase the difficulty of returning to work.

The average annual rate for disabled people making a transition from economic inactivity into employment is 4%, while the equivalent figure for non-disabled people is six times higher.

Disabled people are approximately three times more likely to exit work.

Disabled people have a very low representation in public appointments – the current make-up is just 1 in 20 (5%) across the UK, even though 1 in 5 of the working age population has a disability.

Source: Papworth Trust (2011: 5–7).

The Equality Act now provides wider support for people with disability and includes a duty to make 'reasonable adjustments' to enable staff to continue to work. Indeed, for many, the London 2012 Paralympic Games served as a powerful reminder of what can be achieved when reasonable adjustments are incorporated for a person with disability. Within the workplace, the types of reasonable adjustment which can be made available include making physical adjustments to the workplace; transferring the disabled person to another role; adjusting working hours or place of work; modifying work equipment; providing supervision; providing a reader or interpreter; reallocating some duties where necessary and possible; and allowing time off for treatment or rehabilitation.

Sexuality

It is unlawful within the UK Equality Act to discriminate against someone based on their sexual orientation. Sexual orientation is defined as having a sexual attraction to:

- Lesbians and gay men – persons of the same sex
- Heterosexuals – persons of the opposite sex
- Bisexuals – persons of both sexes.

It is also unlawful to discriminate against any employee and applicant who is undergoing any stage of gender reassignment under medical supervision for the purpose of reassigning that person's sex by changing physiological or other characteristics of their sex.

It is unclear what proportion of the workforce would describe themselves as lesbian, gay, and bisexual employees (LGB), since one of the issues in self-reporting is the fear of potential recrimination or prejudice. Research cited in Bond et al. (2009) by Stonewall suggests that the number of UK employees is approximately 1.7 million. In separate research, the ONS (2011) found that 1.5 per cent of UK adults described themselves as LGB (although 3.6 per cent did not know, or refused to answer the question).

LGB people are twice as likely as heterosexual employees to report that they have been discriminated against, experienced unfair treatment, or experienced harassment or bullying, with those going through gender change very likely to experience discrimination during transition (Equality and Human Rights Commission 2010).

Religion and belief

Religion and belief are covered as 'protected characteristics' within the Equality Act. They are not precisely defined, but can include philosophical belief, and no belief; however, political beliefs are not covered.

The ONS (2011) found that the percentage distribution of beliefs in the UK was as follows: Christian 68.5; Buddhist 0.4; Hindu 1.3; Jewish 0.4; Muslim 4.4; Sikh 0.7; any other religion 1.1; no religion at all 23.2.

As with some other forms of occupational segregation, Bond et al. (2009: 14) cite research from the ONS (2004) which showed that 37 per cent of Muslim men in employment were working in the distribution, hotel and restaurant industries, compared with 17 per cent of Christian men. Sikh, Muslim and Hindu women are also more likely to work in this industry.

Muslims have the lowest rates of employment in the UK, with 47 per cent of men and 24 per cent of Muslim women in employment (Equality and Human Rights Commission 2010).

HIV and AIDS

HIV/AIDS is not specifically covered under UK discrimination, but is an issue in wider global discrimination affecting both the workplace and wider society. Within the UK, a person with HIV/AIDS may be covered by the disability provisions of the Equality Act 2010. However, in addition to the diversity/discrimination issues of HIV/AIDS, it is worthwhile to note that despite the progress in managing HIV/AIDS, there are 1.8 million deaths a year in the world as a result of HIV/AIDS, and the total number living with HIV/AIDS was 34 million – many of whom were from the African sub-Sahara (UN AIDS *World AIDS Day Report* 2011: 6).

▤ CASE STUDY 9.4 ▤

Women and AIDS

According to a UN Report, a young woman is infected with HIV every minute.

HIV has a disproportionate effect on the lives of women: 'It is still the leading cause of death for women of reproductive age, and gender inequalities and women's rights violations are persistent in rendering women and girls more vulnerable to HIV and preventing them from accessing essential HIV services'.

Source: UN AIDS (2012).

Caste

In global diversity, one other notable form of discrimination which has historically affected a large number of people is the caste culture in India.

A report published in 1999 by the UNHCR suggested that, at that time, approximately 160 million people live a precarious existence, shunned by much of society because of their rank as 'untouchables' or Dalits, which means 'broken' people. Dalits are discriminated against, denied access to land, forced to work in degrading conditions, and routinely abused, even killed, at the hands of the police and of higher-caste groups that enjoy the state's protection. Dalit women are frequent victims of sexual abuse. (UNHCR 1999: 1)

Summary

This section has introduced the reader to some of the forms of inequality and discrimination which occur both in developed and developing countries. Some of those forms of discrimination may seem obvious, while others are either far more subtle or may even be outside our personal range of experiences. In whatever form, they remain pernicious to both society and the workplace. The chapter has already seen the efforts which many states are making towards the elimination of discrimination, and you are advised to review how this applies to your own home country. However, in order to illustrate one particular approach to legislation to abolish inequality in the workplace, the chapter will now consider UK legislative approaches.

Legislative response to diversity and equality

In response to the inequalities within the workplace, many governments have involved themselves in support and protect discriminated against groups and individuals, and areas addressed by various UK legislation are covered in Table 9.5 . This section provides a brief overview of UK employment discrimination.

The range of government support varies between voluntary means, to legislation providing both for individual protection in the workplace, and the establishment of bodies and organizations to research and promote minority groups. In particular, the Equality and Human Rights Commission (EHRC) was established in 2007 with the statutory requirement to promote and monitor human rights; and to protect, enforce and promote equality across the

Table 9.5 To show areas of non-discrimination covered by UK legislation as at 2014

Age discrimination	Part-time employees
Pregnancy and maternity	Disability discrimination
Race discrimination	Equal pay
Religion or belief	Fixed-term employees
Sex discrimination	Sexual orientation
Gender reassignment	Marriage and civil partnership
Trade union membership	Rehabilitation of offenders

Source: author.

nine 'protected' grounds – age, disability, gender, race, religion and belief, pregnancy and maternity, marriage and civil partnership, sexual orientation and gender reassignment (Equality and Human Rights Commission 2012). In this role, the EHRC drew together other non-departmental public bodies with statutory responsibilities to promote human rights for women, those with disabilities, and ethnic minorities.

=== PIT STOP: REFLECTIVE ACTIVITY 9.5 ===

Spend some time looking at the range of activities and reports undertaken by the EHRC at http://www.equalityhumanrights.com/

Since 2010, previous UK discrimination law has been integrated into the Equality Act 2010. This legislation drew together a range of discrimination law dating back over 40 years, and introduced some additional provisions. It identifies protected characteristics, which are defined as age, disability, gender, gender reassignment, marriage and civil partnership, pregnancy and maternity, race, religion or belief, sex, sexual orientation. The Equality Act makes the following discriminatory practices and behaviours unlawful.

Direct discrimination

This applies to all protected characteristics. It is treating someone less favourably than another person because of a protected characteristic that they have. For example, failing to recruit a person because they are pregnant.

Indirect discrimination

Indirect discrimination occurs when:

- a provision, criterion or practice is applied to all, and it puts a group with a protected characteristic at a disadvantage when compared with another group
- an individual is put at a disadvantage
- the employer cannot show it to be a proportionate means of achieving a legitimate aim.

Associative discrimination

This means treating an employee less favourably because they associate with an individual who has a protected characteristic.

Perceptive discrimination

This means treating someone less favourably because it is perceived that they have a protected characteristic, whether or not they do: for example refusing to appoint someone because it is thought that they are undergoing gender reassignment.

Victimization

Victimization means a person is treated less favourably because they have made or supported a complaint or raised a grievance under the Equality Act 2010.

Harassment

Harassment means unwanted conduct related to a relevant protected characteristic, which has the purpose or effect of violating an individual's dignity or creating an intimidating, hostile, degrading, humiliating or offensive environment for that individual.

≡ CASE STUDY 9.5 ≡

Harassment and bullying

Harassment and bullying in the workplace may take many different forms, and some of the cruellest is verbal bullying.

However, harassment and bullying may take other forms as well. In the example below, harassment and bullying was verbal, physical, and racially based.

Jones was a 16-year-old of mixed ethnic origin. When he started work, he was immediately subjected to physical and verbal abuse, which included a hot screwdriver, and metal bolts thrown at him. He resigned within a month and successfully claimed racial discrimination.

Source: Jones v Tower Boot Co IRLR 168.

Two additional areas are also covered by the Equality Act:

Occupational requirement

An organization may be able to demonstrate that there is an occupational requirement for an employee with a particular characteristic which would otherwise be discriminatory – for example, an employee with a particular ethnic background, or with a particular religion or belief. In practice, however, this clause is only used on a very limited basis.

Positive action

Positive action may be taken where there are otherwise areas of disproportionate under-representation within the workplace.

However, positive action to support the development of under-represented groups should not be confused with positive discrimination – for example, appointing a woman to a role, irrespective of her competences, skills, and experience, but so as to increase the proportion of women in that group. Positive discrimination continues to be unlawful in the UK.

Claims under the Equality Act do not require an employee to serve an initial period of employment and for most claims the burden of evidence and proof is on the employer to show that discrimination did not happen. Unlike unfair dismissal cases, there are no statutory limits on the levels of financial awards which can be made following a successful claim under the Equality Act. It is therefore important for employers to have effective policies and procedures in place to make clear the standards required, and for those standards to be monitored. Therefore, employers are encouraged to have an equality or diversity policy, and to communicate this to all employees. Claims made arising from discrimination legislation are referred in the UK to the Employment Tribunal Service. Table 9.6 shows the numbers of claims and compensation awarded in the year 2009–2010.

However, the decision to engage with an employer on litigation is not one which can be taken lightly. Even the Equality and Human Rights Commission (2009), the body charged with working to eliminate discrimination, cautions

Table 9.6   To show UK discrimination cases, 2009–2010

Employment Tribunal referral	Number of cases referred	% of all discrimination cases (77, 600)	Maximum/*average* compensation (£)
Equal pay	37,400	58.2	NA
Sex/gender	18,200	23.4	289,167/*13,911*
Race	5,700	7.3	62,530/*12,108*
Disability	7,500	9.6	181,083/*14,137*
Religion or belief	1,000	1.3	20,221/*8,515*
Sexual orientation	710	0.9	47,633/*11,671*
Age	5,200	6.7	144,100/*30,289*

Source: Derived from Employment Tribunals Service (2010).

advisers of potential litigants to consider carefully the effects of submitting claims to employment tribunals:

> Litigation can sometimes even seem a little self-indulgent. Certainly it may mean having to wait a long time before achieving the hoped for victory, whilst losing can be an utterly demoralizing experience. Any litigant should take into account the potential stress to herself or himself (and the rest of the family), as well as making a calm and realistic assessment of the merits of the claim. Emotions can run high in discrimination claims. (EHRC 2009: 3)

So far, the chapter has considered the background to discrimination, its impact on various minority groups, and how legislation may be used to address inequality. The chapter will now consider how organizations and HRM policy respond to some of those challenges.

Organization and HRM response to diversity and equality

Organizations differ in their response to the desire and need to promote equality and diversity, and their reasons for adopting policies in these areas. This chapter has also demonstrated the many areas in which HRM has a legitimate role – indeed a responsibility – to be involved in equality and diversity issues in areas such as career, pay, workplace values and behaviours, legal compliance, workplace ethics, labour force planning and monitoring, extending talent management programmes, corporate social responsibility and learning and development.

The Chartered Institute of Personnel and Development (2007) found that organizations had a range of reasons for introducing equality and diversity policies, and these are summarized in Table 9.7.

Some organizations appear to do very little to address workplace diversity, while others develop policy and actions to the full. Underlying organizational reasons for embracing equality and diversity policies have been identified as the business case for diversity and the social justice case for diversity.

The arguments for a business case relate to human capital considerations, including a wider recruitment selection pool (see Chapter 5), and maximized use of a wide range of different skills and outlooks. For example, Cornelius et al. (2001) summarize the business case as:

1. Taking advantage of diversity within the labour market, so as to reduce the problems associated with recruitment difficulties.
2. Maximizing employee potential, so as to maximize the capabilities of diverse groups in order to maximize organizational performance, and reduce the negative impact on morale which may be caused by the perceived unfairness of prejudice and discrimination.

Table 9.7 To show organizations' reasons for equality and diversity policies by percentage

Driver	Most/very important (%)	Important (%)	Less/least important (%)
Legal pressure	45	6	17
Recruit/retain best talent	30	19	15
Corporate social responsibility	30	26	18
Employer of choice	30	14	17
Makes business sense	31	14	15
Morally right	24	15	21
Improve business performance	16	15	17
Help recruitment problems	19	12	15
Belief in social justice	20	12	14
Improve customer relations	13	15	13
Improve products and service	19	13	12
Improve creativity and innovation	14	14	15
Desire to reach diverse markets	13	11	15
Improve corporate branding	12	13	12
Enhance decision-making	11	15	9
Trade union activities	7	8	17
Respond to market competition	12	10	8
Respond to global competition	9	8	13

Source: CIPD (2007); N = 285.

3. Enhancing the ability to manage across cultures and borders (see Chapters 11 and 12).
4. Creating opportunities and enhancing creativity, with access to new customers and new markets, accessing the knowledge of a culturally diverse workforce (2001: 32–50).

Despite the initial attractiveness and logic of the business case, it has attracted criticism. Dickens (1994) and Kaler (2001) see the rationale for the business case as being essentially narrow and short-term in nature, such as when national and international economic pressures on unemployment are evidenced. Both at government and organization levels, some researchers have questioned the motivations behind the business case. Bradley and Healy comment that 'governments may espouse an egalitarian stance, but only as long as it doesn't interfere too greatly with profits or markets' (2008: 71). Zanoni and Janssens (2004) found that managers tended to see diversity in a very selective and instrumental fashion when managing, appointing, and determining reward, so that 'diversity discourses clearly reflect existing power relations (see Chapter 8) between management and employees' (2004: 71). Similarly, Duncan (2003, 2008) and Forbes (1996) found that any discussion of the business case for organizational age diversity would be secondary to business performance goals.

Noon (2007) challenges the 'fatal flaws' of the diversity business case in ethnic minorities, arguing that the business case is short term, purports to develop an over-rational, and potentially unobtainable, cost–benefit approach to diversity, and is based on flawed assumptions of management rationality. Noon (2007) adds that the business case arguments are based on an underlying assumption that the right to fair and equal treatment needs to be justified on the contingency that equality needs to be good for business and the organization, rather than any social justice arguments. Noon also notes that to assume that managers will behave rationally in pursing the business case for diversity is to ignore that managers are equally capable of reacting with prejudice.

The social justice case aims to address some of the criticisms of the business case. Noon (2007) argues instead that diversity/equal opportunities must be part of the broader social justice agenda. In support of this argument, Noon (2007) cites Zanoni and Janssens (2004) who found that managers used stereotypes to explain difference, and 'were interested only in how such differences could be deployed in relation to organisational goals' (2004: 775). For these reasons, the social justice case gives a wider interpretation of the diversity than the business case, and goes beyond legislative compliance. Instead, the social justice case considers the social, ethical, and environmental arguments, even if the short-term business benefits are less obvious (Dickens, 1994, 1999).

In addition to the business and social justice reasons for introducing a wide range of suitable HRM diversity practices, equality and diversity require substantial training (see Chapter 10) focused both on understanding the principles of diversity and establishing a genuinely diverse workplace culture. Yet Harrison highlights the 'gulf between the rhetoric and reality of managing

Table 9.8 Diversity organization types

Negative	No equality or diversity policy; may act unlawfully; no understanding of the business or social justice cases for diversity and equality
Minimalist	Declares itself as equal opportunity, and has a written policy, but senior managers unlikely to have much interest
Compliant	Narrow business-case orientation to equality and diversity; has policies; most likely to be interested in recruitment processes
Comprehensive/proactive	Emphasizes both the business case and social justice arguments; agenda not just about avoiding discrimination, but promoting and valuing equality and diversity

Source: Kirton and Greene (2005: 205).

diversity in many organisations' (2005: 184). Pointing to the CIPD (2003) Training and Development Survey, she identifies three significant areas where organizations had underachieved in diversity management training:

- That diversity training increased significantly in quantitative terms, but was more likely to do with legal content than with changing skills, attitudes, and emotions related to diversity.
- Little concern to look at diversity in the outside world, and especially in relation to customers.
- [Diversity learning and development] was not extensively evaluated so that its impact and value was hard to determine (Harrison 2005: 184).

Therefore, despite the potential rationales for the business case and the social justice case for organization diversity and social justice, it can be seen that organization practices in these areas may differ from their stated objectives and policies. Kirton and Greene (2005) categorized organization types as negative, minimalists, compliant, and comprehensive/proactive organizations. These are shown in more detail in Table 9.8.

Table 9.9 Percentage of UK workplaces (with 10 or more employees) monitoring workplace equality policies

	Recruitment and selection	Recruitment and selection procedures	Monitor promotions	Review promotion procedures	Review relative pay rates
Gender	24	19	10	11	7
Ethnicity	24	20	10	11	5
Disability	23	19	9	10	4
Age	20	16	7	9	3

Source: Kersley et al. (2006).

There is some disparity in the evidence as to what proportion of organizations actually have equality and/or diversity policies. It is estimated that 73 per cent of UK workplaces have a formal and written equal opportunities policy (Kersley et al. 2006: 236). Separate research by the Chartered Institute of Personnel and Development found that 55 per cent of organizations had a formal diversity strategy, although the figure for public service employees increases to 84 per cent (CIPD 2009: 5). However, Kersley et al. (2006) suggested that even with an equality and diversity policy, employers were unlikely to monitor the impacts of equality policies in any meaningful way, as shown in Table 9.9.

Table 9.10 To show the top ten most frequently asked questions on discrimination to the CIPD August 2012

What is the key legislation that provides protection from discrimination in the UK?

What are the protected characteristics under the Equality Act 2010?

What forms of discrimination are there?

What changes to discrimination law have been introduced as a result of the Equality Act 2010?

How important is an equal opportunities policy and what should it contain?

How does the concept of a comparator work under the Equality Act 2010?

How can an employer justify or defend a discrimination claim?

Can an employer defend a discrimination claim on the basis of an occupational requirement?

Are employers liable for acts of discrimination carried out by employees?Can an employee who has suffered discrimination at the hands of a co-worker sue both the employer and the co-worker?

CIPD (2012).

It is also insightful to consider organizations' motivations for having workplace equality and diversity policies.

> **Kent Fire and Rescue Service is committed to providing services which are accessible to all sections of the community, and to protecting those who are most at risk. We pride ourselves on having well-trained professional staff, and an open culture which values diversity and equality of opportunity in employment. (Kent Fire and Rescue Service, 2012)**

Kent Fire and Rescue Service was subsequently externally assessed and has achieved the Excellent standard of the Fire and Rescue Services Equality Framework, which examines a wide range of equality and diversity issues in the workplace and the services the organization provides to the public. In other organizations, we may be more questioning about organizations' motivations in equality and diversity management, for example, by visiting the Frequently Asked Questions section of the website for the Chartered Institute of Personnel and Development (see Table 9.10). Here, only the top ten questions have been shown: these demonstrate a particular focus on the legalities of workplace discrimination – these are important, although the emphasis of this chapter is that culture plays a more fundamental role to ensure workplace diversity. These findings reinforce Harrison's (2005) earlier assertion that the focus of HRM attention on diversity in many organizations is based on legislative compliance, rather than a genuinely diverse organizational culture.

In concluding this review of diversity and organizations, it is also important to note the important concepts of horizontal and vertical segregation (Kirton and Greene 2005: 54), and the resultant impact on status, pay, training opportunities, pensions, and, in some cases, positions of power within the organization. Vertical segregation refers to the lack of advancement progression once a member of a discriminated against group has joined the organization (for example, the lack of progress for women and the glass ceiling). On the other hand, horizontal segregation refers to some types of job being less accessible for discriminated-against groups (for example, the shortage of women in science or engineering roles), which in turn may exclude them from higher pay or higher-status roles; at the same time, horizontal segregation may find discriminated against groups in lower status and lower-pay roles (for example, ethnic minority or immigrant workers in low-grade labouring or cleaning roles). In both cases, the reasons for segregation may not be the result of clear-cut discrimination, but the outcome of more systemic cultural, societal and historical reasons.

PIT STOP: REFLECTIVE ACTIVITY 9.6

Consider how you would monitor diversity policies within an organization.

You may find that the statistics show that you have a proportionate balance of all minority groups within the organization (gender, age, ethnicity, sexual orientation, belief and disability).

1. By taking into account the issues of horizontal and vertical segregation and pay inequality, what additional information would you require and why?

Compliance with discrimination legislation and the workplace monitoring of key diversity statistics are, of course, important in the workplace. However, this chapter has demonstrated that for truly effective workplace equality and diversity a wider approach needs to be adopted, addressing underlying workplaces values, cultures, and behaviours.

Equality and diversity outlook

Global

The chapter opened with a summary from the International Labour Office on global trends in equality and diversity. The summary demonstrated that across the world progress is being made, but in many states it is slow and patchy. This chapter has seen that the issue of discrimination in the workplace is ever-changing – and that 'new challenges arise where old ones remain at best only partially answered' (ILO 2011: ix).

For an international perspective (see also Chapters 11 and 12) of global trends in diversity, the reader is advised to look at research reviews and reports, especially those published by the ILO and the United Nations, many of which have been cited in this chapter. Within European Union states, the European Union produces a wide range of reviews and reports which are readily accessible. Research is often available on home-country government and government agency websites, and provides a useful starting point for considering the state of research issues in particular countries.

UK

This chapter has reviewed the complexities – and some success – in UK equality and diversity, and also noted that the workplace often reflects inequalities across wider society. The Equality and Human Rights Commission (EHRC) (2010) suggests that there are up to 15 significant challenges facing equality and diversity in the UK (see Table 9.11). As with the discussion on how organizations address equality and diversity, the EHRC's research demonstrates that both for social justice reasons, and for the longer-term economic and social performance of the UK, there are still significant challenges ahead.

Table 9.11   To show significant challenges still faced to achieve equality and diversity in the UK

Issue	Why this is important
Close the differences in health and life differences between the highest and lowest socio-economic groups	Men and women in the highest socio-economic groups live 7 years longer than those in the lowest, and this also reflects the lifetime experience of other disadvantages and health inequalities.
Close the infant mortality gap between ethnic groups	While infant mortality is comparatively rare in the UK, it disproportionately impacts on some ethnic minorities, especially Pakistani and Caribbean babies.
Close the performance gap in education between boys and girls	Boys' educational performance is consistently poorer than girls' in the UK, and potentially damages the skill base for the future economy.
Reduce ethnic and gender segregation in education	Girls are under-represented in some areas of study, which would otherwise lead to well-paid careers (e.g. engineering and physical science). Some students from ethnic minority groups are much less likely to gain entrance to more prestigious universities.
Close the qualification gaps for disabled people	Adults of working age but with a disability are half as likely to have a degree, and lower qualifications directly impact on work and earnings prospects. There is also evidence that disabled students are more likely to suffer disadvantages in learning – for example, through being bullied.
Reduce the disparities in educational performance by socio-economic background	Pupils from lower socio-economic backgrounds are less likely to gain good qualifications and will then face a lifetime of underachievement – this is wasteful of their potential, and wasteful to society. The problem is stated as 'birth not worth'.

Issue	Why this is important
Close the gender pay gap faster and further	While the gap between men's and women's pay has reduced, it remains stubbornly above 10%. It is estimated that better use of women's skills could be worth up to £23bn a year.
Close the ethnic and religious employment and pay gaps faster and further	People from ethnic minorities and some religious groups are less likely to be in work than white British and are paid less when they are in work. For example, 25% of Bangladeshi and Pakistani women work, compared with 75% of white British women; Chinese men earn 11% less on a job-for-job basis; and only 47% of Muslim men are employed.
Close the employment gap for those with disabilities	Work is seen as about being paid but also offers social interaction and well-being. However, disabled people are more likely to be bullied in the workplace.
Reduce hate crime incidence	It is believed that hate crimes are under-reported.
Reduce homophobic, transphobic, disability-related and religiously motivated bullying in schools and workplaces	School children with disabilities, special education needs, or who are gay/lesbian are much more likely to be bullied, with consequences for weaker exam results and employment prospects.
Reduce the rate of rape	It is estimated that there are 85,000 rapes a year in the UK, with less than 20% reported, and lower than expected conviction rates.
Reduce the rate of recorded domestic violence	Women suffer 73% of recorded domestic violence, with serious consequences on the individual, society, and the economy (estimated cost £6bn a year).
Support for carers	25% of women and 18% of men in their fifties are carers. The contribution of unpaid carers is estimated as £87bn a year. There is a need to balance what the economy can afford in care support and the current economic inactivity of those currently providing care support.
Close the 'power gap' in public bodies on all protected grounds	Many public representative bodies are under-representative of the breadth of communities which they serve – especially in religious beliefs, gender, and ethnicity.

Source: EHRC (2010: 42–7).

Conclusion

This chapter has considered the background to discrimination through stereotyping. It has looked at how organizations seek to respond to equality and diversity agendas, and has examined both UK and international examples of workplace discrimination. Overall, we may conclude that while some progress has been made, there is still a long way to go to achieve genuine workplace diversity – even in Europe and the UK, let alone on a more global basis.

The chapter has discussed in some detail issues of diversity based on gender and age. This is not intended in any way to diminish or undermine the importance of other areas of discrimination in any of the other minority/discriminated-against groups which have been identified in the chapter. However, the focus on these two groups has been used to show the depth and complexity of the nature of discrimination.

The future challenge – and opportunity – for managers in organizations, trade unions and employee representatives, and government, is to continue the momentum in achieving greater social justice and business benefit from further developing workplace diversity. Both the international and UK experience is that this can be achieved, but progress is slow. Legislation has its role, but more fundamental, and more challenging, is the need to develop diversity-friendly workplace cultures.

REFLECTIVE ACTIVITY 9.1 REVISITED

A question to challenge our thinking (see the section on the concept and implications of stereotype)

The surgeon was the boy's mother.

The chapter has explained that in the author's experience, less than 10 per cent of respondents answer this question correctly.

1. Why is this?
2. What does it tell us about stereotyping?

Further Reading

For a comprehensive review of the academic research and theory on diversity see:

Kirton, G. and Greene, A.M. (2010) *The Dynamics of Managing Diversity*, 3rd edn. Oxford: Elsevier Butterworth-Heinemann.

The Chartered Institute of Personnel and Development website has a host of useful information and factsheets.

The Equality and Human Rights Commission website has many research reports and publications, and discusses longer term plans for UK diversity.

See http://www3.imperial.ac.uk/events/diversitylecture for the annual Imperial College diversity lecture videos – interesting, informed, and easy to watch.

Various sites, such as the Office for National Statistics, International Labour Organization, the UN Inter-Agency Network on Gender and Equality and Eurobarometer have information and reports on discrimination in the workplace.

For a very useful review of UK equality and diversity, and good practices, see:

Bond, S. and Hollywood, E. (2009) *Integration in the Workplace: Emerging Employment Practice on Age, Sexual Orientation and Religion and Belief*, Research report 36. London: Equality and Human Rights Commission. Available at http://www.equalityhumanrights.com/uploaded_files/research/integration_in_the_workplace.pdf, accessed 4 September 2013.

References

Abrams, D., Eller, A. and Bryant, J. (2006) 'An age apart: the effects of inter-generational contact and stereotype threat on performance and intergroup bias', *Psychology and Ageing*, 21 (4): 691–702.

Achenbaum, W.A. (2005) 'Ageing and changing: international historical perspectives on ageing', in M.L. Johnson (ed.), *Age and Ageing*. Cambridge, Cambridge University Press, pp. 21–9.

Acker, J. (2006) *Class Questions, Feminist Answers*. Lanham, MD: Rowman and Littlefield Publishers.

Allport, G.W. (1954) *The Nature of Prejudice*. Reading, MA: Addison-Wesley.

Alvesson, M. and Due Billing, Y. (1997) *Understanding Gender and Organisations*. London: SAGE.

Arnold, J. (1997) *Managing Careers into the 21st Century*. London: Paul Chapman Publishing.

Barnes-Farrell, J.R. and Piotrowski, M. (1991) 'Discrepancies between chronological age and personal age as a reflection of unrelieved worker stress', *Work and Stress*, 5: 177–87.

Bengston, V.L., Elder (Jr), G.H. and Putney, N.M. (2005) 'The lifecourse perspective on ageing: linked lives, timing, and history', in M.L. Johnson (ed.), *Age and Ageing*. Cambridge: Cambridge University Press, pp. 493–501.

Biggs, S. (1993) *Understanding Ageing: Images, Attitudes and Professional Practice*. Buckingham: Open University Press.

Bond, S., Hollywood, E. and Colgan, F. (2009) *Integration in the Workplace: Emerging Employment Practice on Age, Sexual Orientation and Religion and Belief*, Research report 36. London: Equality and Human Rights Commission. Available at http://www.equalityhumanrights.com/uploaded_files/research/integration_in_the_workplace.pdf, accessed 4 September 2013.

Bradley, H. (2007) *Gender*. Cambridge: Polity Press.

Bradley, H. and Healy, G. (2008) *Ethnicity and Gender at Work: Inequalities, Careers AND Employment Relations*. Basingstoke: Palgrave Macmillan.

Braithwaite, V.A. and Gibson, D.M. (1987) 'Adjustment to retirement: what we know and what we need to know', *Ageing and Society*, 7: 1–18.

Broadbridge, A. and Hearn, J. (2008) 'Gender and management: new directions in research and continuing patterns in practice', *British Journal Of Management*, 19: 38–49.

Brosi, G. and Kleiner, B. (1999) 'Is age a handicap in finding employment?', *Equal Opportunities International*, 18 (5–6): 100–04.

Bruni, A. and Gherardi, S. (2002) 'Omega's story: the heterogeneous engineering of a gendered professional self', in M. Dent and S. Whitehead (eds), *Managing Professional Identities*. London: Routledge, pp. 174–98.

Bytheway, B. (1995) *Ageism*. Buckingham: Open University Press.

Bytheway, B. (2005) 'Ageism', in M.L. Johnson (ed.), *Age and Ageing*. Cambridge: Cambridge University Press, pp. 338–45.

Chartered Institute of Personnel and Development (2007) *Diversity in Business: A Focus for Progress*. London: CIPD.

Chartered Institute of Personnel and Development (2009) *A Barometer of HR Trends and Prospects 2009*. London: CIPD.

Chartered Institute of Personnel and Development (2012) Frequently asked questions on legal issues relating to discrimination. Available at: www.cipd.co.uk/hr-resources/employment-law-faqs/discrimination.aspx (accessed 14/03/2014).

Chasteen, A.L., Schwartz, N. and Park, D.C. (2002) 'The activation of aging stereotypes in younger and older adults', *Journal of Gerontology: Psychological Sciences*, 57: 540–7.

Clance, P.R. and Imes, S.A. (1978) 'The imposter phenomenon in high achieving women: dynamics and therapeutic intervention', *Psychotherapy: Theory, Research and Practice*, 15 (3): 241–7.

Cochrane, K. (2013) 'Interview with Clare Balding, broadcaster and television presenter', *The Guardian*, 12 January: 29.

Cornelius, N., Gooch, L. and Todd, S. (2001) 'Managing difference fairly: an integrated partnership approach', in M. Noon and E. Ogbonna (eds), *Equality, Diversity, and Disadvantage in Employment*. Basingstoke: Palgrave, pp. 32–50.

Coupland, N., Coupland, J. and Giles, H. (1991) *Language, Society, and the Elderly*. Oxford: Blackwell.

Cuddy, A.C. and Fiske, S.T. (2002) 'Doddering but dear: process, content, and functioning in stereotyping of older persons', in T. Nelson (ed.), *Ageism: Stereotyping and Prejudice Against Older Persons*. Cambridge, MA: MIT Press, pp. 1–26.

Davies, E.M. (2011) *Women on Boards*, Department for Business Innovation and Skills, available at http://www.bis.gov.uk/assets/biscore/business-law/docs/w/11-745-women-on-boards.pdf, accessed 29 September 2011.

De Beauvoir, S. (1972) *The Coming of Age*. New York: G. P. Putnam.

Dickens, L. (1994) 'The business case for women's equality: Is the carrot better than the stick?', *Employee Relations*, 16 (8): 5–18.

Dickens, L. (1999) 'Beyond the business case: a three-pronged approach to equality action', *Human Resource Management Journal*, 9 (1): 9–19.

Duncan, C. (2003) 'Assessing anti-ageism routes to older worker re-engagement', *Work, Employment and Society*, 17 (1): 101–20.

Duncan, C. (2008) 'The dangers and limitations of equality agendas as means for tackling old age prejudice', *Ageing and Society*, 28 (8): 1133–58.

Duncan, C. and Loretto, W. (2004) 'Never the right age? Gender and age-based discrimination in employment', *Gender Work and Organization*, 11 (1): 95–115.

Durbin, S. and Conley, H. (2010) 'Gender, intersectionality and labour process theory: une liaison dangereuse', in P. Thompson and C. Smith (eds), *Working Life: Renewing Labour Process Analysis*. Basingstoke: Palgrave, pp. 198.

Employment Tribunals Service (2010) *Employment Tribunal and Employment Appeal Tribunal Statistics (GB) 1 April 2009 to 31 March 2010*, Ministry of Justice,http://www.employmenttribunals.gov.uk/news.htm, accessed 4 July 2010.

Equal Opportunities Commission (2007) *Sex and Power: Who Runs Britain?*Available at https://www.google.co.uk/search?sourceid=navclient&ie=UTF-8&rlz=1T4TEUA_en___GB485&q=Equal+Opportunities+Commission+(2007)+Sex+and+Power%3A+Who+Runs+Britain%3F, accessed 4 September 2013.

Equal Pay Act 1970. London: Her Majesty's Stationery Office.

Equality Act 2010. London: Her Majesty's Stationery Office.

Equality and Human Rights Commission (2009) *About Us*, available at http://www.equalityhumanrights.com/en/aboutus/pages/aboutus.aspx, accessed 16 February 2009.

Equality and Human Rights Commission (2010) *How Fair is Britain: The first Triennial Review*. Available at http://www.equalityhumanrights.com/key-projects/how-fair-is-britain/ accessed on 4 September 2013.

Equality and Human Rights Commission (2011) *Sex and Power,* available at http://www.equalityhumanrights.com/uploaded_files/sex+power/sex_and_power_2011_gb__2_.pdf, accessed on 4 September 2013.

Eurobarometer (2007) *Special Eurobarometer 263, Discrimination in the European Union*. Directorate-General employment, Social Affairs and Equal Opportunities, European Commission. Available at http://ec.europa.eu/public_opinion/archives/ebs/ebs_263_en.pdf, accessed 4 September 2013.

European Commission, Eurostat (2012) *Unemployment Statistics October 2012*, available at http://epp.eurostat.ec.europa.eu/statistics_explained/index.php/Unemployment_statistics#Youth_unemployment_trends, accessed 21 December.

Evetts, J. (2000) 'Analysing change in women's careers: culture, structure, and action dimensions', *Gender, Work and Organization*, 7 (1): 44–62.

Forbes, I. (1996) 'The privatisation of sex equality policy', in J. Lovenduski and P. Norris (eds), *Women in Politics*. Oxford: Oxford University Press, pp. 145–62.

Giele, J.Z. and Elder, G.H. (Jr) (eds) (1998) *Methods of Lifecourse Research*. Thousand Oaks, CA: Sage.

Gold, D.O., Arbuckle, T.Y. and Andres, D. (1994) 'Verbosity in older adults', in M.L. Hummert, J.M. Wicmann and J.F. Nussbaum (eds), *Interpersonal Communication in Older Adulthood: Interdisciplinary Theory and Research*. Thousand Oaks, CA: Sage, pp. 107–29.

Gutek, A., Cohen, A.G. and Tsui, A. (1996) 'Reactions to perceived sex discrimination', *Human Relations*, 49 (6): 791–813.

Harrison, R. (2005) *Learning and Development*, 4th edn. London: CIPD.

Hearn, J. and Parkin, W. (1995) *Sex at Work: The Power and Paradox of Organisation Sexuality*. Hemel Hempstead: Prentice-Hall/Harvester Wheatsheaf.

Home Office (1999) *The Stephen Lawrence Inquiry: Report of an Inquiry by Sir William Macpherson of Cluny, Cm 4262-I, February 1999*. The Stationery Office, available at http://www.archive.official-documents.co.uk/document/cm42/4262/sli-00.htm, accessed 4 September 2013.

International Labour Office (2011) *Equality at Work: The Continuing Challenge*. International Labour Conference, 100th Session 2012, Geneva: International Labour Office. Available at http://www.ilo.org/wcmsp5/groups/public/@ed_norm/@relconf/documents/meeting-document/wcms_154779.pdf, accessed 4 September 2013.

Itzin, C. and Phillipson, C. (1993) *Age Barriers at Work: Maximising the Potential of Mature and Oder Workers*. Solihull: Metropolitan Authorities Recruitment Agency.

Itzin, C. and Phillipson, C. (1995) 'Reviews', *Ageing and Society*, 15 (3): 427–8.

Jones v Tower Boot Co IRLR 168, Court of Appeal.

Kaler, J. (2001) 'Diversity, equality, and morality', in M. Noon and E. Ogbonna (eds), *Equality, Diversity, and Disadvantage in Employment*. Basingstoke: Palgrave, pp. 51–64.

Kandola, R., Fullerton, J. and Ahmed, Y.(1995) 'Managing diversity: succeeding where equal opportunties has failed', *Equal Opportunities Review*, 59: 31–6.

Kent Fire and Rescue Service (2012) *Equality and Diversity, About Us*, available at http://www.kent.fire-uk.org/about_us/equality.aspx, accessed 28 September 2012.

Kersley, B., Alpin, C., Forth, J., Bryson, A., Bewley, H., Dix, G. and Oxenbridge, S. (2006) *Inside the Workplace: Findings from the 2004 Workplace Employment Relations Survey*. Abingdon: Routledge.

Kirton, G. and Greene, A.M. (2005) *The Dynamics of Managing Diversity*, 2nd edn. Oxford: Elsevier Butterworth-Heinemann.

Kirton, G. and Greene, A.M. (2010) *The Dynamics of Managing Diversity*, 3rd edn. Oxford: Elsevier Butterworth-Heinemann.

Kooij, D., de Lange, A., Jansen, P. and Dikkers, J. (2008) 'Older workers' motivation to continue to work: five meanings of age', *Journal of Managerial Psychology*, 23 (4): 364–94.

Leaker, D. (2008) 'The gender pay gap in the UK', *Economic and Labour Market Review*, 2 (4): 19–24.

Levy, B.R. (1996) 'Improving memory in old age by implicit self-stereotyping', *Journal of Personality and Social Psychology*, 7: 1092–107.

Lewis, C. (2005) 'Time to live longer and prosper', *The Times*, T2 (20 October): 3.

Macnicol, J. (2006) *Age Discrimination An Historical and Contemporary Analysis*. Cambridge: Cambridge University Press.

Marshall, J. (1989) 'Re-visioning career concepts: a feminist invitation', in M.B. Arthur, D.T. Hall and B.S. Lawrence (eds), *Handbook of Career Theory*. New York: Cambridge University Press, pp. 275–91.

Marshall, J. (1995) *Women Managers Moving On*. London and New York: Routledge.

Maternity and Parental Leave etc. Regulations 1999. London: Her Majesty's Stationery Office.

Mavin, S. (2008) 'Queen bees, wannabees and afraid to bees: no more "best enemies" for women in management?', *British Journal of Management*, 19: 75–84.

McCann, R. and Giles, H. (2002) 'Ageism in the workplace: a communication perspective', in T. Nelson (ed.), *Ageism, Stereotyping, and Prejudice Towards Older People*. Cambridge, MA: MIT Press, pp. 163–200.

Moen, P. and Han, S.K. (2001) 'Reframing careers: work, family, and gender', in V. Marshall, W. R. Heinz, H. Kruger and A. Verma (eds), *Restructuring Work and the Life Course*. Toronto, Buffalo and London: University of Toronto Press.

Morrison, M.A. and Von Glinow, A.M. (1990) 'Women and minorities in management', *American Psychologist*, 45: 200–08.

Noon, M. (2007) 'The fatal flaws of diversity and the business case for ethnic minorities', *Work, Employment and Society*, 21 (4): 773–84.

Nuessel, F. (1982) 'The language of ageism', *The Gerontologist*, 22: 273–6.

Oakley, J.G. (2000) 'Gender-based barriers to senior management positions: understanding the scarcity of female CEOs', *Journal of Business Ethics*, 27 (2): 321–35.

ONS (2007) *UK Population Age and Gender*, available at http://www.statistics.gov.uk/cci/nugget.asp?id=1651, accessed 20 May 2010.

ONS (2010) *Gender Pay Gap*, available at http://www.statistics.gov.uk/cci/nugget.asp?id=167, accessed 5 July 2010.

ONS (2011) *Integrated Household Survey April 2010 to March 2011: Experimental Statistics*, available at http://www.ons.gov.uk/ons/dcp171778_227150.pdf, accessed 29 September 2012.

ONS (2012a) *Gender Pay Gap Falls to 9.6%*, available at http://www.ons.gov.uk/ons/rel/mro/news-release/gender-pay-gap-falls-to-9-6--in-2012/ashe1112.html, accessed 4 September 2013.

ONS (2012b) *Labour Market Statistics*, available at http://www.ons.gov.uk/ons/index.html, accessed 29 September 2012.

Ozbilgin, M.F., Beauregard, T.A., Tatli, A. and Bell, M.P. (2011) 'Work-life, diversity and intersectionality: a critical review and research agenda', *International Journal of Management Reviews*, 13: 177–98.

Papworth Trust (2011) *Disability in the United Kingdom: Facts and Figures, July 2011*, available at http://www.papworth.org.uk/downloads/factsandfigures_disabilityintheuk_july2011_110721132605.pdf, accessed 29 September 2012.

Part Time Workers (Prevention of Less Favourable Terms) Regulations 2000. London: Her Majesty's Stationery Office.

Pettigrew, T.F. (1998) 'Intergroup contact theory', *Annual Review of Psychology*, 47: 65–85.

Prasad, P. and Mills, A.J. (1997) 'From showcase to shadow: understanding the dilemmas of managing workplace diversity', in P. Prasad, A.J. Mills, M. Elmes and A. Prasad (eds), *Managing the Organizational Melting Pot: Dilemmas of Workplace Diversity*. Thousand Oaks, CA: Sage, pp. 3–27.

Pringle, J.K. (2008) 'Gender in management: theorizing gender as heterogender', *British Journal of Management*, 19: S110–19.

Prior, M. (2013) 'High heels at the Geneva Motor Show' *Autocar*, 13 March: 13.

Rhodes, S.R. (1983) 'Age-related differences in work attitudes and behavior: a review and conceptual analysis', *Psychological Bulletin*, 93: 328–67.

Rothbart, M. and John, O.P. (1985) 'Social categorization and behavioral episodes: a cognitive analysis of the effects of intergroup contact', *Journal of Social Issues*, 41: 81–104.

Schein, V.E., Mueller, R., Lituchy, T., Lu, and Lu, J. (1996) 'Think manager – think male: a global phenomenon?', *Journal of Organizational Behaviour*, 17: 33–41.

Sex Discrimination Act 1975. London: Her Majesty's Stationery Office.

Shen, G. and Kleiner, B. (2001) 'Age discrimination in hiring', *Equal Opportunities International*, 20 (8): 25–32.

Sherif, M. (1956) 'Experiments in group conflict', *Scientific American*, 195: 54–8.

Sontag, S. (1978) 'The double standard of ageing', in V. Carver and P. Liddiard (eds), *An Ageing Population*. Milton Keynes: Open University Press, pp. 72–86.

Steele, C.M. (1997) 'A threat in the air: how stereotypes shape the intellectual test performance of African Americans', *Journal of Personality and Social Psychology*, 69: 797–811.

Steele, C.M. and Aronson, J. (1995) 'Stereotype threat and intellectual test performance of African Americans', *Journal of Personality and Social Psychology*, 69: 797–811.

Sterns, H.L. and Doverspike, D. (1989) 'Ageing and the retraining and learning process in organizations', in I. Goldstein and R. Katze (eds), *Training and Development in Work Organizations*. San Francisco, CA: Jossey Bass, pp. 299–332.

Straw, J.M. (1989) *Equal Opportunities: The Way Ahead*. London: Institute of Personnel and Development.

Stuart-Hamilton, I. (1991) *The Psychology of Ageing*. London: Jessica Kingsley Publishing.

Tajfel, H. (1970) 'Experiments in inter-group discrimination', *Scientific American*, 223: 96–102.

Taylor, P. and Walker, A. (1994) 'The ageing workforce: employers' attitudes towards older people', *Work, Employment and Society*, 8 (4): 569–91.

Turner, A., Drake, J. and Hills, J. (2006) *A New Pension Settlement for the Twenty First Century, Second Report of the Pensions Commission*. London: HMSO.

UN AIDS (2011) *World AIDS Day Report 2011*, available at http://www.unaids.org/en/aboutunaids/, accessed 28 September 2012.

UN AIDS (2012) *Women out Loud*, available at http://www.unaids.org/en/resources/press-centre/featurestories/2012/december/20121211womenoutloud/, accessed 20 December 2012.

UN Radio (2012) 'Aboriginal women in Australia face abuse', available at http://www.unmultimedia.org/radio/english/2012/12/aboriginal-women-in-australia-face-abuse-says-an-aborigine/, accessed 20 December 2012.

UNHCR (1999) *Broken People: Caste Violence Against India's 'Untouchables'*, available at http://www.unhcr.org/refworld/country,,HRW,,IND,4562d8cf2,3ae6a83f0,0.html, accessed 20 December 2012.

Vincent, J.A. (1999) *Politics, Power and Old Age*. Buckingham: Open University.

Walby, S. (2007) 'Complexity theory, systems theory and multiple intersecting social inequalities', *Philosophy of the Social Sciences*, 37 (4): 449–70.

Walby, S. (2009) *Globalisation and Inequalities: Complexity and Contested Modernities*. London: Sage.

Watt, R., McGlone, P., Evans, D., Boulton, S., Jacobs, J., Graham, S., Appleton, T., Perry, S. and Sheiham, A. (2004) 'The facilitating factors and barriers influencing change in dental practice in a sample of English general dental practitioners', *British Dental Journal*, 197 (8): 485–9.

Weyer, B. (2007) 'Twenty years later: explaining the persistence of the glass ceiling for women leaders', *Women in Management Review*, 22 (6): 482–96.

Zanoni, P. and Janssens, M. (2004) 'Deconstructing difference: the rhetoric of human resource managers', *Organizational Studies*, 24 (1): 55–74.

10

DEVELOPING EMPLOYEES AND MANAGERS

Jim Stewart

Chapter Overview

This chapter examines processes and practices in work organizations which aim to achieve and improve desired levels of performance through facilitating learning of employees and managers. It explores some possible meanings of a range of terms associated with those processes and practices and the extent to which, if any, varying terms signal new and different approaches to facilitating learning. The goal of performance improvement itself is also critically examined as an apparently given legitimate aim. The distinction drawn between employees and managers is relevant here, since for the most part managers are of course also employees. At senior levels, managers are seen as agents of owners and as a cadre who serve the interests of those who own organizations. Their role is defined as maximizing the performance of the organization as a whole in order to provide the best returns to owners, and this requires among other things maximizing the performance of employees. The chapter will question this view. Returns are often referred to as the 'bottom line', which is taken from financial statements of private-sector organizations such as company value measured by the balance sheet or profits indicated by profit and loss statements. However, not all organizations operate in the private sector, and we need to be aware that returns can be and are defined and measured in various ways. (See also the discussion of the Balanced Scorecard in Chapter 4.)

Some commonly applied methods of employee and management development will be explored and evaluated for their relevance and potential contribution to the achievement of organization objectives through organization strategy. This analysis will then inform an assessment of the potential and limitations of what is termed human resource development (HRD). The assessment will take account of the relationship of HRD with HRM.

Learning Objectives

- **Explain the meaning of talent management and employee and management development**
- **Evaluate approaches to and methods of employee and management development**

- **Critically evaluate debates on strategic HRD**
- **Analyse the contribution of strategic HRD to organization success in varying contexts**

McDonald's Hamburger University

Nearly everyone knows McDonald's: many however may not know of their Hamburger University. This was one of the first of what are known as corporate universities. McDonald's Hamburger University was founded in 1961 and is still a central part of what McDonald's call their training and development function. The word 'university' is usually associated with education, particularly higher or tertiary education. It is also associated with qualifications, especially Bachelor's and Master's degrees. Despite this association McDonald's Hamburger University is described as their Centre of Training Excellence and is claimed to be 'America's largest training organization'. So the emphasis is on training, which is usually associated with employees learning to be effective in their jobs, in this case within McDonald's. This is achieved by the Hamburger University designing training programmes which are delivered in their restaurants and by online materials. The Hamburger University does also deliver off the job training courses, primarily for current and future managers and franchisees. Since their global expansion, McDonald's have opened Hamburger University campuses across the world including in Sydney, Munich, London, Tokyo, Brazil and Beijing. Among other roles, these campuses support the language and cultural translation of training materials to meet the varying needs of local employees. This expansion of the Hamburger University is perhaps both indicative of and a means for achieving the standardization of product and customer experience that McDonald's is famous for.

Despite this focus on work-related learning and training, the use of the word 'university' and its associations in McDonald's is not without foundation. In the USA, the company has what they term a 'College Credit System'. Through an agreement with the American Council on Education and based on that body's assessment of the Hamburger University's management training and its equivalence to higher education courses, employees can apply for credit against degrees awarded by US universities and colleges. Some of these universities and colleges have already done their own assessment and are part of the McDonald's College Alliance, meaning gaining credit is much speedier with those institutions.

Linking employee training courses to qualifications is not confined to McDonald's in the USA. Macdonald's UK has a long history of awarding National Vocational Qualifications in hospitality, catering, customer service and management. They are also very active in the UK apprenticeship system. In addition, employees in McDonald's UK operations can also access a Foundation Degree in Managing Business Operations. It seems that the usual associations of

(Continued)

(Continued)

the word 'university' have some relevance to and meaning within McDonald's Hamburger University.

Another fact about McDonald's many people may not know is that the company we know today is due to a man named Ray Kroc. The original McDonald's hamburger drive-through restaurant was established and owned by two brothers named McDonald, but it was Kroc who established and grew the global corporation we know today. Kroc is credited with saying: 'If we are going to go anywhere, we've got to have talent. And, I'm going to put my money in talent.' Although Kroc did not himself establish the Hamburger University this quote is part of its rationale, and indeed for McDonald's significant investment worldwide in the education, training, development, learning of employees and arguably, part of the reason for its continued success. This may be an illustration of what is termed Strategic Human Resource Development (SHRD), i.e. the learning of employees being a deliberate part of a business strategy (see Chapter 2). But the quote is also of interest because it introduces yet another word of interest to this chapter: *talent*. The concept of talent is widely applied across all sectors of the economy and across the world in the phrases 'talent management' and 'talent development'. That use raises fresh questions about learning of employees to add to those to do with meanings and associations of the words education, training, development and SHRD. You may wish to consider why and how the words are used in McDonald's as we proceed through the chapter.

See www.aboutmcdonalds.com/mcd/corporate_careers/training_and_development/hamburger_ university.html. Case Study 10.1 raises many questions. These include the meaning of terms such as education, training, talent development and SHRD, and how those meanings differ, if at all. Is education different from training? And is either different from talent development? Do any differences matter? Think about these types of questions as you read the chapter.

Introduction

Many terms have been used to denote the subject of this chapter. For example, in the armed services of many countries and many large private sector organizations the term 'education' was commonly used before and after the Second World War for departments, units, roles and positions responsible for designing and coordinating the provision to prepare new recruits for their roles; in the armed services this included combat. This practice of referring to education was also common in the UK civil service and other government agencies in the same periods. However, in the latter half of the twentieth century the terms 'training' and then 'development' became more commonly used, originally and especially in private-sector organizations. The term 'learning and development' then became popular in all sectors around the turn of the present century. In the same period a separation between employees and management became established in use of the term 'management development'. These terms have more recently been superseded by 'talent' which was adopted as part of the management lexicon in the early 2000s. The concept of talent has been applied to many aspects of HRM, and indeed talent management is argued by some to be a new and alternative approach to managing the employment relationship (Iles et al., 2010). However, the interest in this chapter is confined primarily to talent development rather than talent management.

There is one further term that is of interest, and that is human resource development. As the twentieth century came to its last third, employee development changed yet again to 'human resource development' and management development became 'leadership development'. Human resource development (HRD) is argued to encompass management and leadership development. The term is perhaps more closely associated with HRM, and there have long been debates on the connections and relationship between the two (e.g. McGoldrick and Stewart, 1996). These debates, especially on what exactly constitutes HRD, are not yet settled and perhaps never will be (Hamlin and Stewart, 2011). We will discuss some of the definitions and argued connections in the next section, and this may provide possible answers to some of the questions raised by the Hamburger University case.

All of the terms mentioned so far were and are used to denote the same kinds of processes and practices. These are aimed at and are intended to enable, encourage, facilitate and require individual and organizational learning (Stewart and Rigg, 2011). In all or certainly most organizations resources are allocated to support these processes and practices on the grounds that individual and organization learning are essential if organizations are to survive and prosper. These grounds rest on a simple argument and that is to imagine an organization where no learning occurs; accepting of course that such a situation is possible. Imagine then the armed services of a country where new recruits do not learn how to perform in combat, where they do not learn how to use new equipment and weapons as they are developed by arms companies, where an individual service as an organization, say the British or French or American Army, does not learn and apply lessons of military strategy and tactics from successes and failures in battles and wars. This is of course unimaginable. Therefore, so the argument goes, individual employees and organizations as entities need to learn in order to be effective, to achieve their purpose and objectives, to succeed and to survive and prosper. Investing resources in processes and practices that facilitate learning makes sense since doing so targets what and how learning occurs to ensure it can directly contribute to organization effectiveness, survival and success.

Do different terms then matter? Is a job title of education officer so different to training officer or HRD manager or talent development adviser? The next section will examine this question in relation to HRD and talent development.

Talent, talent development and HRD

The meaning of HRD

The term HRD emerged in the 1960s in the context of what is known as development studies which is concerned with national economic development (Sambrook and Stewart, 2012). It then began to be applied to organization processes concerned with facilitating the learning of employees and, according to some writers, had grown out of what is referred to as organization development (OD) (ibid.). Research conducted on behalf of the American Society for Training and Development argued that HRD actually encompassed OD as well as professional and career development (McLagan and Suhadolnik, 1989). Despite that research and much since, the term HRD still has no settled meaning either in theory or practice (Hamlin and Stewart, 2011). As we have already seen, there are also competing terms; for example 'learning and development' and 'learning and talent development' seem to be favoured by the UK Chartered Institute of Personnel and Development (CIPD) for both qualifications and associated publications (see Stewart and Rigg, 2011, as an example and Stewart and Sambrook, 2012, for a fuller discussion on this point).

Different contexts of practice also seem to favour varying terms; for example 'workforce development' is a common feature of job titles and programmes of learning in public services, especially the National Health Service (NHS). To use the term 'HRD' is in itself to take a particular perspective on one aspect of managing the employment relationship between employers and employees (see Chapter 8). One interesting factor of using the term 'HRD' is that it extends the boundaries beyond the learning undertaken by employees. John Walton, for example, argued that HRD encompasses what he referred to as non-employee development (Walton, 1999); this might include for example agency workers and volunteers in any sector as well as learning provided for the unemployed. Sambrook and Stewart (2010) among others have argued that education, and especially higher education (HE), is a site of HRD practice. A common example is employers sponsoring employees on Foundation, Bachelor's and Master's degrees as well as professional qualification courses in accountancy, marketing and HR, which are commonly provided by universities. And such sponsorship suggests at least that those employers see qualifying their employees as part of their investment in and an activity of their 'training and development' for employees; McDonald's is a clear example of such an employer. This argument means that universities and their staff are practising HRD through both undergraduate and postgraduate degree programmes, whatever the subject.

HRD, training and talent development

Consider the possible differences in meaning between HRD, training and talent development.

Discuss and debate your thoughts with a group of work or student colleagues.

1. What similarities and differences of view can you identify within the group and what are the reasons for these differences?

The argument advanced by Sambrook and Stewart, and that by Walton, reflects in part a definition of HRD offered by Stewart (2007: 66) which states simply that 'HRD is constituted by planned interventions in organisational and individual learning processes'. This definition does not imply or require any form of relationship between an individual and organization, employment or otherwise. However, it does encompass and include any situation where such a relationship exists; employer and employee or university and student, for example. Stewart's definition is based on a view that learning is naturally occurring and continuous and so does not require any organized or formalized activity to make it happen. Such organized and formalized activities are what are termed 'planned interventions' in the definition; courses at colleges, universities or at work for example. Planned interventions can also be less organized and formalized; an impromptu coaching session by a manager to members of a work team, for example, will receive only a small amount of planning but will still have the intention to affect and influence learning. However, the definition offered by Stewart is not the only one available. Hamlin and Stewart (2011) found well over 20 different definitions of the term and their review confirmed previous reviews by for example McGoldrick et al. (2002) that there are a number of competing definitions for HRD.

Based on their analysis of the definitions, Hamlin and Stewart (2011) identified four 'core purposes' of HRD which were included and reflected to varying extents in the 24 definitions they examined in detail. They also identified that 'core purpose' is one of the key factors against which competing definitions vary. The core purposes are, in descending order of frequency in definitions of HRD, 'developing individual knowledge, skills and competences'; 'enhancing human potential and personal growth'; 'improving individual or group performance'; and 'improving organizational performance' (2011: 210). One of these purposes focuses almost exclusively on individuals – it also makes no direct reference to performance. That said, there is an implicit if not explicit link to performance in the definitions extolling that purpose since the expected outcome of developing knowledge, skills and competence is improved individual performance. The group of definitions which focus on enhancing human potential implies a link between individuals and collectives; i.e. personal growth is experienced by individuals but contributes to enhanced human potential. The third purpose has this link but more directly, and also has an explicit reference to performance. It is interesting that the final purpose is the only one to mention 'organization', and that is the one with the least number of mentions in the 24 definitions. Viewing HRD as extending beyond the boundaries of the employment relationship (see Chapter 8) seems to be widely accepted. In summary, definitions of HRD vary in the extent that they link individual learning to performance and individual development to collectives, but it is clear that there are at least assumed links and connections between individual learning and individual and collective performance.

The varying emphasis on performance and on the organization contexts of HRD reflects a long-standing debate in the HRD literature (see also the discussion of possible links between HRM and performance in Chapters 3 and 4). This debate is known as the 'performance' versus 'learning' perspective on HRD (Stewart and McGuire, 2012). This represents the differences between theorists who argue the purpose of HRD is to improve organization performance through improving individual and collective competence, and theorists who argue the purpose is to enhance individuals' growth, development and potential through facilitating their learning (Rigg et al., 2007). The performance perspective is what might be termed a traditional or conventional view of HRD which is associated with long-established understandings of training and training and development as it is practised in work organizations. The performance perspective is also associated with the last two core purposes identified by Hamlin and Stewart, and especially the final one. In contrast, the learning perspective is argued to be a more recent development in theorizing HRD and a reaction to the previously prevailing and dominant performance perspective. The learning perspective is associated with what is termed 'critical HRD' (see below) and emphasizes the emancipating potential of learning for individuals and collectives (see Chapter 13 for a discussion of critical HRM). Learning is seen as providing insight into social and material conditions and as developing the potential to change them to effect improvement. Definitions of 'improvement' in this context are to do with increased autonomy and freedom as social outcomes rather than economic or financial outcomes. Related to this, learning is also seen as a way of increasing choice to individuals in their behavioural repertoires and in their life chances. 'Performance' in the learning perspective is for individuals rather than organizations to define and specify. The learning perspective is most associated with the first two core purposes identified by Hamlin and Stewart and especially the second one. Interestingly, those two purposes were the most common found in the 24 definitions.

One problem with the debate on performance versus learning is that it separates the two purposes as if there was no connection or link. However, most theorists accept that individual learning is a necessary if not necessarily sufficient condition for achieving and improving performance by individuals. And if there is a connection between individual and organization performance, which most theorists also accept, individual learning is also a necessary if not sufficient condition for achieving and improving organization performance. The real difference between the two sides in the debate arises from that connection; i.e. that the purpose of HRD is exclusively to achieve and improve performance as defined and specified by organizations. It should be noted of course that 'organizations' do not define or specify anything. Organization decision-makers, normally senior managers, make those specifications. The key point is that in the performance perspective the purpose of HRD is to improve economic and financial performance, usually of work organizations or nations (see McGoldrick et al., 2002; Stewart and Sambrook, 2012). There is in the performance perspective no inherent value or worth in individual learning and no value or worth exists or is achieved by individual learning unless 'objective' economic and financial gains are realized. Measures such as increased efficiency, productivity and effectiveness (for example indicated by rises in profit and shareholder value at an organizational level or GDP at a national level) are usually used to indicate whether such value and worth have been achieved. Conversely, the learning perspective values individual development and growth as of inherent value, and facilitating achievement and the development of individual potential as worthy in its own right. This leads to an emphasis on personal, social and cultural outcomes being valued in place of, or at least as well as, economic and financial criteria and measurement. (See also the contrast between soft and hard HRM in Chapter 3.) In the learning perspective, measurement of outcomes has a less important place than in the performance perspective, and where measurement is used more 'subjective' criteria such as learner satisfaction or other individually reported benefits are considered valid and significant (McGoldrick et al., 2002).

PIT STOP: REFLECTIVE ACTIVITY 10.2

1. What do you think are the advantages of the performance perspective from the point of view of organization managers?
2. What do think are the advantages of the learning perspective from the point of view of individual employees?
3. Consider the implications of the results of the above for the practice of HRD in work organizations.
4. Discuss and debate your conclusions with a group of work or student colleagues.

Because of the focus on organization performance, the performance perspective is considered to view HRD as being a 'tool' of management justified only by helping to meet managerial goals and objectives, usually expressed in economic and financial measures. The learning perspective is often seen as a rejection of this managerial orientation and so is sometimes associated with what is termed 'critical HRD' (CHRD). More detailed examinations of CHRD can be found in Trehan et al. (2004, 2006) and Rigg et al. (2007). Here it is important to note that many writers on CHRD reject the learning perspective as being 'critical' and so not really a feature of CHRD. This rejection is based on an analysis of the meaning and focus of CHRD as resting on four critiques of traditional, or managerial, perspectives of HRD. We have already examined the first of these critiques, which is that of purpose. The second critique central to CHRD challenges the humanist assumptions informing and underpinning traditional HRD. These assumptions are also shared by the learning perspective and so this disallows the learning perspective as constituting part of CHRD. The assumptions see individuals in purely instrumental terms which leads to notions of 'self-development' and 'personal development' as being both possible and desirable. These two notions are central to the learning perspective, as shown by development of potential being valued as worthy in its own right. However, a more critical analysis of the concept of the individual questions the assumption of a coherent, autonomous, self-directed and independent 'I' which lies at the heart of both traditional and learning perspectives on HRD. Both psychoanalytical and social theory conceptualizations of the self suggest that the self is socially situated and constructed through social relations with others. This being the case, a conceptualization of the self as autonomous and self-directing is both limited and limiting as a basis for HRD practice. The learning perspective shares with CHRD a purpose of human emancipation through learning and development, but it inherently fails as a means of achieving that objective through its invalid assumptions on the nature of the self and human behaviour (Rigg et al., 2007). In any case, concepts such as self-development and personal development have been appropriated by the managerial performance perspective to further the aims and objectives of organizations.

The third CHRD critique is that of representational views of organizations within traditional and managerial perspectives of HRD. Such views are in fact central to the vast majority of research and writing on, and prescriptions for, management and so are not unique to traditional HRD. Most management and related professional practice texts are predicated on such views. Representational views conceptualize organizations as 'things'; that is, organizations are reified. In other words, organizations are made concrete and attributed characteristics such as structures and hierarchies as if they were real in the same sense that objects such as plants, houses and cars are real. But organizations are not objects and neither do they have a concrete existence like that of plants or houses or cars. To the extent that organizations are 'real' and 'concrete' they depend on human beings, i.e. us, making them seem so through our interactions and our individual and collective actions. However, not accepting that we are engaged in creating organizations limits our understanding of and ability to influence and shape them through, among other activities, HRD. CHRD therefore argues for applying a different understanding of organizations as a basis for HRD practice. Some examples of where this will make significant differences include HRD contributions to organization change efforts (Rigg et al., 2007).

The fourth CHRD critique is that of critical pedagogy, again based on both psychoanalytical and social theory. This focuses on the practice of HRD in institutions of education such as schools, colleges and universities as well as in the context of HRD practised in organizations. In that sense, critical pedagogy is 'practical' in that the critique calls for a shift in the power relations between those who teach or train, and those who are taught or trained. It also calls for changes in the curriculum, or content, as well as in the methods of formal learning and development programmes. An associated part of the critique is a call for the development and application of 'critical thinking' and of 'critical reflection' by learners to be facilitated by the content and methods of programmes of learning and development. Within CHRD, critical pedagogy is seen as the primary means through which the aims and aspirations of the other three critiques can best be served and achieved by professional practitioners in all settings and sites of HRD practice. There are however reservations which concern the ethics of developing critical thinking among individuals who may become isolated in the organizations in which they work (Rigg et al., 2007). For example, managers who experience a management development programme designed on the principles of CHRD may return to work with a very different understanding of their organization and their role than that of their colleague managers, their employees and their bosses, and so may become alienated in their jobs.

In summary, we can say that the term and concept of HRD have no settled meaning or single accepted definition. It is however clearly concerned with the learning of individuals and collectives such as groups, teams and organizations. It also has some concern with achieving and improving performance, although there is debate about who decides what and how performance should be measured. This is in part related to HRD also being widely accepted as not being limited to work organizations as the only or exclusive sites of HRD practice. CHRD questions and challenges many of the assumptions which underpin traditional or managerial conceptions of HRD, but can be said to share with them an interest in promoting and facilitating learning. Perhaps we can conclude that HRD is in essence concerned with facilitating learning in perhaps any and all contexts (see Stewart, 2007). So how does this compare with talent development?

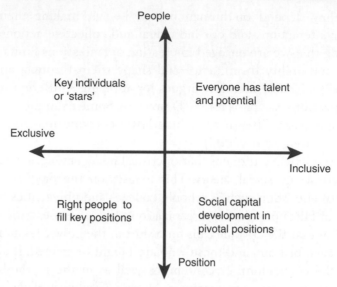

Figure 10.1 Approaches to talent management and development
Source: Iles et al. (2010).

The meaning of talent development

As noted earlier, talent development (TD) is part of the wider notion of talent management (TM). TM itself developed from an analysis and argument that stated a 'war for talent' exists among employers and that this war operated globally (see Chapter 12) as well as nationally (Michaels et al., 2001). A TM strategy commonly consists of focusing on a range of activities to attract, develop and retain employees (Tansley et al., 2007). There are various views on which employees should be targeted in a TM strategy, and this variety is usually characterized by the notions of position and people and of exclusive and inclusive. In the former case the choice is between focusing on particular roles, jobs, occupations or positions in an organization versus focusing on particular individuals who demonstrate either or both of current high performance and future potential. The notion of exclusivity/inclusivity questions whether all or only some employees should be embraced by a TM strategy. These possibilities are captured very clearly in Figure 10.1.

In addition to these questions there are some additional problems with formulating a TD strategy. The first of these is simply defining 'talent'. Most people if asked would have some vague idea of what the word means to them in a generic sense, e.g. a particular ability or aptitude. Thus a talented person possesses that special ability, but that is not really helpful in devising a TM or TD strategy. As Tansley and her colleagues found in their research (2007), a basic starting point in achieving a strategy has to be devising an agreed definition of talent in each particular organization, because talent is always context-specific.

However, they also found that this can be more difficult than it may sound, since people vary in their views of what constitutes talent in any given context. An obvious illustration of this is the aphorism 'beauty is in the eye of the beholder'. Another is the arguments and debates that arise among the professional judges as well as among families and friends about the relative talent of contestants on TV talent shows. Defining talent can be a controversial business.

Additional problems arise when adopting an approach in each of the quadrants in Figure 10.1. In the top-left quadrant only certain individuals will be selected for inclusion in a TD programme, which raises problems of selection for those programmes. Then there are problems for dealing with those not selected who, by definition, view themselves and are viewed by others as 'not talented'. In some organizations this problem is dealt with by keeping secret who is in a programme and who is not, but this then creates problems for those who are in the programme who are not allowed to reveal this to current or former work colleagues; many are not comfortable with such a position. A related problem can arise from what is referred to as 'reluctant talent' (Stewart and Harte, 2010). This refers to individuals who have been nominated or selected for a TD programme but who for a variety of possible reasons do not wish to meet the requirements of the programme. A common example of this is national or international travel to meet the placement or secondment requirements of TD programmes.

The top-right quadrant raises problems of resources to meet the development aspirations of all employees. It also potentially creates the related and additional problem of not being able to meet expectations that may be raised by an inclusive approach. The bottom-left quadrant has a different set of problems. These include first agreeing just which are the key or critical positions in an organization. It is not easy to have your occupation or role or position defined as not critical to success and even less so if you are a senior manager in charge of that function. Assuming agreement is reached, the problem then arises of attracting and retaining the 'best' individuals to fill those positions (see Chapter 5). Once recruited, position-holders have considerable bargaining power and can wield that power in their own interests. Two examples of this phenomenon which can be readily recognized are city traders and professional sports stars, especially footballers in the leading leagues around the world (see the opening case study of Chapter 8). Both examples have seen excessive wage demands being accepted by their employers. This is perhaps one but stark illustration of the 'war for talent'. The final quadrant in the bottom right of Figure 10.1 is to some extent a response to these problems. In the bottom right no position is considered more key or critical than any other. This approach is intended to foster cooperation and collaboration across organization boundaries and so minimize 'silo' mentalities and behaviour. A positive outcome is argued to be the development of what is known as social capital (Iles et al., 2009). However, as with the inclusive approach in the top right quadrant, this can cause resourcing problems as the approach implies a significant investment in TD. This approach can also be the most difficult to implement because of vested interests and organization politics working against true cooperation and collaboration.

▤ CASE STUDY 10.2 ▤

Graduates at Kentz Engineers and Constructors

Kentz Engineers and Constructors is an international company with approximately 7,000 staff in Europe, Africa, the Middle East and Asia. The company provides a range of engineering and construction services. The oil and gas markets are prominent in the work of the company. According to its website (www.kentz.com/careers/graduates), the company 'places a huge emphasis on graduate development and everyone from the CEO downwards is committed to developing graduates in order to allow them to reach their full potential and achieve their career aspirations.' In an article describing Kentz's approach to graduate deployment (O' Donnell et al., 2008) the authors argue that the Kentz model enables the company to help engineering graduates rapidly perform as junior engineers and to be ready to step up to design engineer, field engineer or project engineer. Critical is the provision of mentoring, for example, in part as regards socialization but also in respect of agreeing objectives and standards with the mentee and more broadly monitoring progress through work rotations.

Source: O' Donnell et al. (2008).

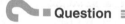 ▪ **Question**

1. After visiting the website www. kentz.com/careers/graduates, how can mentoring help speed up the process of graduate development at Kentz?

Summary

In summary, we can say that TM and so TD emerged as a response to intensifying competition among employers in national and international labour markets. In that sense, TD is basically a competitive strategy in the market for labour. Approaches to TD adopted by employers can and do vary and they do so in an attempt to attract and retain employees critical to organization success, whether because of their personal abilities or because of the positions they occupy, or perhaps in some cases a combination of both.

TD, HRD and strategic HRD

Perhaps because of the potential problems discussed above, surveys suggest a reduction in the number of employers engaging in TM/TD (CIPD, 2011b).

Those that do though focus their TM and TD programmes most commonly on the 'exclusive' and 'people' top-left quadrant; i.e. only some individuals identified as being top performers and/or having most potential are treated as talented and provided with specific TD programmes (ibid.). Such programmes tend to be formalized in the sense that they are closely linked with organization strategy (see Chapter 2), are planned and managed by HR departments, perhaps by TM/TD specialists, and are subject to close monitoring. In this sense, TD can be seen as what others term 'strategic HRD' (SHRD).

SHRD is yet another acronym used in describing and analysing learning and development. The term emerged based on the view that HRD needs to become (more?) strategic. This argument was most ardently supported by John Walton in his 1999 book *Strategic Human Resource Development* and it is an argument that has continued to be advanced. However, HRD itself was previously defined in part by adopting a strategic approach to organizational and individual development (Stewart and McGoldrick, 1996) and that view of the meaning of HRD has been and is still evident in many of the definitions analysed by Hamlin and Stewart (2011). So it is difficult to maintain an argument that there is a meaningful distinction between HRD and SHRD. Walton did draw attention to the useful distinction between SHRD – or HRD itself depending on your position – and HRD strategies. That distinction is accepted by probably every leading writer on the subject. However, the distinction provides little grounds for theorizing a difference between HRD itself and SHRD. Most extant definitions of HRD implicitly or explicitly include a strategic focus for HRD, so it remains debatable whether a supportable distinction can be drawn between SHRD and HRD. We can conclude therefore that the term 'HRD' is accepted to encompass SHRD. That being the case, HRD is strategic in that as applied in work organizations the intended contribution is to support the achievement of strategic goals and objectives. But how does TD differ from HRD, if at all? That question will be considered next (see also the discussion on definitions of SHRM in Chapter 3).

There are three key differences between HRD and TD. The first is simply the contexts of practice. As researched, discussed and practised, TD is confined to work organization contexts. In contrast and as we have seen, HRD encompasses sites other than organizations. Two examples illustrate this. First, HRD includes higher education as a site of HRD practice. It is of course true that some TD programmes include access to support for higher education programmes, but the key word is 'some' and higher education is not of itself encompassed in definitions of TD. The second key difference is that of purpose. We saw earlier that many definitions and meanings attached to HRD do not include organization performance. TD however is clearly and firmly linked to organization performance and strategy. Finally, HRD as practised in work organizations encompasses all employees and influences all forms of learning

(Hamlin and Stewart, 2011). The latter include informal and incidental learning that occurs naturally through work and experience (see Stewart and Rigg, 2011). TD can be and commonly is exclusive and so not always and not necessarily aimed at all employees. In addition, TD programmes are almost by definition formalized and planned and so have little if any focus on informal and incidental learning.

These differences between HRD and TD are significant. However, all of the features of TD can feature in HRD practice, so it could be argued that HRD encompasses TD and that TD is simply one form of applying HRD in work organizations. Therefore, in the context of work organizations, the differences matter little if at all. Approaches to and methods of HRD do not differ from those adopted in TD programmes, as we will see in the following sections, so it seems reasonable to conclude that TD is more of a new term rather than a new concept or practice.

PIT STOP: REFLECTIVE ACTIVITY 10.3

Return to Activity 10.1. As a reminder the task was as follows:

1. Consider the possible differences in meaning between HRD, training and talent development.
2. Discuss and debate your thoughts with a group of work or student colleagues.
3. Consider how your responses and views have changed after reading the chapter to this point. What similarities and differences can you identify?

Developing employees

We will separate this discussion of approaches to and methods of development into those of employees generally and then those for managers. However, it is important to remember that the first case will apply to managers too, and not only because as pointed out earlier, managers are commonly also employees. Talent however is often defined and associated in organizations as leadership (management) ability and TD as preparation for taking up leadership (management) positions (Stewart and Harte, 2010). That provides a reason and logic for separation.

Some general approaches

There is a wide array of options when it comes to selecting appropriate methods to facilitate learning. A number of significant factors help to assess methods and make judgements on which will be most effective in any given situation (Glaister et al., 2010). Some of those factors are listed and discussed below. It is important to understand that the factors cannot make the decision in any kind of mechanistic way; that will always require professional judgement.

A key factor is always the organization context (see Chapter 1) which encompasses a number of related factors. Size and structure will influence the possibilities and limitations of methods. Related to this is the resources available, which will include physical, people and skills as well as financial. For example, a small company with no dedicated HR function may well lack the necessary expertise for direct provision and so will have to rely on external expertise. They may also lack the finance for more expensive methods. Conversely, large multinational organizations such as McDonald's face problems of central control over local delivery, as well as needing to deliver learning in a variety of languages. Resources available reflect the additional organization context factor of management and (organizational) cultural support (see Chapter 11) for learning activities. Senior management will allocate more or less resources depending on their view of the value of learning interventions. They will also influence levels of support provided to learners by colleagues and line managers, i.e. the cultural state of the organization in relation to learning.

Two additional significant factors are the learners themselves and the specific development needs being addressed (Glaister et al., 2010). In the former case, different job categories are likely to demand different methods; e.g. those holding senior positions will not respond the same to methods used for those at entry level. Biographical and demographic differences between learners also need to be taken into account; age and educational level attained for example. Attention also has to be paid to individual circumstances such as care responsibilities outside of work, since standard approaches cannot be assumed to be appropriate to everyone in a particular job. Specific learning needs will demand particular approaches rather than others. Examples of this include whether the need is to develop knowledge or skills; each will require different methods to be effective. Skills also vary, for example between the cognitive, physical or social/interpersonal. While there may be some commonality in methods (e.g. all skill development can be said to require practice), specific methods adopted will vary according to the nature of the skill.

=== PIT STOP: REFLECTIVE ACTIVITY 10.4 ===

1. Consider how these factors will influence TD programmes.
2. Consider how this might relate to varying job categories and, taken together, influence decisions on methods adopted in TD programmes.
3. Discuss your conclusions with a group of work or student colleagues.

The approach adopted will also be influenced by the nature of the TD programme. Most have common elements for all included and so usually this implies significant numbers to be developed. In addition, TD programmes commonly contain a provision for specific individual development and so a method will be limited to that one person. It would make little sense to adopt the same approach in both cases. For example, significant numbers may justify designing and delivering a specific formal course, perhaps delivered by an external partner. Designing a specific formal course would not be justified for a single individual. In that case, the person may attend an established external course if a formal approach is decided. These examples illustrate that there are some general approaches which help to make decisions to fit particular circumstances.

A common choice relates to whether formal or informal methods are adopted. Methods do vary according to degrees of formality; i.e. how much planning and design is involved in providing the learning (Tansley et al., 2007). Courses are considered more formal than coaching, for example. A related choice is whether the learning is provided off or on the job. Off the job is considered to be usually more formal than on the job. To help decision making and to take account of some of the significant factors above, there are some general guidelines that can be applied.

- More formal approaches are generally more expensive
- Off the job approaches are generally more expensive
- On the job methods are more effective in an organization with a culture that is supportive of learning
- The further away from the job that learning occurs, the less effective it will be.

The last point applies because of the 'transfer of learning' problem. Research has shown that learners receiving development away from work can experience problems applying their learning once they are back at work doing their jobs. Research effort has also been applied to discover ways of overcoming this problem (Baldwin and Ford, 1988; Holton et al., 2000). The simple solution to the problem may be thought to have all learning interventions on the job and so there is no need for research into overcoming the problem. However, such research is worthwhile because learning interventions away from work have other advantages that mean they will always be used, so researching how to overcome the transfer of learning problem will help to make those types of intervention more effective.

Some specific methods

This section will discuss three common methods that can and do have an application in meeting a range of learning needs at all levels and most circumstances. They are commonly used in TD programmes and can be utilized for all grades and levels of employees; e.g. professionals as well as managers.

Action learning

Despite that last point, action learning (AL) is commonly associated with facilitating learning and development for managers; in other words, as a management development method. While that was the context of its invention by Reg Revans in the latter half of the last century, it has since been used successfully in a range of contexts (Rigg and Richards, 2008). These contexts include for professions such as accountancy, teaching, nursing and HR management (see Kellie et al., 2010, for one example). At least two business schools in the UK utilize AL in their doctorate in business administration programmes which are delivered to consultants, professionals and academics as well as senior managers. Some of the professions mentioned can also be considered at 'technical' levels in organization hierarchies and so AL can be said to be relevant to technical as well as professional and managerial jobs. It does therefore offer a possible method for developing a wide range of employees, or talent. In addition, it is also suited for use as an internal method with groups of employees, perhaps drawn from varying departments, levels and functions from a single employer. AL is also commonly used on interventions with participants drawn from different employers.

The basic design elements of AL (see Pedler et al., 2005, for a full discussion of AL principles) are first a small group of between four and eight individuals forming what is known as an AL set; a set simply being the group of people. AL can be used for any number of people so long as each individual is allocated to one of any number of AL sets. The criteria for allocating individuals to sets are not universal and can vary depending on the development being addressed. Common criteria include gender, age, job role, functional speciality and hierarchical level, with either similarity or difference being sought in the membership of each set.

The second element is that each individual attempts to solve a real organizational problem during their participation in the AL programme and AL set, and this forms the basis of the individual's AL project. This has to be a problem that matters to the individual themselves and to others in their organization. Revans distinguished between what he called *puzzles* – a question with a single correct answer – and *problems* – a question with a range of possible answers which are not all initially knowable and which will also vary in their effectiveness. AL projects have to address problems and not puzzles. They also have to include 'action' in the organization as a basis of learning and development. Problems addressed in AL projects commonly have some strategic significance to the organization and are commonly aimed at reducing costs and/or improving efficiency or effectiveness (see Pedler et al., 2005).

A third element of AL is the use of reflection as a learning method. This is helped through membership of an AL set and regular set meetings. Sets meet typically for half a day and, depending on the length of the overall programme, usually at weekly or monthly intervals. Individuals are allocated time in each set meeting to report their ideas, plans and progress on their projects and to outline the actions to be taken before the next set meeting. They receive questions and questioning from other set members. So, each member of what Revans called 'comrades in adversity' has, usually, an equal amount of time in each set meeting for them and their project. Being questioned by others supports each individual in reflecting on what and how they are learning (see Pedler et al., 2005).

The final feature of AL is the use of a set facilitator. This role is commonly carried out by a professional who uses skills of observation and an understanding of group processes to facilitate the work and development of the set.

AL sets can be seen as one form of what is called more widely 'communities of practice'. This idea rests on learning being seen as a social rather than an individual process where knowledge, understanding and skills are constructed within, by and through social groups (see Wenger, 1998, for more details). Designing and implementing an AL programme would be one way of encouraging and facilitating the flourishing of communities of practice within an organization. This in turn will help to develop a culture supportive of learning, make continuous learning more likely and support the learning and development necessary for sustained organization performance.

PIT STOP: REFLECTIVE ACTIVITY 10.5

1. Decide on a particular occupation, profession or role.
2. Evaluate the pros and cons of utilizing AL for the selected occupation, profession or role.
3. Assess the relevance of AL for TD programmes.

Coaching

The first point to note about coaching is the popularity of the method with employers in the UK (CIPD, 2011a). Second to note is that it can be and is used to address and provide development for most if not all categories of employees. Managers and supervisors can use the method to develop their subordinates, both individually and in team contexts. In this case, the coaches are internal. As with AL, the method can be and is commonly used for managers at all levels and for professional staff, especially those identified as knowledge workers. Such workers are probably the second-most targeted after managers for TD programmes within either people or position approaches to

TM. When used for managers, coaching can be applied as a management development method for all managers at a particular level, or can be used for just some managers or even just one individual. In those circumstances the coach is usually an external coach/consultant. Such coaching activity is commonly referred to as executive coaching (Peltier, 2010).

There is in theory no job, role or occupation which cannot be a target for coaching as a development method. Individuals occupying the archetypical example low-level job of cleaner can potentially benefit from coaching provided by their line manager, or perhaps by a colleague, with the latter commonly referred to as peer coaching. 'Doing' coaching clearly demands some skills; what is referred to as performance coaching needs the coach to be skilled at observation, questioning and providing feedback. These are skills which themselves can be developed and improved in supervisors and managers so that they can coach their staff to improve performance. As an approach to managing, a coaching style is argued to build a coaching culture supportive of continuous improvement (Whitmore, 2009). Such a style obviously reflects and also develops a learning culture and so is associated with gaining competitive advantage through the continuous development and performance improvement of employees.

Coaching does however extend beyond organizations. Executive coaching is to some extent sought and funded by individuals themselves, perhaps to help further their career. Roles with titles such as personal coach, career coach and life coach suggest demand from individuals as well as organizations. This also reflects the claim that skilled coaches can support development in any area and with any focus, even those where the coach has no personal knowledge, experience or expertise. Whatever the validity of that claim, it is clearly the case that coaching is one of the most widely used methods of development in the UK for both organizations and individuals, and it is certainly popular in TD programmes for all or some participants.

=== PIT STOP: REFLECTIVE ACTIVITY 10.6 ===

1. As with Reflective Activity 10.5, decide on a particular occupation, profession or role.
2. Evaluate the pros and cons of utilizing coaching for the selected occupation, profession or role.
3. Assess the relevance of coaching for TD programmes.
4. Discuss your conclusions with a group of work or student colleagues.

Mentoring

Coaching is concerned with improving immediate or short-term performance. Mentoring focuses more on the medium to long term. Within TD programmes, mentoring is less concerned with performance and more concerned with potential and so is most often utilized for 'talent', defined as those with future potential. As with coaching, it can be easily incorporated into an inclusive approach to TM and so is not only used where talent is defined as exclusive. This to an extent depends however on the degree of formality; mentoring can be totally informal with little or no involvement of HR professionals and mentoring 'pairs' making their own arrangements. More organized and formal use of mentoring will make it more difficult to adopt in inclusive TM because resource implications will arise. Another distinction between mentoring and coaching, or a defining characteristic of mentoring, is a focus on personal growth and a concern with career development (Megginson et al., 2006).

There are many definitions of mentoring. One definition captures the main purpose and nature and was formulated by two of the most influential UK-based authors on the subject: 'help by one person to another in making significant transitions in knowledge, work or thinking' (Megginson and Clutterbuck, 1995: 13). The focus is on how the mentee can move forward in some way. Eby (2010) also makes this clear by referring to mentoring as a 'developmentally oriented interpersonal relationship' (2010: 505). There has been a long recognized distinction in mentoring between the career function of mentoring and the pyscho-social function (Kram, 1983; Stewart and Knowles, 2003). The career focus includes sponsorship, coaching, protection, exposure and visibility and challenging work. The pyschosocial function includes role modelling, counselling and friendship. It is not unusual for a mentoring relationship to initially focus on career development but move in the direction of psychosocial support over time. This might be a typical approach to graduate development and other employees in a TD programme. Among other studies, research by Bozionelos et al. (2011) of MBA students in employment suggested that mentoring was connected with career success.

As suggested earlier, mentoring can be seen as and operate as an informal process for TD. Employees may be responsible for identifying and securing their own mentor. Mentoring processes will also vary according to what is agreed in the mentoring pair. Mentors may or may not receive training and support. More formal programmes will certainly provide the latter and there may well be more structure and control in selecting mentors and allocating/ forming mentoring pairs. There will also be more structure and standardization in how the process operates; e.g. in how much time mentors will allocate and where and how often meetings take place. Whether formal or informal, mentoring is not without criticism in the way the process might discriminate against women and ethnic minority groups (see Chapter 9), or might reinforce the values of dominant groups in an organization (Townley, 1994). This is one reason for formalizing the process to provide more structure and control. Another reason is the rise of TD programmes and the incorporation of mentoring as a development method in those programmes. Formalization also usually makes more use of organizations' competency frameworks or typologies of skills (see Chapter 5). It has also brought about increasing efforts to improve the quality and competence of mentors, with training courses for mentors that utilize a range of tools and instruments (Gilbreath et al., 2008).

As already mentioned, mentoring can have a negative impact in practice; Simon and Eby (2003) found experiences such as sexual harassment, neglect through lack of interest and direction and abuse of power by the mentor over the mentee through intimidation and put-downs. However, there is ample evidence of benefit too; e.g. various studies on mentoring in organizations point to satisfaction and the improvement of careers outcomes (Ragins et al., 2000; Underhill, 2006). In addition, Clutterbuck (2004) showed how benefits are gained by mentees in terms of skills and confidence, mentors gain through the satisfaction of passing on knowledge and the organization gains because of the impact on recruitment, retention, commitment and engagement. Mentoring is often used in management and leadership development, especially in TD programmes. One study (Lester et al., 2011) found a positive impact of mentoring on leadership efficacy – i.e. individuals' belief in their own leadership capability – as well as on actual leadership performance. This confirmed previous studies on the benefits of mentoring on leadership performance (e.g. Rosser, 2005). Returning to the degree of formality debate, some research has indicated that mentoring relationships were not always recognized as such where they operated informally (Welsh et al., 2012). This is important, since mutual recognition was also related to satisfaction. A clear finding from Megginson et al.'s (2006) research was the need to ensure that both mentors and mentees have an idea of what they want from the relationship and this requires a recognition of the relationship as mentoring.

As with coaching, mentoring can also operate within and for group contexts (Mitchell, 1999). Group mentoring can in some cases replace traditional programmes by allowing groups of learners, often considered as high-potential staff, to set learning topics. Each group facilitates its own programme with leaders as advisors (see Emelo, 2011). Another development is the use of ICT and Web 2.0 technologies for e-mentoring. Headlam-Wells et al. (2005) for example showed how e-mentoring for pairs of women helped in career development; other methods of communication were also needed to support the relationships between participants. Part of the case for e-mentoring, as with other forms of what is referred to as e-learning, is often made on the basis of reducing the costs of TD by reducing the need for meeting face-to-face. However, the very presence of participants in the same space may be crucial to the development of relationships.

1. As with the previous activity, decide on a particular occupation, profession or role.
2. Evaluate the pros and cons of utilizing mentoring for the selected occupation, profession or role.
3. Assess the relevance of mentoring for TD programmes.
4. Discuss your conclusions with a group of work or student colleagues.

Developing managers

Much research and writing on TD focuses on developing future leaders and thus leadership development (Tansley et al., 2007, Stewart and Harte, 2010). This reflects organization practice which commonly associates the need to attract, retain and develop talent with providing for future leadership. One point which is important to make is that the terms 'leader' and 'leadership development' are generally used as synonyms for 'manager' and 'management' (Stewart, 2009; Thorpe and Gold, 2010). We use the term 'manager' here as a more accurate reflection of what leadership TD programmes are actually about – developing individuals as current and future managers. Another point to make at the outset is that all of the methods discussed so far can be and are used to develop managerial talent. In fact, they are probably more used for that purpose than for other occupational groups. To an extent the reverse will be true of the contents of this section; i.e. it can and is applied to occupations and roles other than those of managers.

As with the notions of HRD and critical HRD, there is a traditional or conventional view of management development that is open to question. This is illustrated by the assumed purpose, which is to improve organizational performance, however that may be measured. Table 10.1 summarizes the work of Mabey and Salaman (1995) which suggests a range of possible purposes found in practice. Only the first relates to the conventional view. Attending management development programmes at Hamburger University at McDonald's, for example, may be intended by the company itself to meet the second purpose and experienced by employees as meeting the third purpose. Table 10.1 is only one example of research which raises questions about the nature and meaning of managing. There are many arguments and debates which provide reasons from a variety of perspectives to challenge the established or conventional view of management as being a technical and rational activity intended to maximize organization survival and performance (Thomas, 2003; Alvesson and Willmott, 2012). This work obviously has implications for management development and specific research on that practice illustrates some of those implications (see for example Mabey and Finch-Lees, 2008). As well as

Table 10.1 Management development agendas

Type	Description
Functional performance	Focuses on the knowledge, skills and attitudes of individual managers. Assumes an unproblematic link between MD and performance.
Political reinforcement	Focuses on reinforcing and propagating the skills and attitudes valued by top managers. Assumes top managers are correct in their diagnosis and prescription.
Compensation	MD is seen as part of the reward system for managers. Assumes development is motivational and encourages commitment.
Psychic defence	MD provides a 'safety valve' for managerial anxieties. Assumes competitive careers and associated anxieties.

Source: Based on Mabey and Salaman (1995).

management being a problematic concept, that of development can also be less than clear. Lee (2012) provides a clear articulation of the often unstated assumptions that inform varying understandings of and perspectives on the nature and process of development. The fact of variety is significant in itself because as Lee makes clear, development is a complex concept with competing meanings. It is therefore important not to view management development as a simplistic or straightforward process.

Approaches to management development

Despite these difficulties and problems, it is possible to define some possible and common approaches to management development (MD). One typology produced by Burgoyne (see Stewart, 2009) suggests six broad approaches as detailed below.

1. No systematic management development.
2. Isolated tactical management development.
3. Integrated and coordinated structural and development tactics.
4. An MD strategy to implement corporate policy.
5. MD strategy input to corporate policy formulation.
6. Strategic development of the management of corporate policy.

According to Burgoyne's original analysis, approach 1 is most likely to be evident in young and small organizations because in part of what Burgoyne refers to as 'organisation maturity'. Approaches 1, 2 and 3 are probably the most commonly adopted, while approach 4 is likely to be associated with what is currently identified as 'HRM best practice' (see Chapter 3). Perhaps significantly, it also reflects the conventional view of HRM/D being the servant of business strategy. This so-called 'best practice' approach is most likely to be found in large enterprises operating in well-established economic sectors (organizations which are more mature). Examples of these include primary process industries, ICT, financial services, retailing, and public-sector organizations such as those in local government and the health service. Given the first point, size seems to be a significant contingency factor influencing approaches to MD. So, too, does business strategy and, relatedly, the degree of top management support. A final example from the list of influencing factors having an impact is economic sector on approach adopted. The final approaches, 5 and 6, are for most organizations, and according to Burgoyne, aspirational. A key factor in the typology is the link between MD programmes and organization or corporate strategy (see Chapter 2). The final two approaches have the closest link, which is perhaps why they are the least commonly found in practice.

A criticism of this typology is that apart from the first approach, it conceptualizes MD as being planned and organized – formal in other words. This also assumes that such programmes are exclusively when and where learning occurs, or is most efficient and/or effective. An alternative view is provided by Gold et al. (2010). These authors argue that much managerial learning occurs informally and their typology thus has two potential strengths. First, it accommodates dealing directly with informal processes of learning and development. Second, it is limited to three approaches. This makes the typology less conceptually complex and therefore easier to apply to inform practice. The three approaches are described in Table 10.2.

Each of the three types of MD suggested by Gold and his colleagues has particular characteristics which will have implications and consequences for their effectiveness as an approach to MD. Type 1 has the strength and advantage of focusing on and occurring in 'real' work. This focus on 'real' work is a growing trend in approaches to MD, even in the context of increases in investment in formal programmes. However, according to Gold et al. (2010), learning in the type 1 approach can be unconscious, undirected and insufficient. Type 3 overcomes these problems and disadvantages by being planned and therefore directed to serve desired purposes. However, type 3 approaches have their own problems and disadvantages. First, the content of formal programmes may not be relevant to 'real' work. Second, participating managers may experience difficulties in transferring their learning to the work context (ibid.). Both of these disadvantages are associated with the 'distance', both temporal and spatial, between formal learning and work. Gold et al. therefore go on to argue that type 2 approaches have the potential to maximize the advantages and minimize the disadvantages of each of the other two types. This argument relies in part on their contention that the either/or choice of formal or informal approaches is in fact a false dichotomy. This contention, in turn, seems to support the current

Table 10.2 Typologies of management development

Type	Description
Type 1	Informal managerial – accidental process
Type 2	Integrated managerial – opportunistic processes
Type 3	Formal management development – planned processes

Source: Based on Gold et al. (2010).

arguments for 'blended approaches' (see Stewart, 2010). In any case, the work is valuable in emphasizing the actual and potential learning inherent in the everyday experience of carrying out work tasks and activities.

One further factor arising out of the typology is of interest. The authors suggest that a characteristic of both type 1 and type 2 approaches is that 'ownership' of MD processes and activities remains with managers themselves. Type 3 approaches, by contrast, imply ownership by HR professional practitioners. There is therefore in the typology a choice to be made in terms of the relative role and contributions of professional developers and other managers. Type 3 approaches provide professional practitioners with control and ownership. The other approaches do not. This issue of control and ownership is one of the main reasons for advocating type 2 approaches.

PIT STOP: REFLECTIVE ACTIVITY 10.8

1. Identify some possible relationships and connections between organization contingencies and the idea of 'organization maturity'. Think about how a 'mature' and an 'immature' organization might differ in relation to the contingencies (see also Chapter 3 on organization life-cycles).
2. Consider the likely implications for management development practice arising from changes in organization contingencies.
3. Research and access some examples of management development practice from published cases in journals such as *People Management*.
4. Analyse the descriptions provided and categorize the approach adopted in each case according to the Burgoyne and Gold et al. frameworks.
5. Evaluate the utility of both frameworks and decide which is more effective, and for what reasons, in categorizing varying approaches

Some specific methods

There are obvious connections between approaches to and methods of management development. A simple example would be that type 3 approaches in Gold et al.'s typology are likely to be associated with formal programmes of management education and training, while type 2 approaches are likely to incorporate work and job-based methods such as action learning, coaching and mentoring, discussed above. One commonly applied method of MD is to produce frameworks of management competence (Thomson et al., 2001). As Thomson and his colleagues detail, there are a number of different meanings associated with, and methods of development attached to, this concept. It has however been applied within national policy through the work of the former Management Charter Initiative in creating occupational standards and National Vocational Qualifications (NVQs) for management (see Stewart, 1999). These occupational standards provide specifications of 'competences' that managers in various roles and hierarchical levels require to perform their jobs. The meaning of competence and the methodology applied to produce specifications of competence in NVQs have both been heavily criticized (see for example Gold et al., 2010). Some empirical research has claimed to demonstrate improvements in both individual and organization performance through the use and application of management NVQs (Winterton and Winterton, 2002). It is the case that use of management NVQs provides opportunities for the adoption of type 2 approaches because they require the generation and assessment of work-based evidence of competence. It is also true that NVQ-based specifications do not have to be used in competence-based methods of MD. Organizations can and do develop their own frameworks and specifications (Thomson et al., 2001).

Gold et al. (2010) suggest a range of MD methods which, since they focus on combining learning and working and working and learning, enable the application of type 2 approaches. The methods are categorized into three sets as follows:

- Changes in the job:

  o promotion;
  o job rotation;
  o secondments.

- Changes in job content:

  o additional responsibilities and tasks;
  o specific projects;
  o membership of committees or task groups;
  o junior or shadow board.

- Within the job:

  o coaching;
  o counselling;
  o monitoring and feedback;
  o mentoring.

This list explicitly focuses on what might be termed informal methods of MD, which nevertheless are capable of, and perhaps would benefit from, some degree of planning and formalization, as we saw earlier is the case with both coaching and mentoring. The list does, however, exclude off the job and other methods that are normally associated with formalized and planned approaches. Alternative classifications are possible which include these, and a summary of the main methods is listed below (Stewart, 2009):

- group-based methods, e.g. managerial grid;
- e-learning;
- outdoor development;
- in-house courses;
- planned experience outside the organization;
- external courses, qualification or non-qualification based;
- role analysis;
- internal or external seminars;
- action learning;
- performance review;
- development centre;
- career management and development.

The global leader

There is not space here to describe these methods in detail. There is however one further aspect of management development that needs to be mentioned, although it is usually expressed using the word 'leadership'. This is developing what is referred to as 'global leaders'. Turnbull James and Collins (2010) identify at least three problems with this concept. First, what exactly is a global leader? There are a variety of argued answers to this question including a person who can lead (manage) anywhere in the world or a person who can lead (manage) organizations and/or teams who are drawn from and operate in multinational contexts (see Chapter 12). The second problem is the question of whether a competent or skilled leader in any given national context will be competent and skilled in a different national context. If the answer is no then that leads to the third problem, which is the impossibility of identifying any specification of a truly global leader; it is improbable at best that if different competencies and skills are needed in different national contexts any single person will be able to demonstrate them all.

These problems are of course interconnected and are related to a longer-standing problem in leadership research. This is the possibility, or not, of any universal specification of leadership competences. For example, UK NVQs in management are often criticized for conceptualizing competences which are supposed to be relevant in any and all organization contexts; many claimed universal theories and specifications of effective leader behaviour have been found to be flawed (Turnbull James and Collins, 2010). And so the prospect of a universal specification seems at best unlikely. A famous attempt at producing such a specification is that of the GLOBE project (see House et al., 2004). However, that research found that there is a mix of universal and culturally context-specific behaviours considered effective and ineffective in different countries and regions of the world. However, even the commonalities found cannot be termed behaviours of a global leader; they are simply similar behaviours considered to be effective or ineffective in different nations and regions. Notwithstanding this situation, work is still done by both academics and professionals on developing global leaders. The methods such programmes adopt are summarized by Turnbull James and Collins (2010) as follows:

- classroom and action learning projects;
- forming teams of individuals with diverse backgrounds;
- immersion in the country's way of life through foreign travel;
- broaden the outlook of potential global leaders through overseas assignments.

Much of the activity in the first and third of these is aimed at preparation for working in a different single country and so these do not really constitute activity to develop a 'global leader'. The other two sets of activities may be considered relevant to the concept but still have the limitation of the nationalities and countries included in the diverse teams or locations of overseas assignments. The case of McDonald's again illustrates these problems. As well as language translation, training materials need to be subject to cultural translation so as to be applicable in different and varying national contexts. That experience suggests there is little if any current practical possibility of a culture-free 'global leader'.

≣ CASE STUDY 10.3 ≣

A HRD insight into cross-cultural working

The basis of effective cross-cultural working is trust and transparency – and the first step to building that trust is fair and effective recruitment, delegates to HRD 2007 were told by Roland Dubois, CEO of the Industrial and Vocational Training Board of Mauritius.

'It starts there,' Dubois said. 'In Mauritius, people used to be recruited based on their skin colour. But globalization means you now cannot afford not to recruit the best candidate whatever their background.'

In talking about how organizations can promote effective multicultural working, Dubois drew on lessons learned from Mauritius's hybrid population: the 1.2 million inhabitants include Indians, Chinese, Europeans, Africans, Sri Lankans and Bangladeshis.

Mauritius wants to keep attracting more international companies and foreign workers. 'The trend for migration is universal; like it or not people will continue to migrate,' Dubois said, noting that diversity brings challenges. 'The story of Richard Gere and Shilpa Shetty this week caused anger in India,' he said, referring to the much publicized kiss given by the American actor to the *Big Brother* winner. 'It was an example of a lack of cultural awareness.'

In Mauritius, at a national level the government has worked hard to promote diversity and multiculturalism. For example, children are taught many languages in schools so they can learn about each other's cultures. A Ministry of Arts and Culture promotes multicultural activities and every religion has public holidays for religious events.

A similar commitment was also needed at an organizational level, Dubois said. If companies wished to build a high-performance but diverse team they needed to improve communication, emphasize teamwork, ensure equity in recruitment and promote an agreed vision and set of values.

Source: Evans (2007).

 ■ **Question**

1. On a practical level, what could Dubois do when rolling out multicultural programmes to employees at Mauritian companies?

Conclusion

This chapter has provided brief discussions of a number of concepts related to developing employees and managers. These discussions have made clear that the concepts applied in work organizations are neither simple nor without debate and controversy. Application may be commonly treated as unproblematic, but activities which are encompassed by concepts such as HRD and TD require many choices and decisions to be made; i.e. from strategic issues such as level of investment and primary purpose to be pursued to tactical issues such as what methods to employ and for which employees. In addition, the intentions of senior managers may not be realized in practice. For example, an exclusive and people-focused TD programme may bring benefits to the individuals included and to the organization but may also bring disbenefits through the lower motivation, commitment and engagement of those employees excluded. These disbenefits may extend to less effective teamwork and a loss of trust and social capital. Taken together, the disbenefits may outweigh any gains. In any case, the banking and economic crises of 2007 onwards have brought into question the appropriateness of an unfettered pursuit of profit as the only legitimate aim of commercial organizations (see Sun et al., 2011). This experience lends support to critiques of traditional and conventional views of the purpose of management and adds weight to related arguments for the legitimacy of social and cultural objectives to be given attention alongside economic and financial performance.

■ Further Reading ■ ■ ■ ■ ■ ■ ■ ■ ■ ■ ■ ■

Alvesson, M. and Willmott, H. (2012) *Making Sense of Management*, 2nd edn. London: Sage Publications.

Gold, J., Thorpe, R. and Mumford, A. (2010) *Leadership and Management Development*. London: CIPD.

Rigg, C., Stewart, J. and Trehan, K. (eds) (2007) *Critical Human Resource Development: Beyond Orthodoxy*. Harlow: FT Prentice Hall.

Stewart, J. and Riggs, C. (2011) *Learning and Talent Development*. London: CIPD.

Stewart, J. and Rogers, P. (eds) (2012) *Developing People and Organisations*. London: CIPD.

Tansley, C., Turner, P., Foster, C., Harris, L.M., Stewart, J., Sempik, A. and Williams, H. (2007) *Talent: Strategy, Management, Measurement*. London: CIPD.

References

Alvesson, M. and Willmott, H. (2012) *Making Sense of Management*, 2nd edn. London: Sage Publications.

Baldwin, T.T. and Ford, J.K. (1988) 'Transfer of training: a review and directions for future research', *Personnel Psychology*, 41 (1): 63–105.

Bozionelos, N., Bozionelos, G., Kostopoulos, K. and Polychroniou, P. (2011) 'How providing mentoring relates to career success and organizational commitment: a study in the general managerial population', *Career Development International*, 16 (5): 446–68.

CIPD (2011a) *The Coaching Climate*. London: Chartered Institute of Personnel and Development.

CIPD (2011b) *Learning and Talent Development Survey*. London: Chartered Institute of Personnel and Development.

Clutterbuck, D. (2004) *Everyone Needs a Mentor*. London: Chartered Instituted of Personnel and Development.

Eby, L.T. (2010) 'Mentorship', in S. Zedack (ed.), *APA Handbook of Industrial and Organizational Psychology*. Washington, DC: American Psychological Association, pp. 505–25.

Emelo, R. (2011) 'Group mentoring best practices', *Industrial And Commercial Training*, 43 (4): 221–7.

Evans, R. (2007) 'HRD Conference Report', *People Management,* April.

Gilbreath, B., Rose, G. and Dietrich, K. (2008) 'Assessing mentoring in organizations: an evaluation of commercial mentoring instruments', *Mentoring and Tutoring: Partnership in Learning*, 16 (4): 379–93.

Glaister, C., Holden, R., Griggs, V. and McCauley, P. (2010) 'The design and delivery of training', in J. Gold, R. Holden, P. Iles and J. Beardwell (eds), *Human Resource Development: Theory and Practice*. Basingstoke: Palgrave Macmillan, pp. 129–55.

Gold, J., Thorpe, R. and Mumford, A. (2010) *Leadership and Management Development*. London: CIPD.

Hamlin, R. and Stewart, J. (2011) 'What is HRD? A definitional review and synthesis of the HRD domain', *Journal of European Industrial Training*, 35 (3): 199–220.

Headlam-Wells, J., Gosland, J. and Craig, J. (2005) '"There's magic in the web": e-mentoring for women's career development', *Career Development International,* 10 (6/7): 444–59.

Holton, E.F., Bates, R.A. and Ruona, W.E. (2000) 'Development of a generalized learning transfer system inventory', *Human Resource Development Quarterly*, 11 (4): 333–60.

House, R.J., Hanges, P.J., Javidan, M., Dorfman, P.W. and Gupta V. (eds) (2004) *Culture, Leadership and Organizations: The GLOBE Study of 62 Societies*. Thousand Oaks, CA: Sage.

Iles, P., Chuai, X. and Preece, D. (2010) 'Talent management and HRM in multinational companies in Beijing: definitions, differences and drivers', *Journal of World Business*, 45 (2): 179–89.

Kellie, J., Henderson, E., Milsom, B. and Crawley, H. (2010) 'An account of practice: leading change in tissue viability best practice: an action learning programme for link nurse practitioners', *Action Learning Research and Practice*, 7 (2): 213–19.

Kram, K.E. (1983) 'Phases of the mentor relationship', *Academy of Management Journal*, 26 (4): 608–25.

Lee, M. (2012) 'A refusal to define HRD', in M. Lee (ed.), *Human Resource Development As We Know It*. London: Routledge, pp. 13–26.

Lester, P., Hannah, S., Harms, P., Vogelgesang, G. and Avolio, B.J. (2011) 'Mentoring impact on leader efficacy development: a field experiment', *Academy of Management Learning and Education*, 10 (3): 409–429.

Mabey, C. and Finch-Lees, T. (2008) *Management and Leadership Development*. London: Sage.

Mabey, C. and Salaman, G. (1995) *Strategic Human Resource Management: A Reader*. Oxford: Blackwell.

McGoldrick, J. and Stewart, J. (1996) 'The HRM-HRD nexus', in J. Stewart and J. McGoldrick (eds), *HRD: Perspectives, Strategies and Practice*. London: Pitman Publishing, pp. 9–27.

McGoldrick, J., Stewart, J. and Watson, S. (2002) 'Theorising human resource development', *Human Resource Development International*, 5 (1): 343–56.

McLagan, P. and Suhadolnik, D. (1989) *Models for HRD Practice: The Research Report*. Alexandria, VA: American Society for Training and Development.

Megginson, D. and Clutterbuck, D. (1995) *Mentoring In Action*. London: Kogan Page.

Megginson, D., Clutterbuck, D., Garvey, B., Stokes, P. and Garrett-Harris, R. (2006) *Mentoring in Action*, 2nd edn. London: Kogan Page.

Michaels, E., Handfield-Jones, H. and Beth, A. (2001) *The War For Talent*. Boston, MA: Harvard Business School.

Mitchell, H. (1999) 'Group mentoring, does it work?', *Mentoring and Tutoring*, 7 (2): 113–20.

O'Donnell, H., Karallis, K., Sandelands, E., Cassin, J. and O'Neill, D. (2008) 'Case study: developing graduate engineers at Kentz Engineers and Constructors', *Education + Training*, 50 (5): 439–52.

Pedler, M., Burgoyne, J.G. and Brooks, C. (2005) 'What has action learning learned to become?', *Action Learning Research and Practice*, 2 (1): 49–68.

Peltier, B. (2010) *The Psychology of Executive Coaching: Theory and Application*, 2nd edn. London: Routledge.

Ragins, B.R., Cotton, J.L. and Miller, J.S. (2000) 'Marginal mentoring: the effects of type of mentor, quality of relationship and program design on work and career attitudes', *Academy of Management Journal*, 43 (6): 1177–94.

Rigg, C. and Richards, S. (2008) *Action Learning, Leadership and Organization Development in Public Services*. London: Routledge.

Rigg, C., Stewart, J. and Trehan, K. (eds) (2007) *Critical Human Resource Development: Beyond Orthodoxy*. Harlow: Prentice Hall.

Rosser, M.H. (2005) 'Mentoring from the top: CEO perspectives', *Advances in Developing Human Resources*, 7 (4): 527–39.

Sambrook, S. and Stewart, J. (2010) 'Teaching, learning and assessing HRD: findings from a BMAF/UFHRD research project', *Journal of European Industrial Training*, 34 (8/9): 710–34.

Simon, S.A. and Eby, L.T. (2003) 'A multidimensional scaling study of negative mentoring experiences', *Human Relations*, 56: 1083–106.

Stewart, J. (1999) *Employee Development Practice*. London: FT Pitman.

Stewart, J. (2007) 'The ethics of HRD', in C. Rigg, J. Stewart and K. Trehan (eds), *Critical Human Resource Development: Beyond Orthodoxy*. Harlow: Prentice Hall, pp. 59–77.

Stewart, J. (2009) 'Developing managers and managerial capabilities', in J. Leopold and L. Harris (eds), *The Strategic Managing of Human Resources*, 2nd edn. Harlow: FT Prentice Hall.

Stewart, J. (2010) 'E-learning for managers and leaders', in J. Gold, R. Thorpe and A. Mumford (eds), *Gower Handbook of Leadership and Management Development*. Farnham: Gower Publishing Limited, pp. 441–56.

Stewart, J. and Harte, V. (2010) 'The implications of talent management for diversity training: an exploratory study', *Journal of European Industrial Training*, 34 (6): 506–18.

Stewart, J. and Knowles, V. (2003) 'Mentoring in undergraduate business management programmes', *Journal of European Industrial Training*, 27 (3): 147–59.

Stewart, J. and McGoldrick, J. (eds) (1996) *HRD: Perspectives, Strategies and Practice*. London: Pitman Publishing.

Stewart, J. and McGuire, S. (2012) 'Contemporary developments in human resource development', in J. Stewart and P. Rogers (eds), *Developing People and Organizations*. London: CIPD Publishing, pp. 121–43.

Stewart, J. and Rigg, C. (2011) *Learning and Talent Development*. London: Chartered Institute of Personnel and Development.

Stewart, J. and Sambrook, S. (2012) 'The historical development of human resource development in the United Kingdom', *Human Resource Development Review*, 11 (4): 443–62.

Sun, W., Stewart, J. and Pollard, D. (eds) (2011) *Corporate Governance and the Global Financial Crises*. Cambridge: Cambridge University Press.

Tansley, C., Turner, P.A., Foster, C., Harris, L. M., Stewart, J., Sempik, A. and Williams, H. (2007) *Talent: Strategy, Management, Measurement*. London: CIPD Publishing.

Thomas, A.B. (2003) *Controversies in Management: Issues, Debates, Answers*. London: Routledge.

Thomson, A., Mabey, C., Storey, J., Gray, C. and Iles, P. (2001) *Changing Patterns of Management Development*. Oxford: Blackwell.

Thorpe, R. and Gold, J. (2010) 'Leadership and management development: the current state', in J. Gold, R. Thorpe and A. Mumford (eds), *Gower Handbook of Leadership and Management Development*. Farnham: Gower Publishing Limited, pp. 3–21.

Townley, B. (1994) *Reframing Human Resource Management: Power, Ethics and the Subject at Work*. London: Sage.

Trehan, K., Rigg, C. and Stewart, J. (2004) 'Special issue on critical human resource development', *Journal of European Industrial Training*, 28 (8/9): 611–88.

Trehan, K., Rigg, C. and Stewart, J. (2006) 'Special issue on critical human resource development', *International Journal of Training and Development*, 10(1): 2–86.

Turnbull James, K. and Collins, J. (2010) 'Leading and managing in global contexts', in J. Gold, R. Thorpe and A. Mumford (eds), *Gower Handbook of Leadership and Management Development*. Farnham: Gower Publishing Limited, pp. 489–512.

Underhill, C. (2006) 'The effectiveness of mentoring programs in corporate settings: a meta-analytical review of the literature', *Journal of Vocational Behavior*, 68 (2): 292–307.

Walton, J. (1999) *Strategic Human Resource Development*. Harlow: FT Prentice Hall.

Welsh, E., Bhave, D. and Kim, K. (2012), 'Are you my mentor? Informal mentoring mutual identification', *Career Development International*, 17 (2): 137–48.

Wenger, E. (1998) *Communities of Practice: Learning, Meaning, and Identity*. Cambridge: Cambridge University Press.

Whitmore, J. (2009) *Coaching for Performance: Growing Human Potential and Purpose: the Principles and Practice of Coaching and Leadership*, 4th edn. London: Nicholas Brealey Publishing.

Winterton, J. and Winterton, R. (2002) *Developing Managerial Competence*. London: Routledge.

PART 3
*SHRM AND THE
'BIGGER PICTURE'*

ORGANIZATIONAL CULTURE

Crystal Zhang and Paul Iles

Chapter Overview

This chapter provides an important insight into both organizational and national cultures and how these two critical aspects impact upon human resource management in organizations. Chapter 1 introduced the concept of culture and its links to organizational strategy and structure. This chapter further extends the reader's understanding of how organizational and national cultures act independently and jointly within business practices. The chapter begins with a fascinating case study of a United States-owned organization (Wal-Mart) which operates in Argentina.

≣ Learning Objectives ≣

- Define and explore the nature of organizational and national culture, and the interplay between them
- Critically analyse theories of organizational culture, its determinants and effects and its relationship to leadership, ethics and organizational performance
- Understand the importance of organizational and national culture to human resource management
- Critically analyse how organizations can incorporate cultural aspects in managing and dealing with organizational culture

≣ CASE STUDY 11.1 ≣

Wal-Mart in Argentina

When Wal-Mart built its first stores in the Buenos Aires region, Argentina, it strongly pushed its US-based blueprint of low-pricing tactics and shopping traditions; these were rapidly rejected by

(Continued)

(Continued)

most Argentine consumers. After a few years of trial and error, Wal-Mart finally brought about five major business and cultural changes:

1. adaptation of store design,
2. adaptation of products to local tastes,
3. adaptation of shopping culture,
4. adaptation of employment practices and workplace culture, and
5. acceptance of trade unions.

In order to be successful, Wal-Mart adopted a 'hybrid' cultural fusion of North and South American practices after the cultural collision it faced when it first entered Argentina. Wal-Mart encountered many cultural hurdles in fully adapting to the Argentine cultural ways of shopping, buying, and working. By and large, these problems were caused by Wal-Mart's adamant decision to impose its Bentonville (Arkansas) model in Latin America, opting to replicate – rather than modify – the same basic US store model, ignoring local cultures and idiosyncrasies.

It was perceived as arrogant in its approach to Argentina because, for a long time, it was resistant to catering to local tastes before focusing more on cultural sensitivity and local tastes (e.g., metal displays for fish were replaced by ceramic tiles suggestive of long-established Argentine fish markets). Argentine customers are, on average, smaller than their American counterparts, so clothing racks are holding more items in medium sizes and fewer in large sizes. Argentinians mostly buy local food products; consumers are more likely to buy meat, vegetables, fruit, and bread from small shops because customers perceive small shops as retaining the produce freshness that giant chains do not always have. Until Wal-Mart began to sprinkle produce to make them look fresh and adopted other 'freshness' strategies, consumers favoured traditional markets.

'Wal-Mart Argentina' managers – most US Americans – tried to delegate decision-making and control to employees, but were faced with resistance and frustration. In one Wal-Mart store in Argentina, after clocking in every morning employees devoted an hour to chatting with each other (e.g., about what they did the night before, what they ate, where they went for dinner) and discussing the safety and health of their families before getting to work, hallmarks of collectivism (Hofstede 2001). Because the workplace atmosphere and output did not improve over time after the American manager told them to 'cut it out' and go straight to work, the manager reinstated the right of employees to chat for an hour before getting down to work.

Source: Adapted from Matusitz (2014).

 ■ **Questions**

1. How would you use Hofstede (2001) to explain some of these phenomena?
2. What international orientations did the firm adopt 1) initially 2) subsequently (see Chapter 12)?

Introduction

Cross-cultural management is not a new topic; research 'can be traced back as early as the tenth century from the Arab scholar Abu al-Rayhan al-Biruni (973–1048), possibly the earliest pioneer in cross-cultural studies' (Zhang and

Iles 2013: 19). He compared human behaviour and culture as influenced by Zoroastrianism, Judaism, Hinduism, Christianity, Buddhism, Islam and other religions, arguing that all cultures have unique common elements which make them distinct from all other cultures (Rosenthal and Yarshter 1976). The study of culture has remained a vital field in anthropology, psychology and organizational behaviour (OB), analysed and debated by the early anthropologists from the nineteenth century, such as Tylor and Galton.

From the 1950s to 70s, there has been rigorous theoretical development in the anthropology discipline into the understanding of culture. Keesing (1974) distinguished between the *ecological* theory of culture and the *ideational* theory of culture; in the former perspective, culture is conceptualized in terms of *adaptive systems* while in the latter, culture is perceived in terms of cognitive, structural and *symbolic* systems – a distinction which as we shall see remains important in studies of organizational culture. In 1980 the publication of *Culture's Consequences* (Hofstede 1980) 'initiated a fundamental shift in how culture would be viewed and studied, leading to an explosion of empirical investigations into cross-cultural differences' (Zhang and Iles 2013: 19).

Despite globalization (see Chapter 12), national differences, especially in organizational forms, managerial practice and HRM systems, remain pervasive. Why should this be? Cultural arguments give one important explanation of these differences and why they persist, influencing many aspects of organizational behaviour and human resource management.

But what is culture, and why is it such an important driving force in daily life? Why is it important for us to analyse culture? Human beings 'are social mammals who live in social groups; we are also an adapting species, given the diverse civilizations we have created over thousands of years. Each individual has a unique background, history, upbringing and personality. Even though there are common values and behaviours, these differences lead to different forms of social interaction and form the unique identity of a group' (Zhang and Iles 2013: 20). Unwritten rules on 'how to do things round here', how to behave or how to adapt into a group, are referred to as 'culture'. Culture can be represented by symbols, signs, heroes, religions, taboos, laws, rituals, customs etc. How to adapt into a new culture is a fundamental challenge to all human beings, especially with globalization, international migration and the growth of international business. With increasing globalization and social mobility, it is therefore important to understand the origins and historical development of this controversial, paradoxical and evolving concept, and its impact and implications for management theories and practices and HRM in particular (Bird and Fang 2009). It is equally important to equip ourselves, and employees, with the skills, knowledge and competences to be able to thrive in this new era. This chapter will therefore lay the foundation stones for some of the key milestones in research on culture as a concept, before presenting a critical discussion of its value to understanding organizations, organization policies, and HRM research and policy. In the next section we will explore this in greater depth by reference to the contribution of cultural theories to a series of topics of great relevance to HRM, such as enhancing employee motivation, increasing organizational performance, and facilitating successful mergers and acquisitions.

Observing and analysing culture

In one sense, cultural research can be easily conducted: one simply needs to open one's eyes and observe the environment and what to look for in a culture, such as rules, which include both the official and the hidden framework on how to behave, to do things and fit in with the observed culture. However, to understand culture fully, you need tools, models and theories guiding you as to what to look for, and different theories provide different answers to this question!

The concept of culture

Culture is not a material 'thing' that can be touched or held in the hand; it can represent the values of a country, or the elite aspects of a society's achievements, 'as in the use of the term "high culture" to refer to art, classical music and opera, for example, and an appreciation of good literature, music, art and food' (Zhang and Iles 2013:21). The term itself comes from the Latin for 'cultivation', and was introduced into English in the fifteenth century to represent the cultivation of the soul or mind, in the same manner as the cultivation of the land by a farmer. Thus culture in this sense enhances our appreciation of life and is an intrinsic part of it.

Culture from an anthropological perspective

For anthropologists and other behavioural scientists, culture in contrast refers to the full range of learned human behaviour patterns, and more extensive work on cross-cultural studies was carried out in the nineteenth century. The term was first used in this way by Edward B. Tylor, the first Professor of Anthropology at Oxford University, in *Primitive Culture* published in 1871 (note the title reveals an issue colouring much debate on culture: 'different' easily slips into 'deficient', as many people, including researchers, may judge 'different' cultures as 'deficient' ones). Tylor defined culture as 'that complex whole which includes knowledge, belief, art, law, morals, custom, and any other capabilities and habits acquired by man (sic) as a member of society' (Holden 2002: 21). One of Tylor's early works led to the rise of statistical analyses of cross-cultural studies; Sir Francis Galton became the first to introduce the problem of cultural group independence in his work on correlation (Bird and Fang 2009). His critiques on Tylor's study involved claims that the processes of cultural transmission created relationships that cannot be easily disentangled, and cultural groups could not be regarded as truly independent from one another (Bird and Fang 2009).

Another important point is that cultures are dynamic and constantly evolving; for example, the *Oxford English Dictionary* is updated every year, adding new words to reflect the vibrant changes in language and culture. Many 'English' words such as bungalow, shampoo, chintz, chutney, jute, juggernaut, thug, pyjamas and gymkhana originate from Indian languages; others such as tycoon, tea, typhoon or ketchup, come from Chinese languages, reflecting great linguistic hybridization. Acronyms used in text and Internet instant messages, such as OMG, LOL and FYI, were officially added to the dictionary in 2011. Our written and spoken languages, governments, buildings, and other man-made things are the products of culture: they are not culture in themselves but are given meaning by culture. For this reason, 'archaeologists cannot dig up culture directly in excavations; broken pots and other artefacts of ancient people are only material remains that reflect cultural patterns, things that were made and used through cultural knowledge, skills and concepts' (Zhang and Iles 2013: 22).

Similarly, the material things around us represent our culture; artefacts act as reminders and triggers. When people see them, they think about their meaning and hence are reminded of their identity as a member of the culture, and, by association, of the rules of the culture. For example, the Elgin Marbles in the British Museum arouse very different feelings in the British, the Greeks, or the Turks (who first sold them to the British when Greece was part of the Ottoman Empire).

One of the strengths of the 'cultural' perspective is that it reminds us that the social world we inhabit in organizational life is a world of intersubjectivities and 'multiple constructed realities' (Lincoln and Guba 1985: 295); participant actions can be explained by understanding the subjective dimensions of their behaviour (Corbin and Strauss 2008). Such arguments are key to symbolic interactionist (Mead 1934) and social constructionist (Berger and Luckmann 1967) accounts of social and organizational reality. They draw our attention to the role of 'symbols' which act as 'triggers to remind people of rules, beliefs, and expectations; shorthand ways to keep people aligned and indicate status within a culture, including clothing' (Zhang and Iles 2013: 22). In working with the Rover Group in the 1990s, Iles noticed that during their alliance with Honda engineers wore, like everyone else, the same uniform of puce polo shirt and grey boiler suit that symbolized the 'equality of functional contribution' often stressed in Japanese companies. However, they quickly switched to smart suits to indicate their higher status under BMW acquisition, where engineers were now seen as the privileged group, the heart and soul of the company (Eckardt and Matthias 2003). Indeed, they went on to occupy a prestigious, marble-pillared new design and engineering centre. Office decor and layout and non-verbal communication can also act as symbols, e.g. open-plan offices or 'hot desks' as opposed to larger, better-furnished offices being associated with a higher organizational status. The depth of the bow in Japan is tied to status.

Status symbols signal to others the 'correct behaviour' with respect to others in the hierarchy, alerting users of the symbols to follow prescribed behaviours appropriate for their status and position. For example, the BMW logo is an icon representing a high value automobile brand, but that symbolism would be lost on someone not familiar with the cultural symbols.

A danger here is that culture is seen in a deterministic, monolithic way, neglecting possibilities of change, challenge and resistance. If explanations of human action derive from the meanings and interpretations of actors (Gill and Johnson 2010: 61–2), are these not better accessed through qualitative methods and induction, often used by anthropologists? These help us to better understand the meanings and interpretations of participants, rather than the positivist survey methods often employed in the study of organizational culture (e.g. Hofstede 2001). Organizational members use meaning 'in making sense of their worlds and which influence their ongoing social construction and accomplishment of meaningful action' (Gill and Johnson 2010: 62; see also Glaser 1978; Ritchie and Spencer 1994; Alvesson and Deetz 2000). Highly structured methodological approaches like surveys may impose an external logic that distorts access to subjective domains, including cultural meanings. So 'monolithic accounts of "culture" may tend to play up false concepts of fixity and stability, and play down subcultures and conflicting cultures within a given society' (Zhang and Iles 2013: 23). Within discussions of OB a distinction is often made between those who see organizational culture as a variable, a 'part' of the organization (culture is something that an organization has, and is able to manipulate and alter depending on leadership), and culture as 'the same as the organization', a 'root metaphor' for something that the organization is and is created through communication and symbols, or competing metaphors (Smircich 1983; Brewis 2005; Modaff et al. 2011). Hofstede (2001) for example takes a 'culture as variable' stance; national culture is something a nation 'has', an ultimately functionalist and unitarist perspective on culture.

We will next explore how the concept has been used in studies of organizational behaviour and HRM, especially through the concept of 'organizational culture'. One leading definition is provided by Schein (1984: 3), who defines organization culture as

> the pattern of basic assumptions that a given group has invented, discovered or developed in learning to cope with its problems of external adaptation and internal integration, and that have worked well enough to be considered valid, and, therefore, to be taught to new members as the correct way to perceive, think, and feel in relation to those problems. (1984: 3)

Later we will examine and critique this view in more detail, but first we will discuss the concepts of corporate and organizational culture.

PIT STOP: REFLECTIVE ACTIVITY 11.1

1. What are the key elements of Schein's definition of culture?
2. Are there any aspects you have problems with, or disagree with?

Organizational and corporate culture

As Smircich (1983: 339) has noted, the concept of culture has 'been borrowed from anthropology, where there is no consensus on its meaning'. There have been numerous approaches to the definition of organizational or corporate culture, often employing different terminologies. Allaire and Firsirotu (1984: 218–19) argue that from a cognitive perspective, culture can be viewed as 'a system of knowledge, of standards for perceiving, believing, evaluating and acting', while from an ecological-adaptationist perspective, culture can be seen as 'a system of socially transmitted behaviour patterns that serve to relate human communities to their ecological settings', a distinction similar to Keesing's (1974).

Organizational culture can therefore be explored in several ways. Alvesson and Berg (1992) point out that culture can be studied at several *levels*:

- the societal/national level
- the industrial sector level
- the social sector level
- the organizational level
- the functional subculture level
- the social grouping level
- the professional culture/subculture level.

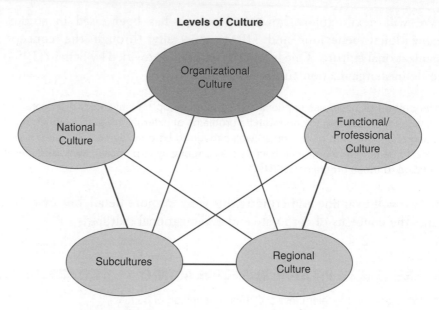

Figure 11.1 Levels of culture

Source: Adapted from Schneider and Barsoux (2003).

Figure 11.1 shows some of these levels and how they might interact with organizational culture in particular.

Our focus in this chapter will primarily be on *organizational culture* and its interaction with *national culture*. Below the level of the organizational culture is the level of the *subculture* – there may be different, perhaps overlapping and interacting subcultures based on department, social group, profession or other interest groups. Professional cultures may extend beyond the boundaries of the organization – e.g. engineers working in the oil industry across many companies may have similar modes of dress, behaviour and worldview that unite them at some level, distinguishing them from, say, accountants or marketers working for the same company as them. For Martin and Siehl (1983), some subcultures can be *enhancing* (committed to the dominant culture's values), others *orthogonal* (accepting of the dominant organizational culture and another non-conflicting set of values) or even *counter-cultures* (directly challenging the main organizational cultural values).

These perspectives on culture do not necessarily imply that corporate cultures are static or monolithic. To the degree that the same patterns of beliefs are shared throughout the company, the culture may be considered a strong one (Saffold 1988). It is also possible that different units within a company may develop subcultures that can be neutral toward, or even conflict with, the dominant culture (Martin and Siehl 1983). Indeed, Lawrence and Lorsch (1967) show that most large companies have distinct subcultures within different functions (e.g., engineering, marketing, R&D, and manufacturing). Meyerson and Martin (1987) take this concept of different paradigms or discourses operating within organizational culture research further by positing three paradigms focused on the concept of 'cohesiveness'. The *integration* paradigm assumes consensus and cohesiveness; culture is a sort of social glue holding the organization together. The *differentiation* paradigm emphasizes subcultures and dissensus, whilst the *ambiguity* paradigm focuses on a lack of clarity, confusion and turbulence within the organizational culture.

As we have seen, 'culture' was originally an anthropological concept. One of the first times it was used in HRM and organizational behaviour was by the British sociologist Turner (1971), who coined the phrase *'the industrial subculture'* to capture similarities across a number of different industrial cases he studied. The 'industrial subculture' was seen in terms of a distinctive set of shared meanings, maintained by socializing new members – new recruits, apprentices etc. – into the subculture. His work was primarily about male manufacturing workers (though he noted the use of gendered job roles, e.g. female secretaries or receptionists). He introduced a number of issues and dimensions around culture that have recurred in later studies of 'organizational culture' (rather than industrial subculture), such as:

- *the use of symbols* to convey meaning – e.g. a 'new culture' may be conveyed through new signs and logos or colour schemes;
- *the importance of rites and rituals* to organizational life; e.g. initiation ceremonies to welcome new recruits (at football clubs new players may have to sing a song, tell a story or perform some action); the role of leaving ceremonies and Christmas parties;
- *socialization and norms* – this refers to standards of expected behaviour such as punctuality, quality, dress code, or formality/informality that are transmitted to new entrants (in German organizations like BMW formal titles and surnames may be used – 'Herr Dr Professor' – whereas in the USA it may be first names, e.g 'call me Bob'; front-line staff in banks may wear a uniform, senior staff a smart suit, whilst in advertising or IT, T-shirts or jeans may be acceptable);
- *transmission of a moral code*: what is considered ethical or unethical behaviour, e.g. stealing company property, gifts and bribes, use of 'hospitality';
- *attempts to manipulate culture* by management or workers – e.g. to make the culture more 'innovative' or 'enterprising' or 'market-oriented' or 'safety-conscious' through training programmes.

The main distinction made in the literature on organizational culture, as we saw in the discussion of culture from an anthropological perspective, is between the view that culture is an *independent variable* to be manipulated and with impacts on dependent variables like organizational performance or quality, separate from other features like structure and technology; and the view that culture is not a variable but a *'root metaphor'* (Smircich 1983). These perspectives can be termed *'culture as variable'* and *'culture as metaphor'*. Both managers and researchers use metaphors or images to understand organizations; here culture is used as a metaphor to define an organization as if it were a culture. The first view sees culture as something that can be changed and manipulated; the second 'metaphor' view analyses manifestations of organizational culture without assuming cause and effect relationships. These two positions broadly resemble *functionalist/adaptive* and *symbolist/ideational* perspectives, discussed in the introduction.

For functionalists, the key question is what function culture plays in organizational survival; cultural elements can be listed and the relationships between them mapped (Schultz 1994). Though not pure functionalist, this approach is shown by Schein (1990) who draws attention to the functions played by culture in organizational problem-solving. Schein (1986) embraced elements of several traditions to define three levels of cultural phenomena in organizations; culture should therefore be analysed at these three levels, that is, *observable artefacts, values* and *basic underlying assumptions*.

1. On the surface are the overt behaviours and other physical manifestations (artefacts and creations).
2. Below this level is a sense of what 'ought' to be (values).
3. At the very deepest level are those things that are taken for granted as 'correct' ways of coping with the environment (basic assumptions). He argued that even though the first two levels reflect culture, only the third is the essence of culture.

Artefacts are observable organizational symbols, signs, dress codes, manners, communication channels, physical layouts, smells, documented records, and statements of philosophies, strategies, and structure, such as the Rover dress code. Some of these are emotion-related, while others are permanent archiveable manifestations of organizational culture. At this level organizational culture focuses on what kind of behaviours and symbols there are in an organization, whilst the next two levels emphasize why those behaviours and symbols exist. Values refer to explicit explanations of those artefacts, while basic underlying assumptions are implicit types of understanding of why artefacts exist and in what way. However, most authors, e.g. Broms and Gahmberg (1983), consider each level to be an important part of the study and understanding of corporate or organizational culture. Schermerhorn et al. (1994) also identified three levels of culture: observable culture, shared values, and common assumptions.

Schein (1992) sees culture in terms of shared values and beliefs influencing and controlling behaviour; a 'functionalist, normative and instrumentally biased conception of culture' (Alvesson 1993: 28). Schein (1992) makes clear his preference for an instrumental, functional approach of value to managers, though also acknowledging the existence of subcultures and diverse perspectives. He also distinguishes between *espoused values* and *values in action*; for example, senior managers may state that innovation, creativity and risk-taking are valued and rewarded (espoused values), but in practice employees who stick by the rules and play it safe may be rewarded and promoted (values in action).

PIT STOP: REFLECTIVE ACTIVITY 11.2

1. In Case Study 11.1, identify examples of artefacts, values and basic assumptions in Wal-Mart.

The 'culture as variable' school finds its main expression in the concept of *corporate culture*, especially its presumed link with organizational performance (see Chapter 3 for a discussion of the link between HRM and organizational performance). Organizational culture is viewed as a construct, 'a theoretical creation that is based on observation, but cannot be observed directly or indirectly' (Driskell and Brenton 2005: 17). Certo and Peter (1988) see organizational cultures as 'sets of shared values and beliefs that organization members have regarding the functioning and existence of their organization' (cited in Wells 2003: 7), linking *shared values and beliefs* of employees explicitly to the success of the organization. For Gordon (1993: 186) corporate culture is 'an organization-specific system of widely shared assumptions and values that give rise to typical behaviour patterns. These systems of cognition and behaviour patterns are transmitted to organizational entrants in formal (e.g., mission statements) and informal ways (e.g., modes of speech)'. Davis (1984) argues that culture is based upon internally oriented beliefs regarding how to manage, and externally oriented beliefs regarding how to compete. The main focus is on the assumptions and values relevant to issues of managing and competing for organizational survival and prosperity (i.e., the values relevant to running the business).

Others in the 'culture as variable' school have put forward other classifications of organizational culture. Handy (1985) following Harrison (1972) distinguishes four types of organizational culture:

- *'Power culture'*: here power is concentrated among a small group or a central figure and its control radiates from its centre like a web. Power cultures need only a few rules and little bureaucracy.
- *'Role culture'*: here power is delegated within a highly defined structure, often a hierarchical bureaucracy with functional departments.

- '*Task culture*': here teams such as project teams are formed to solve particular problems; power is exercised within the team using team members with the expertise to execute tasks, perhaps within a matrix structure.
- '*Person culture*': here individuals such as professionals, researchers and other 'knowledge workers', or partners in professional service firms, may believe themselves superior to the organization, making cooperation and teamwork difficult, though some professional partnerships operate well as person cultures, with each person bringing in a particular expertise and clientele.

However, this model seems as much about organizational structure as culture. Johnson and Scholes (1999) put forward the concept of the '*cultural web*'; again at the centre are deeply-held *core beliefs and assumptions* constituting the organizational paradigm. These guide the other elements of organizational culture, which represent both visible, tangible aspects (*structures* and *control systems*) and less tangible aspects, such as *myths and stories*, *symbols*, *routines and rituals* and *power structures* (Balogun and Hope Hailey 2004). For example, in an engineering company like BMW the paradigm may include an engineering focus and a product, not people, focus. In such a company the power structures may show that professional engineering status is valued (as in our Rover/ BMW example where engineers had a special status and dress code, as well as superior work spaces) and the company may be male-dominated, with an antagonistic union. The organization structure may be hierarchical, with an 'us and them' mentality; control systems may emphasize a lack of open communication; the rites and routines may show a conservative, quality-focused, craft engineering focus; and the myths and stories may emphasize engineering and technical excellence, as in the Audi slogan 'vorsprung durch technik' (Graetz et al. 2006).

Another key concept emphasized in this perspective is *cultural strength*. To the degree that the same patterns of beliefs are shared throughout the company, the culture may be considered a *strong* one (Saffold 1988). Different units within a company may develop subcultures that can be neutral toward, or even conflict with, the dominant culture (Martin and Siehl 1983). A *weak* culture or lack of culture may exist where important assumptions or values are not widely shared in an organization, but vary from individual to individual or unit to unit. In organizations or work groups where there is a relatively great consensus along such measures, that is, where norms are highly crystallized, shared behavioural norms reflect a 'strong' organizational culture and well-defined pattern of underlying values and ways of seeing things. In such organizations, these shared norms are likely to be relatively stable and enduring because they are based on common assumptions and understandings that do not readily change.

Additional aspects of organizational culture include other components and characteristics, such as ideologies, symbols, heroes, rites, and rituals (Deal and

Kennedy 1982), and strategy and goals (Schein 1992). The following attributes seem to shape the organization's culture:

- mission and strategy;
- leadership and management effectiveness;
- communication and decision-making;
- organization design and structure;
- organizational behaviour;
- knowledge and competence;
- business and organizational interventions;
- innovation and risk-taking;
- performance; and
- change readiness.

Deal and Kennedy (1982) identified five elements that comprise organizational culture, including the business environment, values, heroes, rites and rituals, and the cultural network. Chehade et al. (2006) defined seven types of culture as

- passive-aggressive;
- over managed;
- outgrown;
- fits-and-starts;
- just-in-time;
- military precision;
- resilient.

They argued that almost all organizations fall into one or more of these categories.

=== **PIT STOP: REFLECTIVE ACTIVITY 11.3** ===

Using the cultural web to analyse organizational culture

1. Using the cultural web, analyse Case Study 11.1, comparing the core assumptions, myths and stories, symbols, power structures, organization, control systems and rites and routines apparent in Wal-Mart.
2. Use the cultural web to build a framework that represents an organization you work for or have worked for or with which you are familiar, i.e. identify its present state or present situation.
3. Which aspects do you think should change to make the organization more effective (i.e. its preferred or desired future state)?

Symbolist approaches to organizational culture

For symbolists, the key question is what is the *meaning* of the organization to its members? Definitions of the phenomenon, their epistemology and methodology, and their theoretical foundations differ; culture is seen as created as an ongoing construction and reconstruction of meaning, to be studied using ethnographic methods emphasizing interpretation. Culture is context-specific, and not necessarily shared; there may be both shared and non-shared webs of meaning, and the local creation of subcultures.

From an interpretivist approach, social and organizational reality is created through people and the way in which they interpret and view the world, associated with the interpretation of the thoughts and feelings of individuals (Easterby-Smith et al. 2002). For Gammack and Stephens (1994: 73)

> a methodology sensitive to the social and dialogical processes involved in constructing knowledge formulations is seen as appropriate ... rather than viewing knowledge as a disembodied commodity that can be removed from its context for independent analysis, the explicit construction of knowledge is seen as a process meaningful to the knowers involved in producing it.

Analyses of written or spoken text and observations of behaviour (Cassell and Symons 2004) give researchers the opportunity to explore areas in depth with selected individuals, allowing salient points to be followed up to help inform later research (Collis and Hussey 2003).

Both employees and researchers interpret the social world in particular ways through socially constructed versions of reality. The social world is therefore a world of intersubjectivities and 'multiple constructed realities' (Lincoln and Guba 1985: 295). To evaluate the trustworthiness and authenticity of research claims, Guba and Lincoln (1994: 114) argue that different members' realities need to be included and represented in any account; and participant actions explained by understanding the subjective dimensions of their behaviour (Corbin and Strauss 2008).

Meek (1988) points out that organizational culture theorists often borrow ideas from one particular branch of anthropology, the 'structural–functional' paradigm. This sees culture as performing a function; however, this perspective is contested, as we have seen, by other views seeing culture as creating meaning. Symbols have more than merely instrumental meaning (Schultz 1994); for Morgan et al. (1983) a symbol is a sign denoting something greater than itself. In Schein's (1992) terms it may be an artefact with surplus meaning. For Dandridge (1983), symbols are descriptive of the organization, controlling people's energy by inspiration or repulsion, and are system-maintaining; separation rituals like farewell or retirement ceremonies for example. Symbols are socially created, and can include objects, actions, events, utterances, images, rituals, traditions, humour, storytelling and metaphorical images. Dandridge (1983) distinguishes between action symbols (e.g. meetings and behaviour); verbal symbols (slogans, stories and jargon); and material symbols, such as architecture and dress. Organizations have their own languages, with unique terminology, codes and acronyms, often associated with similarities and differences with other organizations. This may become a heated issue in acquisitions; for example, one supermarket may refer to 'roll cages' to describe the vehicles used to transport goods, another 'rollers'. Each 'side' in a merged organization may cling tenaciously to its own language, and use it to indicate who is included in the group and who is excluded.

PIT STOP: REFLECTIVE ACTIVITY 11.4

1. In Case Study 11.1, what is the role of material symbols in Wal-Mart?
2. What is the role of action symbols?
3. What values and assumptions are these expressing?

The 'culture as variable' school also studies symbols such as rites, rituals and ceremonies. However, these are seen here as artefacts, while in culture as metaphor approaches they are seen as processes which configure meaning and make organizational life possible. Here the subjective and emotional aspects of symbols are emphasized, including their role in creating meaning. Smircich (1983) divides the 'culture as metaphor' perspective into three approaches: *organizational cognition* (seeing cultures as networks of meanings functioning as rules or scripts), *organizational symbolism*, and *unconscious processes and organization* (culture as the expression of unconscious processes, as in psychodynamic and psychoanalytic approaches in psychology).

Hatch (1993) has tried to combine Schein (1992) with a symbolist approach, arguing that his 'model of organizational culture as assumptions, values, and artifacts leaves gaps regarding the appreciation of organizational culture as symbols and processes' (1993: 657). She seeks to combine Schein's theory with ideas drawn from symbolic–interpretive perspectives; her new model, cultural dynamics, 'articulates the processes of *manifestation, realization, symbolization, and interpretation* and provides a framework within which to discuss the dynamism of organizational cultures' (1993: 657).

Such processes can work in both directions: proactively and retroactively. In prospective manifestation, assumptions shape values; in retroactive manifestation, values maintain, challenge or change existing assumptions. In proactive realization, values shape artefacts and activities with tangible outcomes; in retroactive realization, artefacts may maintain or reaffirm existing values, or retrospectively challenge them. Realization can be studied through 'the production, reproduction and transformation of artifacts' (Hatch 1993: 998). Symbols can include logos, stories, myths, actions, non-actions, visual images, metaphors, organizational charts, corporate architecture and rites and rituals. Prospective symbolization gives artefacts additional or 'surplus meaning'; retrospective symbolization 'enhances awareness of the literal meaning of symbolized artifacts' (1993: 671). Ethnography or aesthetic techniques, e.g. art or literary appreciation and criticism, are necessary to study symbolic processes; in the prospective mode, symbols maintain or challenge basic assumptions, while in the retrospective mode, assumptions reconstruct the meaning of symbols.

Ravasi and Schultz (2006) discuss a longitudinal study employing symbolist and interpretivist arguments. Organizational responses to environmental changes are seen as inducing members to question aspects of their organization's identity, highlighting the role of organizational culture as a source of cues supporting 'sensemaking' action carried out by leaders as they re-evaluate their conceptualization of their organization. Organizational culture can also act as a platform for 'sensegiving' actions aimed at affecting internal perceptions. The interplay of construed images and organizational culture shapes changes in institutional claims and shared understandings about the identity of an organization, highlighting the influence of organizational culture (particularly the influence of its manifestations) on the redefinition of members' collective self-perceptions. Organizational culture is here seen as a central construct in understanding the evolution of organizational identities in the face of environmental changes.

This study suggests that collective history, organizational symbols, and consolidated practices provide cues to help members make new sense of what their organization is really about, and give that new sense to others. Organizational culture can also help preserve a sense of distinctiveness and continuity, as organizational identity is subjected to an explicit re-evaluation.

▰▰▰▰▰ PIT STOP: REFLECTIVE ACTIVITY 11.5 ▰▰▰▰▰

Think of an organization you work in, have worked in, or are familiar with.

1. What are its dominant symbols (e.g. logos, colour schemes, stories, myths, ceremonies, rites, rituals, heroes etc.)?
2. What would be your interpretation of their meaning?
3. What is your interpretation of the dominant symbols being employed in Case Study 11.1?

The origins, determinants and effects of organizational cultures

Organizational culture researchers recognize that culture has a *historical* element (Kotter and Heskett 1992). What gives rise to organizational culture? Dickson et al. (2000) trace the source of organizational culture to

- values and beliefs held by founding leaders;
- the characteristics of the industry;
- the broader society in which the organization is located.

Often associated with an organization's historical culture is the *founder or early leader* of that particular organization. Schein (1983) posited that the organization's culture begins with the creation of the organization, based on the initial successes of the company and the impact of its founders. Schein (1992) identified three sources of cultural beginnings as:

- the belief values and assumptions of the founders;
- the learning experiences of group members as the organization grows;
- new beliefs, values, and assumptions brought in by new employees as recruits.

Schein (1992) sees leaders as key influences in forming and maintaining culture; entrepreneurs often begin with strong ideas and cultural assumptions which gain critical importance, initially explicitly but later implicitly (Schein 1983).

A strong statement of the importance of leaders and founders to corporate culture is made by Bass and Avolio (1993: 112): 'the organization's culture develops in large part from its leadership while the culture of an organization can also affect the development of its leadership'. While transactional leaders work within their organizational cultures following existing rules, procedures, and norms, transformational leaders *change* their culture by realigning it with a new vision and a revision of its shared assumptions, values, and norms (Bass 1985). Effective organizations require both strategic thinking to create and build the vision of an organization's future, and culture-building by leaders. A vision can emerge as the leader builds a culture dedicated to supporting that vision. The organization culture is the setting within which the vision takes hold, while the vision may also determine features of the organization's culture. Bass and Avolio (1993: 113) claim

in a highly innovative and satisfying organizational culture we are likely to see trans-formational leaders who build on assumptions such as: people are trustworthy and purposeful; everyone has a unique contribution to make; and complex problems are handled at the lowest level possible. Leaders who build such cultures and articulate them to followers typically exhibit a sense of vision and purpose. They align others around the vision and empower others to take greater responsibility for achieving the vision. Such leaders facilitate and teach followers. They foster a culture of creative change and growth rather than one which maintains the status quo.

A key feature is a stress on the constant interplay between culture and leadership as leaders develop mechanisms for cultural development and the reinforcement of norms and behaviours within cultural boundaries. Cultural norms arise and change because of what leaders focus their attention on, how they react to crises, the behaviours they role model, and who they attract to their organizations. Such characteristics and qualities of an organization's culture are taught by its leadership and eventually adopted by its followers. Therefore the organizational culture affects leadership as much as leadership affects culture. A 'strong' organizational culture can prevent top management from increasing personal power at the expense of others. The organizational culture can affect how decisions are made with respect to recruitment, selection, and placement (Chapter 5). However, some argue the influence of leaders on culture is over-rated (Alvesson 1993; Anthony 1994).

Another determining factor of organizational culture is the kind of *industry* the organization operates in. This 'industry effect' is noted by Gordon (1991: 396): 'organizational or corporate culture is strongly influenced by the characteristics of the industry in which the company operates ... companies within an industry share certain cultural elements that are required for survival'. There are three classes of industry variables with the potential for creating cultural elements: *competitive environment*, *customer requirements*, and *societal expectations*. Although a culture may be unique to a company or its subunits, industries and sectors also exert influence, causing cultures to develop within defined parameters. For Gordon (1991: 396) 'because of this relationship, the potential for changing a company's culture is limited to actions that are neutral to, or directionally consistent with, industry demands'.

In terms of the *effects* of organizational culture, several researchers have studied *dysfunctional* organizational cultures and their effects on effectiveness, efficiency, brand and reputation (e.g. Schein 1992). Deal and Kennedy (1982) and Balthazard et al. (2006) identified factors that could lead to organizational culture dysfunction, linking dysfunctional cultural styles to deficits in operating effectiveness and efficiency. Organizational culture might contribute to or detract from dysfunctional behaviour in a variety of ways; leaders play a major role in motivating dysfunctional work behaviour. Gebler (2006) observed that organizations with dysfunctional cultures might also be unethical; organizational culture needed to be managed to eliminate unscrupulous behaviour and promote an ethical culture (Jackson and Ones 2007).

From this viewpoint, leaders in particular can affect how ethical the organizational culture is, as well as its commitment to CSR (corporate social responsibility). Many examples of unethical behaviour are related to ethical leadership (or the lack of it). For Jackson and Ones (2007), leaders have significant opportunities to behave unethically, and may also foster it among others through their own behaviour, promulgating unethical practices as normal business practice. Bass and Avolio (1993: 114) claim that 'leaders need to be attentive to the conservativeness reflected in beliefs, values, assumptions, rites, and ceremonies embedded in the culture that can hinder efforts to change the organization.' They need to modify key aspects of culture, when it is possible to do so, to fit with new directions desired by the leadership and membership of the organization. For example, leaders can invent new rites to replace the old, some of which will symbolize the value of change itself. An example is the ceremonial introduction of a new product or process to replace an older one, or a new logo or name to symbolize a new company created through a merger or acquisition. As organizations move across time, external constraints change, forcing the company to question its deeply rooted assumptions and values. As new members are brought into the organization, they too will often challenge deeply held assumptions, even though organizations often hire people who have similar values to those dominant in the organizational culture. Consequently, it is incumbent upon the leaders in the organization to view the development of assumptions and values as an evolutionary process – a process by which the organization and its membership periodically question its assumptions and change them if the conditions warrant it.

This view of organizational or corporate culture is as a 'variable' that can be manipulated to bring about managerially desired outcomes and sees organizational culture as the '*glue*' that holds the organization together as a source of identity (Bass 1991). However, in decline, organizational culture can also become a constraint or brake on innovation, rooted as it is in the organization's past glories.

To some extent, this work on 'culture as variable' has evolved from concepts of organizational climate, such as climates for safety, diversity or innovation. This concept arose within organizational psychology rather than anthropology, and is usually assessed through surveys in terms of such factors as perceived structure, reward, support and warmth (Reichers and Schneider 1990). The concepts of climate and corporate culture have become somewhat blurred; many articles on a 'quality culture' for instance are really describing climate (Payne 1991) though some distinguish climate (individual-level psychological processes) from culture (unit-level social phenomenon: see Rousseau 1990).

Denison (1996) discusses how organizational culture researchers have begun to apply quantitative survey methods to identify comparative 'dimensions' of culture and how this seems to contradict some of the original foundations of culture research within organizational studies because it bears a strong resemblance to earlier research on organizational climate.

From this perspective, culture is often measured by survey instruments, such as the Organizational Culture Inventory (Cooke and Lafferty 1983), a self-report instrument designed to measure normative beliefs and shared behavioural expectations in organizations. These specify the ways in which all members of the organization – or at least those in similar positions or organizational locations – are expected to approach their work and interact with others. These behavioural prescriptions (and proscriptions) generally are viewed as an important component of group or organizational culture, given that they reflect and are shaped by the basic assumptions and values held in common by members (Siehl and Martin 1984; Schein 1985). The OCI measures 12 sets of normative beliefs or shared behavioural expectations associated with three general types of cultures: constructive, passive-defensive, and aggressive-defensive. These cultural norms are hypothesized to influence the thinking and behaviour of organizational members, their motivation and performance, and their satisfaction and stress. As components of organizational culture, behavioural expectations are considered to be shared and enduring in nature.

Tests of three types of reliability – internal consistency, interrater, and test–retest – and two types of validity – construct and criterion-related – on data provided by 4,890 respondents indicated that the inventory was a dependable instrument for assessing the normative aspects of culture. Factor analysis provided general support for the construct validity of the scales, most of which were related to both individual and organizational criteria as predicted.

Corporate culture perspectives on 'culture as variable' therefore tend to share a number of common themes:

- a focus on the unitary or homogeneous nature of corporate culture (Alvesson 1993);
- a focus on cultures being 'bounded', with relatively impermeable boundaries; culture is coterminous with organizational structure and membership;
- culture gives employees a sense of identity, enhancing commitment and integration (Smircich 1983);
- culture influences individual and organizational performance in an 'instrumentalist' way;
- culture is paradoxically seen both as fairly stable, enduring and static, yet also capable of change;
- a neglect of organizational diversity (Chapter 9) and heterogeneity and subcultures, as well as of competing or disparate interests;
- confusion over whether the concept is meant descriptively – as a real state of affairs – or prescriptively, as a future state to which the organization should aspire.

The most important claim of the 'culture as variable' school is probably that culture can influence both individual and organizational performance; the so-called 'culture–performance link'. In the 1980s, managers were urged to understand, manage and create culture and develop quality cultures, learning cultures, innovation cultures etc. Culture was seen as linked to organizational performance, especially 'strong' cultures. In part, this perspective was related to American disillusion with over-rationalistic management methods and the apparent success of Japanese organizations in the 1980s. This was often attributed to strong cultures binding employees to the organization and enhancing their commitment to it. The 1980s were the heyday of the managing organizational culture, 'corporate culturism' (Willmott 1993, 2013) or 'corporate culturalism' movements (Fleming 2013), though their essentials had appeared earlier in the work of 'human relations' theorists such as Argyris (1967). Their aim was to secure the commitment of employees to corporate goals and values selected and promoted by top management, in order to enhance organizational performance. This reformulated the implicit unitarist assumption 'of an underlying consensus of interest between employers and employees' (Willmott 2013: 448); the active building of strong cultures was seen as engendering employee identification with a few core, managerially endorsed core values. However, many employees and managers may in practice comply outwardly with such values while inwardly remaining sceptical, cynical or resistant to such initiatives; they may also engage in resistance, both overtly through strikes and other disputes or through more covert 'micro-emancipation' actions such as bitching, jokes or the wearing of subversive clothing.

In recent years, the concept of corporate culture has been of less interest to researchers, though implicit in studies of organizational identity (e.g. Ravisi and Schultz 2006, Ravisi and Canato 2013) and interest in individual identity and subjectivity at work (e.g. see Preece and Iles' 2009 study of the identities of chief executives as leaders). Fleming (2013) argues that in an era of capitalist realism and the widespread discrediting of corporations by scandals such as Enron and the banking crisis 'it is difficult to imagine that corporate culturalism might once have mattered'. Willmott (2013: 459) however asserts its continued interest and importance as employees continue to be targeted by 'forms of identification that include Corporate Culturism', though perhaps in mutated forms.

In part, the importance of shared values in many 'culture as variable' perspectives comes from the influence of Japanese management styles (Deal and Kennedy 1982; Peters and Waterman 1982). The importance of organization culture and the acknowledgement of the effects that organizational culture could have on organizational performance became widely appreciated in the 1970s and 1980s. Ouchi's (1981) Theory Z assigned seven values to organizational culture (Moorhead and Griffin 2004). Peters and Waterman (1982) developed the 7-S model with 'shared values' playing a key element, as one of the soft factors giving companies sustained competitive advantage. Shared values act as guiding concepts, fundamental ideas around which a business is built; these must be simple, with great meaning inside the organization even though outsiders may not see or understand them. They act to identify what the organization stands for and what it believes in; a strong organizational culture makes a company successful. Gordon and DiTomaso (1992) consider corporate culture to be the pattern of shared and stable beliefs and values that are developed within a company across time.

Deal and Kennedy (1982) focused on company values, rites, rituals, and communication, concluding that a company's culture strongly influenced its success. Collins and Porras (1997) examined 18 top performing companies, linking strong cultures to organizational performance. According to Coogan and Partners (2006), companies which outperform the norm in their category have specific cultural differences from their underperforming peers. A strong organizational culture has a significant impact on financial outcomes; organizations with strong cultures outperform those with weaker ones, giving incentives for managers to focus on organizational culture as a strategic tool to sustain competitive advantage (Carmeli and Tishler 2005), though very few companies pay sufficient attention to this. Gebler (2006) pointed out that 88 per cent of employees think their managers devoted inadequate consideration to the effects of culture on performance outcomes.

Links between culture and performance

Xiaoming and Junchen (2012) have reviewed much of the literature on the links between organizational culture and performance and its effect on many elements of an organization, including teams, change, ethics (Gebler 2006), strategy, turnover, and fraud. Each element, in turn, influences the organization's performance.

The relationship between organizational culture and corporate performance has been widely studied (e.g. Barney 1986; Kotter and Heskett 1992, 2011; Gordon 1991; Gordon and DiTomaso 1992; Parry and Proctor-Thomson 2003). For Barney (1986), the core values (about how to treat employees, customers, suppliers, and others) foster innovativeness and flexibility in firms, and lead to sustained superior financial performance when linked with management control. These issues are discussed more fully in Chapters 3 and 4.

Many such studies have however been conceptual and anecdotal or used case studies without a formal measurement of either performance or culture (Gordon and DiTomaso 1992). Some research has looked at direct relationships between organization culture and corporate performance. Denison

(1984) established a positive relationship between high employee-participation cultures and corporate performance. Kotter and Heskett (1992, 2011) examined organizational culture and its relationship to organizational performance in 72 companies across 20 industries over 11 years. Corporate performance measures included the average increment of gross income, the increment of staff quantity, the change of stock price and the variation of corporate net income. The question of how the 'culture' of a corporation powerfully influences its economic performance was studied at such firms as Hewlett-Packard, Xerox, ICI, Nissan, and First Chicago. In addition a quantitative study of the relationship between culture and performance in more than 200 companies was used to identify 'shared values and unwritten rules' as influencing economic success or leading to a failure to adapt to changing markets and environments. 'Unhealthy cultures' could emerge, especially in firms which have experienced past success; fundamental to the process of reversing unhealthy cultures and making them more adaptive is effective leadership. Executives in ten corporations worked to establish new visions, align and motivate managers to provide leadership to serve customers, employees and stockholders, and thus created more externally focused and responsive cultures.

However, Kotter and Heskett (2011) challenge the widely held belief that 'strong' corporate cultures create excellent business performance; while many shared values and institutionalized practices can promote good performance, those cultures can also be characterized by arrogance, an inward focus and bureaucracy, undermining an organization's ability to adapt to change. Even 'contextually or strategically appropriate' cultures fitting a firm's strategy and business context do not necessarily promote excellent performance over long periods of time unless they facilitate the adoption of strategies and practices that continuously respond to changing markets and new competitive environments.

Using linear regression and comparisons between 'healthy culture' and 'unhealthy' companies, Kotter and Heskett (1992) put forward a contingency model, arguing that better performing organizations have strong cultures, but only if the culture fits the organization's environment. Better performance is sustained over the long run only if the organization's culture contains change values leading the organization to continually re-adapt, culturally and otherwise, to its environment. For an organization to perform well in the long-term, it must have a culture whose values emphasize care and concern for three constituencies: (1) customers, (2) employees, and (3) stockholders.

One key question about the culture–corporate performance link is the problem of *variable selection*; which variables best measure corporate performance? Efforts to explore the relationship often have methodological weaknesses, such as unknown construct validity, a small number of participating organizations, and respondents who do not represent the entire organization

(Wilderom et al. 2000), as well as lack of agreement by researchers concerning the best way to measure culture. Possible dependent measures include accounting performance (Barney 1986), profit rate, ROA (return on assets), long-term profitability, sales growth rate and so on.

Other studies have used non-financial indices, such as employee satisfaction, customer satisfaction, turnover rate, and quality of products/services, sometimes using Kaplan and Norton (1996) and the balanced scorecard (see Chapter 4) to emphasize the importance of customers, internal business processes, learning and growth measures. Bagozzi and colleagues (2003) divide corporate performance into In-role and Extra-role performance. In-role performance includes sales volume, communication effectiveness and relationship-building; Extra-role performance includes courtesy, helping, sportsmanship and civic virtue.

Ogaard et al. (2005) suggested using financial performance, service quality, resource utilization and revenue management indicators; no single indicator will give a comprehensive picture of organizational performance

Organizational culture is however just one of the many variables that could contribute to explaining performance. Anthony (1994) points out that cultural change is often associated with structural change, making it difficult to attribute successful change to cultural change alone. Pettigrew (1990) points out the difficulties in bringing about cultural change; these include its existence at different levels, its breadth as well as its depth, its taken-for-grantedness, its deep historical roots, its relationship with the distribution of power within the organization, the existence of subcultures, and its interdependence with people, priorities, structure and systems.

Moderators and mediators of the culture–performance link

Other research has examined some variables as moderators or mediators in the relationship between organization culture and corporate performance (Hoffman 2007). A variety of variables have been studied here, including leadership (Ogbonna and Harris 2000; Parry and Proctor-Thomson 2003; Chen 2004), HRM styles (Miah and Bird 2007), human resource flexibility (Ngo and Loi 2008) and organizational commitment (de Brentani and Kleinschmidt 2004; Chen 2004). Communication may also be a mediator or moderator of organizational culture's impact on organizational performance (Garnett et al. 2008).

Organization culture can also itself be a moderator or mediator (Bagozzi et al. 2003). Ogbonna and Harris (2000) claimed that culture is a full mediator between leadership style and corporate performance; while the links between leadership and performance and between culture and performance have been examined independently, few studies have investigated the association between the three concepts. They claim that the relationship between leadership style and performance is mediated by the form of organizational culture present; leadership style was not directly linked to performance but indirectly associated. In contrast, competitive and innovative cultural traits were directly linked with performance (as predicted) while community and bureaucratic cultural traits were not. Both of these cultures are characterized by an emphasis on integration, internal cohesiveness, and the establishment of uniformity (that is, a strong culture); little evidence was found to support claims of a link between cultural strength and performance. Competitive and innovative cultures sensitive to external conditions had a strong and positive impact on organizational performance (Barney 1986, 1991). This suggests that a potential solution to the difficulties associated with changing organizational culture may involve focusing on leadership style. Culture has also been shown to be a mediator between enterprise strategy (see Chapter 2) and organization performance (Arogyaswamy and Byles 1987).

Of course, the relationship between culture and performance is not always positive; Peters and Waterman (1982) pointed out that some excellent companies fail due to 'culture rigidity' (Meyerson and Martin 1987) and culture antecedents and legacies may get in the way of adapting to a new environment rapidly and successfully.

Many studies have supported the importance of culture for organizational commitment in particular (Chen 2004). Bureaucratic working environments may result in negative employee commitment, whereas supportive working environments result in greater employee commitment and involvement. For Chen (2004), the relationship between leadership and organizational commitment is moderated by the organization culture. De Brentani and Kleinschmidt (2004) used the interactions of organization culture and commitment to predict corporate performance. Organizational commitment is unlikely to predict accounting performance directly, but often plays a role as a moderator or a mediator. Chen, Hwang and Liu (2009) considered commitment as a moderator of the effects of leadership on voluntary performance.

As we have seen, researchers have initially put forward a direct positive relationship between organizational culture and performance, hypothesizing that certain types of cultures led to better financial performance (e.g., Barney 1986). Clarity derived from salient shared norms that are strongly enforced would promote greater strategic alignment and goal attainment in strong-culture firms. Denison and Mishra (1995) linked organizational culture attributes such as adaptability to growth and profitability, and Kotter and Heskett (1992) and Gordon and DiTomaso (1992) found that firms emphasizing adaptability and change in their cultures were more likely to perform well over time.

Other studies however have found inconclusive relationships between organizational culture and performance (e.g. Wilderom et al. 2000). Chatman et al. (2012) argue that the relationship between culture and organizational performance is contingent on environmental conditions (see Chapter 1). Strong-culture firms may gain advantages in stable environments but, because of the corresponding social control that promotes conformity among members, may perform worse or less reliably in dynamic environments and during periods of change (Sorenson 2002). Since many organizations operate in dynamic environments, this view suggests that strong cultures may reduce a firm's performance. They claim that previous research has blurred a critical distinction between a culture's *strength* and its *content*, and that there are two distinct aspects of culture strength. One is the degree to which members agree about cultural norms (consensus) and the other is the force (intensity) with which certain norms are held (O'Reilly et al. 1988). Even in dynamic environments, organizations displaying intensity around a certain kind of cultural-norm – one that promotes non-uniform behaviours and adaptability in particular – and which are characterized by higher consensus among members about cultural norms, may perform better than those characterized by lower consensus, lower intensity, or both. Culture as a construct encompasses three dimensions: the content of norms (e.g., teamwork, integrity), how forcefully these are held by organizational members (its intensity), and how widely members agree about the norms within the organization (consensus). Strong cultures will boost performance in dynamic environments if a norm of adaptability is intensely held and if cultural norms are widely shared among members. High-tech firms characterized by higher cultural-norm consensus and intensity about adaptability performed better than those characterized by lower consensus, lower intensity about adaptability, or both.

A particularly influential perspective in this area of culture-performance links has been the concept of 'person–organization fit', particularly the relationship between organizational culture (especially values) and individual values or personality. Education, training, communication, and reward and punishment may all be used to bring about cultural change, as well as recruitment and selection. Increasingly organizations are less interested in matching 'the job' and 'the person' (measured by skills, abilities or competencies) and more interested in the 'fit' with the team or organization (see Chapter 5). In South-West Airlines (Jackson and Schuler 2003) people are selected for their attitudes and 'fit' with the culture, not their skills. The company believes it can change skill levels through training, but not attitudes. Recruitment is carried out using employee networks, and teams of employees, managers and customers participate in the selection process in a 'casting call' type process, as well as testing the profile of applicants against the profile of outstanding employees. The cultural emphasis is on a family feeling, a sense of the underdog battling the majors, and a strong sense of fun.

In W.L. Gore Associates, Inc. (the makers of Gore-Tex: see Bell 2004) the culture aspires to unleash creativity and foster teamwork, showing how inventiveness, commitment, and initiative combined can create business success (www.gore.com). Four operating principles at Gore support these objectives:

Job fit/job demands)	Organization fit/cultural values	Outcomes
Skills		
Abilities		
Knowledge		
Experience	Values	
	Personality	
	Goals	
	Attributes	
		Satisfaction
	Stress	Absence
		Commitment
		Turnover
		Performance

Figure 11.2   Selection, socialization and 'cultural fit'

Source: Adapted from Anderson and Heriott (1997).

fairness; freedom; commitment; and waterline (decisions might be categorized as above or below the waterline, so sharing the burden of risk through consultation). Upon successful selection all new associates are immersed heavily in the Gore culture, tools and processes through a four-day programme. Storytelling is a key element to orientation at Gore; a frequently used tool is a video of Bill and Vieve Gore and many legendary associates discussing the first five years of the company, emphasizing the importance of the culture and how to be successful in it. Every 'associate' (employee) has one or more sponsors: a 'starting sponsor' to help a new associate become comfortable operating in the Gore culture, a 'contribution sponsor' to act as a coach, mentor and advocate and help plan an associate's development, and a 'compensation sponsor' to represent the associate at pay review discussions. If conflict arises between associates, the contribution sponsor acts as a mediator.

Figure 11.2 shows how this concept of 'fit' between individual and organization, especially with organizational cultural values, might work.

For O'Reilly et al. (1991), the *employee–organization culture gap* refers to the extent to which employee self-assessment differs from the employees' assessment of the organization. Employees not fitting with the culture of an organization might find long-term employment difficult, as applicants tend to match their characteristics and values to those of the organization, and some organizations use cultural fit as a means of assessing person–organization fit to select employees or predict retention. This approach comes from Schneider's (1987) claim that 'the people make the place'; organizational culture, climate and practices are determined by the people in the organization through Attraction, Selection and Attrition (ASA) processes. People are differentially attracted to organizational careers as a function of their own interests and values, searching for work environments that fit their personalities and values. Organizations then select people who they think are compatible for many different kinds of jobs. In that way organizations end up choosing people who share many common personal attributes. When people do not fit with a work environment they tend to leave it; a more homogeneous group then stays, making the organization less heterogenous and diverse as time passes.

═══ **PIT STOP: REFLECTIVE ACTIVITY 11.6** ═══

1. What do you see as some of the issues and problems associated with 'selecting for cultural fit'?

Managers have tended to ignore the impact of employee demographics, including gender, longevity with an organization and age, on organizational culture; these and other variables may moderate the relationship between the employee–organization culture gap and performance. Many commentators have noted the existence of distinct workforce generations with differing values; managers and leaders therefore must design ways for the generations to work together and interact. However, despite the current fashionability, especially among consultants, of 'generational' differences in values ('Generation x, generation y, baby-boomers, generation Me etc.) academics are often sceptical of such claims, arguing that they are often age, rather than generation, related, and that generational values do not always vary in the directions predicted (e.g. Parry and Urwin 2010).

Allard (2011) used O'Reilly et al.'s (1991) Organizational Culture Profile (OCP) to analyse the culture–performance link at three similar technical institutes in South Dakota. The OCP contained 54 value statements to capture organizational cultural values. The results indicated a significant negative relationship between the employee–organization culture gap and organizational performance. Employee longevity with an organization moderated the relationship between the employee–organization culture gap and organizational performance; the employee–organization culture gap and organizational performance were stronger for employees who had worked for the company longer than was the case for shorter-term employees. Employee age and gender did not however moderate the relationship between the employee–organization culture gap and organizational performance

Culture at a national level

In the 1994 Hollywood Tarantino crime film *Pulp Fiction*, one of the characters recalls his experiences of Europe: fries with mayonnaise rather than ketchup, beer in bottles rather than plastic cups in cinemas, and the translation of the McDonald's *quarterpounder with cheese* into *Royale with cheese* in France. His partner on screen, amazed by these cultural differences, would probably be even more amazed if he knew that he could order boiled rice instead of fries as a side order for a Kentucky Fried Chicken meal in Asian countries. Food is an intrinsic part of national culture, and differences in food consumption show differences among countries in the world, as we saw in Case Study 11.1.

PIT STOP: REFLECTIVE ACTIVITY 11.7

(adapted from Zhang and Iles 2013: 24)

McDonald's and its international market strategy

McDonald's is a leading global foodservice retailer, with more than 30,000 local restaurants serving 52 million people in more than 100 countries each day. Its logo of 'golden arches' symbolize one of the world's most well-known and valuable brands, and it holds a leading share in the global market of fast-food restaurant segments in virtually every country in which it operates (http://www.mcdonalds.com/corp/about.html).

Looking at its website, what do you think of its marketing strategy in different countries, in terms of how it has adapted its product offering in international different environments?

Ritzer (2005) discusses the 'McDonaldization' of society, where the principles of the fast-food industry such as efficiency, consistency, quantification, and control are universally adopted, contributing to impersonal uniformity, with standardized products: Brazilian children sporting American-style T-shirts and drinking Coca-Cola, Saudi women applying Chanel or Christian Dior cosmetics under their veil, Swedes increasingly eating burritos and tacos at fast-food chains.

Similarly, the concept of 'Disneyfication' may refer to bigger, faster, and better entertainment with a large sense of uniformity worldwide. The term was invented by Bryman (1999) to refer to the internationalization of the entertainment values of US mass culture. However, when Euro Disney went bankrupt in 1994, amid criticisms that the theme park was too American for Europeans, management made appropriate changes to cater to local tastes and renamed the park 'Disneyland Paris', e.g. introducing wine and not requiring French employees to act in such scripted ways (Matusitz and Lord 2013, Matusitz and Palermo 2013). When Disney opened a theme park in Hong Kong in 2005, it was not successful. Hong Kong Disneyland personnel found the 'emotional labour' required too artificial (Adekola and Sergi 2007), with objections to Disney's refusal to let Chinese food inspectors into the park. The attempted Disneyfication of Chinese culture brought about a significant cultural backlash; feng shui principles were not brought into the park, and cast members were concerned about their salary and working conditions.

This case indicates that many organizations are 'cultural hybrids', combining aspects of both the parent country (e.g. the US) and host country (e.g. Hong Kong) culture; a wholesale transfer of practices which may be culturally appropriate in the home culture may not be appropriate in the host culture (see Chapter 12). We will explore this further after looking more closely at national culture.

Over decades, there has been an increase in the movement of people across borders, looking for work and settling down in foreign countries; for example, Britain has had a large movement of immigrants from Second World War refugees from Europe, from Commonwealth colonies in Asia and in the Caribbean, and more recently from Central and Eastern European countries, changing and moulding British culture. The British staple of fish and chips originally came from German Jewish immigrants, and curry is a current part of the British culture (with the Balti having been invented not in India, but in Birmingham).

While the United Kingdom has now devolved into English, Welsh, Scottish and Northern Irish nations and administrations, many European countries have been coming together to form a European Union, an eclectic and complex mixture of differing cultures from the 'cold industrious north' to the 'warm relaxed south' (Zhang and Iles 2013: 25). During the current (2013) financial crisis, cultural stereotypes (e.g. lazy Greeks, bossy Germans and chauvinistic French) have been used by the media as a shorthand, over-simplified way to explain such problems. However, Spain is no longer a country of siestas, and the Spanish working week of 38.4 hours is actually longer than those in Germany (37.7), Italy (38) and France (35.6), showing the persistence of cultural stereotypes.

National clichés are not always true; but national characteristics have been used by researchers as useful approximations to understand culture and national differences, often interpreted as 'cultural differences'. Hofstede's (1991) seminal work on culture used data on IBM employees working in 58 countries, justifying the use of these data on the grounds that he was comparing *like for like*, i.e. for the same position within IBM's branches worldwide, employees will have similar attributes, except for their culture. The differences observed were therefore attributed to culture. Trompenaars and Hampden-Turner (2003) also divided their respondents into countries when devising their own version of 'cultural attributes'. The following sections will now examine the work of Hofstede and Trompenaars and Hampden-Turner on culture and how their theories impact on international relations, trade and organizational policies and practices, including HRM.

The work of Geert Hofstede and its implications for HRM

Geert Hofstede, a Dutch cultural anthropologist, developed a very frequently used set of frameworks for analysing international cultures, defining two types of cultures (Hofstede 1991). The first one (Culture 1) refers to anthropological culture, i.e. civilization, education, literature. Culture 2, on the other hand, refers to broader and more fundamental human processes such as how people greet, eat, demonstrate emotions, and keep a physical distance from others (Zhang and Iles 2013: 26).

Hofstede (2001) has emphasized that 'Culture' is best seen as the set of commonly held and relatively stable beliefs, attitudes and values within an organization (organizational or corporate culture) or society (national or societal culture). These influence the way that organizations implement decision-making, resolve problems, and behave (Hall 1984). Culture is thus, as we have seen, embodied in symbols, rituals and heroes, reflected in organizational communication, manners, dress codes, social rules and norms, and role models. For Hofstede (1980), national culture has values as its central component.

Hofstede initially analysed cultural differences along four dimensions (Hofstede et al., 2010), rating countries on a scale from 1 to 100. A further two dimensions were later added to the initial four. The six dimensions centred on the following theoretical constructs (Zhang and Iles 2013: 26):

Power

Hofstede named this dimension Power Distance (PD or PDI), referring to the extent to which less powerful members both expect and accept unequal power distribution. High PD cultures usually have organizations with centralized, top-down control systems. Low power distance implies organizations displaying greater equality and empowerment. Malaysia, Panama, and Guatemala rated as the highest on the PDI dimension.

Predictability

Hofstede named this dimension Uncertainty Avoidance (UA or UAI). It defines the extent to which a culture values predictability. UA cultures have strong traditions and rituals and tend toward formal, bureaucratic structures and rules in organizational forms. Greece was rated highest here, followed by Portugal and Guatemala.

Self

Hofstede named this dimension Individualism versus Collectivism (ID or IDV). In an individualistic environment, people and their rights are more important than the groups they may belong to, including organizational groups; in a collectivist environment, people are born into strong extended family or tribal communities, and these loyalties are paramount, including in organizations. The US was rated highest in IDV, closely followed by Australia and the UK; many Asian and African countries were rated as more 'collectivist'.

Gender

Hofstede named this dimension Masculinity versus Femininity (MAS), focusing on the degree to which 'traditional' gender roles are assigned in a culture. For example, men may be considered aggressive and competitive, with women expected to be gentler and more concerned with home and family. Japan led the MAS list scores, followed by Austria and Venezuela; Nordic and Scandinavian countries were rated as much more 'feminine' (and interestingly have by far the greatest proportion of women in leading political and economic roles, often with gender-based quotas for board membership, as in Norway – see http://siteresources.worldbank.org/INTWDR2012/Resources/7778105-1299699968583/7786210-1322671773271/Pande-Gender-Quotas-April-2011.pdf).

Time

Hofstede named this dimension Long- versus Short-term Orientation (LTO), focusing on the extent to which the social group or organization invests for the future, is persevering, and is patient in waiting for results. This dimension, also known as Confucian dynamism, was proposed following a Chinese value survey based on traditional Chinese cultural values, representing Confucian values in Chinese and other East Asian societies influenced by Confucianism such as Korea, Vietnam and Japan. As such, China scored highest on this dimension, followed by Hong Kong and Taiwan. A 'long-term orientation' refers to the capacity of social and organizational members to pragmatically adapt traditions to new situations, show a willingness to save, display a thrifty approach to scarce resources, manifest a willingness to persevere over the long term and to subordinate one's own interests to achieve a purpose, and a concern with virtue (Bond 1988). This dimension did not appear in the original work, but was identified as important by Chinese scholars among Chinese employees, and later extended more generally to other societies.

Happiness

Hofstede named this dimension Indulgence versus Restraint; it is a newly added construct, loosely correlated with LTO, and focuses on the gratification of pleasure. In an indulgent society, there is relatively free gratification of 'natural' human desires related to enjoying life and having fun. In a restraint society, strict social norms control and regulate gratification. The US and Western Europe are relatively indulgent societies, while many Asian and especially Muslim countries show more restraint.

Hofstede (1980, 2001) has integrated these earlier dimensions into more general national models: for example, the UK is said to resemble a *village market*, exhibiting low uncertainty avoidance, high individualism and low power distance. Germany on the other hand is a *well-oiled machine*, showing both higher uncertainty avoidance and power distance. France, displaying relatively high power distance, is more of a *pyramid*; and India, the Middle East and many other Asian countries, showing both high collectivism and power distance, seem more like a *family*. These typologies are related to HRM in several ways; for example, recruitment and selection criteria (see Chapter 5) will systematically vary. In the UK, there will be a stress in resourcing on interpersonal, communication and negotiation skills in managers, perhaps assessed through assessment centres and psychometric tests; in Germany, a greater stress on technical competence, assessed through the education/apprenticeship system. For example, Iles noticed that BMW top managers were more likely to have formal engineering qualifications and PhDs than Rover top managers. In France, there is a greater stress on analytical skills and 'elite' potential, assessed through the education system and a background in elite institutions such as the 'grandes ecoles'. In much of Asia, Africa and the Middle East, there is a greater stress on extended family connections. In the Nordic and Scandinavian countries, with their high 'femininity' scores, both genders are more likely to pursue more personally satisfying rather than hierarchically oriented careers, with high value given to work-life balance.

PIT STOP: REFLECTIVE ACTIVITY 11.8

1. In Case Study 11.1, can you see any examples of Wal-Mart stressing different skills from those more common in most Argentinian organizations?
2. To what extent do organizational differences relate to differences in power-distance or collectivism?

In addition, these cultural dimensions seem associated with many other dimensions of IHRM, with organizations from countries scoring high in uncertainty avoidance (e.g. Japan, Germany) being more likely to make extensive use of expatriates (parent-country nationals) to control overseas operations than organizations from countries scoring low in uncertainty avoidance (e.g. the US, UK, the Nordic countries). Such issues are further discussed in Chapter 12.

Hofstede's work has received sustained criticism, especially after the publication in 2001 of the second edition of his original book, e.g. McSweeney (2002), Smith (2002). Hofstede's analysis was carried out on a country-by-country basis; it may not hold in countries where there are strong subcultures based on ethnic origin or geography. There have been many critiques concerning the use of nation-states as the basic unit of analysis (McSweeney 2002; Soderberg and Holden 2002). In Canada, for instance, there is a distinct French Canadian culture in Quebec with quite a different set of norms compared to English-speaking Canada, such as greater collectivism and trade union involvement in employment relations. In Italy, masculinity scores differ between north and south; many would criticize such over-generalizations (e.g. Ailon 2008). Hofstede (1980) appears to assume that national territory corresponds to cultural homogeneity, but China, as with many African countries (except Botswana and Somalia) or India, is not homogeneous, with strong regional differences and many minority ethnic/religious subcultures. There are also problems with the use of some of his concepts, for example, 'individualism' and 'collectivism' differ in meaning in different countries. Japanese employees may be seen to be loyal to their organizations, but Chinese and many Asian or African or Latin American employees may well be more loyal to their families. In China, many employees working in Japanese companies will leave for small pay increases elsewhere, in contrast to Japanese employees. However, both China and Japan adopt the principle of collectivism which differs from Western individualism.

Hofstede himself acknowledges the limits of his model (Hofstede 2011), arguing that cultural research suffers from 'level confusion' or confusion over value differences at individual, national or corporate levels.

PIT STOP: REFLECTIVE ACTIVITY 11.9

(based on Zhang and Iles 2013: 29)

Visit the following link and listen to Hofstede's recent speech (http://www.geerthofstede.nl). Then go to http://geerthofstede.nl/dimensions-of-national-cultures.

To what extent do you think Hofstede's model helps us understand national and organizational cultural differences, such as in Case Study 11.1?

Hofstede's fifth dimension (Confucian dynamism or LTO) has been particularly subject to critique to which Hofstede has responded with analysis of another data set (the World Values Survey) as well as the original Chinese Values Survey (Minkov and Hofstede 2012). Wu (2006) has also re-examined the significance of LTO using Taiwanese and American respondents, demonstrating that work-related cultural values are not static and can be changed over time.

Hofstede's original IBM sample was collected over 30 years before and Wu (2006) argues that there have been influential political, societal and economic changes over the past 30 years, causing changes in people's values.

This has been shown to be particularly true for China, often using a cultural frameworks different from that of Hofstede (2001). Liu (2003) used interview and survey studies in two factories in north-east China. Recent organizational and HR reforms in China such as performance-based reward (see Chapter 7) and lower job security have led to generational differences in assumptions, beliefs and values between first-generation employees hired pre-reform and younger, second-generation employees hired post-reform. Confucian values of harmony and loyalty have influenced the way employees perceive an organization as a symbolic family, amplified by the earlier Maoist-era ideology of 1949–1979 which emphasized group rewards and stressed hierarchy, authority, order, mutual obligations and the provision of benefits in exchange for loyalty. Harmony, long-term relationships, a concern for face, respect and integrity, and the avoidance of direct criticism in interpersonal relationships are also regarded as important (Pye 1992).

However, a recent focus on efficiency, productivity, performance-based rewards, and the decline in job security has threatened these traditions and values, leading to subcultural generational differences. Factor analysis of the survey data revealed five themes: equality, security, loyalty, harmony and bureaucracy. Younger workers however expressed unhappiness with regard to harmony at the expense of poor performance, and differed in their interpretation of the value of bureaucracy, security, stability and loyalty, seeing these in less relational and more conditional, contractual, and calculative or 'transactional' ways.

Li and Nimon (2008) have also shown generational differences among Chinese workers' values, distinguishing between the 'social reform', 'Cultural Revolution', 'consolidation', and 'pre-liberation' generational cohorts. The Cultural Revolution cohort entering the workforce when the manual worker was most privileged was least happy with recent economic reforms and their current position, and more likely to work in state-owned enterprises (SOEs), especially when compared to the younger 'social reform' cohort.

Cultural arguments (such as Hofstede 1980) linking recent strong Chinese economic performance with 'Confucian' values neglect however the ways culture changes – cultures interact with, and influence, each other. Confucian culture also stresses practical realism and pragmatism, and the valuing of practical application (Hofstede 1991). China has always flourished when open to other cultures (e.g., the Tang/Song Dynasties in the early middle ages) compared to periods when it was culturally closed (e.g., the Qing Dynasty in the early modern period). Interestingly, not long ago the same 'Confucian' values were held to be holding back Chinese economic growth – which rather casts doubt on the value of these kinds of explanation!

Other regions have shown similar patterns of cultural change; from the perspective of Hofstede (2001), Arab cultures are seen as masculine, relatively long-term in orientation, and middling on individualism, uncertainty avoidance, and power distance; the family is the cornerstone of social life, with social identity and loyalty oriented to the 'wider' extended family. However, there has been a diminution in size of the typical household and again, like in China, a tendency for younger generations to have a more independent life (Suliman 2006). In much of North Africa, more individualized work values have also emerged (Mellahi and Budhwar 2006). Horwitz (2012) and Kamoche and Newenham-Kahindi (2012) argue that collectivist 'African values' like *ubuntu* (interconnectedness and interdependence) held much more appeal for older, male employees than younger, female ones, indicating that different sections of the workforce, as in China, did not share a common set of cultural values.

In summary, Hofstede's impact on the field has been at least fourfold (Bird and Fang 2009: 140):

1. Theoretically and methodologically, by adopting nation/state culture as the basic unit of analysis, he analysed the concept of culture into more concise and measurable components.
2. He established cultural values as a key factor influencing HRM and organizational behaviour.
3. He enhanced awareness of cultural variations.
4. His paradigm has inspired other scholars and practitioners to carry out large-scale studies of national culture.

Other models of culture: Schwartz, Trompenaars and Hampden-Turner

There has been much interest in understanding how to classify and differentiate cultures ever since the work of Hoftsede (1980), with a variety of approaches including Schwartz (1990) and Trompenaars (1997). Schwartz (1990), building on Hofstede's approach, listed 56 different values intended to be comprehensive and recognized in all cultures, using both individual and culture-level analyses. His main model includes seven dimensions: conservatism, hierarchy, mastery, affective autonomy, intellectual autonomy, egalitarian commitment, and harmony. China for example is characterized by an emphasis on harmony and hierarchy.

In their book *Riding the Waves of Culture* Trompenaars and Hampden-Turner (2003), perhaps the most-cited model after Hofstede (2001), classified cultures along a mixture of behavioural and value patterns, synthesizing 30,000 responses from business executives selected and drawn from 55 countries. They identified seven value orientations, described in terms of alternatives (Zhang and Iles 2013: 30).

1. *Universalism versus particularism*: emphasis on rules and procedures as opposed to relationships. Universalism is focused on developing broad and general rules; when no general rules fit, it finds the best rule. Particularism is about finding exceptions. When no rules fit, it judges the case on its own merits, rather than trying to force-fit an existing rule. In particular, it makes decisions such as who to appoint or promote not on the basis of universal meritocratic criteria of 'best performer' but in terms of particularistic criteria like family or friendship relationships with the decision-makers, as expressed in the Chinese 'guanxi' or connections or the similar emphasis on 'wasta' in many Arab societies.

2. *Communitarianism versus individualism:* individualism is about the rights of the individual, seeking to let each person grow or fail on their own; it sees group focus as denying the individual their inalienable personal rights. In contrast, communitarianism is about prioritizing the rights of the group or society, seeking to put the family, group, company and country before the individual. It sees individualism as selfish and short-sighted. Individualism tends to be competitive, while communitarianism promotes cooperation. Many Asian societies promote communitarianism in the form of team relationships (e.g. in appraisal and reward practices) whilst many Western societies promote individualism in the form of individually-based performance-related pay.

3. *Neutral versus emotional*: neutral societies such as Japan's conceal emotions as opposed to emotional societies like in many African or Latin American countries which show emotions, including at work. Streamlined and machine-efficient cultures such as Germany or Japan prefer a neutral outlook where interactions are objective and detached and where there is a lower chance of emotions confusing issues such as promotion or discipline, assumed to be a characteristic of the colder north-western countries of Northern Europe and America. In contrast, warmer southern European Mediterranean and many Latin American and African countries prefer to conduct business with emotional expression.

4. *Diffuse versus specific cultures*: superficial as opposed to deep relationships, including relationships at work. This is similar to the previous dimension; in diffuse cultures, everything is connected, and this integration helps build a big picture, important for building trust among team colleagues. In contrast, specific cultures prefer to assume that a separation of work and life is the way to success, with an emphasis on separating work from private life.

5. *Achieved status versus ascribed status*: here the focus is on what one does – competence, performance – as opposed to what one is – family, ethnic or class background. Achieved status is about gaining status through performance, assuming individuals and organizations earn and lose status every day, whereas ascribed status is about gaining status through other means, such as seniority or background; it assumes status is acquired by right rather than by ongoing daily performance. It finds order and security in knowing where status is, and where it stays, characteristic of many Asian or African societies, in contrast to the more fluid 'earned' status of many Western societies.

6. *Time as sequence vs. time as synchronization*: time as sequence (characteristic of many Western societies) sees events as separate items in time, sequencing one after another, and finds order in a set array of actions that occur one after the other. Time as synchronization (characteristic of many developing societies) sees events in parallel, as synchronized together, finding order in the coordination of multiple efforts.

7. *Human–Nature relationships*: orientations to nature influence the way we conduct daily life and business. Societies like those of the US and the old USSR that believe they can and should control nature by imposing their will (e.g. on earth, the Arctic, space) are described as inner-directed. In contrast, to believe as many Asian societies influenced by Buddhism or Daoism do that we should 'go with the flow' is to be outer-directed.

══ PIT STOP: REFLECTIVE ACTIVITY 11.10 ══

Look again at Case Study 11.1.

Can you see any differences between the American and Argentinian approaches to work that might be explained by Trompenaars and Hampden-Turner (2003)?

You might want to consider in particular such dimensions as universalism versus particularism, communitarianism versus individualism, neutral versus emotional, diffuse versus specific, and ascribed versus achieved status.

There are some clear similarities to the analysis of Hofstede (2001). According to Dahl (2004), two dimensions are directly consistent with Hofstede's dimensions of collectivism/individualism (especially communitarianism/individualism). To a lesser extent, this is also true of power distance: achievement/ascription describes how status is accorded and appears to be linked to Hofstede's power distance index if it is accepted that status is accorded by nature rather than achievement. Ascription also reflects a greater willingness to accept power distances. However, Hofstede's power index relates not only to how status is accorded, but also to the acceptable power distance within a society, an area that is not touched upon by Trompenaars (1997).

The other dimensions appear to focus more on some resulting effects of underlying value dimensions. Thus the neutral/emotional dimension describes the extent to which feelings are openly expressed, and relates to normative behaviours rather than values. Universalism/particularism describes a preference for rules rather than trusting relationships, and could be interpreted as part of Hofstede's uncertainty avoidance dimension on one side, and to some extent the collectivist/individualist dimension on the other. However, the Human-time relationship would appear to be very similar to Hall's (1984) polychromic/monochronic time perceptions dimension. Finally, the Human–Nature relationship appears to be closely connected with the Human–Nature relationship in Kluckhohn and Strodtbeck's (1961) theory of value.

Trompenaars and Hampden-Turner (2003) have also summarized their cultural factors into a model of corporate culture dependent on organizational affinity to two dimensions (egalitarian versus hierarchical, and task versus person). They assume that differences in national cultures influence the type of corporate culture encountered. The four corporate models (similar to Handy 1985, popularizing Harrison's 1972 model of corporate cultures in terms of role, power, task and person cultures, as we discussed earlier) are:

1. *Incubator* (fulfilment-oriented)
2. *Guided Missile* (project-oriented)
3. *Eiffel Tower* (role-oriented)
4. *Family* (person-oriented).

Each of the types represent a distinct model in terms of the relationship between employees ways of thinking and learning, and attitudes to authority, people, and managing change. These characteristics are summarized below.

Relationships between employees

Family-type organizations show diffuse relationship to an organic whole: Eiffel Towers are characterized by specific roles within a mechanical system of required interactions. Guided Missiles in contrast are characterized by specific tasks in a cybernetic system focused upon shared objectives, while Incubators show diffuse spontaneous relationships which grow organically out of shared creative processes.

Attitude to authority

In Family-type organizations, status is ascribed to parent figures who are close, paternalistic and all powerful; in Eiffel Towers, status is ascribed to superior roles who are distant but still powerful. In contrast, in Guided Missiles status is achieved by project group members who are able to contribute to the articulated goals, while in Incubators, status is achieved by individuals displaying creativity and growth.

Ways of thinking and learning

Family-type organizations display intuitive, holistic, lateral and error-correcting behaviour, in contrast to Eiffel Towers, who show logical, analytical, vertical and rationally efficient behaviours. Guided Missiles are problem-centred, professional, practical, and cross-disciplinary/cross-functional in nature, while Incubators are process-oriented, creative, ad hoc, and inspirational in style.

Attitudes to people

Family-type organizations treat people as family members; Eiffel Towers in contrast see people as human resources to be utilized and exploited; Guided Missiles see employees as specialists and experts; Incubators in contrast see them as co-creators of products and services, irrespective of their role or function.

Managing change

In Family-type organizations, the 'father' (boss, patron) makes changes to organizational direction; in Eiffel Towers, the rules and procedures are changed; in Guided Missiles, the aim of the organization shifts as the target moves; while in Incubators, the focus is on ongoing iteration, improvisation and attunement to a dynamic environment.

In contrast to Hofstede (2001) and the use of large-scale surveys, Trompenaars (1997) used a variety of scenarios and dilemmas (e.g. would you report a friend who had a traffic accident to the police, measuring adherence to universalistic 'yes, the law applies equally to all' or particularistic 'no, he's my mate' values). Can responses to such dilemmas really provide a true picture of these dimensions? Rai and Holyoak (2009) suggest that moral dilemma scenarios are prone to biases originating from the researchers themselves, rather than the respondents, a point initially raised by Hofstede (1996) who questioned the conceptual categories presented by Trompenaars as dimensions, the validity of the model, and the paucity of data used to support these dimensions. Nonetheless, the Trompenaars database is a unique one which, with better analysis tools and refinements, may offer a detailed and accurate interpretation of cultural differences.

Transferring HRM practices across cultural and organizational boundaries

The role of culture, adaptation and hybridization of HRM

Can organizations transfer practices across cultural boundaries? Gamble (2010: 708) argues that cultural differences are often predicted to inhibit parent-country diffusion of HRM practices from corporate headquarters to foreign affiliates, especially to 'culturally distant' countries (e.g. the UK to Morocco compared to the UK to Australia). This would appear to strengthen the need for local responsiveness and isomorphism, but cultural explanations

> cannot account for change over time or divergence within national populations ... they also ignore the potential to implement innovative practices in novel settings ... frequently, 'culture' provides a convenient catch-all 'black box', deployed to explain why MNCs cannot transfer their parent country organizational practices ... in a way that closes off further analysis or explanation. (Gamble 2010: 708)

This should warn us about placing too much faith in static, overly homogenized and over-determined models of culture that neglect the agency of firms and individuals to shape and influence IHRM practices (Zhang and Iles 2013: 34; see Chapter 12) – though not always in circumstances and contexts of their own choosing of course! We need to seek to understand and analyse these actions and interpretations within the social, national, cultural, economic, historical and political context in which they take place.

Cultural hybridism or *hybridization* is another important concept, which we began to explore in terms of the 'transfer' of HRM practices in responding to cultural practices like food preferences to other countries in Case Study 11.1. Hybridization 'is a process, not an outcome, leading to contested but negotiable responses in organizations' (Iles 2013a: 199). Outcomes might include the evolution of hybrid HRM configurations, mixing local indigenous and global or Western practices, rather than the binary categorization into either global or local practices claimed by much of the literature on MNCs. Neither total global standardization nor local adaptation may be observed, but 'complex, dynamic and pragmatic mixes and blends of HRM practices' (Iles 2013a: 199).

Gamble (2010) shows this to be the case with Japanese retail MNCs in China. Here different companies retained different Japanese-style practices – a *'country of origin'* effect – while also adopting different mixes of local Chinese practices – an *'adaptation'* effect. In Japan, the companies 'engaged in many practices considered typical of "Japanese" HRM, such as careful and lengthy recruitment with testing and interviews, the use of the internal labour market for managers, extensive on-the-job training, high levels of customer service (e.g. greeting and farewell ceremonies for customers, with bows and greetings), patriarchal management (older male supervisors of female staff), job security for regular employees, flat salary differentials, and seniority-based pay increases (alongside a trend to increase performance-based pay, though with some differences in emphasis)' (Iles 2013b:227). Some companies were making extensive use of individual bonuses dependent on sales, whilst another had retained Japanese-style seniority pay. Another company was actually phasing this out in Japan itself, but was introducing it into China to off-set turnover and enhance employee retention.

Therefore, in China many modifications were being made to 'Japanese' practices, partly because of cultural differences. The firms in general made greater use of expatriates than European or US ones, with extensive communication back to HQ in Japan, perhaps reflecting high Japanese scores on 'uncertainty avoidance'. Senior positions were all held by Japanese staff. Customer service was however generally emphasized as an even stronger differentiation from local firms, despite its lower value in Chinese culture. At first, both Chinese customers and employees found the customer greetings ceremonies 'strange' and alien, even 'too polite'. This even stimulated historical anti-Japanese feelings, often linked to the Second World War, and Chinese employees did not fully internalize such values. In China, firms felt the need to make many more rules than in Japan, and codified knowledge which was mostly left implicit in Japan, not trusting Chinese workers to 'naturally' show good service, unlike Japanese employees. This value was reinforced with warnings and fines (though Chinese workers resisted bag searches, unlike Japanese ones, who found it normal practice). As in Japan, the firms tried to offer job security for core, regular employees, but Chinese staff showed 'less loyalty', often leaving for higher salaries and promotion. Japanese companies, unlike Chinese ones, also relied more extensively on internal labour markets for promotion as in Japan, but at a faster pace than in Japan. They found that 'promoting by cohort', the Japanese approach, invited other companies in China to poach staff if they did not experience rapid promotion.

There were also other notable differences in China from Japanese practice. Far fewer part-time staff were used, perhaps because of lower Chinese wages; and patriarchal management of male supervisors over female staff was less common in China, in accordance with the less 'masculine' Chinese culture. Many managers and supervisors in China were female, often judged by the companies as better workers. Unlike in Japan, where the norm is for women to leave full-time work on marriage or motherhood, women's full-time employment is promoted in China by nursery provision and grandparent proximity. Companies also often found it hard to replicate Japanese parent-country graduate recruitment schemes, as staff often left quickly, in some cases to Wal-Mart (see Case Study 11.1). Pay systems and sanctions were more explicitly stressed in China, especially performance-related pay, partly due to a lack of trade union opposition in China. Seniority pay was also less commonly used in China, but performance-related pay was more frequently used.

In conclusion, Gamble (2010: 728) claims culturalist explanations

> are shown to be inadequate, individually, to account for the complex patterns of transfer, local adoption, and adaptation in these multinational companies. These findings highlight the value of conceptual bricolage and multi-level analysis for developing explanations that can encompass and explicate complex patterns of hybridization.

In contrast, context-specific, firm-level perceptions of sources of competitive advantage are key motives for transferring practices, though these are constrained by the practices and cultural norms prevalent in local labour markets. Cultural explanations often 'leave us with static, overly homogenized, and over-determined models' which 'neglect the extent of sub-national diversity' (Gamble 2010: 711–2) and 'transfer by multinational companies to transitional economies with high levels of deinstitutionalization illustrates problematic dimensions for various theoretical perspectives' (ibid: 705) not just 'culturalist' explanations, but also institutionalist ones such as national business system explanations (see Chapter 12).

The claim here is that it is increasingly difficult, given rapid change in a dynamic, deinstitutionalizing environment, to identify a recognizable Chinese model of work culture, organization and employment practice, and that various forms of hybrid practice exist. Vo and Hanif (2013) make similar observations with respect to Vietnam.

PIT STOP: REFLECTIVE ACTIVITY 11.11

(based on Iles 2013b: 227–228)

1. Where would you place these Japanese firms?
2. To what extent do these cases show examples of 'hybrid' HRM practices?
3. To what extent are they transferring 'Japanese' practices? To what extent are they local 'Chinese' ones?
4. Do you expect any 'reverse diffusion' of practices back to Japan?

Emphasizing the adaptation of organizations to their societal and cultural (particularly institutional) environments and that the global diffusion and adoption of practices downplays the role of national cultural and institutional differences, such practices are locally interpreted or translated as they diffuse (Czarniawska and Joerges 1996; Iles and Yolles 2002a, 2002b, 2003, 2004; Yolles and Iles 2006). There may be diffusion of a common global language, such as 'empowerment' or 'customer service', but some leeway is left for local interpretation and practice.

For example, consider a global company with espoused cultural values such as impact, customer service, and networking. In some countries 'good customer service' may be signified by the use of first names; in others, hierarchical or job titles. In some 'networking' may signify playing golf with key contacts, in others, joining chambers of commerce, attending sports events or beach barbecues or joining local officials in karaoke and banquets. 'Impact' may signify participative leadership styles in some countries, authoritative direction in others. An over-socialized view of actors leaves little scope for agency in the role actors play as interpreters, synthesizers and hybridizers in the local interpretation and implementation of globally diffused practices.

Such *cultural hybridism* is also found in Latin American organizations; HRM practices within Latin America differ, and the unique context companies operate in needs to be considered, such as 'economic and political instability, the role of the enterprise as a social institution, and the value of the individual within the society' (Davila and Elvira 2009: 8). These authors argue (2009: 3) in contrast that many Latin American organizations have developed a hybrid HRM model combining 'Human Resource Management practices responsive to global competition and traditional Latin American practices derived from cultural work values', challenging traditional 'universal' HRM models (see Chapter 3) as only offering partial explanations in a region where 'multiple contextual elements challenge the use of a single theoretical view' (2009: 182). One example of a hybrid approach to HRM is shown by the small Salvadorean pharmaceutical company Grupo San Nicolas, which also operates in Guatemala, Nicaragua and the Dominican Republic; it illustrates the importance of close family and small group relationships, acceptance of power distance and low tolerance of uncertainty in much of Latin America (Leguizamon et al. 2009). This has influenced the leadership style of the CEO, who adopted locally appropriate practices that put people at the centre of strategy, such as benevolent paternalism, including visits and assistance after a major earthquake, and specific employee benefits such as discounts, educational family scholarships, free medical examinations and group reading sessions, alongside such 'universal' practices as connecting employees with the business, communication, and encouraging intrinsic motivation.

PIT STOP: REFLECTIVE ACTIVITY 11.12

1. How would you use Hofstede (2001) to explain some of the phenomena encountered in Case Study 11.1?
2. Can you point to any examples of:

   i a transfer of policies and practices from HQ?
   ii the adaptation of policies and practices to local culture?
   iii cultural hybridization?

Another illustration of the need for this is shown in the case of international mergers and acquisitions and other kinds of alliances, where both organizational and national culture play key roles.

The role of organizational and national culture in international mergers and acquisitions

In international alliances, two or more firms enter into a formal or informal agreement without fusing; in an *international joint venture*, two or more 'parent' firms create a separate 'infant' entity; in an *international merger or acquisition* or *IM&A*, two or more separate firms fuse to become one entity. Organizations increasingly use IM&As to gain access to new global markets and resources, such as technology, skills and talents (e.g. BP and Amoco, Daimler-Chrysler, Tata-Jaguar-Land Rover etc.). Rover and Honda entered into an alliance in the 1990s, and subsequently BMW acquired Rover. Such resources may be too expensive, or take too long, to acquire, or be impossible to develop internally. In some countries, partnerships and alliances with locals may be the only, or best, way to enter a market, as was the case for many years in China.

We will first look at IM&As before looking at alliances and joint ventures.

PIT STOP: REFLECTIVE ACTIVITY 11.13

(based on Iles 2013c: 108)

1. Look up the following websites on IM&As.
2. Why do you think organizations are increasingly using IM&As?
3. What kinds of problems, especially cultural problems, might they often encounter?
4. What cultural problems can you see in Case Study 11.1?

The Institute of Mergers, Acquisitions and Alliances at http://www.imaa-institute.org/; http://www.imaa-institute.org/statistics-mergers-acquisitions.html; and http://www.imaa-institute.org/publications-studies-mergers-acquisitions-alliances.html?PHPSESSID=6d6f1cafebb1fb754537b449c93e6451

The 'acquisition of organizations, and the coming together of two or more organizations to form a new entity (often from different countries) is becoming increasingly common in a more global, competitive business landscape' (Iles 2013c: 108). Sometimes the acquired business continues as a separate entity, with little initial change to its HR practices and with only gradual changes in structures, processes and personnel (e.g. Asda and Wal-Mart in Taylor 2005; see Case Study 11.1). Other mergers may involve changes, including changes to HR practices, that may be much more dramatic and rapid. In IM&As two or

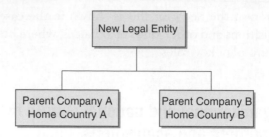

Figure 11.3 An international merger or acquisition
Source: Adapted from Iles (2013c: 109).

more companies agree to join their operations together to form a new company; in an international acquisition, one firm buys a controlling or full interest in another, with the buyer determining how the combination will be managed (Briscoe et al. 2012). Figure 11.3 shows the IM&A process.

Many mergers and acquisitions, as well as alliances and joint ventures, 'fail', in part because they did not take into account people issues and cultural differences between the two organizations. What can HRM do to mitigate such problems and help ensure a smoother merger process?

Institutional factors (see Chapter 12) may also play a part; Rees and Edwards (2009) discuss how these may slow or modify the merger integration process, e.g. the need for works council approval (see Chapter 8) in many EU countries. The 'orientation of a parent in a merger may affect the success of the IM&A – the country of origin effect. In addition, the way that HR issues are handled at local level may show a host-country effect' (Iles 2013c: 110). For example, the UK-based mobile phone company Vodafone – which has grown rapidly through IM&As – found considerable opposition when it acquired the German firm Mannesmann, because such activities are less acceptable in Germany. US, Japanese, French or German firms for example seem to handle HR issues very differently in IM&As; e.g. US firms often prefer 'formal and regular appraisals and a more forceful, hands-on approach to integration, whereas Japanese firms took a slower approach, and French firms tended to operate a system of formal qualifications for promotion and a glass ceiling for non-French managers' (Iles 2013c: 111).

Different approaches to IM&As

Some IM&As may practise a *portfolio* approach, where managers in both companies maintain autonomy; others may require *assimilation* into one culture assigned legitimacy. Some may try *blending*, mixing the best elements of both cultures; others will try to *create a new culture* derived from both parties. Mirvis and Marks (1992) refer to different kinds of post-merger outcome:

1. *Preservation* – here there is no cultural change in acquired company, which retains independence, autonomy and boundary protection.
2. *Absorption* – here there is a large cultural change for the acquired company, assimilating with the acquiring company.
3. *Transformation* – here there is cultural change in both companies to 'break with the past'/establish a new future.
4. *Best of both* – here there is selective combination of the 'best' features of both parties to form a 'merger of equals'.
5. *Reverse merger* – here the acquired company dictates terms.

Another classification framework refers to three main integration approaches (Schwieger et al. 1993); the higher the need for cultural integration, the higher the degree of change required in the organizational culture, identity and HR practices of the acquired company:

1. *Assimilation*: here one party (voluntarily or forced) adopts the identity, culture and practices of the other, replicating the dominant party's HR and other practices and culture as in 'absorption' above, perhaps generating culture clash, hostility and resistance to change, as we saw in Case Study 11.1 where Wal-Mart tried to impose its US-based approaches on the Argentinian worforce.
2. *Novation*: here the combined organization develops new working practices, culture and identity through cultural integration ('best of both' above) or through new and distinctive practices and culture ('transformation' above).
3. *Structural integration*: here units retain their own cultures and identities, as in 'preservation' above; though perhaps avoiding an initial cultural conflict, this may still emerge later.

Around one-third of IM&As are dissolved within a few months or years (Briscoe et al. 2012). It is often argued that cultural differences play a key role here. However, Pucik et al. (2011) argue that the fear of national cultural differences upsetting or derailing IM&As may be exaggerated – recent research has shown that cultural distance may have positive, as well as negative, effects on IM&A performance. Perhaps organizational cultural differences sensitise managers to the importance of culture in IM&As as opposed to domestic M&As, and provide opportunities for mutual learning.

A study of Finnish international acquisitions by Vaara et al. (2012) found that organizational and national cultural differences had different effects in

IM&As. Organizational cultural differences prompted 'social identity building', leading to 'us and them' thinking. The 'parties involved tend to develop a lack of trust and in-group vs. out-group biases, especially given ambiguous and uncertain futures' (Iles 2013c: 110). However, cultural differences can also contribute to helpful learning and knowledge transfer; *organizational cultural differences* may often be positively associated with social conflict, but *national cultural differences* can actually lead to a decrease in conflict, perhaps because of useful complementarities and synergies between the organizations involved (Vaara et al. 2012). In addition, both organizational and national cultural differences were here associated with *knowledge transfer*, implying that national cultural differences may be less of a problem in IM&As than often thought; 'organizational cultural differences may present more challenges to successful IM&As, and national cultural differences may be an asset or resource rather than a problem for organizations' (Iles 2013c: 110).

In Nigeria, 70 previously independent banks were merged to create 19 new banks, leading to large job losses and continued monitoring by the Central Bank of Nigeria (Gomes et al. 2012). Here, *regional* cultural differences were underestimated in many cases, especially those between the mainly Muslim north and the mainly Christian south, over issues like dress code, age of bosses/subordinates, closing times for prayers and regional origins of senior managers in the newly merged bank. Nine banks followed an *assimilation* approach, where one or more of the combined firms adopted – voluntarily or by coercion – the identity, name, culture and policies of one partner. Four however followed a *novation* approach, involving high levels of reorganization and restructuring and often renaming themselves to symbolize 'combining the best of all parties'. Here HRM policies and practices played a particularly important role in successful integration. Three mergers followed a *structural integration* approach, where the original banks maintained high levels of autonomy, identity and separateness. This seemed a particularly common approach when the merging banks came from both the north and south, so as to avoid or mitigate culture clashes. These banks often made extensive use of training and induction to set out a common shared vision and build mutual trust. Fear of job losses seemed to raise stress levels, in-group thinking and perceptions of regional cultural differences among employees, e.g. feelings of 'we're being marginalized or ignored'. Staff who were let go were often helped by the banks to find jobs elsewhere. HR themes emerging in successful mergers included the quality of HRM due diligence, the careful handling of regional cultural differences, the extent and quality of communications employed and the use of integration advisors to smooth the process of integration.

Leaders have a key role to play in culture change in mergers also. Kavanagh and Askanasy (2006) examined mergers between three large multi-site public-sector organizations. The success or otherwise of any merger hinged on individual perceptions about the manner in which the process is handled and the direction in which the culture is changed. Communication and a transparent change process are important, as this will often determine not only how a leader will be regarded, but also who will be regarded as a leader. Leaders need to be competent and trained in the process of transforming organizations to ensure that individuals within the organization accept the changes prompted by a merger.

Conclusion

At the beginning of this chapter we looked at various theories of organizational culture, and at different approaches and classifications (especially between the functionalist 'culture as variable' and the symbolist 'culture as metaphor' approaches). We also discussed the origins of organizational cultures, especially industry and leadership effects, and the consequences of cultures in terms of ethics and corporate performance, noting some problems in methodology and interpretation in many studies.

Gelfand et al. (2007) argue that the study of cross-cultural differences in the workplace 'has a long past but a short research history'. Hofstede, Lewis, Schwartz and Trompenaars among others have paved the way to an appreciation of cultural differences and their impact in a business setting, though 'not without criticisms, such as taking the nation as the unit of analysis, ignoring subcultures, perpetuating stereotypes, and downplaying change, instability and resistance' (Zhang and Iles 2013: 34). The 'valuing diversity' approach argues that cultural differences should be recognized as a resource and an asset for the organization. International mergers and acquisitions dealing with cross-cultural conflicts successfully can improve creativity, innovation and adaptiveness, enhance productivity and improve competitive advantage. It is vital that cultural theories are taken in their context and not applied to other levels for which they were not designed; they 'do not provide a complete analysis of national differences, but may complement other kinds of analysis, such as institutional approaches and national business systems approaches' (Zhang and Iles 2013: 34-35; see Chapter 12).

Later we explored in more detail the interaction of organizational and national culture in such areas as the transfer of HRM practices across organizational and national boundaries and the role of organizational and national culture in international mergers and acquisitions. Here both organizational and national culture play key roles, but also interact in often surprising ways.

Further Reading ■■■■■■■■■■■■■■■■■

Vignali, C. (2001) 'McDonald's: "think global, act local" – the marketing mix', *British Food Journal*, 103 (2): 97–111.

Vrontis, D. and Pavlou, P. (2008) 'The external environment and its effect on strategic marketing planning: a case study for McDonald's', *Journal of International Business and Entrepreneurship Development*, 4 (3/4): 289–307.

References _____

Adekola, A. and Sergi, B.S. (2007) *Global Business Management: A Cross-cultural Perspective*. Aldershot: Ashgate Publishing.

Ailon, G. (2008) 'Mirror, mirror on the wall: culture's consequences in a value test of its own design', *The Academy of Management Review*, 33 (4): 885–904.

Allaire, Y. and Firsirotu, M.E. (1984) 'Theories of organizational culture', *Organization Studies*, 5 (3): 193–226.

Allard, I.N. (2011) *Examining the Relationship Between Organizational Culture and Performance: Moderators of Culture Gap*. North Central University Dissertation, available at http://udini.proquest.com/preview/goid:749945161/?clickandtype=full, accessed 2 October 2013.

Alvesson, M. (1993) *Cultural Perspectives on Organizations*. Cambridge: Cambridge University Press.

Alvesson, M. (2002) *Understanding Organizational Culture*. Thousand Oaks, CA: Sage.

Alvesson, M. and Berg, P.O. (1992) *Corporate Culture and Organizational Symbolism*. Berlin: de Gruyter.

Alvesson, M. and Deetz, S. (2000) *Doing Critical Management Research*. London: Sage.

Anderson, N. and Herriott, P. (1997) *International Handbook of Selection and Assessment*. Minnesota: Wiley.

Anthony, P. (1994) *Managing Culture*. Buckingham: Open University Press.

Argyris, C. (1967) 'Today's problems with tomorrow's organizations', *Journal of Management Studies*, 4: 31–55.

Arogyaswamy, B. and Byles C.M. (1987) 'Organization culture: internal and external fits', *Journal of Management*, 13: 647–59.

Bagozzi, R., Verbeke, W. and Gavino, J.C. (2003) 'Culture moderates the self-regulation of shame and its effects on performance', *Journal of Applied Psychology*, 88: 219–33.

Balogun, J. and Hope Hailey, V. (2004) *Exploring Strategic Change*, 2nd edn. London: Pearson Education.

Balthazard, P., Cooke, R. and Potter, R. (2006) 'Dysfunctional culture, dysfunctional organization: capturing the behavioral norms that form organizational culture and drive performance', *Journal of Managerial Psychology*, 21 (8): 709–32.

Barney, J. (1986) 'Organization culture: can it be a source of sustained competitive advantage?', *Academy of Management Review*, 11: 656–65.

Barney, J. (1991) 'Firm resources and sustained competitive advantage', *Journal of Management*, 17 (1): 99–120.

Bass, B. (1985) *Leadership and Performance Beyond Expectations*. Cambridge, MA: Harvard University Press.

Bass, B. (1990) *Bass and Stodgill's Handbook of Leadership*. New York: Free Press.

Bass, B. and Avolio, B. (1993) 'Transformational leadership: a response to critiques', in M. Chemers and R. Ayman (eds), *Leadership Theory and Research: Perspectives and Directions*. San Diego, CA: Academic Press, pp. 49–80.

Bell, A. (2004) 'Case study 2: W. L. Gore and associates Inc: natural leadership', in G.C. Avery (ed.), *Understanding Leadership: Paradigms and Cases*. London: Sage, pp. 171–187.

Berger, P.L. and Luckmann, T. (1967) *The Social Construction of Reality: A Treatise in the Sociology of Knowledge*. Harmondsworth: Penguin Books.

Bird, A. and Fang, T. (2009) 'Cross-cultural management in the age of globalization', *International Journal of Cross Cultural Management*, 9 (2): 139–43.

Bond, M.H. (1988) 'Finding universal dimensions of individual variation in multicultural studies of values: the Rokeach and Chinese value surveys', *Journal of Personality and Social Psychology*, 55 (6): 1009–15.

Brewis, J. (2005) 'Othering organization theory: Marta Calás and Linda Smircich', *The Sociological Review, Special Issue, Contemporary Organization Theory*, 53 (Issue Supplement s1): 80–94.

Briscoe, D., Schuler, R. and Tarique, I. (2012) *International Human Resource Management: Policies and Practices for Multinational Enterprises*, 4th edn. London: Routledge.

Broms, H. and Gahmberg, H. (1983) 'Communication to self in organizations and cultures', *Administrative Science Quarterly*, 28 (3): 482–95.

Bryman, A. (1999) 'The Disneyization of society', *Sociological Review*, 47: 25–47.

Carmeli, A. and Tishler, A. (2005) 'Perceived organizational reputation and organizational performance: an empirical investigation of industrial enterprises', *Corporate Reputation Review*, 8 (1): 13–30.

Cassell, C. and Symons, G. (eds) (2004) *Qualitative Methods in Organizational Research*. London: Sage.

Certo, S.C. and Peter, J.P. (1988) *Strategic Management: A Focus on Process*. Homewood, Il: Irwin.

Chatman, J., Caldwell, D., O'Reilly, C. and Doerr, B. (2012) 'Organizational culture and performance in high-technology firms: the effects of culture, content and strength', available at http://faculty.haas.berkeley.edu/chatman/papers/Culture%20Paper_FINAL. pdf, accessed 4 June 2013.

Chehade, G., Mendes, D. and Mitchell, D. (2006) 'Culture change for the analytical mind', *Strategic Finance*, 87 (12): 11–15.

Chen, L.Y. (2004) 'Examining the effect of organization culture and leadership behaviors on organizational commitment, job satisfaction, and job performance at small and middle-sized firms of Taiwan', *The Journal of the American Academy of Business*, 5(1/2):432–43.

Chen, T.Y., Hwang, S.N. and Liu, Y. (2009) 'Employee trust, commitment and satisfaction as moderators of the effects of idealized and consideration leadership on voluntary performance: a structural equation investigation', *International Journal of Management*, 26: 127–41.

Collins, J. and Porras, J. (1997) *Built to Last: Successful Habits of Visionary Companies*. New York: HarperCollins.

Collis, J. and Hussey, R. (2003) *Business Research: a Practical Guide for Undergraduate and Postgraduate Students*, 2nd edn. Basingstoke: Palgrave Macmillan.

Coogan and Partners (2006) *HRM Guide*, available at www.hr-topics.com/wire-usa/ organizational-culture.htm, accessed 2 October 2013.

Cooke, R.A. and Lafferty, J.C. (1983), *Level V: Organizational Culture Inventory (Form I)*. Plymouth, MI: Human Synergistics.

Corbin, J. and Strauss, A. (2008) *Basics of Qualitative Research*, 3rd edn. Thousand Oaks, CA: Sage.

Czarniawska, B. and Joerges, B. (1996) 'Travels of ideas', in B. Czarniawska and G. Sevón (eds), *Translating Organizational Change*. Berlin: de Gruyter, pp. 13–48.

Dahl, S. (2004) *Intercultural Research: the Current State of Knowledge*, Middlesex University Discussion Paper No. 26. London: Middlesex University Business School. Available at http://papers.ssrn.com/sol3/papers.cfm?abstract_id=658202, accessed 13 November 2005.

Dandridge, T.C. (1983) 'Symbols function and use', in L.R. Pondy, P.J. Frost, G. Morgan and T.C. Dandridge (eds), *Organizational Symbolism*. London: JAI Press pp. 66-69.

Davila, A. and Elvira, M.M. (eds) (2009) *Best Human Resource Management Practices in Latin America*. London: Routledge.

Davis, S.M. (1984) *Managing Corporate Culture*. Cambridge, MA: Ballinger

Deal, T. and Kennedy, A. (1982) *Corporate Cultures: The Rites and Rituals of Corporate Life*. Reading, MA: Addison-Wesley.

De Brentani, U. and Kleinschmidt, E.J. (2004) 'Corporate culture and commitment: impact on performance of international new product development programs', *Product Innovation Management*, 21(5): 309–33.

Denison, D.R. (1984) 'Bringing corporate culture to the bottom line', *Organization Dynamics*, 13 (2): 5-22.

Denison, D.R. and Mishra, A.K. (1995) 'Toward a theory of organizational culture and effectiveness', *Organization Science*, 6 (2): 204–23.

Denison, T. (1996) 'What is the difference between organizational culture and organizational climate? A native's point of view on a decade of paradigm wars', *Academy of Management Review*, 21 (3): 619–54.

Dickson, M.W., Aditya, R.N. and Chokar, J.S. (2000) 'Definition and interpretation in cross-cultural organizational culture research: some pointers from the GLOBE research program', in N.N. Ashkanasy, C. Wilderom and M.F. Peterson (eds), *The Handbook of Organizational Culture and Climate*. Newbury Park, CA: Sage, pp. 447–64.

Driskell, G.W. and Benton, A.L. (2005) *Organizational Culture in Action a Cultural Analysis Workbook*. London: Sage.

Easterby-Smith, M., Thorpe, R. and Lowe, A. (2002) *Management Research: An Introduction*. London: Sage.

Eckardt, A. and Matthias, K. (2003) 'The internationalization of a premium car producer: the BMW group and the Rover case', in M. Freyssenet, K. Shimizu and G. Voplato (eds), *Globalization or Regionalization of European Car Industry?* Basingstoke: Palgrave, pp. 170–97.

Fleming, P. (2013) '"Down with Big Brother!" The end of "corporate culturalism"?', *Journal of Management Studies*, 50 (3): 474–95.

Gamble, J. (2010) 'Transferring organizational practices and the dynamics of hybridization: Japanese retail multinationals in China', *Journal of Management Studies*, 47 (4): 705–32.

Gammack, J.G. and Stephens, R.A. (1994) 'Repertory grid technique in constructive interaction', in C.M. Cassell and G. Symons (eds), *Qualitative Methods in Organizational Research: A Practical Guide*. London: Sage, pp. 72–90.

Garnett, J.L., Marlowe, J. and Pandy, S.K. (2008) 'Penetrating the performance predicament: communication as a mediator or moderator of organizational culture's impact on public organizational performance', *Public Administration Review*, 68(2): 266-281.

Gebler, D. (2006) 'Creating an ethical culture', *Strategic Finance*, 87: 28–34.

Gelfand, M.J., Erez, M. and Aycan, Z. (2007) 'Cross-cultural organizational behavior', *Annual Review of Psychology*, 5 (8): 479–514.

Gill, J. and Johnson, P. (2010) *Research Methods for Managers*. London: Sage.

Glaser, B. (1978) *Theoretical Sensitivity*. Mill Valley, CA: Sociological Press.

Gomes, E., Angwin, D., Peter, E. and Mellahi, K. (2012) 'HRM issues and outcomes in African mergers and acquisitions: a study of the Nigerian banking sector', *The International Journal of Human Resource Management*, 23 (14): 2874-2900.

Gordon, G.G. (1991) 'Industry determinants of organizational culture', *Academy of Management Review*, 16: 396–412.

Gordon, G.G. and DiTomaso, N. (1992) 'Predicting corporate performance from organizational culture', *Journal of Management Studies*, 29: 783–98.

Gordon, J. (1993) *A Diagnostic Approach to Organizational Behavior* (4th edn). Boston, MA: Allyn and Bacon.

Graetz, F., Rimmer, M., Lawrence, A. and Smith, A. (2006) *Managing Organizational Change*, 2nd Australasian edition. Milton, Queensland: Wiley.

Guba, E. G., & Lincoln, Y. S. (1994). Competing paradigms in qualitative research. In N. K. Denzin and Y. S. Lincoln (eds), *Handbook of Qualitative Research* (pp. 105–117). Thousand Oaks, CA: Sage.

Hall, E.T. (1984) *The Dance of Life: The Other Dimension of Time*. Garden City, NY: Anchor.

Handy, C. (1985) *The Gods of Management* London: Penguin Books.

Handy, C. (1993) *Understanding Organizations*. Harmondsworth: Penguin.

Harrison, R. (1972) 'Understanding your organization's character', *Harvard Business Review*, 4: 119–28.

Hatch, M.J. (1993) 'The dynamics of organizational culture', *Academy of Management Review*, 18 (4): 657–93.

Hoffman, R.C. (2007) 'The strategic planning process and performance relationship: does culture matter?', *Journal of Business Strategies*, 24: 1, 27-48.

Hofstede, G. (1980) *Culture's Consequences: International Differences in Work-related Values*. Beverly Hills, CA: Sage.

Hofstede, G. (1991) *Cultures and Organizations – Software of the Mind*. London: McGraw-Hill.

Hofstede, G. (1996) 'Riding the waves of commerce: a test of Trompenaars' "model" of national culture differences', *International Journal of Intercultural Relations*, 20 (2): 189–98.

Hofstede, G. (2001) *Culture's Consequences: Comparing Values, Behaviors, Institutions, and Organisations Across Nations*, 2nd edn. London: Sage.

Hofstede, G. (2011) 'Dimensionalising cultures: The Hofstede model in context', *Online Readings in Psychology and Culture*, Unit 2. 2 (1): 8.

Hofstede, G., Hofstede, G.J. and Minkov, M. (2010) *Cultures and Organizations – Software of the Mind*, revised 3rd edn. New York: McGraw-Hill.

Holden, N.J. (2002) *Cross-cultural Management: A Knowledge Management Perspective*. London: Prentice Hall.

Horwitz, F.M. (2012) 'Evolving human resource management in Southern African multinational firms: towards an Afro-Asian nexus', *International Journal of Human Resource Management*, 23 (14): 2938–58.

Iles, P.A. (2013a) HRM in Latin America, in P.A. Iles and C. Zhang *International HRM: A Cross-cultural and Comparative Approach* London: Chartered Institute for Personnel and Development, pp. 193–206.

Iles, P.A. (2013b) HRM in China, in P.A. Iles and C. Zhang (eds) *International HRM: A Cross-cultural and Comparative Approach*. London: Chartered Institute for Personnel and Development, pp. 223–238.

Iles, P.A (2013c) IHRM, Culture and Knowledge Flows in International Alliances, Joint Ventures, Mergers and Acquisitions, in P.A. Iles and C. Zhang (eds) *International HRM: A Cross-cultural and Comparative Approach*. London: Chartered Institute for Personnel and Development, pp. 107–23.

Iles, P.A. and Yolles, M. (2002a) 'Across the great divide: HRD, technology translation and knowledge migration in bridging the knowledge gap between SMEs and universities', *Human Resource Development International*, 5 (1): 23–53.

Iles, P.A. and Yolles, M. (2002b) 'International joint ventures, HRM, and viable knowledge migration', *International Journal of Human Resource Management*, 13 (14): 624–41.

Iles, P.A. and Yolles, M. (2003) 'International HRD alliances in viable knowledge migration and development: the Czech Academic Link Project', *Human Resource Development International*, 6 (3): 301–24.

Jackson, H.L. and Ones, D.S. (2007) 'Counterproductive leader behaviour', in S. Werner (ed.), *Managing Human Resources in North America: Current Issues and Perspectives*. London: Routledge, pp. 114–26.

Jackson, S.E. and Schuler, R.S. (2003) *Managing Human Resources for Strategic Partnership*, 8th edn. Cincinnati, OH: Southwestern.

Johnson, G. and Scholes, K. (1999) *Exploring Corporate Strategy*, 5th edn. Harlow: Prentice Hall Europe.

Kamoche, K. and Newenham-Kahindi, A. (2012) 'HRM and knowledge appropriation: the MNC experience in Tanzania', *International Journal of Human Resource Management*, 23: 2854–73.

Kaplan, R. and Norton, D. (1996) *The Balanced Scorecard*. Boston, MA: Harvard Business School Press.

Kavanagh, M. and Ashkanasy, N.M. (2006) 'The impact of leadership and change management strategy on organizational culture and individual acceptance of change during a merger', *British Journal of Management*, 17 (Supp 1): S81–S103.

Keesing, R.M. (1974) 'Theories of culture', *Annual Review of Anthropology*, 3: 73–97.

Kluckhohn, F.R. and Strodtbeck, F.L. (1961) *Variations in Value Orientations*. Evanston, IL: Row, Peterson.

Kotter, J.P. and Heskett, J.L. (1992) *Corporate Culture and Performance*. New York: MacMillan.

Kotter, J.P. and Heskett, J.L. (2011) *Corporate Culture and Performance*. New York: Free Press.

Lawrence, P.R. and Lorsch, J.W. (1967) *Organization and Environment*. Cambridge, MA: Harvard University Press.

Leguizamon, F.A., Ickis, J.C. and Ogliastri, E. (2009) 'Human resource practices and business performance: Grupo San Nicolas', in A. Davila and M.M. Elvira (eds), *Best Human Resource Management Practices in Latin America*. London: Routledge, pp. 85–96.

Lewis, R.D. (2000) *When Cultures Collide: Managing Successfully Across Cultures*. London: Nicholas Brealey Publishing.

Li, J. and Nimon, K. (2008) 'The importance of recognizing generational differences in HRD policy and practices: a study of workers in Qinhuangdao, China', *Human Resource Development International*, 2: 167–82.

Lincoln, Y.S. and Guba, E.G. (1985) *Naturalistic Inquiry*. Beverly Hills, CA: Sage.

Liu, S. (2003) 'Cultures within culture: unity and diversity of two generations of employees in state-owned enterprises', *Human Relations*, 56 (4): 387–41.

Matusitz, J. and Lord, L. (2013) 'Grobalization or glocalization of Wal-mart in the USA: a qualitative study', *Journal of Organizational Transformation and Social Change*, 10(1): 81–100.

Matusitz, J. and Palermo, L. (2013) 'The Disneyfication of the world: a grobalization perspective', *Journal of Organizational Transformation and Social Change*, 10 (3).

Matusitz, J. (2014) 'A giant retailer in Argentina: glocalization perspectives, *International Journal of Organizational Transformation & Social Change* (in press).

Martin, J. and Siehl, C. (1983) 'Organizational culture and counterculture: an uneasy symbiosis', *Organizational Dynamics*, 122: 52–64.

McSweeney, B. (2002) 'Hofstede's model of national cultural differences and their consequences: a triumph of faith – a failure of analysis', *Human Relations*, 55 (1): 89–118.

Mead, G.H. (1934) *Mind, Self, and Society*, edited by Charles W. Morris. Chicago, IL: University of Chicago Press.

Mead, R. (1994) *International Management: Cross-cultural Dimensions*. Oxford: Blackwell.

Meek, L.V. (1988) 'Organization culture – origins and weaknesses', *Organization Studies*, 9 (4): 453–73.

Mellahi, K. and Budhwar, P.S. (2006) 'Human resource management in the Middle East: emerging models and future challenges for research and policy', in P. Budhwar and K. Mellahi (eds), *Managing Human Resources in the Middle East*. London: Routledge, pp. 291–301.

Meyerson, D. and Martin, J. (1987) 'Cultural change: an integration of three different views', *Journal of Management Studies*, 24: 623–47.

Miah, M.K. and Bird, A. (2007) 'The impact of culture on HRM styles and firm performance: evidence from Japanese parents, Japanese subsidiaries/joint ventures and South Asian local companies', *The International Journal of Human Resource Management*, 18: 908–23.

Minkov, M. and Hofstede, G. (2012) 'Hofstede's fifth dimension: new evidence from the World Values Survey', *Journal of Cross Cultural Psychology*, 43 (1): 3–14.

Mirvis, P.H. and Marks, M.L. (1992) *Managing the Merger: Making it Work*. Englewood Cliffs, NJ: Prentice Hall.

Modaff, D.P., DeWine, S. and Butler, J. (2011) *Organizational Communication: Foundations, Challenges, and Misunderstandings*, 2nd edn. Boston, MA: Pearson Education.

Molinsky, A. (2007) 'Cross-cultural code-switching: the psychological challenges of adapting behavior in foreign cultural interactions', *Academy of Management Review*, 32 (2): 622–40.

Morgan, G., Frost, P.J. and Pondy, L.R. (1983) 'Organizational symbolism', in L.R. Pondy, P.J. Frost, G. Morgan and T. Dandridge (eds), *Organizational Symbolism*. London: JAI Press, pp. 3–38.

Moorhead, G. and Griffin, R.W. (2004) *Organisational behaviour: Managing people in organisations*, 7th edn. Boston: Houghton Mifflin Company.

Ngo, H.-Y. and Loi, R. (2008) 'Human resource flexibility, organizational culture and firm performance: an investigation of multinational firms in Hong Kong', *The International Journal of Human Resource Management*, 19: 1654–66.

Ogaard, T., Larsen, S. and Marnburg, E. (2005) 'Organizational culture and performance – evidence from the fast food restaurant industry', *Food Service Technology*, 5(1): 23–34.

Ogbonna, E. and Harris, L. (2000) 'Leadership style, organizational culture and performance: empirical evidence from UK companies', *International Journal of Human Resources Management*, 11 (4): 766–88.

O'Reilly, C., Chatham, C. and Caldwell, R. (1988) *People, Jobs and Organizational Culture*, Working Paper. Berkeley, CA: University of California.

O'Reilly, C.A., Chatman, J. and Caldwell, D.F. (1991) 'People and organizational culture: a profile comparison approach to assessing person-organization fit', *Academy of Management Journal*, 34: 487–516.

Ouchi, William G. (1981) *Theory Z: How American Business Can Meet the Japanese Challenge*. Reading: Addison-Wesley.

Parry, E. and Urwin, P. (2011) 'Generational differences in work values: a review of theory and evidence', *International Journal of Management Reviews*, 13 (1): 79–96.

Parry, K. and Proctor-Thompson, S.B. (2003) 'Leadership, culture and performance: the case of the New Zealand public sector', *Journal of Change Management*, 3: 376–99.

Payne, R. (1991) 'Taking stock of corporate culture', *Personnel Management*, July: 26–9.

Peters, T. and Waterman, R. (1982) *In Search of Excellence*. New York: Harper and Row.

Pettigrew, A. (1990) 'Two constructs in search of a role' in B. Schneider (ed.) *Organizational Climate and Culture*. Oxford: Jossey Bass.

Preece, D. and Iles, P. (2009) 'Executive development: assuaging uncertainties through joining a leadership academy', *Personnel Review*, 38 (3): 286–306.

Pucik, V., Evans, P., Björkman, I. and Stahl, G.K. (2011) 'Human resource management in cross-border mergers and acquisitions', in A.-W. Harzing and A. Pinnington (eds), *International Human Resource Management*, 3rd edn. London: Sage, pp. 119–52.

Pye, L.W. (1992) 'The Chinese approach to negotiating', *The International Executive*, 34 (6): 463–8.

Rai, T.S. and Holyoak, K.J. (2009) 'Moral principles or consumer preferences? Alternative framings of the trolley problem', *Cognitive Sciences*, 34 (2): 311–21.

Ravasi, D. and Canato, A. (2013) 'How do I know who you think you are? A review of research methods on Organizational Identity', *The International Journal of Management Reviews*, 15 (2): 185–204.

Ravasi, D. and Schultz, M. (2006) 'Responding to organizational identity threats: exploring the role of organizational culture', *Academy of Management Journal*, 49 (3): 433–58.

Rees, C. and Edwards, T. (2009) 'Management strategy and HR in international mergers: choice, constraint and pragmatism', *Human Resource Management Journal*, 19 (1): 24–39.

Reichers, A. and Schneider, B. (1990) 'Climate and culture: an evolution of constructs', in B. Schneider (ed.), *Organizational Climate and Culture*. San Francisco, CA: Jossey Bass, pp. 5–39.

Ritchie, J. and Spencer, L. (1994) 'Qualitative data analysis', in A. Bryman and Burgess (eds), *Analysing Qualitative Data*. London: Routledge, pp. 173–94.

Ritzer, G. (2005) *Enchanting a Disenchanted World*, 2nd edn. New York: Sage.

Rosenthal, F. and Yarshter, E. (eds) (1976) *Al-Biruni between Greece and India*. New York: Iran Center, Columbia University.

Rousseau, D. (1990) 'Normative beliefs in fund-raising organizations', *Group and Organization Studies*, 15 (4): 448–60.

Saffold, G.S. (1988) 'Culture traits, strength, and organizational performance: moving beyond "strong" culture', *Academy of Management Review*, 13: 546–58.

Schein, E. (1983) 'The role of the founder in creating organizational culture', *Organizational Dynamics*, 2: 13–28.

Schein, E. (1984) 'Coming to a new awareness of organizational culture', *Sloan Management Review*, 25: 3–16.

Schein, E. (1985) *Organizational Culture and Leadership*. San Francisco, CA: Jossey Bass.

Schein, E. (1986) 'Culture: the missing concept in organization studies', *Administrative Science Quarterly*, 41: 229–40.

Schein, E. (1990) 'Organizational culture', *American Psychologist*, 45 (2): 109–19.

Schein, E. (1992) *Organizational Culture and Leadership*, 2nd edn. San Francisco, CA: Jossey-Bass.

Schermerhorn, J.R., Hunt, J.G. and Osborn, R.N. (1994) *Managing Organizational Behavior*, 5th edn. New York: Wiley.

Schneider, B. (1987) 'The people make the place', *Personnel Psychology*, 40: 437–53.

Schneider, S. and Barsoux, J. (2003) *Managing Across Cultures*, 2nd edn. Harlow: Pearson Education Limited.

Schultz, M. (1994) *On Studying Organizational Cultures: Diagnosis and Understanding*. Berlin: DeGruyter.

Schwartz, S.H. (1990) 'Individualism-collectivism: critique and proposed refinements', *Journal of Cross Cultural Psychology*, 21: 139–57.

Schwieger, D.M., Csiszar, E.N. and Napier, N.K. (1993) 'Implementing cross-national mergers and acquisitions', *Human Resources Planning*, 16 (1): 53–70.

Siehl, C., & Martin, J. (1984) 'The role of symbolic management: how can managers effectively transmit organizational culture?' in J.G. Hunt, D.M. Hosking, C.A. Schriesheim and R. Stewart (eds), *Leaders and Managers,* pp. 227–269. New York: Pergamon Press.

Smircich, L. (1983) 'Concepts of culture and organizational analysis', *Administrative Science Quarterly*, 28 (3): 339–58.

Smith, P. (2002) 'Culture's consequences: something old and something new', *Human Relations*, 55 (1): 119–35.

Soderberg, A.M. and Holden, N. (2002) 'Rethinking cross-cultural management in a globalizing business world', *International Journal of Cross-cultural Management*, 2 (1): 103–21.

Sorensen, J.B. (2002) 'The strength of corporate culture and the reliability of firm performance', *Administrative Science Quarterly*, 47(1): 70–91.

Suliman, A.M.T. (2006) 'Human resource management in the Arab Emirates', in P.S. Budhwar and K. Mellahi (eds), *Managing Human Resources in the Middle East*. London: Routledge, pp. 59–78.

Taylor, S. (2005) *People Resourcing*, 3rd edn. London: Chartered Institute of Personnel and Development.

Trompenaars, F. (1997) *Riding the Waves of Culture: Understanding Diversity in Global Business*. London: McGraw-Hill.

Trompenaars, F. and Hampden-Turner, C. (2003) *Riding the Waves of Culture: Understanding Cultural Diversity in Business*. London: Nicholas Brealey Publishing.

Turner, B.A. (1971) *Exploring the Industrial Subculture*. London: Macmillan.

Vaara, E., Sarala, R., Stahl, G. and Björkman, I. (2012) 'The impact of organizational and national cultural differences on social conflict and knowledge transfer in international acquisitions', *Journal of Management Studies*, 49 (1): 1–27.

Vo, A. and Hanif, Z.N. (3013) 'The reception of Anglo Learning Styles in a transforming Society: the case of American companies in Vietnam', *The International Journal of Human Resource Management*, 24 (18): 3534–3551.

Wells, D.L. (2003) 'The relationship between employee-organisation cultural fit and organisational performance', Doctoral Dissertation, Retrieved from Proquest, UMI Number 3109819.

Wilderom, C., Glunk, U. and Maslowski, R. (2000) 'Organizational culture as a predictor of organizational performance', in N. Ashkanasy, C. Wilderom and M. Peterson (eds), *Handbook of Organizational Culture and Climate*. Thousand Oaks, CA: Sage, pp. 193–209.

Willmott, H.C. (1993) 'Strength is ignorance, slavery is freedom: managing culture in modern organizations', *Journal of Management Studies*, 30: 515–23.

Willmott, H.C. (2013) '"The substitution of one piece of nonsense for another": reflections on resistance, gaming and subjugation', *Journal of Management Studies*, 50 (3): 443–73.

Wu, M.Y. (2006) 'Hofstede's cultural dimensions 30 years later: a study of Taiwan and the United States', *Intercultural Communication Studies*, XV (1): 33–42.

Xiaoming, C. and Junchen, H. (2012) 'A literature review on organization culture and corporate performance', *International Journal of Business Administration*, 3 (2): 28–37.

Yolles, M. and Iles, P.A. (2006) 'Exploring public-private partnerships through knowledge cybernetics', *Systems Research and Behavioral Science*, 23: 1–22.

Zhang, C and Iles, P.A.(2013). 'National difference, culture and IHRM', in, P.A. Iles PA and Zhang C. (eds) *International Human Resource Management: A Cross-cultural and Comparative Approach*. London: Chartered Institute for Personnel and Development, pp. 19–34.

12

MANAGING IN A GLOBAL CONTEXT

Paul Iles and Kate E. Rowlands

Chapter Overview

The aim of this chapter is to review the management of people in an international context and the concept of strategic international HRM through considering research and theory and appropriate conceptual models in International HRM (IHRM). In addition, the implications for a global workforce and global HR practices will also be discussed. We will begin by considering a case study that we will draw upon at various points to illustrate some key principles in IHRM.

Learning Objectives

- **Critically analyse the changing impact of globalization on organizations, and especially on IHRM**

- **Critically evaluate the field of IHRM and different models and approaches to IHRM**

- **Identify approaches to international and comparative HRM**

- **Understand the IHRM policies of the international enterprise, and critically evaluate different approaches to and frameworks in IHRM, with particular reference to host country, country of origin, and firm effects**

- **Discuss the advantages and disadvantages of different orientations to IHRM, with particular reference to regiocentric approaches**

- **Consider and analyse some key theoretical perspectives on institutional theories and national business systems, with particular respect to employment relations and national vocational education and training systems**

- **Appreciate national differences in HRM policy and practice**

- **Evaluate the implications of the above perspectives for international HRM**

International HRM at Extronics China

Rob had been looking forward to his assignment with Extronics China, but soon he was returning to the UK. It had started badly, and then deteriorated. An English electronics engineer with an MSc looking for new challenges, he'd recently married Hilde, a German artist. At a conference Helen, a marketing manager for Extronics, a partner of many leading global pay TV operators, told him they wanted to develop Chinese operations, setting up a joint venture with Kaijun, a local businessman. Recruitment of an engineer was a high priority to enhance client confidence, but excellent marketing and interpersonal skills were also needed. A search firm Cathay Consulting began to look for a credible, technically competent engineer with experience and relevant management skills.

Rob applied and was interviewed; Helen was impressed with his background, initiative and skills. However, neither Rick nor Hilde spoke Chinese, and Hilde only limited English. Rob worked at headquarters for two months before becoming CEO, China. Work problems meant a late arrival, compressing the briefing by the consultant, a Canadian, Jeff, into one day. Jeff's wife – who also spoke no Chinese – took them round Shanghai, mainly to show them the shops, Western restaurants, and tourist sights. No briefing was given on the job itself; Rob was disappointed the expected car was not provided. Cindy, Cathay's resident consultant, had arranged an apartment, but Kaijun had decided that Rob should choose himself. Rob and Hilde seemed very tired, getting angry when told they would have to leave their apartment in a week. Rob was annoyed about house-hunting, transport, and having no time to settle in or relax before work took over. Kaijun thought Rob was turning out to be unsuitable; weren't there other more serious problems to address, such as investment licenses and relationships with government officials?

Rob was also concerned about the amount of administration, government bureaucracy, and the endless meetings and banquets; Hilde quickly stopped going as she did not enjoy them. Rob grew increasingly frustrated, wanting weekends free, something the consultants had promised in their briefings, but these were often taken up with official business. Kaijun began to feel his attitude and commitment were wrong; Hilde made little attempt to socialize.

Rob decided to leave both Extronics and China. Helen was concerned about losses and damage to her, and the company's, brand and reputation. What should she do?

For useful information on expatriation (Iles and Jiang 2013: 247), see:

www.expatexchange.com
www.relojournal.com
www.livingabroad.com
www.dialogin.com
www.brookfieldgrs.com

Source: author.

Introduction

The case highlights some of the key issues in IHRM and demonstrates the crucial importance of recruitment, selection, training, and culture and performance management in particular. The organizational and personal costs of poor selection, training and other HRM decisions may be significant, reducing organizational efficiency and affecting brand, company reputation and business development. We will explore this after first looking at what IHRM is and why it is important before going on to discuss the field and context of IHRM and various models of IHRM.

In the Extronics case you may have identified a number of issues and problems, such as:

- Language and cultural issues
- Expatriate and family adjustment issues
- Housing and welfare issues
- Compensation and living cost issues
- Job and organization issues
- Training and development issues
- Career and repatriation issues
- Performance management issues.

PIT STOP: REFLECTIVE ACTIVITY 12.1

1. So what is IHRM?
2. Why is its study important?
3. If possible, discuss these questions in pairs or a small group, and try to arrive at a consensus view.

Source: Adapted from Iles (2013a).

The field and context of international HRM

The differences between IHRM and domestic HRM lie less in the nature of the activities or functions involved in managing people globally – as with domestic HRM, these involve recruiting, selecting, training and developing, appraising and rewarding staff and in managing the employment relationship – and more with the country in which these activities are carried out and the types of staff involved (Dowling et al. 2008). Is HRM to be applied in the home (domestic) or host (local) country? Is it to be applied to parent-country nationals (PCNs) who are expatriates from the same country as the corporate HQ is located; or host-country nationals (HCNs) who are local staff; or third-country nationals (TCNs), staff from neither the home or host country?

━━━━━━━━━━━━━━ **PIT STOP: REFLECTIVE ACTIVITY 12.2** ━━━━━━━━━━━━━━

1. Look again at Case Study 12.1, and give examples of:

   i   PCNs

   ii   HCNs

   iii   TCNs

IHRM is concerned with the management of human resources in the different national contexts in which they operate. Such contexts are separated by time, distance and culture. There are a multitude of factors which influence HRM such as institutional issues, cultural differences and legislative practices (Harzing 2001b). The differences clearly affect the processes of people management within different nations and regions globally. There are a number of issues which face IHRM due to the cross-cultural nature of the function and cross-boundaries (see Chapter 11). Challenges of where HRM starts and finishes, universal issues of working towards a cohesive HRM perspective across the organization and professionalism and ethical considerations are also important. As companies become more international, there is also the demanding issue of how the human resource can be managed effectively through a difference of geographical sites and across cultures.

IHRM is also driven by the organization's approach to both international strategy and development. A key issue here is the supply of the human resource in terms of the management hierarchy and whether this supply can be consistent and sustained to ensure that global success is not threatened by an inadequate supply of international managers.

IHRM has come to the forefront of debate due to the velocity with which multinational corporations (MNCs) have developed in the last 20 years, driven predominantly through trade barriers being lifted and the impact of globalization. As used here, globalization refers to global interconnectedness and the global diffusion of organizational practices. In and of itself, globalization is not necessarily a monolithic or homogenizing force constraining local cultures to embrace norms, practices, and values; it does not necessarily erode local cultural arrangements altogether, but often results in 'hybrid' practices being adopted or 'cross-vergence' where subsidiaries do not necessarily converge with the HQ or completely diverge from it, but show a mix of global and local practices (Gamble 2010). For example, a US bank in Tanzania can meld some American practices such as performance-related pay with some more collectivistic African practices based on the concept of ubuntu or interconnectedness (Horwitz 2012; Kamoche and Newenham-Kahindi 2012; see

Chapter 2). A company from El Salvador can combine some 'global' HRM practices with more 'locally appropriate' ones such as a paternalistic or personalized leadership style (Leguizamon et al. 2009). A Japanese retail company in China may seek to transfer some 'Japanese' practices such as extensive use of an internal labour market and customer-service training, but reject others such as seniority-based pay as inappropriate for a more fluid Chinese labour market (Gamble 2010).

The management of people from varying cultures and diverse backgrounds gelled together in MNCs is often considered the essential glue for organizational success. In addition, there is also the concern over managing these differences in a cost-effective manner. The challenge here is whether the organization can successfully manage these cross-boundary differences while agreeing HR policies and practices in a way which is coherent throughout the company. HR practices must be sensitive to local factors and critical aspects of national difference, including cultural and institutional differences. There is also the consideration of exploiting the workforce across borders as it may be more cost-effective for an MNC to do so.

This international diversity involves other people management issues, including heightened risks and insecurities and the need for staff to engage more with local and national governments and act as envoys or ambassadors of the company, leading to a complex and challenging approach to human resource management on an international scale and how the effectiveness of such a complex system can lead to competitive advantage. It is often no longer apparent where the economic value lies, as much trade is now facilitated through technology such as email and the Internet, making it more difficult to locate its origin; employees pass initiatives and projects through sites via the Internet, as opposed to attributing it to a specific location. IHRM displays a greater emphasis on the management of diversity because it embodies a varied demographic make-up compared to that on a national level. In addition, there are clearly issues over managing such a multicultural workforce, as the shift from homogeneous societies to a heterogeneous employment world has led to other considerations, such as the increasing importance of ethnicity. The role of the state has also changed due to the influence of globalization; in Malaysia globalization has led to the transformation, if not the end, of the nation state in terms of managing global capital, yet the state still exists as a sociocultural space.

However, this issue, and the extent of globalization generally, can be overstated; there are few state-owned MNCs which operate free from national boundaries and work within the global economic rules (Ferner 1997). The majority of MNCs continue to have their key controls within the parent home country, such as assets, ownership of their employee base and sales (Edwards et al. 2005). The marketplace for IEs has changed from the traditional foundation of the US to becoming a more accessible route for other nations. Currently, there are some substantial international organizations which do not operate from the US operating in 'distinct national business systems' and incorporating their own methods of HRM practice and corporate governance (Morley and Collings 2004).

Multinationals predominantly include US–global firms, European–global firms and Japanese–global firms, though MNCs from the emerging economies such as China, India and Brazil are growing rapidly. For example, Latin American MNCs include the Mexican concrete producer CEMEX, the mineral company CVRD of Brazil, the auto parts company Alfa of Mexico, the Mexican telecoms company TELMEX, the Chilean wine company Concha y Toro, the Peruvian soft-drinks company Grupo Kola Real, and the Venezuelan state-owned oil company PDVSA (Elvira and Davila 2005; Davila and Elvira 2009). Chinese (e.g. the oil company SINOPEC) and Indian investment (e.g. the automobile manufacturer TATA) in Asia, Latin America, Europe, North America and Africa has grown enormously in recent years.

Models of IHRM

International orientation models

HRM was predominantly developed in the West as a distinctive approach to the management of people, process and practice to achieve organizational success within the marketplace, primarily based on the concept that people are human resources who need to be managed strategically to achieve competitive advantage (see Chapters 3 and 4).

According to Jansenns (2001) there are four main approaches to IHR, all reflecting managements' *orientation* to international management:

1. The *exportive approach*: HR best practices are exported from another country.
2. The *adaptive approach*: if the host country has a best practice of HRM that appears to be more efficient, then this process will be adopted.
3. The *integrative approach*, when a number of practices are adopted from various countries.
4. The *synergistic approach* where new HRM practices are formulated through recognizing and integrating approaches from the individual cultures involved.

These policy and practice decisions are adopted in a variety of methods and combinations within IEs; but the first two tend to be more frequently employed.

Another related and influential theory of IHRM is the approach of Perlmutter and Heenan (1979), who (building on Perlmutter 1969) noted that there are four main approaches used by MNCs towards internationalization and IHRM, in terms of how MNCs manage their employee base:

- **Ethnocentric**; the MNC operates predominantly from the parent country and key management and personnel are located within the parent country headquarters. The subsidiaries have little autonomy as strategic decisions are made at headquarters.
- **Polycentric**; the MNC treats the subsidiary as having a 'distinct national entity' with some control over their decision-making ability. These subsidiaries are usually managed by the host country locals or nationals who are rarely promoted to headquarters in the parent country.
- **Regiocentric**; this reflects a geographic approach of the multinational. Here personnel may move outside of their parent countries but normally within a set geographic area or region, such as Europe for example. Managers within these regions are not promoted to head office but often hold a greater autonomy within their field. For example, the Japanese car giant ABCar (pseudonym) has established regional headquarters in several locations, including North America, Europe and most recently Thailand for the Asia Pacific region, seeking to 'regionalize' the staff composition at regional headquarters by drawing on staff from throughout the region (Preece et al. 2013).
- **Geocentric**; the MNC approaches its operation robustly, nationality is not considered, and worldwide success and ability are key for all. There is recognition here of the unique contributions made by each sector of the business. The staffing and managerial positions are available to any key person who demonstrates the skill and capability to perform at a high level and there are no limits as to where they live and work in this respect.

PIT STOP: REFLECTIVE ACTIVITY 12.3

1. What are the advantages/disadvantages of these orientations?
2. Remember that no option is without disadvantages, for the company or employee.

Source: Based on Iles (2013b).

Essentially, these perspectives all involve different advantages and disadvantages, especially trade-offs between global or local advantage, global learning, and integration or responsiveness (Perlmutter 1969). IEs seem to often retain distinctive features, often linked to 'country of origin' (Ferner 1997), despite the impact of globalization and pressures towards 'global convergence' sometimes held to reduce the importance of local contexts (Meyer et al. 2011). IEs need to exploit the differences and similarities in their multiple host locations; this is traditionally seen in terms of the need to balance *local responsiveness* with *global integration* within the overall IE structure (Bartlett and Ghoshal 1989).

Most research 'has focused on the design and implementation of global strategies and the management of the tension between global integration and local responsiveness' (Iles 2013b: 48). Rugman et al. (2011) argue that this fails to recognize the full complexity associated with the adaptation to local contexts – each subsidiary needs to reconcile both parent and local business interests, and different stages of the value chain in subsidiaries will vary in their position on an integration–responsiveness continuum. In practice, few companies pursue fully geocentric HR practices; as labour flows become increasingly intra-regional and cross-regional, does regionalization help firms pursue transnational strategies (Iles 2013b: 48)?

Strategic life-cycle models

These promote the view that HR practices are closely linked to either an organizational or product life cycle, relating IHRM choices to the overall strategy and development of the organization, especially in terms of organizational life cycle (see Chapter 2). Adler and Ghadar (1989) posit various stages in the development of an international organization: *domestic*, *international*, *multinational* and *global*, with implications for the management of personnel from one phase to the other. The first stage, domestic, is concerned with focusing on the home market and exporting outwards. At this point, there is no real cultural impact as the management of the company acts from a primarily ethnocentric perspective and there is no immediate push for considerations of foreign cultures because the company performs predominantly from the home market. This approach may be somewhat arrogant, permitting foreigners to buy 'our product' but not becoming influenced by their culture.

The second phase, international, focuses on the transfer of learning and local responsiveness (Scullion 2005); very different from the first domestic stage because cultural differences in foreign markets play a greater part in securing external relationships within the global marketplace. At this stage, the production, marketing and manufacturing of products in terms of style, product and preference are focused on key markets to ensure success. This approach emphasizes polycentric aspects; Scullion (2005) points out that production is often moved to the relevant country to facilitate these influences.

In the third phase, multinational companies focus on the product becoming globalized to ensure that prices can be kept to a minimum as a form of competitive advantage (Chen 2008). Price is a key issue here; whereas cultural influences play a major part in the international phase, price and lowering costs are key to production within this phase. There is some influence from an internal perspective of global diversity in this phase.

In addition to price and cost advantage on world markets, the final global stage involves quality; the product must be adapted to individual market tastes, styles, designs and specific niche markets in order to be successful. Here cultural sensitivity is imperative, both externally and internally. Adler and Ghadar (1989) move on to outline the relevant skills that may be required for the managers at each of these stages and the links between HRM and strategy.

Evans and Lorange (1989) discuss how a corporation operating in different product markets and diverse sociocultural environments can effectively establish human resource policies, proposing two logics for developing HRM policy on an international scale: product–market logic and sociocultural logic.

According to Evans and Lorange, the different phases of the product life cycle each require a very different type of manager. For example, 'cost-conscious' management may be appropriate at the maturity stage of the life cycle, yet not at the 'emergent' stage. Key skills such as entrepreneurial skills may be crucial at the emerging business stage but of less benefit at the maturity stage. Recruitment and selection, performance appraisal and reward also differ at each stage of the life cycle. Variance in product–market combinations forms part of the specific criteria for an MNC; a very complex approach to HRM. In addition, the two logics model also incorporates a suggestion that managers be allocated into different units, such as corporate, divisional and business unit levels.

Sociocultural logic assumes that an organization operating in various geographic locations, cultures and regions takes staff from differing cultural backgrounds and allocates them to different parts of the business (Minbaeva 2005), leading to a diverse workforce. Evans and Lorange (1989) devised two strategies for managing such cultural diversity. The first, the global approach, coincides with the work of Perlmutter's ethnocentric approach: the organization's culture dominates, so that HRM practices remain standardized and centralized. HRM policies remain uniform, involving 'one approach for all', particularly in terms of recruitment and selection, training and development and promotion. The second strategy, the polycentric approach, involves the responsibility for HRM practice being decentralized, often sitting with subsidiaries. There may be some guidelines directed from the central unit, but generally subsidiary sites are free to interpret HRM in a way that fits or suits their needs, regardless of country or geographic location. In addition, adaptation to the local culture is paramount, and the decentralized approach gives subsidiaries even more scope and potential to take advantage of the market. This approach does not facilitate staff development and movement around the business; as subsidiaries become more influenced by local cultures there is less scope for developing employees who wish to geographically move within the organization.

In addition, Bartlett and Ghoshal (1989) highlight approaches to IHRM on a continuum, with multidomestic at one end phasing through to the transnational solution at the other (which does arguably have similarities to the geocentric approach as described by Ferner 1997). The transnational company is also related to the two logics discussed previously by Evans and Lorange.

Integrative models

Within all the models discussed above it appears that the key to MNC operational success is offering flexible working processes; HRM practices must facilitate the needs of the business to enable the change processes to excel and respond efficiently to demands. DeCieri and Dowling (1989) focus on the international concerns of the MNC, with specific concern for HRM practices which influence strategic activities. The four components involve *exogenous factors, endogenous factors, strategic HRM* and *IE concerns and goals*. The exogenous factor is concerned primarily with the importance of interorganizational relationships and the benefits of these for trade. The endogenous factors include the structure of the IE, entry modes and strategic influence, which in turn link to strategic HRM policies and practices. Exogenous factors have direct influence on the endogenous factors, including SHRM factors as well as IE goals and concerns. The four elements operate in an integral manner, influencing each other to provide an efficient operation. One notable aspect of this model is the effect of strategic HRM on organizational strategy, as this enhances achievement of goals and objectives.

Taylor et al. (1996) identify a specific system for managing people within the framework of the MNC in terms of distinct activities, processes and people management functions aimed at attracting, developing and sustaining the working human resources of the MNC. They also integrate the various HRM systems adopted between the parent and host so that they work in unison to coordinate and control all the people management processes, with the root of the company acting as the dominant element, that is, the parent.

In comparison, Schuler and Tarique (2007) define IHRM models in terms of *outcomes*. The foundation for IHRM lies with one definitive objective for the multinational: to gain a competitive advantage through the management of its people and resources on a global scale. This model demonstrates a clear driver in that the outcome is competitive advantage and success for the organization on a global scale. However, the model fails to consider that the key to success for an MNC can be defined as 'competitive, efficient throughout the world; a locally responsive and flexible business which is adaptable within the

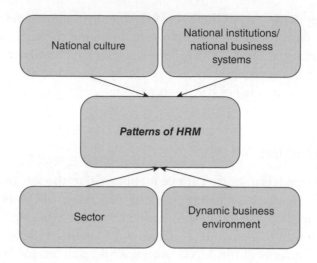

Figure 12.1 International HRM

Source: Adapted from Budhwar and Debra (2001: 6) and Iles (2013b: 44).

short periods of time to a changing environment; and capable of transferring knowledge and learning across globally dispersed units'.

Several features of different HRM models can exist within the same organization, largely dependent on culture and institutions and the distinct nature of the labour market. HRM is concerned with the management of all employment relationships within an organization (see Chapter 8), including all levels of the hierarchy. Budhwar and Sparrow (2002) developed a framework for examining cross-national HRM practices with three main groups of factors: national factors, contingent variables and organizational strategies. Figure 12.1 illustrates this model of international HRM.

- **National factors**: national institutions, commercial sectors and vibrant business environments, which are influenced by national culture.
- **Contingent variables:** include the age, size, nature, ownership and life cycle of the organization, the interests of various stakeholders, HRM practices and trade union presence.
- **Organizational strategies**: policies related to primary HRM functions and the internal labour market (Porter 1985).

Factors determining cross-national HRM practices

Case Study 12.2 helps to illuminate some of these issues and the usefulness of these models.

IHRM challenges in establishing new subsidiaries

FoodCo are a dominant market leader in the food retail sector in Malaysia and have already established over 15 different sites throughout Malaysia. Historically, the company originated in the UK and has since expanded rapidly trading in over 20 countries in total. The expansion has been mainly focused across Europe; however within the last five years FoodCo has gained access to Malaysia, Thailand, and China and also trades as IndeCo in India. As a result of this expansion, the MNC has found it essential to establish head offices in each of the newly appointed countries, so outside of Europe there are a further four central head office bases. This has led to numerous issues for the company, as predominantly London acts as the main focal point for managerial decisions and initiatives throughout Europe. However, as the countries based in Asia Pacific vary much more in terms of language, religion and culture it has been imperative that local offices were established to manage these operations more closely. Being a food retailer the company has also experienced many issues with the product itself, as eating habits, dietary requirements and localized traditions are extremely varied between the Asia Pacific countries by contrast with Europe. As a result, turnover and market penetration have been a struggle for the company because the brand is less known within the countries and locals are wary of trying new foreign brands when it comes to food: also the concept of the supermarket is less familiar. Some market research data have identified that the shopping habits of customers within these regions are very different, as they generally prefer an 'open marketplace' concept. The climate has also influenced shopping habits, as customers are more likely to buy fruit and fresh local products in both their summer and winter months, whereas Europeans during the summer months are prone to buy ice creams and frozen processed products.

As a result, FoodCo decided the company had to get back to 'traditional values', creating a delicate balance between the simultaneous need for centralization and decentralization, and tapping into local expertise, knowledge and experience. FoodCo has attempted to launch more localized initiatives within this geographical area through their recruitment and selection policies, launching an initiative in 2010 called 'Grow your own'. Although much of the senior management team within these countries are expatriates from the UK, the company promoted the need for local talent to be sought through a large-scale recruitment drive. Much of the workforce within the stores were local people who spoke their national language but through this initiative they were exposed to intense training to help identify potential managers and also improve their understanding of the company, brand and expectations of their employer.

Over 45 management trainees were identified, and the company then invested further in these individuals to encourage progression through the ranks. They also encouraged these selected individuals to travel between sites for training to demonstrate the scope and nature of the business across stores, distribution centres and shopping malls. The retention for the programme has so far been over 90 per cent, and a recent staff morale survey carried out across the four countries illustrates that there are many more staff now wishing to progress with the company, and new recruits are joining with the objective of progression and development.

Initially there were some concerns from the hierarchy in the UK head office in terms of whether local nationals could perform these roles to the standard required. This was challenged by again offering UK managers the opportunity to work abroad and support a cross-cultural training programme. It has been key that the UK staff have been involved in the integration of

(Continued)

(Continued)

the new subsidiaries and that they are seen as part of the company as a whole, and not separate entities operating different standards.

The objective now within the company is how they can sustain the growth of their organic management team and how they will continue to attract and also retain talented staff. FoodCo were one of the first retailers to venture into these four countries as a food retailer with the concept of the supermarket, and their goal is to be as big in these countries as they are in the UK. Yet they face fierce competition from new MNCs wishing to adopt their footprint. In addition, local people have resisted the influences of such MNCs in the belief that they will ruin the village environment with its vibrant local marketplace and force bland, Westernized glass buildings into their idyllic landscape. The question here is how will FoodCo maintain and continue to build and expand within such countries with such local resistance?

Source: author.

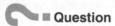 ■ **Question**

1. What main issues, tensions or challenges does this case throw up for IHRM?

Porter (1985) initially linked HR strategies to the three key elements of management strategy, arguing that the use of human capital could be effectively managed if the HR policy was closely linked (see Chapter 3). Huselid (1995) argued that it was not one particular HR policy which aligned to provide a benefit to HRM, but rather a 'bundle of internally consistent HR practices' each with its own underlying logic. Dess and Davis (1984) carried out an extensive study of manufacturing industry which determined that HR and corporate strategy were both structured around typologies and configurations to form an approach to gain competitive advantage. Welch (1994) examined the cross-national function of HRM practices, developing a contingency theory based on an in-depth study of four comparative case studies in Australia, identifying variables which determined the generic functions of specific HRM practices such as recruitment and selection, development and training and compensation and reward, all centred around the expatriation and repatriation of overseas employees (Budhwar and Sparrow 2002). The variables include three elements: contextual, such as the host country legal system; firm-specific, such as the type of industry and culture; situational, such as staff availability and localization issues.

Rowley (1998) suggested that HRM in context is largely influenced by these factors. Khatri (1999) argued that the economic crisis in Asia Pacific in the late 1980s speeded up the process of HRM adoption and influenced the shape of HR policies, from jobs for life and priority given to seniority to contract-based employment and performance-related pay schemes (Sparrow 2002). Hendry and Pettigrew (1992) also suggest that the impact of a dynamic business environment can shape and change the format and direction of emphasis on the HR function.

There are then three areas for examination within IHRM:

1. The influence of factors such as culture and national institutions (see Chapter 11).
2. The variables influencing HR policy and practices, such as the age, size and life cycles of the organization.
3. HR policy/HR strategy – the cost reduction, talent acquisition/improvement, defender strategies for example (see Chapter 3).

Understanding the IHRM policies of the international enterprise

We can use these models in an attempt to understand the IHRM policies of the IE. Internationalization and the effective use of international human resources located outside the home or parent country are major issues affecting enterprises in an increasingly global economy. A key issue is why and how enterprises adopt different HRM policies and practices in such areas as recruitment and selection, training, talent management and career development.

PIT STOP: REFLECTIVE ACTIVITY 12.4

1. What do you think are the main issues affecting enterprise IHRM policy?

An integrative model for studying IHRM at the enterprise level has been put forward by Shen et al. (2005). This tries to move forward from a single factor focus on factors associated with IHRM policy and practice, such as contextual factors, e.g. the well-known Political, Economic, Social, Environmental and Legal (PESTEL), or firm-specific factors such as international strategy, structure, culture, stage of internationalization, mode of internationalization, size, sector, reliance on international markets, top managers' perceptions, or ownership type (see Figure 12.2).

We have adapted this framework to draw particular attention to a firm's international orientation, which is linked to the balance between

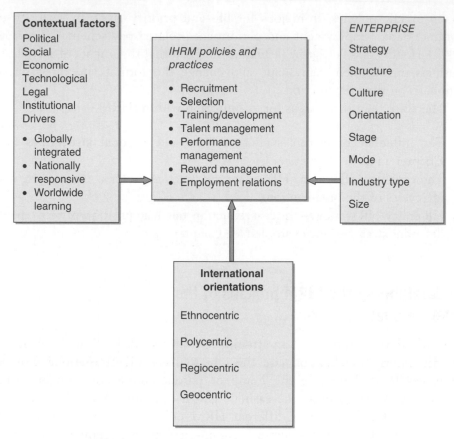

Contextual factors	IHRM policies and practices	ENTERPRISE
Political Social Economic Technological Legal Institutional Drivers • Globally integrated • Nationally responsive • Worldwide learning	• Recruitment • Selection • Training/development • Talent management • Performance management • Reward management • Employment relations	Strategy Structure Culture Orientation Stage Mode Industry type Size

International orientations

Ethnocentric

Polycentric

Regiocentric

Geocentric

Figure 12.2 An integrative IHRM framework

Source: Based on Shen et al. (2005: 373); Budhwar and Debrah (2001), Iles (2013b: 45).

HCNs, PCNs and TCNs (Perlmutter 1969) and life-cycle stage (Bartlett and Ghoshal 1989).

There is empirical evidence for the influence of all of these factors; for example, Shen et al. (2005) found that Chinese companies were affected by all the contextual factors outlined in Figure 12.2. Political factors influenced whether such companies set up operations in a particular country; Hong Kong and Western Europe were seen as relatively safe and stable, for instance. HR policies for Chinese PCNs took account of Chinese values such as respect for age, hierarchy, and 'face'; but morality and peer opinion contributed less to HCN recruitment and appraisal than they did back in China. For HCNs, experience and technical criteria were more influential. Companies did not feel they could transfer local 'Chinese' domestic HRM policies to foreign affiliates, partly because they saw these as socioculturally based within a specific Chinese context, and partly because they saw them as inefficient, and not sufficiently market-oriented! However, political and cultural factors within China limited their ability to change such practices in China itself. Similarly Gamble (2010) found that Japanese retail companies might introduce HRM practices such as more rapid promotion or performance-based pay into their Chinese operations, but found it more difficult in Japan itself due to cultural and legal restrictions.

Economic and legal factors (e.g. local pay rates, legal restrictions) also affect whether the company uses PCNs or HCNs for different positions (Iles 2013b). Firm-specific factors include the firm's international strategy, structure, organizational culture (see Chapter 11) and stage/mode of internationalization which all affect HRM, especially the degree to which domestic HRM policies are transferred or localized to the foreign affiliate. 'Power culture' organizations may be more likely to centralize their management of affiliates than 'role culture-based' ones (Iles 2013b: 46). Firms new to internationalization may use more PCNs; industrial sector type also has an influence, as firms in multi-domestic industries like trading and shipping companies often rely more on PCNs than global industries like electronics, which are more likely to use HCNs. Ownership is now less of an issue for Chinese companies; even state-owned enterprises often now report low interference from government.

─────────────── **PIT STOP: REFLECTIVE ACTIVITY 12.5** ───────────────

1. In Case Study 12.1, what are the advantages/disadvantages of using:

    i   A PCN?
    ii A HCN?
    iii A TCN?

It is important to note that the extent to which the factors identified in Figure 12.2 influence IHRM differs, and that such influence can vary over time. Reliance on international markets may have more influence than labour costs for some companies, but not others with a greater reliance on domestic markets. Some factors may also affect some functions of IHRM more than others; the political, legal and economic environment or the firm's overall international strategy may have a bigger impact on staffing and reward practices than training and development practices, for example, as these may be more affected by the local sociocultural environment.

As noted by Jackson and Schuler (2000), it is now accepted that HRM practices are not globally unique but are socially constructed in individual societies. Horwitz (2012) points out that wherever a business is based and wherever a business employs people, there are understandings that exist for this company to become successful in the marketplace, such as offering the workforce a safe environment to work and a place to thrive and develop with fair and competitive remuneration packages. MNCs must consider different cultures and perspectives of leadership and working for an organization while at the same time working across varying locations and time zones. Other challenges include the decision of when and where to be global and when to be local with limited 'face time' with employees across the organization who demand leadership, communication and inspiration (Doz 1986).

In order for the MNC to become a success both locally and globally there is the need to 'capture skills and expertise from different parts of the corporation and transfer the benefits' (Ferner and Edwards 1995). The strategy for IHRM employs both a local and global context, and the issue faced by the MNC is to challenge and motivate employees to drive the organization forward from a local perspective globally (Bartlett and Ghoshal 1989).

Three variables influence the employee on a local level while working towards achieving the bigger picture on a global level. The first of these is rooted in the psychological contract (see Chapter 13) that an individual will work more efficiently and offer greater loyalty to the multinational if they can identify with the organization, i.e. they will instinctively want to work at their best for the organization. Second, the emphasis placed on supervisory support for the individual is of paramount importance to an employee's motivation towards the organization. Finally, the individual's perceived access to the hierarchy despite nationality and location is critical to organizational identification and psychological bonding.

In contrast to people-based localization, there are also arguments which consider that it depends on the product of the MNC as to whether the company needs to localize. For Luo (2001), localization was considered in terms of three elements: structure, environment and organization. Structure can be divided into factors such as the market competition for the product and demand for the product. The environment would include a consideration of local business practice and culture, and how this could be adopted into the organization. Lastly, the organization element would include a consideration of market penetration of the product, the experience of the MNC within the host country and the understanding or ability to penetrate the local network. In addition, local government policies favourable to localization need to be considered.

As we have seen, one of the environmental/contextual factors in which IEs operate is the local institutional context, which influences many IE HRM policies and practices, as we will discuss shortly. We turn next to examining national differences in patterns of HRM using institutional theory and the concept of *national business systems*. This approach, analysing similarities and differences in HRM systems at the national or regional level, is often called *comparative HRM* (Iles 2013a).

Table 12.1

1. How is HRM structured in individual countries?
2. What HRM strategies are developed by organizations?
3. Do organizations implement such strategies?
4. What are the similarities and differences between HRM systems in different countries?
5. What are the reasons for the similarities and differences?
6. What is the influence of national factors such as culture, government policy and education patterns on national patterns of HRM?
7. Is HRM converging or diverging at a cross-national level?
8. To what extent are HRM models established in Western nations applicable to other parts of the world?

Source: Hendry (1996).

Comparative HRM

Institutionalized and national business systems approaches to employee relations and national HRD

According to Hendry (1996) there are specific questions which comparative HRM researchers pursue, as indicated in Table 12.1.

Institutional perspectives 'see firms and institutions as socially constituted, and reflecting national distinctiveness: dominant national institutions tend to be integrated and mutually reinforcing. National institutional arrangements tend to be robust, demonstrating significant inertia in the face of pressures for changes' (Iles 2013a: 5). Such approaches seek to establish a conceptual framework that allows the comparative study of different national business systems (NBS), allowing cross-country comparisons. As with cultural theories (see Chapter 11) this takes the 'nation' or 'region' as the key unit of analysis, but focuses on a broader range of institutional factors; specific contexts promote distinctive forms of business and market organization, influencing how companies operate (Ferner 1997; Tempel and Walgenbach 2007; Gamble 2010).

Institutionalist analyses focus on macro-level societal institutions, in particular those that govern 'access to critical resources, especially labour and capital' (Whitley 1999: 47), such as differences in the organization and activities of the state, the capital, labour and financial systems, and the route taken by different countries to industrialization and modernization. Lane (1992) for example distinguishes British financial versus German production-oriented capitalism; other approaches use the term 'varieties of capitalism' (Hall and Soskice 2001). These approaches tend to identify just two institutional solutions to coordination – 'liberal market economies' such as those of the US and UK and 'coordinated market economies' such as in Germany and Japan, broadly 'voluntarist' or 'interventionist'. This however misses out most of the world, not neatly fitting into either category! Italy (and many other Mediterranean countries) fit neither model (Baccaro and Pulignano 2011).

There are other approaches to NBS; for example Orru et al. (1997) distinguish 'alliance capitalism', with both horizontal flexibility and vertical efficiency facilitated by the state, as in Japan, from 'familial capitalism', where there are strong horizontal linkages but a comparatively weak state with fragmented interests and weak planning, as in Taiwan. 'Dirigiste capitalism', where there is an emphasis on vertical integration and state leadership, centralized planning and targeted capital flows, is also found, e.g. in South Korea. Nations pursuing such policies would appear on the interventionist (corporatist/centralized) pole. NBS is the term employed by Whitley (1999) in his analysis of such divergent capitalisms and the different paths taken by nations in terms of coordination and control; this is the term we will use here.

However, there are some differences in claims as to what the 'dominant social institutions' actually are; subsystems considered as a significant part of an NBS by some might be excluded by others (Iles 2013a: 6). Lane's framework (1992) for example consists primarily of the state, the financial system, and interestingly for our purposes the system of education and training; this institution we will explore in more depth. To a lesser extent, she also includes the network of business associations and the system of employee relations, which we will also discuss.

For Lane (1992) the most significant national institutions therefore are:

1. The state
2. The financial system
3. The network of business associations
4. The system of employment relations
5. Education and training systems, especially vocational education and training.

The state

This is particularly influential in shaping business systems, exerting both a direct and an indirect influence and shaping other institutional organizations (Lane 1992), such as education, finance, business associations and employment relations systems. Furthermore, the role of the state during industrialization, implementing and enforcing development policies and creating and maintaining a stable and supportive political and economic environment for enterprises, is crucial. German enterprises for example tend to have close relations with banks, insurance companies, and the state, with much evidence of cross-shareholdings and interlocking directorates. Greater commitment to union consultation and worker participation, employee training involving unions and extra-firm bodies such as employer associations, and employment security is also evident, termed 'Rhenish capitalism' by Albert (1993), or the social market model. The USA and UK in contrast give more emphasis to the market, to shareholder interests, and to flexibilty in labour markets.

The financial system

The financial system affects both the ability of the state to support and guide business development and the nature of enterprises' strategic business choices and risk management, as well as relations between banks and firms.

The network of business associations

National differences between associations such as trade associations or chambers of commerce in powers and breadth of functions and services affect enterprise strategy. For example, in Japan business networks link industrial, commercial, and financial firms in complex networks of relationships, creating stable, long-term relationships among them. On the contrary, in Britain, trade associations are not subject to uniform regulation, and often compete for membership. This situation results in lower membership, a less secure financial basis and a voluntarist position, inhibiting the width and depth of functions they are able to perform and leaving firms more institutionally isolated (Lane 1992).

The system of employment relations

National systems of employment relations influence business organization both through their structural relations and through underlying employer–employee relationships (Lane 1992). The strength of trade unions 'directly determines the role of unions in collective bargaining, the effectiveness of conflict resolution, the degree of flexibility in labour deployment, and the nature of negotiated bargains' (Iles 2013a: 7). The national system of employment relations ultimately constrains the strategic choices that enterprises can adopt (see Chapter 8).

Education and training systems, especially vocational educational training

The development and competitiveness of countries are influenced by the nature, scope and quality of their education and training system. There are major differences between nations in the organization and structure of formal educational institutions and their links to labour markets, with consequences for recruitment, promotion and training polices, as well as the division of labour (Lane 1992).

Whitley (1999) compared the role of the state in South Korea and Taiwan in economic development (see also Green et al. 1999; Walter and Zhang

2012). In South Korea, the state directly managed the dominant industrial networks, known as *chaebol*, through agencies and fiscal control (an interventionist position). *Chaebol* are financed by state banks and government-controlled trading companies. On the other hand, the Taiwanese government adopted a more US-style laissez faire attitude towards the development of large firms. Without government support, the difficulty of obtaining bank loans and high bank interest rates, family firms and the business group are the dominant organizational forms throughout the economy, especially in the export industry (Iles 2013a: 8).

Various typologies of institutionalist frameworks and the outputs of these systems exist. They are helpful in comparing an NBS to other systems and in identifying the critical institutions which influence the structure and behaviour of economic enterprises. Some of these differences, e.g. over timescale or collectivism, also reflect cultural differences (see Chapter 11). Whether institutions affect culture, or vice-versa, or whether there is mutual influence, is an open question. Other NBSs, e.g. China and India, will display even more divergence from the US model.

Whitley (1999) identifies three ideal types of NBS (Iles 2013a: 7):

- *Particularistic*: here firms lack trust in formal institutions, with a weak or predatory state: weak collective intermediaries/norms govern transactions, and firms exercise paternalistic authority relationships. This type is characterized by flexibility and *opportunistic hierarchies*; the control exercised by the owner is typically direct and personal; coordination is highly personal and non-routinized; and flexibility is a response to the unpredictable environment. Examples might include family firms, especially in developing countries.
- *Collaborative*: here, interlocking institutions encourage cooperative behaviour, as in Japan and Germany. This leads to 'cooperative hierarchies' and corporatist/interventionist approaches. Owners and managers share authority more with employees and partners; skilled manual workers are typically integrated into the organization as core members.
- *Arm's length*: here there is flexible entry and exit within an institutionalized formal system. Competitive capital markets exist, and the state acts as regulator. Training for example is seen as a matter for individual firm investment, not for coordinated collaboration between the state, employers and unions, as in the USA or UK. This approach leads to 'isolated hierarchies'.

We will now discuss the important institutions of employee relations and vocational education and training in more depth. In *voluntarist* systems, 'employers are fairly free to decide what practices to implement with respect to employment relations and employee voice' (Iles 2013c: 342). In more *interventionist* systems, called '*mandatory*' by Hannon (2011), legislation often forces employers to adopt institutions or mechanisms for employee participation (see Chapter 8). Voluntarist systems include Anglo-Saxon common law countries like the USA and UK, favouring free market policies and an arm's length stance by government. They tend to have limited legal regulation; employee involvement rather than participation is favoured.

However, EU legislation has changed this to some extent in the UK and Ireland; it can be queried whether voluntarist is now the appropriate term here. Marchington et al. (2011: 44) point out that such a characterization is increasingly anachronistic 'as the state has increasingly sought to reconstruct ER institutions'. Though it has largely avoided intervention in employee rights, EU membership has brought legislation on health and safety, labour law, individual employment rights and information and consultation rights.

Mandatory systems 'oblige voice to be exercised through various institutions, more characteristic of many continental European countries' (Iles 2013c: 342). Here it may sit alongside collective bargaining to form a dual system of employment relations. The Germanic system is often regarded here as the ideal type, featuring works councils and rights to information, consultation and co-determination (joint decision making) on many HR matters. There is also mandatory representation of employee interests on supervisory boards of companies above a certain size, appointing and overseeing the activities of the management board, and featuring directly elected employee representatives.

However, the situation in Germany is changing, with recent moves towards more flexible labour markets (Keller and Kirsch 2011). Some companies 'have gone beyond industrial-level collectively bargained agreements, withdrawing from employers' associations to negotiate at company level. Others, like McDonald's, have resisted the representation of employees in works councils' (Iles 2013c: 343).

Co-determination as a form of participation is a distinguishing feature of the German system at both workplace and company levels, with legally established rights for works councils. These are separate from unions, but many works councillors are union members. However, one half of private sector employees are not now covered by them, a figure rising since the 1980s (especially in services, SMEs and eastern Germany). Collective bargaining now mostly takes place at regional and industry levels, but the coverage rate of industry-level agreements has declined and there is an increasing 'tacit escape from collective agreements' (Keller and Kirsch 2011: 211). Though the German system has been characterized by the dual system of collective bargaining and co-determination, only a minority of employees now enjoy both: 'the "duality" of the German system, one of its fundamental characteristics, has gradually been weakened and is disintegrating' (2011: 212) in the wake of 'German reunification, changing modes of production, new forms of employment, and Europeanization and globalization' (Iles 2013c: 343).. Germany is becoming more like the Anglo-American model: 'no longer the prototypical example of highly regulated, well-integrated, consensus-driven employment relations … nevertheless, increasing heterogeneity … or even the dualization between core and peripheral segments of employment is more likely than a wholesale convergence towards the Anglo-American model' (Keller and Kirsch 2011: 221). This process may be referred to as *dualization* or dual flexibility (Eichorst 2012).

Hannon (2011) agrees that globalization and competitive pressures have affected how German works councils function, but this has been uneven and contradictory. There is evidence of a decline in works council presence in companies, especially in services; employer disagreements with works councils over such areas as relocation, employment levels and outsourcing have grown and councils have often made concessions over flexibility to secure jobs. However, trends towards negotiating employment conditions and practices at a company or plant, rather than a sectoral level, have at the same time also strengthened the role of works councils.

Let us now turn to the vocational education and training (VET) system, noting that here there is a danger of over-generalization in these institutionalist explanations; for example, Whitley (1999) claims that Japan and Germany are both examples of collaborative business environments generating cooperative hierarchies, but there are significant differences between the Japanese and the German education and training systems. The development of the internal labour market and in-company training in large Japanese firms, as opposed to the greater support German firms have from the system of education and technical/vocational training focusing on skill development responsive to economic needs, is one example (Lane 1992).

Change in the system, such as in respect of VET, is also difficult to explain. Determinism – seeing the nation-state as hermetically sealed and leaving little scope for international factors, agency or politics – is also a problem, making it difficult to account for the pragmatic adaptations made by Japanese firms in China, and following neither purely Japanese nor Chinese models (Gamble 2010). There may also be transitions from one system to another, as with respect to VET systems. Differences in national human resource development, especially in terms of vocational training and development systems or VET, usefully illustrate this point. Case Study 12.3 shows some of these differences in the VET and national HRD system; Figure 12.3 illustrates this.

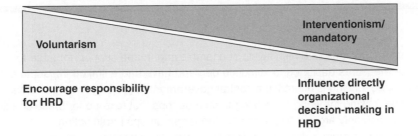

Figure 12.3 Types of VET: voluntarism and interventionism in national HRD
Source: Adapted from Iles (2013a: 10)

≣ **CASE STUDY 12.3** ≣

VET and National HRD in the Czech Republic

Czech VET and national HRD systems have also undergone a transformation (Stewart et al. 2008). There is a very high level of youth participation in post-compulsory education; official estimates of the rate vary, but all put it at above 90 per cent (and as high as 96 per cent), well above the EU average. Participation was at high levels during the Communist era, and has remained at high levels since then, due to the long history of support for the value of education in Czech society.

The wider education system in the Czech Republic is undergoing change, which is centrally designed and driven but relying on local implementation. The need for reform is driven by the requirement to better align the VET system with labour market needs, particularly those of foreign-owned businesses locating in the Czech Republic, and to increase the supply of skilled workers. The Czech economy currently relies heavily on immigrant labour.

Several reforms have been introduced in recent years, modelled on lessons learned and policies adopted in other EU member states, particularly the UK. These reforms therefore bear some resemblance to features of the English post-16 education and training landscape. There has been curriculum reform, focusing more on delivering skills and outcomes relevant to the labour market, including transferable skills, and the introduction of a National Qualifications Framework specifying standards of qualification and assessment as well as the introduction of a National Career Framework, indicating employers' skills needs across different job roles. 'Sector Councils' are to be established, involving employers and other organizations in the design of new curricula, as well as approved assessors to separate training provision from the assessment and verification of qualifications. Human Resource Development Advisory Councils in each region have also been set up.

These reforms have been designed and implemented mainly through EU funding; there is little political will to commit state funds to education, a relatively low proportion of GDP is allocated to the education budget. EU funding is finite, so one of the critical factors is the extent to which the country is prepared to sustain funding for the reforms when the EU investment comes to an end.

It has not yet made consistent use of financial incentives to encourage the participation of either individuals or employers in training, although there is some evidence of incentives being

(Continued)

(Continued)

offered to employers in regions with high levels of unemployment, and support for large foreign companies. Other measures designed to stimulate demand have had a limited impact to date, even when subsidized training is offered; the central government funded re-training courses for unemployed people looking for work, or seeking to change jobs, but take-up for these courses has been very low, with only around 10 per cent of the target groups participating.

The limited impact of such policies therefore illustrates the importance of ensuring that measures to stimulate demand for learning are effectively aligned with employment and social policies.

Source: Adapted from Stewart et al. (2008).

 ■ **Questions**

1. Where does this case fit on the voluntarist-interventionist continuum of national HRD shown in Figure 12.3?
2. How would you try to stimulate demand for VET (Vocational Education and Training)?

Having explored the local environment, especially in terms of institutions and business systems likely to be faced by an IE (International Enterprise), we next turn to how an IE might go about composing an international workforce.

Composing a global workforce

Here we are particularly concerned with the relative advantages of using different categories of staff (e.g. PCNs, TCNs and HCNs) and what factors affect this process of decision making. There are several factors affecting the choice of which orientation and which category of staff to use, as described in Figure 12.2. Factors include the country/region of origin of the company, the nature of the host country, the type of industry sector, the age and performance of the subsidiary, and the type of position to be filled (Harzing 2001b; Reiche and Harzing 2011).

Country of origin effects include Japanese IEs historically using high numbers of PCNs in subsidiary organizations (Collings et al. 2007) and European firms using a higher percentage of TCNs (Harzing 2001a, 2001b). Gamble (2010: 716) found in China that Japanese retail stores 'made greater use of expatriates than comparable European and American firms'. The main role of the HQ IHRM function in Japanese companies is often to manage Japanese expatriates at their subsidiaries, with little involvement in the management of local PCNs. In US firms, senior-level managers are usually included regardless of nationality. Often most or all company presidents are Japanese, and most senior positions also. The explanation often given is that this makes communication and liaison with Japanese HQ easier; in addition, local skill-levels may be seen to be lower. Japanese subsidiaries of US- or European-based firms however are usually headed by Japanese HCNs, who also make up most of the HR positions.

If the home country shows high uncertainty avoidance, like Japan, PCNs may also be used as control mechanisms. Cultural distance may also be a factor; if subsidiaries are located in distant countries, enterprises seem to prefer to deploy PCNs (though they may be less willing to go in these situations!).

In addition, subsidiary characteristics like age, whether it is an acquisition or a new greenfield site, and the performance of the company are all significant factors affecting choice. The longer a subsidiary has been in operation, the fewer PCNs may be used, as the need for control may be diminished in long-standing, presumably successful, affiliates; if acquired, existing local managers may be left in place. Greenfield sites in contrast may be initially staffed with PCNs (Iles 2013b: 53).

There are also industry effects; ethnocentric approaches seem more common in some sectors (e.g. banking and finance) than for example advertising, electronics, or food industries, all multi-domestic industries where cultural responsiveness is important. The host country also has an influence: local education levels, level of risk, and cost of living all have impacts on choice.

So the use of PCNs is most common in Japanese companies, especially in banks, and in Africa/Latin America as a host region compared to Western Europe/North America. PCNs are also most likely to be the financial director, managing director, or CEO of the company. Locals are most likely to occupy the role of HR director, and make up the majority of the workforce.

Before we go about recruiting staff, we need to know what we want them *for*, and what we want them to do. Of particular interest are issues of expatriate management and multinational team management. What are the IEs' motives for recruiting or assigning staff? These motives in part relate to the advantages and disadvantages of employing different categories of international staff.

PIT STOP: REFLECTIVE ACTIVITY 12.6

1. In Case Study 12.1, what were the motives involved in choosing an expatriate?

Edstrom and Galbraith (1977) found three general assignment motives: to fill positions/transfer knowledge; to develop managers; and to develop organizations through creating information networks and socializing both expatriate and local managers into the corporate culture. Motives for international assignments (Gamble 2010; Reiche and Harzing 2011) include:

- To fill positions with qualified competent staff
- To alleviate the problems caused by a lack of suitably qualified, competent locals
- To ensure corporate control/coordination and deliver bottom line results
- To encourage the transfer of knowledge, organizational development and enhancement of information networks, develop a common corporate culture, common policies and practices, increase coordination and control, and build greater corporate loyalty (e.g. Bonache and Brewster 2001)
- To develop international staff to ensure global business objectives
- To facilitate management development by increasing global awareness, giving talented high-potential recruits useful experience, and ensuring career development for high-potential staff.

These motives are not necessarily mutually exclusive – IEs 'may want staff to fulfil several motives simultaneously, say coordinating processes and delivering results while transferring knowledge to the local affiliate and staff and developing locals' (Iles 2013c: 243). Interestingly, German-language work on the issue (Reiche and Harzing 2011) more often stresses direct control and coordination by expatriates as a motive; could this be related to the relatively high German scores on uncertainty avoidance?

Harzing (2001a, 2001b) distinguishes between:

- bears (focusing on surveillance/control);
- bumble-bees (focusing on coordination and socialization); and
- spiders (focusing on developing informal communication networks).

These motives for international assignments are related to the international orientation of the firm, explored earlier (Figure 12.2). Expatriates/PCNs (of course TCNs are 'expatriated' too, but here we will use the term to refer to PCNs) offer a range of advantages as part of an ethnocentric strategy. They are more likely to show their familiarity with headquarters and also more likely to be able to successfully liaise with it, knowing the language and people involved. They probably have a known track record and competence profile, and may be trusted to exercise control over local affiliates on behalf of the corporate HQ. However,

they also come with disadvantages: they are more likely to experience local adaptation and language problems, are expensive (not only high salaries, but travel, training, accommodation, transport, schooling and other costs), host countries may exercise localization pressures on the company to recruit locals (Arabization, indigenization, Africanization etc.) and their family may find adjustment difficult. (Iles 2013c: 43)

PIT STOP: REFLECTIVE ACTIVITY 12.7

1. What problems did Rick and his partner encounter in Case Study 12.1?

This strategy is, as we saw, most commonly used in Japanese companies (perhaps also linked to high levels of uncertainty avoidance) and in banks, perhaps due to control/trust issues; it is also more commonly used in developing regions such as Africa where staff with appropriate skills, education and experience may be harder to find (Reiche and Harzing 2011).

In contrast, locals or HCNs

> also offer many advantages, such as local familiarity, and lower costs (probably lower salaries and no need to incur support costs). In offering locals opportunities, they may be seen as responding to local government pressures for indigenization/localization. However, the enterprise may harbour (not necessarily accurately) doubts about their ability to exercise control on behalf of the company, and their ability to liaise and communicate with HQ may be less, not knowing the people or even the language fluently. (Iles 2013c: 244)

In addition, employing locals may be seen as denying international opportunities for an IE's own PCNs, which may have been a strong employer brand offering in graduate recruitment.

Using TCNs also has its attractions, perhaps as a useful compromise between local and global. TCNs

> are often cosmopolitan career internationals with extensive global experience. They are also likely to be cheaper than PCNs, and may have already extensive host country knowledge. However, there are disadvantages; there may be host country sensitivity to employing certain national groups, and the host country may see this strategy as blocking local opportunities, preventing successful nationalization or localization. (Iles 2013c: 244)

TCNs are most commonly employed in European MNCs.

Factors affecting which choice to make include parent country/company factors, like high uncertainty avoidance. Here, as in Japan, PCNs may be viewed positively as exercising control, and seniority is favoured, especially when operating in culturally distant countries (Gamble 2010). There are also industry effects; financial services are more likely to use PCNs, presumably for control and trust reasons, while the advertising, electronics, and food sectors are more likely to use HCNs, either for reasons of local responsiveness (food, advertising) or because the industry is global, such as electronics (Reiche and Harzing 2011). There are also host country effects: 'PCNs are more likely to be used in countries with low education levels and cost of living. Subsidiary characteristics like age, acquisition status and performance also affect choice; HCNs are more likely in older, more successful subsidiaries and in acquired subsidiaries' (Iles 2013c: 244).

Spider and bumble-bee roles seem particularly important in polycentric subsidiaries with high levels of local responsiveness, and in acquisitions rather than greenfield sites, where the subsidiary may operate quite independent of headquarters, and where the expatriate presence is generally lower (Reiche and

Harzing 2011). Geocentric orientations emphasizing control and standardization tend to make more use of bears, especially expatriates.

For international assignments (IAs), 'it is therefore important to clarify the nature of the job, role or position intended to be filled and its link with the motives for assignment' (Iles 2013c: 244). Is it to:

- Do a technical job?
- Transfer knowledge?
- Develop the individual?
- Develop the organization?

Answers to these questions will influence job analysis: what do we expect from IAs in terms of roles, duties, responsibilities and priorities? This will influence the job description and person specification, identifying the relevant skills, knowledge and other attributes necessary for success prior to departure (see Case Study 12.1).

Issues and problems in international assignments

MNCs often send expatriate workers abroad with the aim of transferring knowledge and ensuring that the set-up of the new subsidiary is successful, based on the expatriate's existing experience and knowledge within the field and ultimately to improve the subsidiary performance (Bonache and Brewster 2001). However, this process is daunting, with mounting pressures from the parent company to ensure the success, competition and long-term longevity of the operation. Familiarization challenges for the expatriate include basic needs such as sociocultural association. Survival in terms of the new subsidiary is critical, yet the barriers of an undeveloped structure and limited institutional knowledge can prevent embedding knowledge which has been rooted at its origin with the parent company.

It has also been suggested that the number of expatriates selected is not of great significance, but the quality of their knowledge, which has been documented through the history of the company, and culture, which is not easily imitated, is of paramount significance (Minbaeva et al. 2003).

The failure of an expatriate to adapt to the local and new environment can be catastrophic in terms of knowledge transfer and embedding those essential skills from the parent company into the host subsidiary: the entire process can be extremely vulnerable and the end product can result in the organizational performance being unproductive. This will create poor coverage on the global corporate scene for the company as a unit, not to mention disastrous complications for a failed subsidiary in a foreign market. Therefore, the business of recruiting and assigning expatriates is an extremely important process which requires a focus and skill to ensure that the right people are indeed recruited for the right job.

Consideration of the person and the skills they must possess to ensure that an international assignment is successful has focused predominantly not only on the skills they possess – such as experience and technical know-how – but also more importantly on their leadership skills or those of their manager to survive and become successful. There is immense pressure on the individual to succeed within the international role in terms of work adjustment and job satisfaction. The elements which act as barriers to this transfer process can include adaptation to new colleagues and a new position yet with corresponding tasks and responsibility, communication and acceptance from the host nationals. These factors can put tremendous stress upon an individual and can be hugely underestimated by the MNC (Collings et al. 2007). Trust within a team can help to mediate transformational leadership. In the context of an international assignment the host country can also moderate this form of leadership style.

Effectiveness of suitable social networks for expatriates is linked to their performance in the workplace. Social networks are defined by the relational ties experienced by the expatriate, linking them with family, friends, colleagues, neighbours, managers and colleagues. There are a number of issues in terms of expatriates feeling comfortable within their social network, particularly as this may be a relatively new network in comparison to that of their home life. This will require that the expatriate adjusts to the new network and indeed to the host culture, which will mean that they may have to adapt their behaviours to the host country culture and in turn their cultural norms.

PIT STOP: REFLECTIVE ACTIVITY 12.8

1. What is the quality of the social networks enjoyed by Rick in Case Study 12.1?

The expatriate can establish a strong social network; this will enhance their performance within the workplace, and expatriate adjustment is a predictor of effective performance. It is not the quantity which acts as the catalyst towards performance enhancement but the uniqueness and clarity of the relationships within the network itself. Is the structure of the network important or is it the resources that cascade through the social ties? For Hechanova et al. (2003), there are a number of clarifying factors which can support the expatriate in developing a social network and reducing stress, such as reducing role ambiguity, increasing an individual's coping strategy and facilitating the induction into new social networks through social support. Adelman (1988) cites a number of benefits that expatriates will gain from having supportive social networks, such as information clarity and understanding, emotional support and the need to coach and counsel one another through experiences. Appraisal support can help them define their own performance goals and the indicators needed to share and celebrate success and clarify new goals within the international role.

Black et al. (1991) highlight three aspects of expatriate adjustment; the first is general adjustment, primarily concerned with the ability of the expatriate to adapt to the new lifestyle in terms of non-work factors such as neighbours, external friendships and community aspects of their social life. The second dimension is concerned with interaction adjustment, focusing on the necessity to interact effectively with host-country nationals, to adapt to their cultures and if need be overcome language and religious barriers. The last dimension, work adjustment, is the need for the expatriate to associate themselves effectively with aspects of the workplace such as colleagues, mentor, subordinates, and line manager.

Alternative forms of international working

Alternatives to expatriate international assignments – typical of ethnocentric companies – are also being used by international enterprises, especially in response to dual-career couple and work–life balance issues which may discourage international mobility (Scullion and Brewster 2001; Mayrhofer and Scullion 2002). Desires to reduce expatriation costs and respond to localization pressures from governments are also generating interest in alternatives to typical expatriation assignments, such as (Iles 2013c: 248):

- *short-term assignments* e.g. postings between 1 and 12 months unaccompanied by family; especially useful for problem-solving/skills transfer
- *international commuting*
- *frequent flying* or business trips for irregular specific tasks
- *home-based managers* focusing on different global markets, but with a global outlook
- *internationally mobile* managers; creating a cadre of career internationals
- *rotating technical professionals* e.g. oil rigs
- *self-initiated international assignments*
- *virtual assignments* e.g. team distribution of international responsibilities through IT, email, social media, video-conferencing etc.
- *inpatriation* i.e. bringing subsidiary staff, whether TCNs and HCNs, to the headquarters to learn and apply parent company operations and culture, transfer knowledge, test suitability, socialize into company culture, and build multicultural teams.

Inpatriates – transfers to headquarters of subsidiary managers – may take on a linking-pin role, especially with regard to the transfer of tacit knowledge and developing a global mindset, but inpatriates may experience status differences and cultural adjustment challenges. Inpatriation is more likely to occur in geocentric companies (or, on a regional basis, in regiocentric companies) (Reiche and Harzing 2011).

These roles all have implications for the type of HRM required and the skills needed. Virtual assignments through international collaboration on projects through videoconferencing, email, and telephone rather than physical travel are becoming more common, but 'face-to-face communication is often still necessary to build and maintain trust and clear up misunderstandings. The use of a greater variety of shorter assignments (troubleshooting, contractual assignments, rotational assignments, knowledge transfer activities, training, personal development, short-term commuters, frequent flyers) is also increasing' (Iles 2013c: 249). Collings et al. (2007) claim that the desire to create global core competencies and cultural diversity of perspectives in the top team has driven this move, as well as the desire to offer career opportunities to high-potential HCNs and TCNs and encourage a bilateral knowledge transfer.

PIT STOP: REFLECTIVE ACTIVITY 12.9

1. Will the development of modern ICT technologies such as social media, videoconferencing, Skype and email make the traditional expatriate assignment disappear?
2. Could they be more extensively used in Case Study 12.1?

Expatriate preparation

Recruitment, selection, training and development

Given the issues often encountered by expatriates, as Case Study 12.1 illustrates, it is imperative to address the question of what IEs can do to support the preparation of expatriates. One area is in recruitment and selection, trying to ensure a better match or fit between expatriates' skills, experience, knowledge and competencies and the demands of the job and organization in order to enhance adjustment.

Yet there is a significant question to be asked here: how is expatriate performance measured? This is contested; as Brislin (2000) indicates, there is no clear definition of what constitutes success and failure for an expatriate. In contrast, Bennett et al. (2000) state that expatriate failure can include a number of themes, such as lost opportunities of the business, delayed productivity due to settling-in periods becoming extended, adjustment differences, poor transfer of management practices, and finally returning home before completion of the objectives of the assignment.

Graf and Mertesacker (2009) suggest assessing intercultural competence as part of a training needs analysis on six measures; their model is based in part on Gertsen (1990). Questionnaire results were here correlated with observations of student behaviour in intercultural exercises. Measures included the Intercultural Sensitivity Inventory and other scales (See Figure 12.4).

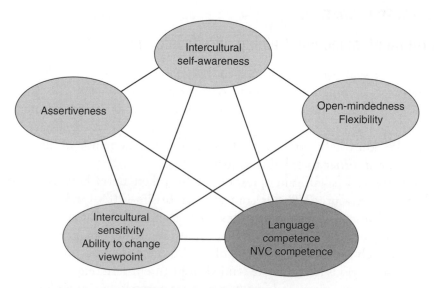

Figure 12.4 Dimensions of intercultural competence
Source: Based on Graf and Mertesacker (2009).

━━━━━━━━━━━━━━ **PIT STOP: REFLECTIVE ACTIVITY 12.11** ━━━━━━━━━━━━━━

See:

http://winfobase.de/lehre%5Clv_materialien.nsf/intern01/A86A0DB8DE3B7D22C12
577B500308A01/$FILE/1%20-%20Intercultural%20Sensitivity.pdf

You may like to assess yourself on this instrument, and discuss your results with your peers in a small group.

See also:

http://mdbgroup.com/idi-background.html

Source: Adapted from Iles (2013c: 247).

These dimensions are now often reflected in the concept of 'emotional intelligence'. Though emotional intelligence, personality traits and interpersonal skills are very important for international selection, in practice most companies still often use technical competence and knowledge of company systems as key criteria (Reiche and Harzing 2011). Personal recommendations via an informal 'coffee-machine system' are common (Harris and Brewster 1999). Here, in a closed/informal system, candidates are not formally evaluated against a formal person specification, but through an informal chat over coffee; the candidate pool is very restricted, and the organization fails to behave strategically.

With respect to expatriates and other IAs selection is often an informal process, but it needs to be treated as formally as domestic selection. In addition, technical skills and previous track record are often given priority, but interpersonal and communication skills and emotional intelligence are equally important.

━━━━━━━━━━━━━━ **PIT STOP: REFLECTIVE ACTIVITY 12.12** ━━━━━━━━━━━━━━

1. Why does international selection in practice differ so widely from best practice recommendations?
2. What examples of poor practice can you identify in Case Study 12.1?
3. What recommendations would you make to improve selection in this case?

Developing intercultural competence

Littrell et al. (2006) have examined the extent to which preparation for expatriate assignment can be supported in terms of cross-cultural training to lead to enhanced performance of expatriates through the learning of social interaction of diverse cultures. However, there are a number of critics of such a process, such as Brewster (1995), who suggests that this form of cross-cultural training does not benefit the expatriate preparation process as the 'goals, contents, effectiveness and process' are limited in a contextual comparison. According to Black and Mendenhall (2007) cross-cultural training for expatriates should be led by social learning theory: experiencing learning of different cultures in the context of expatriation through direct and vicarious-shaped learning experiences of observation, future behaviours and modelling of such behaviours will lead to increased learning and ultimately success in terms of expatriate preparation: the expatriate would have the skills necessary to interact appropriately with local host country nationals.

Case Study 12.1 shows there is evidence of a high cost to using expatriates who often 'fail', leaving early or under-performing. These costs include not just the direct costs of recruitment, travel, support and training, but also the indirect costs to relationships, reputation and brand. These costs are often caused by a failure to adjust on international assignments (Black et al. 1991), leading to poor performance. Earlier, we looked at the role of recruitment and selection in reducing or avoiding such problems; here we look at another strategy, training and development (see also Chapter 10).

PIT STOP: REFLECTIVE ACTIVITY 12.13

Look again at Case Study 12.1.

1. How might training and development have helped?
2. What form of training and development would you recommend, and why?

Oberg (1960) first used the term 'culture shock' to refer to the long-term process of adapting to new cultural behaviours, including physical, biological, and social changes. It is often experienced as a lack of direction, feelings of not knowing what to do or how to do things in a new environment, and not knowing what is appropriate or inappropriate. This feeling of culture shock generally sets in after the first few weeks of coming to a new place.

PIT STOP: REFLECTIVE ACTIVITY 12.14

1. When have you, as a student, traveller or employee, experienced 'culture shock'?
2. If so, what 'symptoms' did you display?
3. How long did it last?
4. What did you do or others do to address it?

Source: Adapted from Zhang and Iles (2013: 265).

Oberg (1960) discussed culture shock in terms of four phases of emotional reactions associated with a U-curve:

1. *The honeymoon*, with an emphasis on the initial reactions of euphoria, enchantment, fascination, and enthusiasm (e.g. 'it's warm, the people are friendly!')
2. *The crisis*, characterized by feelings of inadequacy, frustration, anxiety and anger ('it's not working – I can't make myself clear')

3. *The recovery*, including crisis resolution and learning ('I found myself trying to learn the language – I'm finally communicating!')
4. *The adjustment*, reflecting, enjoyment of, and competence in, the new environment ('I'm enjoying this – it's going really well!')

Oberg's U-curve theory of acculturation was later expanded by Gullahorn and Gullahorn (1963) to include 'reverse culture shock' when the cross-cultural traveller returns back to the home culture. This re-entry stage can be considered as a second cycle of adjustment. For example, perhaps the old boss has retired; colleagues have left or been sacked by new foreign owners; spouse and kids miss the lifestyle; and no-one wants to know about what has been learned.

===== **PIT STOP: REFLECTIVE ACTIVITY 12.15** =====

1. Discuss in groups your personal experience when facing a new and distant culture, or returning to an old one. How much does this echo Oberg's culture shock theory?

Source: Adapted from Zhang and Iles (2013: 265).

Emphasis has also shifted from the description of negative psychological experience associated with stress (Oberg 1960; Gullahorn and Gullahorn 1963) to viewing acculturation as a learning experience (Brislin 1981; Ward et al. 2001) and accounting for the various factors that influence its outcomes. For example, Brislin (2000) suggests the importance of skills in cross-cultural contact, including language and communication skills. Thus the foreigner's efforts to speak the language of the host country, even imperfectly, may be appreciated by the host nationals. Such skill 'stimulates interaction effectiveness during the acculturation process. Since adaptation can be learned as a skill, Brislin suggests cross-cultural training (CCT) can help overcome adaptation difficulties and decrease the possibility of stress' (Zhang and Iles 2013: 266). Intercultural adaptation is a function of uncertainty reduction – the more we know about the unknown ahead, the less the culture shock, and the easier it is to cope (Gudykunst and Hammer 1988), and the experience of culture shock becomes a learning experience (Adler 1991).

Black et al. (1991) provide a useful framework which integrates both acculturation and socialization theories (for expatriates in particular) in the international business context, identifying three categories of pre-departure variables and two post-arrival variables.

The former includes previous experience, pre-departure training and candidate selection. The latter refers to individual skills (i.e. self-efficacy, relation skills and perception skills) and non-work factors (i.e. family adjustment and culture novelty, as we saw in the Extronics Case Study, 12.1).

What is termed 'domestic adjustment' consists of two stages: prior to entry and after entry. Before entering the organization, both individual factors (i.e. accurate or realistic expectations) and organizational factors (i.e. selection mechanisms and criteria – again, poor or missing in Case Study 12.1!) are very important, since they result in anticipatory adjustment. This may be helped by a realistic job preview rather than presenting an over-optimistic picture trying to 'sell' the asignment to the assignee, as we saw in Case Study 12.1 with its depiction of the wonderful opportunities for travel and lesiure!

After arrival, three factors influence adjustment: organizational socialization factors (i.e. socialization tactics), job factors (i.e. role clarity, role discretion, role novelty and role conflict) and organizational culture factors (i.e. organizational culture novelty and social support). These factors all influence the mode and degree of adjustment.

According to Littrell et al. (2006: 356), cross-cultural training or CCT refers to 'the educative processes used to improve intercultural learning via the development of the cognitive, affective, and behavioral competencies needed for successful interactions in diverse cultures'. Culture-specific training usually refers to 'information about a given culture and guidelines for interaction with members of that culture' (Brislin and Pedersen 1976: 6) or training that is 'specific to a particular culture' (Triandis 1977: 21). Culture-general training refers to 'such topics as cultural awareness and sensitivity training that allow one to learn about himself (or herself) as preparation for interaction in *any culture*' (Brislin and Pedersen 1976: 6). Psychological adaptation, social adaptation and motivational orientation can be affected by a number of factors (Ward et al. 2001). In designing CCT, culture distance, language, communication and individual variables (such as interaction with host culture and personal learning style) are all important factors.

Culture/cultural distance refers to how similar two cultures are in terms of dimensions such as language, religion etc. Though geographically close, the USA and Mexico are culturally distant; though physically distant, the UK and Canada are culturally close. Berry (1980) found that variations in stress and culture change patterns were dependent to some extent upon the cultural and psychological characteristics of the culture, and the degree and nature of previous contact with culturally diverse groups. Employees experience lower stress when their culture is more similar to the second culture – e.g. a French expatriate working in Belgium, as compared to a French expatriate in Nigeria. Ward and Kennedy (1999) show that English travellers in Singapore experienced more sociocultural difficulties than Chinese counterparts; Malaysian cross-cultural travellers had more difficulties in New Zealand than in Singapore. For Waxin and Panaccio (2005), cultural distance is negatively related to adjustment, and CCT is an effective method to reduce the presence of culture distance felt by expatriates.

Thus 'cultural distance may have an impact on acculturation; the closer the home culture is to the host culture, the less difficulty or stress is experienced, leading to better adaptation' (Zhang and Iles 2013: 268). Berry (1997) suggests that greater cultural distance implies the need for greater 'culture shedding' and 'culture learning'; perhaps large differences trigger negative inter-group attitudes and induce greater culture conflict, leading to poorer adaptation. CCT may therefore have its biggest benefit, and justify the biggest investment of time and money, when experienced by employees moving to a culturally distant destination as in Case Study 12.1.

In addition to the extent of interaction, Furnham (2004) also suggests that the quality of interaction (e.g. friendship) with the host culture is also important, suggesting another important variable in determining the investment in CCT. If the assignee is going to spend a long time interacting with locals in a position where high-quality interaction is necessary (e.g. as in Case Study 12.1 or a three-year stint for a British expatriate as a B&Q store manager in China; see Gamble 2003), CCT is highly recommended. If the assignment is a one-week technical assignment with little time spent with locals, CCT may not be necessary, or may be quite brief. Friendship networks may form the basis of social capital in social settings, using the goodwill built up between group members. If multinational group members expect that other group members will behave with respect and consideration toward them, then they will be inclined to interpret a cultural error as unintended, the result of not knowing cultural differences in acceptable behaviour, rather than a calculated insult.

Tung (1981) identifies five different training programmes which are complementary to each other and dependent on the type of job and country of foreign assigment. The higher the cultural distance, the more CCT is required. The different training modes (Zhang and Iles 2013: 271) are:

1. *Didactic training.* Delivery of 'factual' training via lectures, briefings, or written materials. Practical information and facts about the host culture are given, such as living conditions and cultural differences (Littrell et al. 2006).
2. *Culture assimilators.* One of the most popular methods of CCT, especially in the USA. A series of scenarios or incidents that normally involve a culture clash or misunderstandings are used to prepare people for interacting with people from a specific culture. Trainees are normally given scenarios and a choice of explanations of a problem; feedback is obtained on the appropriateness of the choice made.
3. *Language training.* This can range from giving basic greetings to fluency in the host language.
4. *Sensitivity training.* This focuses on sensitizing teaching trainees to accept that other cultures have different ways of doing things, preparing assignees to

accept cultural differences and to improve the motivation for interactions with people from the host culture.

5. *Field experience* refers to learning on the job, involving assignments to the host culture directly or to a 'microculture' (such as a local Chinatown or Little India, if the host culture is Chinese or Indian). While microcultures are not exactly identical to the host culture, the experience gained by the trainee is helpful and beneficial for understanding the host culture.

CCT helps prepare staff for potential difficulties during the foreign assignment and form expectations about the job. The theory of *met expectations* proposes that the closer the individual's expectations to the reality encountered, the better the adjustment will be (Wanous et al. 1992). Caligiuri et al. (2001) found that pre-departure training helped provide expatriates with skills for acculturation, helping them form expectations of the assignment; the more realistic these were, the more likely the expectations would be met, leading to better adjustment. Furthermore, in the absence of complete information, staff speaking the language of the host culture may expect the assignment to be easy, leading to potential problems when expectations did not match reality. However, those who do not speak the language may expect a difficult assignment.

Others have put forward alternative models; Black and Mendenhall (2007) have developed a similar framework, but refer to three modes of training and development:

- *Factual* – didactic training in the form of lectures or hand-outs, as in university courses
- *Analytical* – provision of analytical theories and models
- *Experiential* – providing direct interaction with people from other cultures, as in field trips, projects, multicultural action learning, role-plays, and multicultural outdoor development.

They argue that these modes vary both in terms of rigour and the extent to which modelling processes are used (experiential modes use far more modelling than factual ones). When to use which depends in part on the degree of cultural novelty (going to a culturally distant country suggests more experiental methods be used as compared to a close one, where factual briefings may suffice) and the degree of interaction expected with locals (the more expected, the more justification there is for using experiential methods). Gudykunst and Hammer (1983) present a typology of CCT processes (Zhang and Iles 2013: 272) in terms of:

- *methods* of delivery, e.g. didactic (cognitive) vs experiential (emotional/behavioural)
- *content*, e.g. culture-general vs culture-specific.

- *focus*, e.g. work-oriented only, or private-life oriented, or both.
- *arena*, e.g. is CCT delivered in a classroom or training room, or at work, perhaps through on-the-job learning, coaching and mentoring, or 'blending' virtual and face-to-face training ?

===== PIT STOP: REFLECTIVE ACTIVITY 12.16 =====

1. What are the advantages and disadvantages of each of these approaches, in your experience?

We can map these approaches using the axes *'factual vs experiential'* and *'culture-general vs culture-specific'* in Figure 12.5. A 'factual-specific' approach might be a briefing or handout on a specific culture; an 'experiential-specific' approach might involve a bicultural action learning set or reading a novel or biography of a local's experiences; here no-one can predict the emergent outcomes, or what different individuals will make of them. A factual-general approach might involve a general cultural model being presented, e.g. Hofstede (2001); an 'open-general' approach might involve multicultural action learning sets, projects or outdoor training, or reading multiple biographies or novels.

Mendenhall et al. (2004) found lectures, presentations, culture assimilators and discussions to be the most frequently used methods: these were useful for knowledge transfer but less effective in changing behaviour and attitudes and

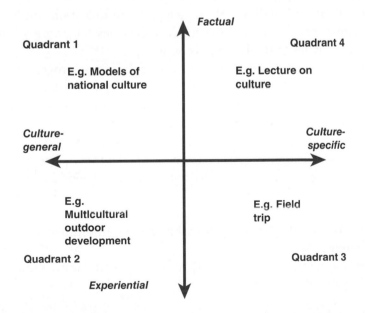

Figure 12.5 Modes of CCT

Source: Adapted from Zhang and Iles (2013: 273).

enhancing adjustment and performance. Pre-departure training, especially imparting basic information, has been found to positively affect the accuracy of prior expectations and subsequent adjustment (Caligiuri et al. 2001). Waxin and Panaccio (2005) found that CCT accelerated the adjustment of expatriates, but that this effect was moderated by prior international experience; CCT had its largest impact on those with little prior international experience. Cultural distance also moderated this effect; CCT tended to have most impact with greater cultural distance between home and the host country. The type of CCT used also had an effect; experiential methods were generally more effective, especially if culture-specific approaches were used.

Examples of CCT include the use of dramas and other simulations in exploring decisions to invest in Mexico or China (Lewis 2005) and 'blended action learning', combining face-to-face action learning sets in five European partner countries and an e-learning platform called the 'Cultural Fluency Club'. These were used to develop cross-cultural skills and cultural awareness by sharing knowledge and experiences of SME leaders (Stewart 2008). Another example is the Executive Training Program (ETP) for European companies in Japan, mixing language training, seminars, company visits, and in-house training in a hybrid blend of experiential and analytical methods in small groups (Lievens et al. 2003).

Chien and McLean (2011) have explored the Taiwan-specific intercultural training needs of US expatriates from the perspective of both expatatriates and locals; a culture-specific approach. Relevant content included knowledge of Taiwan, relationship-building, interpersonal communication, business protocol, legal issues, and living in Taiwan. US colleagues felt more strongly than their local colleagues that all items were needed.

Tung (1981) recommends a mixed or hybrid training programme, combining factual and experiential methods. First, pre-departure training would be offered, including didactic activities and culture assimilators. On arrival, training would change to experiential learning. Finally, at the end of the assignment, didactic debriefings are offered to update the expatriate on the home organization. Tarique and Caligiuri (2004) have developed a three-stage programme of CCT: *pre-departure training*, involving online training needs analysis and briefing; *initial post-arrival training*, using CCT with e-support and coaching; and *later post-arrival training*, using more sophisticated CCT with e-support such as CD-Roms, DVDs, internet/intranet-based training, multimedia and distance/blended learning.

Tarique and Caligiuri (2004: 285) have also put forward some guidelines for designing effective CCT:

- *Identifying the type of global assignment*: Is the position technical, functional, high-potential, or strategic/executive?

- *Determining specific CCT needs*: What is the organizational context, individual needs and level of the assignment?
- *Establishing goals and measures*: To evaluate effectiveness in the short and long term, such as the cognitive, affective and behavioural changes necessary to enhance adjustment and success.
- *Developing and delivering CCT*: Deciding the content, the methods, the sequencing, and which models to use; the mix of didactic, analytical and experiential methods; and whether training is delivered pre-departure, post-departure, or both. Basic didactic information may be appropriate pre-departure, deeper analytical/experiential learning post-departure.
- *Evaluating the programme's success*: Against stated objectives, e.g. adjustment might be measured by interviews, surveys, and appraisal records balancing home (HQ) and host (affiliate) culture data sources; CCT may be integrated with other HR practices, especially recruitment, selection, reward, appraisal and career/talent management.
- *Considering also the training needs of HCNs and TCNs, not just PCNs.*

Other issues include (Briscoe and Schuler 2004):

- Who delivers CCT? Is it the corporate HQ? Regional HQ? Local affiliates? This choice is likely to be related to the international orientation of the firm: polycentric companies may choose local design and delivery, regiocentric ones training design and delivery at the regional level.
- Should each subsidiary/joint venture develop its own CCT?
- Who takes responsibility for CCT? The company? The affiliate? The regional HQ? The individual?
- Should CCT be exported, or employees brought to regional or centralized training centres? Again, this choice is associated with the firm's international orientation.
- Should training be localized, or integrated into a global programme?
- What are the effects of language differences? These may be especially significant if translators are used. For example, 'change management' may be translated not as 'managing change' but 'sack the managers'!

Tung (1981) has developed a comprehensive flow chart for the selection and training of expatriates, proposing that a local national HCN, not a PCN, is the most desirable person for filling the assignment if possible, unlike the situation in Case Study 12.1. However, when not possible, the training needs of the selected employee should be evaluated against several factors:

- Willingness to accept the international assignment
- Degree of interaction required with people from the host culture

- Differences between home and host culture
- Personal circumstances, including family circumstances.

If there is much interaction with the host culture (sales or marketing), or if the cultural difference is very large (e.g. UK and China, as in Figure 12.1), all types of CCT programme should be offered. For smaller assignments, e.g. technical (troubleshooting equipment) or when there are relatively few cultural differences (e.g. Ireland vs UK), didactic/factual training may be sufficient. Personal circumstances should also be considered, such as marital status, gender, family, and location of the assignment (cosmopolitan capital city or provincial town?).

Mendenhall and Oddou (1985) analysed US expatriate training needs into seven different profiles, based on degrees of self-orientation (SO), others-orientation (OO) and perceptual orientation (PO); for each, different training is required. SO refers to the degree to which the assignee engages in activities that represent concern for self-preservation, self-enjoyment and mental hygiene. OO refers to the degree to which they express concern for and a desire to interact with host nationals. Finally, PO refers to the degree to which the assignee understands the nature and reasoning behind the host national behaviour. The seven profiles and suggestions for further development (Zhang and Iles 2013: 275) are:

1. *Ideal expatriate*: high on SO, OO and PO, likely to successfully adjust to the host culture and only require repatriation training.
2. *Academic observer*: high on SO and PO, but low on OO, so not interacting well with the host culture. Suggestions for development are to increase their interactions through language training and simulations such as role plays.
3. *Well-intentioned missionary:* high on SO and OO but low on PO, so misinterpreting situations and lacking in awareness of host culture and values. Suggestions for development are to increase cultural awareness and give practice in interpreting situations, perhaps in role plays or through culture-assimilators.
4. *Type A expatriate*: high on PO, but low on SO and OO, so possesses good intercultural skills but tends to get stressed very easily. Suggestions for development are to give them more culture assimilator training and role plays.
5. *Introvert:* high on SO and PO, but low on OO, so does not interact well and tends to exhibit socially inappropriate behaviours. Suggestions are to improve their language fluency, and help them learn culturally appropriate behaviours through culture assimilator training.
6. *Ugly American* (sic!): high on SO but low on OO and PO; exhibits very high self-confidence but displays poor interpersonal skills, exhibiting

socially inappropriate behaviours. Suggestions for development include culture assimilator and sensitivity training.

7. *Dependent expatriate*: high on OO but low on SO and PO; so good interpersonal skills but gets stressed easily and does not understand the host culture. Suggestions for development are to increase their cultural awareness through models, simulations, role-plays and sensitivity training.

Repatriation training

Many employees may accept foreign assignments in the belief that they will deliver career opportunities and advancement (Mendenhall et al. 2002; Stahl et al. 2002), perhaps drawn from popular press accounts and anecdotal evidence (Fisher 2005). However, the reality may be different; a study of 1001 chief executives in contrast revealed that international experience from long multiple assignments often slowed career advancement (Hamori and Koyuncu 2011). Often only a few employees were promoted when they returned, and most companies did not give post-expatriation employment guarantees (Tung 1998). Up to 50 per cent of returnees were no longer employed by their companies within two years of returning (Black 1989; Stroh et al. 1998), with repatriates often feeling that the new skills and knowledge they had acquired were not valued by the company.

Given the costs of expatriate assignments, it is in the organization's interest to maximize its investment. Thus the final stage of CCT should focus on repatriation training. This is an often overlooked area, especially as it is often assumed that the expatriate returning to the home country would not require any special adjustment. However, repatriation is often not easy, with many employees finding it frustrating and stressful (Mendenhall and Oddou 1985; Shen and Hall 2009) and experiencing reverse culture shock when returning to the home culture. Expatriates often seem to consider their assignment as an exile from the home office, where 'out of sight is out of mind' (Ramsey and Schaetti 1999), fearing that they are being excluded from training, job opportunities, pay rises and promotions. They also experience the (rational) fear that their international experience is not valued by the company (Bolino 2007). Furthermore, many expatriates may consider their accepting the assignments as a 'sacrifice' for the company, for which they expect appreciation in the form of a promotion and pay rises (Stahl et al. 2002).

Thus repatriation training should include the following (Zhang and Iles 2013: 277):

- *Clear career development plans and goals,* so that assignees understand the reasons for the assignment and the benefits of accepting it (Feldman and Thomas 1992). While this should not imply career guarantees, it should provide motivation for a successful completion of the assignment.

- *Regular updates* with the home office, e.g. providing a 'home' mentor (Feldman and Thomas 1992) or granting regular visits back to the home office (Guzzo et al. 1994) to help employees maintain their network of colleagues on their return and increase their awareness of internal career opportunities within the organization.

Although these suggestions are all helpful for increasing the success of repatriation, they also require the organization to be willing and able to use employees' international experience, knowledge and skills. For example, the banking group HSBC has a dedicated programme for international managers. Furthermore, for smaller organizations, the top management team should also have extensive international experience, so that the value of expatriates' knowledge, skills and experience can be properly assessed and utilized (Reuber and Fischer 1997).

PIT STOP: REFLECTIVE ACTIVITY 12.17

Look at the International Management Programme developed by HSBC:

http://www.hsbc.com/1/2/careers/im/about

1. How useful do you think this programme is for preparing employees for global careers?
2. Based on the models and theories, do you think the International Management Programme is likely to be effective for international assignments?

Reward management and compensation

Once international staff – whether PCNs, HCNs or TCNs – have been recruited, selected and trained, their performance will need to be managed and rewarded. The international orientations framework we presented earlier can also be applied to *reward management* (see Chapter 7). Some IEs export their home-country policies to maintain consistency (ethnocentric); others seek to adapt to local conditions (polycentric) or regional conditions (regiocentric). Others may seek to blend different policies and practices together to create a new globally-standardized policy (geocentric). Outsourcing has introduced additional complexities, as have web-based human resource information systems (HRIS) and a greater focus on performance metrics and human capital management. There is a continuing need for IEs to balance a global reward strategy with local conditions. This requires paying attention to and monitoring changing employment and taxation laws, currency fluctuations and special allowances, often requiring advice from specialist consultancies.

Dowling et al. (2008) argue that international reward policies need to:

- Be consistent with the overall strategy, structure and business needs of the IE
- Be able to attract and retain staff in areas of greatest need and opportunity
- Facilitate the transfer of employees in the most effective manner
- Give due consideration to equity and ease of administration
- Meet employee needs for financial protection, advancement, career development, housing, education and recreation.

Of course, there may be contradictions and clashes between these objectives. Some IEs seek to emphasize global mobility through a geocentric strategy; here rewards are expressed in a major global or regional currency, e.g. US dollar or Euro, alongside a set of compensation principles and practices that fit their global strategy and structure. Local subsidiary managers may be granted autonomy to develop base pay, benefits and incentives in line with local standards, but the core principles over performance-based recognition and reward differentiation will remain consistent (Kramar and Syed 2012).

The decentralization of collective bargaining (see Chapter 8) has led to more individualized pay negotiations and the spread of pay for performance schemes in IEs, though effectiveness and acceptance by different parties remain challenges and such schemes are more common for certain groups such as managers and certain countries, such as the USA. The national institutional context, as we have seen, is an important influence, such as the use of tax benefits to encourage profit-sharing in France, or the use of employee stock ownership plans in Japan to encourage long-term commitment. The cultural context (Chapter 11) is also an important factor (Chiang and Birtch 2012). Masculinity for example is often associated with the greater importance of financial, as compared to other, benefits to employees; individualism is associated with a preference for individual-, rather than group-based performance-related pay and less emphasis on need or relationships with co-workers; and uncertainty avoidance (see Chapter 11) is often associated with seniority or skill-based compensation offering more certainty and less variability or risk in pay, as in Japan.

Performance-related or merit pay refers to a policy where an organization gives larger base salary increases to employees receiving higher performance (or merit) ratings than to employees receiving lower ratings (Gerhart and Trevor 2008). The intention 'is to not only motivate the current workforce (incentive effect) but also to increase the attraction and retention of high-performers (sorting effect)' (Iles 2013d: 331). Such policies differ in terms of *pay level* (how much pay) and *pay basis* (how pay is determined); organizations including IEs need to decide whether to pay the same, more, or less relative to competitors, and what criteria to use on which to base decisions (seniority, performance, etc.). Should a single performance-criterion, or multiple criteria, be used (see Chapter 7)?

Merit *bonuses* 'are different in not becoming part of the base salary; other pay-for-performance programmes include profit-sharing, stock plans, gainsharing, individual incentives and sales commissions' (Iles 2013d: 332). Here, measurement can be at the individual, unit (e.g. local subsidiary) plant or organization (e.g. group) level; it can employ results or behaviour-oriented measures. Merit pay operates at the individual level, and often uses behavioural measures. Many employees are covered by hybrid plans, mixing levels and measures in different combinations.

The evidence for the effectiveness of merit or performance-related pay schemes is mixed; as Franco-Santos (2008: 41) points out, 'the effectiveness of an incentive system is closely related to the appropriateness of its performance measures'. If inappropriate measures are used, dysfunctional behaviour may result, such as over-competitive or unethical behaviour and adverse effects on teamwork and the work climate.

IEs, especially geocentric ones, often seek to use a consistent set of performance measures for incentives, but this may not always be appropriate; as Franco-Santos (2008: 51) argues, 'global organizations need to review the unique stakeholder profile and business model of each of the locations where they operate ... when using performance measures incentives as a management mechanism, global organizations should also take into consideration contextual factors such as national culture'. The national culture and institutional context or National Business System all influence the ways in which people perceive the effectiveness and fairness of performance measurement and incentive pay.

One area of current interest here *is executive compensation* in a global context, especially given recent shareholder revolts (the 'shareholder spring') over executive (especially chief executive) pay such as at many banks like Barclays and RBS amid rising concerns with ethical behaviour and CSR. Often the variable elements of pay – so-called long-term incentive awards and deferred bonuses – have soared most, and 'owners and shareholders have become increasingly concerned about what they see as excessive pay increases for directors not justified by company performance, with a rise in the number of protest votes against remuneration practices at companies' annual meetings' (Iles 2013d: 332). Governance reforms and insurer pressure may force all companies to disclose a single figure for realizable remuneration every year in their annual reports.

Haynes (2008: 86) points out, 'what contributes to the disparity in executive pay across countries is not merely individual, firm or industry variables'. Chief executives of firms of a similar size in the same industry do not receive the same rewards, which are much higher in the USA than in other countries. *Institutional* factors such as legal and governance arrangements (for example the German requirement to have employee representatives on the board of large listed companies), ownership patterns, equity markets and the tax system all have an impact, as does culture. Uncertainty avoidance affects preferences for variable pay and its ratio to fixed pay; higher uncertainty avoidance in the home country, as in Japan, is associated with higher ratios of fixed to variable pay and lower total CEO pay. Time horizon is another – short-term time horizon countries like the USA focus on short-term goals, and a high risk of turnover is associated with maximizing CEO reward, whilst long-term horizon countries like Japan focus on longer-term goals and rewards. Egalitarianism is another important factor – more egalitarian home countries like Scandinavian and Nordic countries have higher ratios of fixed to variable pay within the CEO package, and lower total CEO pay, in comparison with inegalitarian countries like the USA.

Global standardization and convergence in IHRM?

The opportunities for IEs to invest in developing countries in particular, as we saw in Case Study 12.2, also lead us to consider the issue of how HRM policies and practices are transferred from the parent country to the host country and what the implications of this transfer process are (Schuler et al. 2004). Are countries becoming more similar in terms of macro-level operations, yet at a micro-level still showing great variance due to the diversity of culture and insitutions?

In the context of the developing country, globalization and the activities of the International Monetary Fund as expressed in 'structural adjustment programmes' have often encouraged or forced governments to shed their public enterprises or at least subject them to a rigorous review of practice to reflect the private sector (Debrah 2007), leading to the privatization of various public enterprises. However, this competiveness and thrust for change on such a robust scale has also demanded that these enterprises update their technologies and become innovative in terms of product and management practice, including HRM. There are several key global influences which have shaped the development of HRM in developing countries such as the global economic force and employment trends; globalization often increases the flow of Foreign Direct Investment (FDI) from developed to developing countries. Although globalization brings with it turbulent pressures, disrupting, changing and transforming HRM, it can also bring opportunities to upgrade, shape and motivate new management methods.

The term 'developing countries' is widely used in academia and also in practice and to some extent has become a generic term; but what is it exactly? A developing country is one which does not follow the structure of an advanced

Table 12.2

Developing countries play an important role within the global marketplace

1. Developing countries act as significant buyers within the global marketplace.
2. Emergent economies are important suppliers of different resources (both natural and human) to industrialized nations.
3. Developing nations are direct competitors to developed countries with lower labour costs.
4. Strategic regional centres for expansion of MNCs.
5. Production sites for MNCs.
6. Capital users, i.e. from private creditors such as international banks, FDI and foreign official government assistance.

Source: Budhwar and Debrah (2001).

industrialized society. Some authors have used other terms to describe a country falling into this category such as *'less developed'*, *'newly industrialized'*, *'third world'*, *'emerging nations'*, *'emerging markets'* and *'transitional economies'* (Budhwar and Debrah 2001; O'Neill 2011). The term developing country will signify a country in the early growth stages of economic development, and which may either be in the process of industrialization or non-industrialized. However, even with this term now defined, there are clearly still differences and variables, as developing countries are in various stages of economic growth (Kanungo and Jaeger 1990; Budhwar and Debrah 2001).

As demonstrated in Table 12.2 developing countries also perform some key functions in the global economy, emphasizing the extent to which developed and developing countries have become interdependent and reliant on each other.

Although there is dependence between the developed and developing countries, there are also concerns here for the transfer of HRM practices. Within a Westernized society, many businesses operate with state of the art techniques and approaches to people management; yet it cannot be an expectation that these practices can be merely adopted by the developing country. Considerations must be given to the unique configurations of varying cultural and institutional factors which exist within the developing country. There is the question here of what HRM practices and policies are relevant for developing countries. How are HRM practices diffused or standardized globally? Are they converging across the globe (Budhwar and Debrah 2001)?

One view discusses the role of the expatriate and how they specifically help the facilitation of knowledge across borders, how expatriates embed new knowledge, the extent to which they use organizational processes to do so and the micro factors within the organization which may promote this facilitation process. Knowledge is 'grafted' through social interaction within the organization and the exchange processes selected to ensure that this transfer is of knowledge useful to the overseas operations (Wang-Cowham 2011).

It is essential that the expatriates offer other skills in addition to technical skills, such as the ability and motivation to perform at a consistently high level, because the work of an expatriate in embedding new knowledge to local employees which has been 'hard-earned' on their part can be extremely demanding. There is also the implication of adapting to the local staffing and localization pressures within the host country (Bonache and Brewster 2001).

The aim of the IE in such a foreign environment is often to overcome such concerns with 'foreignness' and strive to succeed and gain competitive advantage (see Case Study 12.2). Due to the differing nature and culture of the host country it is often a necessity that knowledge is adapted prior to being transferred; however knowledge is often tacit, that is it is deeply rooted within the minds and experiences of individuals and cannot be taught or decoded (Wang-Cowham 2011). This also creates concerns for transfer, as it requires people and human resource practices to transfer it efficiently. The transfer of knowledge across borders can be 'sticky' and it is an easier process to transfer in a domestic format; key constraints with the transferral process include resource costs, absorption costs, transferee fee and those notable dimensions of international adaptation (see Case Study 12.1).

This view has led to the increased importance of the expatriate and their role in embedding knowledge in the subsidiary to ensure success for the performance of the subsidiary organization as a whole. However, with such importance placed on the expatriate, it is imperative that they possess the appropriate skills and competencies to perform such an important role within the emerging business ((Bonache and Brewster 2001; Wang-Cowham 2011).

A number of issues face the multinational in terms of transferring practices and policies between the parent and host subsidiary. 'Institutional duality' exists whereby the MNC and the host subsidiary face differing pressures from those in their own environments. According to Kostava (1996) the greater the institutional distance – described as 'the divergence between the parent and the host subsidiary' – between the IE and the host subsidiary, then the more difficulty the company will have in terms of transferring policy and practice from the parent to the subsidiary.

This transfer has several dimensions, such as the degree of adaptation by the organization or subsidiary in terms of internalization, functionality and directionality (Lawrence and Suddaby 2006). Internalization addresses the issue that transfer is not a complete process in itself and there may well be varying degrees of transfer. In addition this transferral process may become adapted, adjusted or made more flexible to suit the needs of the receptor or in this case the business environment. Indeed, the transfer process may be adapted to suit another framework, be added to fit the requirements of the host environment or even diluted to adjust to a different cultural perspective. The functionality concept addresses whether the transferred practice still suits the requirements of business needs within the host environment. Lastly, directionality addresses the issue that the transfer process does not merely occur between the parent and subsidary only, but it also occurs between other subsidiaries and from subsidiaries to head office or the central head-quarters (Iles and Yolles 2002b).

The NBS approach discussed earlier highlights 'how business continues to be influenced by the national institutional frameworks in which it is embedded' (Tempel and Walgenbach 2007: 2) but 'it downplays the effects of transnational developments on national patterns.' Another 'institutionalist' perspective in contrast, 'neo' or 'new' institutionalism, emphasizes the global diffusion of practices and the adoption of these by organizations, but pays little attention to how such practices are interpreted or 'translated' as they travel around the world (cf. Czarniawska 1997; Czarniawska and Joerges 1996). So 'what is needed is a framework which moves beyond the convergence/divergence dichotomy to capture signs of both global standardization and continued persistence of differences in IHRM' (Iles 2013a: 12).

Neo-institutionalist explanations of the global standardization of organizational forms (Tempel and Walgenbach 2007; Gamble 2010; Iles, Preece and Chuai 2010) seek to explain how global forms of HRM are diffused and standardized. For Tempel and Walgenbach (2007: 2) 'particular organizational forms exist not because they provide an optimal input-output balance, but because they correspond to institutionalized expectations'. The focus is on how organizations attain legitimacy within the institutional environment by adopting its expectations of structure and practice, including IHRM practice.

DiMaggio and Powell (1983) introduced the *homogenization* phenomenon: organizations become increasingly similar to each other as managers try to change them. *Isomorphism* best captures this process: organizations in the same or similar social, economic and political contexts come to resemble each other over time. (Iles, Preece and Chuai 2010). DiMaggio and Powell (1983) distinguish two types of isomorphism: *competitive* and *institutional*. Competitive isomorphism emphasizes market competition and fitness, but IEs also face institutional pressures from government regulators, professional associations like the CIPD in the UK and SHRM in the USA and social networks, competing not only for resources and customers, but also for political power and institutional *legitimacy*.

Three institutional mechanisms influence organizational decision making: *coercive, normative* and *mimetic*. Coercive mechanisms arise from pressures exerted by political contexts and the challenge of legitimacy and from formal and informal pressures exerted by other organizations upon which they are dependent, experienced as force, persuasion, or invitations to collusion (Meyer and Rowan 1977). Normative mechanisms refer to the articulation between management policies and the professional backgrounds of employees in terms of educational level, job experience and craftsmanship; in many cases, the influence of the professions per se can be as strong as that of the state (Iles 2013a: 13). Professional networks, such as professional and trade associations like the Confederation of British Industry or Institute of Directors in the UK, help define and promulgate norms about organizational and professional behaviour, and

> normative mechanisms create pools of individuals who not only share common expectations, but also occupy similar positions across a range of organizations and possess a similarity of orientation and disposition. This normative isomorphism is reinforced by filtering personnel, as many professional career tracks in organizations are carefully controlled and monitored, both at entry and throughout the career path. (Iles 2013a: 13)

Individuals in similar positions across organizations tend to have similar biographies in terms of education, skills, work experience, and ideology, and develop similar patterns of thought about organizational practice; through this global discourse, similar HRM ideas and concepts are diffused globally.

Finally, mimetic mechanisms refer to imitations of the strategies and practices of competitors as a result of uncertainty; these are the mechanisms most often referred to in discussions of management fashion-setting (Abrahamson 1991). Management fashions need to be not only novel but also rational, solving substantive problems for the organization. Management fashions are often developed by fashion-leaders like consultants, academics and leading MNCs, and marketed to 'fashion-followers' such as local companies and SMEs through books, publications, seminars, conferences, websites and training courses. Organizations may model themselves on other similar organizations in their field, generally seen as more legitimate or successful. Later, fashionable novel managerial techniques may be 'diffused unintentionally, indirectly through employee transfer or turnover, or explicitly by consulting firms or industry trade associations' (DiMaggio and Powell 2002: 172). This may occur globally in IEs through the global or regional rotation of staff, and especially through expatriates 'transferring technology'. Employees studying common concepts at university, on education or training courses, reading similar textbooks, and global consultancies preaching a common message may help diffuse such fashions, as well as the deliberate actions of IEs themselves in standardizing operations. Popular management books and the management consulting industry may also aid diffusion (Fincham and Evans 1999).

Isomorphism

> thus results from adopting institutionalized elements, in particular expected structures and management practices. The fashionable practice may become insitutionalized over time as a regular practice, adopted 'ceremonially' perhaps in name only or simply as a re-labelling of an existing practice without substantive change, or rapidly dropped in favour of the next fashion or fad. (Iles 2013a: 14)

Perkmann and Spicer (2008: 812) argue that managers' decisions to embrace new ideas are often informed by collective beliefs about rational or progressive managerial practice, shaped by idea providers such as consultants or gurus; fashionable management concepts may acquire permanence when anchored within field-wide institutions. *Institutional entrepreneurs* such as consultants can also act as active fashion agents, purposefully working towards changing existing or creating novel institutions; for Scarbrough (2002), institutionalization is driven by the 'translation' of practices into specific organizational contexts through the actions of professional groups and consultants: 'Business gurus may legitimate a body of knowledge, large consulting firms will engage in its commodification and colonization, and business schools in due diligence and innovation through critical analysis' (Iles 2013a: 14).

Figure 12.6 shows how this process of isomorphism might work in the IHRM field with specific reference to performance-related pay (PRP), discussed earlier.

However, 'emphasizing the adaptation of organizations to their societal and cultural (particularly institutional) environments, and the global diffusion and adoption of practices, downplays the role of national cultural and institutional differences and how such practices are locally interpreted or translated as they diffuse' (Iles 2013a: 15), as in international mergers, acquisitions and joint ventures (Czarniawska and Joerges 1996; Iles and Yolles 2002a, 2002b, 2003a, 2003b; Yolles and Iles 2006). There may be diffusion of a common global language, such as 'flexibility' or 'engagement', but leaving leeway for local interpretation and practice. In

> some countries good customer service may be signified by the use of first names; in others, titles. In some networking may signify playing golf with key contacts, in others, joining chambers of commerce, attending sports events or beach barbecues or joining local officials in karaoke and banquets. (Iles 2013a: 15)

Creating high impact may signify using participative leadership styles in some countries, but authoritative direction or command and control in

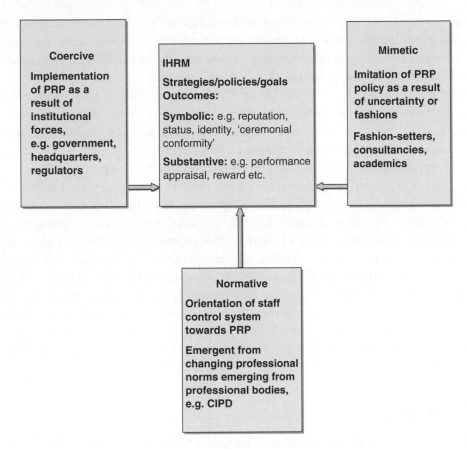

Figure 12.6 IHRM and the new institutionalism in performance-related pay

Sources: Adapted from Boselie et al. (2000), Iles, Preece and Chuai (2010: 140), Iles (2013a: 14).

others. An over-socialized view of participants leaves little scope for agency in the role actors play as interpreters, translators, synthesizers and hybridizers over the local interpretation and implementation of globally diffused HR practices.

Gamble (2010: 728), in analysing the extent to which Japanese retail companies in China 'transferred' home practices, claims that existing theories

> are shown to be inadequate, individually, to account for the complex patterns of transfer, local adoption, and adaptation in these multinational companies. These findings highlight the value of conceptual bricolage and multi-level analysis for developing explanations that can encompass and explicate complex patterns of hybridization.

In particular, context-specific, firm-level perceptions of sources of competitive advantage are key motives for transferring practices, but these are constrained by the practices and norms prevalent in local labour markets. Some companies transferred home-country 'Japanese' practices such as job security for core employees, alongside greater reliance on internal labour markets and Japanese-style customer service. However, they did not often transfer other 'Japanese-style' practices, such as part-time employment, careful recruitment, slow promotion, seniority pay or use of male rather than female supervisors. Some companies did however try to transfer some Japanese-style practices. In China, staff fines and bonuses were often used, absent in 'high-commitment' Japan. 'National' level explanations, whether cultural or institutionalist, 'leave us with static, overly homogenised, and over-determined models' which 'neglect the extent of sub-national diversity'(Gamble 2010: 711-12). In addition, in many developing economies 'transfer by multinational companies to transitional economies with high levels of deinstitutionalization illustrates problematic dimensions for various theoretical perspectives, including influential neo-institutionalist models' (ibid: 705). It is increasingly difficult, given rapid change in a 'deinstitutionalizing' environment, to discern a recognizable 'Chinese model' or 'Vietnamese model' of work organization and employment practice; various forms of 'hybrid' practice exist, as in many African and Latin American countries, combining 'foreign' and 'local' practices in different combinations.

Conclusion

This chapter began by critically analysing the changing impact of globalization on organizations, and especially on IHRM, and discussed the field of IHRM and different models and approaches to IHRM, especially orientation and life cycle models. It sought to identify and distinguish approaches to international and comparative HRM in order to help understand the IHRM policies of the international enterprise, and critically evaluate different approaches to and frameworks in, IHRM, with particular reference to host country, country of origin, and firm effects.

The chapter then discussed the advantages and disadvantages of different orientations to IHRM and analysed some key theoretical perspectives on institutional theories and national business systems, with particular respect to employment relations and national vocational education and training systems. The purpose was to help appreciate national differences in HRM policy and practice and evaluate the implications of the above perspectives for international HRM. A particular focus was on composing an international workforce, recruiting and selecting international managers, developing cross-cultural competence, and delivering cross-cultural training programmes to enhance adjustment and performance. It also considered reward management in a global context. It concluded by discussing whether there was global convergence or divergence in IHRM policies and practices, and used neoinstitutionalist theory to discuss how IHRM policies and practices might diffuse and be transferred globally.

■ Further Reading ■■■■■■■■■■■■■■■■■■■■■■

Brewster, C., Sparrow, P., Vernon, G. and Houldsworth, E. (2011) *International Human Resource Management*, 3rd edn. London: Charted Institute for Personnel and Development, pp. 67–89.

Briscoe, D.R., Schuler, R. and Claus, L. (2009) *International Human Resource Management; Policies and Practices for Multinational Enterprises*, 3rd edn. Routledge Global Human Resource Management Series. London: Routledge, pp. 155–98, 286–312.

Edwards, T. and Rees, C. (2011) *International Human Resource Management; Globalization, National Systems and Multinational Companies*, 2nd edn. Harlow: Pearson, pp. 50–67, 120–39.

Lundby, K. and Jolton, J. (2010) *Going Global; Practical Applications and Recommendations for HR and OD Practitioners in the Global Workplace*. San Francisco, CA: Jossey-Bass Publications, pp. 113–75.

Rao, T.V. (2004) *Performance Management and Appraisal Systems; HR Tools for Global Competitiveness*. London: Sage Publications, pp. 125–67.

Schuler, R., Jackson, S.E., Sparrow, P. and Pool, M. (2008) *Performance Management Systems; A Global Perspective*. Abingdon: Taylor and Francis, pp. 3–154.

Ulrich, D., Brockbank, W., Younger, J. and Ulrich, M. (2012) *Global HR Competencies*. Maidenhead: McGraw-Hill Books, pp. 55–175.

References

Abrahamson, E. (1991) 'Managerial fads and fashions: the diffusion and rejection of innovations', *Academy of Management Review*, 16 (3): 586–612.

Adelman, M. (1988) 'Cross-cultural adjustment: a theoretical perspective on social support', *International Journal of Intercultural Relations*, 12: 183–204.

Adler, N. and Ghadar, F. (1989) 'Strategic human resource management: a global perspective', in R. Reiperl (ed.), *Human Resource Management: An International Comparison*. New York: Walter de Gruyter, pp. 235-60.

Adler, N. (1991) *International Dimensions of Organizational Behavior*, 2nd edn. Boston: PWS Kent Publishing.

Albert, M. (1993) *Capitalism Against Capitalism*. London: Whurr.

Baccaro, L. and Pulignano, V. (2011) 'Employment relations in Italy', in G. Bamber, R.D. Lansbury and N. Walles (eds), *International and Comparative Employment Relations: Globalisation and Change*. London: Sage, pp. 138–68.

Bartlett, C. and Ghoshal, S. (1989) *Managing Across Borders: The Transnational Solution*. Boston, MA: Harvard Business School Press.

Bennett, R., Aston, A. and Colquhoun T. (2000) 'Cross -cultural training: a critical step in ensuring the success of international assignments', *Human Resource Management*, 39 (2/3): 239–50.

Berry, J.W. (1980) 'Acculturation as varieties of adaptation', in A. Padilla (ed.), *Acculturation: Theory, Models and Some New Findings*. Boulder, CO: Westview, pp. 9–25.

Berry, J.W. (1997) 'Immigration, acculturation and adaptation', *Applied Psychology: An International Review*, 46: 5–68.

Black, J.S. (1989) 'Repatriation: a comparison of Japanese and American practices and results', *Proceedings of the Eastern Academy of Management Bi-annual International Conference*. Eastern Academy of Management: Hong Kong, pp. 45–9.

Black, J.S. and Mendenhall, M.E. (2007) 'A practical but theory-based framework for selecting cross-cultural training methods', in M.E. Mendenhall, G.R. Oddou and G.K. Stahl (eds), *Readings and Cases in International Human Resource Management*, 4th edn. New York: Routledge, pp. 219–45.

Black, J.S., Mendenhall, M. and Oddou, G. (1991) 'Toward a comprehensive model of international adjustment: an integration of multiple theoretical perspectives', *Academy of Management Review*, 16 (2): 291–317.

Bolino, M.C. (2007) 'Expatriate assignments and intra-organizational career success: implications for individual organizations', *Journal of International Business Studies*, 38: 819–35.

Bonache, J. and Brewster, C. (2001) 'Knowledge transfer and the management of expatriation', *Thuderbird International Business Review*, 43 (1): 145–68.

Boselie, P., Brewster, C. and Paauwe, J. (2009) 'In search of balance – managing the dualities of HRM: an overview of the issues', *Personnel Review*, 38 (5): 461–71.

Brewster, C. (1995) 'Towards a European model of human resource management', *Journal of International Business Studies*, 26 (1): 1–21.

Brewster, C. and Bournois, F. (1991) 'Human resource management: a European perspective', *Personnel Review*, 20 (6): 4–13.

Briscoe, D.R. and Schuler, R.S. (eds) (2004) *International Human Resource Management*, 2nd edn. London: Routledge.

Brislin, R.W. (1981) *Cross-cultural Encounters*. London: Pergamon Press.

Brislin, R.W. (2000) *Understanding Culture's Influence on Behavior*, 2nd edn. London: Thomson Learning Inc.

Brislin, R.W. and Pedersen, P. (1976) *Cross-cultural Orientation Programs*. New York: Gardner.

Budhwar, P. and Debrah, Y.A. (eds) (2001) *Human Resource Management in Developing Countries*. London: Routledge.

Budhwar, P. and Sparrow, P. (2002) 'An integrative framework for determining cross-national human resource management practices', *Human Resource Management Review*, 12: 377–403.

Caligiuri, P., Philips, J., Lazarova, M., Tarique, I. and Burgi, P. (2001) 'The theory of met expectations applied to expatriate adjustment: the role of cross-cultural training', *International Journal of Human Resource Management*, 12 (3): 357–72.

Chen, R. (2008) 'The cost of doing business abroad in emerging markets and the role of MNC parent companies', *Multinational Business Review*, 16 (3): 23–40.

Chiang, F.F.T. and Birtch, T.A. (2012) 'The performance implications of financial and non-financial rewards: an Asian Nordic comparison', *Journal of Management Studies*, 49 (3): 538–70.

Chien, T.-C. and McLean, G.N. (2011) 'Intercultural training for US business expatriates in Taiwan', *Journal of European Industrial Training*, 35 (9): 858–73.

Collings, D., Scullion, H. and Morley, M. (2007) 'Changing patterns of global staffing in the multinational enterprise: challenges to the conventional expatriate assignment', *Journal of World Business*, 42 (2): 198–213.

Czarniawska, B. (1997) 'Learning organizing in a changing institutional order: examples from city management in Warsaw', *Management Learning*, 28 (4): 475–95.

Czarniawska, B. and Joerges, B. (1996) 'Travels of ideas', in B. Czarniawska and G. Sevón (eds), *Translating Organizational Change*. Berlin: de Gruyter, pp. 13–48.

Davila, A. and Elvira, M.M. (eds) (2009) *Best Human Resource Management Practices in Latin America*. London: Routledge.

Debrah, Y.A. (2007) 'Promoting the informal sector as a source of gainful employment in developing countries: insights from Ghana', *International Journal of Human Resource Management*, 18 (6): 1063–84.

De Cieri, H. and Dowling, P.J. (1999) 'Strategic human resource management in multinational enterprises: theoretical and empirical developments', in P.M. Wright, L.D. Dyer, J.W. Boudreau and G.T. Milkovich (eds), *Research in Personnel and Human Resources Management: Strategic Human Resources Management in the Twenty-first Century*. Supplement 4. Stamford, CT: JAI Press.

Dess, G.G. and Davis, P.S. (1984) 'Porter's generic strategies as determinants of strategic group membership and performance', *Academy of Management Journal*, 26 (3): 467–88.

DiMaggio, P. and Powell, W. (1983) 'The iron cage revisited: institutional isomorphism and collective rationality in organizational fields', *American Sociological Review*, 48 (2): 147–60.

DiMaggio, P. and Powell, W. (2002) 'The iron cage revisited: institutional isomorphism and collective rationality in organizational fields', in C. Calhoun, J. Gerteis, J. Moody, S. Pfaff and I. Virket (eds), *Contemporary Sociological Theory*. London: Blackwell, pp. 175–92.

Dowling, P.J., Festing, M. and Engle, A.D. (2008) *International Human Resource Management*, 5th edn. London: Thomson Learning.

Doz, Y (1986) *Strategic Management in Multinational Companies*. Oxford: Pergamon Press.

Edgar, F. and Geare, A. (2005) 'HRM practice and employee attitudes: different measures – different results', *Personnel Review*, 34 (5): 534–49.

Edstrom, A. and Galbraith, J. (1977) 'Transfer of managers as a coordination and control strategy in multinational organizations', *Administrative Science Quarterly*, 22 (2): 11–22.

Edwards, T., Almond, P., Clark, I., Colling, T. and Ferner, A. (2005) 'Reverse diffusion in US multinationals: barriers from the American business system', *Journal of Management Studies*, 42: 6.

Eichhorst, W. (2012) *The Unexpected Appearance of a New German Model*, IZA Discussion Papers 6625. Bonn: Institute for the Study of Labor (IZA).

Elvira, M.M. and Davila, A. (eds) (2005) *Managing Human Resources in Latin America*. London: Routledge.

Evans, P. and Lorange, L. (1989) 'The two logics behind human resource management', in P. Evans, Y. Doz and A. Laurent (eds), *Human Resource Management in International firms*. Basingstoke: Palgrave, pp. 144–61.

Feldman, D.C. and Thomas, D.C. (1992) 'Career management issues facing expatriates', *Journal of International Business Studies*, 23 (2): 271–94.

Ferner, A. (1997) 'Country of origin effects in multinational companies', *Human Resource Management Journal*, 7: 19–37.

Ferner, A. and Edwards, P.K. (1995) 'Power and diffusion of organizational change within multinational enterprises', *European Journal of Industrial Relations*, 1 (2): 29–57.

Fisher, A. (2005) 'Offshoring could boost your career', *Fortune*, 151 (2): 36.

Fincham, R. and Evans, M. (1999) 'The consultants' offensive: reengineering – from fad to technique', *New Technology, Work and Employment*, 14 (1): 32–44.

Franco-Santos, M. (2008) 'Performance measurement issues, incentive application and globalization', in L. R. Gomez-Mejia and S. Werner (eds), *Global Compensation: Foundations and Perspectives*. London: Routledge, pp. 41–56.

Furnham, A. (2004) 'Performance management systems', *European Business Journal*, 16: 83–94.

Gamble, J. (2003) 'Transferring human resource practices from the United Kingdom to China: the limits and potential for convergence', *International Journal of Human Resource Management*, 14 (3): 369–87.

Gamble, J. (2010) 'Transferring organizational practices and the dynamics of hybridization: Japanese retail multinationals in China', *Journal of Management Studies*, 47 (4): 705–32.

Gerhart, B. and Trevor, C. O. (2008) 'Merit pay', in A. Varma, P. Budhwar and A. DeNisi (eds), *Performance Management Systems: a Global Perspective*. London: Routledge, pp. 67–80.

Gertsen, M. (1990) 'Intercultural competence and expatriates', *Journal of Human Resource Management*, 4: 341–61.

Gold, J.R., Holden, P.A., Iles, J. Stewart, and Beardwell, J. (eds) (2009) *Human Resource Development: Theory And Practice*. Basingstoke: Palgrave.

Graf, A. and Mertesacker, M. (2009) 'Intercultural training: six measures assessing training needs', *Journal of European Industrial Training*, 33 (6): 539–58.

Green, F., Ashton, D., James, D. and Sung, J. (1999) 'The role of the state in skill formation: evidence from the Republic of Korea, Taiwan and Singapore', *Oxford Review of Economic Policy*, 15 (1): 82–96.

Gudykunst, W.B. and Hammer, M.R. (1983) 'Basic training design: approaches to intercultural training', in D. Landis and R. W. Brislin (eds), *Handbook of Intercultural Training: Issues in Theory and Design*, vol. 1. Elmsford, NY: Pergamon, pp. 118–54.

Gudykunst, W.B. and Hammer, M.R. (1988) 'Strangers and hosts: an uncertainty reduction based theory of intercultural adaption', in Y. Kim and W.B. Gudykunst (eds), *Cross-cultural Adaption*. Newbury Park, CA: Sage, pp. 106–39.

Gullahorn, J.T. and Gullahorn, J.E. (1963) 'An extention of the U-curve hypothesis', *Journal of Social Issues*, 19: 33–47.

Guzzo, R.A., Noonan, K.A. and Elron, E. (1994) 'Expatriate managers and the psychological contract', *Journal of Applied Psychology*, 79 (4): 617–26.

Hall, P.A. and Soskice, D. (eds) (2001) *Varieties of Capitalism: the Institutional Foundations of Comparative Advantage*. New York: Oxford University Press.

Hamori, M. and Koyuncu, B. (2011) 'Career advancement in large organizations in Europe and the United States: do international assignments add value?', *International Journal of Human Resource Management*, 22 (4): 843–62.

Hannon, E. (2011) 'International and comparative employee voice', in T. Edwards and C. Rees (eds), *International Human Resource Management: Globalization, National Systems and Multinational Companies*, 2nd edn. Harlow: Pearson FT Prentice Hall, pp. 229–52.

Harris, H. and Brewster, C. (1999) 'The coffee machine system: how international selection really works', *International Journal of Human Resource Management*, 10 (3): 488–500.

Harzing, A.W. (2001a) 'Of bears, bumble-bees and spiders: the role of expatriates in controlling foreign subsidiaries', *Journal of World Business*, 36 (4): 366–79.

Harzing, A.W. (2001b) 'An analysis of the functions of international transfer of managers in MNCs', *Employee Relations*, 23 (6): 581–98.

Haynes, K.T. (2008) 'Executive compensation in an international context: the role of formal and informal institutions', in L.R. Gomez-Mejia and S. Werner (eds), *Global Compensation: Foundations and Perspectives*. London: Routledge, pp. 86–99.

Hechanova, R., Beehr, T.A., Christiansen, N.D. (2003) 'Antecedents and consequences of employees' adjustment to overseas assignment: a meta-analytic review', *Applied Psychology*, 52: 213–36.

Hendry, C. (1995) *Human Resource Management: A Strategic Approach to Employment*. London: Butterworth Heinemann.

Hendry, C. (1996) 'Continuities in Human Resource Processes in Internationalisation and Domestic Business Management', *Journal of Management Studies*, 33 (4): 475–494.

Hendry, C. and Pettigrew, A. (1986) 'The practice of strategic human resource management', *Personnel Review*, 15 (5): 3–8.

Hendry, C. and Pettigrew, A. (2002) 'Patterns of strategic change in the development of human resource management', *British Journal of Management*, 3 (3): 137–56.

Hofstede, G. (2001) *Culture's Consequences: Comparing Values, Behaviors, Institutions, and Organizations Across Nations*, 2nd edn. Thousand Oaks, CA: Sage.

Horwitz, F.M. (2012) 'Evolving human resource management in Southern African multinational firms: towards an Afro-Asian nexus', *International Journal of Human Resource Management*, 23 (14): 2938–58.

Huselid, M. (1995) 'The impact of human resource management practices on turnover, productivity, and corporate financial performance', *Academy of Management Journal*, 38 (3): 635–72.

Iles, P.A. (2013a) 'International HRM, national differences and the transfer of HRM', in P.A. Iles and C. Zhang C (eds) *International Human Resource Management: a Cross-Cultural and Comparative Approach*. London: Chartered Institute for Personnel and Development, pp. 1–17.

Iles, P.A. (2013b) 'Globalisation and IHRM policies at the enterprise level', in P.A. Iles and C. Zhang (eds), *International Human Resource Management: A Comparative and Cross-Cultural Approach*. London: Chartered Institute for Personnel and Development, pp. 37–53.

Iles, P.A. (2013c) 'Employment relations and employee voice in a global context', in P.A. Iles and C. Zhang (eds), *International Human Resource Management: a Comparative and Cross-Cultural Approach*. London: Chartered Institute for Personnel and Development, pp. 335–52.

Iles, P.A. (2013d) 'Global Reward Management, Organizational benefits and employer branding', in P.A. Iles and C. Zhang (eds), *International Human Resource Management: A Comparative and Cross-Cultural Approach*. London: Chartered Institute for Personnel and Development, pp. 319–33.

Iles, P.A. and Yolles, M. (2002a) 'Across the great divide: HRD, technology translation and knowledge migration in bridging the knowledge gap between SMEs and universities', *Human Resource Development International*, 5 (1): 23–53.

Iles, P.A. and Yolles, M. (2002b) 'International joint ventures, HRM, and viable knowledge migration', *International Journal of Human Resource Management*, 13 (14): 624–41.

Iles, P.A. and Yolles, M. (2003a) 'Complexity, HRD and organization development: towards a viable systems approach to learning, development and change', in M. Lee (ed.), *HRD in a Complex World*. London: Routledge, pp. 25–41.

Iles, P.A. and Yolles, M. (2003b) 'International HRD alliances in viable knowledge migration and development: the Czech Academic Link Project', *Human Resource Development International*, 6 (3): 301–24.

Iles, P.A., Preece, D. and Chuai, X. (2010) 'Is talent management a management fashion in HRD? Towards a research agenda', *Human Resource Development International*, 13 (2): 125–46.

Iles, P.A. and Jiang, T. (2013) 'Employee resourcing', in P.A. Iles and C. Zhang (eds), *International Human Resource Management: a Cross-cultural and Comparative Approach*. London: CIPD, pp. 241–61.

Jansenns, M. (2001) 'Developing a culturally synergistic approach to international human resource management', *Journal of World Business*, 36 (4): 429–42.

Kamoche, K. and Newenham-Kahindi, A. (2012) 'HRM and knowledge appropriation: the MNC experience in Tanzania', *International Journal of Human Resource Management*, 23: 2854–73.

Kanungo, R.M. and Jaeger, A.F. (1990) 'Introduction: the need for indigenous management in developing countries', in A.M. Jaeger and R.M. Kanungo (eds), *Management in Developing Countries*. London: Routledge, pp. 1–23.

Keller, B.K. and Kirsch, A. (2011) 'Employment relations in Germany', in G. Bamber, R.D. Lansbury and N. Wailes (eds), *International and Comparative Employment Relations: Globalisation and Change*. London: Sage, pp. 196–223.

Khatri, N. (1999) 'Emerging issues in strategic HRM in Singapore', *International Journal of Manpower*, 20 (8): 516–29.

Kostova, T. (1996) 'Transnational transfer of strategic organizational practices: a contextual perspective', *Academy of Management Review*, 24 (2): 308–25.

Kramar, R. and Syed, J. (2012) *Human Resource Management in a Global Context: A Critical Approach*. Basingstoke: Palgrave Macmillan.

Lane, C. (1992) 'European business systems: Britain and Germany', in R. Whitley (ed.), *European Business Systems: Firms and Markets in their National Contexts*. London: Sage Publications, pp. 64–97.

Lawrence, T.B., and Suddaby, R. (2006). Institutions and Institutional Work. In S. Clegg, C. Hardy, T.B. Lawrence and W.R. Nord (eds), *The SAGE Handbook of Organization Studies*, 2nd edn. London: Sage, pp. 215–54.

Legge, K. (1995) *HRM; Rhetoric and Realities*. Basingstoke: Macmillan.

Leguizamon, F.A., Ickis, J.C. and Ogliastri, E. (2009) 'Human resource practices and business performance: Grupo San Nicolas', in A. Davila and M.M. Elvira (eds), *Best Human Resource Management Practices in Latin America*. London: Routledge, pp. 85–96.

Lewis, M.M. (2005) 'The drama of international business: why cross-cultural training simulations work', *Journal of European Industrial Training*, 29 (7): 593–8.

Lievens, F., Van Keer, E., Harris, M. and Bisqueret, C. (2003) 'Predicting cross-cultural training performance: the validity of personality, cognitive ability and dimensions measured by an assessment centre and a behavior description interview', *Journal of Applied Psychology*, 88 (3): 476–89.

Littrell, L. N., Salas, E., Palye, M. and Riedel, S. (2006) 'Expatriate preparation: a critical analysis of 25 years of cross-cultural training research', *Human Resource Development Review*, 5: 355–88.

Luo, Y. (2001) 'Determinant of local responsiveness: perspectives from foreign subsidiaries in an emerging market', *Journal of Management*, 27: 451–77.

Marchington, M., Waddington, J. and Timming, A. (2011) 'Employment relations in Britain', in G. Bamber, R.D. Lansbury and N. Wailes (eds), *International and Comparative Employment Relations: Globalisation and Change*. London: Sage, pp. 36–61.

Mayrhofer, W. and Scullion, H. (2002) 'All equal? The importance of context empirical evidence about male and female expatriates from the German clothing industry', *International Journal of Human Resource Management*, 3 (5): 815–36.

Mendenhall, M. and Oddou, G. (1985) 'The dimensions of expatriate acculturation: a review', *Academy of Management Review*, 10 (1): 39–47.

Mendenhall, M., Kuhlmann, T., Stahl, G. and Osland, J. (2002) 'Employee development and expatriate assignments', in M. Gannon and K. Newman (eds), *The Blackwell Handbook of Cross-Cultural Management*. Oxford: Blackwell Publishers, pp. 155–83.

Mendenhall, M., Stahl, G., Ehnert, I., Oddou, G., Osland, J. and Kühlmann, T. (2004) 'Evaluation studies of cross-cultural training programs: a review of the literature from 1988–2000', in D. Landis and J. Bennett (eds), *The Handbook of Intercultural Training*. Thousand Oaks, CA: Sage, pp. 129–44.

Meyer, J. and Rowan, B. (1977) 'Institutionalized organizations: formal structure as myth and ceremony', *American Journal of Sociology*, 83 (2): 340–63.

Meyer, K., Mudambi, R. and Narula, R. (2011) 'Multinational enterprises and local contexts: the opportunities and challenges of multiple embeddedness', *Journal of Management Studies*, 48 (2): 235–52.

Minbaeva, D.B. (2005) 'HRM practices and MNC knowledge transfer', *Personnel Review*, 34 (1): 125–44.

Minbaeva, D.B., Pedersen, T., Bjorkman, I., Fey, C.F. and Park, H. J. (2003) 'MNC knowledge transfer, subsidiary absorptive capacity, and HRM', *Journal of International Business Studies*, 34 (6): 586–99.

Morley, M.J. and Collings, D.G. (2004) 'Contemporary debates and new directions in HRM in MNCs: introduction', *International Journal of Manpower*, 25 (6): 487–99.

Oberg, K.(1960) 'Culture shock: adjustment to new cultural environments', *Practical Anthropology*, 7: 177–2.

O'Neill, J. (2011) *The Growth Map: Economic Opportunity in the BRICs and Beyond*. London: Penguin.

Orru, M., Biggart, N. and Hamilton, G. (eds) (1997) *The Economic Organization of East Asian Capitalism*. Thousand Oaks, CA: Sage.

Perkmann, M. and Spicer, A. (2008) 'How are management fashions institutionalized? The role of institutional work', *Human Relations*, 61 (6): 811–44.

Perlmutter, H. (1969) 'The tortuous evolution of the multinational corporation', *Columbia Journal of World Business*, 1: 9–18.

Perlmutter, H. and Heenan, D. (1979) *Multinational Organization Development*. Reading, MA: Addison-Wesley.

Porter, M.E. (1985) *Competitive Advantage*. New York: Free Press.

Preece, D., Iles, P.A. and Jones, R. (2013) 'MNE regional head offices and their affiliates: talent management practices and challenges in the Asia Pacific', *International Journal of Human Resource Management*, 24 (18): 3457–77.

Ramsey, S.J. and Schaetti, B.F. (1999) 'Reentry: coming "home" to the unfamiliar. Repatriates may feel like strangers in a strange land', *Mobility*, available at http://www.transitions-dynamics.com/reentry.html.

Reiche, S. and Harzing, A.W. (2011) 'International assignments', in A.W. Harzing and A. Pinnington (eds), *International Human Resource Management*, 3rd edn. London: Sage Publications, pp. 185–226.

Reuber, A. and Fischer, E. (1997) 'The influence of the management team's international experience on internationalization behaviors of SMEs', *Journal of International Business Studies*, 28 (4): 807–25.

Rugman, A., Verbeke, A. and Yuan, W. (2011) 'Reconceptualising Bartlett and Ghoshal's classification of national subsidiary roles in the multi-national enterprise', *Journal of Management Studies*, 48 (2): 253–77.

Scarbrough, H. (2002) 'The role of intermediary groups in shaping management fashion: the case of knowledge management', *International Studies in Management and Organization*, 32 (4): 87–103.

Schuler, R.S., Tarique, I. and Jackson, S.E. (2004) 'Managing human resources in cross-border alliances', in S. Finkelstein and C. Cooper (ed.), *Advances in Mergers and Acquisitions, Volume 3*. Bingley: Emerald Group Publishing Limited, pp. 103–29.

Scullion, H. (2005) *International HRM: a Critical Text*. London: Palgrave.

Scullion, H. and Brewster, C. (2001) 'The management of expatriates: messages from Europe', *Journal of World Business*, 36 (4): 346–65.

Shen, J., Edwards, V. and Lee, G. (2005) 'Developing an integrative IHRM model: the contribution of Chinese MNEs', *Asia Pacific Journal of Business Review*, 11 (3): 365–84.

Shen, Y. and Hall, D. (2009) 'When expats explore other options: retaining talent through greater job embeddedness and repatriation adjustment', *Human Resource Management*, 48 (5): 793–816.

Schuler, R.S. and Tarique, I. (2007) 'International human resource management: a North American perspective, a thematic update and suggestions for future research', *International Journal of Human Resource Management*, 18 (5): 717–44.

Stahl, G.K., Miller, E.L. and Tung, R.L. (2002) 'Toward the boundaryless career: a closer look at the expatriate career concept and the perceived implications of an international assignment', *Journal of World Business*, 37 (3): 216–27.

Stewart, J. (2008) *A Blended Action Learning Programme to Develop Cross-cultural Skills for SME Leaders*. Paper presented to British Academy of Management, Harrogate, UK, September.

Stewart, J., Johnson, S., Iles, P.A., Gold, J. and Devins, D. (2008) *World-class Comparisons in HRD*. Research report. Leeds: Learning and Skills Council.

Stroh, L.K., Gregersen, H.B. and Black, J.S. (1998) 'Closing the gap: expectations versus reality among repatriates', *Journal of World Business*, 33 (2): 111–24.

Tarique, I. and Caligiuri, P.M. (2004) 'Training and development of international staff', in A.W. Harzing and J. van Ruysseveldt (eds), *International Human Resource Management*. London: Sage, pp. 283–306.

Taylor, S., Beechler, S., and Napier, N. (1996) 'Toward an integrative model of strategic international human resource management', *Academy of Management Review*, 21 (4): 959–85.

Tempel, A. and Walgenbach, P. (2007) 'Global standardization of organizational forms and management practices? What new institutionalism and the business-systems approach can learn from each other', *Journal of Management Studies*, 44 (1): 1–24.

Triandis, H.C. (1977) 'Theoretical framework for evaluation of cross-cultural training effectiveness', *International Journal of Intercultural Relations*, 1: 19–45.

Tung, R.L. (1981) 'Selection and training of personnel for overseas assignments', *Columbia Journal of World Business*, 16 (1): 8–78.

Tung, R.L. (1998) 'American expatriates abroad: from neophytes to cosmopolitans', *Journal of World Business*, 33 (2): 125–44.

Walter, A. and Zhang, X. (eds) (2012) *East Asian Capitalism: Diversity, Continuity and Change*. Oxford: Oxford University Press.

Wang-Cowham, C. (2011) 'Developing talent with an integrated knowledge-sharing mechanism: an exploratory investigation from the Chinese human resource managers' perspective', *Human Resource Development International*, 14 (4): 391–407.

Wanous, J.P., Poland, T.D., Premack, S.L. and Davis, K.S. (1992) 'The effects of met expectations on newcomer attitudes and behaviors: a review and meta-analysis', *Journal of Applied Psychology*, 77: 288–97.

Ward, C. and Kennedy, A. (1999) 'The measurement of sociocultural adaptation', *International Journal of Intercultural Relations*, 23: 659–77.

Ward, C., Bochner, S. and Furnham, A. (2001) *The Psychology of Culture Shock*, 2nd edn. London: Routledge.

Waxin, M.F. and Panaccio, A. (2005) 'Cross cultural training to facilitate expatriate adjustment: it works', *Personnel Review*, 34 (1): 51–67.

Welch, D. (1994) 'Determinants of international human resource management approaches and activities: a suggested framework', *Journal of Management Studies*, 31 (2): 139–64.

Whitley, R. (1999) *Divergent Capitalisms: the Social Structuring and Change of Business Systems*. Oxford: Oxford University Press.

Yolles, M. and Iles, P.A. (2006) 'Exploring public–private partnerships through knowledge cybernetics', *Systems Research and Behavioral Science*, 23: 1–22.

Zhang, C. and Iles, P.A. (2013) 'Cross-cultural training and international HRD', in P.A. Iles and C. Zhang (eds) *International Human Resource Management: A Cross-Cultural and Comparative Approach*. London: Chartered Institute for Personnel and Development, pp. 263–79.

THE FUTURE OF HR

Linda Holbeche

Chapter Overview

This chapter addresses the perennial question: what is the future of HR? In addressing this question the author considers perspectives from leading HR writers and provides a personal perspective on some of the themes discussed earlier in this book. These include some key elements in the development of HRM theory and the reported gaps between theory and practice (Legge, 2005). The author re-evaluates the added value debate in the light of contemporary contextual changes, arguing that these developments to a large extent may determine the outcome of the 'future of HR' debate. This, she argues, highlights the need for theorists and practitioners to develop a more coherent and critical approach to the development of theory and practice, together with a shared understanding of the purpose of this applied discipline and an HR agenda that better supports mutual gains for both the organization and employees.

≣ Learning Objectives ≣

- **To explore key milestones in the development of HRM theory and HR functional practice**
- **To consider the implications of changes in the global business environment for the definition of 'added value', drawing on key findings from eminent HR writers across the globe**
- **To consider where HR goes from here in the light of these developments**

Introduction

In this final chapter I shall argue that it was a combination of economic and political factors in the 1980s that led to the development of human resource management (HRM) theory and practice. Since then HRM has also emerged as a pervasive theme in the literatures of organizational behaviour, strategic management, business policy, international and intercultural management. These context factors also led to calls for greater accountability in all functional areas of business, including what was previously known as 'Personnel'. As an applied discipline, HRM is therefore still relatively 'young' and as yet the nature of HRM is contested, with various traditions and multiple perspectives and no overall theory of HRM. There is however some consensus that HRM is a business concept reflecting a mainly managerial view of the employment relationship, with theory, policies and practices geared to enabling organizations to achieve flexibility, competitive advantage and high performance through people. Ulrich (1997) for instance emphasizes the role of the HR function in creating 'value' for business and its stakeholders (see Chapter 4).

Almost since HRM came to prominence as the preferred international discourse to frame employment management issues and as a field of practice within organizations, 'it is nearly unanimous that HR can and should add more value to corporations' (Lawler, 2005: 165). In recent times, pressure on HR functions to create added value has led to the outsourcing of many of HR's basic transactional functions (Cascio, 2005) in order to save costs and to free up HR functions for more strategic contributions which are slow to materialize. Moreover, the process of HR transformation often tends to be expensive and poorly executed. This has led many commentators to question whether HR's future is essentially transactional, or whether HR is capable of a more strategic contribution and what value this would bring.

In reviewing the question of HR's 'added value', the author will consider contemporary debates about the nature of added value required from HR in the light of today's context trends, pressures and challenges.

=== **PIT STOP: REFLECTIVE ACTIVITY 13.1** ===

1. What are your perceptions of the HR profession and its strategic capabilities?
2. Think of an organization with which you are familiar. To what extent is the HR function perceived as a strategic asset?

Key milestones in the development of HRM

Since this chapter considers the 'future of HR', it is perhaps fitting to set this in context by reconsidering HRM's origins, journey and current stage of development before making predictions based on contemporary trends.

Jacques (1999) argues that the origins of HRM can be found in the ideas which emerged between 1900 and 1920 from the historical conjunction of scientific management, the employment managers' movement and industrial psychology. Over the last 30 years HRM has emerged as a global discourse and has become a recognized semiotic for 'modern people management' (Paauwe, 2007: 9). It is now a pervasive theme in the literatures of organizational behaviour, strategic management, business policy, international and intercultural management. Critical scholar Keenoy (2009: 466) argues that HRM, which began as a local US cultural artefact, has emerged as a global naturalized discourse which informs the social practice of international corporations. In recent years there has been a growing contribution to HRM theory development from various European and international centres of scholarship, especially in Australia and India.

The predominant view implicit in American models of HRM is unitarist, i.e. it assumes that employees and employers are united in the common endeavour of achieving business success. Influential US thinkers on HRM include Beer et al. (1985) and Fombrun et al. (1984) whose prescriptive and normative 'matching model' emphasized the importance of a tight fit between human resource strategies and the overall (and predominantly short-term) strategies of the business (see Chapter 3). This model proposes that employees are a resource that should be treated as other business resources, to be managed in line with, and for the benefit of, the business. Moreover, this model suggests that the management of human resources is a stand-alone function which reacts to the needs of the business as opposed to taking a shaping role and planning growth. In terms of employee relations, this US-based HRM mostly favours individual rather than pluralist perspectives, though the Harvard model (Beer et al., 1985) recognizes the need to address the concerns of various stakeholders.

The gradual consolidation of HRM (in organizations), into the general repertoire of managerialism, is the outcome of a complex and paradoxical cultural process. On the one hand, HRM appears to have become less coherent, less centred, more dispersed and insubstantial when compared with other technical specialities of management such as strategy or marketing. In spite of this appearance, though, HRM has become a very strong cultural programme capable of extending its range to emerge as one of the most significant grounds of managerialism itself (Costea et al., 2007). Delbridge and Keenoy (2010) point out that since mainstream HRM became the dominant discourse relating to management practice from the mid-1980s on, what Keenoy (1997) terms 'HRMism' has enjoyed 'unparalleled success'.

Neo-liberalism

It could be argued that a significant spur to the early development of HRM was the broader economic backdrop of the 1980s and the promotion by the Reagan government in the US and the UK government led by Margaret Thatcher of neo-liberal economic theory – which advocated the development of free markets and flexible labour (Friedman 1977). This followed a prolonged period of industrial unrest, economic stagnation and crisis, out of which grew a new and invigorated global capitalism underpinned by a political commitment to new forms of market, in particular to knowledge and service-based industries such as the financial services industry (Marquand 2008; Gamble 2009). The Thatcher government was determined to advance economic growth by deregulation and reducing union power which was seen as a barrier to economic success, as outlined in Chapter 8 on the employment relationship.

A period of economic expansion began, based mainly on knowledge-based work. The 1990s were a period of significant industrial and organizational restructuring. Much traditional manufacturing capability migrated away from mature economies to parts of the developing world. Technology enabled a general evolution of office work in the 1990s as a result of the far-reaching organizational changes taking place in the banking industry, linked to the introduction of new generations of information and communication technologies (ICT) (Bain et al. 2002). Back office operations were being centralized and a new form of 'front-line' facility was being developed in the form of 24-hour, customer-servicing call centres.

Mainstream management theory since the 1980s has sought to advance business practice. In order to advance the new economic order, business schools offering executive education and MBA programmes were established on both sides of the Atlantic to develop more professional forms of management. Free market principles and managerialism were also increasingly applied to public sector institutions under 'New Public Management'. Since the Thatcher era, various UK governments have continued to promote regulatory and employment legislation reform to support free trade and stimulate economic growth.

The development and expansion of HRM since the late 1980s as an offshoot of managerialism, at the expense of personnel management and industrial relations (see Chapter 8), reflects the perceived political need to expose all parts of the UK economy to the values of business, and for HRM to achieve a closer functional relationship between the needs of business and 'human resource' practices. This overtly unitarist and managerialist framing of HRM represents a legitimizing management point of view which has progressively edged out pluralist perspectives on the employment relationship, including what are described as 'traditional' personnel management or old-style industrial relations (Francis and Sinclair 2003; Wright and Snell 2005). Mueller and Carter (2005) argue that the discourse of HRM is closely intertwined with the shift in power relations between employers, managers, employees and trade unions from the early 1980s onwards. They propose the notion of an 'HRM Project' which includes not only language but also HR practices, boundary-spanning linkages, and external agents such as regulators and financial institutions.

Much of what became mainstream HRM theory development was influenced by the resource perspective of the firm (Barney, 1991), outlined in Chapter 3. HRM's main purpose was conceived as alignment with business strategy – in order to make cost-effective and efficient use of 'human resources'. HR functions were to secure compliant and productive workforces, aligned to the needs of business. In particular, HR functions were to assist business in achieving labour flexibility and reducing workforce costs. Boxall (1996) argued that human resource advantage consists of two elements. The first is the potential to create commitment among an exceptionally talented supply of 'human resources' through the management of mutuality (or alignment of interests) while the second is to develop employees and teams so as to create an organization sustainably capable of learning across industry cycles (see Chapter 10).

The individualism implicit in HRM has assisted the development of labour flexibility from the employer perspective (see Chapter 6). Widespread restructurings during the 1990s had destabilized the traditional white-collar employment relationship and undermined the psychological contract based on reciprocal employer–employee expectations of loyalty and hard work in exchange for job security and gradual promotion based on seniority. This came to be seen by employers as an obstacle to flexibility. The 'new deal' on offer from employers was no longer about job security but instead proposed 'employability' in exchange for performance (Herriot and Pemberton 1995). New means of assessing performance – in the form of performance management (see Chapter 7) – were introduced. In the UK, collective employee relations practices, such as collective bargaining involving unions, have largely been replaced by individualized HR practices (Beardwell and Holden 2001), as outlined in Chapter 8. Without collective protection, an individual could only show dissatisfaction with the organization by leaving their employment. This does not wield any power; only if there was a mass exit of employees would the organization investigate the cause (Farnham 2002).

Psychological contract

In examining the changing power dynamics within the white-collar employment relationship over the past two decades in particular, a number of researchers – both mainstream and critical – have used the term 'psychological contract' to describe what is implicit within the employment relationship in terms of reciprocity and exchange. Because psychological contracts involve employee beliefs about the reciprocal obligations between themselves and their employers, they can be viewed as the foundation of employment relationships (Shore and Tetrick 1994; Rousseau 1995). Various scholars suggest that it is the psychological contract that mediates the relationship between organizational factors and work outcomes such as commitment and job satisfaction (e.g. Guest and Conway 1997; Marks and Scholarios 2004).

There are two main definitions of the psychological contract. The first, which is described by Herriot and Pemberton (1995) as the 'classic' definition, derives from the work of Argyris (1960) and Schein (1978). This refers to the perceptions of mutual obligation, held by the two parties in the employment relationship, the employer and the employee (Herriot et al. 1997). According to the second definition, which is based on the work of Rousseau (1989: 122), the psychological contract is:

> An individual's belief regarding the terms and conditions of a reciprocal exchange agreement between the focal person and another party. A psychological contract emerges when one party believes that a promise of future returns has been made, a contribution has been given and thus, an obligation has been created to provide future benefits.

In this definition, the psychological contract is formulated only in the mind of the employee and is therefore about 'individual beliefs, shaped by the organization, regarding terms of an exchange between individuals and their organization' (Rousseau 2001: 2).

In terms of underlying constructs, there remains no overall accepted definition of the psychological contract and this exchange relationship is very complex and dynamic, with a wide range of factors shaping employee perceptions of how they experience the deal. However, there is consensus that psychological contracts extend beyond legal contracts to the beliefs or expectations an individual and an employer might hold toward the other. In other words, psychological contracts relate to individuals' beliefs regarding reciprocal obligations: what obligations the employee owes the employer and vice versa. When one or other party is perceived to have reneged on their obligations towards the other, the psychological contract is thought to be 'breached', or in the case of severe breaches, 'violated'.

By the end of the twentieth century, changes to work organization were putting the white collar employment relationship under strain. Thus, according to the 'conventional' white-collar psychological contract, in exchange for loyalty and performance from employees, employers were expected to provide secure employment and for some at least the possibility of promotion up hierarchical career ladders. According to the new deal (Herriot and Pemberton 1995), job security is replaced by employability; instead of loyalty, employees are expected to demonstrate commitment and performance. The extent to which HRM practices perpetuated the old deal expectations, which were usually doomed to disappointment, is open to question. What might be concluded however is that in the new work culture from the mid-1990s on, the balance of interests and obligations implicit in the old psychological contract was becoming lopsided, often with deleterious effects for employees (Sennett 2006).

Today it could be argued that the risks in the employment relationship now lie largely with employees whose ability and willingness to be flexible, and to continuously develop themselves in order to increase their employability, may be the crucial determinant of their career success. As a consequence rather than by design, flexible competence instead substitutes for short life-cycle jobs (Sennett 2006). People who can adapt, and who have the behavioural and cognitive competencies associated with flexibility, find themselves, rather than their roles, taking on the characteristics of permanent or core employees. Those without such competency face the prospect of downgraded or outsourced roles.

Given this context, the ability of individual employees to manage their own career and other employment interests seems to depend largely on the relative degree of bargaining power individuals can exercise in the employment market, with low-skill workers having low bargaining power. The decline in trade unionism in the UK and US has left many employees with little collective employment protection (see Chapter 8). The increasing reliance on individuals to manage their own employment, careers and skill development makes for severe vulnerability among those with least financial and educational capital (Virgona et al., 2003). Since 2004 many organizations requiring flexible labour have preferred to employ highly skilled migrant workers from EU accession states on short-term contracts. As Britain has progressively moved towards becoming a high skills knowledge- or service-based economy, there have been growing gaps in life opportunities between 'knowledge workers' and people with few or low work skills.

Moreover, as developing economies such as China's and India's also pursue high-skill/high-pay economic policies, the UK's ability to compete on the basis of highly skilled knowledge and service work may come under increasing strain (Brown et al. 2010b), potentially driving down the value of high-skill work. With the rise of an increasingly mobile global talent pool, employment gaps may increase between those workers who can command their price in their labour market and others who struggle to find any work at all.

PIT STOP: REFLECTIVE ACTIVITY 13.2

1. Given the changing nature of the employment relationship as outlined in this chapter, what are the key HR issues that are likely to arise in future?
2. What does this mean for the nature of HR's future role and contribution?

Critical HRM

Alongside mainstream theory, critical management studies (CMS), critical HRM (CHRM) and critical human resource development (CHRD) studies include a variety of perspectives. CMS is a disparate field encompassing critical versions of postmodernism (Alvesson and Deetz 2005) and radical humanist approaches (Burrell and Morgan 1979). Much critical management and HRM scholarship derives from a Marxist perspective (see Chapter 8). For instance critics point out the different interests of employers/executives (representing 'owners' and shareholders) and those of employees, especially with respect to the way employers use technology to gain complete control of the labour process, increase flexibility and drive down costs, often at the expense of employees. Other critical scholarship derives from the industrial relations tradition within which HRM was seen as 'part of a system of employment regulation in which internal and external influences shape the management of the employment relationship' (Bach and Sisson 2000: 8) as argued in Chapter 8 on managing the employment relationship.

According to Watson (2010), CMS's motivating concern is the social injustice and environmental destructiveness of the broader social and economic systems that these managers and organizations serve and reproduce, rather than focusing simply on the practices of managers themselves. For Watson the common core of what CMS offers to mainstream management theory is deep scepticism regarding the moral defensibility and the social and ecological sustainability of prevailing forms of management and organization.

Managerialism and performativity

A key tenet of much critical management scholarship is that managerialism involves an abuse of power, either by government, or by the professional manager class (Grey 1996). The wholesale shift in power towards 'managers' since the 1980s reflects the dominance of organizational interests within the employment relationship (Parker 2002). Moreover, according to Deetz (1992: ix) the increased influence of management may be interpreted in terms of a 'corporate colonisation of the lifeworld' in that all cultural and institutional forms become progressively subsumed within the logic of capitalism.

With its development of pervasive management controls, aided and abetted by technology, managerialism is often represented as an updated version of an older tradition embodied in the work of Frederick Winslow Taylor (Terry 1998: Pollitt 2003) which has been pushed as a form of social domination (Clarke and Newman 1997). Moreover, because the Anglo-American forms of global capitalism have been dominant since the 1980s, 'rational' managerialism has to some extent become an international phenomenon. While the full extent of the application of Taylorism (or scientific management) in Britain is debatable, nevertheless the spread of managerialism across many sectors appears incontestable.

Thus critics see HRM, an offshoot of managerialism, as a significant contributor to the deliberate shaping of a neo-liberal new work culture characterized by flexibility, work intensification and performativity. Mainstream HRM approaches are thus a managerial tool for controlling and managing the workforce in ways which are designed solely to meet business needs but which appear less directive than the command and control structures of previous decades. Many critics highlight the contrasts between HRM rhetoric and the reality as experienced by employees (Legge 1995, 2005). For example, Sennett (1998: 28) describes 'high performance work practices', such as teamworking, as 'the work ethic of a flexible political economy' since it relies on 'the fiction of harmony' and stresses mutual responsiveness at the expense of original thinking.

More specifically, practices that are grouped in the mainstream HRM literature under 'performance management' (Armstrong and Baron 1998; Beardwell and Holden 2001), as outlined in Chapter 7, have a strong shaping function on employee subjectivities and, from a critical management perspective, form part of an array of means of securing management domination over work. This term roughly denominates a varying set of HRM practices – appraisal interviews, 360-degree feedback, competence assessments, performance-related pay, peer appraisal, and others – that are aimed at managing the job performance of individual employees, tied together by 'a strategic and integrated approach' (Armstrong and Baron 1998).

In contrast to the views put forward by prescriptive mainstream accounts of performance management that emphasize the development of innate qualities of individuals, critical scholars argue that the prevailing paradigm is in fact one of performativity and the degrading instrumentality that this assumption engenders. Thus employees are encouraged to self-regulate their attitudes and behaviours to be consistent with business needs. Indeed, through the use of such practices the subject is in fact reconstituted by means of a set of linguistic concepts which graft performativity in the self, discursively re-constituting people's behaviour in line with local organizational objectives yet simultaneously reinforcing the notion of a free, autonomous individual (Keenoy 1997, 1999; Du Gay and Salaman 1992; Keenoy and Anthony 1992; Iles and Salaman 1995; Legge 1995; Fournier and Grey 2000; Deetz 2003).

This discursive shaping of the individual project emphasizes the relational and constructed nature of the self, embedded in social (power) relations. So in performance appraisal discussions for example, as employees recount and evaluate their work experiences and ambitions, they do so in a situation where they are observed and judged by others (Townley 1994, 1998). They create a narrative of their experience using the discursive resources of the local organizational context (Alvesson 2003), with all the intricacies and implicit values embedded within these resources. Potentially, this has important effects on the way in which people look upon their working life. In this way, it is argued, the subject's conception of the employment relationship shifts away from former collectivist ideas toward a more individualist version, where the primary responsibility for performance lies with the employee, continually free to 'opt out' if they so please.

The commoditization and commodification of white-collar work

Many critical scholars also argue that technological advances have been used to accelerate the commoditization of routine white-collar work. Commoditization is the process by which goods that have economic value and are distinguishable in terms of attributes (uniqueness or brand), end up becoming simple commodities in the eyes of the market or consumers (Rushkoff 2005). Thus Bain et al. (2002) consider that the technology-enabled call centre labour process represents new developments in the Taylorization of white-collar work because it enables a combination of target-setting and monitoring in real time which makes management control of the labour process more complete.

Moreover, changes in industrial organization and the pursuit of labour flexibility since the late 1980s have resulted in specific jobs and tasks having a shorter lifespan than in the past. Technology has enabled the growth of outsourcing, flexible work arrangements such as working from home and 'nonstandard' work (e.g. casualization or the 'contingent workforce'). Reported employer motivations for using casual labour include the pursuit of flexibility (see Chapter 6), dealing with high-peak production periods and providing specialist skills (Vanden Heuval and Wooden 1999), but there is also considerable employer interest in offloading employee responsibility, risk, management and training burdens (Watson 2003). Hall et al. (2000) also found that decisions to employ casual workers were considerably influenced by economic rationalist thinking which focuses on product rather than people, and engages with managing suppliers in preference to participating in 'non-core' activity.

In addition, critics point out that managerialism also favours the commodification of professional work. Commodification (which first appeared in the *Oxford English Dictionary* in 1975 but has its origins in Marxist political theory) describes the process by which something which would not normally be seen as 'goods' such as ideas, becomes a commodity and is assigned a value. Hence it describes how market values can replace other social values including a modification of relationships, formerly untainted by commerce, into commercial relationships in everyday use.

In the current era of knowledge capitalism, companies are attempting to increase surplus by reducing the cost of knowledge work through a technology-assisted process of knowledge-capture that Brown et al. (2010a: 16) call 'Digital Taylorism':

In order to reduce costs and assert proprietary rights, companies are experimenting with new ways to move from knowledge work to working knowledge; that is, from the idiosyncratic knowledge that a worker has and applies, to working knowledge, where that knowledge is codified and routinised, thereby making it generally available to the company rather than being the 'property' of an individual worker.

In short new technologies have increased the potential to translate knowledge work into working knowledge, leading to the standardization of an increasing proportion of technical, managerial and professional jobs that raise fundamental questions about the future of knowledge work and occupational mobility.

As a result, even highly skilled and professional forms of work are potentially exploitable by managements as commodities, leaving workers de-skilled and with less control over their 'knowledge capital'. It is possible that economic recovery will lead to fewer jobs, as advances in technology allow companies to replace manual and intellectual labour with automation and artificial intelligence. Increasing numbers of knowledge-based jobs may become 'hollowed out' and, in the global auction for scarce talent (Brown et al. 2010b), individuals who might previously have been deemed well-paid 'knowledge owners' may find themselves rendered dispensable as their knowledge is codified and systemized. Not surprisingly, for many white-collar knowledge workers, the employment relationship has become more transactional in recent years.

Since many critical management theories are based on democratic principles of equity and social justice, and because their purpose is not to advance managerialism and HRM but rather to draw attention to their limitations and consequences for employees, these critical schools of thought are often considered impractical and tend to be treated with scepticism within organizations and business schools.

═══════════ **PIT STOP: REFLECTIVE ACTIVITY 13.3** ═══════════

1. To what extent do you consider that critical perspectives are incompatible with improving practice?
2. What could be the challenges – or benefits – for HR practitioners who choose to adopt a critical HRM perspective?

The added value debate

The definition of what constitutes added value and how this is achieved by HR thus depends on the observer's perspective. Within mainstream HRM discourse the dominant emphasis is generally placed on how to make HRM more effective in achieving managerial interests. Yet despite this, the value of the HR function has been questioned within the business community from the outset, often for its lack of relevance and value with respect to implementing strategy. The massive restructurings of organizations in the 1990s and changing organizational critical success factors led to new expectations for human resources and the call for changing roles and capabilities of HR professionals. The search for academic and business credibility is therefore a common characteristic of both the discipline and the field of practice within organizations. In particular HR functions within organizations have been under pressure to transform and become 'strategic' in order to create added value.

However, there is no overarching definition of 'strategic' HRM (SHRM) (see Chapter 3). It has been variously defined as:

- 'a human resource system that is tailored to the demands of the business strategy' (Miles and Snow 1984: 36).
- All those activities affecting the behaviour of individuals in their efforts to formulate and implement the strategic needs of business (Schuler 1992).
- The pattern of planned human resource deployments and activities intended to enable the forms to achieve its goals (Wright and McMahan 1992).
- SHRM also emphasizes the implementation of a set of policies and practices that will build an employee pool of skills, knowledge, and abilities (Jackson and Schuler 1995) that are relevant to organizational goals.

SHRM is concerned with top management's attention and approach to HRM as a critical strategic dimension affecting firm performance. According to Guest's (2002) typology, SHRM is distinguished by its emphases on:

- People as a source of competitive advantage.
- The integration of people management plans, policies and practices with business strategy.
- Proactive line management.
- Action on organizational and people issues at the most senior levels.

This can be regarded as a general approach to the strategic management of human resources in accordance with the intentions of the organization and the future direction it wants to take (Boxall 1996). It is concerned with longer-term people issues and macro-concerns about structure, quality, culture, values, commitment and matching resources to future need.

How does HR add value?

The attempt to understand and prove added value is a characteristic of this applied discipline. From the 1990s on HR functions have used measurement to ensure, or prove, that HR strategies are aligned to business strategy, often using frameworks such as the Balanced Business Scorecard and Investors in People to focus HR efforts on key aspects of people practice and establish 'value added' in the form of 'human capital', as discussed in Chapter 4. It might be argued that this focus on measurables may have made the HR function somewhat insular, focused on its own processes, and that the emphasis on numbers may have reduced the status of people as employees to that of resources.

HRM and performance

As discussed in Chapter 3, a plethora of academic studies have looked for links between particular HR and employment management practices and business performance (Huselid 1995; Becker and Gerhart 1996; Delery and Doty 1996; Patterson et al. 1997). However, there is as yet no overall theory of performance, nor of how specifically HRM impacts on performance. Early US-based strategic HRM literature (e.g. Delery and Doty 1996; Huselid and Becker 1996; Wright and Snell 1998; Welbourne and Cyr 1999) examined the relationship between HR and firm performance outcomes in large samples of firms, but they did not specifically study how HR practices directly affect intangibles. Thus within the mainstream there is a strong focus which continues to this day on how to forge ever-tighter links between HR work and firm financial performance (Huselid 1995; Guest et al. 2003; Wright et al. 2005; Fleetwood and Hesketh 2006).

Theorists take different positions with respect to how HR practices actually impact on organizational performance, and there is a dearth of longitudinal studies to establish whether and how HR practices do lead to high performance outcomes. For instance, a contemporary debate exists about the links between 'employee engagement' and performance outcomes. It is assumed that it is engaged employees – who are aligned with organizational goals, willing to 'go the extra mile' and act as advocates of their organization – who are most critical to business success. That's because high performance theory places employee engagement or 'the intellectual and emotional attachment that an employee has for his or her work' (Heger 2007: 121) at the heart of performance, especially among knowledge workers. Yet many scholars argue that engagement is a poorly defined concept and the many available studies of engagement tend to be carried out by consultancies.

Employee engagement has been linked in various studies with higher earnings per share, improved sickness absence, higher productivity and innovation – the potential business benefits go on and on. For instance, Gallup Consulting report (2010) that companies with world-class engagement have 3.9 times the earnings per share growth rate compared with organizations with lower engagement in their same industry, while a Corporate Leadership

Council (CLC) study found that companies with highly engaged employees grow twice as fast as peer companies. A three-year study of 41 multinational organizations by Towers Watson found those with high engagement levels had a 2–4 per cent improvement in operating margin and net profit margin, whereas those with low engagement showed a decline of about 1.5–2 per cent.

The employment relationship (see Chapter 8) between the individual and the organization provides the context in which employee engagement is created. The state of employee engagement is characterized as a feeling of commitment, passion and energy, which translates into high levels of persistence with even the most difficult tasks exceeding expectations and taking the initiative. At its best, it is what Csikszentmihalyi (1998) describes as 'flow' – that focused and happy psychological state when people are so pleasurably immersed in their work that they don't notice time passing. In a state of 'flow' people freely release their 'discretionary effort'. In such a state, it is argued, people are more productive, and more service-oriented, less wasteful, and more inclined to come up with good ideas, take the initiative and generally help organizations achieve their goals than people who are disengaged.

At face value, improving employee engagement should therefore be a key aspect of HR strategy. This brings us to one of the key discussions within contemporary HRM theory and practice (see Chapter 3): what is the best way to achieve this – through best practice or best fit approaches?

Best practice or best fit?

Much of the added value debate over the last 20 years has centred on how HR strategy aligns with business – is there a universal set of HR practices which can be applied in any circumstance (best practice) (Pfeffer 1998) or should the approach taken be contingent on organizational circumstances (best fit)?

Marchington and Wilkinson (2008) point out that the mainstream's predominantly prescriptive tradition used to be the dominant approach in the literature, stemming from the domain of personnel management. Best practice approaches are essentially vocational in character, and they examine and prescribe the 'best' tools and techniques for use by practitioners. For instance Pfeffer (1998) identified seven best practices:

- Employment security
- Selective training
- Self-managed team or teamworking
- High pay contingent on company performance
- Extensive training

- Reduction of status differences
- Sharing information.

To these might be added other best practices such as employee participation or on-the-job development – the list is potentially long and best practice approaches continue to be promoted today, particularly in the consultant-led literature. However, as Wright et al. (2005) point out, most of these best practice developments in the academic literature have come from communities of scholars focusing on their own particular countries or regions. In the UK Guest and others identified clusters of HR practice which appear to impact on business performance through HR outcomes such as employee commitment, but the precise composition of practices within these clusters which lead to effective outcomes appears to depend on situation and context, rather than being a universal prescription.

Others argue that the effect of HR practices depends very much on the specific (internal and external) context. The search for keys to the 'black box' (i.e. knowledge of exactly how HR impacts people to drive market value) has been pursued by Purcell et al. (2003) amongst others, though in these analyses there is a greater recognition that the right 'fit' of HR practice to firm situation is more effective than universal best practice. Increasingly UK theorists advocate the use of evidence for the claims HR might make for its value-added contribution with analytical HR (Boxall 2007) and evidence-based HR (Briner 2007; Hirsh and Briner 2010).

The development of HRM and SHRM theory to date has largely been a UK and American/Australasian phenomenon. Even within UK markets there is debate about whether the principles of individualism endemic to US culture apply to the wider British culture (Armstrong 2008: 16). Brewster (1995) proposed a European model of HRM based on the assumption that European organizations operate with limited autonomy because the internal constraints on HRM included union influence and employee involvement in decision-making through various bodies such as workers' councils, as discussed in Chapter 8. With respect to international HRM theory (see Chapter 12) – defined as 'HRM issues, functions and policies and practices that result from the strategic activities of multinational enterprises and that impact the international concerns and goals of those enterprises' (Scullion 2005: 356) – other theoretical models have been developed (Scullion 2001; Brewster et al. 2005) which recognize the importance of linking international HRM strategy with the strategic evolution of the firm. Wood (1999) makes a distinction between four different 'fits': internal, organizational, strategic and environmental.

More recently, more intense competition among organizations at the national and international level, and the emergence of new markets such as the BRIC countries (Brazil, Russia, India and China), have raised interest in comparative human resource management studies (Budhwar and Sparrow, 2002), addressing the configuration of HRM in different national contexts (see Chapters 11 and 12). Comparisons are typically made on the four different approaches: economic, environmental, behavioural and open systems (Nath, 1988). An important strand of comparative HRM is the cultural perspective. Hall (1976) argues that a useful way of understanding cultural differences derives from the notion of high- and low-context societies. In high-context societies such as in Japan and Arab countries, the meaning of communication largely derives from facial expressions, setting and timings, while in low-context Northern European cultures, more explicit and clear forms of communication are preferred. In contrast, Hofstede (1980) argues that cultures can be categorized according to four distinct cultural value distinctions – power distance, uncertainty avoidance, individualism/collectivism and masculinity/femininity – which have become embedded in society over long periods. Although Hofstede's distinctions were criticized for their limited statistical derivation and for the assumption of the slow evolution of cultures, nevertheless these values are popularly used in understanding cultural differences in managerial intentions and behaviour.

Aycan (2005) has studied the effect of culture on the design and implementation of HRM policies and practices, and while in general scholars agree that some HRM policies may contain universal elements, specific HRM practices will vary since they are culture-bound (see Chapter 11). For instance Budhwar and Khatri (2001) found that, with respect to recruitment strategies, collectivist cultures seem to prefer the use of internal labour markets in order to promote loyalty to the firm. Scholars who embrace the culturalist approach argue that it would be very difficult for a multinational company to successfully apply common HRM practices in different national cultures, e.g. implementing an individualistic HRM system (e.g. merit-based pay and promotion) in a collectivist culture (Ramamoorthy and Carroll 1998).

Some national cultures could be said to be undergoing a more rapid transformation than Hofstede assumed, given the effects of globalization and technological advances. For instance Sarawagi (2010), discussing HRM issues at a number of Indian firms, found that managers are forced to think globally, which can be difficult for those who are used to operating in vast, sheltered markets with minimum competition from domestic or foreign firms. Sarawagi argues that in the Indian context, to cope with the challenges of maintaining workforce diversity, motivating employees, communication, performance management, competency development etc., firms will need to undergo a transformation from rigid hierarchies to flat, more flexible structures; from family-centric and secretive to dispersed ownership, open-mindedness and sharing; from caste-ridden and superstitious to rational thinking and a vibrant style for handling issues.

'Hard' vs 'soft' HRM

There is ongoing debate about how best to align people with business needs, with mainstream HRM practices variously described as hard and soft (Storey, 2001) in the way they seek to align HR strategy and people's behaviour with the specific nature of an organization's competitive strategy (see Chapter 2). For instance the rhetorically dominant soft 'high performance', 'high commitment' or 'high involvement' HRM approaches aim to develop highly committed and flexible people and tend to be associated with knowledge work, where employees know more than managers about the work and managers can thus only monitor and evaluate the outcomes of work.

Typical soft HR practices include rewarding commitment with promotion and a degree of job security, and a participative leadership style that forges a commonality of interest and mobilizes consent to the organization's goals (Hutchinson et al. 2000). The premise is that if employees identify and engage with the organization they will produce high performance in most contexts. The language of mutuality ('people are our greatest asset') implicitly encourages employees to commit to the organization and to furthering its aims. The underlying premise of such approaches is that employees are passive objects to be moulded into appropriate attitudes and behaviours. In contrast the hard or control-based model of HRM links with strategy and the role of HRM in furthering competitive advantage. It relates to the ways in which management attempts to monitor and control employee role performance and focuses on cost reduction and containment. Hard theorists tend to argue that HR practices should be contingent on context.

Throughout the 1990s and 2000s the quest for the elusive overall theory of HRM (Huselid, Purcell, Guest) has continued, as discussed in Chapter 3, as has the debate about how exactly HR impacts on performance, whether through best practice or best fit approaches. Watson (2010) argues that the earlier best practice emphasis has been revived in much of the writing on what is now called 'HRM', most notably in influential works by Pfeffer (1998) and Ulrich (1997).

Most SHRM research focusing on fit (alignment) has failed to find a positive effect for the fit between HR and firm strategy (e.g. Arthur 1994; Huselid 1995; Delery and Doty 1996). On the other hand some SHRM researchers (e.g. Cascio 2005; Cascio and Boudreau 2008) continue to talk about the importance of alignment/fit between HR practices and firm strategy, as discussed in Chapters 2 and 3. However, rather than looking at fit between generic firm strategies (e.g. brand leadership) and generic HR practices (e.g. soft commitment-based HR versus hard control-based HR), newer models are becoming more specific. For example, alignment comes from HR practices that are aimed at fostering/supporting the same organizationally relevant outcome (e.g. all aimed at customer service). This research contrasts with the earlier SHRM fit studies that focused on generic HR practices and generic strategies.

'Hard' HRM – as control mechanism

In contrast to the soft models of HRM, the hard version of HRM focuses on cost reduction and containment, links with strategy and the role of HRM in furthering competitive advantage (see Chapter 3). HR functions are responsible for ensuring that organizations are legally compliant with respect to employment and also that performance is appropriately managed, measured and rewarded. In this respect managerial controls are at their most obvious in practices grouped in the mainstream HRM literature under 'performance management' (Armstrong and Baron 1998; Beardwell and Holden 2001), the formal use of which has grown steadily over the last two decades (Bach and Sisson 2000), especially in medium-sized and large organizations. The processes of target-setting, performance appraisal and performance-related pay are usually designed by HR practitioners (see Chapter 7).

While prescriptive mainstream accounts of performance management often stress the development of innate qualities of individuals, critical scholars in contrast have long argued that the prevailing paradigm is one of performativity and a mechanistic view of people as assets or liabilities. From a critical management perspective, these form part of an array of means of securing management domination over work, since they reduce worker autonomy while exposing individuals to subtle forms of control as people are encouraged to 'work on self' (Townley 2004) to comply with organizational requirements. The use of 'competencies' and other behavioural indicators to distinguish between people's behaviour and capability usually leads to a highly prescribed definition of 'performance' and 'contribution':

> Management implies and reproduces compartmentalization and fragmentation as a means of mastery and control. For, in order to be managed, the totality of physical and social processes, whether within limited instrumental contexts or in society as a whole, needs to be broken down into narrow domains that can be inspected, measured and handled. (Kallinikos, 1996: 37)

Thus, from a critical perspective, mainstream HRM approaches are a managerial tool for controlling and managing the workforce in ways which are designed solely to meet business needs but which appear less directive than the command and control structures of previous decades.

'Soft' HRM discourse

The discourse of HRM is an alignment tool in its own right. Soft mainstream HRM practices – variously described as 'high performance', 'high commitment' or 'high involvement' HRM – are based on the assumption that if employees identify with the organization they will produce high performance. The underlying premise of such approaches is that employees are passive objects to be moulded into appropriate attitudes and behaviours. The language of mutuality ('people are our greatest asset') implicitly encourages employees to commit to the organization and to furthering its aims.

Critics contrast the rhetoric of mutuality implicit in soft high commitment HRM (Legge 2005) with the organizational practices of hard or control-based HRM, including managing by fear and cost-cutting (Keenoy 1990; Caldwell 2003). In their analysis of HRM's contribution to the flexibilization of further education (FE) in the 1990s, Esland et al. (1999) describe the agenda pursued by HRM as follows:

> Our central contention is that, in spite of its emphasis on employee development and the importance of skill enhancement through training, HRM is often perceived by both managers and those 'managed' as a means of reducing an organisation's human resource costs and of increasing 'flexibility' in staffing. (Blyton and Morris 1992 in Esland et al. 1999)

Esland et al. point out that, in FE, HRM achieves these aims in two ways: first by enabling teaching inputs to the learning process to be redefined as a variable cost, so that greater output can be achieved for less. Second, HRM is capable of being deployed as a disciplinary instrument for the identification of 'underperformance' or inadequate commitment among employees, if necessary as a basis for downsizing, redundancy or casualization (Cunningham 1997). These conflicting HRM priorities – of organizational identification and control/cost-reduction – may create cognitive dissonance for some practitioners.

Thus, echoing Keenoy (1990, 2009), HRM has something of a 'wolf in sheep's clothing' about it. These approaches include 'leadership', performance-related pay and other 'high performance work practices', such as teamworking, which Sennett (1998: 28) describes as 'the work ethic of a flexible political economy' since it relies on 'the fiction of harmony' and stresses mutual responsiveness at the expense of original thinking.

PIT STOP: REFLECTIVE ACTIVITY 13.4

1. Which approaches to HRM (hard or soft; best practice, best fit) are you most comfortable with, and why?
2. From a 'best fit' perspective, which approaches would be more appropriate in different circumstances, e.g. redundancy situations?

Common criticisms of mainstream HRM

Thus perceptions of added value vary according to the eye of the beholder. As Lawler points out, HR generally is assumed not to add sufficient value. Here are some of the common criticisms both of mainstream HRM theory and of HR practice within organizations.

Theory–practice gap

Though an applied discipline, one of the common criticisms relating to mainstream HRM is the gap between theory and practice. Storey et al. (2009) point to not only the value of linking theory and practice, but also to the relative lack of such connectivity in reality and thus the need for this application. As Guest (1987: 505) notes, 'there is a danger of confusing "management thinkers" with management practitioners and assuming that because human resource management is being discussed, it is also being practised'.

Conversely HR practitioners are sometimes inclined to enthusiastically embrace fads of consultancy-led theory, such as becoming deeply committed to the methodologies and underpinning theory e.g. of particular survey providers. Moreover, many practitioners are generally still too busy 'doing personnel' to make a more strategic contribution to their organizations.

HR transformation

Another common criticism relates to the nature, process and effects on stakeholders of HR functional transformation. Yet since the late 1990s HR leaders have responded to critics by trying to become business partners who add value and help implement business plans. The HR functional roles framework developed by Ulrich (1997) has been regularly adopted within large organizations as a functional design model (i.e. business partners, shared services, centres of expertise and corporate centres). Transactional work is increasingly commoditized, shared services are often outsourced and Human Resource Information Systems (HRIS) are used to enable manager and employee 'self-service'.

While the concept of business partnering is widely accepted within the HR profession, the political issues arising from HR transformation can reduce the effectiveness of the resulting service. For instance, while SHRM theory suggests that HRM should really be delivered by line managers, in practice line managers are often ill-prepared for dealing with what they see as the extra responsibilities for people management now devolved to them by HR. Moreover HR practitioners are generally assumed by line management to lack sufficient business acumen to be true strategic 'partners' with respect to aligning HR practices to business strategy, and many studies suggest that HR 'business partners' soon revert to their previous generalist roles.

The professional development of HR practitioners has to date perhaps focused too exclusively on 'core' HR activities, processes and issues, and it is only in recent times that moves been made to strengthen the business aspects of the curriculum for HR professional qualifications. Indeed CIPD and other developers of HR professionals propose that practitioners should develop 'business savvy' (McGurk 2012). The roles of strategic business partners (SBP) in large organizations have typically been through several iterations, often resulting in HR leaders playing the strategic (SBP) role, while more junior business partners generally work alongside line management as internal consultants on change and other projects typically linked to short-term organizational problem solving.

Moreover, though often considered a '90s issue', the general lack of a seat for HR at boardroom tables may reflect how the function's value is perceived by management. Some pundits as early as the 1990s were predicting that HR would in future have mainly an operational role. Throughout the last two decades the popular press has continued to characterize the HR function as ineffective, an obstacle to change, overly bureaucratic and failing to add strategic value. Cascio (2005) argues that unless HR is able to improve its own calibre, capacity and credibility, HR risks being excluded from participation in 'big stuff' and will become a discounted function. Ulrich argues that HR should focus on the 'deliverables', i.e. the outcomes which will add value to the business, rather than on the 'do-ables' which risk diluting strategic impact.

So where does HR go from here?

It could be argued that context factors will once again play a significant part in determining the nature and role of HR in future. As global business competition shifts from efficiency to innovation and from enlargement of scale to creation of value, the strategic use of human resources becomes increasingly relevant. Yet the perceived gap between rhetoric and reality when it comes to HRM highlighted by Legge (2005) and Keenoy (1990) is reported to be getting wider in the fast-changing global context (Storey et al. 2009). This refers not only to the 'knowing-doing gap' highlighted by Pfeffer and Sutton (1999) but also to the significant inconsistencies between theory and the so-called 'reality' of life in organizations. These context changes are leading to a widespread transformation in the nature of business, work and workforces such that the 'new normal' is likely to be very different from in the past. How HR prepares their organizations to thrive in the new environment will to a large extent determine how value is defined and also the exact nature, purpose and role of HR in future.

New working practices and a 'new' workforce

In particular, advances in technology have led to new methods of manufacturing, distributing and selling goods across time and geographical boundaries. Technology has also enabled changing organizational forms, outsourcing and new working practices such as remote working and virtual teams of people from different cultural and economic backgrounds working together. Managers may increasingly find themselves responsible for the output of people who may not be directly employed by their firm, who work in different time zones and whom they may rarely meet face-to-face.

Changes brought about by the digital revolution in particular will have a deep impact on the way businesses are organized and the ways people look at work. While many of these changes may benefit individuals, some may be detrimental to employees' health and personal lives. For instance new technologies, especially ICT, not only enable flexibility but also work intensification because the use of Internet technology and emails has led to increased workloads and shorter lead times. Work can be, and is, carried out from anywhere, leading to a blurring of boundaries between work and other aspects of life for many people. Thus unitarist thinking in the digital era may prove unsound because what is good for the organization may not prove good for the health and well-being of employees.

With demographic changes and global 'talent' shortages in some occupations HR is charged with finding, attracting and retaining the people needed for business success. HR functions are also typically expected to lead on developing employee engagement strategies as part of the retention and performance effort. As workforces become more diverse, many of the assumptions about what will attract, retain and bring the best out of people need to be revisited. In particular, stereotypical generational differences may lead to the need for different forms of 'employee value proposition'. Lettink (2012) for instance argues that a future workforce encompassing five generations will want a career lattice that caters to individual needs. Workers will move fluidly between companies and assignments, bringing their own devices and applications, and will expect to use them in the enterprise (see Chapter 6). Moreover, employees will expect to be consulted and involved in decisions that affect them and expect that their voices will be heard and responded to by management. Given that Hamel and Breen (2007) among others argue that styles of management are out of date, HR has a key role to play with respect to ensuring that leadership and management practice is fit for the future.

Recession and growth

It could be argued that the recession brought into sharp focus some underlying trends with respect to work and employment. Throughout the economic downturn organizations have downsized and restructured, with an ever-greater focus on flexibility, cost and efficiency. The ongoing social and political impacts of the global economic crisis – including the eurozone crisis, corporate scandals, excessive executive rewards and rewards for failure – have highlighted many of the deficits of the short-termist ways of doing business endemic to contemporary forms of capitalism. It could also be argued that the way HR professionals have operated throughout the recession will affect their ability to help their organizations return to growth.

When the recession began, many HR professionals were struggling with ongoing credibility and status problems, and the recession may prove to be a pivotal point in how HR's added value is perceived. The HR function may be at its most useful in terms of value added during times of industrial crisis and recession – when downsizing and industrial relations issues need managing – while in 'normal' times, HR is often depicted by line managers as a constraint on doing business ('the function that says no'). The way HR professionals responded to the recession is likely to have impacted on perceptions of their status and effectiveness. Lawler et al. (2011) point out that when HR has been actively involved in downsizing the function may be seen as less credible, if as a result, companies subject to significant cost reductions are not able to perform as well as they did before the recession. Similarly, if HR leaders have been preoccupied with reorganizing their own function or have failed to provide good answers to the tough talent management questions the recession raised, they are likely to be seen as poor business partners.

On the other hand the recession also created a situation where executives in a large number of organizations developed new competencies and capabilities and changed their strategies. Then they needed to make corresponding changes in the compositions and sizes of their workforces. Lawler et al. (2011) argue that HR professionals who were able to lead and contribute to realigning the strategy, talent and competencies of an organization and stepped up to the plate in the way they responded to these changes, would be seen as operational drivers who helped reduce costs and strategic drivers who helped reshape their organizations' business strategies. If so, HR executives may have taken advantage of opportunities to demonstrate their value and to significantly improve their reputation and credibility as well as that of the HR function.

Changing service delivery and workforce models in English local authorities

Local government in England is operating within ever shrinking budgets, yet demand for its services – which range from refuse collection to social care and teaching – continues to grow. The cost-constrained environment is forcing local councils to rethink what services are provided (beyond the statutory) and how these are delivered. Many councils are euphemistically in a 'strategic holding position' on this as they struggle to maintain services without a fundamental rethink of the 'how'. A spectrum of possible service and service delivery options exists, ranging from conventional service delivery by a council's own directly employed workforce through to a commissioner-led model by which services are delivered on behalf of the council through third parties in various forms of outsourcing or partnering arrangement. Thus the nature of the way local authorities deliver their obligations to council tax payers and service users will be somewhere along the following dimension:

Conventional service delivery _____ Commissioner-led

While commissioning and its associated activities – such as contract design, procurement and contract management – are not new in the local government context, two things make today's situation different from the past:

- the range of services that the government hopes will be commissioned
- the sophistication of the contracting models used (Blatchford and Gash, 2012).

If alignment is to be tight, the HR strategy needs to mirror the strategic intent reflected in service delivery models. The workforce planning implications of each service delivery model will differ and will affect the size and nature of workforce required. In a purely commissioner-led model, it is conceivable that workforces could shrink significantly and the skills required by retained staff would change dramatically. For example, employees working in commissioner hubs will need to work effectively across organizational boundaries, demonstrate sophisticated partnering skills, and be able to manage the risks inherent in delivering outcomes through third-party providers, such as if a provider's business fails. Similarly, some local authority functions and centres of expertise could themselves embark on traded futures, becoming suppliers of services to other client organizations. People working in these 'consultancy' operations will need commercial skills of a high order and are likely to be on different terms and conditions from conventional local authority employment contracts.

Moreover, given the context, the cultures of local authority organizations will need to become 'change-able', i.e. agile, flexible, innovative and sustainably effective in scenarios of ongoing change. The traditional bureaucracies and hierarchies of many public-sector institutions are generally not set up for corporate agility, a concept more readily applied in commercial contexts. This is the ability of a business or institution to adapt rapidly to changes in the business environment in efficient, productive and cost-effective ways. An agile organization is able to gain competitive advantage, or provide relevant and cost-effective services by intelligently, rapidly and proactively seizing opportunities and reacting to threats.

The organization's need for flexibility may also be in tension with that of employees for job security and for many employees whose traditional 'psychological contract' – of permanent, full-time employment with some degree of job security – may be under threat, these may be worrying times. Many council employment models have relatively low flexibility except among the low-grade female workforce. If the only alternatives on offer are some form of flexible work contract, 'permanent' full-time employees may perceive these as risky because flexible contracts are often the first to be cut when savings need to be made. Employees may perhaps more readily adjust to more flexible ways of working if they believe that the changes are in line with the public service ethos and in harmony with employees' own values, rather than driven by the need to cut costs alone.

This transitional period is potentially an exciting and unparalleled opportunity for HR to really make a strategic contribution to delivering benefit to service users. Yet in the current cost-cutting context, there is a distinct risk that HR will be required to provide only a procedurally driven transactional service. If this were to happen, the far greater strategic contribution of the 'HR with attitude' service will be wasted, and, as one strategic director of a major local authority commented,when interviewed by the author, 'A lot of corporate services get chopped as overheads and yet we need them.'

It is therefore vital to get across the message about the value HR can bring before it is too late to do so. And if HR wishes to move beyond administration to deliver strategic value and enhance its reputation, it must act as an effective credible activist, pushing well beyond the basics to develop impactful HR policies and initiatives which deliver institution-wide benefits that are also locally relevant.

Source: author.

=== PIT STOP: REFLECTIVE ACTIVITY 13.5 ===

1. What do you consider are the greatest challenges now facing English local authority organizations in delivering their services to users?
2. In what ways could HR bring the greatest value in these circumstances?
3. What skills will HR require to deliver this value?
4. What is the best way to get the message across about the value HR can bring?
5. You may wish to discuss with other colleagues and compare your answers with the HR 'deliverables' outlined in the section below.

What kind of 'deliverables' are fit for the future?

For Cascio (2005) HR must drive the business forward, rising to the challenge of adding and creating value. Ulrich and Smallwood (2005) argue that a new human resource measure of return on investment (ROI) is *return on intangibles*. This perspective is consistent with an 'investor-literate' approach to HR because intangibles such as innovation represent the hidden value of a firm and are becoming an increasingly important portion of a firm's total market capitalization (Ulrich and Smallwood, 2005: 137). These authors propose that HR needs to ensure that HR activities positively impact intangible value, as reflected in the premium the market is willing to pay above a firm's earnings and book value. My own view is that aligning HR only to short-term business plans risks reducing rather than adding value because this thinking may encourage a cost/efficiency orientation at the expense of building the capabilities required for future success.

Increasingly HR and business leaders define organizational effectiveness beyond traditional financial outcomes to include sustainability – achieving success today without compromising the needs of the future. Sustainable growth will require organizations to have the capabilities to succeed over time, i.e. to be well-governed, agile, flexible, innovative and customer-focused; and also able to attract and retain the key people on whom business success depends. Both the CIPD and SHRM have also embraced the notion that HR's purpose should be defined as producing sustainable performance. In their 'Next Generation HR' report (Sears, 2011), the CIPD proposes that HR should be 'future-proofing' cultures, moving from them from 'healthy' cultures to 'agile' cultures. The CIPD also argues that HR should exercise stewardship, acting as organizational 'guardians and commentators' on ethical matters. I would go further.

While agreeing with these propositions to some extent I would argue that organizational agility – synonymous with strategic capability, short decision-cycles, effective processes and implementation, teamwork and impermanent structures – is only practicable when built on 'healthy' cultures. Given that future business success, particularly but not exclusively in the knowledge and service economies, depends heavily on the talent, goodwill and discretionary effort of people, I argue that the purpose of HR should be redefined as about building *sustainably healthy and effective* organizations conducive to high performance through people – i.e. focusing on attracting, developing and retaining the 'right' people and building organizational cultures in which those people want to work and are able to give of their best. This agenda thus inevitably requires a strategic response from HR functions: HR must be operationally effective in the here and now but with future capability-building in mind. The relevant HR deliverables derive from this purpose.

Designing the target workforce model to fit the target operating model

HR must ensure that organizations have the right numbers of the right types of people in the right places at the right times (Dyer and Ericksen 2006). Working out the talent implications of the shifting definition of strategic success requires HR to look ahead at business, work and labour market trends, using strategic workforce planning to anticipate future shortages and plan for tomorrow's workforce today by redeploying and deliberately building vital competencies as well as sourcing future talent. HR should initiate conversations with stakeholders to develop scenarios relating to future workforce models. This would typically involve looking at the external drivers for change and asking:

- Are we sufficiently prepared for the future?
- What would be the impact if we don't address these?
- In particular, how would these affect our ability to attract and retain our key employees?
- What skills would our employees need to succeed in this environment?

US theorists Boudreau and Ramstad (2007) argue that HR should be considered a 'decision science' and propose that a key intangible deliverable for HR is 'talentship', which includes talent segmentation, or identifying pivotal talent pools where the quality and/or availability of human capital makes the biggest difference to strategic success. This requires analytical and modelling capability, or the ability to access this and use data insightfully, in order to produce relevant scenarios from which choices about the size, shape and nature of future workforce can be made. HR can help clarify the key roles in the value chain, seek to understand how the transition will impact on the types of workforce required for the future and put in place the support and policies required. They can build vital competencies through development and redeployment as well as sourcing future talent externally.

The value of this ability to translate HR into strategic planning should not be under-estimated and is becoming increasingly mainstream. As Bolton and Isaacson (2012: 3) point out:

> We know the primary driver of value creation from the HR function is a combination of accurate and predictive information, business-driven and business driving strategy, solid service delivery and valuable business partnering – all engineered to be an integral and holistic part of the execution of business strategy.

Of course in pursuit of a tight fit with strategy, as proposed here, HR risks embracing a mechanistic approach to workforce planning which does not lend itself to a dynamic context. Nor should workforce planning be undertaken as an offline activity delivered by experts.

Instead HR should work closely with the line to identify pivotal roles and people risks, to estimate for example the cost per day when operating without a key player, and put plans in place to minimize people risks. This should help HR to support managers to be more intentional in how they manage people. Roles should of course be aligned to strategy and the definition of 'mission critical' roles is likely to change in the new context. In that respect role segmentation is helpful. Do all roles contribute equally to strategic execution? Which contribute more, or less? For strategic roles the aim should be to build skills and experience; core (operational) roles should be protected and talent management should be applied as much to roles that shape the customer/ service user experience as to future senior management roles. Supporting roles should be streamlined while misaligned roles should be redirected. Role segmentation can enable better decisions, lead to meaningful development programmes and the targeting of communication mechanisms and employee engagement initiatives. It should also allow better reporting and data analysis across multiple variables, for instance of the state of the talent pipeline.

For many HR teams this kind of contribution is relatively new ground. Again, HR practitioners do not themselves need to be expert analysts, but they must find ways of accessing such capability and of developing meaningful insights from evidence that can enrich decision-making.

Attracting, managing and retaining key talent

HR's core responsibility is to define, plan for, acquire, engage, develop, deploy, lead and retain the talent needed for success. Given the changing context, it is important to review all related processes to ensure they are fit for purpose. For instance, even though many organizations will continue to downsize for the foreseeable future, most may also wish to continue to recruit new external talent. 'Employer brands' will need to be refreshed to take account of the changing context and the specific aspirations of today's more diverse, multi-generational workforces. More flexible approaches to resourcing will be needed to enable organizations to quickly deploy and then redeploy resources, talent and skills/knowledge. Options are likely to include increased use of partnering, through which HR seeks to secure knowledge assets and talents from outside the organization that can be drawn upon to mobilize a response. Such partnerships enable knowledge and skills to be migrated into the organization but require careful third-party management.

More generally the retention of key talent is likely to become the more significant future talent challenge (see Chapter 5). Recruitment firms are aware of wide-scale pent-up career frustration across most UK sectors in today's tight labour markets and predict that, as soon as these improve, there is likely to be significant employee turnover in particular sectors. Risk management and retention plans should be applied to people and jobs where key knowledge and skills are in short supply. Career routes should be redefined and people should be helped to develop the skills and competencies they really need, especially in new roles. An agile workforce is multi-skilled and focused on the customer.

Performance management processes should be simple to use, provide line of sight to how people's roles fit with company strategy and effective as a means of ensuring ongoing feedback and development. Taking a fresh look at what is rewarded may indicate some oddities in reward systems which should be ironed out – such as rewarding only individual 'siloed' performance while company values explicitly encourage collaboration and customer-centricity. It will be important to provide forms of recognition and non-financial benefits that matter most to people, stabilizing and sharing the benefits.

Building a sustainably agile and resilient workforce

HR's aim should be to build employee agility, resilience *and* engagement and performance. An agile workforce is engaged both in their work and with the organization. For reasons discussed here and elsewhere, such as the lessening of job security, in many contexts there is low employee morale and employee engagement has become the holy grail.

Improving employee engagement involves more than carrying out engagement surveys. It requires a holistic organization development (OD) perspective. HR professionals should create a dialogue on how to make their organization a better place to work, get to grips with the key issues for specific groups of employees and target meaningful action at areas which are likely to unblock key barriers to engagement. Since a deep, shared belief in the organization's core values and beliefs is thought to be key to both resiliency and employee engagement, HR can help ensure for instance that people have a clear line of sight to the organization's core purpose through the work they do. HR should work closely with line managers, placing a special focus on improving employee engagement, diagnosing and improving the root causes of employee disengagement and also re-skilling employees more generally for employability. The aim should be to make employee engagement a daily focus for managers rather simply an annual survey process. Developing effective employee well-being strategies can help people to cope with the demands made of them and will show staff that they are valued.

Strengthening organizational productivity and performance

Since many studies suggest that line managers have a major impact on employee performance and engagement, HR should aim to build line management capability to bring out the best in (knowledge) workers. HR can help line managers to build high performance climates, though there is no cut and dried formula for this. In general this is about helping managers understand when and how to involve employees *and* when to direct them; how to achieve the right blend of effective leadership *and* management together with employee authority, accountability and empowerment. HR can help identify and remove barriers to performance and engagement by training managers as coaches and building a coaching culture. HR can ensure that managers design roles in which employees have scope for some autonomy and opportunities to grow, and value employees as individuals.

As organizations increasingly operate beyond their own boundaries, HR can help enable cross-boundary partnership working, for instance by clarifying accountabilities, skill and manager capability requirements, developing teams and communication strategies. Learning and development interventions (see Chapter 10) can be targeted at helping people improve their ability to collaborate across organizational boundaries as they work/manage in partnerships or matrix structures. Performance management, reward and recognition systems (see Chapter 7) can provide a line of sight to business strategy and reinforce a culture of collaboration, service and innovation. The aim should be to develop a sense of shared leadership in which employees are proactive, committed and delivering what is needed.

Managing and supporting change

HR is generally expected to support change projects, and many of the key change activities required are well within HR's core remit. These include retaining key talent, handling redundancies and other exits, supporting line managers, ensuring effective communications, re-engaging the 'survivors', combining action and learning and defining the new employment relationship. More generally, HR can help create a climate for change by equipping people for change, with new skills and a sense of purpose and progress, preparing people for new roles, coaching line managers and helping people feel valued.

Increasingly senior HR practitioners are also expected to lead change projects, including redesigning and integrating organizations, yet HR functions generally are reported to be poor at change management (Ulrich 2008). This is clearly an area where HR needs to up to its game to be perceived to add value in future. Being able to manage change projects will require HR to have an understanding of at least of some of the core principles of the fields of organization development and design, internal communications, marketing etc. While HR practitioners do not themselves need to be change experts, they must be able to work in partnership with specialist practitioners in these disciplines. For HR practitioners who have become expert advisers in conventional HR processes, some elements of the personal transformation required may be uncomfortable.

Carrying out some basic research into the kinds of working practices used by other organizations (from any sector) can be informative in clarifying change goals and designing effective change processes. For example, how are other organizations implementing more agile working practices? What support will be needed for employees and managers if people are required to work more flexibly and/or remotely? How does this agility permeate mindsets? What are the implications for the kinds of workspace required, technology support, training and development etc.? How can strong drivers to reduce costs also be used to transform the organization into a more collaborative and exciting place to work? How can the physical, psychological and environmental aspects of the change journey be eased for all concerned?

HR should focus on building constructive employee relations (see Chapter 8) as the bedrock of change, working directly and with trade unions, with communications characterized by genuine employee involvement and voice. Organization development activity should be targeted at behavioural change, with leaders and HR role-modelling organizational values. HR can also ensure greater coherence between change projects through stimulating knowledge-sharing across the organization.

Building very strong, innovative and adaptive organizational cultures

Management literature is replete with definitions of high performance, agile and sustainable organization models. For instance the characteristics of high-performance organizations as described by Clemmer (1992) and others include:

- *Intense customer and market focus*. The organization is designed in such a way that it allows daily contact with customers by both front-line staff and line managers with internal systems, structures and processes facilitating this. Support systems are designed to enable employees to meet the needs and demands of the customer, rather than being designed for management and bureaucratic purposes.
- *Teamwork*. Operational and improvement teams are highly autonomous and decentralized, with teams able to adapt the way they work to better serve their customers. High-performing organizations tend to have flatter organizational structures, with fewer people whose role is purely about 'leading, directing and developing'.
- *Partnering and working across boundaries*, with people learning and collaborating with other teams. Focused professionals with specific skills can be drawn on throughout the organization.

While structural and process characteristics such as these are important, in post-recessionary times increasing emphasis is being placed on how organizations can achieve *sustainable* high performance in a context where the role and purpose of business may be increasingly questioned. Thus cultural factors (see Chapter 11) such as organizational agility, ethics, the nature of organizational purpose and the alignment of individuals to organizational values are increasingly considered high performance characteristics.

From the resource perspective of the firm (Barney, 1991), four characteristics of resources and capabilities – value, rarity, inimitability and non-substitutability – are important in sustaining competitive advantage (see Chapter 3). Birkinshaw (2010: 16) argues that the shift towards a knowledge economy enhanced by the 'Information and Communication Technology Revolution', means that firms 'succeed not just on the basis of efficiency, but also creativity and innovation'.

From the resource perspective, collective learning in the workplace on the part of managers and non-managers, especially on how to coordinate workers' diverse knowledge and skills and integrate diverse information technology, is a strategic asset that rivals find difficult to replicate. Adaptive, agile cultures are thus characterized by flexible mindsets and practices, the ability to efficiently and quickly acquire, build, share and apply knowledge to critical priorities, and also to rapidly deploy resources across boundaries (Meredith and Francis, 2000). In such cultures knowledge-sharing and innovation are the norm. The need to manage risk is balanced by the ability to stimulate innovation, with bureaucracy kept to the minimum *and* appropriate checks and balances.

However, agility without resiliency is unlikely to be sustainable. Resiliency at an organizational level is about the robustness of systems; the capacity for resisting, absorbing and responding, even reinventing if required, in response to fast and/or disruptive change that cannot be avoided (McCann et al. 2009). At the individual level, resiliency is reflected in personal resilience, or the ability to thrive and perform despite ongoing change, uncertainty and confusion. Both agility and resiliency are needed if the organization is to have adaptive capacity or 'change-ability' (Holbeche 2005).

HR has many means at its disposal to reinforce the desired direction of travel. Thus it can provide thought leadership on how to innovate through people, fostering innovative products, services and ways of working. HR should focus on developing constructive employee relations and employee communications characterized by genuine involvement and 'employee voice' (see Chapter 8). These are key to stimulating a change-able, innovative culture. HR can help unblock key structural and process barriers to agility and resilience, support managers to manage the effects of change on people, help people adapt to new ways of working and embed new, more agile working practices. HR can also align career incentives and reward to new behaviours such as innovation. The aim should be to build employee agility, resilience *and* engagement and performance.

Building leadership agility

Leadership capabilities and behaviours are critical to harnessing the firm's human assets and have a disproportionate impact on organizational effectiveness (Francis et al. 2011). Bringing about culture change requires business leaders and HR to understand the current culture, break established patterns and challenge sacred cows. Leaders must be able to manage ambiguity, reconcile seeming paradoxes and also provide clarity and coherence to others.

Succession planning and talent management processes should be under-pinned by a clear understanding of what future senior leaders need to be capable of in future, and how they will need to exercise leadership in specific contexts. Pfeffer (2005) argues that today's leaders need new mental models. For instance, building a more sustainable, change-able organization will require managers and leaders at all levels who can manage the short term with the long term in mind, switching out of the cycle of short-term reactivity and taking a more proactive, anticipatory and shaping approach in order to create real opportunities for organizations. HR can help managers to improve their 'sense-making' skills – to better manage uncertainty and ambiguity, develop innovative business models and create and sustain an openness to change. Companies such as Standard Chartered Bank are experimenting with new approaches to developing leaders which can help managers cope with paradox and ambiguity.

HR can also help develop engaging (MacLeod and Clarke, 2009) and ethical leaders and managers who are able to create a sense of shared purpose and provide a strong strategic narrative about the organization – where it's come from and where it's going; who can focus people and structure the organization and its tasks so that people can get on with what matters; who actively lead culture change and who demonstrate values-based leadership even, or especially, during today's difficult times.

The focus however should not be exclusively on developing future top leaders but also on developing shared or distributed leadership at all levels, so that the organization becomes better able to rapidly mobilize and harness the initiative, insights and energies of all its employees.

Conclusion

So with respect to the future of HR, several trends seem significant. Since study after study confirms that people issues are at the forefront of CEOs' minds, it seems likely that the responsibility for employing, leading and managing people will become more obviously 'owned' by the business as a whole rather than HR. The general trend towards fragmentation of HR structures according to the Ulrich framework is likely to continue, i.e. as an insourced or outsourced service centre working alongside business partners and centres of excellence using a project-based approach to respond to changing circumstances that affect the workforce. Some pundits predict the 'consumerization' of HR in which managers and employees will expect direct access to HR on their smart devices, thereby cutting out HR as the middleman. I consider this scenario quite plausible, though I would argue that the new normal makes a more strategic form of contribution from HR even more important than ever. To enable focus this may require separating out operational and strategic HR functions, with the former addressing short-term requirements with the longer-term in mind and the latter's focus more on the long-term organizational requirements and opportunities, on bringing about change and building organizational capabilities, including leadership. However, in order to have the licence to deliver such a strategic contribution senior HR practitioners (who may increasingly be drawn from many business and functional backgrounds) must be credible with senior management, usually as a result of business acumen, deep insight into people and organizations, shrewd advice and operational excellence.

With respect to how HR practitioners will gain credibility in future, the general consensus among UK-based 'HR leaders' (Holbeche 2009) is that HR must be a business partner and put business needs ahead of those of employees. I argue that such one-sided priorities are ultimately unsustainable. In future a better balance will need to be struck between the needs and outcomes of business and those of employees and other workers, if organizations are to consist of people united in a common endeavour. The HR function should lead on creating a more equitable, adult–adult employment relationship between employers and employees – in which benefits and risks are more mutual for employers and employees – as the foundation for more genuinely sustainable performance in fast-changing times. In such a scenario the 'deal' for employees will be based on *mutual* obligations and needs, trust *and* flexibility, empowerment and accountability, support *and* challenge, performance *and* development, shared risk, shared gain and win–win outcomes. Creating a more level playing field and a sense that 'we are all in this together' may require more challenging approaches to reward strategies, in particular executive pay. Indeed, the 'new normal' times may require HR to shift from both the unitarist thinking and the adversarial industrial relations of the past and to proactively develop new forms of pluralist employee relations (see Chapter 8).

As HR practitioners engage in such forms of strategic contribution, they will inevitably transcend the conventional disciplinary boundaries. Indeed a greater confluence of HRM/HRD with organizational development and design, statistics and analytics, internal communications and marketing is increasingly evident in contemporary attempts to identify the impact of HR practices, develop more agile organizational cultures and attractive employer brands. Perhaps the key capability required by HR leaders aiming for a more strategic contribution is influence, earned through customer insight, confidence and effective delivery and based on personal integrity and political acumen. Such contributions are about thought and practice leadership about how to produce contexts where people can give of their best and be fairly treated.

For HRM as a field, there are some slight signs of rapprochement between some mainstream and critical HRM theorists (Paauwe 2007; Spicer et al. 2010). Practitioners themselves could make closer links between theory and practice by adopting the 'thinking practitioner' approach of actively experimenting with their own practice and seeking evidence for what works in their own context, rather than relying largely on consultancies and academics. For this they need 'a capacity for reflection on their intuitive knowing in the midst of action' (Schön 1983: 8–9) which they can use to cope with the unique, uncertain, and conflicted situations of practice. This is about taking stock of one's own values, and being willing to challenge practice which appears unethical, inappropriate or unfair.

Moreover, as Watson (2010: 918) points out, the critical study of HRM should be developed and strengthened:

> to help counter the tendency for HRM academics to act, in effect, as 'best practice' advisors and legitimacy-givers to corporate interests (suggesting to employers which employment management practices to adopt in order to increase corporate 'competitive advantage', for example).

It could indeed be argued that this chapter demonstrates this particular tendency highlighted by Watson: on the one hand to be critical of mainstream theory; on the other to accept the dominant business paradigm of competitive advantage as the justification for advocating HR practices which reflect the supremacy of business interests in the employment relationship. I would counter this argument by suggesting that critical practitioners have choices in how they approach their roles, and that the job of the author as I see it is to raise readers' awareness of some of the choices they may have. These may include opportunities to advocate more progressive practices to help redress seeming imbalances in the employment relationship.

In particular practitioners can help close the theory–practice gap by developing a more critical edge to theory in practice – by, for instance, not just seeking great learning methodologies but also challenging the 'givens' of what Ramdhony (2012) considers the constructionist epistemology that permeates mainstream human resource development theory. This involves looking at the broader system and at what may be influencing current business and organizational practice, with a view to finding better ways forward that are also practical. Practitioners should also question their own language and assumptions, develop a clear perspective on what they are trying to achieve and pursue this with confidence while accepting that ambiguity and unpredictability are inherent characteristics of human systems. If HR practitioners can achieve this, it is more likely that HR will be acting in a leadership capacity and be better able to build healthy and effective organizations that people want to be part of and are willing to do their best work for.

═══ PIT STOP: REFLECTIVE ACTIVITY 13.6 ═══

1. As you reflect on the key messages in this book, which have most resonance for you? Which most closely match your own beliefs about what effective HRM is about? With which do you disagree, and why?
2. To what extent have your own initial ideas about HRM theory and practice changed in the light of reading this book?
3. How will you translate your insights into practice?

■ Further Reading ■■■■■■■■■■■■■■■

Francis, H., Holbeche, L.S. and Reddington (2012) *People and Organisational Development: a New Agenda for Organisational Effectiveness*. London: CIPD.

Holbeche, L.S. (2009) *HR Leadership*. Oxford: Butterworth-Heinemann.

Sears, L., Bird, S., Clake, R., Sassienie, J. and Robinson, V. (2010) Next *Generation HR*. London: CIPD.

Wong, W. and Sullivan, J. (2010) *The Deal in 2020: A Delphi Study of the Future of the Employment Relationship*. London: The Work Foundation.

References

Alvesson, M. (2003) 'Beyond neopositivists, romantics, and localists: a reflexive approach to interviews in organizational research', *Academy of Management Review*, 28: 13–33.

Alvesson, M. and Deetz, S. (2005) 'Critical theory and post-modernism: approaches to organisation studies', in H. Willmott and C. Grey (eds), *Critical Management Studies: A Reader*. Oxford: Oxford University Press, pp. 60–106.

Argyris, C. (1960) *Understanding Organizational Behavior*. Homewood, IL: Dorsey Press, Inc.

Armstrong, M. (2008) *A Handbook of Human Resource Management Practice*. London: Kogan Page.

Armstrong, M. and Baron, A. (1998) *Performance Management: The New Realities (Developing Practice)*. London: CIPD.

Arthur, J.B. (1994) 'Effects of human resource systems on manufacturing performance and turnover', *Academy of Management Journal*, 37 (3): 670–87.

Aycan, Z. (2005) 'The interplay between cultural and institutional/structural contingencies in human resource management practices', *International Journal of Human Resource Management*, 16 (7): 1083–19.

Bach, S. and Sisson, K. (eds) (2000) *Personnel Management: A Comprehensive Guide to Theory and Practice*. Oxford: Blackwell Publishers.

Bain, P., Watson, A., Mulvey, G., Taylor, P. and Gall, G. (2002) 'Taylorism, targets and the pursuit of quantity and quality by call centre management', *New Technology, Work and Employment*, 17 (3): 170–85.

Barney, J.B. (1991). 'Firm resources and sustained competitive advantage', *Journal of Management*, 17: 99–120.

Beardwell, I. and Holden, L. (2001) *Human Resource Management: A Contemporary Approach*, 3rd edn. London: Financial Times Management.

Becker, B. and Gerhart, B. (1996) 'The impact of human resource management on organizational performance: progress and prospects', *Academy of Management Journal*, 39 (4): 779–801.

Beer, M., Spector, B., Lawrence, P., Quinn, Mills, D.Q. and Walton, R. (1985) *Human Resource Management: A General Manager's Perspective*. New York: Free Press.

Birkinshaw, J. (2010) *Reinventing Management: Smarter Choices for Getting Work Done*. Chichester: Wiley.

Blatchford, K. and Gash, T. (2012) *Commissioning for Success – How to Avoid the Pitfalls of Open Public Services*. London: Institute for Government.

Blyton, P. and Turnball, P. (1992) *Reassessing Human Resource Management*. London: Sage Publications.

Bolton, R. and Isaacson, K. (2012) *Designing Next Generation HR*. London: KPMG.

Boudreau, J.W. and Ramstad, P.M. (2007) *Beyond HR: The New Science of Human Capital*. Boston, MA: Harvard Business School Publishing.

Boxall, P.F. (1996) 'The strategic HRM debate and the resource-based view of the firm', *Human Resource Management Journal*, 6 (3): 59–75.

Boxall, P.F. (2007) 'Human resource management: scope, analysis and significance', in P. Wright, J. Purcell and P.F. Boxall (eds), *The Oxford Handbook of Human Resource Management*. Oxford: Oxford University Press, pp. 1–16.

Brewster, C. (1995) 'Towards a "European" model of human resource management', *Journal of International Business Studies, 26 (1): 1–21.*

Brewster, C., Sparrow, P. and Harris, H. (2005) 'Towards a new model of globalising HRM', *International Journal of Human Resource Management*, 16 (6): 949–70.

Briner, R. (2007) *Is HRM Evidence-based and Does it Matter?* Opinion paper OP6. Brighton: Institute for Employment Studies.

Brown, P., Lauder, H. and Ashton, D. (2010a) *Praxis 4: Skills are Not Enough: the Globalisation of Knowledge and the Future UK Economy*. London: UK Commission for Employment and Skills

Brown, P., Lauder, H. and Ashton, D. (2010b) *The Global Auction: The Broken Promises of Education, Jobs and Rewards*. New York: Oxford University Press.

Budhwar, P.S. and Khatri, N. (2001) 'A comparative study of HR practices in Britain and India', *International Journal of Human Resource Management*, 12 (5): 800–26.

Budhwar, P.S. and Sparrow, P.R. (2002) 'An integrative framework for understanding cross-national human resource practices', *Human Resource Management Review*, 12 (3): 377–403.

Burrell, G. and Morgan, G. (1979) *Sociological Paradigms and Organizational Analysis*. London and Exeter: NH. Heinemann.

Burrell, G. and Morgan, G. (2008) *Sociological Paradigms and Organizational Analysis: Elements of the Sociology of Corporate Life*. Farnham: Ashgate Publishing. (Originally published in 1979.)

Caldwell, R. (2003) 'The changing roles of personnel managers: old ambiguities, new uncertainties', *Journal of Management Studies*, 40 (4): 983–1004.

Cascio, W. (2005) 'From business partner to driving business success: the next step in the evolution of HR management', in M. Losey, S. Meisinger and D. Ulrich (eds), *The Future of HR*. Chlichester: Wiley/Society for HRM, pp. 159–63.

Cascio, W.F. and Boudreau, J. (2008) *Investing in People: Financial Impact of Human Resource Initiatives*. Upper Saddle River, NJ: FT Press.

Clarke, J. and Newman, J. (1997) *The Managerial State: Power, Politics and Ideology in the Remaking of the Welfare State*. London: Sage.

Clemmer, J. (1992) Firing on all Cylinders: the Service/quality System for High-powered Corporate Performance, 2nd edn. Kitchener, ON: The Clemmer Group.

Costea, B., Crump, N. and Holm, J. (2007) 'The spectre of Dionysus: play, work, and managerialism', *Society and Business Review*, 2 (2): 153–65.

Csikszentmihalyi, M. (1998) *Finding Flow: The Psychology of Engagement with Everyday Life*. New York: Basic Books.

Cunningham, B. (1997) 'The failing teacher in further education', *Journal of Further and Higher Education*, 21 (3): 365–71.

Deetz, S. (1992) *Democracy in an Age of Corporate Colonization: Developments in Communication and the Politics of Everyday Life*. Albany, NY: University of New York.

Deetz, S. (2003) 'Reclaiming the legacy of the linguistic turn', *Organization* 10: 421–9.

Delbridge, R. and Keenoy, T. (2010) 'Beyond managerialism?', *The International Journal of Human Resource Management*, 21 (6): 801–19.

Delery, J.E. and Doty, D.H. (1996) 'Modes of theorizing in strategic human resource management: tests of universalistic, contingency and configurational performance predictions', *Academy of Management Journal*, 39 (4): 802–35.

Du Gay, P. and Salaman, G. (1992) 'The cult(ure) of the customer', *Journal of Management Studies*, 29 (5): 615–33.

Dyer, L. and Ericksen, J. (2006) *Dynamic Organizations: Achieving Marketplace Agility through Workforce Scalability*, CAHRS Working Paper #06-12. Ithaca, NY: Cornell University, School of Industrial and Labor Relations, Center for Advanced Human Resource Studies, available at http://digitalcommons.ilr.cornell.edu/cahrswp/454

Esland, G., Esland, K., Murphy, M. and Yarrow, K. (1999) 'Managerializing organizational culture', in J. Ahier and G. Esland (eds), *Education, Training and The Future of Work*, vol. 1. Milton Keynes: Open University/Routledge, pp. 160–85.

Farnham, D. (2002) *Employee Relations in Context*, 2nd edn. London: CIPD.

Fleetwood, S. and Hesketh, A. (2006) 'High performance work systems, organisational performance and (lack of) predictive power', *Journal of Critical Realism*, 5 (2): 228–50.

Fombrun, C.J., Tichy, N.M. and Devanna, M.A. (1984) *Strategic Human Resource Management*. New York: Wiley.

Fournier, V. and Grey, C. (2000) 'At the critical moment: conditions and prospects for critical management studies', *Human Relations*, 53 (1): 7–32.

Francis, H. and Sinclair, J. (2003) 'A processual analysis of HRM-based change', *Organization*, 10 (4): 685–706.

Francis, H., Holbeche, L.S. and Reddington, M. (eds) (2011) *People and Organisation Development: A New Agenda for Organisational Effectiveness*. London: CIPD.

Friedman. A. (1977) 'Responsible autonomy versus direct control over the labour process', *Capital and Class*, 1 (1): 43–57.

Gallup Consulting (2010) *What is Your Engagement Ratio?* London: Gallup Organization Ltd.

Gamble, A. (2009) *The Spectre at the Feast: Capitalist Crisis and the Politics of Recession*. London: Palgrave Macmillan.

Grey, C. (1996) 'Towards a critique of managerialism: the contribution of Simone Weil', *Journal of Management Studies*, 33: 591–612.

Guest, D., Michie, J., Conway, N. and Sheehan, M. (2003) 'A study of human resource management and corporate performance in the UK', *British Journal of Industrial Relations*, 41 (2): 291–314.

Guest, D.E. (1987) 'Human resource management and industrial relations', *Journal of Management Studies*, 24 (5): 503–21.

Guest, D.E. (2002) 'Human resource management, corporate performance and employee well-being: building the worker into HRM', *The Journal of Industrial Relations*, 44 (3): 335–58.

Guest, D.E. and Conway, N. (1997) *Employee Motivation and the Psychological Contract*. London: Institute for Personnel and Development.

Hall, E.T. (1976) *Beyond Culture*. New York: Anchor Press/Doubleday.

Hall, R., Bretherton, T. and Buchanan, J. (2000) *'It's Not my Problem'. The Growth of Non-standard Work and its Impact on Vocational Education and Training in Australia*. Adelaide: National Centre for vocational Education Research.

Hamel, G. and Breen, B. (2007) *The Future of Management*. Boston, MA: Harvard Business Press.

Heger, B.K. (2007) 'Linking the employment value proposition (EVP) to employee engagement and business outcomes: preliminary findings from a linkage research pilot study', *Organization Development Journal*, 25 (2): 121–31.

Herriot, P., Manning, W.E.G. and Kidd, J.M. (1997) 'The content of the psychological contract', *British Journal of Management*, 8: 151–62.

Herriot, P. and Pemberton, C. (1995) *New Deals: The Revolution in Managerial Careers*. Chichester: Wiley.

Hirsh, W. and Briner, R. (2010) *Evidence-based HR: From Fads to Facts?* London: Corporate Research Forum.

Hofstede, G. (1980) *Culture's Consequences: International Differences in Work-related Values*. Beverly Hills, CA: Sage.

Holbeche, L.S. (2005) *Understanding Change: Theory, Implementation and Success*. Oxford, Butterworth-Heinemann.

Holbeche, L.S. (2009) *HR Leadership*. Oxford: Butterworth-Heinemann.

Huselid, M. (1995) 'The impact of human resource management practices on turnover, productivity, and corporate performance', *Academy of Management Journal*, 38 (3): 635–72.

Huselid, M. and Becker, B.E. (1996) 'Methodological issues in cross-sectional and panel estimates of the human resource–firm link', *Industrial Relations*, 35 (3): 400–22.

Hutchinson, S., Purcell, J. and Kinnie, N. (2000) 'Evolving high commitment management and the experience of the RAC call centre', *Human Resource Management Journal*, 10 (1): 63–78.

Iles, P. and Salaman, G. (1995) 'Recruitment, selection and assessment', in J. Storey (ed.), *Human Resource Management: a Critical Text*. London: Routledge, pp. 202–33.

Jackson, S.E. and Schuler, R.S. (1995) 'Understanding human resource management in the context of organizations and their environment', *Annual Review of Psychology*, 46: 237–64.

Jacques, R. (1999) 'Developing a tactical approach to engaging with "strategic" HRM', *Organization*, 6. 2: 199–222.

Kallinikos, J. (1996) 'Mapping the intellectual terrain of management education', in R. French and C. Grey (eds), *Rethinking Management Education*. London: Sage, pp. 36–53.

Keenoy, T. (1990) 'HRM: a case of the wolf in sheep's clothing', *Personnel Review*, 19 (2): 3–9.

Keenoy, T. (1997) 'Review article: HRMism and the languages of representation', *Journal of Management Studies*, 34 (5): 825–41.

Keenoy, T. (1999) 'HRM as hologram: a polemic', *Journal of Management Studies*, 1 (36): 1–23.

Keenoy, T. (2009) 'Human resource management', in M. Alvesson, T. Bridgman and H. Willmott (eds), *The Oxford Handbook of Critical Management Studies*. Oxford: Oxford University Press, pp. 454–72.

Keenoy, T. and Anthony, P. (1992) 'HRM: metaphor, meaning and morality', in P. Blyton and P. Turnbull (eds), *Reassessing HRM*. London: Sage, pp. 233–55.

Lawler III, E.E. (2005) 'From human resource management to organizational effectiveness', *Human Resource Management*, 44, 2: 165–9.

Lawler III, E.E., Jamrog, J. and Boudreau, J. (2011) 'Shining light on the HR profession', *HR Magazine (USA)*, 56 (2): 38–41.

Legge, K. (1995) Human Resource Management: Rhetorics and Realities. London: Macmillan.

Legge, K. (2005) *Human Resource Management: Rhetorics and Realities; Anniversary Edition*. Basingstoke: Palgrave-Macmillan.

Lettink, A. (2012) What is the future of HR? Employment Intelligence blog XpertHR, posted 27 February, accessed 28 February.

MacLeod, D. and Clarke, N. (2009) *Engaging for Success: Enhancing Performance through Employee Engagement*. London: The Department of Business, Innovation and Skills.

Marchington, M. and Wilkinson, A. (2008) *HRM at Work: People Management and Development*. London: CIPD.

Marks, A. and Scholarios, D. (2004) 'Work life boundary, reciprocity, and attitudes to the organization, the special case of software workers', *Human Resource Management Journal*, 14 (2): 54–74.

Marquand, D. (2008) *Britain Since 1918: The Strange Career of British Democracy*. London: Orion Books.

McCann, J., Selsey, J. and Lee, J. (2009) 'Building agility, resilience and performance in turbulent environments', *hrps online journal*, 32 (3): www.hrps.org/resource/resmgr/p.../hrps_p_sissue32.3_mccann_et.pdf

McGurk, J. (2012) *Business-savvy: Giving HR the Edge*. London: CIPD.

Meredith, S. and Francis, D. (2000) 'Journey towards agility: the agile wheel explored', *The TQM Magazine*, 12 (2): 137–43.

Miles, R.E. and Snow, S.S. (1984) 'Designing strategic human resources systems', *Organization Dynamics*, 16: 36–52.

Mueller, F. and Carter, C. (2005) 'The "HRM project" and managerialism: or why some discourses are more equal than others', *Journal of Organizational Change Management*, 18: 369–82.

Nath, R. (ed.) (1988) *Comparative Management: a Regional View*. Cambridge, MA: Ballinger.

Paauwe, J. (2007) 'HRM and performance: in search of balance', inaugural address as Professor of Human Resource Management at the Department of HR Studies at Tilburg University.

Parker, M. (2002) *Against Management: Organization in the Age of Managerialism*. Cambridge: Polity Press.

Patterson, M.G., West, M.A., Lawthorn, R. and Nickell, S. (1997) 'Impact of people management practices on business performance', *Issues in People Management*, 22, London: Institute of Personnel and Development.

Pfeffer, J. (2005) 'Changing mental models: HR's most important task', *Human Resource Management*, 44 (2): 123–8.

Pfeffer, J. (1998) *The Human Equation: Building Profits by Putting People First*. Boston, MA: Harvard Business School Press.

Pfeffer, J. and Sutton, R. (1999) *The Knowing-doing Gap: how Smart Companies Turn Knowledge into Action*. Cambridge, MA: Harvard Business School Press.

Pollitt, C. (2003) *Managerialism and the Public Service: The Anglo-American Experience*, 2nd edn. Oxford: Blackwell.

Purcell, J., Kinnie, N. and Hutchinson, S. (2003) *Understanding the People and Performance Link: Unlocking the Black Box*. London: Chartered Institute of Personnel and Development.

Ramamoorthy, N. and Carroll, S. (1998) 'Individualism/collectivism orientations and reactions towards alternative human resource management practices', *Human Relations*, 51 (5): 571–88.

Ramdhony, A. (2011) *A Conceptual Expansion of Critical HRD: Towards a Post-reflective Understanding of HRD?*, Conceptual Paper. Edinburgh: Edinburgh Napier University.

Ramdhony, A. (2012) 'Critical HRD and organisational effectiveness', in H. Francis, L.S. Holbeche and M. Reddington (eds) *People and Organisational Development: a New Agenda for Organisational Effectiveness*. London: CIPD, pp. 161–79.

Rousseau, D.M. (1989) 'Psychological and implied contracts in organizations', *Employee Responsibilities and Rights Journal*, 2: 121–39.

Rousseau, D.M. (1995) *Psychological Contracts in Organizations*. Thousand Oaks, CA: Sage.

Rousseau, D.M. (2001) The Boundaryless Career; a New Employment Principle for a New Organizational Era. Oxford: Oxford University Press.

Rushkoff, D. (2005) 'Commodified vs commoditized', available at http://zomobo.net/Douglas-Rushkoff, accessed 21 July 2008.

Sarawagi, V.K. (2010) *Challenges in Modern Human Resource Management, A Project Report by a Student of IMS, Ghaziabad*. Ghaziabad, India: Institute approved by AICTE, Government of India.

Schein, E. (1978) *Career Dynamics: Matching Individual and Organizational Needs*. Reading, MA: Addison-Wesley.

Schön, D.A. (1983) *The Reflective Practitioner – How Professionals Think in Action*. New York: Basic Books.

Schuler, R.S. (1992) 'Strategic human resource management: linking people with the needs of the business', *Organizational Dynamics*, 21 (1): 18–32.

Scullion, H. (2005) 'International HRM: an introduction', in H. Scullion and M. Linehan (eds), *International HRM: a Critical Text*. London: Palgrave, pp. 3–21.

Scullion, H. (2001) 'International human resource management' in J. Storey (ed.), *International Human Resource Management: A Critical Text*. London: Thompson Business Press.

Sears, L. (2011) *Time for a Change: Towards a Next Generation HR*. London: CIPD.

Sennett, R. (1998) *The Corrosion of Character, Personal Consequences of Work in the New Capitalism*. New York: W. W. Norton.

Sennett, R. (2006) *The Culture of the New Capitalism*. New Haven, CT: Yale University Press.

Shore, L.M. and Tetrick, L.E. (1994) 'The psychological contract as an explanatory framework for the employment relationship', in C.L. Cooper and D.M. Rousseau (eds), *Trends in Organizational Behaviour, vol. 1*. Chichester: Wiley, pp. 91–109.

Spicer, A., Alvesson, M. and Karreman, D. (2010) 'Critical performativity: the unfinished business of critical management studies', *Human Relations*, 62 (4): 537–60.

Storey, J. (ed.) (2001) *Human Resources Management: A Critical Text*, 3rd edn. Stamford, CT: Thomson Learning.

Storey, J., Wright, P.M. and Ulrich, D. (2009) *The Routledge Companion to Strategic HRM*. London: Routledge.

Terry, L.D. (1998) 'Administrative leadership, neo-managerialism, and the public management movement', *Public Administration Review*, 58 (3): 194–200.

Townley, B. (1994) *Reframing Human Resource Management: Power, Ethics and the Subject at Work*. London: Sage.

Townley, B. (1998) 'Beyond good and evil: depth and division in the management of human resources', in A. McKinlay and K. Starkey (eds), *Foucault, Management and Organization Theory*. London: Sage.

Townley, B. (2004) 'Managerial technologies, ethics and management', *Journal of Management Studies*, 41 (3): 425–45.

Ulrich, D. (1997) *Human Resource Champions: The Next Agenda for Adding Value and Delivering Results*. Boston, MA: Harvard Business School Press.

Ulrich, D., Broadbank, W. and Johnson, D. (2008) *HR Competencies: Mastery at the Intersection of People and Business*, Alexandria, Virginia: Society for Human Resource Management (SHRM)

Ulrich, D. and Smallwood, N. (2005) 'HR's new ROI: return on intangibles', *Human Resource Management*, 44 (2): 137–42.

Vanden Heuval, A. and Wooden, M. (1999) *Casualisation and Outsourcing – Trends and Implications for Work-related Training*. Adelaide: NCVER.

Virgona, S., Waterhouse, P., Sefton, R. and Sanguinetti, J. (2003) *Making Experience Work*. Adelaide: NCVER.

Watson, T.J. (2003) 'Ethical choice in managerial work: the scope for managerial choices in an ethically irrational world', *Human Relations*, 56 (2): 167–85.

Watson, T.J. (2010) 'Critical social science, pragmatism and the realities of HRM', *The International Journal of Human Resource Management*, 21 (6): 915–31.

Welbourne, T.M. and Cyr, L.A. (1999) 'The human resource executive effect in initial public offering firms', *Academy of Management Journal*, 42 (6).

Wood, S. (1999) 'Human resource management and performance', *International Journal of Management Reviews*, 1 (4): 367–413.

Wright, P.M. and McMahan, G.C. (1992) 'Theoretical perspectives for SHRM', *Journal of Management*, March: 215–47.

Wright, P.M. and Snell, S.A. (1998) 'Towards a unifying framework for exploring fit and flexibility in strategic human resource management', *Academy of Management Review*, 23: 756–72.

Wright, P.M. and Snell, S.A. (2005) 'Partner or guardian? HR's challenge in balancing value and values', *Human Resource Management*, 44 (2): 177–182.

Wright, P.M., Gardner, T.M., Moynihan, L.M. and Allen, M.R. (2005) 'The relationship between HR practices and firm performance: examining causal order', *Personnel Psychology*, 58 (2): 409–46.

NAMES INDEX

SUBJECT INDEX

executive coaching, 365
executive compensation, 484
expatriate workers, 148–9, 466–72, 481, 487
expectancy theory, 80, 238–9
Extronics China, 441–2

'false positives' and 'false negatives'
    amongst business propositions, 51
Family Friendly Working Hours Taskforce,
    191–2
family-type organizations, 421–2
fashionable management ideas, 489–90
feminism, 315–16, 321–2
financial data, 123–4
Finland, 175, 429–30
'fit' between HR and strategic objectives, 126,
    131, 517
'flexible firm' concept, 194
'flexible specialization', 191
flexible working, 183–219, 236, 272, 505, 507;
    business benefits, 192; constraints on
    implementation of, 217–18; definition of,
    187, 218–19; employees' perspective on,
    195–8; examples of, 187–8; HRM
    perspective on, 186–92; reasons for
    increased interest in, 190–2
flexitime, 188, 215–16
fluid intelligence, 167
'focus' strategy, 76
FoodCo, 451–2
'forced distribution' in reward management,
    245–6
Ford Motors, 64, 127–8
founders of organizations, 399
Foxconn, 290–1, 300
France, 278, 282, 285, 287, 415
fuel tanker drivers' dispute (2012), 294, 300
functionalism, 392–3
future of HR, 501–36

game theory, 60–1
gender roles, 414
General Electric, 45
General Motors, 64
generational differences, 410, 417, 522
Geneva Motor Show, 307
Germany, 86, 279–82, 285, 292, 415,
    458, 461–2, 484–5
'glass ceiling', definition of, 318
global economic crisis, 523
global leaders, 373–4

globalization, 7, 51, 271, 281, 288, 443–4,
    462, 485
'glocal' approach to recruitment, 158
Glowhome Housing Association, 122–3

goal-setting theory, 237–8
Gore Associates, 408–9
Grupo San Nicolas, 426

happiness, 414–15
harassment in the workplace, 330
'hard' HRM, 85, 232, 273, 517–19
Harvard model of HRM, 82–3, 232, 503
headhunters, 159–61
'hidden value' of an organization, 117
hierarchy of human needs, 237
high-performance work systems (HPWS), 185,
    196, 509, 513, 517–19, 531
HIV/AIDS, 308–9, 327
homeworking, 188, 200–2
homogenization of organizations, 488
homosociality, 314
hotel sector, 90–2
HOYER UK, 296–7
HR Balanced Scorecard, 103, 125–6
HSBC Bank, 482
human capital theory, 236
human–nature relationships, 420–1
human resource accounting (HRA), 103, 117
human resource development (HRD), 349, 535;
    core purpose of, 351–2; definition and use
    of term, 350–2, 355
human resource (HR) function, 7–8, 19, 23, 27;
    effectiveness of, 128–30; evolving nature of,
    105–8; perceptions of, 521
human resource information systems
    (HRIS), 520
human resource management (HRM), 232, 272;
    criticisms of, 520–1; definition of, 8, 73,
    105; development of, 501–7; first use of
    term, 9; micro perspective on, 75; models
    of, 9–11; and organizational performance,
    513–14; quest for overall theory of, 517
human resource practice transfer across cultural
    and organizational boundaries, 423–7
human resource practitioners, professional
    development of, 521
Hungary, 210–11
hybridism and hybridization, cultural, 423, 426
'hygiene factors', 237
hyper-competition, 42

IBM, 64, 412, 417
ideational theory of culture, 385
ideological perspectives, 278–81
incentive pay, 249–50
India, 415, 516
individualism, 152, 275, 284, 300, 413–16,
    419, 505, 510, 515; definition of, 286
induction programmes, 145
industry effects, 400, 463

516; expatriate staff of, 466–7; HRM practices of, 445–6, 449; stages in development of, 447–8

'real options' method for evaluating strategy, 38
Really Best Foods, 101–2
recruitment advertising, 143, 155–6
recruitment and selection (R&S), 21; fairness in, 143, 150; good practice in, 141–7, 150, 153, 160–7, 171, 176–9; strategic approach to, 153, 176–8
Red Digital Cinema, 94–7
'red ocean' strategy, 59–62, 65
references from former employers, 144
reinforcement theory (Skinner), 237
religion, discrimination based on, 326–7
repatriation training, 481–2
research and development, 50–1, 64
resiliency, 532
resource-based view (RBV) of the firm, 23–4, 45–6, 77–8, 83, 505, 532; in practice, 88
RETCO, 258–62
retrospective symbolization, 397–8
reward: determinants of, 239–41; elements of, 247–9
reward management, 226, 229, 234–6, 241, 262, 482–5; definition of, 230; strategic approach to, 256–7
reward mix, 256
reward strategy, 226, 229–30, 248–9, 257–8, 534
reward systems, 242, 262, 529–30; best practice for, 230–1; contingency approach to, 230; legal constraints on, 240
rites and rituals, 391, 397
Rochester, NY, 116
role segmentation, 528
Rover Group, 387–8, 394, 415, 427

Saudi Arabia, 277
scalability of a business, 38
scientific management, 196, 233, 508
Securitas, 133–4
security of employment, 83–4, 87
segregation, *horizontal* and *vertical*, 336–7
selection interviews, 144, 162–5
self, conceptualizations of, 354
senior managers 152; rewards for, 79; role of, 346, 361
sensitivity training, 473
server companies, 56
'Seven S' model, 17, 403–4
sexuality, discrimination based on, 326
'shamrock organisations' (Handy), 195
shared-services model of business organization, 107, 115
shared values, 403–5
shareholder-dominant HR, 78–81
sharing of resources, 43–4

short-listing for recruitment, 144
Silicon Valley, 87
'Six Sigma' approach to quality, 117
social constructionism, 387
social justice, 334–5, 338
socialization, 391
'soft' HRM, 81, 83, 232, 273, 517–19
South Africa, 72–3
South Korea, 459–60
Southwest Airlines, 24–5, 408
Spain, 412
staff turnover rates, 80
stakeholder-orientated approaches to HRM, 78, 81–2
Standard Chartered Bank, 533
start-up companies, 51
states, 277–8, 281, 458–9
status, *achieved* and *ascribed*, 420
status symbols, 388
stereotype threat theory, 312–13
stereotyping, 162–3, 306, 308, 311–13, 334, 412, 522
strategic analysis, 34, 36–7
strategic business partners (SBPs), 521
strategic business units (SBUs), 44–5
strategic goals/objectives, 9, 13
strategic HRD (SHRD), 359; as distinct from HRD strategies, 359
strategic HRM (SHRM), 20–3, 72–93, 112–16, 131, 241; core elements of, 131; definition of, 74, 112–13, 512; practicalities of, 75–8, 113–16; rise of, 74–5
strategic planning, 104, 232
'strategic reward' concept, 226, 229–35, 239, 242, 250, 256–8, 262; aims of, 235; definition of, 229–31
strategy: definition of the concept, 15–16, 30; *emergent* and *espoused*, 74; formulation and implementation of, 34–7; *see also* business strategy; corporate strategy
subcultures, 390–1
subsidiary companies, 487–8
substitute products, 40
Subway franchise, 31
sustainable performance, 526, 531–2
SWOT analysis, 36
symbolic interactionism, 387
symbolic power, 283
symbols, 387, 391–2, 396–8; *see also* status symbols
synergies, 43–4, 53

tacit knowledge, 46, 487
Taiwan, 460, 478
takeovers, 80